THE STORY OF
ALDERSHOT

By the same writer :

HERALDRY IN WAR : Formation Badges, 1930-45.

BADGES ON BATTLEDRESS : Post-War Formation Signs.

THE WELLINGTON STATUE

Erected at Hyde Park Corner in 1846,
re-erected in Aldershot in 1885.

THE STORY OF

ALDERSHOT

A History and Guide to Town and Camp

BY
LIEUT.-COLONEL HOWARD N. COLE
O.B.E., T.D.

ALDERSHOT
GALE & POLDEN LIMITED
1951

*First Published in the Year
of the Festiival of Britain,*
1951

MADE AND PRINTED IN GREAT BRITAIN BY GALE AND POLDEN
LIMITED AT THEIR WELLINGTON PRESS, ALDERSHOT, HAMPSHIRE

TO THE PEOPLE OF ALDERSHOT—OF
YESTERDAY AND TODAY—WHO HAVE
MADE THE ALDERSHOT STORY

TO ALL RANKS OF THE BRITISH ARMY
WHO HAVE MADE THE MILITARY
PATTERN OF ALDERSHOT THROUGHOUT
THE YEARS

AND . . .

TO MY WIFE AND DAUGHTERS, JANET
AND LINDA, WHO MADE MY ALDERSHOT
HOME A HAPPY ONE

CONTENTS

ACKNOWLEDGMENT

Every photograph reproduced to illustrate this volume, covering the period 1899-1950, has been taken, except where otherwise acknowledged, from the records of the Photograph Department of Messrs. Gale & Polden Ltd., whose operators have, throughout the years, recorded photographically the events in the Town and the Camp. All these photographs are the copyright of **Gale & Polden Ltd.**

ILLUSTRATIONS

THE BOROUGH OF ALDERSHOT

ALDERSHOT is first mentioned in our history as a hamlet in the Crondall Hundred.

As the years passed the hamlet grew into a small village community, and it was this village which expanded into the "mushroom town" which grew up on the boundaries of "The Camp" when it was established in 1854.

The town's civic life dates from 1857, for in that year a Local Board of Health was formed as the local authority. By the passing of the Local Government Act of 1894 the Local Board assumed the dignity of an Urban District Council, and on 23rd March, 1922, the Charter for the Incorporation of Aldershot as a Municipal Borough was signed by His Majesty King George V.

FOREWORD

by

HIS WORSHIP THE MAYOR OF ALDERSHOT ALDERMAN LIEUTENANT-COLONEL H. D. TANNER, o.b.e., j.p.

It is a privilege for me to be granted the opportunity of writing a foreword to the chapters in this book which provide the civic history of the town of my birth.

The history of Aldershot has previously been assumed by many to have commenced when the British Army made its home here, but those who read this book will now have the pleasure of absorbing an authentic story starting from much earlier days.

The citizens of Aldershot are provided for the first time with a comprehensive history of their Borough, and for this they will always be indebted to the writer, Lieut.-Colonel Howard Cole, whose many hours of diligent study and painstaking research have made possible the publication of this fine volume.

If this book proves a storehouse of knowledge to the historian, if it teaches those indifferent to history to read more about the towns of Britain, I know that the aim and the desire of the writer in framing it will be fully accomplished.

H. D. TANNER,
Mayor.

The Mayor's Parlour,
  Aldershot.
December, 1950.

MILITARY ALDERSHOT

FROM 1855 to 1856 Aldershot was officially designated "The Camp at Aldershot." This was changed in 1856, and from then until 1870 it was known as "The Division at Aldershot." From 1870 until 1901 it was known as "Aldershot District," and from then until 1904 as "First Army Corps." In 1904 it was designated "The Aldershot Command," by which title it was known until 1940 when it became, once again, "Aldershot District," which is its title at the present day.

FOREWORD

by

MAJOR-GENERAL W. A. DIMOLINE
C.B., C.B.E., D.S.O., M.C.

General Officer Commanding Aldershot District

ALDERSHOT is known as the home of the British Army; and as the thirty-fifth General Officer to command in Aldershot, I am happy to commend this book to all in search of an authentic and detailed history of Aldershot during the last century.

It will make a particular appeal to soldiers, for during this period the life of the Town has been intimately bound up with the life of the Camp. From Aldershot and its environs British and Commonwealth soldiers have trained and mobilized for their varied duties at home and abroad in peace and in war. They continue to do so, since Aldershot still remains the largest military station in the Commonwealth.

The research and preparation which the writing of this history has entailed have been a labour of love. The author has been closely connected with the Army for the last twenty-four years and is now commanding an Anti-Aircraft Regiment of the Territorial Army in Aldershot.

W. A. DIMOLINE,
Major-General.

HEADQUARTERS,
ALDERSHOT DISTRICT,
December, 1950.

INTRODUCTION

IN compiling a history of Aldershot, the first decision to be taken by the writer is the date at which it is best to start, for Aldershot has links with the distant past, as is proved by the existence in the vicinity of prehistoric earthworks—Caesar's Camp and Batt's Hog Stye in Claycart Bottom.

The first known mention of Aldershot in our history is in the will of King Alfred in A.D. 885, in the description of the Crondall lands bequeathed to his nephew Ethelm. Other early records dated 1248, 1276, 1281, 1316 and 1334 make mention of Aldershot, and there is considerable detail in the Crondall Customary of 1568. The first record of Aldershot Manor is in 1481, whilst the earliest registers of our Parish Church date from 1571.

All this deals with the original hamlet of Alreshute, Alreshete or Alreschate—later, as it was known a hundred years ago, the village of Aldershott.

The writer is then faced with another problem. Shall the history of Aldershot be confined to the history we can touch, the history which exists around us today in "The Camp" and Town—the great military centre which was established in the early fifties of last century, and the town which, in consequence, came into existence and developed in step with the growth of "The Camp"—the Aldershot of today? Even so, what should be taken as the date of the birth of modern Aldershot? 1852, the year of the military reconnaissance of the area? 1853, the year of the Government decision to establish "The Camp" and in which over twenty-five thousand acres were sold to the War Department? or 1854, the year in which the first loads of building materials arrived for the construction of "The Camp"?

All factors considered, it has been finally decided that this history should cover the span of a century, 1850 to 1950, as this period covers the whole era from the time when Aldershot was but a small village, which had changed but little in the preceding centuries, to its metamorphosis to the greatest military centre of the whole Empire and the busy, prosperous, ever-growing Borough of Aldershot of today.

Few towns have such a history of growth and development, coupled with a name which is now world famous—a name proudly associated with British feats of arms. For here, in our town, and in the expanse of heathlands which bound the Borough, the British Army has trained for its great tasks, ranging from its participation in the major conflicts of the past hundred years to minor operations in distant outposts of the Empire, internal security and imperial policing in every corner of the globe. Aldershot is admittedly not alone in its history of expansion and progress; other towns, too, can claim a similar record of growth from such small beginnings, especially those which grew in consequence of the advance of industrialism and the development of commerce during last century. But Aldershot's growth has been unique. No natural resources, no mineral deposits, no centre of communications, no growth in consequence of proximity to great neighbours, brought into existence the Aldershot of today. Aldershot owes its existence to one factor, and a great factor at that—the British Army, and the establishment of "The Camp at Aldershot" in 1854.

For almost a hundred years the life of Aldershot has been bound up with the Army. That is so today, for a great tradition has been established—a tradition which will be maintained; but, in addition, Aldershot is desirous of growing to full stature, with eventually all the amenities and facilities of a county borough. Aldershot is an ambitious borough. It is today a thriving and progressive business centre. It is also anxious to make the town the centre, in every sense of the word, of the north-eastern portion of Hampshire.

As this book closes for press these plans for development of the area, with the extension of the existing Borough boundaries and thereby the establishment of a county borough, have not yet come to fruition. It is perhaps appropriate, therefore, to conclude this historical record of Aldershot in 1950, covering a period of one hundred years, before the leaf is turned to open another new chapter in the history of the Aldershot of the future.

The scope of this book covers, in fact, territories beyond the confines of the existing Borough boundaries, but this was inevitable, for this is a history and survey of "The Camp" as well as the town, and a portion of the former lies within the boundaries of the Farnborough Urban District Council.

This book has been compiled with two main objects. Firstly, to place on permanent record, as a book of reference, something of the history of Aldershot as a Military Station—the greatest in the British Empire—and as a growing and progressive Borough which, although its development dates back but a few years less than a century, has its roots much deeper in the past. Secondly, to record *now* something which will not only serve as a guide to the Aldershot of today, but will in the years to come give an insight into the Aldershot of 1950.

Generally speaking, people pay little attention to the value of contemporary history. The details of current events are not visualized as being of value and interest to the future. Too quickly do current records and tangible evidence come to be regarded as old, out of date, and unwanted, and too quickly one has to fall back upon memories and scattered evidence.

Some of the material which has gone into the compilation of this book has been published before in the local Press, and in various guide books to the Borough, but where now can anyone put his hands upon a comprehensive history or guide? Hoarded newspapers and old guide books eventually found their way to the dustbins. The great paper salvage drives during the late war destroyed for ever much that had, for several generations, been kept with care. Over eighty years have passed since the last full history of Aldershot was written, and most copies of the books written in the fifties and sixties of last century have long since disappeared. Surely the time had come, before it was too late, to produce this volume. To many of the older residents of Aldershot there may be little that is new concerning their town in the following pages, but this book has been compiled for today and for the future, and should be accepted for this reason.

One of my main sources of information has been the files of *The Aldershot News*, from which a considerable amount of material has been drawn, more particularly the Special Numbers which have been produced from time to time—namely, the Diamond Jubilee Supplement of June, 1897; the General Buller Number of November, 1900; the Coronation Numbers of August, 1902, and June, 1911; the Special Charter Day Edition and the Charter Day Supplement of June, 1922; selected Special Aldershot Shopping Week Supplements and the paper's Golden Jubilee Number of June, 1944. In addition, I have made use of the Official Guides published by Messrs. Gale and Polden in 1904 and 1909, and "Aldershot Calling," published in 1946.

Although *The Aldershot News* files go back only fifty-six years there is a wealth of information in their pages, for during that time there have been many interesting articles and references to the early history of the town and camp, many of them from the pen of the late Mr. E. J. Sercombe, Editor of *The Aldershot News*, 1914-1945.

In addition, I have consulted numerous books, files and other references in libraries and museums and in the possession of several older residents of the Borough. I have also made a point of visiting every place of interest in the Borough to which reference is made in

Chapter VIII; and this, perhaps, has been most interesting of all, for it has taken me into the clock tower of the Cambridge Hospital, to the underground passage of the Royal Pavilion, the belfry of the Parish Church, the plinth of the Wellington Statue, along the stretches of the Canal, to the summit of Caesar's Camp, to every hilltop vantage point, to every church and public building, to private houses, to factories, into basements and attics—in fact, to everywhere where first-hand knowledge could be obtained; whilst for earlier details my research has taken me to the British Museum, the Public Record Office, the Royal Library at Windsor Castle, the War Office, the Royal United Service Institution, the Institution of Royal Engineers at Chatham, to Winchester and a number of other places where I might pick up a thread and confirm or find new details.

Every effort has been made to ensure correctness of fact and detail, and it is hoped that I have achieved this object. In a work of this nature, however, I am aware that there may be omissions which should have been included, and for these I apologize to the reader, but it is hoped that the work will be accepted as the best record I have been able to compile from the sources available and as a tribute to all those who have made up the history of Aldershot throughout the years.

There have been many other reasons which led me to the task of compiling this record of our town. I have a friend, an Aldershot resident of over ten years. Last year I took him for his first drive through "The Camp," taking him to the top of Thorn Hill, to the base of the Wellington Monument, to the Royal Garrison Church and through "The Camp" roads, pointing out the memorials and other items of interest. He was amazed and most interested. He had never before ventured off the bus route running along Queen's Avenue.

I met another friend, a Regular officer stationed here for nearly two years. His knowledge of Aldershot, he admitted, was confined to High Street, Wellington Street, my office and the route to the station. I took him through the Manor Park; we spent half an hour in the Parish Church, we drove on to the Swimming Pool and through the residential area of the south of the town—up through Ayling Lane, along Church Lane West and finally to the Municipal Gardens. He saw an Aldershot that he did not know, an Aldershot which to him had not existed. "I thought," said he as we left St. Michael's Church, "that the town finished just over the railway and in any case there was nothing to see anyway." This short introduction gave him an entirely different viewpoint on the town in which he was stationed.

Many hundreds of thousands of people in this country know Aldershot—or at least so they say. Hundreds of thousands have visited

Aldershot—but when? and for what? As soldiers during the last two wars, or to the Aldershot Tattoo, the Aldershot Show or to the football ground; but what do they know of the town and camp and its history of progress and development? One does not see much in an evening off duty from a barrack block or an adjacent camp; one's outlook is limited in a private car or motor coach driving through with a "Red Car Park" label on the windscreen or on a walk from the Recreation Ground to the station on a winter's Saturday afternoon with one's fellow-supporters of the Away Team.

But for the national and sporting events held in Aldershot there are but few visitors to the town other than those engaged in commerce or those visiting friends or relations stationed in "The Camp." Added to this, Aldershot has been bypassed by the compilers of many guide books. Reference to the town and camp is usually dismissed in a few lines, and some of these have been of a critical nature and not encouraging to the visitor.

The history of modern Aldershot has been one of rapid progress. As will be seen, at first it was composed of nothing but a heterogeneous collection of people who could minister to the wants of "The Camp." There was no civic unity or pride; there was in fact, as will be seen, no constitutional body to administer its needs or guide its future. Great credit is due to those public-spirited and far-seeing few who in 1857 took steps to establish the first Local Board, and to those who have followed through the years, imbued with the same spirit of public service, who have striven for the improvement and progress of the town. From the obvious disadvantages of its early growth, Aldershot today has grown to a Borough of standing, progressive and well able to hold its own in competition, if necessary, with other towns of similar size and status. The same may be said of "The Camp." No finer military establishment of its size exists. Nowhere else will the soldier find such facilities and amenities in a large garrison. There are many who prefer to serve in single-battalion stations and who claim divers advantages of such over Aldershot and the like, but for a purely military area Aldershot provides much to commend itself.

It is for the readers of this book to judge for themselves if the criticisms of Aldershot which have been made from time to time are entirely justified.

I have derived considerable pleasure from the necessary research conducted for the compilation of this book, and I am proud to have been but a tiny piece in the military mosaic of Aldershot in the past twenty-four years—as an R.H.A. driver bending low over the necks of the wheelers as we swung round in a cloud of fine sandy dust to "Action front" near Cocked Hat Wood; as a young bombardier riding down Wellington Avenue under the shade of the chestnut trees in bloom to await the order "Battery—Dismount"; on the square at Waterloo Barracks; as a Territorial Sapper Subaltern directing a Sound Locator crew "on target" on a searchlight site on Burn's Plain, below Caesar's Camp; as a war-time Staff Officer industriously making notes from the description given by a more senior Staff Officer on the performance of the new Churchill tanks demonstrating their capabilities amid the sand and scrub of the Long Valley near Miles Hill; and finally as a Territorial C.O. marching from Beaumont Barracks with Aldershot's own Anti-Aircraft Territorial Gunner Regiment *en route* to their first post-war camp.

Since the war, when I became a resident, I have learned more and more about Aldershot, and I hope that this book may be taken as a tribute to the people of the town of my adoption.

This morning, walking through the Manor Park, I could hear the familiar rat-tat-tat of light machine guns echoing across from the direction of Caesar's Camp ranges. This evening, as the pealing of bells which had been ringing from the tower of our fine old Parish Church was stilled, I stood below the tall elms lining the centuries-old footpath leading to Croft Road, and, from the distant barracks, the sound of a bugle was borne on the wind. These are the sounds of Aldershot, the voice of the town and camp, sounds which have been familiar for nearly a hundred years—the church bells for almost five centuries. There is something of the spirit of Aldershot in the bells, the bugles and the sound of small-arms fire. They are calls to service and to action and to progress, and—Aldershot is a progressive town.

HOWARD N. COLE.

ALDERSHOT,
December, 1950.

ACKNOWLEDGMENTS

FIRSTLY, I have the honour to acknowledge the gracious permission of His Majesty The King to make use of material from the Royal Archives at Windsor Castle in the compilation of this book.

I am also indebted to Major-General W. A. Dimoline, C.B., C.B.E., D.S.O., M.C., General Officer Commanding Aldershot District, and Alderman Lieut.-Colonel H. D. Tanner, O.B.E., J.P., Mayor of Aldershot, for reading the proofs and for contributing their Forewords; Alderman G. Roberts, J.P., Deputy Mayor of Aldershot, for assisting me in various ways during his years of office; Mr. D. Llewellyn Griffiths, O.B.E., Town Clerk of Aldershot, for his help at all times, and for his permission to quote from "Aldershot and the War"; and to Sir Owen Morshead, K.C.V.O., D.S.O., M.C., the Librarian, Windsor Castle, and Miss Mary Mackenzie, M.V.O., for assistance in my research. I also record my thanks for and appreciation of, the assistance afforded me by my colleague, Mr. Ivan Smith, Editor of *The Aldershot News*, in making available for reference all the existing file copies of that paper. My thanks are due to my friend Mr. E. A. Deverell, former Editor of *The Aldershot News*, who also made material available for reference and who assisted me in checking detail in the proof; to Lieut.-Colonel Dymott, the Librarian of the Prince Consort's Library, whose assistance with the old Ordnance Survey maps of the area has been invaluable; to Colonel F. C. W. Fosbery, Chief Engineer, Aldershot District, and Lieut.-Colonel D. S. Blunt, R.E., C.R.E., South Aldershot (1948-1950), for their help in providing the answer to several inquiries regarding "The Camp"; to Canon W. A. Challacombe, of Farnborough, for his permission to quote from "Jottings from a Farnborough Notebook," by the late Mrs. Jessie Challacombe; the Rev. A. L. E. Hoskyns-Abrahall, Vicar of Aldershot, who allowed me to peruse the Parish Records and checked my details and description of the Parish Church; the Rev. Alan Cook, Vicar of Holy Trinity Church, and the Rev. A. G. Kick, M.C., Minister of the Methodist Church in Grosvenor Road, who assisted me in reading the sections devoted to their churches; Major R. Maxwell Lefroy, J.P., of Crondall, for his permission to quote from "Some Historical Particulars of the Parish of Crookham, Hants," by the late Grace Lefroy, C.B.E.; Dr. and Mrs. J. H. Gibson, for their assistance and interest and checking detail in the proofs, and to Dr. Gibson for permission to quote from his history of the Parish Church of St. Michael the Archangel; Mr. Tom C. McCall, Deputy Minister of the Department of Travel and Publicity of the Government of Ontario, for the information supplied by him and his Department concerning Aldershot, Ontario; Major T. M. Hunter, the Canadian Army Historical Liaison Officer of the Canadian Army Liaison Establishment in London, for his assistance in providing details regarding Aldershot Camp, Nova Scotia; the Director of News and Information of the Department of the Interior of the Government of Australia and the Premier and Chief Secretary's Department of Queensland, for the information they provided concerning Aldershot, Queensland; Mr. G. A. Broomfield, of Virginia Water, for the information he gave me concerning Mr. S. F. Cody's early flying days; Mr. S. H. Wheble, of Southmead Road, for providing information regarding the Aldershot Home Guard, in which he served as Second-in-Command of the 27th (Hampshire) Battalion; Mr. C. J. Loveridge, of St. Michael's Road, for the material concerning the Aldershot Fire Service during the 1939-1945 war; Mr. Harry Lloyd, who made his family papers available for reproduction and assisted me over certain details; Mr. Albert Shaw, the former Borough Rating Officer; Mr. Walter Finch, of Ayling Barn, who placed his library and family records at my disposal; Mr. C. J. Harland; Mr. John Russell, of Messrs. Alfred Pearson & Co., for his assistance in searching out details of certain land and properties from old sales sheets, etc.; Mr. W. Viggers, of Highfield Gardens, who provided me with the material concerning the bells of the Parish Church; Lieut.-Colonel E. A. Oldfield, for permission to refer to and reproduce the illustration from the History of the Army Physical Training Corps ("The Army Gymnastic Staff, 1860-1914"); Mrs. Cottrill, the County Archivist of Hampshire; Lieut.-Colonel Alfred H. Burne, D.S.O., M.C., Editor of The Gunner; Major T. J. Edwards, M.B.E., F.R.Hist.S., author of "Military Customs"; Mrs. Joan Marshall, General Manager of the New Basingstoke Canal Company Ltd.; Mr. T. W. Hill, Vice-President of the Dickens Fellowship; the Deputy Keeper of the Records, and his Staff, of the Search Department of the Public Record Office; the Controller of His Majesty's Stationery Office, for permission to quote from "The History of the Great War—Order of Battle of Divisions" (Part III A); Messrs. Warren & Son Ltd., Printers and Publishers, of Winchester, and the Hampshire Record Society, for permission to refer to and quote from the archives of the Society, and in particular "The Crondall Records" (Part I—Historical and Manorial); the proprietors of the *Illustrated London News*, for permission to refer to and quote extracts from their early issues with particular reference to the details of the Wellington Statue and the building of the Royal Pavilion, Officers' Club House and "The Camp"; the proprietors of *Punch*, for permission to quote from and refer to extracts from their issues of 1884; the Institute of Historical Research, for permission to quote from the "Victoria History of the Counties of England" (Volume IV); the Department of National Defence, Ottawa, for permission to refer to and quote from "The Canadian Army at War" (No. 1—The Canadians in Britain); Mrs. George Bambridge, daughter of the late Mr. Rudyard Kipling, Messrs. A. P. Watt & Son, and Messrs. Methuen & Co. Ltd., for permission to reproduce the lines from Mr. Rudyard Kipling's works appearing with some of the illustrations (from "Gunga Din" ("Barrack Room Ballads"), from "Tommy" ("Barrack Room Ballads)," from "M.I." ("Five Nations") and from "Back to the Army Again" ("The Seven Seas")); Mr. F. W. Smith, director of Messrs. Wm. May & Co. Ltd., Aldershot, for permission to refer to and quote from William Sheldrake's "Guide to Aldershot" (1859); Mr. A. E. Jenkins, Director of the Woodbridge Press Ltd., Guildford, for permission to reproduce the two lithographs of Aldershot Camp, 1859, and to refer to and take extracts from "Sketches of the Camp at Aldershot," published by Andrews and Lucy, of Farnham; Mr. William E. Totman, Managing Director of Rock Bros. Ltd., London, E. 6, for permission to reproduce the early steel engravings of Aldershot Camp, *circa* 1859, and the reproductions from "Rock's Album of Aldershot," *circa* 1879; Mrs. G. S. Davidge, of Coronation Road, and Miss M. E. Dalziel, of Park Road, for their assistance in research work and preparation of the manuscript; and to my friends Major P. B. Fox, M.B.E., Mr. Henry Phillips, of Wellington Street, and Mr. G. C. Williams, of Brighton Road (to whom I owe a special debt of gratitude), for their assistance in checking proofs and details. Also to all those members of the Staff of Gale & Polden Ltd. who in their various departmental functions have assisted in the production of this book in The Wellington Press.

I also gratefully acknowledge, to the publishers and owners of the copyright as stated, the permission granted me to quote from the following works:

"Aldershot and All About It," by Mrs. Young (Routledge & Kegan Paul Ltd.).

"Aldershottana, or Chinks in my Hut" (Ward, Lock & Co. Ltd.).

"An Introduction to Field Archæology as Illustrated by Hampshire,"
by Dr. J. P. Williams-Freeman, M.C. (Macmillan & Co. Ltd.).

"From Midshipman to Field-Marshal," by Field-Marshal Sir Evelyn
Wood, V.C. (Methuen & Co. Ltd.).

"Flying," by Claude Grahame White (Chatto & Windus Ltd.).

"George, Duke of Cambridge, A Memoir of His Private Life," by
Edgar Sheppard, C.V.O., D.D. (Longmans, Green & Co. Ltd.).

"Hark Back," by Colonel Wilfrid Jelf, C.M.G., D.S.O. (John Murray).

"My Early Life," by the Rt. Hon. Winston Churchill, C.H., M.P.
(Odhams Press Ltd.).

"Rock's Album of Aldershot" (Rock Bros. Ltd., London).

"Sixty Years a Queen," by Sir Herbert Maxwell, M.P., and Alfred C.
Harmsworth (The Amalgamated Press Ltd.).

"The Prince Consort," by Roger Fulford (Macmillan & Co. Ltd.).

Murray's Handbook for Travellers in Hampshire (John Murray).

The Times (1884).

The Dictionary of National Biography (Oxford University Press).

The Concise Oxford Dictionary of English Place Names, by Eilert
Ekwall (Oxford University Press).

"The History of Aeronautics in Great Britain," by J. E. Hodgson
(Oxford University Press).

"The Old Flying Days," by Major C. C. Turner (Sampson Low,
Marston & Co. Ltd.).

"The Parish Church of St. Michael The Archangel, Aldershot," by
Dr. J. H. Gibson (The British Publishing Co. Ltd., Gloucester).

"The Story of a Short Life," by the late Mrs. Horatio Ewing (The
Society for Promoting Christian Knowledge).

"The Civil War in Hampshire," by the Rev. G. N. Goodwin (John
& Edward Bumpus Ltd.).

"The Military Life of H.R.H. George, Duke of Cambridge," by
Colonel Willoughby Verner (John Murray).

"Wellington," by Richard Aldington (Wm. Heinemann Ltd.).

"County Typographies—Hampshire" (1875) (Kelly's Directories Ltd.).

The Times History of the War, Vol. I, 1914 ("The Times").

I have made every effort to trace the author and owner of the
copyright of each work to which I have referred in this book, or
which has been consulted in its preparation, and have done my
best to ensure that full and complete acknowledgment has been made.
If I have unwittingly infringed the rights of any, I tender them my
apologies and crave their kind indulgence.

HOWARD N. COLE.

ALDERSHOT,
December, 1950.

"Fair be all thy hopes
And prosperous be thy life in peace and war."

Henry VI, Act II.

CHAPTER ONE

A HUNDRED YEARS AGO
1850

A HUNDRED years ago, Aldershott, as it was then spelt, was almost unknown. The area was described as "a vast stretch of common land, unbroken for miles by any sign of habitation." It was regarded as a somewhat dangerous locality, for the stretch of the London to Winchester turnpike road between Bagshot and Farnham*—now known as the Farnborough Road—was the scene of highway robberies. There were many stories of highwaymen intercepting coach travellers on this lonely road which cut through the heath and waste lands of Aldershott, marked by small groups of tall, lonely pines. Both the notorious Dick Turpin and "Springheeled Jack" are said to have operated in the area, the former having his headquarters near Farnborough,† possibly in the old cottages in the grounds of Vine Cottage, which was for many years known as "Bagman's Castle."‡

The following extract taken from a Hampshire Directory published in 1852 describes Aldershott: "a parish 3½ miles N.E.N. of Farnham, the County Court town. Acres 4,070. Population 875. Post Office at W. Chuter's; letters are delivered at 8 a.m. and despatched to Farnham at 5.30 p.m."

The same directory listed the "Principal Residents" as Mr. Reuben Attfield, Charles Barron Esqr, Rev. Henry Cary, M.A., and Captain Newcome; and the "Commercial" residents as nine farmers, namely, Richard Allden, William Herrett, John Kimber, Robert Lloyd, Richard John Stovold, George, James and William Robinson, and George Gosden, who was also a grocer; two innkeepers—George Foulkner of the "Red Lion" and Henry Webster of the "Beehive"—and a blacksmith, Henry Howe.

---

* The road undoubtedly traversed on 22nd December, 1648, by King Charles I, under escort by Parliamentary troopers commanded by Major Harrison, *en route* from Hurst Castle to Windsor—the first stage of his journey to London to face his trial. The King spent a night at Farnham before riding on to Bagshot.
† "Jottings from a Farnborough Notebook," by Jessie Challacombe (Gale & Polden Ltd.) (1923).
‡ See pp. 23 and 39.

I

The only houses were in the neighbourhood of St. Michael's Parish Church, which dated from the twelfth century, and these included Aldershot Lodge, the Manor House, Elm Place and Aldershot Park. Other houses are shown in the plan of the Aldershot Manor Estate issued with the sale sheet of the Manor House when it was sold by auction in 1831, and these were in what are now Church Road and Church Hill, which leads down to Aldershot Green, which was then known as "Aldershott Street" and was the centre of the community around the present-day section of High Street by the Green. This same plan shows that the rest of the area of the estate, west and north of the Manor House, comprised meadow and woodland. Several farms with their houses and outbuildings were shown, including Park Farm, Ayling Farm and another at West End.

The main groups of cottages were around the Green, then owned by one Pharo* ; in Drury Lane, now called Windmill Road, which then led to the Windmill, on Windmill Hill, lying between Waterloo Road and Windmill Road ; and by the "Dog Kennels" in Weybourne Road.

The social life of the villagers centred around the "Beehive" and the "Red Lion." Both inns exist in name today in the present public houses, the former at the junction of Pound Road and High Street and the latter at the corner of Brighton Road and Ash Road. There is an old story* associated with the "Red Lion" which goes back many years even before the days of the building of "The Camp." It is the story of the "Tinker's will." One Sunday evening after a service at the Parish Church a few of the villagers adjourned to the "Red Lion." Whilst talking over their ale, a noise was heard outside, and the wailing of someone obviously in distress. Looking out it was seen to be a travelling tinker who had obviously been taken ill. The man was carried into the inn, but it was obvious that his end was near, and he expressed a desire to make his will. This he was able to do shortly before he died. By his will he stipulated that his barrow and its contents should be sold and the amount realized added to that in his possession. After the deduction of funeral expenses the balance should be distributed among the twelve poorest men and six poorest women in the parish. Those assembled at the inn carried out his wishes. The barrow and contents were sold for £5 and this was added to the money he was carrying—in all some £25. The funeral expenses were nearly £8 and this left a balance of £17 15s. for disposal. Then arose the question of how the money was to be distributed and who was to benefit by the bequest. Those who had been at the inn

---

* "Traditions about Aldershot," by C. S. Herve (W. Straker & Co., London) (1881). Mr. Herve lived at Flagstaff Villa, Grosvenor Road, which stood opposite the present Imperial Hotel.

on the night of the tinker's death, who were incidentally among the leading villagers of the day, decided to form themselves into a committee, and the following day settled down—at the inn—to go fully into the matter. The news of the meeting and its object had travelled, and the committee were besieged with numerous claimants for participation in the bequest. The committee found that they had undertaken a difficult task, and so, as the morning wore on, it occurred to the self-elected chairman that it would help their deliberations if they partook of refreshment, so ale was called for ; and at the suggestion of a committee member, so also was bread and cheese ordered, and then churchwardens and tobacco. As the committee were giving their time to the problem of distributing the bequest, it was generally agreed that it was perfectly fair for the refreshments to be paid for out of the tinker's money, and so this was done.

Still more claimants arrived. Still the committee continued their deliberations until late in the afternoon, when they felt the need for more substantial refreshment, and a course dinner was ordered and duly eaten at the expense of the tinker's bequest. Whilst they were eating their meal the crowd of claimants were also refreshed with ale and bread and cheese whilst they waited, and so in this manner the evening drew in, and finally the landlord announced that all the drink in the house had been consumed except for a 36-gallon cask in the cellar. The chairman immediately ordered this to be brought up, insisting that there were still further claimants who had not partaken of refreshment. At this stage the committee, who were by then feeling the strain of the day's labour, were reinforced by two local farmers who had arrived to help them, and their arrival led to further discussion. When late in the evening the Vicar arrived to find out what was really going on, he was somewhat taken aback and remonstrated with the assembled company, finally inquiring how much of the bequest was left. The chairman peered into the cash-box and announced that there was only sixpence left, "and," he suggested, "as the charitable funds of the parish cannot benefit very considerably from it your reverence might drink to the memory of the poor tinker." This the Vicar was persuaded to do, and so the tinker's bequest was spent.

The larger residences in Aldershot already had, by 1850, an interesting history. The first record of Aldershot Manor is in the year 1481, when a conveyance* was drawn up on 26th December for the sale of the house by "John Awbery of Aldershot, Gent., to Richard Newbrigge, Vicar of the Parish Church of Farnham, to John Brown, Clerk, Clerk to the King's Chancellory, and to Richard Balche, of Farnham, Cloth Maker," in which he referred to "My Manor of

* In the possession of the Hampshire Record Office, Winchester.

Aldershot and appurtenances in the counties of Southampton and Surrey." Payment was to be made of £126 over a period of years to the Prior of the House of Salutation in London (The Charterhouse). In the "Victoria County History of Hampshire"* there is mention of the Manor in the year 1537 "when Thomas Saunders and Henry White, clerk, dealt with it by recovery."† In 1599 Robert White, of Aldershot Manor, died, by which it appears probable that it had been bequeathed to him by his father, Sir John White, of Aldershot, Alderman of the City of London, who died in 1573. Robert White divided the Manor between his two daughters, Ellen, wife of Richard Tichborne, and Mary, wife of Walter Tichborne, a brother of Richard. Ellen surrendered her share of the Manor to her sister, who died in 1640, the Manor passing into the hands of her son and heir, Benjamin Tichborne. Benjamin died without issue, some time before 1661, for by that year the Manor had passed to the possession of his brother Francis, who died in 1671, and the estate passed on to Sir John White, until his death in 1701. The association of the families of White and Tichborne with Aldershot is perpetuated by the family memorials in the Parish Church of St. Michael the Arch-angel.‡

In 1712 James Tichborne mortgaged Aldershot Manor to Samuel Johnson, and in 1720 to Sir Charles and George Vernon. In 1788 the Manor became the seat of Godfrey Clarke, and in 1787 it was dealt with by fine between William Assheton and Francis Penyston, the latter being mentioned in 1816 as the holder.

The Manor was offered for sale by auction in 1831, and a copy of the sale sheet and plan are reproduced in J. A. Eggar's book, "Life and Customs in White's, Cobbett's and Kingsley's Country." The sale particulars read :

In Hampshire on the borders of Surrey. Eligible Estate, copyhold of inheritance and being subject to a nominal fine only, may be considered as freehold, the Land Tax has been redeemed. It is known as Aldershot Halimote Manor House and Estate situated in rural village of Aldershot, about 3 miles from market-town of Farnham, 9 from Guildford, 10 from Godalming and 36 from London ; it comprises a substantial built residence which by a moderate outlay might be rendered equal to the accommoda-tion of a family of first respectability, with pleasure grounds at the extremity of which a Church is discovered, garden, orchard, rookery, hop kiln, numerous farm and outbuildings and 115 acres

* "Victoria County History of Hampshire," Vol. IV, p. 3 (1911).
† The "Crondall Records," Part I (Warren & Son Ltd., Winchester).
‡ See p. 286.

of rich land laying very compact, 40 of which are fine grazing and forms a Park of great beauty surrounding the house, the remainder is arable and wood, in a high state of cultivation. The Estate is pleasingly studded with ornamental timber, giving a park like appearance. Also the Manor of Aldershot Halimote with all its Rights, Privileges and Immunities. A Court is held, various quit Rents receivable and a Game-keeper has been usually appointed. The Manor extends over about 3,000 acres of fine sporting country abounding with game and there are three packs of fox hounds in the neighbourhood; and will be sold by auction, by Mr. George Robins at the Auction Mart, opposite the Bank of England on Thursday the 14th day of July 1831 at 12 o'clock.

The whole property was bought at the auction by a Mr. Buckle, of Farnham, and later Mr. John Eggar inherited the property from Mr. Buckle, his uncle by marriage.* In 1842 Mr. Eggar sold the Manor and forty acres of parkland adjoining the house to a Mr. Bridges for £2,500 and the remainder of his property to his brother, Samuel Eggar. About 1847 the Manor House and grounds were purchased from Mr. Bridges by Captain G. Newcome, R.N., who died in 1884, leaving the estate to his widow. On the death of Captain G. Newcome's widow the Manor House was bequeathed to his nephew, Major Henry George Newcome, and when he died in 1895 it passed into the hands of his wife, who sold the House and Park to the Aldershot Urban District Council in 1920.

The Manor House which exists today was built in 1670. The original Manor House, known as Aldershot Place Mansion,† was on the site of the present-day Aldershot Park, near which traces have been found of the foundations of an ancient castellated mansion, said to have been visited by King John and Queen Elizabeth. Some parts of the walls, the portcullis and the drawbridge remained until the latter part of the eighteenth century, together with traces of the moat and fishpond which existed until they were obliterated by the construction of the present-day Bathing Pool. During the period of

* *Vide* "The Life and Customs in White's, Cobbett's, and Kingsley's Country," by J. A. Eggar (great-nephew of John Eggar) (Simpkin Marshall).

† There are references to Aldershot Place in the account book of a Mrs. Sarah Forbes, now in the possession of the Hampshire Record Office at Winchester. In this book is a note dated 17th November, 1732, recording an agreement she made with Francis Miller to pay half the Church and Poor Rate and all the window tax on Aldershot Place by bringing 5,000 peat (turfs) into her stables at Aldershot for her use. There is also a note concerning advice received from "Brother Cole" (of the Coles of Liss family) that forty fish would be enough to stock the moat, that they should be eleven inches long and ninepence or tenpence apiece. On 3rd July, 1736, there is another entry in the account book showing outgoings for the Church and Poor Rate on the house.

C

ownership by Mr. Charles D'Oridant in the eighties, the pond was described as a "fine sheet of water in the centre of the grounds abounding with fish of all fresh water descriptions." The present-day Aldershot Park Mansion, now the property of the Borough Council, was built in 1850 and was owned by Mr. Charles Barron.* The house and estate were later sold to Mr. John Black and afterwards to Mr. Charles D'Oridant. The last private owner was a Miss Kennedy, who sold the property to the Borough Council in 1920.

Other buildings in the Aldershot of 1850 which exist to this day are Aldershot Lodge and Elm Place, both in Church Lane East, the former having a history which has been traced to medieval days. The latter, built in the seventeenth century, was for many generations the home of the Allden family and later the residence of Mr. Richard Simmonds, a member of the Aldershot Urban District Council for many years.

Rock House, originally called Rock Place, in Sandford Road, was built about 1850. This was then the property of a Mr. Tom Hughes. Park Farm House, built in the early part of the nineteenth century, now stands between Haig Road and Wolfe Road, surrounded by the houses of the Chrismas Estate, which was built on the farmlands in 1930. The house, today the residence of Councillor S. N. Chrismas, has been in the possession of the Chrismas family since its purchase by Mr. William Chrismas from a Mr. Hugh Sears in the seventies. Park Farm, together with Holly Farm, was sold by auction in June, 1894, the former then being described in the notice of sale in *The Aldershot News* as a compact estate "with residence, extensive agricultural buildings and hop kilns and four pieces of hop, pasture, arable, and orchard land containing about 30 acres." Manor Cottage, which stands at the junction of High Street and Waterloo Road opposite Manor Park, bears the date "1851."

The next oldest houses to the Manor House are undoubtedly the old "Fox and Hounds" inn,† better known as the "Dog Kennels," situated on the Weybourne Road opposite the south end of Ayling Lane. These houses date from the Tudor or early Stuart period and were constructed of massive oak beams filled in with wattle and daub. Threatened by demolition in 1924, they were saved by the intervention of Mr. Walter Finch, of Ayling Barn. They were renovated, bricks

---

* One-time proprietor of the Pavilion Hotel, Folkestone.

† Owned in the eighteen-eighties by one Browning, who dispensed, it is recorded, "good ale, brewed from Hampshire malt and Farnham hops," for the delectation of such wayfarers who in summer time chose to take shelter under the "arboured benches" or in winter in the warmth of the "cozy old-fashioned ingle nook" —"Traditions about Aldershot," C. S. Herve (W. Straker & Co., London) (1881).

replacing the daub and wattle, but the old oak beams remain as they were when the houses were first constructed. It was here, in February, 1675, that (local legend has it) Nell Gwynn gave birth to an illegitimate son of Charles II.*

Other old buildings which existed a hundred years ago in the original Aldershot village have, as the years have passed, fallen before the tools of the demolition gangs as the town has grown, developed and progressed.

In 1850 the present-day Wellington Street was known as Lloyd's Lane, named after the farmer Robert Lloyd. It ran through fields of rye and potatoes and was so narrow that two carts could not pass each other. The last thatched cottage in what today is the centre of the town was demolished in 1895 and stood facing a large sand-pit in Wellington Street at the end of the Arcade which runs from Victoria Road. In 1850 it was the only house in Lloyd's Lane. Robert Lloyd, who died in 1855, was the head of the well-known Aldershot family which by 1850 had already been established in the area for over sixty years. In 1792 Robert Lloyd purchased his first acre of land for market gardening in what today is Wellington Street. The following was the deed of purchase:

---

* In his book, "Traditions about Aldershot" (W. Straker & Co., London) (1881), Charles S. Herve recorded the story of this local belief from material he collected from the "prattle of sundry old men and women, together with the semi-historical record of an old bank clerk named Piper, a pensioner of the eminent banking firm of Messrs. Knight of Farnham." He records how in February, 1675, Nell Gwynn was travelling between Portsmouth and London, accompanied by "two hand maidens and two servants in plain livery." Near Farnham the party was met by one Master Vernon, a staunch Cavalier, the son of a Royalist landowner who lived in a mansion between "Batchetlea [Badshot Lea] and Aldershot" (Aldershot Park Mansion). Vernon had been commissioned by the King to escort Mistress Nell between Farnham and Guildford. The route from Farnham led along what today is Weybourne Road. It was dark and raining and the King's mistress was showing signs of distress and fatigue. Immediate shelter was necessary and, although Aldershot Park and the Manor House were near by, it was decided to seek the shelter of the "Fox and Hounds" inn. The same evening a boy child was born to Mistress Nell, but born dead, owing doubtless to the lack of medical attention ; although the two servants had been sent off at the gallop through the night to find a surgeon, only the local village midwife, known as "Mother Squalls," was available to minister at the birth.

The little body was enclosed in a box and taken away the same night by "Jem May," "Mother Squalls' " son, accompanied by Master Vernon. Through the rain and darkness they went to Aldershot Parish Church, where a grave was dug by a yew tree in the churchyard. The body was covered by Vernon's cloak, and the grave filled in and covered to hide the appearance of the turned soil.

Vernon then rode to London to inform King Charles of the facts, and five days later the little cavalcade left the "Fox and Hounds" to resume the journey to London. The secret, although known to a dozen men and women, was well kept, the escort and others concerned doubtless being well rewarded for their silence in keeping the Royal secret.

THE MANOR AND HUNDRED ⎫ A view of Frank Pledge
OF CRONDALL IN THE   ⎬ Court Leet* and Court
COUNTY OF SOUTHTON   ⎭ for the Manor there
                            holden the 30th day of
October in the Thirty Third year of the reign of our Sovereign
Lord George the Third King of Great Britain and so forth and
in the year of our Lord 1792 before C. T. Herley Esq. Serjt.
at law Steward there.

At this Court came Robert Lloyd and claimed to be admitted
to all that—one cottage and two parcels of land late one parcel
containing by estimation one acre in Aldershott formerly called
Temples by virtue of an absolute surrender made by James
Coules out of court and since the last Court and entered and
recorded at this Court to whom the Lords of the said Manor by
the said Steward granted seizen TO HOLD to him his heirs
and assigns for ever according to the form and effect of the said
surrender and according to the Custom of the Manor and Hundred of Crondall YIELDING the accustomed rents, burthens
and services before due and of right accustomed and be paid
                            s d
for a fine 6d. and for an Heriot 2–6 and was admitted Tenant
and did his Fealty saving the right of Samuel Smith Mortgagee
of the said premises.

                    Exd.
                        C. T. HERLEY
                                Steward.

In 1855 Robert Lloyd's son Richard purchased "two roods and
twenty two perches" of adjoining land for £50 from one James
Reeves, and in June, 1857, purchased a further 77 feet of land facing
Wellington Street and 55 feet facing Victoria Road for the sum of £30.
In the early fifties Grosvenor Road was but a rough cart-track running
across Twynham's Field—the pastures adjoining Twynham's Farm.
Victoria Road was a footpath which traversed "Clerk's Land"—the
land of the Parish Clerk, now the Municipal Gardens—with fields on
either side known as Barn Field, Appleton's Field and Eight Acres
Field. These fields with much of the adjoining property were owned
by Mr. Richard Allden, and adjoined that owned by Mr. Eggar to the
south and the farm-lands of Mr. Stovold—the present-day West End.
The present-day Municipal Gardens, which formed part of the Parish
Clerk's land, occupy an area referred to in the Crondall Customary
of 1568, wherein it states :

---

* A local Court especially concerned with the maintenance of the Frank pledge—
a surety entered into by ten men, or a "tithing," to be responsible for any of their
number in a Court of Law (Meiklejohn).

That there is a parcel of lande caulled Claversden, containing by estimation 12½ acres, and one croft caulled The Clerke's Croft, containing by estimation 2½ acres, which severall parcells have bene taken out of all the severall yarde landes within the said Tythinge; and by Th' assent of the Lord of this Mannor and Hundred, and of the tenauntes within the same mannor and hundred, have bene allwayes past rembrance of man lymitted and appoynted to the maintenaunce and fyndinge of a clarcke, within the parishe churche of Aldershotte for the tyme beinge; for which the said parishe church doth pay yearelye unto the lorde of this manor, by eaven portions at the feasts of the aforesaid, fourpence.*

In 1850 High Street was but a track leading from Ash, through "Aldershott Street," through the present-day site of the Cavalry Barracks and the West End to the London–Winchester turnpike road. It is recorded that in the West End the cart ruts were so deep that wheels sank into them up to the axles.

Such was Aldershot village immediately prior to the purchase of the adjoining land by the War Department and the subsequent establishment of "The Camp." The population in 1852 was only 875. In the "Victoria County History of Hampshire" it is said of Aldershot that "previous to 1855 it was one of the most pleasing and picturesque hamlets in Hampshire, consisting of the Church, the two important houses called Aldershot Manor and Aldershot Place, two or three farmhouses, and the village green."

Aldershot Church was then described as "an ancient structure of mixed architecture, with a brick tower and three bells. The perpetual curacy, valued at £64, being in the patronage of Frederick Eggar, J. Andrews, J. Allden and W. Tice, Esqrs., and in the incumbency of the Rev. James Dennett, who had a good Parsonage House, which was repaired in 1825, at the cost of £400." The benefice had been augmented some years previously with a Parliamentary grant of £1,800.† The tithes belonged to St. Cross Hospital, at Winchester, but were leased to the patrons of the Church. At that time the poor parishioners had the interest of £30, left by a Mrs. Raleigh Viner,‡ and vested with the Overseers.

The only building standing on the land now occupied by the War Department property, stretching northwards from the town, was the old Union Workhouse, then in use as a Union School for pauper children. The building exists to this day as the District Pay Office,

---

* "The Crondall Records," Part I (Hampshire Record Society) (Warren & Son Ltd., Winchester).
† This may have given rise to the local legend recorded on p. 288.
‡ See p. 287.

lying back from Hospital Hill. One can well imagine this bleak, lonely
building a hundred years ago, standing among the bracken, heather
and gorse of the rising heathland, far removed from the few houses
in "Aldershott Street."

The country to the north and west of Aldershot was barren waste
heathland, undeveloped, uncultivated and in the main untraversed, a
wide expanse of poor sandy soil, covered with gorse, heather and
bracken. There were but few trees, the plantations of firs which break
the landscape today being of comparatively recent growth. Aldershot
village stood as an outpost of civilization on the borders of this
expanse of wild and windswept heathland, traversed only by the
London–Winchester turnpike road, and with only six buildings
between the village and the "Tumbledown Dick" inn at Farnborough :
Heath Villa,* by Hungry Hill, the White House, on Dollys Hill, the
Union Workhouse, the "Row Barge" inn, by the Wharf Bridge over
the Basingstoke Canal, "Bagman's Castle," and a large country house
by Cockadobby Hill. To the east and south, however, lay more
green and cultivated lands, dotted with farms, market gardens, pastures
and hop-fields ; the country between Ash, Tongham, Badshot Lea
and Farnham being a farmers' hop-growing area. It was this agricultural industry which led to the opening, in 1849, of the railway from
Guildford to Farnham, through Ash Green and Tongham, which
until 1870 was the nearest railway station to Aldershot.

---

* Referred to in Queen Victoria's Journal (14th May, 1859) as "Heath House."
This house was demolished about 1860-1 when Anglesey House was built on the
site, as the residence of the Cavalry Brigade commander. See p. 299. (Royal
Archives, Windsor.)

CHAPTER TWO

HISTORICAL ALDERSHOT

A.D. 885-1850

SUCH was Aldershot a hundred years ago, but, as has been seen, the town has links with the past far deeper than most people realize. Unfortunately, Aldershot in its earlier days was not very significant, and in consequence has been overlooked in many historical records, compared with other villages in the vicinity, which have secured lasting references in the national archives. However, even if Aldershot's history is obscure, it is, all the same, of ancient origin. Apart from early records, its antiquity is proved by the existence of its Parish Church, parts of which date back to the twelfth century, whilst its archives go back to the year 1571. The presence of the church itself is sufficient evidence of the fact that at the time of its establishment there must have been a community of sufficient size to warrant the appointment of a minister to serve their spiritual needs.

One of the most striking features of Aldershot is the remarkable number of ways in which the name of the hamlet, village and town has been spelt throughout the ages. There are records of nineteen ways of spelling the name : ALRESHETE (*circa* 1248, the first mention in "The Crondall Records"), ALDRESHOLT, ALRESHUT, ALRESHUTE, ALRESSHUTE, ALRESHOTT, ALRISCHOOT, ALRESHATE, ALRESCHATE, ALDERSHATE, ALDERSHUT, ALDERSHUTE (fourteenth century) ALDER-SCHOTE, ALDERSHARE (*circa* 1575), ALDRISSHOT, ALDRISSHOTT, ADDER-SHOT (*circa* 1642-1645),* ALDERSHOTT (*circa* 1667-1850) and ALDERSHOT.†

In a map of "Hant-shire" published in 1627 in Speed's Atlas, Alder-shot is spelt "Aldershate" and shown by the then conventional sign for a church ; and Saxton's map of the South-Eastern Counties (1575) shows it as "Aldershare."

There is even inconsistency in the spelling of the name in maps

---

* *Vide* "The Civil War in Hampshire, 1642-45," by The Rev. G. N. Goodwin (J. & E. Bumpus) (1904).

† It is interesting to note that in the official documents relating to the purchase of the War Department lands, the village is spelt "Aldershot," but in Press reports *circa* 1854-1860 it is spelt "Aldershott."

issued by the same publisher within the course of a few years. In the map of Surrey published by Richard Blome in 1667 the spelling is "Aldershott," but in another map by the same cartographer published in 1673 it is shown as "Aldershot," whilst Robert Morden's map of 1688 reverts to the spelling "Aldershott."

However, Aldershot, in all its forms of spelling throughout the ages, means "wood of alders," derived from the Old English "alorsceat." The word "sceat" is recorded in Eilert Ekwall's "Concise Oxford Dictionary of English Place Names" as a piece of cloth, quarter of the earth, corner, or strip of land, whilst "alor" is the name which has now become "Alder." Place names having firstly a tree or plant name developed into meaning a piece of land left untilled and overgrown with trees or plants, or even a belt or piece of woodland or park between arable land. The word "sceat" varies in Middle English sources, appearing as "shet," "shat," "shute" or "shite," which accounts for the many varied spellings which have appeared. The word "alorsceat" has been recorded prior to the Norman Conquest. It may well be concluded from these facts that the first habitations in Aldershot were erected near a belt or copse of alder trees in the area whence the original hamlet took its name.

The suffix "shott" dates from Anglo-Saxon times when cultivated land around small communities was divided into acres—a day's ploughing—and then grouped into "shots" consisting of from twelve to thirty acres or more according to the cultivated area of the village or hamlet. This suffix "shot," however, prevails today only in the area around the Borough within a radius of some fifteen miles (i.e., Bagshot, Bramshot, Badshot Lea, Cowshot and Ewshot).

The district of Aldershot can provide a record of human activities from earliest times. The gravels of the river terraces of the Wey and the Blackwater have furnished a wealth of Palæolithic flint weapons and implements, whilst the surface soil has yielded a great number of flint implements of later stages of human endeavour and culture, the Solutrean, Aurignacean and Magdalenian phases being represented. The round tumuli which are to be seen in several places represent Neolithic and Bronze Ages.

In 1828 two brothers named Lefroy,* when snipe shooting in Bourley Bottom, discovered a hoard of 101 gold coins, one of which bore the name of Eligius, moneylender of the Merovingian kings between the years A.D. 628 and A.D. 641.

Early entrenchments exist on the range of hills to the south and

---

* Mr. Charles and Mr. Anthony Lefroy, of Ewshot House, then lads of eighteen and sixteen, members of the Lefroy family who were the Lords of the Manor of Ewshot.

west of Aldershot. Among these are two important prehistoric earthworks : "Caesar's Camp," the large promontory fortress, and "Batt's
Hog Stye," in Claycart Bottom, which is of a later but still prehistoric
date. This is a small square enclosure with rounded corners and four
surrounding ramparts* and three ditches. It may well have been the
homestead of an early Celtic chieftain. Dr. Williams Freeman, the
archæologist, has expressed the opinion† that Batt's Hog Stye was
the homestead of a chieftain who lived in the early Iron Age. Batt was a
Saxon hobgoblin akin to "Lob-lie-by-the-fire,"‡ and Dob or "Dobby"
was the old English name for a goblin, from which the tumulus
known as Cockadobby Hill opposite the Queen's Hotel, Farnborough, is said to have been named.

Caesar's Camp, according to the records and documents relating
to the Hundred of Crondall, recalls the Roman occupation, but
authorities on the subject insist that Caesar's Camp is of greater
antiquity and that it dates from the time of the early Britons. The
older name for this prehistoric earthwork, said to date from the early
Iron Age, was Bricksbury. The name "Caesar's Camp" was given
to it, and other similar earthworks, by eighteenth-century antiquaries.

It has been asserted that the original inhabitants of the area were,
about three centuries before the arrival of Julius Caesar, driven north
and exterminated by the Belgæ, who, crossing the Rhine into Gaul,
later crossed the Channel, landing near Southampton, pushed north
and overran Hampshire, expelling the Segontiaci, a tribe then inhabit-
ing North Hants and part of Berkshire ; and that it was the Belgæ who
first fortified Caesar's Camp as an outlying defensive point. It is,
however, certain that prior to the Roman invasion in 55 B.C.§ Caesar's
Camp was an outlying fort separating the territories of the Belgæ
and the Regni tribes. The entrenchment on Caesar's Camp is of
irregular shape with triple vallum and is probably early British. It
has been suggested‖ that it may have been occupied by Alfred before
his defeat, in A.D. 894, of the Northmen at Farnham.

---

* There are only three or four earthworks of a similar nature and pattern in
the country.

† *Vide* "An Introduction to Field Archæology as illustrated by Hampshire,"
by Dr. J. P. Williams Freeman, M.D. (Macmillan & Co. Ltd.) (1915).

‡ "Lob-lie-by-the-Fire—the Lubber fiend, as Milton calls him—is a rough kind
of Brownie or House Elf, supposed to haunt some north-country homesteads."
—"Lob-Lie-by-the-Fire," by Juliana Horatia Ewing (George Bell & Sons) (1874).

§ The only relics in Aldershot of the Roman occupation which have been found
are potsherds of the third century A.D. which were found by Dr. J. H. Gibson in
a garden near the Parish Church, where he found traces of what appears to have been
a small pottery. In a field which existed at the rear of Church Hill was a small
pond which may well have been the source of the clay used by the potters.

‖ *Vide* Murray's Handbook for Travellers in Hampshire, 1894, and "Sketches of
'The Camp' at Aldershot" (Andrews & Lucy) (1858).

The Rev. Canon Francis O'Farrell, O.B.E., L.D., Rector of St. Joseph's Roman Catholic Church, who died in 1942, devoted much of his time to archæological research in the Aldershot area, and it is due to his interest and his labours that considerable evidence of local life in the Iron, Bronze and Stone Ages was brought to light. It was Father O'Farrell who made many of the discoveries which have given us an insight into early civilization within the present-day boundaries of the Borough.* His research took him on to the War Department lands to the west of the Farnborough Road, turning to the beds of gravel in the locality in searching for the earliest forms of flint instruments. The deposits of gravel covering the plateaux of Bricksbury, Hungry Hill and Caesar's Camp are prehuman and have never been found to contain hand-made instruments. The only other local gravel deposits are those which mark the old Wey–Blackwater river which are found on the eastern edge of the Borough, and these gravels should contain Palæolithic implements of the types found in abundance in the Farnham pits of the same old river.

A considerable period of time is accepted as separating such a stage of human civilization from that of the flint implements which are found on or near the present surface of the soil and those which belong to the Neolithic Age. Up to the year 1910 Father O'Farrell had heard reports of Neolithic implements having been found in the neighbourhood, but there is only one known specimen in existence—an arrowhead which was found on Redan Hill by a schoolboy in that year.

The uncultivated War Department lands to the west of the Farnborough Road, which for the great part have never been cultivated, had been regarded as worthless as an area for research despite the presence of Batt's Hog Stye, but in May, 1910, Father O'Farrell during one of his walks noticed in the sand near Brown Loaf Hill an object which he thought to be an old Martini-Henry rifle bullet. He picked it up out of the sand and found it to be an undoubted implement of flint, what is styled a "fabricator," used in the secondary flaking of other flint implements. He immediately made a systematic search over every bit of waste ground in the vicinity, and within a few days was rewarded with the discovery of a hammer-head, used for primary flaking, a broken arrowhead, and several worked flakes.

The next stage in Father O'Farrell's research was to establish that the few specimens he had obtained, and the quantity that he began to find, were not stray pieces dropped in the locality, but that the implements had actually been made in the area. He obtained several series of flakes

---

* Vide "A Contribution to the Prehistoric Archæology of Aldershot," by the Rev. F. O'Farrell (Official Guide to the Borough of Aldershot, 1929).

struck from the same block, and found that some of them could be fitted again to one another. In several places were accumulations of "pot boilers," showing where man had lived and cooked his food, and there were definite "factories" where he made his implements. These sites were mainly in the area of the Caesar's Camp ranges and on and about the cliff edge of Caesar's Camp.

A solitary specimen of a flint implement was found in 1911 by Father O'Farrell on Sunny Hill, near the Royal Pavilion, and this is the only evidence of Palæolithic man which has so far been discovered in the Borough.

The net result of Father O'Farrell's discoveries and research over a period of years from the beginning of the century was that some thousands of flakes and hundreds of implements were collected. The majority of the implements were "scrapers" of various forms and sizes ; cores and cones used as planes were fairly frequent ; arrowheads of different types also occurred, but were rare. Some implements were worn with use, but others were in fine condition, whilst some had been cast aside half made, spoiled by some flaw or bad flaking. These implements were varied and it was difficult to decide to what particular phase of human culture they belonged. The particular tract of land on which they were found has been practically unaltered for ages. The 600-ft. plateau adjoining Caesar's Camp has been there since before man came into existence, and therefore evidence of every possible phase of human culture may conceivably be found upon it. The sandy slopes and "bottoms" have been more or less the same since the oldest Palæolithic ages came to an end. Flint implements are indestructible so far as sub-aerial influences are concerned, therefore every particle of flint ever used by man is still there and all ages of culture may be represented. Experts whom Father O'Farrell consulted were inclined to see in some cases resemblance to Aurignacean and Solutrean types ; many seemed to correspond closely to those found in France at Bruniquel, of Magdalenian type; whilst some were clearly Neolithic.*

*   *   *   *   *

The first record of Aldershot in our history is in King Alfred's will (*circa* A.D. 880-885), wherein he bequeathed Crondall to Ethelm, his nephew, Aldershot being included in the bequest.

Aldershot was included in the Hundred of Crondall, which was formed from the north-eastern portion of Hampshire and comprised some thirty thousand acres of land ; the boundaries being defined as

---

* *Vide* "A Contribution to the Prehistoric Archæology of Aldershot," by the Rev. F. O'Farrell (Official Guide to the Borough of Aldershot, 1929).

running along the Hartford Bridge Flats—between Camberley and Hartley Wintney—and following the course of the River Blackwater to Ash Bridge (Bryda's Ford) and thence round by Aldershot to Crondall.

In A.D. 975 King Edgar* gave the Hundred of Crondall to the monastery of the Cathedral Church of Winchester as "a perpetual pension for the support of the monks dwelling therein." The Hundred of Crondall was originally placed under the supervision of the Rector of Crondall, but in the course of time had to be provided with several chapels in the outlying districts of the "hundred," and subdivided into "tithings." In later years the districts of these chapels were redesignated "parishes" instead of "tithings." The chapelry of Aldershot had no subdivisions although it contained exempted lands belonging to Waverley Abbey.†

The Hundred of Crondall remained under the control of Winchester until the dissolution of the monasteries in 1539, when it was surrendered to King Henry VIII. Two years later, however, the King granted Crondall to the newly constituted Dean and Chapter of Winchester Cathedral.

During the years of Cromwell's Commonwealth (1649-1660) the land was seized by Parliament, but in 1661, following the return to the throne of King Charles II, it was restored to the Dean and Chapter, with whom it continued for two hundred years until 1861, when, like other church property, it was vested in the Ecclesiastical Commission.

During the long period from A.D. 975 until the middle of last century the Aldershot tenants were represented by their "tything men," who attended the Bishop's Court at the Lawday House‡ and the Prior's Court at Crondall twice a year, at Lady Day and at Michaelmas. The Aldershot tenants had the right of grazing for their cattle on the common land, the cutting of turf for fuel and of bracken for litter, the peat turf being in great demand for fuel in the manufacture of coarse local pottery.

It is strange that Aldershot is not mentioned in the Domesday Book,§ for it is mentioned, as Alreshete, in the Patents Roll of 1276† and even earlier; in 1248 in the Compotus Roll,† which shows, among the outgoings of the "Crundal Manor," "Fifteen shillings for fifteen ploughers in Halle, Bramshete, Sewode *and Alreshete* for ploughing released in winter"; whilst among the perquisites of the Manor

---

* Reigned A.D. 959-975.
† "The Crondall Records," Part I.
‡ Situated on the Odiham Road, at the junction of the roads from Hale and Upper Hale and the road which runs northwards out of Farnham.
§ *Vide* the description of the "Corondel Hundret" in the Domesday Survey.

of that period were "ten shillings for the tithing of Alreshete that it may present sentences of the Crown."

In the Court Roll of 1281,* which recorded the proceedings of the Manorial Courts held by the Prior of St. Swithun's, it is recorded that "The Tithing of Alreshate was find five shillings because it did not come as it was summoned to the Hundred (Court) of the Term of S. Martin," and further that "Avice, who was the wife of Hugh the Miller, comes and surrenders into the hands of the lord one messuage and a virgate of land in Alreschate." In 1300 it is on record that Aldershot paid a heavier tax than either Cove or Farnborough.

Alreshute is again mentioned in 1316 as being part of the Hundred of "Crundal," belonging to the Prior of St. Swithun's, Winchester.

In the Custumal and Rental Rolls of St. Swithun Priory, Winchester, of 1287* there are a number of references to "Alresshate," several entries listing the "holders of a virgate"† and referring to the rent and conditions of holding the land. Typical of these entries are the following : "William of Cranemore holds ten acres of encroachment in payment, therefore of 4/- at the feast of St. Michael, and he shall find one man for one day in the autumn for the Lord's harvest day service" ; and "Adam de Estfelde holds one virgate† of land on payment of 2/- at the feast of St. Michael and 9½d. for pondpany and half a churchscot of white wheat and two hens for churchscot and one hen against Christmas and five eggs at Easter, and he shall perform the services in every respect as Warden and Purveyor."

Among the thirty-seven land-holders mentioned in this Custumal Roll were Adam, the Clerk ; Elias Wilde ; Hugo, the Miller ; John Aylward ; Matildis de Cranemore ; William, the Carpenter ; Warren le Achatour ; Ralph and Robert le Wychare and Richard Tongham, who with others held between them some eighty acres of land.

The Crondall Customary has preserved to this day the name of every tenant of the Manor in the sixteenth century and the names of their holdings, some of which have survived until today. This Customary of the Manor of Crondall was shaped in the form of an indenture with a series of schedules setting out the lands of the tenants, their holdings and its acreage, its rents and other services. This document was drawn up as a result of the uncertainty which existed regarding the tenures and customs of the Manor of Crondall after the establishment in 1541 of the Dean and Chapter of Winchester. In order to put an end to the uncertainty, approval was given to the drawing up of a new Customary showing the name of every tenant, with the name of his holding, and its acreage, and the rent and services

---

* "The Crondall Records," Part I.
† A virgate was between 24 and 30 acres.

he owed; and each tenant agreeing, on a day, surrendered his holding to the Steward and had re-seising of it under the new agreement. This was effected on 16th October, 1569, and it detailed how the land in the "Tithing of Aldrisshott"* was let, and shows that the sum total of rents arising from the tithing was £16 14s. 5d. Here is a typical entry from the Customary† :

> John White, Knight.‡—To the same court there held on the day and year above named, came John White, Knight, who holds in like manner according to the custom of the manor, a meadow called Pryse meade, containing one and a half acres of land with oppurtenances in Alreshott. . . . And now in the aforesaid Court the said John White, Knight, surrendered the aforesaid meadow with oppurtenances into the hands of the lord, with the intention that the lord should re-grant the aforesaid meadow to the said John White, Knight, his heirs and assigns, according to the custom of the manor in the aforesaid indentures specified and declared. Paying there for yearly to the said Dean, etc., 8d. and the other burdens and services therefor due by the said indentures And he shall give to the lord as a heriot according to the form of the said indentures, nothing, because it is not heriotable. And in like manner the heirs and assigns of the said John White shall give to the lord as a fine when it falls 2s., and not more. And the same John gave to the lord as a fine for such entrance thereupon had 2s., and for a heriot, nothing. Which aforesaid fine the lord of his special grace pardoned and re-gave him and he did fealty to the lord and was admitted tenant thereof.

Two copies of this valuable and historic document exist to this day. One is in the possession of the Dean and Chapter of Winchester Cathedral, the other was until recent years held by the Church Wardens of the Aldershot Parish Church. This copy was discovered in 1857 by Mr. Francis Joseph Baigent in an old chest in the belfry of the Parish Church of St. Michaels, where its existence had been forgotten. When the chest was opened, with the help of a blacksmith, beneath

---

* The following place names within the parish are recorded in the Crondall Customary (1568): Home Grove, Owle's Hole, Le Clarck's Lane Ende, Rough Grove, Gallowe Hill, Cranmore Wood and a heath called Hopcoxe.—"Victoria County History of Hampshire."

† "The Crondall Records," Part I.

‡ Sir John White was born at Farnham, the sixth son of Robert White, of Farnham. He was Master of the Grocers' Company, A.D. 1555-6; Sheriff of the City of London, 1556-7; Lord Mayor of London, 1563-1565, during which time he was knighted; Alderman of Cornhill, 1566-1571; Member of Parliament for the City, 1571-2; Treasurer of St. Bartholomew's Hospital, 1549; President of Bethlem and Bridewell, 1568-1573, and of Christ's Hospital and Surveyor General of Hospitals, 1572-3. He died and was buried in Aldershot (see p. 287)—"The Parish Church of St. Michael the Archangel, Aldershot," by Dr. J. H. Gibson (The British Publishing Co. Ltd.) (1948).

an immense cobweb thick with dust, from the churchwardens' bills and memoranda in the chest it was evident that the chest had not been opened for a very long period. The Customary was, it is recorded, "in a fine state of preservation."* The document passed into the custody of Mr. Richard Eve, the Vestry Clerk,† who claimed the official right of holding it. The Customary was later taken into the custody of the Aldershot firm of solicitors, Messrs. Herrington & Carmichael, who presented it to the Borough Council in 1947 to hold on trust for the people of Aldershot. Arrangements were made for the historic document, which is composed of thirty-three large skins of parchment, to be cleaned and preserved by the Keeper of Manuscripts at the British Museum.‡

The Parish Church of St. Michael the Archangel dates from the twelfth century, although its origin is certainly of an earlier date as it has been recorded that a "chapel of ease" was built at Aldershot in the early eleventh century. The chancel of St. Michael's is clearly of twelfth-century construction of chalk and ironstone. The earliest registers of the church go back to 1571. From a much earlier date, however, Aldershot was served from the Crondall Church. The earliest known record occurs during the episcopacy of William of Wykeham, 1367-1398, but it is considered probable that a church existed long before this date.

The old records of the Parish Church§ date from 1571, and there are three books, the first covering the period 1571 to 1719, in which baptisms are recorded from 1571, burials from 1581, and marriages from 1590. This book ends with the entries dated May, 1719. The second book, which embraces the years from 1714 to 1796, includes marriages from 1714 to 1754 and three marriages of previous years

---

* "The Crondall Records," Part I.
† "The Vestry" was an authority, in Aldershot, until 1927. It survived under the ancient Vestry Act by which any ratepayer, regardless of creed, was entitled to attend meetings of the Vestry of the Parish Church, and at these meetings this authority was empowered to transact certain local affairs, and to elect the "People's Churchwarden" of the Parish Church. This Vestry Council was a relic of antiquity which survived long after the formation of the local Board of Health (1857), the Urban District Council (1894), and, even later, the Borough Council. One of its functions was the election of the members of the Burial Board. The meetings were on occasions attended by a considerable number of townspeople, but there were many occasions when but a handful of residents were present, empowered under the ancient act to control, in some directions, the destinies of the town. Another function was the making of the Poor Rate, the Vestry Clerk forwarding it to the local authority. The Poor Rate was merged into the General District Rate on the abolition of the Vestry. The Vestry authority in Aldershot was abolished on 1st April, 1927, under the Rating and Valuation Act, 1925.
‡ The Customary is now on view in the Municipal Buildings (see page 306).
§ Vide "The Hampshire Parish Records," Vol. II, edited by W. P. W. Phillimore and S. Andrews (1900), which lists all marriages in Aldershot, extracted from the Parish Records, 1590-1812 (The Hampshire Record Society).

which had been omitted from the first volume, burials from 1718 to
1796, and baptisms from 1720 to 1794. This second book is badly
written and the spelling is bad; a number of pages have been torn
out, but it has been thought (by the Hampshire Record Society) that
they may well have been blank pages. The third volume of records
covers the period 1754 to 1812.

The Parish Church is composed of four parts : The present-day
Lady Chapel, originally the main chancel of the village church—the
stone tracery of the windows is variously dated from 1270 to the early
fourteenth century; the tower, built of red brick and dating from
about 1600—one of the bells bears the date 1611; the south aisle,
built in 1865 when the church was enlarged following the increase in
population; and the main aisle, chancel and north aisle, which were
built in the early part of this century. In the course of enlargements
and rebuilding portions of the original twelfth-century building have
been replaced.

*   *   *   *   *

Although there is no record of any major engagements at Aldershot
between the Royalists and Parliamentary forces during the Civil War,
there is no doubt that skirmishes and patrol activity took place in
the vicinity. At the outbreak of war Farnham Castle was held for
Parliament by George Wither. During his absence whilst seeking
more active assistance from Sir Richard Onslow, who commanded the
Roundhead forces in Surrey, the Castle was occupied by Royalists
under Sir John Denham. He in turn was driven out by Sir William
Waller, who continued to hold it for Parliament as a depot for troops
and stores. Farnham was the Parliamentary base for the siege of
Basing House, and during this time there were numerous minor
encounters in the area between the opposing forces, one recorded
engagement, thought to be in the area of Aldershot Common, taking
place on 27th January, 1645. On this day a hundred and twenty men
of Goring's Horse "sallied forth from Basing House and attacked
two small troops at Crondall and Addershot [Aldershot]."* Many
of the Parliamentary troops escaped, owing to their being quartered at
scattered farmhouses, but the Royalists must have been well pleased
with the result of the engagement, for it is recorded that fifty men and
forty horses were captured, including a Lieutenant, two Cornets and
a Quartermaster.

In the Prince Consort's Library there is preserved a stone shot, a
little larger than a cricket-ball, dating from this period, which supports

---

* "The Civil War in Hampshire, 1642-45," by The Rev. G. N. Goodwin (J. & E.
Bumpus) (1904).

the records of actions in the area. The shot was found in 1863 on Eelmoor Common buried three feet below the surface.

The first military association, as we know it, with the Aldershot area was in 1792 during the manoeuvres which were held in the district. A camp was established on Beacon Hill to the west of Caesar's Camp for troops participating in the exercises. The success of the manoeuvres and the suitability of the ground undoubtedly led some sixty years later to the establishment of the camp at Chobham, and the subsequent Government decision to purchase land in the area for a permanent military training area. The 1792 manoeuvres were among the first of their kind and set a pattern which was later adopted for many "sham fights," manoeuvres, exercises and schemes, as they have been known throughout the years, in the Aldershot area.

The troops taking part in this early exercise were commanded by the Duke of Richmond, the Master-General of Ordnance, and the force was composed of two regiments of cavalry, the 10th[*] and 11th[†] Light Dragoons, two brigades of infantry, the 1st Brigade composed of the 2nd[‡] and 3rd[§] Regiments of Foot and the 2nd Brigade made up of the 14th[||] and 29th[¶] Foot ; in addition were two batteries of Artillery and a Military Train. A camp was established for this force on 23rd July, 1792, at Wickham Bushes, south of Easthampstead. On the 27th the troops moved to a camp at Hartford Bridge, and on the night of 31st July/1st August moved to a camp on Beacon Hill to the west of Caesar's Camp. The troops remained there until 4th August, when they returned to Wickham Bushes for a Royal Review on the 6th. The exercise was completed and camp broken two days later.

* * * * . *

In a map of the area[**] prepared by W. Eaden, "Geographer to His Majesty the King and H.R.H. The Prince of Wales," which was published in July, 1792, by W. Faden, of Charing Cross, and described as a "Plan of the country round Bagshot showing encampments of H.M. Forces Commanded by His Grace The Duke of Richmond," Aldershot village is shown, together with Aldershot Place, the Parish Church and Ash Bridge. The present South Camp area was marked as Windmill Clump, whilst the Long Valley area was described as Aldershot Common.

---

* Now The 10th Royal Hussars.
† Now The 11th Hussars (Prince Albert's Own).
‡ Now The Queen's Royal Regiment.
§ Now The Royal East Kent Regiment (The Buffs).
|| Now The West Yorkshire Regiment.
¶ Now The 1st Bn. The Worcestershire Regiment.
** A copy of which is preserved in the Prince Consort's Library.

D

Across this common was a series of posts which marked the route to Aldershot from the west. It was along this track that droves of cattle and sheep were driven from the West of England and Wales to London, a practice which continued for several years after the establishment of "The Camp," the drovers thereby avoiding the main roads and traversing a track in order that the herds might graze on the way and at night. This old route led into Aldershot by way of a track which exists today in the road between the Royal Pavilion and the Royal Garrison Church. The route continued through Cargate and down to "Aldershott Street" and on to the Ash Road, past North Town and on to Ash, and so towards Guildford. Alternatively a less frequented route led along the south of Aldershot Park, across the Blackwater, and along Green Lane, Tongham, to Ash Green.

*   *   *   *   *

The first record of the population of Aldershot was in 1725, when James Forde, Minister of Aldershot, in response to a questionnaire sent to all clergy by the Bishop of Winchester in which he asked "About what number of souls according to the best information you can muster do you suppose to be in your parish ?" reported the number in his parish to be "six score and fifteen."* By 1801 the population had risen to 494. In the ten years from 1801 to 1811 the number was increased by only four. In 1821 the total population was 525 and ten years later 665, and by 1841 it had increased by twenty.

The first Sunday school was established by the Rev. Christopher Thurger between 1820 and 1824 in a building erected opposite the site of the present parish hall. The first perpetual curate—the Rev. Reginald Rabbit—was appointed to the Parish Church in 1828.

In John Gorton's Topographical Dictionary of Great Britain and Ireland, published in 1833, Aldershot is noted as being situated 3¾ miles north-east of the "Parish Town of Farnham," and having a population of 525. Aldershot village is described as "a parish in the Basingstoke Division of the Crondall Hundred a chapelry to the vicarage of Crondall," the living being a perpetual curacy and donation in the archdeaconry and diocese of Winchester in the patronage, dated 1829, of John Andrews, Esq., "and others."

The annual poor rate valuation was £15. It is interesting to find on record that at one time a rate of 2½d. in the £ sufficed to produce all the money required for the upkeep of the village, and even in the early days of the last century the rate varied from that sum to 1s. 3d., although there is a record of a rate of 9s. in the £ having been levied

---

* "Victoria County History of Hampshire," Vol. IV.

in 1804 for the relief of the poor. In 1831 a rate was made "for the composition money of the parish of Aldershott in the County of Southampton of all persons in the said parish liable to do statute work on the highways, with the annual value of their lands." The total rate for the year was £9 8s. 10½d., of which only £8 3s. 10½d. was collected. In 1836 a rate of 10d. in the £ was made "for the repair of the highways for the parish of Aldershott in the County of Southampton." In 1839 a 5d. rate produced the sum of £38 19s. 4d., whilst two years later the rate collected was £78 8s. 5d.; but ten years later, in 1851, the authorities called for only £42 1s. 3d. from the landowners to meet all expenditure.

An interesting map of North West Hampshire, published on 1st May, 1816, shows Aldershot (the village being spelt with one "t"). The map was engraved at the "Drawing Room" of the Tower (of London), under the direction of Colonel Mudge, by Benjamin Baker and assistants, the writing being executed by one Ebenezer Bourne. The map shows Aldershot Place, North Lane, West End, Windmill Clump (the Windmill Hill of today), the White House, which stood in the area of Dollys Hill just off the Farnborough Road, and the "Row Barge" inn near the Aldershot Wharf on the Basingstoke Canal. The same places are marked in the Ordnance Survey Map of 1821, and in addition the brick-and-wood cottage with wooden stables and outhouses standing today in the grounds of Vine Cottage in the Farnborough Road below Blandford House is shown marked as "Bagman's Castle"; an ironical title associating it with the local belief that it was used as a highwayman's "hideout." There is also a large house shown at the junction of what today is Government House Road and the Farnborough Road.*

In 1841 a large-scale map (three chains to an inch) of the Parish of Aldershot was drawn by J. Streat of Ash to mark all the tithe parcels of land in the parish. This old map, which is still in existence, is signed by F. O. Martin, the Assistant Tithe Commissioner, and bears the certificate of the Tithe Commissioners, William Blamire and Richard Jones, who certified this map to be a copy or plan of the map referred to in "the apportioning of the Rent Charges in lieu of Tithes in the Parish."

The tithe parcels of land, which are numbered up to five hundred (number 500 being Aldershot Green), were all within the area bounded by the Blackwater on the south and east and on the west the turnpike road, with the exception of a few parcels in the area of Claycart

---

* Until the building of Government House this area was known as "The Guard's Enclosure," for it was on this site that regiments of the Brigade of Guards used to camp during training.

Bottom, where a brick kiln is marked. The northern boundaries of the tithe parcels run on a general line from Claycart Bottom to Deadbrook Pond, running just north of the Union Workhouse.

Eleven farms are shown on the map; they are unnamed, but are identified as Ayling Farm, West End Farm, Manor Farm, Boxall's Farm, Parkhouse Farm, Park Farm, Yew Tree Farm, North Farm, Holly Farm, Sheeling Farm and Herrett's Farm, and there are a number of scattered small buildings in the Pavilion Road area.

Only four roads are marked: Cranmore Lane is shown as Cranmer Lane, North Lane, Malt House Lane (Lower Newport Road) and Church Lane; and the other named places are the Parish Church, the Manor House, Aldershot Lodge and Place, the "Red Lion" and the "Row Barge" Inn, on the turnpike road, whilst Rowhill's Copse is marked as "Rough Hills Copse."

In 1841 the parish contained some 2,700 acres of heath and common land, 731 acres of arable land, 19 acres of hop fields, 530 acres of meadow land and pastures, 130 acres of woodland and 20 acres of buildings and gardens.*

*   *   *   *   *

Although obscure, and without any place of note in our nation's history, Aldershot had throughout the centuries been one of the countless little villages which went into the pattern of England. Self-supporting agriculturally and producing grain and hops from its cultivated land for sale in the Farnham markets, our predecessors had played their part in our national life in peaceful, undisturbed and undeveloped surroundings. They lived in a small community, their lives closely identified with the families of the first large homes. They worshipped at our Parish Church, and brought up their families to follow in their footsteps in the close-knit life of a typical small English village, depending upon its own labours for its existence.

Little did the villagers of Aldershot in 1850 dream of the great change which was to come but four short years hence!

---

* County Topographies: "Hampshire." Edited by E. R. Kelly, M.A., F.S.S Kelly & Co., London) (1875).

CHAPTER THREE

THE ESTABLISHMENT OF "THE CAMP"

1854-1862

It was in 1853 that a decision was reached by the Government to make use of the extensive heath and common land in the Aldershot area for military training purposes. This decision was the outcome of the dissatisfaction expressed in ministerial and military circles regarding the inadequate facilities then existing for the training of troops, and also the fact that expense would be saved by concentrating troops in heath and moorland instead of paying out compensation after exercises in cultivated areas.

It must be realized that prior to the establishment of the camp at Aldershot in 1854 no garrison or camp existed in the whole country for the concentration or training of troops on a large scale. The British Army at home were stationed in recognized long-established garrisons, most of which had been military centres from earliest times, and the garrisons occupied castles, forts and similar old defensive installations. London, Chatham, Hounslow, Dover, York, Plymouth, Pembroke, Portsmouth, Windsor, Woolwich, Edinburgh, Dublin and Chester were all such garrisons, none of which, with the exception of Woolwich and Hounslow, offered much in the way of training facilities, and until the establishment of the permanent camp at Aldershot there had, with the exception of Dublin, never been sufficient numbers of troops concentrated in one area to permit even Brigade field days. Troops not stationed in such recognized garrisons were quartered in the main cities and county towns, for the most part in small detachments, billeted on the civil population. During the Napoleonic Wars, Hythe had been developed as a military camp, and here were concentrated the regular and militia units in preparation to resist any invasion from the Continent. From Hythe the garrisons for the chain of coastal Martello Forts were drawn, and "The Camp" became a permanency, but this was inadequate for the needs of the Army by the middle of the last century.

As part of the training programme for the Army in 1852 a camp was established at Chobham Common, under the direction of Lord Hardinge, who had succeeded the Duke of Wellington as Commander-in-Chief of the British Army, and exercises were conducted in the area of the Chobham Ridges. The idea of such a camp in which troops "might be tested" had been taken up by the military authorities at the suggestion of the Prince Consort.* The highly satisfactory results of this experiment led to a further examination of the possibilities of the establishment of a permanent camp in the area, and this idea was pressed on the Government by Queen Victoria and the Prince Consort, which resulted in the decision to acquire the tract of land which became Aldershot Camp.†

The establishment of the Chobham Camp had been the result of a survey of the Aldershot area and the surrounding district in 1851. Lord Hardinge examined the ground again in 1853 and stayed during his visit at the "Red Lion," for he wrote‡ from there to the Prince Consort on 26th August, 1853, to say he had ridden over the ground from the slopes of Caesar's Camp to the Canal, and that this area was admirably adapted for an encampment for a Division, reserving all the rest of the ground for the purpose of manœuvres. He had experienced some "heavy squalls," he wrote, but on the whole made a very satisfactory reconnaissance. He also referred to several meetings which had been held in the neighbouring parishes for an Enclosure Bill to be passed.

It was shortly after this that Lord Hardinge's notice was drawn to an Act of Parliament proposing the enclosing of twenty-seven commons and waste lands. Such an Act was a danger to any scheme for obtaining land for military training. This was foreseen by the Commander-in-Chief, who made strong representations to the Government recommending that the ground in the Aldershot area should be purchased for a permanent camp. The Government's original plan had been for the purchase of such land in the Reigate area, as this was considered to be better, from a strategical viewpoint, being immediately to the south of London, between the Metropolis and the Kent and Sussex coast and along the line of the North Downs, the main features in the tactical defence of London against an invading

---

* *Vide* "Life of His Royal Highness the Prince Consort," Vol II, p. 487, by Sir Theodore Martin, K.C.B. (Smith, Elder & Co.) (1879).

† "On major questions of Army Organization—such as the development of the Camp at Aldershot and the selection of the site—the Prince played a decisive part." *Vide* "The Prince Consort," by Roger Fulford (Macmillan & Co.) (1949).

‡ Royal Archives, Windsor.

army from the Continent. Land in the Reigate area was not, however, finally considered suitable.*

On 26th September, 1853, Lord Hardinge wrote a memorandum* on the subject of a permanent camp in the Aldershot area, the object of the paper being to show that "the experiment of collecting two Divisions of troops of 8,000 men each in succession at the Camp at Chobham" had shown "in a degree, which justified the recommendation" that he made "that a waste tract of Ground for a permanent Camp should be purchased by the Government, it being quite out of the question to rely upon hiring similar tracts of waste lands from year to year." Lord Hardinge went on to refer to the fact that at every session Acts of Parliament were passed enclosing these barren commons, and twenty-seven enclosures proposed on 20th August, 1853, in one Act contained clauses which included the parishes of Chobham, Aldershot and Farnham. "Not being in the House of Commons," Lord Hardinge added, "I was not aware of what was proposed. . . . The difficulty of purchasing or hiring ground for military purposes is thus increasing rapidly," and he went on to say that at the moment of writing a large proportion of the infantry could not "even be instructed in Ball Cartridge firing, on account of the difficulty of finding proper ranges."†

The memorandum† continued to advocate the purchase of land for a permanent camp, suggesting that a tract of 8,000 to 10,000 acres could probably be purchased for £80,000 to £100,000, and that for five months of each year Brigades and Divisions could be "encamped or hutted or put in temporary Barracks at moderate expense." "Every Continental Army (even those of second and third rate powers)," he added, "makes a point of affording to their troops this essential advantage."

"The purchase of 10,000 acres at and around Aldershot would enable the military authorities to concentrate a large body of troops in the best possible position, and to a certain extent correct the danger of dispersion by a cheap and useful system of concentration," added to which there was the advantage of having a central training establish-

---

* In Lord Hardinge's memorandum of 26th September, 1853, he set out the merits of the Reigate area as it afforded "very great facilities for moving troops rapidly to Dover, Brighton, Portsmouth, or any intermediate points on the coast, and eventually to Exeter and Plymouth through Salisbury, but," the note concluded, "there are no waste lands at Reigate and a scanty supply of water. It is impossible to acquire the ground." As the next best position for the camp "for collecting troops for covering the capital and affording speedy reinforcements for the Southern Counties" he recommended "the extensive heaths of Aldershot, Farnham and Ash" (Public Record Office : War Office Correspondence, Out-Letters (W.O.3) 326).

† Public Record Office : War Office Correspondence, Out-Letters (W.O.3), 326.

ment for the Militia, who could "from May to September be encamped and hutted for the period of 28 days' training intermingled with Battalions or Brigades of the Line."

The ground in the Aldershot area was, Lord Hardinge considered— for he notes that he visited the area in August, 1852, and in March and April of 1853—"admirably adapted for the assembly of a large military force, from the interior moving to and from London by two railways in direct communication with Portsmouth, Chatham and Dover ; for all purposes of strategy it is one of the most important points that could be selected, with an ample supply of water at all seasons. The tract of land is therefore suited for a permanent camp of Instruction in peace and of concentration in War. . . . I do not believe," the memorandum concluded, "that any waste land possessing the great advantages of Aldershot from its position can be found in any other of the Maritime Counties. . . . I now very earnestly request the consideration and sanction of the Government to the proposed purchase of the Lands."

Lord Hardinge's visualization of the permanent accommodation at Aldershot was at that time confined to barracks for three regiments of Infantry, two regiments of Cavalry, two troops of Horse Artillery, a company of Sappers and Miners and a Commissariat Establishment, but he recommended that a larger number of troops might be encamped at Aldershot during the summer ; "the men changing from Barracks to Tents every fortnight," and that "the arrangements made as at Chobham so that 2 or 3 Divisions of 10,000 men each might be exercised there during the 4 to 5 months of Summer."

Lord Hardinge in his memorandum* called for the preparation of a plan and estimates to be placed before the Government following the vote of £10,000 allocated in the Ordnance Supplementary Estimate for the year.

A scheme of military training, on a scale never before attempted in the country, was carried out in the summer of 1853. Some twenty-five thousand troops of all arms were assembled in the Aldershot area, a considerable part of this force being under canvas or in bivouacs around Aldershot. Lord Seaton was in command of the exercises, with the Duke of Cambridge in command of the cavalry.

The value of this training in 1853 was without doubt inestimable, and the experience gained in the manœuvres was put to good account in the following year when our Army saw action against the Russians in the Crimea.

The success of these exercises, in addition to the difficulties which had arisen in negotiation for the purchase of land at Reigate, had led

* Public Record Office : War Office Correspondence, Out-Letters (W.O.3), 326.

Lord Hardinge to make his recommendation that the extensive heath and waste lands of Aldershot, Ash and Farnham were admirably suitable for the assembly of a large body of troops. Lord Hardinge's report and recommendations were fully supported by the powerful influence of the Prince Consort, who took an active interest in all aspects of Army organization and who played a decisive part in the adoption of the scheme for the establishment of "The Camp" and the selection of the site.* On 5th December, 1853, Lord Hardinge wrote† to the Prince stating that he hoped shortly to report progress ; "Knowing the very deep and successful interest which your Royal Highness takes in this matter, and how much the Army will be indebted to your Royal Highness for this permanent and admirable camp of instruction."

It was on 11th January, 1854, that Lord Hardinge reported that the proprietors of Aldershot Heath extending over twenty-five thousand acres had agreed to sell the land at £12 an acre. The Treasury approved the sum of £100,000 being included in the Army Estimates‡ for the purchase of land at Aldershot for the establishment of a permanent camp. The total sum spent on the purchase of land—between seven and eight thousand acres—up to 31st March, 1861, was £144,656, this sum being apportioned between the owners of the property and those entitled to cut turf from the commons.

A memorandum§ on the use of the camp written by Lord Hardinge at Horse Guards on 22nd May, 1854, makes interesting reading.

> It is not necessary [he wrote] to advert to the military advantages obtained by the purchase of the tract of waste land at Aldershot for a Camp of Instruction.
> It is desirable however in occupying that piece of ground to render it as generally useful for all Military purposes as possible.
> It should be made available for the assembly of a Body of Troops in Peace or War and the troops should be able to occupy the Buildings which may be constructed in Winter as well as Summer.
> The Barrack accommodation towards the Maritime Counties has been greatly reduced.‖ In 1808 after the Battle of Trafalgar accommodation, as will be seen, was 95,527 men and in 1854 is for 21,197.

---

* *Vide* "The Prince Consort," by Roger Fulford. (Macmillan & Co.) (1949).
† Royal Archives, Windsor.
‡ The figure quoted in the memorandum prepared by the Accountant-General's Office, 13th July, 1855 (see p. 43). (Public Record Office : War Office Correspondence, Out-Letters (W.O.3), 326.)
§ Public Record Office : War Office Correspondence, Out-Letters (W.O.3), 326.
‖ The total number of troops quartered in 1808 in the "Maritime Counties" of Kent, Sussex, Hampshire, Essex, Suffolk and Norfolk was 95,527, made up of 8,731 Cavalry and 86,796 Infantry. By 1854 the number of troops in the same area had been reduced to 21,197, of which there were 1,618 Cavalry and 20,579 Infantry.

The construction of the Buildings therefore on the score of the health of the troops should be such as to ensure their warmth in the severest winter.

On this account it would be inexpedient to attempt the hutting system which can only be advantageously resorted to on any great and sudden emergency.

Low wooden sheds on weak foundations are damp and unhealthy and can only be occupied in the Summer season—and their construction although cheap at the outset is found in the end to be very expensive by the frequency of the repair required.

I therefore assume that it is for the advantage of the service at all times and under all circumstances that the Buildings should be constructed of such strength and materials that they should be calculated to last for at least 30 or 40 years—that the pillars of iron and principal beams of wood should be so simple that if a barrack such for instance as that proposed by Lieut.-Colonel Jebb, is found to answer these conditions, the material parts could be made up, if suddenly required, at any of our great stations and put up or taken down rapidly.

It is assessed that this description of Barrack can be built for £20 or £25 a head including Officers Quarters, Mess House etc. etc. whilst a Permanent Barracks in Masonry will cost £50 and £70.

It therefore appears very desirable that an immediate system of Building Barracks for troops should be adopted on this occasion of finding accommodation for troops at Aldershot, and that a Committee of Ordnance Officers, with Colonel Jebb, Lieut.-Colonel Tulloch (of the Statistical Branch of the War Office), Colonel Torrens Assistant Quarter Master General should be assembled as was proposed to have been done last year since which Colonel Jebb has built a small Barrack at Portland which practically exhibits the system, which he considers can conveniently and cheaply admit of extension at many stations in Great Britain.

Lord Hardinge then went on to refer to the action of the Belgian Government some seventeen years previously in providing a long Military Camp of temporary barracks at Beverloo, and how this in 1849-50 had become a permanent camp with brick-built barracks. He went on to say that we should derive advantage from their past experience and recommended that an Engineer Officer should be sent to Belgium to inspect their large camp and that a request should be made through the Belgian Minister to afford facilities for the inspection of the camp and be "favoured with sight of the Printed Plans and Printed Estimates and Reports."*

---

* It would appear also from records available that a visit was made to France with the similar object of learning from past experience, for in a letter from Horse Guards to the Ordnance Office dated 14th October, 1854, reference is made to a report on the French encampment at Boulogne (Public Record Office ; War Office Correspondence, Out-Letters (W.O.3), 326).

The war with Russia which was declared on 27th March, 1854, had a permanent effect upon the destinies of Aldershot. War broke out soon after the completion of the initial purchases of lands. Among those who foresaw the future of Aldershot as a permanent training ground for the Army was the Prince Consort, who pointed out in various memoranda to the War Office the importance of securing its retention. "Put permanent buildings on the land," urged the Prince, "and the country will never be allowed to sell it. . . . The state of popular feeling engendered by the war is such," he added, "that you can now ask Parliament for anything you want. Strike while the iron is hot." This advice was acted upon and the senior officers, accompanied by Surveyors and Engineers who had arrived at Aldershot in the winter of 1853, marked out the sites of the permanent barracks now known as Wellington Lines.*

On 22nd August, 1854, General Yorke, writing† on behalf of "the General Commanding in Chief" from Horse Guards to a Colonel Munday for the information of the Duke of Newcastle, drew attention to a memorandum dated 26th September, 1853, drawn up by Lord Hardinge, "recommending that ground for a permanent camp should be purchased by the Government," and setting out the "reasons which have induced the purchase of the ground around Aldershot" ; adding that plans had been sent to the Ordnance Department for them to proceed with the proposed barracks for "three Regiments of Infantry, two troops of Horse Artillery and one Company of Sappers and Miners," and also to prepare plans for "two Regiments of Cavalry on the Peace Establishment."

Work on the permanent barracks was commenced in September, 1854, and completed in 1859. The sites for the barracks were plotted by Colonel Sir Frederick Smith, of the Royal Engineers,‡ who was in charge of the construction of "The Camp," with Captain J. H. Freeth, R.E.,§ as his executive officer and Mr. Baker, of the R.E. Works Service, as Clerk of the Works ; whilst the officer appointed by the War Office to draw up the plans for the barracks was Captain

---

* The barracks flanking Wellington Avenue—Waterloo (for Artillery), Talavera, Salamanca and Badajos, and the Cavalry Barracks formerly named East, West and South Cavalry Barracks, subsequently designated Warburg, Willems and Beaumont Barracks respectively.

† Public Record Office: War Office Correspondence, Out-Letters (W.O.3), 326.

‡ Then commanding R.E., South-Western District, with his office at Portsmouth.

§ Captain James Holt Freeth, commissioned in Royal Engineers, Second-Lieutenant, 12th December, 1834, was promoted Captain, 1st March, 1846, and became Colonel, R.E., 2nd December, 1862. (*Vide* Hart's Annual Army List, 1873.)

R. M. Laffan.* In addition to the permanent barracks, a large hutted camp as originally planned was built to house Militia battalions mobilized, following the passage of an Act of Parliament to call out and embody Militia following the declaration of war. Previous to the passing of this Act the Militia could only, with the exception of annual training, be called out for service in the case of invasion or imminent danger of invasion. The original intention had been to quarter the Militia units in the barracks vacated by the Regular troops embarked for the Crimea, but most of this accommodation was needed for the housing and training of recruits who flocked to the colours, prompted by the patriotic indignation against Russia, the enthusiasm and public warlike spirit and the £10 cash bounty paid to all recruits. In consequence of the influx of recruits to the Regular Army, the Militia had to be billeted upon the civilian population, which gave rise to general dissatisfaction and prompted the authorities to take steps to speed up the provision of accommodation in Aldershot Camp to house some 20,000 men.

The Aldershot Camp project was fully considered by a special committee under the chairmanship of Major-General Sir Frederick

---

* Captain R. M. Laffan, R.E. (later Major-General Sir Robert Laffan, K.C.M.G., Governor and Commander-in-Chief, Bermuda), was at that time a Deputy Inspector-General of Fortifications at the War Office. He is mentioned in a letter dated 2nd August, 1855, from the Commander-in-Chief to the Inspector-General of Fortifications (Lieutenant-General Sir John Burgoyne, K.C.B.), when Laffan was referred to as "one of the R.E. officers responsible for the plans and construction of the Infantry Barracks . . . the plans having been submitted by Laffan in accordance with the suggestions of the Committee appointed by Lord Panmure."

Robert Michael Laffan, who later in his career became C.R.E. of Aldershot (1866-1872), was responsible for many improvements in the camp, including the planting of trees and the laying of turf. When the Queen's Parade was changed to Queen's Avenue in the early nineties, the former parade ground was named Laffan's Plain in his memory. Laffan was born in Skehana, Southern Ireland, on 21st September, 1821, and entered the Royal Military Academy in September, 1835. He was gazetted to the Royal Engineers on 5th May, 1837. After two years at Chatham he served in South Africa, where he organized the Engineer requirements of the expedition to relieve Colonel Smith and the Natal Garrison, then beleaguered by the Boers under Pretorius. He next served in Mauritius, and was promoted to Captain in May, 1846. Returning to England, he was posted to Belfast as C.R.E., later becoming Inspector of Railways under the Board of Trade. In the autumn of 1852 he was sent to Antwerp and Paris to report on the fortifications, and in 1854 he was again in France to report on the organization of the French War Ministry. It was in this year that he was appointed C.R.E., London District. Despite his military activities, however, he found time to stand for Parliament, and from 1852 to 1857 he represented the Borough of St. Ives in the House of Commons.

Laffan's first association with Aldershot was whilst he was at the War Office in an R.E. Staff appointment in 1855-1859. He next served in Portsmouth (1859-60), in Malta 1860-1865, and Ceylon (1865), returning in 1866 to be C.R.E. at Aldershot. On leaving that appointment he served in Gibraltar (1872-1877), and on the 27th April, 1877, was appointed Governor and Commander-in-Chief, Bermuda, and promoted Major-General in October, 1877. He died in Bermuda on 22nd March, 1882. (R.E. Journal, Vol. XII; Dictionary of National Biography.)

Smith, R.E., set up by the Inspector-General of Fortifications, and the handwritten memoranda* and copy letters in the old files* of the Ordnance Board make most interesting reading. Typical of these are the following letters, which prove that matters were dealt with in an expeditious manner, which is also an indication of the importance attached to the establishment of the camp.

ORDNANCE OFFICE,
LONDON.
1st December, 1854.

SIR,

I am requested by the Committee on the Aldershot Encampment question to report to the General Commanding in Chief the necessity of a General Hospital being constructed at Aldershot for the troops to be encamped there and suggest that the Director General of the Army and Ordnance Medical Departments be requested to give an opinion as to the proper site for such Building having a regard to the relative intended sites of the Barracks for the Cavalry, the Artillery and the Infantry. The Committee beg to recommend that one General Riding School of large proportions should be erected for the use of the three Regiments of Cavalry and the Artillery in such a locality as Viscount Hardinge may be pleased to point out, and they are also desirous of bringing under His Lordship's consideration the propriety of a Chapel for the Troops being erected at Aldershot with a residence for an Army Chaplain.

I have the honour to be,

(*Signed*) FREDERICK SMITH.
Major-General and President.

MAJOR-GENERAL YORKE,
HORSE GUARDS.

HORSE GUARDS,
1st December, 1854.

SIR,

Having laid before the General Commanding in Chief your letter of this date on the subject of the Building to be erected at Aldershot, I am directed by his Lordship to state that he very much prefers the system of Regimental Hospitals to having one General Hospital for all the troops that may be assembled there,

* Public Record Office : War Office Correspondence, Out-Letters (W.O.3), 326.

and he therefore requests that there may be a hospital constructed for each Regiment.

Lord Hardinge approves of a General Riding School of large proportions being erected for the use of the three Regiments of Cavalry and the Artillery, and he requests that you will be good enough to fix upon the site which you consider best for the purpose.

With regard to the Chapel Lord Hardinge considers the question of its construction as well as of a residence for the Chaplain may be postponed for the present reserving a site for the purpose.

In conclusion he desires me to express his hope that the contracts for all the buildings at Aldershot may be so formed as to insure their completion, under heavy penalties within the year 1855.

I have the honour to be,

Sir,

Your obedient humble servant,

C. YORKE.

GENERAL SIR FREDERICK SMITH.

A Memorandum* signed by Lord Hardinge at Horse Guards, dated 26th February, 1855, recorded that :

The Ordnance Department have received orders from the Secretary of State for the War Department to erect huts for 20,000 militia on the ground at Aldershot lately purchased by the Government.

I went down the day before yesterday and met Major-General Sir Frederick Smith, R.E., by appointment and it is decided that Huts should be erected for 12,000 men on the South side and 8,000 men on the North side of the Basingstoke Canal.

The roads round the huts will be settled by me and the Quarter Master General whenever Sir Frederick Smith will be so good as to call upon me at the Horse Guards.

The Ordnance Solicitor will have to enter into communication with the owners of the Basingstoke Canal.

We shall probably require wharfs for coals, forage and various other articles.

The lighting of the chief avenue to the Camp by lamps or gas must also be taken into consideration by the Ordnance Department.

Small Guardhouses will also be required and for so large a body of raw undrilled troops there must be a few officers of the Staff lodged at one end of the Huts who can have their offices adjoining to Sleeping Huts so as to be close to the troops ; and

---

* Public Record Office : War Office Correspondence, Out-Letters (W.O.3), 326.

with easy access with the Commanding Officers and Adjutants of the Militia, and one room for the General Officer Commanding, so that he and his staff may in all weathers be transacting their daily duty as in any large garrison and ready to give orders with the least possible delay.

The Ordnance Department will see the necessity of having one or two Barrack Masters to take charge of Barrack furniture and supplies of fuel, the supplies of food, forage etc. and I need not enter upon the plan that should be taken up without delay by the Commissariat Branch of the War Department.

(*Signed*) HARDINGE.

P.S.—All details about stores for warming officers rooms, cooking places covered in for officers and men and stables for officers horses as close as may be convenient are details which the Barrack branch of the Ordnance Department will of course well consider and decide upon. The Probability is that the Hut Barracks may be required to be occupied during the winter months.

* * * * *

Building operations had commenced prior to the outbreak of war. The first loads of building materials, sent to the site by the civilian contractors—Messrs. Haywood & Nixon—arrived at Aldershot on 15th February, 1854. Whilst the permanent brick buildings were being constructed, a hutted camp of some twelve hundred wooden huts was built on the ground now known as Stanhope and Marlborough Lines.

The original proposal for the layout of "The Camp" was for huts to be built on either side of the Farnborough Road, but after discussions between Lord Hardinge and Major-General Sir Frederick Smith it was decided to construct "The Camp" on the east side of the Farnborough Road and north and south of the Basingstoke Canal. The original contracts were drawn up for the provision of 1,260 huts. The huts were built of Memel and Niger fir, and cost approximately £150 each.* Eight hundred of these huts were built for the accommodation of twenty-four men each; the remainder were for officers' quarters, administrative offices, stores, mess rooms, kitchens, hospitals and other installations.

Some of the huts had been completed in North Camp by May, 1854, and the first troops to arrive in Aldershot to occupy them marched into the camp on 7th May, 1854. These were five officers† and

---

* The huts were subsequently roofed by felt, an estimate of £6,726 10s. being approved by the War Department on 28th March, 1855 (War Office Correspondence, Out-Letters (W.O.3), 326).

† Including the Medical Officer.

103 other ranks of the 94th Regiment (later the 2nd Bn. Connaught Rangers*), who marched to Aldershot from Windsor. A week later a battalion of London Militia—The Tower Hamlets—arrived, and the following week a Surrey Militia battalion.† Throughout May, June, July and August more and more troops poured into Aldershot. These were in the main Militia battalions who had volunteered for service in the Crimea. Some units stayed but a short while before marching away again to the waiting transports at Portsmouth which were to bear them to the Black Sea and the theatre of war.

Amid the coming and going of troops bound for the Crimea, the construction of "The Camp" progressed—both the permanent barracks in Wellington Lines and the hutted camps. Men and materials poured into the area, into "The Camp," and into the mushroom town that was springing up along "The Camp" boundary. Every inducement was offered by the contractors to labourers to urge them to press on with the construction of the accommodation so urgently required. The cost was not considered, and fabulous wages were paid to all classes of skilled workmen and unskilled labourers. The financial gain was an attraction to many, and carters, herdsmen and other agricultural workers left the farms for miles around to work as builders' labourers in "The Camp."

Among the many attracted to the remunerative work on "The Camp" was Isaac Lamb, who was born and brought up on the Duke of Wellington's estate at Strathfieldsaye. A fine, strapping young man, he worked in the camp for eight years as a labourer and tinsmith, walking every day from Dipley near Mattingley and back again in the evening. Until coming to Aldershot he had worked as a farm labourer at 18s. per week, but his wages whilst working in the camp were at one time £1 per day.‡

The nearest railway line and station were at Tongham, and as the supply of materials increased so did the number of carters daily thronging the station yard to carry bricks, timber and builders' stores to "The Camp" sites and the R.E. yard which was established on the site of the present-day Princes Gardens and the Municipal car park. It was near this site, on a cold winter's day in November, 1853, that an officer with a small party of N.C.Os. and men of the Royal Engineers had arrived and pitched a few tents—the first troops to arrive on the

---

* Disbanded on 31st July, 1922. The 1st Bn. Connaught Rangers was the old 88th Regiment.

† This battalion mounted the first Guard of Honour at the Royal Pavilion on the occasion of Queen Victoria's first visit to Aldershot. During the Crimea War the battalion sent 400 men as volunteers to Regular units.

‡ Isaac Lamb, who later lived in Pinewood Road, Ash, died at the age of 103 in Farnham Infirmary, in 1923.

NORTH CAMP, ALDERSHOT

circa 1859

The view depicted above was drawn on stone by H. Prosser, lithographed by S. Straker of 80 Bishopsgate, London, and published by Andrews & Lucy of Farnham. It is from the high ground which now forms the terrace of Government House, above the old Camp Nursery. The white house to the left, which stood opposite Cockadobby Hill by the Bridge Gate toll post, where the Queen's Hotel now stands, is shown on the Ordnance maps of 1856, but the house does not appear on the map of 1873, having been demolished in the intervening years. The road in front of the huts is the old London–Winchester turnpike road, now the Farnborough Road. The road between the huts is now Evelyn Woods Road, at the top of which stands the Marlborough Lines Garrison Church, erected on its present site in 1856 as a temporary church—it had been constructed for shipment to the Crimea as a prefabricated hospital.

E

SOUTH CAMP, ALDERSHOT

circa 1859

The view depicted in the lithograph above was sketched by H. Prosser, lithographed by S. Straker of 80 Bishopsgate, London, and published by Andrews & Lucy of Farnham. It is from the high ground now forming the terrace of Blandford House, the former residence of the General Officer Commanding Aldershot District.

On the extreme right in the distance is the Royal Pavilion before the plantations of trees grew. The next large building is the Officers' Club House. The tree-lined road running diagonally to the crest of the hill is the old London–Winchester turnpike road, now the Farnborough Road. The rows of wooden huts stand on the sites of the present-day barracks—Gibraltar, Albuhera, Barrosa, Corunna and Maida—whilst at the lower end of the rows of huts is the line of the Basingstoke Canal.

The large building on the skyline on the left of the view is the Roman Catholic Garrison Church of St. Michael and St. Sebastian, which stands, its exterior unchanged, to this day. The group of three huts by the flagstaff was the Headquarter Offices of "The Division at Aldershott" standing near the site of Scott Moncrieff Square. The staff appearing above the top of the left-hand line of huts is the 40-ft. gambol weather-vane of the Observatory and Meteorological Station, which was set up at this point, 325 feet above sea level. The meteorological readings at this time were taken by an orderly of the Medical Staff Corps, John Arnold, and the readings published in "The Times" and the "Aldershot Military Gazette." On the crest of the hill are the huts which were erected for use by the Commander-in-Chief and the Secretary of State for War.

site of what was to become the greatest military centre in the Empire. The site of their camp was the present-day car park by Princes Gardens; it was bleak, open heathland, the only building in sight being the old Union Poor House.* Soon the tents were replaced by wooden huts and the R.E. yard took shape. Until the time that this yard was demolished in 1929, the buildings erected for the Royal Engineer Department staff remained known to all as the "R.E.D. Huts."

It was a hectic period. One can visualize the scene in the area now occupied by Princes Gardens, the Ritz and Empire Cinemas, and High Street: the R.E. Yard, stacked high with standards of timber, high piles of bricks, and with dumps of tools outside the low wooden sheds; the unmade roads running either side of the dump crowded with traffic, mainly heavy horse-drawn carts and drays moving slowly forward, laden with building materials, in the direction of the East Cavalry Barracks or Talavera Barracks; then, rising some six to twelve feet from the foundations in bright new yellow bricks, the future outline of the barracks could be seen by the towering scaffolding; empty carts creaking slowly back towards the dump from the rough beaten tracks leading up past the old Union Workhouse to the wooden huts of South Camp. On fine days the sandy dust from the uneven, unmade, rutted roads rose in clouds as the wheeled traffic trotted or trundled by. In the rain the dust and rough tracks soon churned into a chrome-coloured mud, the rain running away down the tracks of the present-day High Street in rivulets. Looking away towards where the present-day Police Station stands, one sees the continuous stream of carts wending their way from Tongham Station with yet more building materials.

The line of buildings on the south side of High Street from the present-day Queen Hotel to Woolworth's has not yet taken shape. Building is in progress—scaffolding rises from where bricklayers are already at work with bricks and mortar. Two or three buildings are almost complete and the ground floors are already occupied. There are gaps between the buildings under construction, gaps which are spaces, some still vacant, with scrubby bushes and trodden-down bracken and gorse; other spaces are occupied by low wooden huts, some roofed over with tarpaulin, some with zinc sheets. Here is the start of High Street, Aldershot, for these new buildings, huts and shacks are the forerunners of the shops, businesses and licensed houses which later formed the vista of Aldershot's trading centre facing "The Camp." Already this community is providing the needs of the soldiers, the workmen and labourers. There are general stores and beer shops: bonneted women seated beside stalls and baskets

---

* See p. 322.

E

of fruit and vegetables ; bearded labourers seated on benches outside beer shops ; soldiers, young and old, in scarlet or rifle green tunics or in undress uniform, with the circular small-crowned forage-caps or wearing the heavy grey-caped greatcoats of the day ; smocked and long-coated civilian carters ; short-sleeved labourers. Shakoed, scarlet-coated sentries with long bayonets on their smooth-bore muskets* stand guard over a newly arrived consignment of Engineer stores around which bare-footed, long-petticoated children are playing with two rough-coated ownerless dogs. Two mounted officers are trotting by, saluted by a tall, heavily bewhiskered N.C.O. A high-wheeled gig is driven by a bearded, frock-coated contractor with a "stove-pipe" hat, accompanied by an officer with mutton-chop whiskers and in the long dark-blue undress uniform tunic, followed by a mounted orderly leading an officer's charger. The moving men, horses, carts and gigs move up and down in a swirl of fine dust amid the cries of the foremen gangers or the hawkers, the orders of N.C.Os to parties of marching troops, and the sound of the brassy bugles from the parade grounds outside the huts in the distance at South Camp.

Such is the picture conjured up by the descriptions of the busy industrious months following the first steps in the establishment of "The Camp" and the growth of Aldershot town from the scattered, sleepy village, set down on the fringe of the heath and moor lands, which had existed undisturbed through the passage of the centuries.

Mention has been made of the presence of the beer houses which were very soon established by enterprising civilians to cater for the needs of the many hundreds of troops and workmen, who found the need to slake their thirst after the long day's work or to use them as their only place of relaxation. There had originally been but three inns in the area,† but so great was the demand that the number of inns and beer houses increased with rapidity.

When "The Camp" was planned and the War Office acquired the land there were but very few buildings in the area, practically the whole of the country between the Parish Church and the "Tumble-down Dick" inn‡ at Farnborough being common or waste land.

---

* The old percussion muzzle-loading rifles were still the weapons of the infantry-man, and were still referred to by the older N.C.Os. as "Firelocks." The Miné rifle was adopted just before the Crimea, but even so some units embarked for the campaign armed with the old weapons.

† The "Beehive" and the "Red Lion" in the village and the "Row Barge" on the turnpike road.

‡ This inn is reputed to have been built in the reign of Henry VIII, and so named to commemorate the downfall of Richard III ; another school of thought attributes the name to a commemoration of the downfall of Cromwell's Commonwealth, which he left in the hands of his son Richard ; whilst a third opinion is that the name was adopted after the execution of one of its most notorious patrons, namely, Dick Turpin, the highwayman.

There was, however, the large country house standing in what today are the Government House grounds opposite Cockadobby Hill, and the Bridge Gate Toll Post, and the old buildings, now in the grounds of Vine Cottage, which were shown on the map of 1821 as "Bagman's Castle." On the 1856 map these were marked as "Poverty Place," possibly owing to the fact that, with the passing of the highwaymen who used it as a base for operations along the turnpike road, the residents fell on less prosperous days. There was also a small isolated inn situated near the toll gate on the Farnborough Road, about half-way between the present-day Officers' Club and the Wharf Bridge over the Basingstoke Canal, where in the map of 1856 a Timber Wharf is marked, denoting the fact that the old Farnham Wharf,* which was soon to be renamed Aldershot Wharf, was used to off-load timber from the barges for the building of the huts of the camp. The inn was called the "Row Barge" or "Houghton's Inn," after the name of the innkeeper. Until the opening up of "The Camp," James Houghton had made his living by catering for the travellers on the London–Winchester turnpike road and from the bargees operating on the Basingstoke Canal, which had been opened in 1778† with a wharf then called the Farnham Wharf, constructed in 1788 by the present-day Wharf Bridge on the Farnborough Road, and by accommodating sportsmen from London, to whom he also acted as guide, who came to shoot over the waste land, and more especially for the snipe shooting on Cove Common, which at that time was an excellent snipe bog.

With the construction of "The Camp" and the arrival of troops and highly paid labourers, the "Row Barge" became a very valuable property and, as may well be imagined, it did a roaring trade and was undoubtedly a "gold mine" for Houghton. In February, 1855, James Houghton signed an agreement with the "Offr. Comdg. R.E." for the hire of a room at the inn for the use of the Engineer Department, it having been reported by Captain Freeth, R.E., on 4th February that the "Row Barge" was the only place at which a room suitable for an Engineer office could be obtained. The room was 27 feet long by 15 feet broad, and was let at "one pound per week, coals are extra, of four shillings a week." The inn later became the temporary headquarters of the General and his staff, and, before the establishment of messes, officers used to go to the inn for meals, the speciality being

---

* The old wharf was still used for this purpose as late as 1920. In this year the canal was still navigable along the Aldershot reaches, and timber consigned to Messrs. W. & L. Edgoose, of Aldershot, was unloaded there.

† The Basingstoke Canal, which extends thirty-seven miles from Basingstoke to near the junction of the River Wey with the Thames, was constructed between 1778 and 1794. (See p. 358.)

a "cut of the joint"—a luxury for those living under canvas or in temporary hutments.

The trade at the inn continued to increase as officers, labourers and troops multiplied. It was the proud boast of the landlady that she drew a barrel of beer in fifty minutes and kept up the rate all day. The evenings saw this isolated inn surrounded by crowds of soldiers and workmen, the numbers sometimes running into several hundreds.

On the completion of "The Camp" and the establishment of messes and canteens it was decided that the "Row Barge," which was then situated on Government land, had served its purpose. Notice to quit was served on the innkeeper. The six-month period of notice finally expired and Houghton showed no signs of moving. His refusal to comply with the notice eventually led to the dismantling of the inn by a party of Sappers, who removed the roof, and this at last had the desired effect.

Houghton was not the only civilian who plied his trade within the boundaries of "The Camp." A Mr. Nichols, of Farnham, set up a small printing press in a hut in South Camp as "The Printer to the Camp," a Mr. Boulter ran a canteen in "F" Block in South Camp, a Mr. Farr opened a tobacconist business near by, and Trufitt's hairdressing saloon* was established by the pontoon bridge over the canal.

On 8th August, 1855, the Electric Telegraph Department of the South Eastern Railway issued printed notices, signed by Charles V. Walker, Engineer and Superintendent of Telegraphs, which were posted up, notifying the fact that

> On August 9th, and until further notice, a Messenger will leave the Ash Station for the Post Office at the Camp at 7.0 a.m. and at 1.0 and 6.0 p.m. ; and will carry up to the Post Office or to any place *en route*, to the Post Office, Telegraph Messages, free of posterage. The signal W. M. is to be given with messages to go up by next Messenger in other cases they will be sent up by an Express Messenger in the usual way. A Messenger will leave the Post Office at the Camp for Ash Station at 8.0 a.m. and at 2.0 and 7.0 p.m. and will carry down to the Station free of posterage all Telegraph Messages that are deposited at the Post Office.

In April, 1855, Lieut.-General Sir William Knollys† was selected

---

* Trufitt's hairdressing saloon exists, in name, to this day, the present building occupying the same site, by the Iron Bridge in Queen's Avenue.

† Sir William Knollys was born in 1797, eldest son of General William Knollys, eighth Earl of Banbury. He was educated at Harrow and Sandhurst and was commissioned when little over sixteen years of age as an Ensign in the 3rd (Scots) Guards. He was almost immediately sent with a draft to the Peninsula, and saw action at the crossing of the Bidassoa and the Adour and at Bayonne. In 1814 he

to command "The Camp" at Aldershot. The General had recently returned from a mission to France, where he had been investigating the French Army's organization of their commissariat and transport, which had proved superior to our own in the Crimea. Previous to this he had in 1854 been promoted Major-General and appointed Governor of Guernsey. General Knollys's appointment to Aldershot was without doubt at the instigation of the Prince Consort, who thought highly of the General, for at the time when he was commanding the Scots Fusilier Guards in 1850 it was he who had initiated the Prince into British military procedure, and under General Knollys's guidance and instruction the Prince had learned much from his attachment to the regiment during parades and field days in Hyde Park. At this time the Scots Fusilier Guards were held to be one of "the best drilled, disciplined and organized in the British Army."

Work on "The Camp" had continued throughout 1855, and on 25th April of that year Lieut.-General Sir William Knollys visited "The Camp," touring it with Major-General Sir Frederick Smith, of the Royal Engineers, and making the administrative arrangements for the quartering of a thousand more men due to arrive on 1st May. Among the buildings under construction at the time were the Royal Pavilion for the use of Queen Victoria, the site of which had been chosen and marked out by the Prince Consort, and special huts located in areas between Stanhope Lines and the Farnborough Road for the Secretary of State for War, the Commander-in-Chief of the British Army, the Adjutant-General and the General Officer commanding "The Camp."

General Knollys assumed his Command on 14th May, 1855, and by 1st June there were four Militia battalions in the camp, and by May the following year there were one cavalry regiment, the Royal Dragoons, three Regular infantry regiments, the 19th, 80th and 95th Regiments,* and six regiments of Militia, the Cavan, Worcester, Sussex, Hereford, Antrim and the Royal South Gloucestershire.

---

returned to England, but directly after Waterloo went with a draft to join his regiment in Paris. He was adjutant of the Scots Guards in 1821, Lieutenant-Colonel in 1844, and Colonel of the Regiment in 1850. (Dictionary of National Biography, Vol. XXXI.)

General Knollys was thought of highly by Queen Victoria. In her Journal, on 19th April, 1856, she wrote that great praise was due to him (for his work at the Camp), "who manages everything so well"; and again on 16th July, 1856, she wrote to him "who does everything so well and so quick" (Royal Archives, Windsor).

* The 19th Regiment, later the 1st Bn. The Green Howards (Alexandra, Princess of Wales's Own Yorkshire Regiment); the 80th Regiment, later the 2nd Bn. The South Staffordshire Regiment; the 95th Regiment, later the 2nd Bn. The Sherwood Foresters (Nottinghamshire and Derbyshire Regiment).

Although Lord Hardinge was the Commander-in-Chief of the Army, the principal moving spirit behind the plans for the co-ordinated training of troops was the Prince Consort, and from him General Knollys received every support. The army of the day lacked cohesion, and General Knollys had been charged with forming his staff, organizing the troops into Brigades and Divisions, and initiating the organization of the Departmental Corps—Commissariat, Transport, Stores and Medical. The General had at the outset an uphill task, and it is recorded* that "he found it necessary to instruct, with his own hands, some of the first arrivals in 'The Camp' in pitching tents, and while sharing with them a tent life, to teach them the elementary duties of soldiers in the field."

There were many delays in the construction of "The Camp." The initial accommodation was scheduled for completion by 15th April, 1855, but by the 18th of that month only about half of the huts had been erected. Although it had been decided that "The Camp" was to be a permanency, the huts in North and South Camps were erected firstly to accommodate the troops engaged in the establishment of "The Camp," and the number was increased as a war-time measure ; they were not intended as permanent quarters. Even so, it is recorded that when they were dismantled nearly forty years afterwards to make way for the present-day brick-built barracks, the foundations were found to be most substantial and most of the woodwork still strong, weatherproof and sound. The thoroughness of the work on these "temporary" huts may well have had something to do with the delay in the completion of "The Camp" in the scheduled time. Many of the contracts took six months to complete instead of two as visualized. The cost was greatly in excess of the original estimate of £120,000 for accommodation of 20,000 men. The total cost, which included the Royal Pavilion, administrative offices, the police station† and other accommodation added to the original specifications, was £476,892.

An office Memorandum‡ prepared on 13th July, 1855, by the

---

* Dictionary of National Biography, Vol. XXXI.

† Aldershot Camp was, and still is, so essentially military that it is interesting to note that on 1st February, 1856, the Prince Consort inspected the Hants Constabulary, under the command of Captain Harris, at Aldershot. The police station and police quarters must have been of considerable size, for it is recorded that "His Royal Highness admired the appearance of the men, as likewise the condition of their horses . . . ; he afterwards went round the huts, stables, stores, etc., the whole of which met with his approval" (*vide Illustrated London News*, 2nd February, 1856). A plan of the proposed buildings shown on a map of 1856 indicates a large police station at the south-east corner of the South Cavalry Barracks above the "Rifleman" public-house, but the site was changed to a position on the west of the Farnborough Road, below the Royal Pavilion.

‡ Public Record Office : War Office Correspondence, Out-Letters (W.O.3), 326.

Accountant-General's Office gives some interesting figures concerning expenditure. In the year 1854-5 the amount voted for the purchase of land for the camp was £100,000, and out of this the imprest granted to Mr. Bannister, the Solicitor to the Ordnance Board, in 1854-5 and 1855-6 on account of purchase of land was £101,312 1s. 9d., which showed an excess of expenditure of £1,312 1s. 9d., and even so there was a note to the effect that it was "understood that this amount increased upwards of £20,000 by purchases not already completed."

In 1854-5 the amount voted in the Army Estimates for 5,000 huts to be erected in Aldershot and elsewhere was £175,000, of which £37,687 17s. 3d. was spent at Aldershot, whilst out of the sum of £125,000 voted for similar expenditure in 1855-6 £92,835 14s. 8d. was spent on the camp.

Originally planned for twenty thousand troops, this number was subsequently reduced to just under eleven thousand five hundred by reducing the number of men in each hut from twenty-four to twenty-two and by the conversion of a large number of huts to other uses.

Despite the vast building project of Aldershot Camp, the return of the Army from the Crimea presented the War Office with an accommodation problem. During the summer months Aldershot had provided ample and adequate quarters, but the winter of 1856 brought problems which prompted H.R.H. The Duke of Cambridge to write on 3rd December, 1856,* to the Secretary of State for War, Lord Panmure :

> The present state of the weather has again made me feel most anxious about the position of the troops at Aldershot. I confess I do not think that it is at all desirable that a large body should be there assembled during the winter, and I should greatly prefer to send them into winter quarters. . . . I hear that the officers dislike Aldershot very much, a feeling which I believe is further shared by the men. The want of occupation during the long winter nights is the great drawback. . . .

Continuing, the Duke, however, expressed the view that he would not like to disturb the then new system of concentrating troops by Brigades and Divisions, for if once that scheme were broken it might be abandoned, added to which he appreciated the expense which would have been involved in moving troops into winter quarters.†

Lord Panmure, the Secretary of State for War, in acknowledging the Duke's memorandum in March, 1857, and referring to his final recommendations, informed him that he had passed this to the

---

* "The Military Life of H.R.H. George Duke of Cambridge," by Willoughby Verner, Vol. I, p. 123.
† Ibid, p. 126.

"Military Committee," saying that he felt that it would "do much to sustain the Camps," and this had the effect of finalizing the decision to retain Aldershot as a permanent camp and garrison.

The camp boundaries were in 1856 much as they are to this day, but in that year the bounds for troops were laid down in a General Order :

The following places being in a ratio of being within two or three miles from the South Camp, will till further orders, be the bounds for the troops in Command. The Major General commanding confidently hopes the extensive range permitted to the men will not lead to disorderly behaviour on their part which would necessitate a narrower boundary. All men found without a pass signed by their Commanding Officer beyond the places designated, will be apprehended. The Corps of Mounted Police are mostly stationed at short distance beyond the bounds here laid down and will be called on to exercise under a system of patrol communicated to them, an efficient supervision over all the bounds surrounding all the camp.

The bounds are fixed as follows :

To the North West to the Pye-Stock Hill and bridge—the bridge not to be crossed from Pye-Stock Southwards—along the right or eastern bank of the brook to the wood, along the enclosure to the west corner of Caesar's Camp—Caesar's Camp not to be crossed, and to form the South-west boundary; from Caesar's Camp along the track to the Farnham Road; along the Farnham Road as far as the cross roads at the village of Sheat, and no further in that direction to the southward ; to the eastward the boundary will be Bagshot Green* and the railway bridge at Tongham, the northward to the Greyhound public house and no further than Ash Church ; from the Greyhound public house and junction of the canal and railway, to the railway gate, to the North Camp ; the Canal in that direction towards Michel's post, is out of bounds ; on the Farnborough Road, the Tumbledown Dick public house to be the limit and the Cross-roads beyond the Tumbledown Dick to be out of bounds.

The Major General Commanding desires that the Commanding Officers of Regiments will take measures to cause these orders to be thoroughly understood by the officers, and by them explained to the soldiers.

By Order.

* * * * *

The Royal Pavilion, originally known as the Queen's Pavilion, situated off the Farnborough Road opposite the West Cavalry Bar-

---

* Badshot Lea.

racks—Willems Barracks—is today secluded by a plantation of firs and unseen from the main road. This Royal residence, without doubt the most unpretentious of any in the United Kingdom, was designed and built in 1855 in the style of a pavilion as a temporary residence for Queen Victoria whilst visiting "The Division at Aldershot." It was constructed with the idea of its being a modest camp residence. The site and design were chosen by the Prince Consort, and it is recorded that Queen Victoria "was delighted with its simplicity, the charming views from its windows, and its seclusion," and that she found pleasure in painting some of these views during her visits to Aldershot.

The original site of the Pavilion was to the north-west of the camp and had been selected by the Prince Consort. This site was not, however, considered by the military authorities to be entirely suitable and they made alternative proposals. On 2nd April, 1855, accompanied by Lord Hardinge, Major-General Sir Frederick Smith and Lieutenant Nicholson, R.E., the Prince Consort inspected a number of these sites before deciding on that upon which the Pavilion was built. It is recorded that the Prince, well satisfied by the final choice, insisted on its being marked out before the party left the site, and that Lieutenant Nicholson, following the Prince's instructions, rode around

The Royal Pavilion, 1866.

Reproduced by kind permission of Rock Bros. Ltd., London, E.6.

the site armed with a bundle of pea-sticks, dropping them at intervals to mark the boundary.

"It is very satisfactory to me," wrote Major-General Sir Frederick Smith to the Inspector-General of Fortifications, after the Prince Consort's visit, "to state that the Prince seemed much pleased" with the progress of the camp. He had also taken a practical interest in the accommodation that was being built. In a demi-official letter* to Lieut.-General Sir John Burgoyne, K.C.B., from Captain Freeth, R.E., dated 5th April, 1855, which opened with "My dear General," Freeth referred to the Prince's visit, stating that he had made suggestions for better ventilation of the huts by an adjustment to the roofs, and that this was therefore passed on for the General's consideration.

The site of the Queen's Pavilion was on a small hill overlooking the Long Valley, Caesar's Camp and the areas then scheduled for the construction of the first permanent barracks. On this eminence it was in an exposed and dominating position, a fact not realized today in view of the thickly wooded surroundings of firs and larches and rhododendron bushes. The construction of the Pavilion was commenced in June, 1854, by Mr. George Myers, one of the contractors engaged in the building of "The Camp," after the first task, the removal of ground to a depth of eleven feet to obtain the level plateau necessary for the building, had already been completed.

It was on 10th June, 1855, that Queen Victoria first visited Aldershot, accompanied by the Prince Consort and General Sir William Knollys. Following an inspection of "The Camp" and a review of the troops—mostly Militia battalions—the Royal party partook of refreshments at the Pavilion, work having been pushed forward by the contractor to complete the building sufficiently for the occasion. The meal was served in a large circular tent erected alongside the building, the meal having been prepared and sent to Aldershot from Windsor.

The Queen visited Aldershot again the following month when she formally opened "The Camp," but it was not until April, 1856, that the Queen first stayed at the new Royal residence. This was on the occasion of the completion of "The Camp," when, accompanied by the Prince Consort and members of the Royal Family, the Queen arrived at Farnborough Station and drove to "The Camp," where she exchanged the carriage for her favourite charger and inspected the 14,000 troops then stationed in "The Camp," who presented a front of a mile and a half. The Queen and the Royal party stayed the night at the Royal Pavilion, a description of which appeared in the

---

* Public Record Office : War Office Correspondence, Out-Letters (W.O.3), 326.

report of the occasion published in the *Illustrated London News* dated 26th April, 1856 :

Her Majesty and the Prince Consort slept in "The Camp" during Friday night, in the building which had been erected for the use of the Royal Family. . . . It is situated to the south of the South Camp about half a mile from the Basingstoke Canal, and about the same distance to the east of the Winchester road. The building forms three sides of a square, and in its ground-plan resembles Buckingham Palace as it used to be before the late improvements. It has another point of resemblance also to its London compeer, viz.: it is bald, cold and ugly to an extreme. The whole Pavilion is built entirely of wood. We believe that, except in one or two cases for the foundations, not a single brick has been used for the whole structure. The entrance is from the south. On the ground floor is a breakfast-room, sitting-room, good sized dining-room and saloon. The upper rooms are of course all used as bed-chambers and dressing-rooms for the Royal family. The two wings are for the different noblemen and Ladies in attendance upon her Majesty. The walls and ceilings of the different apartments are all formed by canvas stretched on frames and papered over. On every side there is merely a waste boggy moor, dreary and repellent in its aspect. In the distance are the black huts of "The Camp," quite in keeping with the moor on which they stand ; and in the foreground is a long narrow piece of muddy water called the Basingstoke Canal, into which occasionally the waters of the surrounding bogs drain.

H.R.H. The Duke of Cambridge, however, had different views, for on 19th April, 1856, he entered in his diary* : "Breakfasted with the Antrim Rifles† and went up to the Queen's Pavilion. It is really very nice and nicely furnished and fitted up."‡

The Duke had travelled to Aldershot to join the Royal party for the review of all troops in "The Camp." The following description of the occasion is taken from a contemporary account§ under the title of "The Review at Aldershott."

All the regiments turned out before ten o'clock. Each corps was inspected by its regimental officers, and then, moving by sections of four, they quitted "The Camp" by various routes leading along the Winchester road to the south. After marching over the wild, rough moorland for about three miles, the troops

---

* *Vide* "The Military Life of H.R.H. George, Duke of Cambridge," by Willoughby Verner, Vol. I, p. 25.

† A Militia battalion.

‡ The Queen, too, later expressed her liking for this residence, for in her own Journal, on 23rd August, 1859, she wrote : "Left the dear cozy Pavilion at Aldershot with regret" (Royal Archives, Windsor).

§ *Illustrated London News*, 26th April, 1856.

approached a broad eminence of considerable extent, called "Caesar's Camp." In some parts the sides are so steep as to be almost precipitous, and the ditches and banks are as well defined as if dug within the last twenty years. The summit of this relic of our conquerors* is from forty to forty-five acres in extent. On the plateau extending from the summit of this camp the troops halted in lines of brigade, and in this position awaited the arrival of the Queen.

Her Majesty left the Pavilion on horseback shortly before eleven o'clock, and rode directly to the review ground. The Prince Consort and the Duke of Cambridge accompanied the Queen on horseback, and the Princesses followed in a pony phaeton. Sir Frederick Smith, R.E., Viscount Hardinge, General Knollys, Brigadier General Hutchinson, Colonel Grey, Lord Alfred Paget, etc., were in attendance on the illustrious party. As the Queen approached the line the whole of the regiments presented arms and lowered their colours, the united band playing the National Anthem. Her Majesty first inspected the whole line, after which the forces were divided into brigades and marched into position as if for the purpose of repulsing a flank and rear attack of an enemy. One brigade was detached along the Winchester road, and, after making a considerable detour, wound round by another part of the heath and took up its position in open column of companies on the right flank of the steep Roman camp. It there threw out a detachment of skirmishers, while the rest of the troops were moved on the hill formed the centre of the position taken up, and extended down its left flank in line, with skirmishers in front, and support in column.

The Royal party having dismounted on an elevated position, General Knollys put himself at the head of the troops, and the mimic engagement began by a sharp skirmishing fire from the Rifles on the right flank of the position. After a few minutes the skirmishing became hotter, and ran along the centre and left. The Rifles kept up this fire for some time, but at last gave way, and were driven in on the right flank. The brigade stationed in the rear immediately supported them by deploying into line, and, after closing up more to their centre, began a file firing. They were, however, not able to maintain their ground, and supports were despatched from the centre to cover their retreat. As this manoeuvre exposed the force on the hill to be taken in rear, these troops were compelled to shift their front. The skirmishers were called in from the centre of the position—the Roman Camp*—and the centre and right fell back at double time, only covering their movements with the Rifles, who broke up and skirmished in beautiful order. The centre and right of the force then fell back nearly a mile, retreating in regular lines, with supports in

---

* The popular supposition that Caesar's Camp dated from the Roman occupation.

open column. Each ditch and bank was lined by skirmishers to cover the backward movement, and each regiment and brigade took ground to the rear and left of their former position. By these manœuvres the left wing of the force, which had not yet been in action, was left to bear the enemy's attack, while the right and centre reformed up in their rear. The left wing accordingly sent out its skirmishers while their main body advanced to the crest of a ridge, taking ground still more to the left. As fast as the left wing moved, the right and centre sent up spare regiments to extend its front, till a line was formed of upwards of a mile in length. This now opened file fire, and for about ten minutes the rattle was deafening, and dense masses of smoke obscured the sky. When the smoke had cleared off the defeated right and centre wings had formed another extended line in support of the left, with powerful reinforcements in the rear. This display of force was overpowering, and the enemy, presumed to be daunted, pursued their success no further.

A keen wind and slight mist, which threatened heavier rain, terminated the engagement earlier than was originally intended. During the evolutions the troops marched and countermarched a considerable distance, and over this ground the Royal party followed on foot, over hills and across valleys. When the engagement was over, the troops formed in continuous line of open columns of companies, and marched past her Majesty. The appearance of the men, while executing this manœuvre, reflected the highest credit upon all the officers connected with the management of "The Camp." The Royal party now rode back to the Pavilion, and after partaking of luncheon, returned to Farnborough station, and from thence by train to London.

On 7th July, 1856, Her Majesty was again in residence at the Royal Pavilion,* accompanied by the Prince Consort, the Prince of Wales, the King of the Belgians, Prince Oscar of Sweden, the Comte de Flanders, the Duke of Cambridge and Lord Panmure, the Secretary of State for War. The occasion was that of the Royal inspection of the Brigade of Guards and other troops then stationed in Aldershot on their return from the Crimea.

A contemporary account† described the events on the following day :

A brilliant field day which had been arranged for July 8th, 1856, was greatly marred by miserable weather. The Royal party, which included the King of the Belgians and Prince Oscar of

---

* It was during the Queen's sojourn at the Pavilion on this occasion that, whilst giving audience with the Prince Consort to Lord Hardinge, the latter was seized with a paralytic attack. He was carried away to his hut, and taken to London on the following day. This seizure led to his resignation from the post of Commander-in-Chief, and shortly afterwards to his death.

† *Vide* "Life of His Royal Highness the Prince Consort," by Sir Theodore Martin, K.C.B., Vol. III, p. 497.

Sweden, had passed the night at the Pavilion. The ground was soaked, and there seemed no chance of the weather clearing.

The troops, however, turned out with alacrity. It was a small matter to them after the hardships of the Crimea.

The Queen arrived on the ground in a close carriage, in attendance upon which rode Prince Albert, the Prince of Wales, the King of the Belgians, the Comte de Flanders, the Duke of Cambridge, and Lord Panmure, all in military uniform. After the usual evolutions had been gone through, a happy break occurred in the weather.

Then followed a scene of unusual interest. The Crimean regiments advanced and formed three sides of a square around the royal carriage. The officers who had been under fire, together with four men of each company and troop, advanced; the Queen's carriage was thrown open, and her Majesty addressed them in the following terms :—

"Officers, non-commissioned officers and soldiers :

I wish personally to convey through you to the regiments assembled here this day my hearty welcome on their return to England in health and full efficiency. Say to them that I have watched anxiously over the difficulty and hardships which they have so nobly borne, that I have mourned with deep sorrow for the brave men who have fallen in their country's cause, and that I have felt proud of their valour which, with their gallant allies, they have displayed on every field. I thank God that your dangers are over, while the glory of your noble deeds remains. But I know that should your service be again required you will be animated with the same devotion which in the Crimea has rendered you invincible."*

No sooner had her Majesty concluded this brief address than a cry of "God save the Queen" sprang to every lip. Helmets, bearskins, and shakos were thrown up into the air, the Dragoons waved their sabres, and a shout of local acclamation caught up from line to line rang through the ranks. It has been described as a grand and spirit stirring sight, full of interest, and not to be witnessed without deep emotion.

Referring to the Queen's speech, H.R.H. the Duke of Cambridge recorded in his diary for 8th July, 1856 : "The Queen made a beautiful address to the troops after they had marched past in splendid style. Nothing could be more beautiful than the manner in which all went off with the exception always of the weather, which was dreadful. . . ."

The Queen remained in residence at Aldershot for over a week, and in a letter† to the Duke of Cambridge dated at Osborne on 19th July,

---

* *Vide* "Life of His Royal Highness the Prince Consort," by Sir Theodore Martin, Vol. III, p. 497.

† "The Military Life of H.R.H. George, Duke of Cambridge," by Willoughby Verner, Vol. I, p. 117.

1856, she wrote: ". . . we had a charming field day on Thursday, which I enjoyed more than any I ever saw, and was on horseback for four hours amongst the troops, the day was beautiful, and the troops marched admirably. We saw the 18th Royal Irish arrive in camp yesterday, the men in excellent order. Altogether we spent a most agreeable time at Aldershot."

On 21st July she wrote* to the King of the Belgians: "We had a delightful sojourn at Aldershot—much favoured by fine weather. The first day, Wednesday, the wind was too high for me to ride, but the second (Thursday) we had one of the prettiest and most interesting field days I ever remember—I rode about everywhere and enjoyed it so much."

Among the troops in Aldershot at this time was the German Legion, numbering some two thousand, and there were several clashes between the 1st Regiment of Jägers and the British regiments in the camp. Details of the disturbances were not given by the military authorities, and in consequence rumour was rife and what had happened was no doubt exaggerated, and this led to the matter being raised in the House of Commons. The matter was sufficiently serious for General Knollys to report details to the Commander-in-Chief (H.R.H. The Duke of Cambridge), who gave orders for the immediate transfer of the German troops to another camp.†

On 14th May, 1859, Queen Victoria and the Prince Consort, accompanied by the Princesses Alice and Helena, arrived in Aldershot. They inspected the new Cavalry Barracks and in the evening a dinner party was held in the Royal Pavilion.

On the next day, a Sunday, the Royal party attended Divine Service in the military church in South Camp—the old iron church below Thorn Hill. On the Monday the entire garrison, under command of General Knollys, composed of three infantry and one cavalry Brigade, mustering, according to a contemporary account,‡ "11,270 bayonets and 1,300 sabres, and inclusive of the Engineers and Military Train found a total of over 13,000 officers and men and eighteen guns," moved out into the Long Valley. "A series of brilliant manœuvres was then carried into execution," the account continues, "after which the troops marched past the Queen in brigades . . . the united bands of each Brigade playing as the different regiments passed by." The Prince Consort, it is recorded,§ wore the uniform of a "Colonel of the Rifles."‖

* "The Letters of Queen Victoria," Vol. III (John Murray) (1907).
† "George, Duke of Cambridge," by Edgar Sheppard, Vol. I, p. 180.
‡ *Illustrated London News*, Vol. 34, p. 516.
§ "The Military Life of H.R.H. George, Duke of Cambridge" by Willoughby Verner, Vol. I, p. 97.
‖ The Rifle Brigade (Prince Consort's Own).

He was mounted and, with the Duke of Cambridge, rode about the field, evincing great interest in the evolutions of the troops. After the march past the Royal party returned to the Pavilion for lunch before leaving "The Camp," the Queen and Princesses in an open carriage drawn by four greys, for Farnborough Station, where a special train awaited them for the return to London.

An Ordnance Survey map published (at a price of 5s.) on 1st October, 1856, from a survey carried out in 1854-5 by Captains Cameron and W. D. Grossett, of the Royal Engineers, and published by Lieut.-Colonel James, R.E., F.R.S., M.R.I.A., Superintendent of the Ordnance Map Office, Southampton, shows in addition to detail of the growing village of Aldershot, the early stages of the development of "The Camp." The hutted barracks of both North and South Camp are shown in detail, as also the R.E. offices which stood on the site of the present-day Princes Gardens and the Ritz and Empire Cinemas.

The Royal Pavilion is shown as "The Queen's Pavilion." The hut of the General Commanding "The Camp" is shown on Stannon Hill by Stannon Clump in the area at the top of the Gun Hill of today, whilst the hut occupied by the Minister of War during his visits to "The Camp" is shown by Red Hill Clump in the area now occupied by the terraces of married quarters in the rear of the main blocks of Badajos Barracks. The first permanent barracks are shown, namely, Badajos, Salamanca and Talavera, but at the time the map was drawn the Cavalry Barracks on the south side of Wellington Avenue had not been built.

The light railway which was constructed on the initiative of, and at the expense of, Mr. Myers, the contractor, to convey building material to the site of the permanent barracks is shown on this map as running off from the London and South-Eastern Railway from Guildford to Farnham near Bin Wood, east of Tongham. The line ran from here north-west in a curve crossing the Ash Road between the present-day sites of the "Greyhound" inn* and the "Bricklayers' Arms," the latter inn probably taking its names from its patrons of those days. From here the line swept round to cross North Lane south of Thorn Hill by Thorn Hill pond and thence parallel with High Street to run along at the rear of the present-day Waterloo, Talavera and Salamanca Barracks, to end just short of the Farnborough Road at the rear of the main blocks of Badajos Barracks.

The growth of Aldershot as a military station between 1854 and 1859 may be judged from the following details of the Staff and troops in the years 1858-9. In 1858 the Headquarters Staff was composed of the General Officer Commanding, Lieut.-General Sir William

---

* Marked on the Ordnance Map of 1856.

The Royal Pavilion, Aldershot, 7th July, 1856, from the original water-colour by G. H. Thomas in the Royal Collection at
Windsor Castle.

Reproduced by gracious permission of H.M. The King.

The view, looking east and south-east, from the terrace of the Royal Pavilion, 16th July, 1856, from the original water-colour by G. H. Thomas in the Royal Library, Windsor Castle.

Knollys. His A.D.Cs. were Captain E. W. Blackett, of the Rifle Brigade, and Lieut. W. Palliser, 18th Hussars. The A.A.G. was Colonel J. Stewart Wood, C.B., R.A.; the D.A.A.G., Captain St. G. M. Nugent, 96th Regiment*; the A.Q.M.G., Colonel J. Clarke-Kennedy, C.B., 18th Regiment†; D.A.Q.M.G., Captain T. Young, 22nd Regiment.‡ The Assistant Commissary-General was Captain H. Robinson, and "The Camp" Quartermaster was Captain R. Brennan, Land Transport Corps.

The Aldershot Cavalry Brigade, which included the Regiment stationed at Hounslow, was commanded by Major-General J. Lawrenson. His A.D.C. was Captain H. D. W. Lyon, of the 2nd Life Guards, and Captain D. T. Godman, of the 5th Dragoon Guards, was the Brigade Major. During the summer training season the Cavalry strength was made up to two Brigades. In 1859 these were composed of the Heavy Brigade—1st Life Guards, 4th Royal Irish Dragoon Guards and 5th Princess Charlotte of Wales's Dragoon Guards—and the Light Brigade, made up of the 10th Prince of Wales's Own Royal Hussars, 11th Prince Albert's Own Hussars and the 15th King's Hussars. There were four Infantry Brigades in "The Camp": the 1st, commanded by Major-General Lord Paulet, C.B.; the 2nd, commanded by Major-General the Hon. A. Spencer, C.B., of the 44th Regiment§; the 3rd, under the command of Major-General J. Laurence, C.B., of the Rifle Brigade; and the 4th, which was under canvas at Rushmoor for summer training, commanded by Colonel Lord Paulet, of the Coldstream Guards.

The Royal Artillery were commanded by Colonel F. Philpotts; the R.H.A. being under the command of Lieut.-Colonel W. P. Radcliff and the Field Batteries under the command of Lieut.-Colonel H. P. Goodenough. The Royal Engineers were commanded by Colonel F. E. Chapman, C.B., the Medical Department by Inspector-General Dr. Gibson, C.B., and the Commissariat Department was supervised by Major K. Osborne, Assistant Commissary-General.

* * * * *

At this time the Headquarters offices of "The Camp" were situated in a series of wooden bungalows near the top of Middle Hill. One of these huts stood until the early 1920's in the west centre of "A" Square, Stanhope Lines, and was the hut occupied as an office by the Duke of Connaught when he was a Staff Officer in Aldershot. The residence of the Senior Royal Engineer Officer was Vine Cottage,

---

* Now the 2nd Bn. The Manchester Regiment.
† Afterwards The Royal Irish Regiment (disbanded 31st July, 1922).
‡ Now The Cheshire Regiment.
§ Now The 1st Bn. The Essex Regiment.

F

which stands to this day, although derelict, below Blandford House on the Farnborough Road.

One of the features of South Camp was the Sebastopol Bell and the Time Gun, which stood at the top of Gun Hill, the hill taking its name from the gun, which was fired at one o'clock and at half-past nine each evening—the first as a time signal, the latter also a signal for all troops to return to their quarters. In the late seventies, when the Cambridge Hospital was built, the gun was removed to a site on Thorn Hill, opposite the main entrance to the Military Cemetery, a little to the right of the last house standing today in Thornhill Terrace. The practice of firing the gun was not discontinued until the 1914-1918 war. For many years a gunner was detailed for the firing duty, and as the hours approached he would walk up from Waterloo Barracks to carry out this twice-daily task. In latter years the gun was fired electrically to coincide with the Greenwich time signal, the co-ordination of timing between Greenwich and Aldershot being by a special telephone line via the Aldershot Telephone Exchange through Stanhope Lines Post Office.

Situated near the Headquarters offices, a sentry, posted at this point, struck the hours on the Sebastopol Bell. The bell, which was mounted under a wooden canopy, had been brought home from the Crimea. In the Royal Library at Windsor Castle is a painting showing the bell on its original wooden mounting, which is of a different construction to that depicted in an engraving of the Gun Hill bell, dated 1869. This bell was taken down from its site near the present-day R.A.M.C. Officers' Mess and re-erected, in 1879, in the Clock Tower of the Cambridge Hospital, where it remains to this day. This bell was one of a pair ; the other was taken to Windsor in 1868 and was erected by Messrs. Stainbank, of Whitechapel, in the Round Tower of the Castle, where it hangs to this day above the main stairway.

These two bells are shown in an engraving published in the *Illustrated London News* of 23rd February, 1856, which illustrated a collection of captured Russian guns and mortars, brought home as trophies of war from the Crimea, then resting in Dial Square at the entrance to Woolwich Arsenal.* The bells, which were ornamented and with representations in relief of saints thereon, came from the Clock Tower of the Church of the Twelve Apostles at Sebastopol.†

The Prince Consort's continued interest in Aldershot was of a practical nature. It was at his suggestion that plantations of trees were planted along the boundaries of and on the military lands to intercept

---

* On 19th February, 1856, Queen Victoria noted in her diary that she had seen and inspected the bells at Woolwich (Royal Archives, Windsor).

† The bells each weighed 17 cwt. 1 qr. 21 lb. and were cast by Nicholas Samtum of Moscow.

the clouds of dust* which swept over "The Camp" from the Long Valley and Laffan's Plain. The avenue of chestnuts along Wellington Avenue was also planted at his instigation.

The Prince Consort's Library, situated off the Farnborough Road near the junction with Knollys Road, was built in September, 1859, and completed in June, 1860, at a cost of about £2,000, which was defrayed by the Prince Consort, reflecting his interest in literature and the arts.†

The appointment of a Librarian appears to have presented some difficulties at the time. Sir C. Phipps wrote‡ from Buckingham Palace on 3rd July, 1860, to Colonel F. E. Chapman,§ confirming arrangements made by the Prince Consort with Major Elphinstone for a Corporal Weston, R.E., to take charge of the Library at a wage of £35 per annum.

Unfortunately, two days after his arrival in Aldershot on 24th September, 1860, he was "seized as a deserter" from the Inniskilling Dragoons. It would appear that he had been watched, for some time, by a person jealous of his success in obtaining a good appointment, and that this person had come the whole way from Chatham to make the disclosure.

In a memorandum‡ from Major H. C. Elphinstone, R.E.,‖ he stated that Corporal Weston had been highly recommended and had excellent testimonials and an exemplary character. He had deserted from the Inniskillings in 1854, but had served six years in the R.E. without an offence of any kind.

Until a successor could be found, General Pennefather placed a Sergeant Wellington, R.E., in charge, but "as his knowledge of languages did not extend beyond limited extent of English," the services

---

* Even as late as 1898 Murray's Handbook for Travellers in Hampshire makes reference to Aldershot suffering from "a plague of dust in summer."

† The Library was opened in September, 1860, and a General Order was issued from Horse Guards, dated 14th September, 1860, signed by James Yorke Scarlett, then Adjutant-General to the Forces : "In announcing," read the Order, "to the Officers of the Army and Militia the opening of the Library at Aldershot, presented for their use by H.R.H. the Prince Consort, the Duke of Cambridge congratulates them on this additional proof of the interest which the Prince Consort takes in their welfare, and commends to their especial care the preservation of a gift so graciously bestowed, and so highly beneficial to the Service" (Royal Archives, Windsor).
A Return of Expenditure by the Prince Consort between 1857 and December, 1861, on the Library amounted to £4,183 3s. 4d., this having been spent on the building, furnishing, the grounds, purchase of books, maps, prints of military costumes, bookbinding and the pay to attendants (Royal Archives, Windsor).

‡ Royal Archives, Windsor.

§ Colonel F. E. Chapman, C.B., R.E., later to be General Sir Frederick E. Chapman, G.C.B., Inspector-General of Fortifications (1870).

‖ Major H. C. Elphinstone, V.C., C.B., later Colonel Sir Howard C. Elphinstone, V.C., K.C.B., C.M.G., A.D.C. to the Queen (1877).

of Lieut. Eustace of the 49th Regiment were accepted, and this enabled the Library to be first opened on 5th October, 1860, as planned.

Further suitable applicants for the post of Librarian were considered, among them a Sergeant of the 18th Hussars, four N.C.Os. of the Royal Engineers and a Sergeant of the 49th Regiment.* Sergeant G. Gilmore of the 49th was finally selected at a wage of £36 per year exclusive of regimental pay.† Knowledge of languages was considered essential to the post, and although Gilmore spoke fluent German he was sent to Jersey to learn French.

Gilmore's appointment as Librarian was confirmed on 18th May, 1861, in a letter written from Horse Guards by the Military Secretary.

Gilmore retired in 1891, on a pension, and was succeeded by Q.M.S. Bex, of the 1st Bn. The Devonshire Regiment. Bex retired in January, 1903, and another serving soldier was selected by the Aldershot Military Society.‡ At this time, however, the War Office ruled that the post should no longer be held by a serving soldier, and so Mr. Bex was invited to return to the post as a civilian. This he did, holding the office of Librarian until 1923. From 1924 to 1930 a retired officer, Mr. George Henson Hewitt, held the post.

On 1st July, 1859, the Victoria Soldiers' Library was opened by General Knollys.§ This Library was started with seven hundred and twenty volumes, the gift of Queen Victoria. These books came from libraries of the hospitals and recreation huts established in the Crimea ; they were rebound and were evenly distributed between two Soldiers' Libraries, the one in Aldershot and the other in Dublin, as the two leading military centres in the British Isles. The whole cost of the libraries was defrayed from the Privy Purse. The Library was housed in a group of wooden huts situated on the crest of Queen's Avenue in South Camp.. The first Librarian was one Sergeant Moss. Libraries and Reading Rooms were also provided on the scale of one

---

* Now the 1st Bn. The Royal Berkshire Regiment.

† Royal Archives, Windsor.

‡ The Aldershot Military Society was formed on 23rd December, 1887, at the instigation of the D.A.A. & Q.M.G., Major E. Hutton (later Lieutenant-General Sir Edward Hutton) with the object of "stimulating professional interest by reason of an augmented library (in 1887 it comprised only 2,160 volumes, many of which dated from 1860), and occasional meetings for the purpose of holding discussions and lectures on the current military topics of the day" (Royal Archives, Windsor).

§ When the Library was opened the principles for its management were laid down in a letter dated 28th April, 1857, addressed to General Knollys by the Adjutant-General. The Library was to be called the "Victoria Soldiers' Library" and was to be under the supervision of a "Committee of Officers of the Division," unlike the Barrack Libraries, which were managed by the War Office. The Victoria Library's books were under the "exclusive control" of the Commander-in-Chief,

per battalion, General Knollys, in a memorandum to Captain Laffan, R.E., stating that twenty-one such Reading Rooms were sufficient at the time.

The spiritual needs of the garrison were catered for in the early days by three churches ; all were built of wood and iron, and two of these are standing and in use to this day. It had been agreed in a letter from the Ordnance Board to the Inspector-General of Fortifications, dated 14th April, 1855, that two churches were to be built in the camp. "The Buildings," it read, "are to be erected on the plan of a covered Railway Station, and are to have no galleries and nothing in them except forms." The letter instructed the Inspector-General of Fortifications to prepare plans and estimates for two large buildings for divine worship. In a memorandum in the same Ordnance Board file is a note in the form of a reminder : "Write to Lord of Treasury," it reads, "to request sanction for an expenditure of £4,416 for two chapels at the Camp at Aldershot approved by the 'Minister at War.' "*

One of the first churches to be erected in "The Camp" was the "Iron Church," which was built some half a mile from "The Camp" just north of the site now occupied by the Municipal Recreation Ground on the rising ground below the Ordnance Depot, and so called from the fact that it was built of cast iron and wood, supported on iron columns which formed the nave and aisles ; its windows were painted glass, and the church was described as "particularly light and elegant." It was generally known to the troops as the "Tin Tabernacle," and its location was known as the "Dustbowl." The church was moved in 1866 to the site now occupied by St. Andrew's Garrison Church by the bridge over the canal in Queen's Avenue.

The Roman Catholic Church of St. Michael and St. Sebastian, near the Cambridge Hospital, remains today as it did when it was first built, constructed of wood as is also the Marlborough Lines Garrison Church in Evelyn Wood's Road, North Camp, which is of similar appearance to the Roman Catholic Church in Stanhope Lines. The Marlborough Lines Church was built by a firm of contractors, Messrs.

---

the use of the Library was "unfettered," and maintained at the Queen's expense, the Queen replacing worn-out books and adding new volumes from time to time.

In May, 1881, General Sir Daniel Lysons found the Library to be in an "unsatisfactory state" on account of the "age of the books and discomfort of the room." (Some of the books which had been sent out to the Crimea were still in use, and also some of the "Bullock Trunks" in which they had been conveyed were being used for storage.) This he reported to the Queen, who approved the reorganization of the Library, its transference to a new room (in Salamanca Barracks) and a grant of £20 per annum for upkeep. A new Committee was appointed, the President being Colonel W. B. Gossett, R.E., with Colonel J. Jago of the 2nd Bn. Highland Light Infantry, and Major H. Knollys, the R.A. Brigade Major, as Secretary (Royal Archives, Windsor).

* Public Record Office   War Office Correspondence, Out-Letters (W.O.3), 326.

Lucas Brothers, on the orders of the Surveyor of the War Department, who received instructions to proceed "with all dispatch in the construction of the church to the drawings and specifications approved by Mr. Monsell and Colonel Bruce."

The Military Cemetery, which lies between Thorn Hill and Peaked Hill, was enclosed in 1856. In 1870 the Cemetery became the responsibility of the senior R.E. officer in "The Camp." The Protestant portion of the cemetery was consecrated by the Bishop of Winchester on 1st November the same year. The mortuary chapel was built in 1879.

A Fire Station was established in "The Camp" as soon as most of the huts were built—a very necessary precaution with the wooden huts built closely together in blocks, when an outbreak of fire, fanned by the winds blowing across the open country, could have proved disastrous. Portable iron screens mounted on wheels were provided in each block of huts which, in the event of fire, could be run between the huts in order to cut off and localize the fire in an effort to prevent it spreading. The Fire Station was equipped with two manual fire-engines. The station stood near the site of the present-day Headquarter Offices, and outside stood a large alarm bell. The door-step of the station was, curiously enough, an old tombstone which disappeared during the rebuilding of "The Camp" and was never traced.

The R.A.S.C. Establishment was constructed between 1855 and 1861. The Commissariat depot, built adjacent to Thorn Hill, was composed of a large bakery, a slaughter-house, stores and administrative offices. The bakery and some of the huts were destroyed by fire on 25th April, 1857, the damage being estimated at £2,000.

The first military gymnasium was built in South Camp in 1861. This followed a War Office decision that the training of the soldier should be extended beyond formal drill evolutions and weapon training and that the physical aspect of the soldier's education and training was to be improved. In 1860 a Major Hammersley and twelve non-commissioned officers, selected from various units, underwent a course at the gymnasium at Oxford University, following which they were sent to Aldershot to become the nucleus of the Army Gymnasium Staff, and the first gymnasium in the Army was built.

A visit to the permanent barracks in 1860 is described in "Sketches of the Camp at Aldershot." The barracks built "for the especial benefit and accommodation of the Royal Artillery"—now Waterloo Barracks—were described as occupying three large structures facing south, the whole designed to accommodate "two troops of Horse Artillery." At the rear of the buildings was the large quadrangular parade ground, surrounded by "schools, magazines ; gun and tumbril sheds and harness-makers', tailors' and farriers' shops." The buildings

The Military Cemetery, Thorn Hill, 1866.

Reproduced by kind permission of Rock Bros. Ltd., London, E.6.

for men and horses were arranged as stables on the ground floor and barrack rooms above, reached from the outside by steps, and a balcony six feet wide.

The Infantry Barracks* were described as

> ... somewhat extensive, each one being composed of two structures facing each other, about forty or fifty feet apart and connected by a roof of glass strengthened with iron. Each of these structures is three stories high and on each floor are ten rooms, each capable of holding twenty-five men. The means of reaching the upper floors is by stairs leading on to balconies on either side of the avenue. These balconies are about ten feet wide. The space between each structure constituted a parade ground, and being, as before stated, covered by a roof of glass,† is admirably suited to the purpose, as the men can go through their daily routine of discipline as well on wet as on fine days, being up to their ancles [*sic*] in mud, or drenched with rain.

---

* Badajos, Salamanca and Talavera Barracks.

† These glazed roofs were removed in the early nineteen-hundreds after a series of accidents, some of which proved fatal, due to troops falling through the glass whilst engaged in cleaning. It was also said that there were accidents due to acts of bravado by soldiers trying to cross from one building to another on the girders.

The Cavalry Barracks* are described as "more commodious in character" than those of the Artillery, and in referring to the Riding Schools the author describes them as being of "some architectural beauty, and, in point of size and accommodation reputed the finest in England."

These Riding Schools exist today, but, sad to relate, shorn of their former glory. The tan has gone ; it went soon after the departure of the horses when mechanization of the cavalry took place in the years immediately preceding the late war. Rough concrete floors now cover the ground where six or so generations of cavalry troopers obediently answered the Riding Master's commands. In Beaumont Barracks,† mostly silent until the evenings, stand 3.7 anti-aircraft guns, a predictor and a radar set. Soldiering has undergone a more drastic change in the past twelve years than ever before in military history.

The hutted camp‡ was divided into blocks systematically arranged and intersected by roads. The blocks were identified by alphabetical designation : "A" Block, "B" Block, etc.—a system which obtains in the Army today, be it a Nissen hutted camp of the 1939-45 vintage or the lines of an overseas cantonment. Each block in the original camp was designed for the accommodation of a regiment. The block was composed of twenty-two huts, each accommodating an equal number of men, plus four officers' huts, one of which was allotted to field officers, the remaining three huts being subdivided to accommodate eight officers—captain and subalterns. In addition to this officers' quarters and barrack-room accommodation, the block contained huts for messes, cook-houses, a school room, quartermaster's office, regimental stores, bread and meat stores, armourers' shop, shoemakers' and tailors' shop, a wash-house, a canteen, a married men's room, a women's wash-house, a hut for officers' servants, and stables.

The hutted barrack rooms were singularly comfortless. Light was provided by oil lamps and later a few open gas jet burners.§ Heat was

---

* Willems, Warburg, and Beaumont Barracks.
† Now the Headquarters of Aldershot's Territorial Anti-Aircraft Gunners—667 Heavy A.A. Regiment, R.A. (T.A.) ; 354 Engineer Equipment Workshop, R.E.M.E. (T.A.); and a Company of 310 Bn. (Southern Command) W.R.A.C. (T.A.). (See p. 319.)
‡ The Barrack Master of the Camp at this time was Major T. Smith, a Peninsular War veteran, who wore the Military General Service Medal with eleven clasps, brother of General Sir Harry Smith. The Barrack Master's Staff consisted of a Captain, two clerks and twenty Barrack Sergeants.
§ Estimates for lighting the huts and barracks with gas were obtained on 13th July, 1855. Until then oil lamps had been the only illumination in the whole camp.

provided from strictly rationed coal stoves* in the centre of each hut. The officers' huts were divided to accommodate six officers in separate compartments, two compartments sharing the same door. Each room had a small window, a fireplace,† an enormous coal box, a small iron bedstead; and the military "yardstick" of furnishing, many will observe, has changed but little in the past hundred years, except that the universal stove has replaced the fireplace of the early fifties and electric light has taken the place of the candle or oil lamp.

In the opening chapter of an amusing book published in 1856 under the title of "Aldershottana, or Chinks in my Hut,"‡ the author describes the accommodation in "The Camp" in a letter to a college friend :

> If you laughed at my folly [he wrote] when I abandoned "Academus' sacred shades" and went soldiering in the militia, I dare say your mirth will be increased as you peruse the following pages. . . . There is little that is new or interesting to be said about the obscure village or desolate heath of Aldershott . . . but there is something to be told about the life we lead . . . when I was quartered in a hut full of cracks and chinks, I flattered myself that I would have had a leisure hour now and then. . . . I un- packed my books, arranged my classics upon a shelf, but the first night I spent in my hut dispelled and routed for ever those pleasing illusions . . . my hut, and the blocks of huts being so craftily constructed as to reverberate and re-echo to every sound from that occasioned by the falling of a pin's head upon the floor to the slamming of doors and windows. Of the eight loose boxes (or delectable chambers nine feet by nine) under one roof-tree, seven in my block were occupied by racketty young fellows Whose pleasure it was to make the "welkin ring" with songs and shouts and maudlin harmony. . . . Negro melodies, demand- ing a chorus, were the favourite pieces. Any performer, who at any time by day or by night took it into his head to "roar a catch" or "howl a verse" of "Old Dan Tucker," "Buffalo Gals"

---

* The stoves, with their flues poking out of the wooden walls, were regarded as a source of danger from fire, and this was the subject of a letter dated 30th July, 1855, and marked "immediate," addressed to Major-General Sir Frederick Smith from Captain R. Laffan, R.E. The stoves were later replaced by brick fireplaces (War Office Correspondence, Out-Letters (W.O.3), 326.)

† Brick fireplaces were installed in the place of stoves on the final recommenda- tion of Lord Hardinge and an additional expenditure of £11,777 11s. 4d. was voted for the building of fireplaces and chimneys, the contract going to Mr. George Myers (who built the Queen's Pavilion) (*vide* letter from the Director-General of the W.D. Contracts Department, 22nd November, 1855) (War Office Corre- spondence, Out-Letters (W.O.3), 326).

‡ "Aldershottana, or Chinks in my Hut," was published by Ward, Lock & Co. Ltd., in 1859. The first edition was dedicated to "The Zealous and Chivalrous Officers of that Noble Army of Volunteers The Militia of Great Britain and Ireland in whose hands the safety, honour and welfare of the realm reposed during the war."

or "Toll the Bell for Nelly" was sure to be sustained by his
neighbours at once, and presently the whole strength of the block,
vocal and instrumental.

In comparison with the officers' quarters in "The Camp," which
have changed but little as far as hutted camp accommodation is concerned, the difference between the accommodation for married soldiers
then and the married quarters of today is perhaps the change of the
greatest magnitude. In the fifties of the last century the married
soldiers of the regiment married "on the strength"—*i.e.*, the small
proportion who were permitted by regulations to mix their domestic
with their regimental lives—were allotted but one hut in the regimental block, which was shared, for example, by ten married couples,
plus perhaps twelve or more children of varying ages, a rug, rough
blanket or ragged sheet forming the only screen between the beds ;
the space along the centre of the hut between the foot of the beds
being "common ground," festooned by washing drooping from lines
running the length of the huts.

The wives lived a communal life under conditions which by modern
standards are indescribable, but no worse, it must be realized, than
that which was the lot of many thousands of civilian wives in the
crowded cottages and terraced rows of dwellings in the mean streets
clustered around the factories of the then new industrial centres of
the Midlands and the North and the narrow by-ways of the old cities.
Under the conditions described above the soldier and his wife were
happy to live, raise families and take part in the lives of the regiments.
To many of the women even this type of life was of a higher standard
than that from whence they had come ; many a weary mile in most
cases, from the hovels of Houndsditch, the crofters' huts of the Highlands, the peat-smoked dwellings of County Kildare, the small thatched
cottages of the shires, or in some cases farther still from the small
ports and garrison towns of the colonies or elsewhere where the soldier
had served his country. These soldiers' wives shared this communal
existence, with only a semblance of privacy. They prepared meals,
assisted in "The Camp," did laundry work, were the seamstresses of
the regiment, and raised their children to grow into the healthy
youngsters with whom "The Camp" abounded.

Early photographs of "The Camp" show the huts built closely
together, with lines of washing strung between them. Between the
huts were the unmade camp roads which threw up clouds of dust in
the summer and became quagmires in the winter. Attempts were,
however, soon made to improve conditions and the appearance of the
hutted camp. Gardens were dug between the huts and small shrubberies planted where possible.

Education of the soldier at Aldershot in the early days of "The Camp" was not neglected. Each block had its school hut and reading rooms were established by many regiments. The following rules from the Reading Room of the Herefordshire Militia in South Camp make interesting reading, as similar rules can be seen to this day.

1. Papers and books are to be read in the room and not taken away.

2. Privates to pay twopence a month, non-commissioned officers threepence a month.

3. No swearing, drinking, gambling, card playing or loud talking allowed.

4. Pens, ink and paper provided free of cost.

5. Chess, draughts and dominoes allowed.

6. Members, if sick, are allowed, when in hospital, writing paper, etc.

The cook-houses were large iron huts. Around the rooms were benches for the cooks to work in preparing the meals. The centre was occupied with large iron slabs on which the pots and pans were placed. Fires beneath the iron slabs had their outlet through small flues connected to a large central chimney.

The ration scale was one pound of bread and three-quarters of a pound of meat, which included the bone, fat and waste. All other food was provided out of the modest pay of the soldier, which in the case of privates of infantry was a shilling a day, with twopence a day extra for cavalrymen.

The story of North Camp really belongs to Farnborough, for the boundary between the areas of the Aldershot Borough Council and the Farnborough Urban District Council runs across "The Camp" from the Farnborough Road across Queen's Parade to the north of the Aldershot Military Stadium. This boundary, however, did not exist when "The Camp" was established; the whole of the military area has always been described as Aldershot; and it is now possible that it may not be many years before the boundary line is lost by the joining of Aldershot and Farnborough as part of a new County Borough.

North Camp developed along the same lines as South Camp with hutted barrack blocks set out along the line of the present-day Lynch-ford Road. The cavalry barracks were at the end of the line opposite what was described in a contemporary account as a "large and showily painted Hotel"—the predecessor of the present-day Queen's Hotel—at which it was said first-class accommodation existed for "both man and beast." The hotel was erected in 1855 by Mr. Hemmings, the contractor for the construction of North Camp, on the site of a nursery garden near the toll gate on the turnpike road.

North Camp was constructed simultaneously with South Camp; it was, like South Camp, composed of low huts, and so the large high-walled Military Prison which was built of wood in 1855* dominated that portion of "The Camp." With the rebuilding of North Camp with permanent barracks the prison was shut in and today it is obscured by the neighbouring buildings. The Military Prison and Detention Barracks, familiarly called "The Glasshouse," took this name from the fact that the main roof over the three-storeyed prison blocks was of glass.

As in Aldershot, a thriving business community sprang up along the northern boundaries of "The Camp"; the appearance of Lynchford Road being similar to that of High Street, Aldershot, with its fair sprinkling of beer houses and inns which are in evidence today, chief among which is the wooden-fronted "Elephant and Castle" public-house at the top of Queen's Avenue. South Farnborough did not, however, develop to the extent of Aldershot, the commercial enterprise confining its activities to the area situated along the bounds of "The Camp."

North Camp was then, as it is today, separated from South Camp by the stretch of grass now occupied by playing fields, the Aldershot Military Stadium and Queen's Parade, so named from the fact that it was here that Queen Victoria held many of her inspections of the garrison. Queen's Avenue, the long, straight road leading from Hospital Hill to Lynchford Road, Farnborough, was laid about this time, and the first avenue of trees planted. The road crosses the canal near St. George's Church. Before the bridge was built the canal was crossed at this point by a pontoon bridge which was constructed by the Sappers at the opening of the camps, and kept in use until the bridge was built some years later. The pontoon bridge was closed at eight o'clock on winter evenings and at 9.50 p.m. in the summer, and every night the open grassland between North Camp and the canal was dotted with "red-coats" who had preferred the amenities of North Camp or the beer of South Farnborough converging, often at the double as time was short, on the pontoon in order to "catch the last boat," as it was generally referred to. Failure to make the bridge before closing entailed the walk up to the Wharf Bridge on the Farnborough Road.

Of the life of the camp, Mrs. Ewing wrote† that the soldier's life was "one of exceptionally hard work . . . with no small proportion of

---

* The present brick building was constructed in 1870.
† "The Story of a Short Life," by Mrs. J. H. Ewing. (S.P.C.K.) (1885).

the hardships and even risks of active service" with "none of the more glorious chances of war." The soldier might die of "sunstroke on the march, or contract rheumatism, fever or dysentery under canvas, without drawing Indian pay and allowances," and ruin a uniform "as rapidly as in a campaign, and never hope to pin a ribbon over its inglorious stains."

The "haters of the Camp" said it was ugly, dusty and crowded, that it was neither town nor country and had the "disadvantages of each without the merits of either"; it was unshaded and unsheltered; the lines were monotonous and yet confusing. The huts let in the frost in the winter and the heat in summer; they were stuffy and draughty.

Admitting some hardships and blunders, "defenders of the Camp" fell back on statistics as witness to the general good health of the troops, avowing that the breezes were bracing and that this particular part of the country would qualify as a health resort. Added to this, the camp was within easy reach of town, and if one did not think the country lovely and the neighbourhood agreeable one must be hard to please. At night the airs that "fanned the silent Camp were as dry and whole-some as by day, that the song of the distant nightingale could be heard there, and finally that from end to end of this dwelling-place of ten thousand men, a woman might pass at midnight with greater safety than in the country lane of a rural village or a police-protected thoroughfare of the metropolis."

The best defence of the camp was that it was a camp: "military life in epitome with all its defects and all its charm."*

As will be appreciated, there was really little to amuse or entertain the growing population of "The Camp." It was not always con-venient or possible to travel to Farnham† to dine at the hotels and join in the social life of that town. Credit was due therefore to the enthusiasts who established the theatre and encouraged amateur theatricals in "The Camp." A large hut, capable of seating five hundred, was subscribed for by officers of the units stationed in camp, fitted with a stage, cushioned seats, an orchestra pit and "green rooms." The scenery, which was sixteen feet in height, was painted by the principal scene painter to the Drury Lane Theatre. The hut, situated in South Camp, was opened in April, 1856, and was called later, following Queen Victoria's visit to a performance on 6th November, 1856, the "Theatre Royal." The first performance given in the theatre was on the evening of 12th May, 1856, when "The Printer's

---

* "The Story of a Short Life," by Mrs. J. H. Ewing (S.P.C.K.) (1885).
† The neighbourhood of Farnham, it was recorded, was "much benefited by the establishment of 'The Camp'," and lodgings were "exorbitantly dear." *Vide Illustrated London News*, 7th June, 1856.

Devil" was presented by the officers of the Worcestershire Militia and was patronized by General Knollys. This was the forerunner of many well-presented productions which proved very popular and were well attended by the officers, sergeants and their wives. The male roles were played in these productions by officers and the female parts by professional actresses. The theatre was managed by a committee of officers. Lieutenant Crossman of the Hants Militia was stage manager, and the secretary was an officer of the Royal Dublin Militia, Captain Shaw.

Cultural entertainment was not, however, confined to theatricals, and an amateur choral society was formed about the same time, called the "Aldershot Musical Society," with four ladies and a considerable number of men described as "all very creditable performers." This Society gave a number of concerts, well presented and well attended, performed, it has been written, "with great *éclat*," with "music of the highest order" made up of selections from Mozart, Rossini, Meyerbeer and other popular composers. Prompted by the success of these amateur efforts, the choir of the Royal Military Schools, Chelsea, gave concerts of "both sacred and secular" music in the South Camp Church, accompanied by bands of the various regiments, including the 2nd Battalion of the Rifle Brigade.

Everything possible was done to cultivate these forms of entertainment and every encouragement given to those whose enthusiasm prompted or led the development of these activities.

Organized sport was almost unknown; some cricket was played, and there is record of some fairly rough-and-tumble boxing, whilst quietly arranged prize fights took place in secluded spots in the Bourley area and in the Fox Hills.

It was due to the general conditions prevailing in "The Camp" that the Officers' Club on the Farnborough Road was first erected in 1858 near the site of the old "Row Barge" inn. The Club was built by the enterprise of a London wine merchant, who obtained permission from the War Department on certain conditions. The Club was found most useful, especially for officers to take their meals before the establishment of messes. Its outward appearance at the time was described as "not unlike a mission church," for it was built of corrugated iron with a central hall with wings either side. Some years later the Club was bought by the War Department and turned over to the Aldershot Division for administration. The following description of the Club is taken from the *Illustrated London News* soon after it was opened in 1859 as "The Royal Aldershott Club House" :

This splendid accommodation has just been provided at "The Camp" at Aldershott, by Mr. Thos. M. Stapleton, who, jointly with Major Chambre, the Honorary Secretary to the Committee, were the original projectors of the Aldershot Club. H.R.H. Prince Albert has visited the building, and suggested some additions and improvements, which have been carried out by the proprietor without any extra cost of subscription to the members. The Prince, who appeared much interested on the subject, at the solicitation of Lord Torrington, consented to become patron of the Club, and gave permission to attach the title of "the Royal Aldershott Club." By the unremitting exertions of Major Chambre, we understand that upwards of 400 officers of "The Camp" have already given their signatures as subscribers. The General commanding, Major-General Knollys, immediately on the officers expressing their wishes on the subject to him, forwarded the proprietor's request, together with a letter of rules and regulations prepared by Major Chambre, to Lords Hardinge and Panmure who immediately gave the ground for the purpose of the Club, with permission for its erection, with a lease at a nominal rent for thirty-five years.

The building has been constructed by Mr. S. Henning, of Clift-House Works, Bow. It is of large dimensions, being 82 feet front, and 130 feet deep; and contains a reading-room, 80 by 30 by 20 feet high; coffee-room, 50 by 26; fencing-room, 40 by 30; and three billiard-rooms, card-room, and smoking-room, each 26 by 20; and numerous offices of all descriptions.

It was commenced on 28th July, 1859, and ready to receive the furniture on 28th August (being just one month from the commencement), and during that time several additions were made to the original design to meet the Committee. The decorations, designed by Mr. Henning, are chaste and appropriate, and have been well carried out by Mr. Connor, of Fenchurch Street. The carpet for the principal room has been designed expressly for the purpose, and contains upwards of four hundred yards. The room is handsomely lighted up (for the present) by three or more chandeliers of forty-eight lights each, till the arrangements shall have been completed for gas. The cuisine is admirably fitted up by Jeakes & Co., with all the modern improvements, regardless of expense. The building has altogether a unique and imposing appearance, is perfectly dry, and fit for immediate occupation.

The total cost, with fixtures and furniture, will exceed £4,000. The Officers, by their arrangement with the proprietor, avoid all risk or liability, as the whole responsibility and expenses of every kind devolve on him. It is intended to have racket, quoit, and cricket grounds attached for the use of the members.

The Club was described by a writer in the late fifties* as a "rendez-vous of all the choice spirits of 'The Camp,' where politics and matters

---

* *Vide* "Sketches of 'The Camp' at Aldershot" (Andrews & Lucy, Farnham) (*circa* 1858).

connected with the turf are discussed with equal energy and gusto, where all grave questions such as 'what do you intend to do with yourself tomorrow, old fellah ?' are debated and settled, and where all pleasure parties and practical jokes are arranged." The Club at this time was "a very comfortable looking and tastefully decorated erection, painted green and white and, to judge from the quantity of glass, well supplied with light. In front is a spacious lawn approachable by gates from the road, and in the centre is a long upright pole on the top of which floats jauntily the Union Jack." The narrator describes the activities inside the club : "a party deeply immersed in a game of billiards," whilst in other parts of the club were a larger number of "England's gallant sons studying *Punch* or perusing *The Times* or *Morning Post* as the case may be" ; in another part of the club "a knot of young blades are improving themselves by an animated discussion as to the best means of placing a sack on the top of the chimney of old Major Plumkin's hut, because if that praiseworthy object could be attained it would just serve the 'crusty old buffer' right. . . ."

In November, 1863, the Club was the scene of the court-martial of Colonel Thomas Crawley of the 6th Dragoon Guards, who was brought home from India to face a charge, following the death of a sergeant-major of the regiment at Ahmednuggur in Deccan, and of being guilty of undue severity whilst the N.C.O. was under arrest. The large club-room was converted into a court-room for the purpose, and 150 witnesses, mainly drawn from the regiment, were also brought home to attend the court-martial. The trial, which attracted at the time considerable public attention, opened in the middle of November and dragged on for a month. At its conclusion the Colonel was found not guilty of the charges brought against him, and he was honourably acquitted.

The growth of Aldershot and the great military camp naturally aroused considerable public interest, and the closely printed national Press of the day devoted many a column to detailed descriptions of the progress of "The Camp" and reports of the Army's activities. In closely set small type the journalists dealt with every aspect of the life of the Army in Aldershot, publishing full accounts of every exercise, arrival, departure or development, with the full designation of units and the names of their officers, and with colourful descriptions of the troops and the events in which they participated. Among the best descriptive contemporary accounts is an interesting article which appeared in the popular magazine *All the Year Round*, which was edited by Charles Dickens. This article has been republished on two occasions in the past twenty-five years in the local Press, and each time it has been attributed to Dickens himself. The style is in fact the style of

H.M. *Queen Victoria reviewing the First or Grenadier Regiment
Foot Guards on their return from the Crimea.*

Reproduced from R. Ackermann's "Costumes of the British Army."

Lieut.-General Sir William T. Knollys, first General Officer Commanding
"The Camp at Aldershot."

Reproduced by kind permission of the G.O.C. Aldershot District.

The south approach to Aldershot Camp, circa 1855.
Reproduced by kind permission of Rock Bros. Ltd., London, E.6.

General view of the Camp looking east, 1855.
Reproduced from "Aldershot and All About It."

[Copyright : H.M. The King.

H.M. *Queen Victoria addressing her troops on their return from the Crimea, 8th July,* 1856. *The scene is in the valley below Hungry Hill. From the original water-colour by G. H. Thomas in the Royal Collection at Windsor Castle.*

Reproduced by gracious permission of H.M. The King.

[Copyright : H.M. The King.

Married quarters of the Rifle Brigade, Aldershot, 1856, *from the original water-colour by G. H. Thomas in the Royal Library, Windsor.*

Reproduced by gracious permission of H.M. The King.

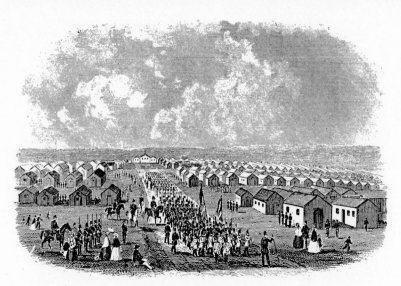

South Camp, Aldershot, circa 1855.

North Camp in 1866. *The central road is now Evelyn Woods Road, and the tall building in the distance is the Marlborough Lines Garrison Church.*

Engravings reproduced by kind permission of Rock Bros. Ltd., London, E.6.

The interior of an officer's hut, circa 1859.

Reproduced from "Aldershot and All About It," by kind permission of the Publisher.

George Housman Thomas (1824-1868) (five of whose original water-colours from the Royal Library, Windsor Castle, are reproduced in this volume) began his career as a book illustrator. He supplied the *Illustrated London News* with sketches of the defence of Rome by Garibaldi, and was retained on the staff of that journal. He was employed by Queen Victoria to make a series of drawings of many events with which she was associated and of many places in which she was interested, including a series of "The Camp at Aldershot." (*Bryant's Dictionary of Painters and Engravers.*)

The Officers' Club, circa 1859.
Reproduced by kind permission of the "Illustrated London News."

Church. South Camp. Aldershott.

The old "Iron Church," which originally stood on a site near the present-day Aldershot Recreation Ground and was moved in 1866 to the site now occupied by the Garrison Church of St. Andrew in Queen's Avenue.

Officers of the 1st Bn. The Royal Regiment (The Royal Scots), Aldershot Camp, July, 1863.

Talavera, Salamanca and Badajos Barracks, circa 1856. The foreground is the area now occupied by Princes Gardens, the Empire Cinema and High Street.

Dickens, written as one would expect from his great pen—a detailed account of what the writer saw, his experiences and his impressions, which appear to be not entirely favourable to the military organization and administration of the day or in fact to the soldier himself.

Charles Dickens's references to soldiers in his works are not numerous, despite the fact that he lived through the times of the Crimean War, the Indian Mutiny, the American Civil War and other conflicts on the Continent. Dickens was three years old when the Battle of Waterloo was fought and he was brought up in a period tired of war. A large section of the nation was ready to forget military glory and devote itself to civil reform and regeneration. Dickens belonged to this party. He was a lover of peace, although he also appreciated the necessities of force and he admired our fighting forces,* for he put one of his sons, Walter (who died on service in Calcutta, in 1863), into the Army, and another, Sidney (who was buried at sea in 1867), into the Navy.

Military pomp made no appeal to Dickens ; military honour alone gave him satisfaction and pride. He was strongly critical of Army administration, as he was of all departmental administration ; he criticized this on several occasions in his works. In his "Miscellaneous Papers" is an article dated 1857 called "Stores for the 1st April," and this is strongly critical of the administrative organization in the Crimea and the Black Sea bases.† It was perhaps natural, therefore, when the article on Aldershot written in 1859, taken from Dickens's own magazine, was republished, that it was generally assumed that he was the writer who had actually visited Aldershot and "The Camp." It must, however, be borne in mind that all the articles in *All the Year Round* were unsigned, which also led to this assumption. There is no record of the authors of these unsigned articles, and Charles Dickens the younger, who was intimate with his father's editorial work and assisted him very often, went through the complete file of *All the Year Round*, with the aid of F. G. Kitton, and identified all the articles that had undoubtedly been written solely by Charles Dickens ; the results of this close scrutiny were published in "The Minor Writings of Charles Dickens," 1900. The article on Aldershot is not included in this list, and so the writer must remain unknown, but it has now been established that it was not the work of the great novelist himself. The writer of the article, who visited "Aldershott" and "The Camp" as the guest of an officer of the Antrim Rifles in July, 1859, recorded his impressions, which were of a practical and critical nature and not

---

* "Immortal Memory," by T. W. Hill, p. 205, *The Dickensian*, 1941.
† J. Cumings Walters writing in *The Dickensian*, 1915, p. 201.

H

tinged with the romanticism which coloured the descriptions of other contemporary writers.

The following is an extract from his descriptions of "The Camp" :

. . . I reach the brow of the hill in the dark, leaving the row of lights of the mushroom town beneath me, and behind me, and coming upon the long, silent, black lines of huts, varied and divided by broad gritty roads of stony gravel, and surmounted by a wide semicircle of streaky orange horizon in front.

Before I have found out the line of huts, and the particular "block" in which I am to pass the night, I am challenged half a dozen times by half a dozen sentries, but as I reply, according to my instructions, "A friend," I am not arrested, run through the body, nor shot through the head.

I pass a few glimmering lights in hut windows, and a few murmuring huts, where the men are divided off in small parties to sleep, and find my lodging on the tented field at last.

Lieutenant Hongwee's quarters (like the quarters of every subaltern) are not sufficiently commodious to accommodate two persons with comfort ; but that young and promising officer is taking his turn as the captain of the watch (a twenty-four hours' guard-house duty which falls to his lot, perhaps, once in six months), and I have full permission to usurp his bed. If any difficulty should occur (which is not anticipated), I am furnished —no doubt, against strict military rule—with the "parole" and "counter-sign." "Romsey" will carry me through anything (except officers' practical jokes) up to the solemn midnight hour, and "Stockport" will be of equal service to me at any time afterwards.

After being disturbed by a variety of noises throughout the night, the clanking of arms, and the talking of the men on guard in the adjacent guard house, the squabbling of the sentry when he took a drunken straggler into custody, and the mysterious humming of the telegraphic wires, which stretch across the line of "The Camp," and form a gigantic Aeolian harp ; the dweller in the hut is thoroughly awakened at five o'clock a.m. by the sound of bugles arousing the men for the day. The officer seldom makes his appearance before the hour of ten a.m. having nothing to do before the parade duty at eleven a.m., but the men are considerately beat into bed at the almost infantine time of half-past nine at night, and they are punctually beat in the morning to be stirring with the lark.

The hut of a subaltern may be described in its outline as part of a coal-shed, a corner in a black, tarred wooden block that is all ground floor. These are built of rough, unseasoned planks, too thin to keep out the cold in winter, or the heat in summer. The temperature, even at five o'clock on a July morning, is that of a bakehouse shortly after the batches of bread have been drawn. The sun finds means to come through the slender roof, if it does not appear in actual beams upon the floor.

The taste of a young officer may lead him to decorate this cupboard in any variety of style, but the size of the area to be decorated will impose a limit on his fancy. There is room for a small iron bedstead, a table, a washstand, a chest of drawers, and two chairs ; which will leave about a square yard of flooring for exercise and the toilet. A fireplace and one small six-pane window complete the fittings of these huts, which look like the lodgings let to single young men about Stepney, at two shillings a week, or the summer-houses that used to be erected in the grounds of the market-gardeners at Hoxton.

A "block," as it is called, contains six compartments, each one of which is considered to be sufficient for a sub-officer's sleeping quarters. A captain takes two of these cupboards ; and a field officer the whole block of six.

Standing upon the brow of the hill at the highest part of the South Camp (on the other side of which lies Aldershot Town), and looking towards the north, the whole encampment lies in a hollow bow before you. At your side is the hut of General Knollys, the Commander-in-Chief at "The Camp" : who saw a night attack about five and forty years ago. The ostensible design of Aldershot is the practical education of the soldier and his officer.

The huts of the South Camp are arranged in alphabetical lines, or rows, for the sake of easy reference, and they stretch down the gravelly slope, towards the north, in many broad black parallels for full half a mile, until they reach the sandy flat that lies between them and the North Camp, on the further ascent. This flat is divided by a canal that is crossed by a pontoon bridge supported by tubs ; the real artillery glowing red pontoons lying high and dry at the side, looking like gigantic German sausages of a light and brilliant hue. A winding gravel pathway crosses this desert for nearly a mile, and then you enter the corresponding black lines of the North Camp huts, which look thinner from the distance, and ascend for another half mile upon a more moderate slope.

A line of these huts, in which, perhaps, the officers and men of two different corps may be quartered, is constructed in divisions, each one of which is exactly like all the rest.

There is a bread-hut, a meat-hut, and a library-hut ; a men's school-hut, a children's school-hut, which latter looks like the national schools in many small villages. There are a number of officers' sleeping-huts, placed back to back, and also a number of men's sleeping huts, in the same position. There is an orderly hut, and a guard-hut, the latter provided with several cool though dismal cupboards, that are called cells, in which are confined the refractory privates who have fallen under the too tempting dissipation of Aldershott Town. There is the women's wash-hut, at which strap pedlars' carts, that are passing through the country, are observed to stand, without any visible driver, for a very long period of time ; there is the family hut, for the married men, and the long canteen, facing the yellow, burning, gravelly road, where the soldier indulges in a little half-baked conviviality during the middle of the day. There is the armourers' hut, a brick edifice, with a fluted zinc roof ; the shoemakers' hut : in which a number of soldiers are at work, with cobblers' shirts, and military legs ; and there is the tailors' hut, where our future field-marshals are sewing on a button, or repairing a yawning rent. There is a hut that is labelled "Ablution," which is very good language for a building containing a long bench and a number of bowls, where the common soldiers go to wash. There is an officers' mess-room hut : a long, black wooden building containing many small windows adorned with crimson curtains ; and there is a non-commissioned officers' mess-room hut, in which the corporals and sergeants are accustomed (when single men) to refresh their exhausted bodies. There is a cook-house hut, a fair-sized fluted zinc building, which is filled with steaming ovens, containing many shapes of beef, a roaring furnace, a number of perspiring half-military greasy cooks, presided over by a stiff corporal who orders the addition of a little salt, or the uncovering of a pannikin, as if he were leading on to glory. From the open doors of this dinner magazine is wafted a fragrant breath of onions and cabbage : a perfume that carries you in imagination to some of the back streets of Paris on the noon of an August day.

At the back of the cook-house is the Quartermaster's store hut, a precisely similar fluted zinc building, that looks like a railway goods depot, being devoted to boxes, packages, and bags. The hospital huts are placed by themselves, being distinguished by white-painted doors. They hold about a dozen beds each ; and some of the French circus-like Pierrot convalescents are lounging about them. These are the main features of a line of huts, at any part of "The Camp."

Still standing upon the hill by the General's hut, and looking across "The Camp," you can see to your right, towering above the huts, the shed-like church of the South Camp, and, further on, the shed-like church of the North Camp ; the white, gleaming, cup-shaped tent of the Royal Artillery, who are roughing it under canvas, and in the distance, across the common, an enclosed racket-ground, which looks like a large stone dust-bin. To the extreme left are the distant tents of the guards, brought out in pleasant relief against a green background of foliage. Trees are by no means plentiful at or near Aldershott Camp, any more than grass, and very few of the hot, dusty elevations can boast of a top-knot, or a whisker of verdure.

I pursue my survey, by walking through "The Camp," and discover a telegraph-office hut, a fire brigade hut, a post office hut, and a luggage office hut. The latter belongs to the South Eastern Railway Company, who are commencing great railway works in connection with their line to this Camp, an important, although a quiet, and, as far as the country is concerned, an inexpensive step on towards the perfection of the national defences. Close by this building is a privileged yard, conducted under military law, for the hire of Broughams, dog-carts, and the ubiquitous Hansom. There are certain camp-followers which dog the steps of the soldier, wherever he goes, from the General-in-Chief, to the lowest private in a regiment.

Towards nine o'clock in the morning the sounds of many military bands of music begin to be heard, and the shrill whistle of the fife comes from the open windows and doors of huts, as well as the more mellow tone of the clarionet. Bodies of men, in different uniforms, appear in oblong masses upon the burning stony slopes, and artillery soldiers driving heavy waggons or field trains, pass along the cross-roads from side to side. Heavy dragoons in thick, muddy, unbraced trousers, and very dirty shirts, with bronzed faces, chests, and arms, appear with pails and cans from behind the tarred huts, and disappear again. A company of bugle-youths plunge out from a side lane, followed by a little girl child, who strides widely to keep step with them. Children play about the red hot gravel, regardless of sun-stroke, amusing themselves, in one instance, with a worn-out shako. Stern warriors are seen through laundry-hut windows, nursing babies amongst the baskets of clothes, or drinking tea out of large blue saucers. Other stern warriors come out attired in all the regulation glory of thick, warm, close-fitting costumes, with the glass standing at one hundred degrees in the shade—even keeping to that wonderful instrument of military torture, the immortal stock. For two hundred years this ingenious, unbending variation of the old cravat has gripped the soldier by the neck, and there is no prospect, at present, of its relaxing its hold. It has many things to recommend it. When a regiment, from over-work, or an insufficiency of food, presented a sickly appearance, by obliging the men to tighten the stock as much as they could bear without suffocation, a ruddy glow was produced in the face, and every sign of a full habit of body. These instruments of clothing, before now, have been made of black horse-hair, tolerably hard, and transformed into a collar as firm as iron by the insertion of a slip of wood, which, acting on the larynx, and compressing every part of the neck, gave the eyes a wonderful prominence, and the wearer an almost supernatural appearance of healthy vigour. The present military stock is not quite as bad as this, although it is bad enough.

A squad of raw, unformed lads is marched out for drill, showing the material that the recruiting sergeant has driven together with the Queen's shillings, in default of better youths, or men. They drop out of the ranks, even on an ordinary field-day, and on real and active service they would die, like children, at the roadside. They have been plucked too early for the game of war, and they are as worthless as all untimely fruit.

A sombre looking soldier is walked slowly down one of the lines, carrying a bag in one hand and a can in the other, and followed by a shabbily dressed woman, who is nursing a sleeping child. His head is bent down, and he has no remark to make, as she pours some low, ceaseless story of wrong and suffering into his ear.

By this time I thought it right that I should pay a visit of condolence to my friend, Lieutenant Hongwee, who had been compelled to pass the night in dismal communion with a whisky bottle, at the regimental guard-house of the Royal Antrim Rifles. I looked round the apartment. Two windsor chairs (the ever-lasting regulation chair all through the army), a dirty table, a fireplace, and deal shelf, were all the furniture. A bit of composite candle had burnt out and guttered down in a champagne bottle, and the shutter of the window at one end of the hut was kept open with a short rusty poker. The bare walls were ornamented with fancy cartoons, mottoes, and initials, drawn by idle, yawning heroes, with pieces of burnt wood ; and the few pegs that were intended to support any superfluous outdoor military gear, were cut to pieces with sword-thrusts. The floor was blackened with accumulated dust, and the whole place, which was about ten yards long and five yards broad, looked like a good dry skittle ground, without the skittles.

"My poor friend," I said, with compassion, looking at a tin machine that resembled a number of large shaving pots and boxes rolled into one, "what have we here ?"

"Don't allude to it," he said, with a sudden spasm ; "you see my dinner-pan."

"Your what ?" I asked.

"My dinner pan," he answered. "To add to the needless torment of the wretched officer on guard, his messman—his club steward, whom he liberally pays—declines to send him his proper food. His regimental servant goes up to the mess-room, and brings down the concrete structure now before you. The bottom of the can contains the soup, a greasy broth ; a box above contains potatoes and peas floating together in more greasy broth ; the next step in the pyramid is another box, full of a dry and leathery grilled beef-steak ; and the apex is a metal pill-box containing pepper and salt."

The first thing we did, when the guard was properly relieved, and an unfortunate Highland ensign was imprisoned in the place of Lieutenant Hongwee, was to visit Truefitts'. Truefitt's is a living example of how a good fight may be won by combination, courage, and determination. Who would care to live without his "toilet club" ? The great barber has got his hut—his little oasis of luxury—firmly planted in the desert, under the constant patronage of military men, far more than the constant regulation of military law. Faithful camp-follower—true and reliable as the Hansom cabman, he is found, in the hour of danger, at his post. What would the regulators of the British Army do without such a comforting retreat ?

Passing out of this fragrant warehouse in the desert, on our way to visit one of the encampments, we came upon half a dozen artillerymen, who were undergoing the punishment of "pack-drill." They were the drunken prisoners of last night, who, after being tried before their superior officers in the orderly room, were condemned for a certain time to walk the day in the full heat of the sun, in their heaviest marching clothes, and with their full marching "kit" upon their backs. They had now been walking up and down for some time, and their legs seemed to give way in their heavy jack-boots.

Going across the black lines of huts, our ears were suddenly saluted with a terrific outburst of military melody, and looking in one of the quartermasters' store-rooms, we found about thirty men and boys of all sizes, furnished with sax-horns of curious shape, and ophicleides as large as pumps, blowing up the roof with a popular quick-step march. The conductor, with the most vigorous action, was endeavouring to keep them in order, as they stood amongst the boxes and packages of their temporary practising room. One short-necked, full-blooded performer, whose back was towards me, caused his neck to contract and expand in such an extreme manner, while supplying his unwieldy instrument with air, that I expected every moment to see him burst, and his head drop out of sight into his opened body. I never saw anything like it, except the left cheek of an old Trumpeter, which from long use and from being nothing but thin skin, used to sink into a hole when his instrument was at rest, and blow out in an almost transparent bladder when he began to play.

Leaving this close-packed hall of harmony, we made our way to the theatre, a building that stood fairly in our road to the canvas quarters of the artillery. A wooden hut, with several entrances, looking like a travelling show that has squatted upon common land ; an audience portion, capable of seating about a

hundred persons ; an orchestra, like a large tank ; a stage such
as is generally run up during a violent private theatrical fever
in a back drawing-room ; and a property-room, in which the
hollow mockeries of the drama are combined with the solid
realities of a habitation and a laundry, comprise nearly all that
need be described of the well-known Theatre Royal, South Camp,
Aldershott. It was manned, during the day, by one male attendant,
who managed it as if it had been a ship, heaving up the scenes
like sails, and putting it in trim working-order for the performance
of the evening.

A quarter of an hour's walk brought us, at last to the Royal
Artillery encampment. There was a large square enclosure full
of horses, like a horse fair, railed in with ropes and stakes, and
surrounded by an irregular line of tents. A man in military
trousers and a dirty shirt—the amateur blacksmith of the regiment—was hammering out a horse-shoe upon an anvil, which
stood full and unprotected on the sand, under the noon-day sun.
Not far from this workman was a camp fire, over which was
cooking the dinner of the men. A couple of narrow ditches,
first cut in the earth in the form of an equal cross, and then filled
full of wood, furze, or any dry rubbish about, that will burn ; a
covering of sheet iron strips placed over these ditches ; a peat
chimney built in the centre, for the purpose of drawing the fire
below ; the wood of furze set alight, and the kettles, like pails,
placed along the iron plates on the side where they are most
likely to avoid the smoke and boil the quickest ; and the rough
and ready camp oven is complete. When the lids of the pail-kettles
are lifted up, bushels of potatoes, spongy masses of cabbage, and
irregular blocks of heavy pudding, like lumps of clay, are boiling
and bubbling away ; and one glance of the glaring mid-day sun
seems to stir up the broth as much as the hidden, choking fire
below.

"That is the elegant kind of picnic," said Lieutenant Hongwee,
"which we are often required to assist at : with this difference,
that we are marched twenty miles away to some solitary spot,
kept out for several days and several nights under canvas, and
made to kill our meat before we eat it, or feed upon blackberries,
like the Children in the Wood."

I saw that this was a tender subject, and made no reply, but
contented myself with observing the other features of "The
Camp."

Most of the men were having a short rest under the tents,
being disposed of in the same manner as they sleep at night.
About a dozen were lying together on straw, with their heads
resting on their great-coats at the lower circumference of the
tent, and their feet meeting together at the pole in the centre,
like the spokes of a wheel. At a given word of command, they

all started up, and went to work with their horses, looking more like dirty gipsy ostlers than the clean and clipt soldier who parades the London streets.

The tent of a sub-officer, to which we were invited, was not remarkable for any luxury, except the luxury of being a lodging for one. The sand at the bottom was covered over with a layer of green leaves, and a sprinkling of straw ; the occupant's soap, and towel, and brush were lying on the top of a tin box ; his small looking-glass was on the ground, leaning against the side of the tent ; he had made a reclining couch of one portmanteau, a money-box to hold loose silver of another, and he had still another huge, black, drum-like box to offer a friend. He was quite a gipsy king, in his tent.

As we sat looking out of the mouth of the tent across the Artillery encampment, and past the lower end of the North Camp, we could see a thin winding lane of scarlet, that looked like a row of poppies in a field. There were a few black patches (the blue Artillerymen and the green Riflemen) studded about the sandy flat of common, with here and there a few white stragglers, probably the Stirlingshire militia, or some Foot Guardsmen in flannel undress jackets ; but the scarlet patches prevailed in that direction ; and, looking further, we saw the white peaks of another range of tents.

"The Guards are as badly off there as you are here," said Lieutenant Hongwee, alluding to the scarlet patch and the distant tents, and addressing the gipsy king.

"Worse," returned the gipsy king, "infinitely worse. We only came from quarters at Woolwich at the dull time of the year ; but those poor fellows have just been sent down from London in the height of the season, to be placed under canvas at once. Canvas is a capital thing properly applied—when it means a dancing tent on a lawn at Fulham—but canvas at Aldershott is a far less agreeable affair."

We sauntered slowly towards the Rifle mess-room for breakfast ; Lieutenant Hongwee rather despondingly, and I rather disposed to condole with my friend and companion.

The mess-room was a long, airy building, very lofty for "The Camp," with a small ante-room in front, and having the mysteries of the cooking department concealed by a chocolate-coloured cloth curtain stretching right across the apartment near the back. The long dining-table and sideboard were well covered with food, and the chairs were the everlasting Windsor regimental pattern. To give a dining-room aspect to these rough companions, they were covered with a padded leather seat and back : a contrivance which each officer provides himself, and carries about with him from one station to another.

"Is this a fair specimen of your ordinary day ?" I inquired, as we proceeded with our morning repast.

"It is : with the exception of a few field-days, and our penal servitude under canvas. We rise about ten a.m.; we show upon parade for about an hour ; and after twelve, until the bugle sounds to dress for mess, at seven, we have no settled occupation whatever."

"There is a club-house built in the South Camp, is there not ?"

"There is, but with a lofty rate of subscription, almost prohibiting the entrance of poor subalterns. When there, you can only read, play at billiards, or talk. Most men, like myself, who get five or six shillings a day, spend twice as much as they earn, and that without indulging in any particular extravagance. As most things are done by mutual and equal subscription, the pressure of the service outlay falls heaviest upon the junior members. The major, or colonel, who sits opposite to me at dinner, pays no more to the mess fund than I do."

"You have field sports for your amusement, which need not cost anything."

"No one cares for them. A few men use the racket-ground ; but very few. Rowing up the canal is a favourite recreation ; to drink beer at a public-house, where they profess to keep an 'officers' room,' and then to row back again. The common soldier is better off than we are, for he has his town and his concert-rooms ; but we can do nothing except wait wearily for the welcome summons to mess."

My vehicle, on its road to the North Camp railway station, rolled me past trucks of camp furniture, past cabs containing field officers, past solitary scarlet soldiers who stood like lonely poppies in the meadows, past other scarlet soldiers who wound slowly along the drab and dusty lanes, and past a group of boy children in green uniform, coming through a hedge, who looked as if the very cradles of the country had been emptied for their contents to be pressed into the ranks. I broke into another crowd of soldiers at the station, and plunged into my carriage, glad to be whirled away.

* * * * * *

In different vein is the following extract from "Sketches of 'The Camp' at Aldershot," published in 1858 by Andrews & Lucy, Booksellers and Stationers of Farnham, which gives a more romantic view of "The Camp," written as it is in the characteristic prose of the Victorian novelist.

Who has not heard of "The Camp" at Aldershot ? That great scene of animation and activity, that stupendous practical military school, with its multitudes of men surrounded by all the paraphernalia of war ; its Royal Pavilion, its churches and schools,

its theatres and clubs, its thousand huts, its commissariat, its
daily routine of discipline and its grand field days when its troops
engage in mimic warfare—frequently in the presence of royalty—
when its valleys resound, and its hills echo with the sombre
booming of ordnance, the sharp and incessant popping of musketry, and ominous clang of bayonet and sword, the tramp of
cavalry, the measured tread of infantry, the hoarse sounding
trumpet, the mellow bugle, the romantic pibroch, the shrill fife
and spirit stirring drum, when may be seen the sturdy Guards-
man, the kilted Highlanders, the dusky Rifleman, the powder-
stained Artilleryman, the dashing Cavalryman and the fiery
charger impatiently champing his bit ; the bright accoutrements,
the polished helmet and the gleaming sabre glittering and flashing
in the resplendent sunbeam. While at intervals may be discerned,
floating proudly in the breeze, old England's time-honoured
Banners, torn by many a foeman's shot in America, the Peninsula,
China, India or the Crimea—Banners which have been planted
as the symbol of victory on many a hard fought and bloody field,
and on the walls of many a stone-girt city deemed impregnable—
Banners which have serenely flapped over thousands of England's
brave and dauntless sons, whose hearts have ceased to beat, and
who have found their resting place in a stranger's land.

Who on visiting "The Camp" has not been struck with the
desolate grandeur of the scenery around it ? The succession of
hill and valley covered with purple heather or stunted gorse
which may be seen stretching far, far away and lost to view, only
in the blue horizon ; or when the pale moon pours her silvery
beams around, gradually dies away in gloom and darkness ; or
who has stood on Caesar's Camp in the "witching hour of night"
and has not felt an indescribable sensation pervade his breast
when contemplating the sublime scene around him. The thrilling
silence, broken only by the measured tread of the watchful
sentinel, the sleeping thousands below him, among whom are the
veteran hero who has fought in India, scaled the heights of Alma,
or mingled in the fearful hand-to-hand struggle at Inkerman and
the weary recruit who is passing a restless night, having discovered
that military life is not so desirable as he once imagined it to
be, and lamenting that he ever left his father's home. While
thus the beholder is indulging in reverie, he is irresistibly led
back to the time when a thousand years ago the wild desolate
eminence on which he is standing was the stronghold of an army
under Alfred the Great ; when instead of a peaceful slumberer,
each man was impatiently awaiting the first streak of light in the
eastern sky to meet in deadly conflict the invader of his country,
and fall if need be in the defence of his liberty and home and when
that morning came instead of the mimic warfare, the plains around
were strewn with slain and the haughty Dane completely routed.

The scenery around "The Camp," as was noticed before, is grand and bold, especially south, south-west and north-east; on the south-east, east and north-west it savours more of rural beauty and simplicity, particularly on the eastern side, where may be seen, about three miles distant, a wide range of wooded country forming a pleasing contrast with the barren heath which intervenes, while among the foliage the weather beaten and time honoured spire of Ash Church rises quietly and serenely. . . .

Such was the "Camp at Aldershot" in its early days, which owed much to the direction of the first G.O.C., General Sir William Knollys, who was succeeded in this appointment in 1860* by General Sir John Pennefather, C.B.,† who had commanded the first Brigade of the 2nd Division in the Crimea at the crossing of the Alma, and had taken over temporary command of the Division at Inkerman. General Pennefather took over an established camp and was able to direct his activities to the training of the troops and to the general improvement of Aldershot as the premier military station in the country.

---

* On leaving Aldershot General Knollys became President of the Council of Military Education, a body formed at the instigation of the Prince Consort. He later became Gentleman Usher of the Black Rod in the Royal Household and died on 23rd June, 1883, in Westminster Palace.

† General Sir John Lysaght Pennefather, third son of an Irish parson of Tipperary, was born in 1800 and entered the army as a cornet of the 7th Dragoon Guards in 1818, later transferring to the 22nd (Cheshire) Regiment. He served in the Scinde Campaign of 1843, commanding his regiment, which distinguished itself at Meanee and Hyderabad. General Pennefather commanded in Aldershot until 1865. He died in 1872. (Dictionary of National Biography.)

CHAPTER FOUR

THE DEVELOPMENT OF MILITARY ALDERSHOT

1863-1902

"It may be conceded to the credit of the Camp that those who lived there thought better of it than those who did not, and that those who lived there longest were apt to like it best of all."—Mrs. Julia Horatia Ewing in "The Story of a Short Life" (1885).

FROM the end of the Crimea War, with which the establishment and early history of Aldershot Camp are so closely identified, "The Camp," as has been seen, steadily developed, and this progress has gone on unceasingly. The plateau on which "The Camp" stands is on an average 250 feet above sea-level, a singularly healthy situation. Improvements and additions have been made through the passing years, from the planting of trees along "The Camp" roads and around the parade grounds—who has not been impressed with the sight of the chestnut trees in bloom in Wellington Avenue, or the vista from the crest of the road by the Maida Gymnasium of the avenue of trees of Queen's Avenue ?—to the more domestic but important installations of the drainage system, the sewage works at Camp Farm, the water supply from Bourley Water Works, the construction of roads and the building of permanent barracks throughout "The Camp." The planting of the trees along the roads and parade grounds was carried out, it is said, at the instigation of Queen Victoria, who, with the welfare of her troops at heart, had commented upon the lack of shade afforded for troops under training and whilst marching through "The Camp." Most of the trees were planted during the time the Duke of Connaught was the G.O.C., and chestnuts were selected in view of their quick growth.

This progress was a continuous process ; as each year passed by, the pattern of the present "Camp" took shape* as the permanent buildings and roads gradually took the place of the huts and other temporary structures, and "The Camp" tracks and footpaths became the roads we know today.

---

* In March, 1866, Queen Victoria made her first visit to Aldershot since the death of the Prince Consort in 1861, and she noted in her journal that the "place has increased wonderfully . . . all the same and yet all changed" (Royal Archives, Windsor).

In addition to the land required for the actual camp, a considerable amount of land was purchased by the Government for the training areas. These extended from the Farnborough Road westward to Fleet, Crondall and Crookham, including the Long Valley, Laffan's Plain, Cove Common, Bourley and Ewshot. Eight hundred acres were purchased from Mr. C. E. Lefroy, the Lord of the Manor of Ewshot, and this area included that bounded by Ewshot, the "North Horns" inn at Crookham, Cocked Hat Wood, and Caesar's Camp.

It was of this area Mrs. Julia Horatia Ewing wrote, in "The Story of a Short Life,"* this description :

> Take a Highwayman's Heath. Destroy every vestige of life with fire and axe, from the pine that has longest been a landmark to the smallest beetle in smoking moss. Burn acres of purple and pink heather, and pare away the young bracken that springs verdant and not spare the broom, whose more exquisite yellow atones for its lack of fragrance. In this common ruin be every lesser flower involved : blue beds of speedwell by the wayfarer's path, the daintier milkwort and rougher red rattle, down to the very dodder that clasps the heather ; let them perish and the face of Dame Nature be utterly blackened ! Then : shave the heath as bare as the back of your hand, and if you have felled every tree, and left not so much as a tussock of grass or a scarlet toadstool to break the force of the winds, then shall the winds come from the east and from the west, from the north and from the south, and shall raise on your shaven heath clouds of sand that would not discredit a desert in the heart of Africa. By some such recipe the ground was prepared for that Camp of Instruction.

The acquisition of additional land became necessary in order to have available a larger area for the training of troops ; field days and "sham fights," as they were called, being a regular feature in the life of the units stationed in "The Camp." Typical of such is the field day described in the *Illustrated London News* of 2nd October, 1869 :—

> Yesterday week the troops at Aldershott Camp were again actively exercised in the movements of a field-day. Although the division under the command of Lieutenant-General the Hon. Sir James Yorke Scarlett, G.C.B., has been considerably shorn of its strength by the recent departure of various crack corps for winter

---

* "The Story of a Short Life," written by Mrs. Ewing and published in 1885 by the Society for the Promotion of Christian Knowledge (S.P.C.K.).

The young hero of the story, Leonard, stayed with his uncle, a barrack master who lived in a wooden hut by the "Iron Church," set in a small garden, fenced about with simple trellis work of crossed fir poles. Here the boy lived, until his early death, absorbed, in his short life, by soldiers and the military atmosphere of the camp, which is described throughout the book in vignettes of army life as seen through the eyes of a small boy.

quarters at other stations, it is still sufficiently strong in infantry to make a respectable appearance in the field. This force of infantry, consisting of eleven battalions, in complete marching order, formed up on the Queen's Parade, North Camp, in line of continuous columns, facing west, for field manœuvres. Shortly before eleven o'clock, Lieutenant-General Scarlett, accompanied by Major Roerdansz, of the Prussian Army ; Colonel Newdegate, Assistant Adjutant-General ; Colonel Gamble, C.B., Assistant Quartermaster-General ; Captain Home, Deputy Assistant Quartermaster-General ; Captain Milligan and Lieutenant Knollys, Aides-de-Camp ; and other officers of the staff and division, arrived on the ground, and was received with the general salute. The Lieutenant-General, having inspected the ranks, proceeded with the above-mentioned officers to the saluting base, and saw the troops march past in open columns of grand divisions. Having passed the saluting base, companies were formed from grand divisions ; the troops then counter-marched, and went past *en masse* of columns at quarter distance, and from the original flank in brigades, in lines of contiguous columns, preceded, in each case, by brigadiers, field officers, and bands, the rear brigade with arms at the trail. They then formed line to the left, facing east, on the left battalion of brigades ; retired in line about a hundred yards, halted and fronted ; advanced in direct echelon of battalions from the left, at ten paces distance ; changed front to right on the right brigade, right thrown back ; advanced about fifty yards and halted ; advanced in direct echelon of brigades from the right about sixty yards ; formed line on the right battalion of the right brigade, left thrown back ; then deployed and formed a general line on the right companies of battalions, facing east ; formed quarter distance on the right companies of battalions ; formed line of contiguous columns, and then marched to quarters, at which they arrived about one o'clock. While the infantry was being exercised, the artillery and cavalry—consisting of "A" Battery, "C" Brigade Royal Horse Artillery, and "B" Battery, "B" Brigade, the 7th Dragoon Guards, and the 6th Inniskilling Dragoons—were put through numerous field movements peculiar to those branches of the service, in the Long Valley.

Rifle ranges were laid out below Caesar's Camp and in Rushmoor Bottom, whilst farther afield ranges were constructed at Ash Common and Pirbright Common. The Caesar's Camp ranges were constructed in the late fifties and were described as a "rifle gallery" which was "a long wooden erection with rooms at each end where the sons of Mars can sit or stand at ease and smoke their meerschaums (pipes) between the time appointed for the performance of their duties." It was at Caesar's Camp ranges that the first meetings of the Army Rifle

Association were held. These meetings, held in July or August, lasted three to four days and attracted many regimental teams. The annual A.R.A. meeting continued to be held at Aldershot until 1885,* when with the opening of the National Rifle Association ranges at Bisley, the annual meeting was transferred to that venue. Up to the eighties there were also Artillery ranges between Cove Park and Bourley Bottom, but with the increasing range of more modern weapons the ranges ceased to be used, the Gunners' practice camps being established on Salisbury Plain. In the early maps of "The Camp," magazines are shown on Smallshot Hill, near the canal, where the R.A.S.C. establishment now stands, and on the slopes of Thorn Hill below the cemetery.

It must be realized that for amusement of any description the Army in Aldershot had to be self-supporting, and sport of all natures began to play an important part in the life of the garrison.† Many excellent sports grounds which exist today were laid out in the latter part of last century, and this encouraged the development of all ball games as a popular recreation for all ranks.

The Annual Army Athletic Sports Meeting was also established in the late sixties. These popular exhibitions of military skill extended over two days, usually about the end of June. The meeting was held on the Recreation Ground behind the Royal Garrison Church, the events including tent-pegging, cutting the lemon, sword versus bayonet and tug-of-war and other competitions of a military nature, which in those days took precedence over the track events which are the main features today. The meeting was always an attraction to the garrison and to the public, the ground being thronged with visitors seated under the awnings of the gaily decorated marquees, watching the events and listening to the military bands. Towards the end of the century the Army Athletic Club established a sports ground on the site of the present-day Military Stadium, and this became the recognized venue for the main athletic meetings.

Tweseldown Race-course was opened in 1867 for steeplechasing,

---

* The medals awarded by the A.R.A. in these days bore a representation of the famous equestrian statue of the Duke of Wellington which was erected in Aldershot in 1885.

† At a meeting held on 27th November, 1859, at the Centre Block, Permanent Barracks, thirteen officers (four Captains and nine subalterns) formed themselves into a Club "for the promotion of athletic exercises," which it was agreed should be called the "Knickerbocker Club," and this Club thrived up to 1868, by which time it had some 450 members. By 1862 its activities had increased and it was decided that it should be managed by a President and a Committee of six members. The first President was Lieut.-Colonel Lord Bathurst, of the Grenadier Guards. In the Club rule book of that year it was stated that the entrance fee was 5s. and that members were "particularly requested to wear the Club Dress when playing Knickerbocker Club matches."

The bell brought from Sebastopol, in its original position overlooking the huts of South Camp, from the original water-colour painted in 1856 by G. H. Thomas, now in the Royal Library, Windsor Castle.

Reproduced by gracious permission of H.M. The King.

The Sebastopol Bell and the Time Gun, with the Meteorological Station, surmounted by the 40-ft, Gambol Vane, as they stood at the top of Gun Hill in July, 1869.

Reproduced by kind permission of Rock Bros. Ltd., London, E.6.

I

Wellington Avenue in July, 1866, with the Royal Garrison Church of All Saints at the top of the road, Warburg and Willems Barracks on the left and Salamanca and Badajos Barracks on the right.

The Royal Artillery Barracks, South Camp, August, 1869, the foreground being the area now occupied by High Street.

Engravings reproduced by kind permission of Rock Bros. Ltd., London, E.6.

The Centre Road (now Queen's Avenue) approaching North Camp, July, 1866. The large building on the right is the Marlborough Lines Garrison Church.

The Centre Road (now Queen's Avenue) looking towards South Camp, July, 1866. The "Red Church" is seen on the extreme right, whilst the large building on the left is the Roman Catholic Church of St. Michael and St. Sebastian.

Engravings reproduced by kind permission of Rock Bros. Ltd., London, E.6.

At the Town end of Hospital Hill, circa 1860. The central building is the old Union Poor House, now the District Pay Office. The buildings on the left are now married quarters of Salamanca Barracks. The fountain in the foreground stood within the confines of Talavera Barracks until after the 1914-1918 War, when it was so damaged in a traffic accident that it was removed.

Reproduced by kind permission of Messrs. Wm. May & Co. Ltd., Aldershot.

The Headquarter Gymnasium, Wellington Lines, Aldershot, 1866.

Reproduced by permission from "The History of The Army Physical Training Corps," Pt. I.

The "Red Church," the Royal Garrison Church of All Saints, in the seventies.

The Cranbrook Gymnasium from Queen's Avenue, circa 1870.
Reproduced from "Rock's Album of Aldershot" by kind permission of Rock Bros. Ltd., London, E. 6.

The South Cavalry Barracks (Beaumont Barracks) from the junction of Farnborough Road and Chetwode Terrace, circa 1880.

Salamanca and Badajos Barracks and the Avenue Road (Wellington Avenue), circa 1880.
Reproduced from "Rock's Album of Aldershot" by kind permission of Rock Bros. Ltd., London, E.G.

The Royal Review at Aldershot, 1880, *from the original water-colour by Godefroy Durand in the Royal Library, Windsor.*

Reproduced by gracious permission of H.M. The King.

although the first steeplechase in the area on record took place on the 30th March, 1857. Flat races were also held around Queen's Parade. A contemporary account describes this meeting as extending over two days about the end of July; they were largely attended by "the neighbouring gentry, officers and soldiers of the garrison and their numerous friends, the sport being considered sufficiently good to tempt many of the bookmaking fraternity." The distance around the course was nearly two miles, with a straight half-mile run-in alongside and parallel with the Farnborough Road, where stands and stalls were erected each year for the convenience of the public. The Ordnance Survey map of Aldershot of 1873 marks a race-course around the Queen's Parade with mile posts and a starting-post, and this was still shown on the maps of 1898, the course crossing Queen's Avenue, then shown as Cranbrook Road, just north of the Iron Bridge and running in a rough circle for just over a mile around the area below Smallshot Hill and where the Aldershot Military Stadium stands today.

The Basingstoke Canal played an important role in the recreation of the garrison. A boathouse was built on the site of the old Farnham Wharf by Wharf Bridge on the Farnborough Road, and any summer evening would find the waters alive with skiffs and punts, soldiers at the oars, their ladies in the stern. Recognized swimming "pools" were established and also an angling club. In winter time skating was a popular pastime. The winters of last century appear to have been more severe than today, for the ice seems always to have been thick enough to permit skating on the canal.

The Royal Garrison Church of All Saints, familiarly known as "The Red Church" from the red bricks of its structure, stands at the top of Wellington Avenue, originally known as "The Avenue Road," in six acres of ground, and now screened by the growth of the firs and larches planted in the grounds when the church was built in 1863. It was consecrated on 29th July of that year. In 1866 the "Iron Church" was moved from Thorn Hill to a site by the Canal bridge in Queen's Avenue, where it remained until 1924, on the site of the present-day St. Andrew's Church of Scotland.

The Cambridge Hospital, which stands in a dominant position on the rising ground overlooking the town, was built in 1879 at a cost of £45,000* by the Aldershot builders, Martin, Wells & Co.

The Ordnance Store Depot—the Field Stores of today—was also completed in 1879. The Mortuary Chapel of the Military Cemetery on Peaked Hill was also built in the same year, and on the Ordnance

---

* "Victoria County History of Hampshire," Vol. IV (1911).

K

Survey Map of 1873 an Observatory is marked on the site of the present-day Officers' Mess of Albuhera Barracks.

Government House, formerly the residence of the General Officers Commanding and now used as "A" Mess of H.Q., Aldershot District, is situated among a plantation of firs on the Farnborough Road, near the Queen's Hotel and facing the huts of Blenheim Barracks. The house was built in 1883 at a cost of £8,000; it was first called Cove Park. Prior to the building of Government House, the General Commanding was accommodated in a large wooden bungalow which stood in secluded grounds in South Camp. Similar bungalows had been built in the area between Salamanca Barracks and the Prince Consort's Library for the Secretary of State for War, the Commander-in-Chief of the British Army and the Adjutant-General—a fact which indicated the importance attached by the War Office to work being carried out in Aldershot.

The wooden hut barracks were built in the fifties as temporary accommodation and were not expected to last more than twenty years. At the end of forty years some were still serving their purpose, although it was fully realized that they were insanitary and inconvenient for the military needs of the day. The contractor had in 1855 guaranteed the huts for thirteen years, so the work had been well carried out, but the annual maintenance had, by the eighties, reached a sum of some £7,000 a year.

It was in November, 1881, that practical steps were first taken to convert the hutted camp into permanent barracks. This project had been under discussion for some years, but it was not until then that the first two brick-built buildings were constructed in North Camp, at a cost, it is recorded, of £1,300, replacing the old wooden huts. This was followed by the replacement of the hutted accommodation of three battalions by brick buildings of bungalow style. In 1882 a further £10,000 was expended, and in 1883-4 the same figure was allotted for reconstruction and development. The existing roads remained and the brick buildings gradually replaced the wooden blocks. These brick buildings are in use today. It was finally decided to rebuild the whole of the hutted camp, and this was finally accomplished during the period that the Duke of Connaught was in command of the District—1893-1898—and cost several million pounds.

Field-Marshal Sir Evelyn Wood, V.C., G.C.B., G.C.M.G., was appointed to command the Aldershot Division in 1889, and it was he who had strongly recommended the immediate reconstruction of South Camp and the replacement of the remaining huts in North Camp by brick buildings, but constructed on improved lines. Sir Evelyn Wood had for many years been striving for the recognition of the

"Company System," and as the outcome of practical experience of this organization advocated the building of the new barracks in company blocks. This plan was, after some considerable discussion, eventually approved. Whilst G.O.C., Sir Evelyn Wood sited all the barracks built in "The Camp," which cost some £1,500,000 between 1889 and 1893. In his reminiscences "From Midshipman to Field Marshal " he records that the Adjutant-General and the Inspector of Fortifications, who came to Aldershot to criticize the plans for reconstruction before they were approved, told the G.O.C. that in London they did not like the scheme at all, but after their visit were in complete agreement with the General's views.

Later, Sir Evelyn Wood wrote : "When the plans, prices and execution were questioned in the House of Commons the Secretary of State appointed a committee of Civilian Architects and builders, who reported that the Royal Engineers had made good plans, the contractors had done their part satisfactorily and the country had obtained full value for its expenditure."*

Sir Evelyn Wood had been acutely aware of the necessity for the rebuilding of "The Camp," having, as he recorded, known "the wretched accommodation provided for the troops, neither wind nor rainproof, having been quartered in the North and South Camps twenty years earlier" when he had served in Aldershot as a Regimental Officer. It was also Sir Evelyn Wood's recommendation that each barrack should be named—the names to commemorate a famous British victory—and this proposal was adopted, but only after repeated applications.

The barracks then in Stanhope Lines were named after famous battles of the Napoleonic Wars—Albuhera, Mandora, Corunna, Maida and Barrosa—as were also those in Wellington Lines—Talavera, Badajos, Salamanca and Waterloo.† In Marlborough Lines, North Camp, the barracks took new names from the victories of Marlborough's Campaigns (1704-1709)—Blenheim, Malplaquet, Oudenarde, Tournay and Ramillies.

Aldershot can claim to a certain extent to have been the home of military aeronautics, for it played a great part in its early development. Lieutenant G. E. Grover, R.E., who has been described as "the father of Military aeronautics," began his investigations and experiments as far back as 1862. Sixteen years passed before the first official experiments and trials with balloons were carried out at Woolwich, under the

---

* "From Midshipman to Field-Marshal," by Field-Marshal Sir Evelyn Wood, V.C. (Methuen & Co. Ltd.) (1906).

† The East, West and South Cavalry Barracks in Wellington Lines remained so named until just before the 1914-1918 war, when they were named Warburg, Willems and Beaumont respectively.

direction of Captain J. L. B. Templar, of the 2nd Middlesex Militia. In 1882 the Balloon Equipment Store was transferred to the School of Military Engineering at Chatham and a Balloon Establishment was formed.

Aldershot's first association with military ballooning was in the summer of 1889, when a Balloon Detachment took part in the manœuvres of that year. In the following year the Balloon Section of the Royal Engineers was formed and established in South Camp near the Canal. In 1892 the balloon factory and school were moved to the R.E. Establishments in Stanhope Lines, and here two years later the balloon factory was established, under the direction of Lieutenant-Colonel Templer, where it remained until 1905, when the Balloon Section, R.E., and the factory were moved to Farnborough, to the present site of the Aerodrome and the Royal Aircraft Establishment.

Aldershot's association with the pioneer days of ballooning is commemorated today by a small plaque on the wall of a building in the R.E. Establishment.*

St. George's Garrison Church in Queen's Avenue was built in 1892, the foundation stone being laid by Queen Victoria in June of that year.

In 1893 the first Army Boxing Championships were held, the ring being set up in the open near the present District Headquarters building. The value of physical training in the Army became more fully appreciated in the latter years of last century, and the demands on the staff and accommodation of the small military gymnasium in Wellington Lines which had been established in the early sixties led to the building of the present-day Army Physical Training School buildings in Queen's Avenue. The "Big Gym," which took the place of the original "Cranbrook Gymnasium," was opened in 1894. The original Gymnasium was situated in what today is the centre of the Military Stadium, and up to the end of the century Queen's Avenue was called Cranbrook Road.

The Louise Margaret Hospital for women and children, which adjoins the Cambridge Hospital, was built in 1898, during the time that H.R.H. The Duke of Connaught was commanding Aldershot District, the Hospital being named after the Duchess of Connaught, who took a deep interest in its building and its work.

The Swimming Bath in Queen's Avenue was opened in 1900 as a result of the efforts of Colonel the Hon. John Scott Napier, C.M.G., who was appointed "Inspector of Gymnasia" in 1897. Prior to the construction of the Swimming Bath, the only facilities for swimming were the Basingstoke Canal or the Cove Reservoir. The Swimming

* See p. 339.

Bath was built by the "private enterprise" of Colonel Napier, who, unable to obtain help from Army sources, drew up the plans and obtained nearly £12,000 for the project from the funds of the Royal Military Tournament.

*   *   *   *   *

It was in 1885 that the famous equestrian statue of the Duke of Wellington, which had previously adorned the top of the triumphal arch at Hyde Park Corner, was brought to Aldershot and re-erected on its present site on Round Hill off the Farnborough Road.

As will be seen from the inscription on the plaque on the plinth of the statue, it was originally erected in London one hundred and three years ago, and it is perhaps not out of place to give the history of this well-known Aldershot landmark.* In August, 1836, Mr. Matthew Coles Wyatt's equestrian statue of George III was placed on its pedestal in Cockspur Street, where it stands to this day. Among the admirers of this statue was a Mr. Thomas Bridge Simpson, a Common Councillor, of Leadenhall Street, who was so impressed that he wrote to the sculptor proposing the erection of a bronze equestrian statue of the Duke of Wellington in the City of London.

A fund was raised in the City and a committee formed. At this committee it was suggested that Sir Francis Chantrey be also asked if he would undertake the task, and finally the commission was given to him instead of Mr. Wyatt. Although Sir Francis died, the work was completed by a Mr. Weekes and erected on the anniversary of the Battle of Waterloo, 18th June, 1844, in the position in which it stands to this day facing the Royal Exchange.

Whilst this project was proceeding, Mr. Simpson made proposals to erect a larger statue of the Duke in the West End of the Metropolis, and a second committee was formed in May, 1838, called the "Wellington Military Memorial Committee," who raised a fund by subscription of £14,000. This committee resolved to commission Mr. Matthew Coles Wyatt to undertake the task, as he was regarded "in every respect entirely qualified to be entrusted with the execution of the proposed equestrian statue."

The Duke of Rutland, chairman of the committee, obtained the Queen's permission and the sanction of the Treasury to proceed.

It was proposed that the statue should be erected on the top of the Triumphal Arch at Hyde Park Corner which was built, to the designs of the architect, Mr. Decimus Burton, in 1828 at public expense and

---

* This story of the statue (pp. 89-97) is based on the contemporary accounts published in the *Illustrated London News*.

described as a "Corinthian Portal," as one of the entrances to the grounds of Buckingham Palace. The proposal that the statue of the Duke should be placed on the top of the arch met with considerable opposition, the architect strongly opposing the suggestion on the grounds that it would be out of place. In this he had a number of supporters, and this opposition led to parliamentary support and the whole question caused considerable discussion.

Mr. Wyatt, however, continued with his work in preparing designs, drawings and models, which were accepted, and eventually a wooden model was erected on the arch in August, 1838. Final sanction to the whole scheme was given after nation-wide interest had been aroused.

The work was entirely executed at Mr. Wyatt's studio at Dudley House in the Harrow Road, the statue being modelled by Mr. Wyatt and his son, James Wyatt. The model was commenced in May, 1840, and occupied the artists for nearly three years, the amount of plaster of paris exceeding three tons. The statue was modelled on a turn-table twenty feet in diameter which revolved on forty rollers. This in itself weighed several tons. The size of the model required pre-cautions to ensure its entirety, and a large wooden beam formed a backbone with traverse timbers akin to the ribs of a ship. In order that the sculptors could reach the different parts of the statue, a travel-ling stage with an adjustable floor was built. For the casing the plaster model was lowered into a pit in a specially built foundry. The statue was cast in bronze, which was melted in two great furnaces : one was capable of melting twelve tons at a time, but as this was insufficient the second furnace was constructed to melt twenty tons.

In consequence of the size of the statue, thirty men were employed in this operation. The body of the horse and lower limbs of the Duke were cast in two pieces and the remainder of the statue in a further six sections, the portions being joined together partly by screw bolts and partly fused together. The legs of the horse were cast in solid bronze to carry the great weight, and the rest of the statue was from one to three inches thick.

The dimensions of the statue were as follows : Girth around horse, 22 ft. 8 in. Girth of legs of horse, 5 ft. 4 in. Distance from horse's hock to ground, 6 ft. Distance from horse's nose to tail, 26 ft. Length of horse's head, 6 ft. Length of each ear, 2 ft. 2 in. The whole weighed forty tons.

It was finally decided that the site for the statue should be the top of the Triumphal Arch at Hyde Park Corner. Great preparations were made for the transportation of the statue from Mr. Wyatt's studio to the site, and the whole project aroused considerable public interest.

The occasion was marked by great ceremony and military pageantry.

The finished statue was first hoisted by blocks and tackle and scaffolding from the pit in the foundry, the roof of which had first to be removed, and moved on to an immense low wooden carriage which was specially constructed at H.M. Dockyard, Woolwich. This huge vehicle weighed twenty tons, with wheels ten feet in diameter.

The statue was moved to its site on the morning of 29th September, Michaelmas Day, 1846, "to the entire satisfaction," it was recorded, "of all parties interested in the event." The day was bright and fair and "greatly heightened the brilliancy of the processional form in which the statue was conveyed to its destination." Vast crowds watched the removal of the statue. Seats and stands were erected along the route via Paddington Green, Edgware Road and Park Lane to Hyde Park Corner, and every roof and window was filled with sightseers.

H.R.H. The Duke of Cambridge, accompanied by the Grand Duke of Mecklenburg Strelitz, visited Mr. Wyatt's studio to inspect the statue on its carriage before the move.

At 9.30 in the morning the military detachments who were to participate in the ceremony assembled in the Harrow Road. These troops included the 2nd Life Guards, Grenadier and Coldstream Guards, and two companies of the Scots Fusilier Guards.

The statue was moved from the studio at 10 a.m., the carriage hauled by a hundred men of the Scots Fusilier Guards in fatigue dress. As it emerged on to the road it was greeted by enthusiastic cheers from the crowds of sightseers.

Twenty-nine horses crowned with laurel leaves were then harnessed to the carriage. These horses came from a firm of brewers and were driven by ten sturdy draymen, one of whom, Mathias Butcher, who had been discharged from the Army in 1820, wore the Waterloo Medal. The procession moved off as the clock on Paddington Green struck midday. It was a brilliant procession, with the bands of the three regiments of Foot Guards, with regimental detachments numbering 500 guardsmen, the 2nd Life Guards riding at the head and the rear of the procession, with twenty troopers under command of Captain F. M. Martyn riding on either side of the statue on its carriage. The hundred men of the Scots Fusilier Guards who had hauled the statue from the foundry, and a party of fitters and riggers from the Royal Woolwich Dockyard, also marched in the procession. As the procession moved off the bands played "See the Conquering Hero Comes" amid the cheers and acclamations of the great crowds.

Hyde Park Corner was reached at 1.30, the arrival of the statue being watched by many thousands, including members of the Royal Family. It was drawn alongside the scaffolding which had been erected by the arch for the purpose of hoisting it up by means of blocks, tackle and winches. The scaffolding was 115 feet high and took 200 loads of timber. The preparation for the hoisting took several hours and it was almost 4 p.m. before the ropes were ready in position. It was decided that it was too late that day to complete the task, and the statue was raised the following day by a party of Dockyard riggers by means of cables fixed under the body and legs of the horse. It took six hours to remove the statue from the car and hoist it into position.

The final fixing of the statue to the top of the arch was carried out by the riggers and a party of masons the following day, Thursday, 1st October.

In 1882 attention was focused on the urgent town planning problems of Central London, and among these the question of the future of Hyde Park Corner demanded immediate attention to meet the ever-increasing tide of traffic. The question was discussed in Parliament and the Government plan proposed a widening of the thoroughfares of this congested area by taking in part of Constitution Hill and the Green Park. One of the main problems in this plan was the removal of the great triumphal arch—the Wellington Arch—opposite the London residence of the Duke of Wellington, Apsley House, surmounted by the colossal equestrian statue of the Duke of Wellington.

The statue had in some quarters never been regarded as entirely suitable or quite in place. Even before the death of the Duke there had been agitations for its removal. There were letters to the Press ; the question was discussed in the House. Parliament agitated for its removal ; the Prime Minister supported the proposition, and Queen Victoria too was in agreement. The Duke of Wellington, however, resented these suggestions and regarded the proposals, which had been made for "purely æsthetic reasons," as a personal slight.* He was adamant in his views, and the statue was not moved during the Duke's lifetime. Thirty years had passed from the time of the Duke's death in 1852 before this question was raised again.

Public interest in the whole question of the removal of the statue is reflected in the many references and cartoons which appeared at the time in *Punch*. When the statue's removal was first mooted in a parliamentary speech on the Hyde Park improvements, a full-page cartoon appeared in *Punch* depicting Wellington looking down at Mr. Shaw Lefeuvre—then Minister of Works—who is shown climbing up to the statue on a ladder waving a Notice of Removal. The cartoon bore the caption, "Hey ? What ? Coming down ? Why certainly, and don't put me up again." In the same issue of *Punch*†

---

* "Wellington," Richard Aldington (Wm. Heinemann Ltd.) (1946).
† *Punch*, 8th April, 1882.

appeared a satirical playlet in verse under the title of "Don Shaw-Vanni and the Statue" or "The Virtuous Lothario and His Happy Thought." The dramatis personæ were Don Shaw-Vanni (of the Office of Works), Il Commendatore (Il Duco de Ferro) and Leporello (of Fleet Street), and the scene was set in "an unsecluded spot in a Green Park."

In July, 1883,* another *Punch* cartoon depicted the statue, after its removal from the arch, standing on a wooden tray, its sides shored up, and with long grass growing up all around. The body of the Duke is shown broken off at the waist, and the reins and sword are broken ; children are playing on and around the statue. The caption to this reads "What the statue will come to if left where it is much longer," and referred to the then undecided future of the statue following its removal from the arch during the time that it stood, shored up, at the corner of the Green Park.

The statue was described as an "unsightly object," but its removal and possible demolition offended the public sentiments, for the memory of "The Duke" was still green. The question was taken up by King Edward VII (then Prince of Wales), who took a keen and practical interest in the structural improvements of the Metropolis.

On 8th January, 1883, the Prince wrote to Mr. Gladstone, the Prime Minister, recommending the removal of the arch to a new position at the top of a retrenched Constitution Hill, the removal of the Duke's statue and its replacement by a quadriga, and the erection of a new and small statue of the Duke on the original site of the arch, which would then stand in the centre of the widened thoroughfare. "As regard the old (colossal) statue of the Duke," wrote the Prince, "I would suggest that it should not be broken up but removed to Aldershot, where it would be highly valued by the Army—and would serve as an example to all time. General Reilly informs me that this could be done as a matter of ordinary service by the Royal Artillery without any further cost to the Government than the expense of billeting the men engaged during the days occupied by the transit."

Mr. Gladstone replied immediately accepting the Prince's proposals and the scheme was put into operation. The Triumphal Arch was moved in 1883 to the position it occupies today at the top of Constitution Hill. The Prince's proposal for the surmounting of the arch by a quadriga was not, however, carried out until 1912, after his death, when the quadriga, by the sculptor Captain Adrian Jones, was erected as a monument to his memory. A small statue of the Duke was erected on the original site of the arch at Hyde Park Corner, where it remains to this day, and the large equestrian statue was moved to Aldershot.

* *Punch*, 7th July, 1883.

The site in Aldershot for the re-erection of the statue was chosen on 23rd February, 1885, by the Prince of Wales, H.R.H. The Duke of Cambridge and the Earl of Rosebery. The Duke of Cambridge noted the occasion in his diary : "Went with the Prince of Wales, Rosebery and others to Aldershot, where we found our horses and went to select a site for the large statue of the Duke of Wellington, removed from Hyde Park Corner. We saw the statue in parts, quite uninjured by the removal, and found a very good position not far from the Queen's Pavilion and the Church, on a natural mound, where we all agreed in thinking it would look very well."*

Work on the removal of the statue from the top of the arch commenced on 25th January, 1883. A frame of iron girders and scaffolding was erected and the removal conducted under the supervision of Mr. F. T. Reade, of the Institute of Civil Engineers, and Messrs. John Mowlem & Co., the contractors. The statue was brought down in a succession of slight descents by means of hydraulic jacks and tackle. The work of removal occupied six weeks, and the statue, resting on a steel platform, was finally drawn away from the base of the arch by powerful locomotives.

The future of the statue was still under discussion, and various sites were suggested—Chelsea Hospital, Portsmouth, Wellington College, and St. James's Park, within the railings, facing The Horse Guards Parade, in the position occupied today by the Guards 1914-1918 War Memorial, or at Aldershot. This last site was the final unanimous recommendation of a special committee formed at the invitation of the Prince of Wales, with the sanction of Queen Victoria,† to advise the Chief Commissioner of Works, Mr. Shaw Lefeuvre, and included the second Duke of Wellington, Lord Hardinge, the Earl of Northbrook, Lord de L'Isle and Dudley, and Baron Ferdinand de Rothschild. The committee came to the conclusion that no other site offered the same advantages as that of Aldershot. "On national and military grounds," this appeared to be the most appropriate position that could be chosen. "At Aldershot the figure of the great Duke could be highly appreciated by the whole army, among whom it was considered most fitting that the statue should find a permanent home."‡

On 24th April, 1883, the first stage of the journey from its old site was undertaken, but it was removed only 150 feet, to rest on the edge

---

* "The Military Life of H.R.H. George, Duke of Cambridge," by Willoughby Verner.
† *The Times*, 22nd April, 1884.
‡ *The Times*, 28th March, 1884. It was undoubtedly due to the Prince of Wales that Aldershot was chosen as the site for the statue, the suggestion having been made by the Prince over a year before when he wrote to Mr. Gladstone on the matter.

of the Green Park outside Apsley House. This was effected by laying a tramway from the arch to the new position, strong steel rollers being placed underneath the iron cradle, on which the statue rested shored up by girders, and being pulled along by an engine. In this new position the statue remained for some considerable time whilst there was still further discussion as to its final destination.

On 5th August, 1884, it was announced that the statue was ready for removal.* It had been cut into seven parts to facilitate its removal. A special carriage was constructed at Woolwich of heavy timber, 19 feet long by 8½ feet broad, with wheels at the rear 8 feet in diameter. The removal commenced at 1 a.m. on the night of 6th/7th August, it having been decided to effect its removal at a time when it would not interfere with public traffic. The head and tail of the horse were first removed upon a railway trolley, drawn by three horses, and then the body of the statue was placed on the specially constructed carriage, drawn by "four powerful horses." It was stated that the parts of the statue would proceed to Aldershot by stages.† On 11th August it was announced‡ that the statue had arrived safely at Aldershot and had been "deposited at the military stores close to the South Camp"§ pending its re-erection on a suitable pedestal in Aldershot.

The work of re-erection of the statue was entrusted to Messrs. Martin, Wells & Co., one of the well-known Aldershot builders and contractors of the day, who raised the statue to the elevated position on the summit of Round Hill, facing the south-west overlooking the entrance to the Long Valley, directly opposite the Queen's Pavilion. It was at the time intended to heighten the effect, although even at that time the monument already presented a very striking sight, by the addition of a number of cannons placed at the base of the pedestal so as to form a framework; several of these cannons were already in position at the time of the handing-over ceremony. The statue was the subject of a letter dated 20th August, 1885, from King Edward VII (when Prince of Wales) to his friend, Alfred Montgomery. The following is a passage from the letter and is taken from Sir Sidney Lee's Biography of King Edward‖ :

"We had a very pretty and successful military ceremony at Aldershot yesterday when I handed over to the General Officer Commanding the troops there (Lieut.-General Anderson) the old statue of the great 'Dook.' "

* *The Times*, 5th August, 1884.
† *The Times*, 7th August, 1884.
‡ *The Times*, 11th August, 1884.
§ The Field Stores of today.
‖ "King Edward VII—A Biography," by Sir Sidney Lee (Macmillan & Co, Ltd.) (1925).

The Prince of Wales and the Duke of Connaught, accompanied by Prince George and Lord Arthur Somerset, had arrived in Aldershot on the afternoon of 18th August. That evening the Prince inspected the statue and made arrangements with Lieut.-General D. Anderson, then commanding the Aldershot Division, for the military parade which was to be held the following day at the express wish of Queen Victoria to mark the occasion of the handing over of the statue to the Aldershot Division.

The ceremony took place at 12.30 p.m. on 19th August and lasted about three-quarters of an hour, and was described in a contemporary account as "one of the prettiest ceremonies that has ever been witnessed in Aldershot." The ceremony followed an inspection by the Prince of Wales of the 2nd Bn. The Rifle Brigade, which was held at 9 a.m. on Rushmoor Common, and later an inspection of the 10th Hussars on the Queen's Parade.

Representatives from every unit in Aldershot were on parade for the official handing over of the statue by the Prince of Wales. The troops were formed up in a half-circle, facing west, at the base of the statue ; in addition to the unit representatives were two companies of Infantry, two squadrons of Cavalry, a battery of Royal Horse Artillery, and one company from the Medical Staff Corps and the Commissariat and Transport Corps. The Infantry were formed up in front of the Cavalry and Artillery. "Vast numbers of spectators," it was recorded, "had assembled on the rising elevation near the Farnborough Road, and the bright uniforms of the military intermingled with the sombre colours of the attire of the civilian spectators, with a background formed by the woods, presented a striking and picturesque sight."

The Royal Party was received by Lieut.-General Anderson. The General made a brief speech. The Prince of Wales replied, and then a Royal Salute of twenty-one guns was fired, the massed bands of the 1st Brigade playing at the same time the National Anthem.

The troops that had taken part in the ceremony then marched past the Prince, who took the salute at the base of the statue.

The Divisional Staff headed the march past, and included the Commander of the Aldershot Division, Colonel C. N. Robinson, A.A. & Q.M.G. ; Colonel R. Harrison, C.B., C.M.G., Royal Engineers ; Lieut.-Colonel E. H. Satorious, V.C., the D.A.A. & Q.M.G. ; Major-General Sir D. C. Drury Lowe, K.B.E., the Commander of the Cavalry Brigade ; Major R. Chalmer, D.D.A. & Q.M.G. ; Major Parry Okeden and Lieutenant C. Fergusson, A.D.C. to the Cavalry Brigade Commander. The Staff were followed by the R.H.A. Battery, under Major G. W. C. Rothe, with their, then new, 12½-pounder guns ;

then the 7th Queen's Own Hussars, under Lieut.-Colonel Drew; the 10th Prince of Wales's Own Hussars, under Lieut.-Colonel E. Wood, C.B.; "V" Battery of the 1st Brigade, Royal Artillery, led by Major Maclaverty. Then followed Major-General W. Cooper, the Commander of the 1st Infantry Brigade, with the 1st King's Own Lancaster Regiment led by Colonel Twentyman and the 2nd Royal Highlanders under command of Colonel Farrington. Then came Major-General Dunne, Commander of the 2nd Brigade, with the 1st Leicesters led by Colonel Utterson, the 3rd Royal Fusiliers commanded by Colonel Hough, the 2nd Rifle Brigade under Lieut.-Colonel Slade, the 1st Wiltshires commanded by Lieut.-Colonel Gream, and the 5th Rifle Brigade under Colonel Maxwell; the Commissariat and Transport Corps, led by Captain E. S. M'Murray, and the Medical Staff Corps detachment under Surgeon-Major Ray.

The march past concluded the ceremony. The Royal Party lunched at the Royal Pavilion and returned to London by special train later in the afternoon.

The following order was issued by Lieut.-General Anderson the next day:

> H.R.H. The Prince of Wales, having on behalf of Her Majesty The Queen entrusted the statue of the Duke of Wellington on Round Hill to the charge of the Aldershot Division, the Lieut.-General Commanding places the statue under the care of the Colonel Commanding Royal Engineers, who will direct that it be periodically inspected by an Officer of the Corps.

*   *   *   *   *

It was in August, 1885, that the 22nd Middlesex Volunteers (The Central London Rangers)* carried out their annual training in Aldershot. There was nothing unusual about a Volunteer Battalion going to camp in Aldershot, but attention was on this occasion focused on this London Volunteer Unit, commanded by Lieut.-Colonel W. J. Ault, for they had with them a "battery" of Nordenfeldt guns with which they trained with the special permission of the Commander-in-Chief. This was the first occasion that machine guns were employed with troops in the United Kingdom. Among those keenly interested in this training was Lord Wolseley, who strongly advocated the use of machine guns. The guns used by the 22nd Middlesex had five barrels and were fired from a carriage designed by Martini-Henri. Detailed reports were made of the firing and mobility performances of the gun and upon its employment as an infantry support weapon. The

* Today The Rangers, The Rifle Brigade (Prince Consort's Own).

results of this training led to the subsequent adoption of the Gatling and Hotchkiss machine guns by the Regular Army.

It was also in August, 1885, that the first exercises in long-distance signalling by heliograph were carried out in the Aldershot area, under the direction of Major Thrupp, then Inspector-General of Army Signalling. The base of operations was on Hungry Hill, and from here contact was made with helio detachments at Hindhead and on Merrow Downs, the rate of signalling being thirty words in two and a half minutes.

Royal interest in the Army led naturally to the sustained Royal interest in "The Camp" at Aldershot which, as has already been seen, was evinced by the regular visits of Queen Victoria and the Prince Consort in the early days. As the century progressed this interest increased and Aldershot became the scene of many brilliant reviews, inspections and other military ceremonies. With the exception of the capital and Windsor, no other part of the country can surely have seen so many Royal visits both by our own Royal Family and the rulers of foreign countries and states.

On 19th May, 1874, the Tsar of Russia visited Aldershot and inspected 15,000 troops on parade, by whose bearing and turn-out, it was recorded, he was most impressed.

Twenty thousand men were on parade on 28th June, 1875, when the Prince and Princess of Wales, accompanied by the Empress Eugénie and the Sultan of Zanzibar, visited "The Camp" to inspect the "Division at Aldershot" prior to manœuvres. The Prince Imperial was, at the time, attached to one of the Field Batteries quartered in Waterloo Barracks.

On 2nd July, 1886, a Royal Review was held in the Long Valley, culminating with a march past near Tweseldown Race-course; 14,000 troops took part in the review, Queen Victoria taking the salute from her carriage. The Queen returned to Windsor at the conclusion of the parade, but the remainder of the Royal Party, which included the Prince and Princess of Wales, the Duke and Duchess of Connaught and the Duke of Cambridge, remained in the area to watch the manœuvres which were carried out and lasted until eight o'clock in the evening.

The following year saw, on 9th July, 1887, one of the largest and most impressive parades, on the occasion of Queen Victoria's Jubilee Review. A force of two Army Corps was assembled in the Long Valley: four Divisions of Regulars, under the command of Lieut.-General Alinson, and five Divisions of Volunteers, with seven Regular Cavalry regiments in two brigades and eighteen batteries of Artillery, under command of the Duke of Cambridge.

On 7th August, 1889, the Kaiser visited Aldershot *en route* from London to Portsmouth at the conclusion of a state visit to Queen Victoria. A grand field day had been arranged in the area of the Fox Hills, 26,000 troops participating in the "sham fight"—including nine regiments of Cavalry, six R.H.A. and fifteen field batteries and four brigades of Infantry. At the conclusion of the operations this force marched past the Kaiser, who watched them keenly and with enthusiasm.

Her Imperial Majesty the Empress Frederick of Prussia visited Aldershot on 15th May, 1894, driving to "The Camp," with a mounted escort from the 9th Lancers, from Bagshot, where she had been the guest of the Duke of Connaught.

The Empress was entertained to lunch at Government House and then made a tour of the barracks. They first paid a visit to the then new Army Gymnasium, where they watched a class undergoing instruction and a demonstration class engaged in Swedish drill. The Empress then visited the Cambridge Hospital, passing through the wards, and then proceeded to Gun Hill along the Avenue Road— the Wellington Avenue of today—to the Royal Pavilion. The troops, in walking-out dress, formed up in the vicinity of their quarters and lined the whole route. Two days later Queen Victoria was in Aldershot and saw 12,000 troops in review order on parade on Laffan's Plain. It was on this occasion of the Royal visit that the first Torchlight Tattoo in Aldershot was held in the grounds adjoining the Royal Pavilion, and was attended by the Queen, accompanied by Prince and Princess Henry of Battenberg. The idea of the Tattoo emanated from the Duke of Connaught, who entrusted the arrangements to Major Mainwaring, of the 2nd Bn. Royal Welsh Fusiliers. The Queen, it was recorded, "expressed her pleasure and interest in the picturesque proceedings and remained until the end of the long programme."

A Royal welcome was given by the Duke of Connaught and the Aldershot Division during the first week of June, 1895, to Shahzada Nasrullah Khan, who was visiting England as a representative of his father, the Ameer of Afghanistan. The Royal visitor arrived at the Farnborough station and from there travelled in an open carriage with a mounted escort of the 9th Lancers and drove to Laffan's Plain. The Shahzada was accompanied by the Prince of Wales, the Duke of Cambridge and Lieutenant Prince Francis of Teck in the uniform of the 1st Royal Dragoons. The Afghan prince wore, according to a report in *The Aldershot News*, "what, it would appear, is his military ceremonial uniform which was of scarlet, richly ornamented with gold facings ; his head covering was a kind of astrakhan fez ; across his left shoulder he had a blue sash." The Shahzada was escorted to

Laffan's Plain to witness a scene "brilliant beyond adequate description." The arrival of the troops on the parade ground had been watched with great interest by the crowds that had gathered. "Flashing scarlet moved in all directions to take up positions and martial music filled the air from a dozen bands," read the description of the parade published in *The Aldershot News*, "while the quick rat-a-plan of the drums beat on the air, mingled with the bugle march of the Rifle Brigade, whose black* battalion moved over the grass in solid sections. A boom of guns fired the salute heralding the approach of the royal visitors. To add to the general scene the Balloon Section, Royal Engineers, became in evidence in mid-air, a balloon circling majestically above the parade." "Seldom," it was recorded, "had so representative a section of the British Army been gathered together in Aldershot. As far as the eye could see arose a forest of steel and pennons of the Lancers."

There were 17,700 troops on parade. The Royal Party moved slowly along the line, the Shahzada "eyeing critically the Regiments as he passed," a number of whom were wearing the medal for the Afghan War, 1879-80, and the bronze star for Lord Roberts' famous march from Kabul to Kandahar. The troops were seen at their best in the review, and "many a heart thrilled as corps after corps of gallant fellows rode or marched proudly past."

The "Right of the Line"—the Royal Horse Artillery, with E, J, and the "Chestnut" Battery† looking as serviceable and smart as they are well known to be. The Cavalry Division in two brigades were led by their G.O.C. The 2nd Life Guards in their steel cuirass led the way, the Life Guardsmen as usual presented a magnificent appearance, the 9th Lancers looked particularly well, and were followed by the Royal Scots Greys, whose squadrons evoked much admiration. The Light Brigade composed of Hussars followed. The 3rd King's Own Hussars in their blue busby bags and white plumes gave a pretty contrast to the well-known yellow of the gallant 4th, who also made a magnificent show. The 8th Hussars with the red busby bags were small in number but smart in appearance. Then came the Field Batteries, the R.E. mounted detachment, followed by the Guards Brigade, who marched past like walls of stone. Then followed the remainder of the Aldershot Division and with them marched detachments of the Portsmouth Volunteer Brigade, which included the 1st Volunteer Battalion of the Hampshire Regiment. "The Shahzada," it was recorded, "glanced along the gleaming mass, but his impassive face betrayed no thought, although the eyes of his bearded attendant officers gleamed with enthusiasm."

---

* Referring to the colour of the uniform of the Rifle Brigade.
† "A" Battery, R.H.A.

The review concluded with a gallop past by the Royal Horse Artillery.

The Shahzada smiled at the grand sight of the galloping horses passing him in a flash, the infantry meanwhile had assumed their original formation in line and at a signal advanced in review order and gave a Royal salute to the strains of the National Anthem.

The Line at a move outwards from the centre disclosed the Cavalry Division drawn up for the charge and also the sight of a solitary "fizzer wallah,"* who undertook to do business at the rear of the line, he found himself in the dangerous position of being in the centre of the Division of Cavalry about to charge, an Aide-de-Camp further bewildered the old man who broke into a trot amid great merriment.

The Heavy Brigade advanced at the charge and on the trumpet note broke into a gallop, pulling up 30 yards from the Shahzada, who was immensely delighted. The Light Brigade followed in similar fashion the line being perfect and the whole incident smart beyond praise. Both Brigades brought a round of applause from the spectators. The thunder of the hooves, the excited horses and the earnest faces of the troopers was a sight to remember and made a deep impression on the visitor.

At the conclusion of the review the Royal visitors were entertained to luncheon by the Duke and Duchess of Connaught at Government House.

In August, 1894, the German Kaiser, Wilhelm II, visited Aldershot. He had been appointed by Queen Victoria Colonel-in-Chief of the 1st Royal Dragoons†—the first foreign sovereign to be accorded such an honour—and expressed a wish to appear on parade with "his" regiment. A Royal Review and an extensive field day were arranged for the entertainment of the Royal visitor.

At that time the Royal Scots Greys formed part of the 1st Cavalry Brigade at Aldershot. The Royals were at Shorncliffe and they were moved to Aldershot for the occasion, and it was then decided to bring the 6th Inniskilling Dragoons over from The Curragh‡ and so re-form for the occasion the Union Brigade of Waterloo fame.

Aldershot prepared a royal welcome for the Kaiser's two-day visit on 13th and 14th August, 1894. The Town station was decorated with

---

* Sherbet vendor. There were always a number of sherbet, sarsparilla and mineral water traders plying their business around the camp, with their hand- or pony-drawn carts which always followed the troops on parade or manœuvres.

† The Royals had the distinction of always recruiting tall men. During the period 1887-1891 the Commanding Officer would not accept recruits under six feet, and it is recorded ("History of the Royal Dragoons, 1661-1934," by C. T. Atkinson) that whilst stationed in Aldershot in 1886-1889 the regiment was nicknamed "The Aldershot Guards."

‡ Dublin.

L

strings of flags in which the Prussian colours predominated. The platform was laid with crimson cloth which continued through the ticket office to the station yard. The station walls were hung with green and white draperies fringed with red and gold ; the fascia was decorated with shields and flags. At the sides were banks of ferns and palms. A line of Venetian masts with fluttering flags was erected on either side of the road leading to a triumphal arch which spanned the road from the corner of Arthur Street. The arch was made of evergreens and heather laid on red and white draperies. Beyond this, a huge banner was stretched across the road bearing the words "A joyous Welcome."

The Kaiser arrived at Aldershot Town station in a special train from Portsmouth, which backed into the "Up" platform. Here he was received by a guard of honour mounted by the Northumberland Fusiliers* as he alighted from the train, wearing the uniform of a Colonel of the Royal Dragoons and the blue ribbon of the Order of the Garter. He was received by the Duke of Connaught as G.O.C. the Aldershot Division, who wore full General's uniform, with the yellow sash of the Prussian Order of the Black Eagle. Senior officers of the Division and the War Office representatives, headed by General Sir Redvers Buller, V.C., then Adjutant-General of the Forces, were then presented to the Kaiser.

During the German Emperor's inspection of the guard of honour, the German officers of his personal staff, all in blue uniforms with gold and silver lace and pickelhaube helmets, were introduced to the British officers. Among the German officers were three Generals and Major Von Moltke, a nephew of the famous Field-Marshal. On leaving the station the Kaiser mounted a "richly caparisoned horse," held by an attendant in blue and silver livery, and rode forward to inspect the mounted escort of the 1st Royal Dragoons, under the command of Colonel Tomlinson, which was lined up in the station yard. "The scene," wrote a reporter in *The Aldershot News*, "was now an extremely brilliant one, the prancing horses, the bright hues of the uniforms, the glitter of gold lace and decorations, the glint of silver and the flashing of steel forming a grand spectacle." The cavalcade then formed up, led by a troop of The Royals ; then came the Emperor, the Duke of Connaught and Captain Carr-Ellison, in command of the escort. The route of the Royal visitor led along Station Road, Victoria Road, Wellington Street and High Street, the shops and houses on either side of the route gay with flags, bunting and bright draperies and lined with crowds of townspeople.

---

* The regiment became the Royal Northumberland Fusiliers in 1935, the title "Royal" being granted in commemoration of the Silver Jubilee of King George V.

The cavalcade continued up Wellington Avenue to Laffan's Plain.

The whole Aldershot Division, of some 12,000 men, had by nine o'clock been on parade* on Laffan's Plain, with the R.H.A. on the right of the line; the massed Cavalry Brigade and the Brigades of infantry drawn up in a solid array, battalions divided by six paces and brigades by twenty. Long lines of private carriages were drawn up facing the parade and the ground was lined with hundreds of spectators. The arrival of the Kaiser with his mounted escort was heralded by the booming of guns firing the Royal Salute from Pavilion Hill, and the German Imperial Standard was run up at the saluting base by the Royal enclosure, which was guarded by a detachment of mounted troops and the 20th (Artists) Middlesex Rifles.†

The Royal cavalcade rode up and down the lines of troops whilst the Kaiser carried out his inspection of the parade in line, and, on his return to the saluting base, the whole division marched past to the stirring music of the massed bands.

After the march past, the Artillery and Cavalry wheeled and formed up at the extreme west of the parade, the mounted troops moving in the rear of the marching infantry. Then they came past the saluting base at the trot and, finally, at the gallop. Of this *The Aldershot News* wrote:

> Never has a more impressive sight been seen on Laffan's Plain. The pace was terrific as the heavy masses swept down the plain. The bands were playing and the brilliant rays of the sun lit up the shining helmets of the mounted troops, gilding the tips of the lances and burnishing the brasswork of the guns and harness. On they came, horses and men welded together. Not a man was unhorsed and so rapid, so brilliant, was the rush, that only a confused memory of magnificent action and gorgeous colour remained in the minds of the spectators. Even the apathy of an

---

* The regiments on parade were: "F," "G" and "P" Batteries, R.H.A.; the Royal Horse Guards (who on this occasion were not wearing their breastplates); 1st Royal Dragoons; Royal Scots Greys; 4th Hussars; 6th Inniskilling Dragoons; 9th Lancers; the 1st, 13th and 77th Field Batteries of the 1st Division R.A.; the 4th, 38th, 41st and 61st Field Batteries of the 2nd Division R.A.; the Telegraph Company and 23rd and 26th Companies, R.E.; the Guards Brigade (3rd Grenadiers, 2nd Coldstreams and 1st Scots Guards); and the 1st Northumberland Fusiliers, 1st Lincolnshire Regiment, 1st Argyll and Sutherland Highlanders and 4th Rifle Brigade, 1st West Yorkshire Regiment, 2nd Royal Welsh Fusiliers, 1st Wiltshire Regiment, 2nd Leicestershire Regiment, 2nd Cheshire Regiment, the Highland Light Infantry, 2nd Leinster Regiment and 2nd Worcestershire Regiment, together with the Departmental Corps Detachments.

† A Volunteer unit, later the Artists Rifles (28th London Regiment) (T.A.) and today the 22nd (Special Air Service) Regiment (Artists) (T.A.), who were undergoing Annual Training at Aldershot at the time of the Kaiser's visit.

Aldershot crowd was stirred* and a cheer, not loud, but deep and earnest, burst from the onlookers.

The whole parade then re-formed and, on the order of the G.O.C., advanced in review order with marvellous precision, the whole line advancing to within fifty paces of the saluting base, where, halting, the Royal Salute was given with colours dipped and the massed bands playing the National Anthem. Thus concluded one of the most brilliant reviews held in Aldershot.

The Kaiser lunched that day in the Mess of the 4th Rifle Brigade, of which regiment the Duke of Connaught was Colonel-in-Chief. Later in the day he visited the Empress Eugénie at Farnborough, where he took tea on the terrace, and the Scots Greys gave a musical ride in the grounds. In the evening a dinner and reception in the Kaiser's honour was held at Government House.

On the following day the Emperor rode out to watch a field day conducted in the area between Cove Common and Beacon Hill, on which an assault concluded the exercise. The Kaiser lunched at the Royal Artillery Mess in Waterloo Barracks, and that evening the Royal visitor attended an Army Boxing Meeting in the "Big Gym" and later dined in the Mess of the Scots Greys. At 10 p.m. that evening the Kaiser prepared for his departure from Aldershot, and, leaving the Mess, drove to the Town station with a mounted escort of The Royals.

The Royal procession drove through the town to the station, which was illuminated by 3,000 lamps hung in strings along the station building's platform and along the approaches. In the centre of the station frontage there was a huge eight-pointed star formed of green and amber lamps, whilst the windows on either side were traced in ruby and amber lights. The whole station glittered with the twinkling lights that crossed and recrossed the platform, the ticket office, and

---

* It will be appreciated that, living as they did in daily contact with the colourful Army, and with numerous grand parades and great military spectacles taking place regularly within easy walking distance of their homes and businesses, the people of Aldershot were not so inspired or impressed by such parades as would have been those to whom they would have presented something new, unique and thrilling. There appears also to have been little or no encouragement for visitors from afar, and no facilities to assist visitors to attend the spectacular military events of the day which took place in "The Camp." Comment on this fact was made by the editor of *The Aldershot News* after the Kaiser's visit. "For a tawdry show on Lord Mayor's Day in London," he wrote, "there are excursions from every quarter of the kingdom. . . . At Aldershot, where the flower of the army is to be seen under splendid conditions in all its strength, it is considered sufficient if the local [railway] companies run a few specials from the neighbouring towns and adjacent villages." Nearly thirty years were to pass, however, before Aldershot did, on the occasion of the magnificent Tattoos, become a centre on which hundreds of special trains and thousands of cars and coaches converged to see the glory of British Arms displayed in Rushmoor Arena.

the whole frontage. The example of the railway company was followed throughout the town, and most of the hotels, traders and many householders lit their premises in similar style so that the whole route from the Cavalry Barracks to the railway glittered and sparkled with the countless lamps which were strung along the buildings and across the streets, whilst fireworks were let off on the open ground off the route. Thousands of spectators lined the streets. The Kaiser's special train, in which his compartment was specially fitted with figured cream satin upholstery, moved out of the station soon after 10.30 p.m. amid the salutes, the music of the bands and the cheering of the crowds.

Aldershot, Camp and Town, had given a terrific reception to the Queen's grandson in the two crowded days he had spent with the Army. The Kaiser himself had undoubtedly been honoured, flattered and considerably impressed not only by the welcome he had received and by the arrangements which had been made, but by the discipline, organization and high standard of the British Army ; but there is no doubt, as he had sat on his charger watching the Aldershot Division march past, he realized with some self-satisfaction that whereas before him was the cream of the British Army at home, concentrated in one single Division, he in his own country could have paraded over ten times that number with ease, and would then have only had but a third of the strength of the German Army.* It may well be that the mind picture he had retained of that day on Laffan's Plain, when the confident, proud and well-disciplined Aldershot Division marched past, flashed before him when, in August, 1914, he bitterly referred to our "contemptible little army" which, although he had seen, he did not understand.

A fully illustrated report of the Kaiser's visit was published in *The Aldershot News*, and a copy was printed on yellow satin and presented to the Kaiser through the German Ambassador. Another copy printed on pale blue satin was presented to the Duke of Connaught, then the G.O.C., Aldershot.

Queen Victoria continued to pay annual visits to Aldershot and 1895 was no exception. Her Majesty arrived by train at Farnborough on Friday, 12th July ; she was met by the Duke of Connaught and the Duchess of Connaught, who was accompanied by Prince Arthur and the Princesses Margaret and Victoria, the Queen being accompanied by Princess Louise, Prince Victor Napoleon and the Prince and

---

* It was then laid down in the German Constitution that every man capable of bearing arms belonged to the army for seven years—three with the colours and four on the reserve (and with five further years in the Landwehr). In 1894 the German Army was composed of twenty Corps and the total strength was 486,983, including 538 battalions of Infantry and 434 batteries of Artillery (*vide* "*The Times History of the War*," Vol. I, 1914).

Princess Henry of Battenberg. Prince Henry was wearing the uniform
of the Isle of Wight Volunteers,* of which he was Honorary Colonel.
The Queen travelled to Aldershot in an open carriage drawn by four
greys ridden by postilions, with outriders in the scarlet Royal liveries.
The Queen travelled with a mounted escort of the 3rd King's Own
Hussars.

The Royal procession formed up at Farnborough, and as it drove
past Cove and Farnborough Commons a Royal Salute was fired, near
the Swan Hotel, by a battery of Royal Horse Artillery. The route
continued past the Queen's Hotel and along Cranbrook Road to the
Army Gymnasium, where a display was given by the Army Gymnastic
Staff on the Army Athletic ground. At the conclusion of the display,
the Queen drove to the Royal Pavilion, where she was received with
a Royal Salute by the guard of honour of the 2nd Worcestershire
Regiment.

On Saturday, 13th July, the Queen reviewed the Aldershot Division
on Laffan's Plain. The main roads to "The Camp" were busy at a very
early hour with pedestrians and vehicles moving towards the scene
of the review. By one o'clock people were thickly clustered on all
the points of advantage at the ropes around the parade ground. The
enclosures were filled with carriages of every sort. Troops converged
from North and South Camps on to the scene, and parading Cavalry
and Artillery moved into position by Eelmore Marsh. "When the
Brigade," wrote a reporter in The Aldershot News, "had been dressed,
the whole line stood at ease, and for some minutes spectators had time
to take in the beauties of the scene. To visitors unaccustomed to the
pomp and display of Royal Aldershot a review of this kind was most
striking."

The Commander-in-Chief and his staff went out along the roadway
and met the Royal procession driving from the Pavilion with an escort
of Royal Scots Greys. As the Royal carriage drew up at the flagstaff
erected at the saluting base, the infantry in line of quarter column
came smartly down to the present and the massed bands played the
National Anthem, the Queen bowing her acknowledgment. The
Queen, it is recorded, wore the sombre black dress of her mourning
attire, relieved by white trimming in her bonnet and a cream-coloured
sunshade.

The review lasted until nearly one o'clock, the troops marching
past the saluting base and the review ending with the gallop past by
the Royal Horse Artillery and the two brigades of Cavalry.

* The 5th Volunteer Bn. The Hampshire Regiment, later the 8th (Isle of Wight
Rifles) (Princess Beatrice's) Bn. The Hampshire Regiment (T.A.), today the 42
(Mixed) Heavy Anti-Aircraft Regiment, R.A. (T.A.).

On 1st July, 1897, the great Diamond Jubilee Review was held at Aldershot. Twenty-seven thousand troops were on parade under command of the Duke of Connaught, composed of two brigades of Cavalry, four divisions of Infantry, two brigades of Militia and Colonial troops. It was an impressive sight. "The Queen was much pleased, and well she might be," wrote H.R.H. The Duke of Cambridge in his diary.* "I never saw a finer parade at Aldershot."

It was a spectacle without precedent. Tens of thousands of spectators thronged on to Laffan's Plain. Accompanying the Queen were more members of the Royal Family than had ever before been seen together in Aldershot at one time. There were the Prince and Princess of Wales, the Duke and Duchess of York, Princess Victoria of Wales, Prince and Princess Charles of Denmark, the Empress Frederick of Prussia, the Duke and Duchess of Connaught, Prince Henry of Battenberg, the Duchess of Albany, Princess Aribert of Hainault, Princess Victoria of Schleswig-Holstein, and the Duke of Cambridge. On the stands were Indian princes, Ministers from the Colonies, and from nearly every state in Europe, peers, ambassadors, envoys and military and naval attachés of all nations.

The following description of the parade is taken from a contemporary account of the proceedings† :

> The Military Review at Aldershot on the 1st of July was a more modest affair than the military parade in the Diamond Jubilee celebrations in London, but the quality of the troops employed imparted a distinction to the function which went far to compensate for their smallness in numbers. Judged by Continental standards our Army is insignificant in size, but it must always command respect. Its traditions are splendid, and its recent achievements completely satisfactory. Some of the foreign Princes who were present with the Queen at Aldershot on July 1 had seen ten times as many soldiers in review, but it is safe to say that not one of them had ever seen a finer body, man for man, than the 28,000 British troops gathered on Laffan's Plain. The presence among these of detachments from so many British Colonies added a significance to the proceedings that could not have been paralleled at a Military Review anywhere else in the world.
>
> About a quarter-past four o'clock the Queen drove up in a carriage. The troops were arranged in the shape of three sides of a great rectangle, Her Majesty occupying the centre of the vacant side. A Royal Salute was given, and then commenced

---

* "George, Duke of Cambridge," Edgar Sheppard, Vol. II (Longmans, Green & Co. Ltd.) (1906).

† "Sixty Years a Queen," by Sir Herbert Maxwell, Bt., M.P. (Harmsworth Bros. Ltd.) (1897).

the march past. The honour of marching in the van had been assigned very properly to the Colonial troops, consisting of 434 cavalry, 184 artillery and engineers, and 423 infantry.

The troops which followed represented almost every branch of the regular army and made a splendid show. But here, as in the Jubilee Procession itself, the Colonial contingent attracted the greatest share of attention. To see gallant horsemen and steady marching infantry in picturesque unfamiliar uniforms from every Continent all following the same flag and serving the same Queen was to receive a new and inspiring impression of the Empire. The red spaces on the map of the earth's surface we had known from childhood's day to represent portions of our own Empire but the impression was a vague one until we saw Canadian, Australian and South African, actually under arms in defence of their and our Queen, as much as of their own distant homes. It was then brought home to us, with startling effect, how great is the birthright of every Briton, how great the privileges attaching to such citizenship—and how great the responsibilities. These men came to us, not in gratitude for any priceless advantages we have bestowed upon them—for we have done nothing of the kind—but simply because their blood is the same as ours, their traditions the same, and their sympathies. We are still well able to take care of ourselves ; but who shall say that the Old Country may not one day need the strong right arms of her children across the seas ?

The Review was brought to an end with the defiling past of the infantry. A splendid effect was produced when the infantry gave the Royal salute, and then burst with one accord into shouts of cheering—bonnets and busbies being thrown up into the air or waved frantically on bayonet points. The Queen returned to Windsor the same evening, and the Jubilee celebrations proper were over.

The Queen again visited Aldershot in July, 1898. Soon after her arrival she presented colours on the Queen's Parade to the newly formed 3rd Battalion of the Coldstream Guards. On the following day the Queen drove to Tweseldown to inspect the 15th Hussars, and in the afternoon a grand review—the last Royal review at Aldershot under the Duke of Connaught's command—was held on Laffan's Plain. On the departure of the Queen the following day, the route from the Royal Pavilion to Lynchford Road, Farnborough, was lined each side of the road by troops standing at attention in close order.

Queen Victoria's last visit to Aldershot was on 28th June, 1899. "Her Majesty," read an account in The Aldershot News, "appeared greatly changed, infirm, bent and tottering. Leaning heavily upon the arm of an Indian attendant, she walked slowly down the ramp of Farnborough station, where the Duke of Connaught and Sir Redvers

Buller were in readiness to receive her." On this occasion all the proceedings were as brief as possible, and the Royal visit lasted only three hours, so ending the long association of the great Queen with Aldershot—the Aldershot she had seen in forty-three years grow from the rows of huts standing on the exposed heathlands to the established home of the British Army—and the soldiers in whose welfare she had taken so deep an interest in her long and glorious reign.

*   *   *   *   *

By the latter years of the nineteenth century, as a result of the construction of the permanent barracks which had replaced the old huts and of the policy of concentrating troops, brought in from old and unsuitable garrisons and stations elsewhere in the United Kingdom, in a unified and organized command, the numbers of troops in the two camps, which then covered an area of about seven square miles, increased considerably. According to an official return made in 1898,* there was in Aldershot accommodation for 585 officers, 19,647 men and 4,358 horses. The total accommodation in the Command, which included Woking, Pirbright and other nearby stations, was sufficient for 21,200 all ranks.

The late Colonel Wilfrid Jelf, in his reminiscences some fifty years later,† wrote :

> They were good days those in the early nineties in Aldershot. . . . There was a glamour which is gone, a romance of dash and colour, an atmosphere of the beau sabreur, which was part of everyday life . . . in the daily walks across the old Canal, over the Queen's Parade and into the North Camp Gardens we were kept alive to the identity of every regiment in the station by the gay uniforms which were met with everywhere and were recognizable half a mile away, on mounted orderlies busily trotting about with leather dispatch bags, parties at drill and soldiers "walking out" . . . it was soldiers, soldiers everywhere. . . . The weekly routine included attendance at Church Parades in the little tin church by the canal bridge, route marches in marching order, sham fights and field days in the Fox Hills, Reviews and Queen's Birthday Parades in all the full dress glories of Ceremonial and on Laffan's Plain. And there was colour, colour, colour all the way.

The 4th Hussars arrived in Aldershot from Ireland in 1894 and were quartered in Warburg Barracks, the East Cavalry Barracks, the main gate of which faces High Street. It was to this regiment in March of the following year that a Second-Lieutenant W. S. Churchill was

---

* *Vide* Murray's Handbook for Travellers in Hampshire, 1894.
† "Hark Back," Colonel Wilfrid Jelf, C.M.G., D.S.O. (John Murray) (1935).

gazetted from the Royal Military College Sandhurst, and so commenced the association with Aldershot of our great war-time Prime Minister, who fifty-three years later was to receive the Honorary Freedom of the Borough from the hands of the Mayor "in appreciation of the unique and most distinguished service rendered by him on behalf of the Nation in the prosecution of the War."*

In his book "My Early Life,"† Mr. Winston Churchill recalls his joining the regiment and the long hours spent in the Riding School, at stables and on the barrack square doing his "stiff and arduous training" as a "Recruit Officer." This initial training lasted six months, during which time he "rode and drilled afoot with the troopers and received exactly the same training as they did." He recalls the severity of the riding school training :

> Mounting and dismounting from a bare backed horse, at the trot or canter ; jumping a high bar without stirrups or even saddle, sometimes with hands clasped behind one's back ; jogging at a fast trot with nothing but the horse's hide between your knees, brought their inevitable share of mishaps. . . . Many a time did I pick myself up shaken and sore from the riding school tan and don again my little gold braided pork-pie cap, fastened on the chin by a boot-lace strap, with what appearance of dignity I could command, while twenty recruits grinned furtively but delightedly to see their officer suffering the same misfortunes which it was their lot so frequently to undergo.

This was typical of the life of the young cavalry officer in Aldershot at the time. Later there came the field training in the Long Valley and on Laffan's Plain, and it was here that the future Prime Minister of the most momentous years in our nation's history learned his first lessons in soldiering ; and it was from Aldershot that he set out to taste his first experience of war—in Cuba, during the Spanish operations against the Cuban rebels.

As has been the case in every war since the Crimea, troops from Aldershot have been among the first to mobilize and move overseas on active service, both in major wars and in many minor campaigns and operations in all parts of the Empire.

The Zulu War of 1879 took troops from Aldershot to participate in the expedition against Cetewayo. It was on 12th February, 1879, that it was decided to send a force to Natal, and this included the 1st Dragoon Guards, two Field Batteries, a Company of R.E. and the

---

* See p. 246.
† "My Early Life," by The Rt. Hon. Winston Churchill, C.H., M.P. (Odham's Press Ltd.).

91st* and 94th† Regiments, then stationed in "The Camp." The units were inspected on 18th March by the Duke of Cambridge, and shortly after they left to embark at Southampton.

The outbreak of war with Egypt in 1882 took a large portion of the garrison at the outset. On 2nd August, 1882, the Duke of Cambridge visited "The Camp" and inspected the 4th Dragoon Guards, the 19th Hussars, two Field Batteries R.A., the 50th,‡ 74th,§ and 87th‖ Regiments, mounted police and "the military train," then mobilizing for service in the campaign. The force that left Aldershot was finally inspected on the Queen's Parade by the Duke of Connaught.

The war in Egypt was followed by the campaign in the Sudan, 1885-1889, and finally by the campaign of 1896-1898, and the majority of troops which took part in these operations, firstly against the Mahdi and then the Khalifa, passed through Aldershot *en route* to the theatre of war.

On 14th February, 1884, the 20th Hussars, the Commissariat and a General Hospital were inspected on Queen's Parade by the Duke of Cambridge before they left for the Sudan ; and on 25th September, 1884, he was again in Aldershot inspecting on Queen's Parade the Cavalry element of the newly raised Camel Corps, composed of 43 N.C.Os. and men from every Cavalry regiment in the country, which was formed for service in the Sudan campaign at the request of Lord Wolseley.

The Ashanti Expedition, 1895, drew upon the troops in "The Camp" and a Special Service Corps was formed and mobilized in Aldershot in 1895 for service in that campaign. This Corps was formed of specially selected detachments from eleven different regiments to form a composite unit, and in addition to these the Corps included units for the Base and the Lines of Communication of the force : Royal Engineers, including men from the "1st Division Telegraph Bn. R.E.," the A.S.C., the Ordnance Store Corps, the Medical Staff Corps and the Army Pay Department.

The first detachments left Aldershot at the end of November. The men were wearing service blue serge, white helmets with puggarees, and were armed with Martini-Henry carbines and Elcho sword bayonets. The men marched to Aldershot down to the station, where they were seen off by an enthusiastic crowd.

---

* Later 1st Bn. The Argyll and Sutherland Highlanders (Princess Louise's).
† Later 2nd Bn. The Connaught Rangers (disbanded 31st July, 1922).
‡ Later 1st Bn. The Queen's Own Royal West Kent Regiment.
§ Later 2nd Bn. The Highland Light Infantry.
‖ Later 1st Bn. Royal Irish Fusiliers (Princess Victoria's).

"When the train moved away from the Town station," wrote an *Aldershot News* reporter, "there was a call for three cheers for our departing comrades, and right lustily did all present, soldiers and civilians alike, respond to the call . . . as the train steamed away."

The Special Service Corps of the composite battalion, totalling some 250 all ranks, left Aldershot on 6th December to embark at Liverpool. The Corps paraded on Corunna Barracks Square and was inspected by the Duke of Connaught before marching off to the Government Siding to entrain, headed by the bands of the 2nd Bedfordshire Regiment,* 1st Royal Scots Fusiliers, 2nd Rifle Brigade, and the drums of the 1st Manchester Regiment. Prince Henry of Battenberg, who later died of fever during the campaign, an officer of the King's Royal Rifles, drove to the station with Princess Beatrice and the Duchess of Connaught to join the Corps. The train drew out to the strains of "Auld Lang Syne," played by the three bands.

The following description of the departure of troops from "The Camp" is taken from Colonel Wilfrid Jelf's reminiscences† of his early life in Aldershot :—

> Always in the early hours the regiments would march through the camp on their way to the station. . . . In the half light the blue or scarlet tunics with the foreign service symbol of white helmet seemed to enhance the atmosphere of parting and farewell. The crowds of friends accompanying them, the tearful faces trying to smile, here and there a father in the ranks carrying his child as a last privilege—it all hurt a good deal. Those traditional tunes played by the bands seemed to carry a special significance : "The Girl I left behind me"—many of them indeed !—"Will he ne'er come back again ?" Bringing to mind the hazards of the climate for which the regiment might be bound. And that grandest and most soul-stirring of all old lilts "Should auld acquaintance be forgot . . . for auld lang syne" dying away over the crest of the slope leading down to Aldershot Town.

Aldershot's value as a great military centre was demonstrated during the South African War (October, 1899–May, 1902). Within a few months, over 60,000 men had been mobilized, equipped and dispatched to the Cape. Following the departure of the Regular troops, the garrison accommodated the mobilized Militia battalions and Imperial Yeomanry companies, trained and equipped them, and, together with drafts of Regular details, kept up the steady flow of reinforcements to the theatre of war. The Field Stores and Mobilization Stores handled

---

* Later the 2nd Bn. The Bedfordshire and Hertfordshire Regiment.
† "Hark Back," by Colonel Wilfrid Jelf, C.M.G., D.S.O. (John Murray) (1935).

the issue of countless tons of war material. In the early days of
mobilization it was quickly discovered that Aldershot could carry out
this task with every satisfaction, and in consequence "The Camp"
grew and was enlarged to keep pace with the increasing flow
of troops. It is recorded that during the "drill seasons" an
army of 30,000, exclusive of units of the Volunteer Force, was
quartered in Aldershot, and to ease the accommodation problem
hutted camps were erected at Frimley and Ewshot. The Ewshot
Camp was built on ground that originally formed part of the estate
of the Lord of the Manor of Ewshot. It was sold to the Government
in 1876 by Mr. C. J. M. Lefroy. It was here that an Artillery Camp
was established which later became a permanent station for Field
Gunners.

Several units had already left Aldershot in the weeks immediately
preceding the outbreak of war ; they were the 6th Dragoon Guards,
2nd Royal West Surrey Regiment, 2nd Somerset Light Infantry, and
the 2nd Scottish Rifles. The first regiment to leave Aldershot for
active service after the first shots had been exchanged was the 1st
Northumberland Fusiliers, who entrained amid great enthusiasm and
a rousing send-off from the Government siding on 23rd September,
1899, together with fifty telegraphists of the Royal Engineers and a
detachment of the Army Service Corps. Other regiments stationed in
"The Camp" which were among the first to depart were the 12th
Lancers, 2nd Royal Fusiliers, 2nd West Yorks, 2nd Devons, 2nd Black
Watch, and 1st Durham Light Infantry.

The departure of troops from Aldershot at the outbreak of the South
African War was a complete contrast to when they went overseas at
the outbreak of the 1914-1918 war, when all in the Aldershot Command
disappeared in a night, and the same secrecy of troop movements
which was observed in the 1939-1945 war.

A considerable number of the men were army reservists who had
been recalled to the colours. It was the first occasion on which the
whole of the Army Reserve had since its inception been fully mobilized. Most were married men who had been called away from their
wives and children. They considerably swelled the population of
the garrison and were swayed by that deep emotion of "Today we
live, tomorrow we die," which at times caused some lively scenes
in the town. But to witness the marching and demeanour of a battalion
when the morning came for their departure, either from the Town
station or Government siding, was to see a magnificent body of
soldiers and men, of mature age and thoroughly trained, fit to meet
any enemy. The sight was enhanced by the fact that they were all
dressed in khaki drill and wore khaki topees. Khaki serge was only

introduced during the South African War, and worn in the latter stages of the campaign. The mobilized battalions marched from "The Camp" to the stations, with bands playing stirring tunes, to cheers of spectators; and from the ranks came shouts of "Where's Kruger?" and the singing of "Good-bye, Dolly Gray" and other popular songs of the day. Weeping women accompanied some of the men, and scenes at the station were both exhilarating and moving.

At the time troops left for South Africa the Government siding was an open space with the exception of the entrance gate, which was closed when the troops entered the siding. An open embankment sloped down to the platforms. A wire fence was at the top of the embankment. This was patrolled by Military Police, but many girls and women, wives and sweethearts, got through or over the fence to run down the embankment to reach the troops on the platform. The police did their best to stop them, not always successfully, and as the crowded troop train moved slowly out, with the bands playing "Auld Lang Syne" and patriotic airs, men leaned from the carriage windows to take their last farewells.

For weeks Aldershot was the scene of great military activity with the continual movement of troops, horses and stores; the streets echoed with martial music and patriotic demonstrations by soldiers and the civilian population. Flags and bunting were displayed everywhere in honour of the departing troops. The theme songs of the days—and nights—were "Good-bye, Dolly, I must leave you" and, above all, "The Soldiers of the Queen." Train after train chugged away. Chalked on the sides of the trucks were the slogans "Aldershot to Pretoria" and "Watch out, Kruger!"

Before the end of the war, on 31st May, 1902, over a hundred thousand troops had passed through Aldershot *en route* to South Africa. Battalions came and went; men, horses and war material were provided through the Aldershot military machine in such numbers and quantities as had never before been known. As division followed division, emptied barracks filled up again, Militia taking the place of the Regulars, who in turn left, after training, for the Cape. Yeomanry by the thousand passed through "The Camp" to a total of over 23,000 by the end of the war. In all over 50,000 Infantry, 34,000 Cavalry, 4,000 Gunners, 2,500 Sappers, 3,000 Army Service Corps and 4,500 R.A.M.C. went out from Aldershot to the theatre of war, together with Mounted Infantry and Cyclist Companies and the 3rd Balloon Section, R.E.

At the outbreak of war, General Sir Redvers Buller, the G.O.C. in Aldershot, was selected to command an Army Corps of 48,000 men as Commander-in-Chief of the South African Field Force. General

Buller had been appointed to Aldershot in October, 1898. For some years before, as Adjutant-General at the War Office, he had had his finger on the pulse of Aldershot and had created a mobilization plan which he himself was to implement. Secret instructions were issued in September, 1899, to prepare, and on 7th October the orders came to mobilize. The town and camp echoed to the tramp of marching men and the music of the bands. Five days before the first troops moved to the ports of embarkation General Buller left Aldershot and sailed from Southampton to the Cape.

While in Aldershot General Buller had gained the esteem and confidence of all ranks, and the admiration of the townspeople; and after a year's service in Natal and the Transvaal, directing and leading the operations at Colenso, the Tugela River, Spion Kop, Monte Cristo, Pieters Hill and finally the relief of Ladysmith, he returnd to England and Aldershot, and the town and camp gave him a great reception. There was a semi-military reception at Aldershot Town station when the beflagged train bearing the General from Southampton arrived, and in the station yard he received the official welcome from the Town. The station was gaily decorated with flags and bunting, and grandstands had been erected. A guard of honour of the 1st Dragoon Guards in full-dress uniform, 450 strong, with their red-plumed brass helmets, lined the route from the station gates to the corner of Victoria Road. A reception committee had been formed and a formal address of welcome was made by the Chairman of the Urban District Council, to which General Buller replied. At the conclusion of the ceremony the General entered his carriage with Lady Buller, his daughter, and A.D.C., but before they could drive off members of the Aldershot Fire Brigade, in their blue uniforms and brass helmets, who had been placed in position beforehand, moved forward and at a signal from their Superintendent unharnessed the horses, seized the traces, and commenced to draw the General through the streets amid the enthusiastic cheers of the crowd. The carriage was drawn through the dense, cheering crowds in the decorated streets of the town to the Headquarters Offices in Stanhope Lines. The route through the town was decorated by masts on both sides of the roads, draped with bunting and surmounted by gilded crowns, with ferns and flowers tied to the masts and with festoons of evergreens and bunting spanning the streets on which messages were emblazoned, "Welcome to our Gallant General," "Welcome Home," "He obeyed the Empire's Call," and "The Nation Thanks You." The route through Victoria Road was lined by 450 men of the Queen's Bays in full dress, whilst the length of Wellington Street and High Street to Wellington Avenue was kept by the 7th Queen's Own Hussars. The

whole route through Stanhope Lines was flanked by troops drawn
from every regiment in the garrison. Never before or since has
Aldershot accorded such a welcome to a homecoming officer. It was
typically an expression of the national spirit and sentiments of the day;
this particular day in Aldershot being called "Buller Day," the
memory of which lasted in the town for many a year.

CHAPTER FIVE

THE GROWTH OF THE TOWN
1854-1902

ONE can well imagine the immediate effect on the people of Aldershot
—one can visualize the discussion and conjecture and rumour which
evolved around the sole topic of the day—as soon as it became generally known in January, 1854, that Samuel Eggar had sold the heathlands adjoining the village to the Government, and that Aldershot
Heath had been selected for the largest camp ever established for the
Army. To a great extent the villagers of Aldershot had led sheltered
lives cut off from the rest of the country. As was general in those days,
many were born, lived their whole lives and died in the parish without
venturing farther afield than Farnham or Ash, the greatest event
of their recent years having been the walk through the fields to Tongham to see the first train pass through on the line which had been
laid in 1846.

For many, Guildford was the largest town they had ever visited,
the great City of London had been seen by but a few, and the one or
two villagers who had ventured farther afield, especially those who had
been to "furren parts," were regarded with respect and awe by their
fellows. The Aldershot villager had for generations been a man of
the soil, living in a rustic community, gaining his livelihood from the
hop-fields, market gardens, and the small mixed farms which had given
security to the self-supporting village community. The great change,
far greater than many could conceive, which was about to take place
in their lives was one beyond the ken of those who talked long hours
over the future as they sat in their cottages, or, with their tankards
of ale, on the fireside benches in the "Red Lion" and the "Beehive,"
where the men gathered to talk over the forthcoming events.

"I seed four gentlemen in uniform ridin' up past the Poor House
at noon," says an elderly gardener, putting down his pewter pot.
"They'm stopped up top o' Red Hill an' was a-walkin' around."

"Eh," adds a ruddy-cheeked yokel, wearing the traditional smock
of his calling, "an' they stopped up at Houghton's* for breakfast. I

* Houghton's inn, the "Row Barge," on the turnpike road.

was a-talkin' with a soldier who was a-lookin' after the 'osses ; he says he come from Portsmouth an' they officers was Engineers from the forts."

"I wonder how many soldiers they'll be a-sending down here," comments a wiry individual, wearing a rabbit-skin cap.

"'Undreds of 'em, so they say," says a voice from the inglenook, "'orse, foot and guns an' all. You mark my words, you won't know this village when they've built this camp."

How true was that observation, but how many of those villagers assembled over their ale in the old inn, lit by the firelight and the flickering oil lamp which hung from the beams, realized how great the change would be ?

The future was discussed in the Vestry when older residents, wondering what the next year would bring, appealed to the Vicar to find out what the building of "The Camp" would really mean. The question was debated over the port after dinner in the large residences where the local gentry met to talk over the news.

"My son, who has a friend at Horse Guards,"* says one of the company, gently pushing the decanter along the mahogany table, "tells me the whole thing is of a temporary nature ; it's just a question of having a number of huts for the men whilst they are here engaged in their training."

"Yes," adds another, leaning back in his high-backed chair, "they tell me that that camp they had on Chobham Ridges† was such a success that they want more men to be exercised in their calling instead of rotting away in the old garrisons."

"I heard," adds a third, "that the Prince has had a lot to do with the scheme. Perhaps he found himself that you want a bit more room than Hyde Park can provide if you're going to form squares with a brigade."

And so it went on, but no one could visualize then that the name of the village was in a short space of time to become known all over the world. It was then a far cry from the quiet rustic village to what was to become the greatest military garrison—the home of the British Army.

It is obvious that there was some local concern at the amount of land being taken over by the War Department, and equally so some concern in the Government Departments over the excessive sums demanded by private owners for land subsequently required after the initial purchases had been made. It was also not clear as to the extent and location of the lands to be acquired for the camp. This led to a letter being addressed to the Prime Minister, Lord Palmerston, by

---

* The Headquarters of the Commander-in-Chief in Whitehall.
† The camp at Chobham, 1852.

Lord Winchester, Lord-Lieutenant of the County of Southampton, when called upon to give his views on the exorbitant sums required by landowners. A letter* was addressed on 13th October, 1854, to the Secretary of State for War by the Prime Minister's Secretary, in which he was instructed to request that he would "move the Board of Ordnance to inform his Lordship in what county or counties the land at Aldershot is situated which the Board desires of purchase," adding that on receiving this information Viscount Palmerston would inform the Lord-Lieutenant.

The rights of the landowners in the area were taken into consideration in all the War Department plans, and there is record of a Committee of Landowners being formed to discuss matters with the Government Departments concerned. The roads and paths to and from Aldershot ran diagonally across the W.D. lands, and the occupation of the area to the north of Aldershot by the camp raised the problem of communications, the construction of new roads for the convenience of the local residents, and the making good of old tracks which had become the main routes. The following letter* from Mr. C. C. Bannister, the Solicitor to the Board of Ordnance, to Mr. J. Wood, the Secretary of the Board, gives an insight into negotiations:—

Office of Ordnance,
15th March, 1855.

SIR,

On the 6th of September last at a meeting of the Aldershot Commoners, Mr. Clutton on the part of the Ordnance agreed to purchase the Commoner's rights for £28,822 19s. 0d. and to make certain roads at the expense of the Ordnance. The amount of Purchase money to be paid was at the rate of £12 an acre for the common land, specified in a plan produced at the meeting.

The Lord of the Manor claims the right to receive in respect of his Manorial Rights for such part of the Common is copyhold the price of enfranchisement the amount of which is not ascertained at present but which cannot exceed £2,400.

Mr. Clutton in agreeing to give £12 an acre considered that he was paying the full value of the fee simple and that the Copyholders would be liable to pay the amount of the enfranchisement to the Lord of the Manor. The Copyholders on the other hand say they considered that they were to receive £12 an acre clear of deduction and that the Ordnance were bound to settle with the Lord of the Manor for his Rights.

The Committee appointed by the Commoners refuse to carry out the agreement until the point in dispute is settled.

It now therefore remains for the Board of Ordnance to say whether they will concede the point or take the case to a Jury.

* Public Record Office : War Office Correspondence, Out-Letters (W.O.3), 326.

It is clear that a Jury will not award a larger sum than the Ordnance have agreed to give, but they may possibly award to the Commoners a less sum on account of the great increase in the value of the land in the neighbourhood of the camp since the commencement of the Government operations there.

There is one ingredient in this case which should not be over-looked. One of the roads which the Ordnance have agreed to make would be extremely inconvenient and is highly objected to by the Chief Royal Engineer. If the Ordnance agree to settle with the Lord of the Manor the Commoners will waive their rights to the Road in question, thus the expense of making the road will be saved to the Government, and what is of far more importance, the inconvenience of having the road at all will be obviated.

On a careful consideration of the whole of this case, and view-ing the effect it may have on matters still unsettled, I am induced to advise the Board to complete the purchase with the Commoners at the price agreed taking upon itself the payment to the Lord of the Manor which cannot exceed £2,400 and may be consider-ably less.

I remain Sir,
Your obedient servant,
(*signed*) C. C. BANNISTER
(*The Ordnance Solicitor*).

J. Wood, Esq.,
Secretary,
Ordnance Office.

Agreement on local problems was finally reached, and on 21st July, 1856, an Act of Parliament was submitted to the Queen* to "extin-guish certain Rights of Way and to stop up certain roads and paths near the Camp at Aldershot." For whereas "certain open or common lands and some enclosed lands" in the several Parishes of Aldershot, Yateley, Farnborough, Crondall and Farnham had already been pur-chased under the Powers of several previous Acts of Parliament† and were then "vested in Her Majesty's Principal Secretary of State for the War Department with perpetual succession upon Trust for Her Said Majesty and Her Successors," and had been "appropriated for" and were in use as a military camp and "for the instruction and training of troops in the science of War and their duties relating thereto" for which compensation had been paid "for the Rights in the Soil, and for the commonable and other Rights in and over all the said open or common lands which were purchased" and were then vested in the

---

* Victoria Regina, Cap LXVI. (Printed by George Edward Eyre and William Spottiswoode, "Printers to the Queen's Most Excellent Majesty," 1856.)

† Acts of Parliament of 1842, 1843, 1854 and 1855.

Secretary of State for War. The Act then referred to "certain Roads, Paths and Rights of Way now existing in Burgh and across the open or common Lands and the said enclosed Lands respectively" which it was intended should be included in the War Department property, for "if they were suffered to continue would very much interfere with and impede the useful purposes intended to be effected by the formation of the Military Camp and would be greatly detrimental to the Public Service," and it was therefore considered expedient that all the roads, paths and rights of way on the W.D. land respectively, except the turnpike road leading from Farnham to Bagshot and the road leading thereto from Aldershot, and another road leading to the turnpike road at a point opposite Heath Villa from the "Entrance of a Lane called Cranmore Lane" should be stopped up.

"May it therefore please your Majesty," read the Act, "that it may be enacted, and be it enacted by the Queen's Most Excellent Majesty by and with the advice and consent of the Lords Spiritual and Temporal and Commons, in this present Parliament assembled and by the Authority of the same." The area covered was then listed and described, and powers given for the Principal Secretary of State for the War Department to stop up, or cause to be stopped up, "all the said several roads Paths and Ways respectively" and laid down that public notice should be given of the stopping up of the roads by advertisement in the *London Gazette* and in "some local Newspaper published or circulated in either of the said counties of Southampton and Surrey and also on the church door of the said several parishes respectively."

An Agreement, bearing the date 31st May, 1856, was drawn up between a Committee of Landowners of the various Parishes who had held a meeting on 28th September, 1855, and the War Office, in which it was agreed that the War Department should make a good road thirty feet wide along what is now Chetwode Terrace and Sandford Road from turnpike road to West End Farm and make up several other roads. It was also agreed that within twelve months of the passing of the Act the Secretary of State for War at the time should "provide and set out upon the Lands of the said Principal Secretary a sufficient occupation or Farm Road of the width throughout of thirty feet at the least, for the use of horses, carts and carriages, commencing at the North End of Sandy Pit Lane* in the said Parish of Aldershot and running thence in a Northward and Eastward direction along the boundary of the Lands there now vested in the said Principal Secretary to a point where that Boundary meets the said Turnpike Road and also a sufficient occupation or Farm Roads for horses, carts and carriages

* The Sandford Road of today.

commencing from the North End of Yew Tree Hatch Lane* in the
said Parish of Aldershot and running thence in a Northward direction
from the said Village of Aldershot to the said Turnpike Road and
also a sufficient occupation road, etc., commencing from the North
end of Lloyds Lane† in the said parish, then in a Northward direction
to join the said road leading from the said village to the said Turnpike
Road," and another road commencing from Sandy Pit Lane near to the
farm buildings of West End Farm to run northwest and westward
terminating by a junction with the turnpike road "at a point lying thirty
five chains or thereabouts to the South of the Milestone on that Turn
pike Road denoting three miles from Farnham."

The establishment of "The Camp," as has been seen, had far-reaching
effects on the village of Aldershot. "The Camp" shaped the destiny
of that small community and shaped it rapidly by the sudden influx
of troops, workmen, bricks, mortar and timber. A mushroom town
which was likened to a prosperous Australian mining camp or a Col
onial settlement rather than a garrison town in the United Kingdom
sprang up immediately on "The Camp" boundary, speedily changing
the quiet life of the villagers, and providing a thriving community of
traders and increasing the population week by week. About 3,000
workmen were employed in the construction of "The Camp." Many
of them had to find lodgings in Farnham and adjacent villages, and to
accommodate others large huts were built. When the work commenced men were paid by the week and they worked all day on Saturday, until after a big strike in London in 1865 when the men were
paid by the hour, a mechanic earning 5d. or 6d. an hour and
labourers 3d. to 3½d.

The trade of the "town" was carried on in a few small cottages and
huts near the point where the "Elephant and Castle" public-house
stood‡; this was one of the many licensed houses built in the early
days of "The Camp." This trading centre was for the most part
composed of huts. One of them had an upper storey in which two
important businesses were carried on : Mr. John Denny, said to have
been the oldest trader in Aldershot, carried on his shoemaking trade
on the ground floor, whilst a chemist dispensed prescriptions in the
upper storey, which was reached by a ladder.

The only hairdresser's shop was a hut on wheels and it was moved
according to fluctuations of trade. Later it was converted into the
first photographer's studio in the town. The duties of undertaker were

* The southern portion of the Grosvenor Road of today.
† The Wellington Street of today.
‡ The public-house was later closed by the Licensing Justices, but the building
still stands at the corner of Sebastopol Road and High Street.

performed by a publican living at the "Hampshire Hog," who carried on the oddly assorted callings with profit to himself and, it is recorded, the satisfaction of his customers. There was no dairy and milk was bought direct from the farms, the price of skimmed milk at West End Farm being a penny a quart. There were plenty of birds, rabbits and game in the woods and copses around the village which found their way to the tables of those who were equipped with the old muzzle-loading shot-guns, whilst there were vegetables and fruit in abundance from the expanding market gardens which grew to meet the demands of the ever-increasing population, the garden produce being sold direct to the consumers from the garden or taken up and displayed in the straggling market area of stalls, booths and shanties which clustered by Wellington Street.

The one policeman of the town was a lame man and was also the town crier. One of the first civil "processions" recorded in the town's history was on the occasion when the town crier was presented with a new bell. Four more lame men were called in to hold a canopy over the crier, and then, with his new bell, he was marched around the town.*

The life of the town was somewhat wild and lawless and stories of ghosts and witchcraft were generally believed. An old woman who lived in a hut situated near the "Dog Kennels"—the "Fox and Hounds Inn"—in Weybourne Road was blamed for many dark doings, and the story was told of one of the late Mr. Allden's horses whose mane was mysteriously plaited night after night by an unseen hand. One after another of the local inhabitants took their turn watching, but always without success; some noise would cause them to turn their heads and they would discover that the hand had been at work. The apparition of a spotted cow which was alleged to have appeared at midnight between the Ash Bridge and Tongham was also the cause of much horror and wild conjecture.

The construction of the wall around the Cavalry Barracks which extends from the junction of Wellington Avenue and Barrack Road along Alexandra Road and Chetwode Terrace to the Farnborough Road and down to the west end of Wellington Avenue, with barrack gates facing High Street, Chetwode Terrace and the Farnborough Road, led to the belief that the whole camp was to be enclosed, and this in turn led to considerable speculation as to where the main entrance or entrances would be. In consequence speculative builders and new traders opened up and developed several parts of the new

---

* This town crier's bell was passed on for several years, and the bell to this day is in the possession of Mr. W. F. Holderness, whose grandfather was the last town crier of Aldershot, in the seventies.

town in the hope that the sites they had chosen would prove to be the most suitable and valuable.

The development of the town in its early days was patchy in consequence.* It was described as "somewhat disjointed and of unconnected appearance." There were four points of development, according to the speculations of those who sought the most prominent positions to open up their business. It was thought that Middle Hill would be the central road into "The Camp," and the shops sprang up at the corner of Wellington Street and High Street. Others felt that Ordnance Road (then called Commissariat Hill) would be the centre, and so Artillery Terrace was built. Some went farther afield, convinced that the main camp entrance would be in the West End, and building commenced in Pavilion Road. Finally, the speculative builders and traders concentrated at the upper end of High Street facing the East Cavalry Barracks, and from these four points the town was gradually linked up.

The troops returning from the Crimea had accumulations of pay to draw upon; many had for the first time in their lives more money to spend than they knew what to do with, and much of this was spent on drink. The canteens and beer houses were run by civilians, who took good care that the money passed over their counters.

The scenes which were witnessed in the town caused much alarm to the law-abiding townsfolk. Violence and vice reigned after dark in certain quarters of the area bordering High Street, and it was considered unsafe to venture out alone at night.

That the earliest days of the town's history were none too creditable was due as much to the lawlessness of the civilian elements as to the lack of efficient control on the part of the military, and the name of Aldershot was held in disrepute. Writing on "The Pioneers of Soldiers Institutes" in 1892, Miss Sarah Robinson, of the Portsmouth Soldiers' Institute, wrote of Aldershot of the early sixties : "At Aldershot from 14,000 to 18,000 troops would be stationed at one time. Four Army Scripture Readers laboured within 'The Camp,' but outside there was not one safe place of resort. A perfect network of public houses, dancing saloons and 'vile houses' entrapped the soldier who went in any direction outside his own lines : the emissaries from these dens could even go into 'The Camp' to entice the men. . . ." An official report, however, written in 1860 for the information of Parliament, by Captain Alkington-Jackson, who described the town as "made up of drinking hells of the worst class," aroused the towns-

---

* "A great deal is required to place the town in a desirable state," wrote William Sheldrake, the proprietor of *Sheldrake's Military Gazette*, in 1859. "Streets must be paved, water laid on and drainage effected."

people to protest, a public indignation meeting being held to deny the charges in the report.*

Prior to the building of the Police Station in 1869 and Court House in High Street, justice was dispensed in the town by Captain Newcome, the Lord of the Manor and the first Magistrate, in the large assembly room on the first floor of the Royal Hotel, where delinquents were brought up for trial. The law-breakers were often taken up to the Manor House to be charged and remanded for the next session at the local "Court," this procedure, it is recorded, being often conducted by the Magistrate from the window of his house, from which he was wont to shout, "And what have you been up to? Don't come here again or else I'll give it to you!" or "You're all remanded; take 'em away, Sergeant!"

The general conditions of the growing town gave, at this time, rise to some alarm among the military authorities, and Deputy Inspector-General J. B. Gibson,† of the Medical Staff Corps, drew attention to this in a report he prepared on 28th October, 1856, addressed to Lieut.-Colonel J. Clark-Kennedy, the A.Q.M.G. of the Division at Aldershot, for the information of Lieut.-General Sir William T. Knollys.

> The health of the troops [he wrote] is seriously endangered, indeed is actually suffering in consequence of the disgustingly foul state of the village of Aldershot to which the men resort every evening in large numbers. For about half a mile eastwards of the huts occupied by the officers of the Royal Engineers there is a succession of Public Houses, small shops and butchers slaughter houses without any sewers or drainage whatever. Everything that should be carried away by such means or collected in cess pools flows, or is thrown into the road ditch, which is thus converted into a large open sewer that emits a most offensive, pestilential effluvia in the evenings and at night, especially in front of Barret's Military Hotel, "The Elephant and Castle" and in the immediate neighbourhood of "The Beehive," particularly at the Butcher's premises and at the small pond of stagnant water adjoining the stile into Mr. Newcome's Park which receives the drainage of all the shops.

It had been ascertained that in none of the numerous new houses built or being built at the time had any provision been made for cess-

---

* Sixty years, however, wrought great changes. In 1912 it was recorded in *The Aldershot News* that the morals of the town compared favourably with any other place, and at the annual Licensing Sessions a splendid tribute was paid to its sobriety, order and morals. "Whatever may be said by those who do not know Aldershot," read the report, "those who are acquainted with it know it as one of the most orderly towns in the country: in fact, seeing that at its gates are some 20,000 young men, many of them at the most impressionable age of a young man's life, Aldershot is a remarkably well-conducted town."

† Dr. Gibson had served in the Crimea as Surgeon to the 17th Lancers.

pools or drainage except in the "contemplated" Victoria Street, where it was intended that a small barrel drain should be laid down the centre, but then it would discharge into the open. The method of disposal of slops, dirt and excrement which were not thrown into the road was to dig a pit in some part of the premises, which, owing to the sandy nature of soil, led to percolation. The whole area was becoming saturated with "most poisonous agents" which were detrimental to the health of inhabitants and troops. "In the past week," the report added, "four soldiers died of fever in South Camp."

The report recommended that urgent steps should be taken to cleanse the village and to enforce the construction of proper drainage, as it was a danger to troops and this danger would undoubtedly get worse.

Following this report, a case was put before the Bench of Magistrates in Aldershot by Colonel J. Clark-Kennedy, who was accompanied by the Assistant Solicitor of the War Department. Strong protests were made and it was suggested that the magistrates acted in the matter. Although appreciating the importance of the matter, it was not in their power, however, to interfere. Colonel Clark-Kennedy also mentioned the disgraceful and disgusting conditions of the lodging houses in the vicinity of the camp, and, fully admitting the evil, the magistrates agreed to appoint an "Inspector of Lodging Houses" to control the conduct of these establishments.

Money was made rapidly and spent as recklessly. Many a tragedy and romance was enacted, but as time went by the town began to take on a more orderly atmosphere both in its development and its population.

The permanent barracks today lining Wellington Avenue, in 1859 still a continuation of Aldershott Street and the old Ash Road, were then faced by "a number of stores, eating houses and tippling shops of which last description there are sufficient at 'the Camp' to furnish a large town."*

"The eating houses and stores," it has been recorded,* deserved to be noticed "as part and parcel of the Permanent Barracks," for it was there the workmen employed at the works were for the greater part fed, clothed and lodged ; while it was reserved for "the public houses and beer-shops to become the area for the same individuals to drink, gamble, quarrel and fight."

There were, the account adds, eating and public-houses of different grades. There was excellent accommodation for the "fast young man" to obtain his "mock turtle, boiled lamb and mint sauce, goose, fowl

---

* *Vide* "Sketches of 'The Camp' at Aldershot" (Andrews & Lucy) (1858).

game, pastry, sherry, or port," as well as facilities for the "bricklayer's paddy" to buy his "rasher of rusty bacon." For the former there were also opportunities for him to "play at billiards, drink champagne, and smoke his weed till he gets intoxicated, and then imbibe soda-water till he revives" ; whilst the artisan or labourer could "drink his common four-penny, smoke his unpretending pipe, and arrive at any *finale* suitable to his temperament,"* which in Victorian politeness of prose implied that he could finish the evening "fighting drunk" with fellow-worker or redcoat, sink quietly into alcoholic slumber in a corner of the bar of one of the many beer houses, or sing himself hoarse at one of the several pseudo music-halls in the square half-mile of the "town."

The term "store" was used in its most comprehensive form, for the traders of Aldershot of that day were, if nothing else, versatile : a chemist for whom photography was a side line, taverner and pawn-broker, "news-vendor" and barber. The stores, it is stated, were not the most "cleanly or best arranged places in the world," but the account adds that "respectable and commodious business premises" had been "recently erected by private speculators, in lieu of those dirty huts, for the comfort and accommodation of which, thousands were obliged to be thankful in the summer and winter of 1856."

* * * * *

In the first military Ordnance Survey map of the area, published in October, 1856, considerable detail of the old village and the new town is shown.

St. Michael's Church and the Parsonage, on the site of the existing Vicarage, are shown ; also the Manor House, Elm Place and Aldershot Place. Church Lane is marked, and some detail of the original Aldershot Village. There is a smithy at the foot of Church Hill facing Aldershot Green. A number of wells are recorded, two at the rear of the "Beehive" inn, another in High Street near Crimea Road, and a number of others scattered over the whole area of the present town.

In the North Lane area Sheeling Farm, North Farm, and Holly Farm are shown, hop kilns and a malt kiln are shown by Herrett's Farm, and Malt House Lane (Newport Road) is marked. At the south end of North Lane is Ash Bridge House. On the site of Ivy Cottages, then called Newland Cottages, facing Aldershot Green, a pottery is marked. Parkhouse Farm and Deadbrook Farm are also indicated. Deadbrook Pond is marked, and at that time it was a sizeable stretch of water. Other places which are recorded and remain in name in

---

* *Vide* "Sketches of 'The Camp' at Aldershot" (Andrews & Lucy) (1858).

one form or another are Smokey Hole ; Heron Wood, with a Keeper's Lodge, in the area now covered by Hicketts Copse, which lay between Manor Road and Hillside Road ; Cargate Copse ; Boxalls Farm ; Ayland (now Ayling) House, the open country below, which is marked as "The Grove" ; Rock Place (now Rock House), in Sandford Road ; and West End Farm House. A fairly large pond is shown at the corner of Cranmore Lane, opposite West End Farm. There was a brick and tile works and a clay pit in Cranmore Lane just opposite the site of "Alverstoke," and the area each side of Cranmore Lane is marked as hop-fields.

At the top of North Lane stood a small house known as "Woodbine Cottage,"* the garden of which adjoined the railway embankment when it was built in 1870. The present-day Grosvenor Road is shown as far as where the Five Arch Bridge now stands, after which it disappears into a track, and is marked as "Yew Tree Hatch Lane."

There was a Police Station in Mount Pleasant Road, and the present-day Recreation Ground is marked as such. White House, on Dollys Hill, just off the Farnborough Road, which was marked on the 1816 map of the district, is also shown in this map.

On a map of "Aldershot Royal Military Camp and Town" dated 1859, the following residences are shown : Aldershot Lodge, Elm Place, Parsonage House (the Vicarage of St. Michael's Parish Church), and Manor House. The Manor Park pond was then quite large and extended into a stream which ran down from Cook's Bottom (the Recreation Ground). The School at the foot of Redan Road is indicated as "Normal School." The Gas Works and the Recreation Ground in High Street are also shown, whilst at the top of Redan Hill is "Aldershot Fort"—no longer in existence. Five public-houses are indicated by names : the "White Lion" (Lower Farnham Road), the "Prince of Wales" (at the junction of Lower Farnham Road and Ash Road), the "Lord Campbell" (Ash Road), the "Beehive" (High Street) and the "Florence Nightingale" (Aldershot Green)† ; all of which, with the exception of the latter, exist to this day. On the War Office copy of the map a beer-house called the "Alma," in North Lane, has been marked in in ink.

Only a few roads are named, and these are Cranmore Lane, Church Lane, West End Lane, North Lane, Malt House Lane (now Newport Road), Cambridge Road, Union Street, Low Road (now Eggars Hill)

---

* This cottage, which in later years was occupied by a W.D. Warden, was demolished in 1946 when the lower Redan Road Housing Estate (Ainger Close) was built.

† Behind Ivy Cottages, then called St. George's Square.

and Victoria Road. The present-day site of Lloyds Bank was a small forage yard with outbuildings and a pond. This was the property of a Mr. Vinson, who combined the occupations of farmer and forage contractor.

The town is indicated by rows of houses along High Street from the "Beehive," behind which was a pottery, to the entrance to the East Cavalry Barracks (Warburg Barracks) and between Victoria Road and High Street.

Around the area opposite the bottom of Redan Road were the shops of W. Martin, a grocer; E. Davies and G. Langrish, butchers; Mr. Angel, a draper; and Boulter's Hotel* (on the site of the present-day Fricker's Hotel). Mr. D. Bateman's establishment—forage merchant and contractors and corn chandlers—is shown at the top of Redan Hill, facing Aldershot Fort. Campbell House, then the residence of a Dr. Shoolbraid, is shown in High Street, facing Manor Park.

Between Wellington Street and Crimea Road in High Street were Jones' stores; Sheldrake's printing establishment; the Alliance Hotel; J. Davis, baker; Copeman and Lacy, grocers; J. Wilson, grocer; the Royal Exchange Hotel; H. Harris, chemist; Mr. G. H. Reutish, surgeon; and L. Shearman, ironmonger. In Wellington Street were the George Hotel; Anthony's tea warehouse; Sowden & Sons, drapery warehouse; C. Storry, fishmonger; and T. Martin, builders and iron-mongers.

An old photograph taken in Wellington Street in 1858 shows it to be a residential area. At the corner of Little Wellington Street, on the site now occupied by the tobacconist Holderness, is a grocer's shop bearing on its fascia-board the name of "Sumpster," and the trade description "Tea and Grocery." This was the business of a Mr. N. Sumpster. On the opposite corner is a private house which bears a board "Harland—Builder." The remainder of the houses are private residences with the front doors opening on to the side walk. The road is cobbled, and in the distance one can discern a bench before one of the houses, where the occupants could sit to watch the leisurely life of the Wellington Street of those days.

Between Grosvenor Road and Wellington Street the shops and establishments in High Street included the "Queen" inn; H. W. Hayes, military furniture stores; Dr. Wilson's house; H. Gray, tobacconist; Sheldrake's cricket, racket and toy repository; and White's military stores. Barnard's Army and Navy Hotel is shown among a group of

---

* Named after Mr. Boulter, who opened a canteen in South Camp in 1855. In 1859 John Boulter was advertising "The trade, messes and families supplied on the most liberal terms in 4½, 9 and 18 gall. casks," and also that a billiard table was "kept private for officers."

houses in the area of Kings Road, below the wall of the South Cavalry Barracks (Beaumont Barracks).

The "History, Gazetteer and Directory of Hampshire and the Isle of Wight," published in 1859, records the "seats of nobility" as : "Captain G. Newcome, Manor House," and "Charles Barron, Esq., Aldershot Place." Charles Barron was a London wine and spirit merchant, with offices in Pall Mall, who made several journeys each week to the metropolis ; one of the pioneers, therefore, of the business-men who made their homes in Aldershot while conducting their businesses in London.

The directory describes Aldershot as "a large village," continuing :

It had only 875 inhabitants in 1851, but since the establishment of the military camp in 1855 its population, exclusive of soldiers has increased to more than 3,000 souls and it now has about 20 taverns and 40 beer houses, though in 1854 it had only two public houses. The Dean and Chapter of Winchester are the Lords of the Manor, but a great part of the cultivated lands belong to Barron, Newcome, Elstone, Allden, Eggar, Tice and other families, some of them freeholders, but mostly copyholders. The Manor House is pleasantly situated in parklike grounds, and is now the seat of Captain Newcome.

There were two Post Offices, one in "The Camp," run by a Mr. Charles Buckland, where money orders were "granted and paid," and the letters were sent via Farnborough Station ; the other was at the premises of Messrs. Allen & Co., the druggists* at the corner of Wellington Street and High Street. Henry Allen, the founder of this firm, came to Aldershot from Basingstoke in 1857, and opened his business at that time in the fourth largest building in the new town. It was in 1868 that Henry Allen took Mr. Lloyd into partnership, founding the firm of Allen & Lloyd.

The Directory listed in detail the residents and traders of the town. Among them are names of businessmen and houses well known to this day :

ALDERSHOTT PARISH DIRECTORY, 1859. Allen & Co.,* druggists ; Thos. Attfield, parish clerk ; Wm. Barnett, gas fitter ; Chas. Barron, Esq., Aldershott Place ; F. C. Birch, builder and contractor, The Wharf ; Chas. Brown, fly proprietor ; Chas. Buckland, Camp P.O. ; Wm. Burle, wharfinger and coal merchant ; Wm. Burns hosier and cap maker ; Colonel Chapman, R.E. ; Edw. Chiddall, ale and spirit merchant ; Wm. Collins, earthenware mfr. ; Jane Davies, tobacconist.

---

* Now Allen & Lloyd (Chemists) Ltd.

Rev. Jas. Dennett; John Ellis, farm bailiff; Evan Evans, greengrocer; Emanuel Finch, builder and undertaker*; Chas. Goodchild, fishmonger; Thos. Goodchild, architect; Mrs. Gosden, Brooke House; Henry Gray, tobacconist; Robert Harris, druggist; Geo. Hedley, gas engineer.

C. B. Hewett, corn dealer; Thos. Hughes, toy dealer*; Wm. Jones, hosier and tailor; Geo. Stott Lincoln, cabinet maker; Richard Lloyd, gardener; Lyon and Cohen, tobacconists and rag dealers; John Martin, builder and contractor; Wm. Hy. Masters, tobacconist; John Miller, hairdresser; Rd. Moir, scripture reader.

Geo. Newcombe, Esq., Manor House; John Parsons, greengrocer; P. Payne, hairdresser; Jas. Pharo, coal dealer; Wm. Pimm, cabinet maker; Rev. Dr. Rule (Wesleyan); Wm. Sheldrake, bookseller; John Shoolbraid, surgeon; Major T. Smith, barrack master; Thos. Stearman, glass and china; Chpr. Storry, fishmonger; Caroline Taylor, schoolmrs; Henry Tistin, musical instrument maker; T. Vinson and Son, corn dealers; Alfred White, timber mert., The Wharf; Ths. White, tailor, draper, etc.*; Andrew Wilson, surgeon†; J. Burdon, builder and carpenter.

Messrs. Thomas White & Co.'s business had been established in 1856 by Mr. Thomas White, who came from Hartley Wintney. In Wellington Street he opened a wooden hut hastily erected to supply drapery and outfitting goods to troops returning from the Crimea and the increasing civil population, but a shop in High Street was built as soon as labour and materials were available.

FARMERS: Richd. Allden, Elm Place; Jas. Elstone, Aldershot Ldg.; Wm. Herrett, Villewoods; Hugh Sears, Prowtings; Thos. Smith, Halliwood Farm; Rd. Jno. Stovold, Halings Hill (Ayling Hill); Hy. Twynam, Tiligs Farm.

---

* The firms founded then are still in business in the town.

† It would appear that the medical profession advertised itself in these days, for in 1859 in "Sheldrake's Guide" Dr. Wilson, described as "Surgeon and Accoucheur &c." (formerly of Woodbine Cottage, Aldershot, now of High Street, three doors from the Queen Inn) "begs respectfully to inform the public that he has added to his profession that of a chemist and druggist, and has specially engaged a duly qualified gentleman to conduct that department and attend in his absence, where the most pure and fresh Drugs can always be obtained, and prescriptions correctly prepared, and for emergency at any hour of the night. At the surgery," the advertisement continued, "can be had all the French remedies in use, as well as the English, Dr. W. being in correspondence with the best houses in Paris. Dr. Wilson may be consulted in his Surgery every morning till 11 a.m. and after 6 in the evening. Advice on diseases of the Eye, Ear and Skin, every Sunday, from 1 till 2 o'clock in the afternoon. Dr. W. trusts," the announcement concluded, "from an extensive experience at home and abroad, of upwards 27 years, that parties may rely on proper attention, and hopes to merit public patronage."

INNS AND TAVERNS : "Alliance," Thomas Pagett ; "Army and
Navy,"* Jas. Barnard ; "Beehive,"* Horner ; "Boulter's,"
Jno. Boulter (and auctioneer) ; "Cambridge,"* — ; "Crimea,"*
Edw. Benham ; "Elephant and Castle," Edw. Tomkins ; George
Rodwell ; "Iron Duke," Henry Keen ; "New Inn," Edward
Hill ; "North Town," Wm. Strong ; "Pavilion," Edward Dozell ;
"Prince of Wales,"* Thomas Manning ; "Queen,"* Haratio
Tuddenham ; "Red Lion,"* George Falkner ; "Royal Camp,"*
Charles Wm. Heaps ; "Royal Exchange,"* Wm. C. Roberts ;
"Royal Hotel," Chas. Tilbury† ; "Royal Military," Edw. Edm.
Elsley ; "Victoria,"* John Williams ; "White Horse," Fredk.
Hughes.

BAKERS : Jas. Barnard, Benham and Stiff,‡ Jno. Dallman,
Jane Davies, Jetten and Hickley, Ed. Wellock, James West.

BEERHOUSES : Hy. Alexander, Fras. Bartlett, Mary Bentley,
Jas. Biddle, Mary Brake, Ths. Brannan, Jonathan Broadbent,
Chas. Brown, John Browning, Jph. Byrne, W. Cade, Jas. Clarke,
John Cooper, Has. Henry Corston, Chs. Coxhead, Mark Davis,
Js. Eastwood, Henry Elkins, Samuel Emerson, Chs. Falkner,
Geo. Garrett, Wm. Goy, Geo. Gwynn (and provision dealer),
David Harris, Wm. Haslett, Edw. James, John Kemp, Geo.
Kimber, Robt. Lawes, Fredk. Lee, Chas. Luff, W. Marshall,
John Morgan, Geo. Norcutt, Henry North, Mich. Parsons, Thos.
Peacey, Wm. Pike, Charles Robinson, Edw. Strange.

BLACKSMITHS : George Goodchild, Edw. Hutton.

BUTCHERS : Lewis Bromham, Edw. Davis, James Greenwood,
Hy. Hawkins, George Langridge, John Williams, Wm. Williams.

CARPENTERS AND WHEELWRIGHTS : Wm. Cade, Emnl. Finch,‡
Chs. Gunner, John Kimber, Robt. Lawes, Athr. Lunn, Robert
Row.

DRAPERS : Athr. Angell, Edn. Collier, John Logan, Sowdon
and Stone.

GROCERS : Anthony and Martin, Dnl. Bateman, Fdk. Beldham,
Chas. Bone (and farrier), Jno. Chiddell, Copeman and Lacy,
Jno. Dallman, Edwin Holderness, Esthr. Hughes, Jetten and
Hickley, John Logan, Walker Read, John Shears, Wm. Smith,
Ed. Snowden, Chs. Sumpster, Fredk. Edwin Webb, Hy. Webster,
John Wilson, Samuel Woolveridge.

IRONMONGERS : T. Harmer, Hy. Poppleton, Ts. Stearman.

SADDLERS : Alfred Patrick, Rd. Henry Smitham.

---

* Licensed to this day.
† In 1859 Charles Tilbury, the proprietor, advertised in "Sheldrake's Guide,'
"C.T. wishes to draw the attention of the public to this Hotel which is replete with
every comfort and convenience. Dinners for large and small parties on the shortest
notice. An ordinary every day at one o'clock. Wines and Spirits of the finest quality.
Good Stabling and well aired beds."
‡ The firms founded then are still in business in the town.

The Parish Church, Aldershot.
Circa 1870.

Aldershot Town Cricket Club, circa 1870. The ground is that on which Holy Trinity Church now stands. The houses in the background are in Victoria Road.

Wellington Street, decorated for the occasion of Queen Victoria's Jubilee Celebrations, 1887. The building on the right is the Royal Hotel, demolished in 1932, but that on the left, then occupied by Messrs. Allen & Lloyd, still stands.

General view of Aldershot Town from Middle Hill, circa 1870.

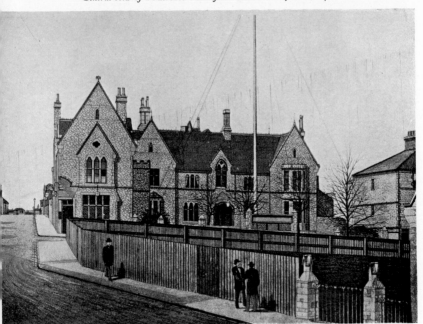

Miss Daniell's Soldiers' Home, circa 1875, *the ground behind the hoarding being later occupied by the Wesley Hall.*

*The Aldershot Institute in the latter years of last century. Note the unsurfaced roads, the trees
and residential houses of Victoria Road.*

The Aldershot Volunteer Fire Brigade in the nineties.

The general scene at the official opening of Aldershot Cottage Hospital by H.R.H. The Duchess of Connaught and Strathearn, 28th July, 1896.

Balloon practice by the Balloon Section, Royal Engineers, in the Long Valley in the nineties.

Mr. S. F. Cody's first flight, Laffan's Plain, May, 1908.

Mr. Cody's aircraft, British Army Aeroplane No. 1, on Laffan's Plain, September, 1908.

A military funeral passing along Station Road, circa 1910 *(prior to the building of the Aldershot Hippodrome on the site behind the hoardings).*

The 2nd Bn. The Worcestershire Regiment arriving in Aldershot in March, 1913, *after seventeen years' service overseas.*

SHOEMAKERS: George Ball, Wm. Bartram, John Denny, Danl. Fraser, John Gordon, Thos. Green, Jas. Knight, Jph. Magnus and Henry, Chs. Robinson, Wm. Shill.

WATCHMAKERS: James Green, John James, Fras. Phillips, Mos. Phillips and earthenware dealer.

Aldershot's first newspaper appeared on Saturday, 6th August, 1859. It was the *Aldershot Military Gazette*, and was founded by Mr. William Sheldrake,* who made his home in Aldershot on leaving the Coldstream Guards, with whom he had served as a colour-sergeant in the Crimean War, and who established a bookseller's, printer's, and stationer's business at No. 47, High Street.† The paper was subsequently renamed *Sheldrake's Military Gazette* and later the *Aldershot Gazette and Military News*.

Aldershot Market, situated between Wellington Street and High Street on the site of the present-day Market Arcade, was opened in 1859 by General Knollys, and here for over half a century everything, from a packet of pins to a live goat, was sold from the stalls.

The first bank in the town, the West Surrey Bank, was also opened in this year on the present-day site of the premises of Messrs. Kingham & Co. at the junction of Victoria Road and Grosvenor Road; and by this year the town's first theatre, the Apollo Musical Hall,‡ had been built on the site of the present-day Grosvenor Hotel at the junction of Union Street and Grosvenor Road.

Among the most prosperous trading enterprises which grew up with the town were the second-hand clothing and uniform businesses which flourished from the fifties until the middle eighties. Up to 1885 soldiers were permitted to retain discarded uniforms and to sell or dispose of them as they pleased. In consequence a trade was carried on in the sale of uniforms to the satisfaction of both dealers and vendors. Private soldiers had but few privileges or perquisites, and there was much criticism and discontentment when an order was issued that henceforth old uniforms were to be returned to W.D. Stores. This order led to the closing of many of the second-hand dealers' shops which had been until then a feature of the town.

It was in the autumn of 1859 that the first steps in the cultural

* The author of "A Guide to Aldershot," which he also printed and published in 1857.

† Today the offices of the Aldershot Chamber of Commerce, in which hangs a large coloured print depicting Queen Victoria receiving men of the Coldstream Guards at Windsor on their return from the Crimea. This picture was presented to the Chamber by the late Mr. Edgar Sheldrake in memory of his father, the founder of *Sheldrake's Aldershot Gazette*.

‡ The theatre was originally called "The Victory" and afterwards the "Theatre Royal," and was run by a Mr. C. Atkins and later by a Mr. Henry Steele. It was burnt down in 1889.

O

development of the town were made. Proposals were made for the opening of an Institute. A meeting was held, attended by a number of young men desirous of becoming members of a "literary and scientific" institution, and Mr. Thomas White promised a donation to further the project and lent a house in Union Street for the start of the Institution, which opened in November, 1859, under the name of "The Aldershot Institution for Mental Improvement and Social Recreation." By December there was a membership of over a hundred, and in January, 1860, an inaugural meeting was held under the presidency of the Patron, General Knollys, the G.O.C., who told his audience that on entering the village five years previously, the only place he could obtain refreshments was at the "Row Barge," whilst the only place he could find a bed was the "Beehive," and that there was not a butcher in the place.

*   *   *   *   *

Aldershot can without doubt claim to be England's cradle of military aviation. It was in July, 1863, that a Balloon ascent was made from the Queen's Parade by a balloonist—Henry Coxwell*—who made the ascent, accompanied by Captain F. Beaumont and Lieutenant G. E. Grover of the Royal Engineers, with the object of demonstrating the use of the balloon for reconnaissance in watching the movement of troops. It has been recorded that he finally landed in the town, dislodging bricks and mortar from the housetops as the cradle and its ropes were dragged over the roof-tops. Thirty years later, Aldershot was the scene of the first manœuvres in which military balloons participated, and the year after the R.E. Balloon School was opened in South Camp ; but sixty years were to pass before the first aeroplane flight in Aldershot was to take place, when "Colonel" Cody flew his biplane from Laffan's Plain.†

When "The Camp" was first established, the nearest railway stations to Aldershot were at Farnborough, on the London and South Western Railway Company's line, and at Farnham, on the South Eastern Railway Company's line, which ran from Guildford to Farnham with stations at Wanborough, Ash Green and Tongham, this line having been opened in October, 1846. No public transport, however, existed between the stations and "The Camp." By 1856 some enterprising private speculators had opened up a public service between

---

* Henry Coxwell (1819-1900), youngest son of Comdr. J. Coxwell, R.N., was one of the pioneer balloonists. In 1854 he published a book entitled "Balloons for Warfare," and for thirty-four years dating from 1851 he devoted his activities to the task of rendering the balloon of practical use for both scientific and military purposes. *Vide* "The History of Aeronautics in Great Britain," J. E. Hodgson (Oxford University Press) (1924).

† See p. 173.

Farnham and South Camp with a horse-drawn omnibus which had been withdrawn from service in the London suburbs. The omnibus did the journey in half an hour, via Hale, entering South Camp near the present-day junction of the Farnborough Road and Chetwode Terrace. The commencement of this service, coupled with the fact that Farnham was an attraction to many, led to the opening up of a number of new taverns along the route. Mrs. Young in her book "Aldershot and All About It" (1857), says that sixteen taverns sprang up between "The Camp" and the Farnham railway in a single year (1856).

For those who wished to travel farther afield four-in-hand coaches plied from Aldershot to Guildford via the Ash Road, Tongham and the Hog's Back, where passengers could transfer to the London coaches.

The following details of this service are taken from an old notice board (2 ft. by 18 in.) which hung on the yard wall of the Royal Hotel until the time of its demolition in 1930 :

ALDERSHOT, GUILDFORD & LONDON COACH

This coach leaves the Royal Hotel at Aldershot every Saturday at 2.30. Meeting the London Coach at the White Hart, Guildford, which leaves at 4 p.m., arriving at Hatchett's, Piccadilly, 7 p.m. Fares : To Guildford, 3s. Return journey, 5s.

Proprietor : J. KNEE.

Tongham was actually the nearest station to the newly formed camp and town, and so it was to Tongham that the building materials and supplies were sent by rail for the construction of "The Camp," the first permanent barracks and the new town which was growing up. As has been described, these materials were conveyed from Tongham by road in an endless stream of horse-drawn carts winding their way slowly down to the Ash Road, along "Aldershott Street" and the High Street of today.

This method of transport was, however, soon superseded to a great extent by the use of a single track light railway,* which was laid from the main line east of Tongham station, and this ran below Thorn Hill and along the rear of the barracks facing Wellington Avenue. The light railway, described as a "tramway" remained in existence until the construction of the permanent barracks of Wellington Lines and the hutted South Camp had been completed.

In November, 1860, when street tramways were still something of a novelty, an American tramway speculator, a Mr. Train, visited Aldershot, advocating the building of a tramway to connect Aldershot with Farnborough. He addressed public meetings, lectured at

---

* See p. 52.

the Aldershot Institute, and did his best to gain support for his proposals. This he did to some extent, but the project failed. The question was again raised in 1871 by a Captain Fowler, and the matter was
resurrected again in 1894, but the tramway was never laid.

The following contemporary description of Aldershot town appeared in Charles Dickens's magazine *All the Year Round*, and is taken
from an article by a contributor who visited the town in July, 1859.

Whatever Aldershott may have been in the former history of its
country, it is now a place which the British soldier has thoroughly
taken by storm. He has squatted (in obedience to superior orders)
upon its peat and sandy common; he has pitched his white tents
in groups upon the scanty patches of grass, until they look, in
the distance, like conjurors' cups arranged upon a green baize
table; he has had planted his long black rows of dwarfed wooden
huts down the gravelly slopes, like streets in the early days of
some English colonial settlement; and he has had built a long
and lofty range of clean, new yellowbrick barracks* which over-
shadow the little mushroom town that has risen up hurriedly to
meet and trade with them.

Along the High-Street of this military village runs a single line
of railway, devoted to the carriage of coal and building material
for the large barrack streets that are still being erected for the
accommodation of future cavalry regiments. Every hour of the
day a train of luggage trucks is panting along this tramway, and
the only wonder is, that the driver who conducts the engine is
not attired in some variety of military undress costume. The
omnibuses that come in at intervals from the different railway
stations are more often loaded with scarlet horses in the shape of
non-commissioned officers, than with the dingy-coated civilian
who is always smoking the pipe of peace. The old familiar face
of the Hansom cab is seen in the one main street of this mushroom
village, as well as its companion vehicle that runs upon four
wheels. A little search will discover a well-stocked stable-yard
as full of these metropolitan conveyances as any cabman's mews
in town.

The old red-brick poor-house† has been taken possession of—
has been legally purchased, I suppose, from the parochial authorities—as an hospital for invalided soldiers. Walking in a small
dusty garden, or sitting on benches under the shadow of the side
walls, are a number of convalescents, dressed in light blue serge
trousers, jackets, and night-caps, which make them look like
comic performers of the Pierrot class in a circus of French horse-
riders.

The mushroom village does not seem able to increase its

---

* Talavera, Salamanca and Badajos Barracks—Wellington Lines.
† Now the District Pay Office on Hospital Hill.

buildings accommodation fast enough. Twenty thousand
men (the number at present stationed in barracks, huts, and tents)
require amusement; to say nothing of the officers, who require
various little luxuries, and furniture for their quarters. Scaffold-
poles, and unfinished brickwork are seen sprouting up at each
end of the straggling mile of shops and houses, while the ringing
of trowels and the noise of hammers striking nails into wooden
planks mingle with the incessant roll of drums from the barracks
and the blowing of bugles from "The Camp" beyond an intervening hill. Certain enterprising speculators are not content to
wait for the slow, substantial work of bricklayers and stonemasons
and they have erected little roadside zinc structures in which to
carry on their commerce, imported from an emigrant's house
depot in London in a few hours, and put up in a single night.
The wooden shed is not unrepresented in the town, any more than
in "The Camp," and the whole line of houses*—large small—
is joined together in some places with clothes' lines of dangling
stockings and shirts. Bright, new, glaring shops are opened for
active business before they are painted or finished; and the stock-
in-trade of one furnishing draper† (the chief warehouseman in
the place) has fairly oozed out into the road.

The titles of most houses have a warlike character, and those
who do not advertise themselves as being "by appointment to
'The Camp,'" attract attention by sticking up "Sebastopol"
or "Waterloo House," the "British Hero," and the "Crimean
Arms." The road in front of these places is either the dusty highway which has few traces of country left; a patch of mangy common which still exists to show the miserable little plot of village
that answered to the name of Aldershott half a dozen years ago,
or a layer of egg-shaped stones thrown down in a swampy piece
of ground before the crowded doors.

Towards evening the British soldier comes out to be amused.
If he is quartered in the barracks, or the huts, and is not under
canvas, nor yet upon guard, he is at liberty up to half-past nine
p.m., at which time he is summoned back to his quarters by the
firing of a gun, and the sound of regimental bands. A special
order will allow him to enjoy the seductive gaieties of the town
long after this time, but these privileges are granted to very few.
If he neglects to return to his disconsolate regiment at the appointed period, he suffers for it the next day, and several following
days, by the extra exertion of "pack drill," if not by a more severe
punishment; for the shadow of the hateful "cat" still hovers
over the pet military settlement, still comes up through the dust
and theatrical glory of a sham field-day, still dims the brightness
of the medal and the cross.

---

* Now High Street.
† Messrs. Thomas White & Co. Ltd.

About seven o'clock p.m. the British soldier rushes into the mushroom town of Aldershott for entertainment, and the mushroom town of Aldershott responds most vigorously to the call. The private soldier is able to save about threepence halfpenny or fourpence out of his thirteenpence a-day, and this, by a mutual arrangement with some comrade who is on duty for that particular night, is swelled into sevenpence or eightpence. A party of six men will sometimes club together, making a common fund of their individual savings, and this will give the one man out the command of about two shillings.

When two or three thousand soldiers are prowling about, with only two or three hours of time before them, and only fourpence each in their pockets, it is not surprising that a number of beer-shops should strive to commend themselves to their notice.

There are wooden beer-shops, and brick beer-shops, central public-houses (those immediately opposite the leading barracks, and the road over the hill into "The Camp"), and zinc beer-shops; pitched at the extreme end of the present town-line. There is a very primitive, early Australian mingling of occupations exhibited in some of these mushroom taverns, and while it is probable that you could have your hair properly cut by some of the landlords who draw a rather muddy ale for the refreshment of the British soldier in his hours of relaxation, it is certain one public-house displays an announcement in its windows about photographic likenesses being taken within at a moderate price. There have been many combinations over the tavern counter before this, but it was reserved for Aldershott to get rid of the conventional sandwich which has hitherto—for fourpence—gone with the glass of ale, and to substitute a doubtless highly artistic portrait in its place.

No tavern, however small, has the boldness or the folly to attempt to attract the British soldier, without providing him with a room in which he can either sing, or hear singing—can either dance, or be amused by professional performers who dance. To obtain this very necessary hall of entertainment nearly every back garden has been covered over with a rude, temporary structure, having something to "The Camp" hut in its composition, and something of the travelling show. Those houses that have been denied the advantage of a back garden are driven to erect a side building, which sticks out, like a large wen, from the main establishment. Some have pressed the first-floor rooms into this semi-theatrical service, and a small stage with a very hastily-painted back scene, and two wings of forest-trees, like nothing known by botanical students, are erected at one end of the largest apartment, covering about the same space as a very small shop-front, and being approached by a short flight of movable steps. In these rooms the British soldier assembles in happy, half-drunken, beer-table rank and file, and in the intervals between the appearance of the "infant Teresa," who has just gone through the Highland fling, and the appearance of "Madame de Pumpadoor, the great English soprano," he is gratified by witnessing a solemn amateur hornpipe performed by a corporal with two medals dangling from his breast, whose motions are directed by the harmony of an ear-piercing fife and jingling piano, and whose bronzed and bearded face, when he leaps up every now and then, disappears amongst the "flies," like the automaton skeleton's head in the street Fantoccini theatre.

Not far from this entrancing temple of recreation on the first floor is another temple on the ground floor, the programme of whose entertainments, placed upon a board outside the door, in coloured, ill-drawn letters, comprises singing, hornpipes, and Ethiopian serenading up to the military time of half-past nine, and "dancing after gun-fire." Looking through the open door into a kind of tent, with a stage at the bottom, you see a solid square of military audience, the scarlet coatee of the Guards relieving the half-naval blue hussar-like uniform of the Royal Artillerymen, and the more sombre green dress of the regular Rifle Corps. The undress cap which these latter soldiers wear in their hours of ease contrasts very favourably with that fearful shako, whose body is like a patent leather crucible or pipkin, and whose summit, at the fore part, is ornamented with a round mossy black ball, that looks like a property apple placed upon the bonnet of Tell's (theatrical) child, and which must be a fruitful source of temptation as a target to those who are anxious to try their skill with the rifle. Heavy as the leather shako is, when weighed in the scale against other purgatorial penal hats, it must certainly be considered light and airy by the side of the artillery rough beaver headgear. This drum-shaped military hat, which looks like a lady's hand muff, is heavier and warmer than even the immortal grenadier's cap. They are all a protection against sun and rain, and they all need a protection against themselves.

The attraction of these two concert-saloons are not sufficient to silence the voice or dim the lustre of the Apollo Music Hall,* which, having the rather unpromising frontage of a labourer's cottage (part of the original village), suddenly invested with a liquor and music license, and being separated from the main road by the mangy bit of swampy common before alluded to, is compelled to hang out rather prominent signs of the entertainments and conviviality to be found within. A chandler's shop, not far from this abode of melody, has set up a tap of drinkable beer, and though it has not yet been able to bud into the full honours of the Aldershott music halls, it is not without a little knot of

---

* On the site of the present-day Grosvenor Hotel at the junction of Union Street and Grosvenor Road.

patrons bearing the true military stamp. The eggs, the bacon, tea and cheese, and the loaves of bread, are huddled in a heap in a small window and a few shelves on one side of the shop, while all the available space on the other side is turned into a small red-curtained tap-room. The stray child who goes to this mongrel shop for its mother's breakfast or tea is introduced with gaping mouth into all the humours of rollicking military canteen life, and is made to take a sip out of a mug of ale by a staggering hero in a scarlet coat, while its packet of grocery knick-knacks is being prepared.

The British soldier is not entirely of a musical turn, and though he is seen through many tavern-room windows standing up against a fireplace, with his eyes fixed upon the ceiling, in a rapt and enthusiastic manner, singing a sentimental song for the amusement of his comrades, or leading a wild chorus in which they are all endeavouring to join, he likewise haunts the road-side in little knots, which look, at a distance, like beds of geraniums, and he marches in along the dusty main road in groups of ten or twelve, as if he had been for an evening walk to Farnborough, or some adjacent town.

Scarlet does not always consort with scarlet, nor green with green ; and a Stirlingshire militiaman, in his white jacket, plaid trousers, and Scotch cap, relieves the monotony of colour by walking between two green riflemen and an artilleryman in blue.

A close examination of the many passing sunburnt faces shows how largely the Irish peasant has, at some time or another, taken the Queen's shilling, as well as the agricultural operative of our provincial farms and fields. The Scotsman is there, in spite of his reputed caution and love of money ; and the Yorkshireman is sometimes content to forget his proverbially assigned keenness, and to mount guard, fire cannon, and practise with the sword. . . .

Mingling with these men for a moment, but hurrying by them with the dignity of a heavy day's work done, and done well, and the sense of another heavy day's work to follow tomorrow, will be half a dozen stonemasons and bricklayers, speeding home with their empty dinner-basins swinging in handkerchiefs from their hands. No signs of fraternity are exchanged between these soiled and powdered labourers and the steady red, white, blue, and green groups of lounging heroes whom they pass. They each belong to different worlds, and they know it.

The principal resort of the "crack" soldiers and the non-commissioned officers (corporals, sergeants, sergeant-majors, and such like) is a crimson music-hall* attached to the principal hotel in the mushroom town. This place is well ventilated by numerous windows that open on a small side street, and is fitted up with a

---

* The Red, White and Blue Music Hall in High Street, opposite the Police Station yard.

stage, the chief object at the back of which is a clear faced, full sized circular clock. The moment the hands of this clock draw near half-past nine p.m. the amusements (consisting chiefly of singing) work up to a climax ; allusion is made to the approach of "gun-fire" from the stage ; an acrobat boy, in crimson leggings and spangled body, makes himself very busy in washing the empty glasses of the drinkers ; while his father, a middle aged acrobat, in a precisely similar dress, is extremely active in performing the duties of a waiter. The leading comic singer having sung his popular song, for that night, to an almost exclusively military audience, comes down from the stage to exchange congratulations all round, with his scarlet and blue admirers (after the style so much in fashion at distinguished London music-halls) ; the hands of the stage clock reach the expected period, the gun fires, the bugles sound, a brass band at the opposite barracks begins to play, the soldiers slowly disperse, having a quarter of an hour's grace before them ; and a long interval takes place in the amusements of the crimson saloon, until its civilian patrons begin, somewhat later, to assemble.

Following the last military straggler, I pass a little knot of artillerymen, who are taking an affectionate leave of two young ladies (without bonnets) at the corner of the street, and ascend the gravelly hill before me, on which stand the huts of the staff-officers of "The Camp."

*   *   *   *   *

An Ordnance Survey Map published in 1869 shows the disappearance of the light railway which was constructed to supply building materials for "The Camp," and the White House on Dollys Hill, off the Farnborough Road, which appeared on the 1816 and 1856 maps, had also disappeared. The 1869 map showed the development of the town, the most noticeable feature of which was the number of inns recorded, many of which have now ceased to exist. In addition to the "Beehive" and the "Red Lion" are the "Elephant and Castle"* near the bottom of Sebastopol Road, the "White Horse," the "Queen's Head," the "Heights of Alma"* in Waterloo Road ; the "White Lion," the "White Hart," the "Albert Hotel," the "Crimea," the "Lord Campbell," the "Imperial Standard," the "Indian Heroes" in Grosvenor Road ; the "Garden Gate," the "Jolly Farmer" in Ash Road ; and the "Brickmaker's Delight,"* situated near a brick kiln off Ayling Lane. Several brickfields are shown in Cranmore Lane, Boxalls Lane, and behind the "Garden Gate" in Church Lane.

The top of Redan Hill is shown as the "Redan Battery" and the conventional outline of a fort or redan is clearly marked. It would

* No longer in existence.

appear from this that this was a defensive post for the protection of the south-eastern approach to "The Camp," or alternatively a saluting battery. The former suggestion is probably correct as a similar fort is marked on the map on Hungry Hill, and this would have formed a defensive post to the south-western approach. Both Redan Hill and Caesar's Camp are dominating features from which an uninterrupted field of fire could be brought to bear, and the value of these sites for look-outs is ideal, giving a clear view in all directions for many miles. Redan Hill, now called Redan Road, obviously took its name from the battery at the top of the hill above the tunnel through which the railway now runs. Bateman's Cottages, on Redan Hill, are shown on this map ; Holly Cottage, near the site of the present-day Labour Exchange ; whilst in the Ash Road, Campbell House, Cross House, Ash Bridge House, Brook House and Oak Villas are shown. Ivy Cottages are marked as Atlas Cottages.

In the Lower Farnham Road are a group of small houses marked as Poyle Cottages. In Victoria Road, Albert Villa, Arthur Villa and Havelock House are shown ; whilst the West Surrey Bank is shown at the junction of Victoria Road and Grosvenor Road—then marked as Bank Street—on the site now occupied by Messrs. Kinghams & Co., the Estate Agents.

The old houses in Weybourne Road opposite the "Duke of York" are marked as "Aldershot Buildings," and the cottage now known as Vine Cottage near the Traction Company's Sports Ground is shown as Aldershot Cottage.

The only buildings in Cranmore Lane are a group of buildings marked as West End Villas.

On Greenham's Hill facing the Farnborough Road between Pavilion Road and Chetwode Terrace, stands a large building marked as a Lock Hospital. The building was originally a police station and was used as such until 1861. It later became a W.D. Store until it was condemned and demolished. It was shown on the maps of Aldershot as late as 1888, but there is no trace of the building today.

Another Ordnance Survey Map published in 1875 shows further development of the town and changes. The major change was the showing of the London and South-Western Railway Line from Woking via Ash Vale through Aldershot, under the Redan Hill, and on to Farnham. The map shows Aldershot station, which was opened in 1871.

Cargate Reservoir is marked in addition to all the main features shown on previous Ordnance maps. A number of new streets were named, including Waterloo Road, Union Street, Wellington Street, High Street, Wyndham Street, and in North Town, Queen Street,

Alexandra Street and Denmark Street, which were erecte
lating builder from Brighton, who, remembering possib
of the building of Kemp Town in the early years of the
Brighton developed rapidly in the days of the Regenc
rows of terrace houses in North Town. Grosvenor R
as Bank Street. Alexandra Road is shown under the name of Union
Road. The Alexandra Music Hall is shown adjoining Miss Daniell's
Soldiers' home (marked as "Soldiers Institute") on the site of the
present-day Alexandra Cinema. A police station is marked as being
located in Barrack Road between Warburg House and the Main
Entrance to the East Cavalry Barracks. The Redan Gardens make their
first appearance on the map of Aldershot, and the forts on Redan Hill
and Hungry Hill are marked as "Redoubts." In addition to the numerous inns which appeared on previous maps, the "Prince Albert"
and the "Pavilion Hotel" are shown.

In a map of the town published in 1888 by Gale & Polden Ltd., at
their Brompton Works, Chatham, five years before the firm moved to
Aldershot, considerable development is shown in the North Town
area, which is described on the map as "New Town."

There was an advertisement on the folder of this map for Church-
wards' Hotel (now the Victoria Hotel) in Victoria Road, calling attention to its good stabling and the fact that light dinner ale was provided
at 1s. per gallon, and light dinner wines at 1s. per bottle. The advertisement carried an announcement of a series which the hotel could
also provide—"Gentlemen's Wines bottled and stacked at their own
residences."

Aldershot's civic life dates from 1857. On 4th November of that
year a meeting was held at Tilbury's Hotel, afterwards the Royal Hotel,*
of the local Board of Health. Previous to this, Aldershot was a rural
area administered by the Farnham Highway Board. The formation of
the Local Board of Health was the outcome of a petition presented to
Parliament for the application of the Public Health Act to Aldershot,
and Mr. Hugh Sears of Park Farm House and Mr. John Elstone of
Aldershot Lodge were appointed to conduct the election.

At the first meeting of the Local Board, Mr. Richard Allden was
elected Chairman,† the other members being Mr. Charles Barron, of
Aldershot Place; Mr. J. Elston, of Aldershot Lodge; Mr. R. J.

---

* The Royal Hotel no longer exists. It stood on the site at the corner of Union
Street, Wellington Street and High Street, now occupied by Burton & Co. Ltd.
and Woolworths.

† Mr. Richard Allden was a member of one of the oldest families in Aldershot.
They had farmed in the vicinity for many years. It was Mr. Allden who later gave
the land upon which Holy Trinity Church now stands. During his life he was a
generous benefactor of the town in many ways.

Barrett, Mr. B. Nicholls, Mr. H. Sears and Mr. G. Trimmer, all of Farnham; Mr. S. Terry; and Mr. Thomas White, founder of the firm of Thomas White & Co. Ltd. Mr. Richard Attfield acted as Clerk. Three military representatives were subsequently added to the Board; these were War Office nominations, the first three officers being General W. T. Knollys, the General Officer Commanding "The Camp at Aldershott," Lieut.-Colonel J. C. Kennedy and Captain T. Murray.

The first meeting of the fully constituted Board was held on 6th April, 1858, when a Mr. Potter was appointed Clerk to the Board, whilst a Mr. Marshall assumed the appointments of Rate Collector, Surveyor and Inspector of Nuisances.

For ten years the meetings of the Board continued to be held at Tilbury's Hotel. In the latter part of 1868, offices were taken in Victoria Road, the premises now occupied by Messrs. Foster, Wells & Coggins, and it was from these offices that the affairs of the town were transacted for many years.

For the first two years election to the Local Board of Health was by nomination, but in September, 1850, the first election was held.

In 1851 the population was 875. The town grew rapidly from 1854 onwards, and soon the population numbered over three thousand, many people having rushed to the new rising town to establish themselves in trade. At the census of 1861 the population numbered 16,720, of which 8,965 were military personnel. The civil population had grown in ten years from 875 to 7,755. Probably no other town in the country could claim such rapid expansion. This increase of nearly seven thousand in the short space of ten years was remarkable, but possibly not quite so in the light of the rapid growth of Aldershot from a small village to the thriving, growing town which developed in step with the influx of the military and the enlargement of the permanent camp.

In 1860 the Aldershot Burial Board was formed at a Vestry Meeting held on 31st October.* The Board's first meeting was held on 16th November, 1860, under the chairmanship of Mr. J. Elston, and on the 30th of that month a Mr. Murless was appointed Clerk at "a salary of £20 per annum." The cemetery was formed in the same year at the foot of Redan Hill in the area then known as "Bedford's Field." Two chapels, conjoined, one for the Church of England and one for Nonconformists, were erected in the year the cemetery was opened. The cemetery was enlarged in 1886 at a cost of £1,700, and further ground was purchased in 1894 at a cost of £1,054.

---

* The members were Messrs. Richard Allden, James Alstone, John Boulter, William Jones, John Hickley, Hugh Sears, Richard Stone, Thomas Manning and William Sheldrake.

There was at this time a sizeable Jewish community in the town. By 1858 a temporary Synagogue had been established at No. 24 High Street, and in 1864 the Burial Board were approached by the Jewish congregation with a request for the sale of a portion of the cemetery, which was to be divided from the remainder, and with a separate entrance to be maintained by the Jewish community. This was agreed to and approval granted by the Home Secretary. Two tablets, one in Hebrew, the other in English, were fixed on the gate pillars inside the cemetery to commemorate the consecration of the ground.

In October, 1861, a public meeting was called by Mr. William Reavell* to discuss a proposal for the building of a Presbyterian church in the town. In consequence of the decision made, a site was purchased in Victoria Road for £210, a tender for building of £1,835 was accepted, and in 1863 work on the church commenced. It was completed and opened on 9th of February, 1869, the first minister being the Rev. Robert Campbell. The frontage of the church is treated in Italian style architecture, flanked on each side by a square tower. The entrances to the church are under a piazza set on arches supported by columns at the top of a flight of five steps. The galleries within the church were built at a cost of £272 and first used on 11th February, 1872.

The first Gas Company in the town was formed as a private enterprise by Mr. John Eggar and in 1865 became known as the Aldershot Gas Consumers' Company. The following year saw the incorporation of the Aldershot Gas and Water Company,† which took over the works and property of the Consumers' Company.

As has been seen at the opening of "The Camp," Aldershot was dependent upon Farnborough and Tongham for its nearest railway stations.

The need for better rail communication was obvious, and in 1865 a company was formed for the construction of a line into "The Camp." The scheme was objected to by the London and South-Western Railway Company, who induced the promoters to withdraw their proposals on condition that a Bill was presented to Parliament for attaining the object in a more satisfactory manner. Approval was obtained later in the year for a line to be constructed to Aldershot, the railway to branch off the main line through Pirbright and Aldershot

---

* Late Chairman of the Local Board, William Reavell was born on the 21st March, 1836; he came to Aldershot in the fifties and took an active interest in local affairs. He died at the age of 85 on the 14th of June, 1921.

† The Company's name was changed in 1909 when it became the Aldershot Gas, Water & District Lighting Company. It was changed again in 1931 to the Mid Southern District Utility Company and the following year became the Mid Southern Utility Company.

and on to Farnham. Work was started on the line, which included the boring of the tunnel under Redan Hill, and it came into use on 2nd May, 1870. Aldershot station was built early in 1870 and at that time stood amid green fields, there being a large market garden at the corner of The Grove, on the site of Gale & Polden's Works, and there were houses in Station Road. A footpath led from the station across the fields to High Street, for the area from Victoria Road, which then had houses only on the north side, to the station was but an open field. When opened the railway had a double track as far as Aldershot and a single line on to Farnham. The double line was opened a few years later. The railway service consisted of eight trains a day to Waterloo and six from London to the town. The fastest train of the day left Waterloo at 11.30 a.m., reaching Aldershot at 12.40 p.m. In May, 1879, the South-Eastern Railway Company extended their line to Aldershot with Guildford and thereby making direct rail communication possible with the South Coast and linking with the Great Northern Railway. A month later the South-Western Railway Company completed their line between Ascot and Aldershot via Frimley, thereby affording another link between the town and other lines of communication in the network of railways which were being laid throughout the country.

The Government siding was built in 1890, the permanent way being constructed with rails brought home from the Sudan after use during the campaign of the Egyptian Expeditionary force (1885-1889). The siding was extended during the South African War in 1899 and 1900 to deal with the increased volume of military traffic.

* * * * *

It was in 1872 that it was decided that there was a need for another church in the town. This was considered necessary firstly owing to the increasing population, and secondly, as the Parish Church of St. Michael lay to the south in the rural area outside the more populous area. A committee was formed and the decision reached that a new church, dedicated to the Holy Trinity, should be erected in the town centre. The site of Holy Trinity between Arthur Street and Victoria Road was given by Mr. Richard Allden. A subscription was raised to cover the expenses of building this new place of worship, and the foundation stone was laid by the Bishop of Winchester on 16th October, 1875. The church was consecrated on 14th October, 1878.

One of the most imposing churches in Aldershot is the Methodist Church situated in Grosvenor Road. Work commenced on this church in 1874 and it was opened in October, 1876. The church was sited on the high ground above the centre of the town, and, with its hundred-foot tower, this edifice dominated the town when seen from the distance of Redan Hill and, farther still, from Caesar's Camp and the Hog's Back.

The year 1872 saw the construction in Queen's Road of a temporary Roman Catholic Church of corrugated iron which was brought to Aldershot from Southampton. Until this time the Roman Catholics of the town made use of a disused public-house in what was then known as Hillary Terrace, now part of Alexandra Road. This had been in use since 1869, when the Roman Catholic Mission was opened at the instigation of the Catholic Bishop of the Diocese, The Right Rev. Dr. Grant. Prior to this date the civilian Catholics of the town were dependent upon the Catholic Military Chaplains of the Garrison for the ministrations of their religion. The Iron Church was replaced in 1912 by the present-day Church of St. Joseph's, built in Romanesque style on the same site, and the Iron Church removed to its present site in Belle Vue Road.

*   *   *   *   *

It was in January, 1872, that the Aldershot School Board first met in the Assembly Rooms. The Board considered at its meeting on 2nd May, 1872, the question of taking over the "Florence Nightingale" public-house in St. George's Square for use as a school, but when inspected it was recorded in the minutes of the meeting that "the buildings were found to be in such a dilapidated condition that unless the owner would be disposed to put them in a thorough state of repair, and which they learn from his agent that he declines to do, they cannot recommend a tenancy upon any terms." The Board's first school was in North Town.* This was Mrs. J. Paine's School, which was taken over by the Board on its formation, and in the same year (1872) the

---

* Prior to this time there were in the town a number of private schools. A Mr. Tom Randall kept a school in a room above the "Nag's Head" in North Town, and there was a school in Denmark Street on the site of the Havelock Hall, the head-mistress being a Mrs. Marsh; this school closed on the opening of the Newport Road School.

In Victoria Road, at No. 84, was a "School for Young Ladies" which was later "opened by Mrs. Marsh, at which she was assisted by her two daughters" described as "three very prim little ladies, familiar figures in Aldershot, walking sedately arm-in-arm." Also in Victoria Road, at one time, were Mr. Bentley's Commercial School, at Rose Villa, Mr. Cullen's Collegiate School, Mrs. Coffee's School (originally opened by a Miss Brocklehurst who was followed by a Mrs. Parrott) and Mr. Sheffield's School. In Grosvenor Road was Mrs. Austin's "School for Girls," and Mr. Russell's School. In Birchett Place was Mrs. Dalloway's School and in Queens Road Mrs. Martin's. All these private schools, which were typical of many which existed before the itroduction of compulsory education, were con-ducted in private houses and were the only educational establishments which existed for the greater portion of the population. A few desks or tables, a blackboard, some standard primers, "readers" and "copy" books were all the equipment that was needed, but it was owing to these pioneers of elementary education that many were able to make their start in life equipped, at least, with a sound knowledge of the "three Rs" (Reading, (w)Riting and (a)Rithmetic).

Church of England School at the bottom of Redan Road, built in 1854 was taken over. Previous to this there were only the Parish Church School and two private schools. In 1867 the teacher at the Church School was a Miss Greenwood, and it is recorded that the school fees were 4d. In the following year, on 24th November, the Board opened a school at West End, and in June, 1874, a third school was opened at the East End of the town. St. Joseph's Roman Catholic School had been opened in 1869.

*   *   *   *   *

In 1879 the Royal Pavilion was occupied by the Duke of Connaught when, after his wedding, he came to reside in Aldershot until Bagshot Park was ready for his occupation. On the occasion of the arrival of the Duke and Duchess in Aldershot on Saturday, 14th June, 1879, it is recorded that the Chairman of the Aldershot Local Board, Mr. W. Reavell, presented a "handsomely illuminated address of welcome" to the Duchess on behalf of the town, which read "we not only welcome you as the bride of a son of our well-beloved Queen but as the bride of a soldier who has endeared himself to the whole Army by the zealous way in which he has devoted himself to the duties of his honourable profession." A report of the occasion records that "the streets of Aldershot were lavishly decorated, triumphal arches were erected, and the school children lined the footpaths." A guard of honour of the Rifle Brigade, of which the Duke of Connaught was Colonel-in-Chief, was mounted at the gates of the Pavilion.

*   *   *   *   *

It was in 1880 that once again the need for an Institute was felt, the original Institution having closed down some years previously. A house known as Eagle House was purchased and served for six years as an Institute, but in 1884 it was considered necessary to obtain a more permanent building. Plans developed slowly, but a site was purchased in Victoria Road, and the foundation stones of the Aldershot Institute of today were laid in September, 1886, by the Rt. Hon. George Sclater-Booth, M.P. for North Hants, and Mr. Richard Allden. The building was opened in January, 1888, by Colonel Birch.

To meet the needs of the district from the Gas Works to North Lane, and North Town to Aldershot Stubbs, an iron Mission Church was erected near the site of the present St. Augustine's Church in 1880 and licensed by the Bishop of Winchester.

It was in 1883 that work commenced on the Baptist Tabernacle in Upper Elms Road. It was not completed until 1886.

The original lay-out of "The Camp" included a police station which was built on the west of the Farnborough Road just below the Royal Pavilion. It was here that the first Petty Sessions were held on alternate Mondays. When the present-day police station, court house, and police quarters were built in 1869 the old police station was converted in 1861 into a Lock Hospital, but later became a military store house. The Bench of Magistrates who sat at the Aldershot Petty Sessions first sat at the original police station and afterwards, until the opening of the present court house, in the long meeting room in the Royal Hotel.

Up to 1881 the town's water supply was obtained from wells, but in that year the Aldershot Gas and Water Company made borings into the chalk below the super-strata on the Lower Farnham Road.

By the eighties the face of the town had begun to change. The business quarter, in the area bounded by High Street, Grosvenor Road, Victoria Road and Station Road, had begun to expand, and shop fronts took the place of the bay windows of the villas in the residential streets. Larger and more commodious business premises were built, taking the place of the two-storeyed shops and residencies of the late fifties. The present-day Lloyds Bank building at the corner of Gordon Road and Victoria Road was built in 1881, together with other larger buildings which became necessary with the development of the town as a business and trading centre.

At this time the home of the Lloyd family was in Wellington Villa, which lay back from Victoria Road opposite the Victoria Hotel. In 1896 this house was demolished to build the present-day Arcade which runs from Victoria Road to Wellington Street. The building of the Wellington Street end necessitated the demolition of the last thatched cottage in the town centre, which was situated on the site of Nelson & Goodrick's shops at the Arcade entrance. The Westminster Bank building at the corner of Wellington Street and Victoria Road was also built in this year.

The development of the town was to a great extent centred between the railway station and High Street. In the seventies Church Lane East was still but a narrow country lane with high banks and hedges, whilst Church Hill was but a footpath running down by the boundary of the grounds of the Manor House.

The year 1887 saw the formation of the Aldershot Volunteer Fire Brigade, which, with the exception of one full-time professional officer appointed in 1926, continued as a voluntary body, composed of some 26 officers and men, until 1939. In the early days the Fire Brigade was equipped with a horse-drawn engine, but as years passed by, improved fire appliances were maintained, affording protection not only for the town but for the villages of Ash, Tongham and Seale. The town's first fire station was near the top of Victoria Road. The "station" was just large enough for the engine to be wheeled in by hand, and the horses were stabled in a mews at the rear of the buildings.

P

The foundation stone of Aldershot Cottage Hospital, at the corner of Church Lane East and St. George's Road, was laid in 1896 by the Duchess of Connaught and the Hospital was opened by her in the following year.

At the time of the establishment of "The Camp" all postal work was conducted from the post office at Farnborough, owing to its proximity to the railway. The first post office in Aldershot was opened in a cottage opposite the "Beehive," and a Mr. Brittle used to drive over from Farnham with his pony and trap to collect the mail and take it to Farnborough. Before arriving in Aldershot he collected mails at Seale, Tongham and Ash, and as he drove along the Ash Road he used to blow a small horn to call out the cottagers *en route* with their mail. A sub-office was eventually opened in High Street at the corner of Wellington Street in the premises then occupied by Mr. Allen, the chemist, the founder of the firm of Allen & Lloyd. This sub-office was later moved to a shop owned by Mr. Rattray in Wellington Street. When Aldershot became a head office, a post office was built in Victoria Road, the premises occupied today by Messrs. Bides, the florists.

The business of the Aldershot Post Office steadily increased and larger premises became necessary. In 1898, the post office moved to the corner of Birchett Road and Gordon Road, the premises occupied by Messrs. Phillips Bros. This move was of a temporary nature, for the site of the existing G.P.O. at the corner of Station Road and Victoria Road had already been acquired. The present G.P.O. was completed and opened in 1902.

During the latter years of the nineteenth century the town grew considerably, the population increasing year by year. By 1871 the civilian population had increased to 11,675, the total of civilians and military being 21,682. Ten years later the civilian inhabitants had increased to 12,875 and the military population was 7,280. In the next ten years to 1891 the numbers of civilians remained more or less stationary, but the number of troops increased to 12,954. By 1901 the civil population was 16,726 and the military 14,248.

Another indication of the town's development may be seen from the records of the former Mid Southern Utility Company. In 1874 the quantity of coal carbonized was 2,000 tons ; by 1906 this had reached a yearly figure of 26,000 tons. In 1882, 20,000,000 gallons of water had been provided at the waterworks ; by 1906 this had increased to 400,000,000 gallons annually.

The Theatre Royal* was built at the corner of Birchett Road and

---

* The lessee of the Theatre was Mr. Clarence Sounes, who came to Aldershot after many years' touring on the stage ; he had made his first appearance at the Theatre Royal, Drury Lane, in 1880. He died in October, 1921.

Gordon Road in 1891 after the old Apollo Music Hall at the top of
Union Street had been destroyed by fire in 1889. The Theatre Royal
was enlarged in 1901.

One of the features of Aldershot is the number of institutes for the
use of soldiers. The need for such was realized soon after the establishment of the permanent camp. The pioneer of these institutes was
Mrs. Daniell, who founded, in 1862, the Aldershot Mission Hall and
Soldiers' Home and Institute, now generally known as Miss Daniell's
Soldiers' Home. Mrs. Daniell, an officer's widow, realized the necessity of providing some place of relaxation for the soldiers other than
the public-houses and saloons which abounded in the town. She
first established a small Soldiers' Home in a house she rented in Artillery Terrace, and then set to work to raise the funds required for the
building of the Institute which stands today at the junction of Barrack
Road and Edward Street, the foundation stone of which was laid by the
Earl of Shaftesbury on 11th February, 1863, the Institute being opened
on 11th October in the same year. The Soldiers' Home was the forerunner of many, and can be said to have been the first step towards
the Official Army Welfare Services of today. When the home was
originally opened it was felt that ladies could not make such a place
their home and that a Council of Management, composed of officers
and their wives, representatives of the town and a small staff of voluntary workers, could manage the Institute. It would appear that
this arrangement was not entirely satisfactory, for twelve months later
Mrs. Daniell was back in Aldershot, with her daughter, and here she
settled, devoting her life to the work of the Home.

In June, 1875, the Grosvenor Road Soldiers' Home, adjoining the
Wesleyan Church, was opened, this Institution taking the place of a
smaller building erected by the Wesleyans some years previously.
When the new building was opened the original "Home" was taken
down and re-erected in Lynchford Road, Farnborough, and opened
in August, 1875, as the "North Camp Soldiers' Home." The Church
of England Soldiers' Home was opened in 1880 in hired rooms in
Union Street, at a rent of £25 per year. This Home came into being
as a result of the efforts of Major J. Clisham, who had suggested the
establishment of such a home, with rooms for men to stay in when
"on pass," outside "the Camp" ; Colonel Walker, the local President
of the Army Guild of the Holy Standard ; and the Rev. J. Pickance,*
who spared no effort to turn these ideas into an accomplished fact.
Proposals for the opening of the Home had been made some years
earlier. In 1875, at the Church Congress at Stoke-on-Trent, the Rev.

---

* The Rev. J. Pickance was born on 23rd March, 1845, and was ordained at
St. Philip's, Battersea, in 1872. He died in Aldershot in 1921 (see p. 276).

J. C. Edghill, then a Chaplain to the Forces, and later Chaplain-General, appealed for "clergymen to open their pulpits, and laymen their pockets, to enable us to build a soldiers' home in Aldershot." The present Church of England Soldiers', Sailors' and Airmen's Institute in Victoria Road was built in 1883 by Messrs. Martin, Wells & Co., and was opened and dedicated by the Bishop of Winchester on Michaelmas Day in the same year. In 1889, Lima House, later re-named Openshaw House, adjoining the Institute, came on to the market and was purchased and incorporated into the Institute. The Gordon Chapel at the top of the building was added in 1890.

In May, 1882, the Army Coffee Tavern Association opened "the Royal Army Coffee Tavern" at the top of Queen's Avenue facing Lynchford Road for the use of the men in Marlborough Lines, North Camp. Prior to the opening of this building, a large corrugated iron hut had been used by the Association on the same site as a temporary Refreshment and Recreation Room. This hut was offered to the Church of England Soldiers' Institute, and was brought to Aldershot. It was erected at the rear of the Institute, facing Birchett Road. Twenty feet at the rear of the hut were cut off and converted into a bath house, becoming the first place in Aldershot where a soldier could obtain a bath. The hut was one of the first public halls in the town, and became known as the "Tin Hall."*

* * * * *

In the early years of "The Camp" the military authorities provided but few means of recreation for the troops, and to a great extent the soldier sought relaxation either in the canteens, in the barracks, or in the public-houses of the town. Each evening military picquets patrolled the streets of the town, and the tramp of marching feet of anything from four to ten men, the flicker of their lantern in winter bobbing up and down as it swung along in the grip of the leading file, and the sharp orders of the N.C.Os. were a feature of the "night life" of Aldershot. There was no 10 p.m. closing of the public-houses ; midnight was the normal time, or in the side streets until the last customer had shouted his cheery good night, or had been pushed outside by the publican with a "You've 'ad enough, me lad," or "Aint you got no-where to sleep ?"

The Military Police were responsible for the behaviour of troops in the town, and they saw to it that any soldier misbehaving himself in the streets was quickly removed by the picquets to the nearest guard room. The picquets were doubled on pay nights, and sometimes when the *esprit de corps* of some units was such that men took it upon themselves

---

* The "Tin Hall" stood on the site of the present-day car park behind the Church of England Soldiers' Institute in Victoria Road. The hall was pulled down in 1935.

to prove their superiority over the men of another regiment or battery. This was in the days when most regiments were known among the rank and file by traditional nicknames, some of which were not always acceptable to the regiment concerned, dating back as they often did to some obscure incident, a generation past, in some far-flung camp, garrison or in the field. "'Ullo," says a stalwart red-coat to his pals, as he looks into a public bar at a group similarly dressed but with different badges and facings, "'eres the old 'Flatfeet Fusiliers'!" "What d'yer mean?" comes the rejoinder from one of the other group, "Flatfeet! You'll bloomin' well take that back"—and so very shortly there was another job for the town picquet.

The Cardwell Reforms of 1871-2 revolutionized Army life and this had its effect on Aldershot. Up to that time all men enlisting in the Army did so for twenty-one years, with the result that a high proportion of the men were nearing middle age and many were hard, sometimes wild and rough veterans, and heavy drinkers; and as Kipling later wrote, "an' if our conduct isn't always what your fancy paints, well, single men in barracks don't grow into plaster saints." It must be admitted in retrospect that the soldier of those days was not without an excuse for his conduct, for he was undoubtedly the victim of a system; for year after year he went through the same routine, and for those without imagination and ambition, the future held but little, and so he lived for the day, or in Aldershot for the night in the town, and he was apt to "break out" on pay nights as a change from what to many was a dull and changeless existence. Under the Cardwell system, short service was introduced, firstly for twelve years with the colours and nine with the reserve, and later for twelve years, of which only seven were with the colours. This brought about a great change and attracted a different type of recruit, who gradually replaced the hardened old soldier which Aldershot had known for nearly twenty years.

The system of town picquets was maintained up to the period just before the 1914-1918 war, when the G.O.C., Lieut.-General Sir Horace Smith-Dorrien, issued an order to the effect that he intended to withdraw all picquets and to place the troops on their honour to behave themselves in the streets of the town. This had excellent results and brought about a great change.

*   *   *   *   *

The first rate laid down by the first Local Board of Health in 1858 was 1s. in the £, and this produced £207. At that time the rating was divided, the Local Board making their own rate quite apart from any rates made by the Overseers of the Poor, who then did much of the work later done by the Board of Guardians, whose duties were transferred to the County Council in 1932. By 1868 the rateable value of the town had increased to nearly £20,000. The local Board rate was still 1s. in the £, and the total sum collected was £874 9s. 9d. Two years later the rates commenced to rise; in January, 1870, the rate was increased to 1s. 4d., and in June of the same year a similar rate was made.*

At that time all the canteens in "The Camp" were assessed on the same basis as the property in the town. On all the other barracks and buildings in "The Camp" the Government paid a lump sum in lieu of rates.

Records show that in the eighties there were a large number of empty properties in the town, the result no doubt of speculative building twenty years before vacated by those whose ties with the town were ended at the completion of their work in its construction and that of "The Camp," and the fact that during the Sudan Campaign there were at one period only two Regular battalions in "The Camp."

It was the year 1892 which decided Aldershot's future as a flourishing business centre. In this year the Government decided to rebuild the whole camp. Up to that time, with the exception of the permanent barracks along the line of High Street and Wellington Avenue, and the brick-built blocks in North Camp, "The Camp" was still composed of the wooden huts erected at the time of the Crimea. This large part of "The Camp" was always regarded as temporary and in consequence businessmen and speculators were wary of putting money into buildings and other development plans until the future of this large portion of "The Camp" was decided upon.

The decision to rebuild entirely the large portion of the old camp was the deciding factor which made businessmen realize that there was a big future for the town, and Aldershot entered upon a second period of expansion and development.

The year 1894 marked a number of important developments in the life of the town. The passing of the Local Government Act of that year converted the Local Board to the Aldershot Urban District Council, the membership of which was increased from nine to twelve, and as the result of application to the County Council was further increased on 10th August, 1903, to fifteen, with three military representatives in addition. The original twelve members of the Urban District Council, under the chairmanship of Mr. W. T. Robertson, were Dr. H.

---

* The assessable value of the town has increased considerably. In 1830 it was £847 9s. 0d., today it is £298,501. Up to 1856 the value increased gradually, the figure in that year being £3,196 16s. 0d. By 1868 it was £18,681. In 1870 it had increased to £23,550 8s. 0d. In 1880 it was £28,954 8s. 8d. and by 1900 the figure had risen to £115,691 2s. 5d., figures which give further proof of the rapid growth of the town.

Coghlan, Mr. W. Clinton, Mr. Richard Eve (the Vestry Clerk), Mr.
S. Friend, Mr. Caleb Hall, Mr. T. B. Jeffries, Mr. J. Lazareck,* Mr.
J. May, Mr. Arthur Smith,† Mr. A. Wells and Mr. Henry Wells.

The development and growth of Aldershot, together with its
importance as the great military centre of the British Isles, gave rise
at this time to the view that the town should be accorded the dignity
of a Borough. It was in the year that the Urban District Council was
formed that this step was advocated by *The Aldershot News*, its founder,
Mr. T. Ernest Polden, and Mr. Henry Wells, J.P., offering to bear
the expense of promoting the Charter. Nothing came of these proposals at the time and it was felt that the time was not then ripe for
the adoption of the scheme ; and although from time to time the proposal was renewed, practical steps were not taken until 1917.

The streets of the town were still badly lighted, as they had been for
many years ; flickering gas lamps and pale oil lamps fixed at street
corners sufficed to light the citizen on his way after dark. But in 1894,
a specimen street lamp was erected by the Incandescent Light Company
in Station Road, and as a result of this trial, steps were taken to adopt
lamps for erection in other main thoroughfares.

The first Aldershot Carnival, with the object of raising funds in aid
of Aldershot Hospitals, was held in the same year, and this became
a popular and well-organized annual event, with fancy dress parades,
a procession, another torchlight procession at night and a Carnival
Ball. The Carnival was such a success as a social function that it
for many years became a regular institution in the town. It was also
in 1894 that the Parish land was purchased by the Council from the
churchwardens and overseers. After some considerable argument
and discussion over the price to be paid, settlement was finally reached
and plans passed for the construction of the Municipal Buildings and
Gardens. In the same year the Council were discussing proposals for
a tramway to be built between Aldershot and Farnborough, but this
project was abandoned.

The only public transport in the town and between Aldershot and
Farnborough was horse buses which plied between the Queen Hotel
in Grosvenor Road and the Queen's Hotel at Farnborough.‡ There

---

* A jeweller and pawnbroker whose name may still be seen on the business
premises occupied at No. 77, High Street.

† Later to be, in 1922, Aldershot's Charter Mayor.

‡ A horse bus service was run through "The Camp" by a Mr. James Doe from
the North Camp Hotel to Aldershot Town station, with a bus yard near the Stanhope Lines Post Office. One of the drivers was one William Cullen, who died in
November, 1919. He had been one of the first twenty men to enlist in the 100th
Regiment—the Leinster Regiment (Royal Canadians)—when it was raised in Canada
in 1858. After twelve years' service with the regiment he had come to Aldershot,
and drove one of the horse buses until the service was discontinued.

were no set time-tables, the buses moving according to the will and
pleasure of the drivers.

Mail coaches were still in operation. In March, 1894, the G.P.O.
even decided to reintroduce a pair-horse van for parcel deliveries in
the area, one route running from Guildford through Aldershot to
Farnham and thence to Farnborough.

The association of the well-known military printers and publishers,
Gale & Polden Ltd., with the Borough of Aldershot dates from 1893,
when the Company opened a branch of the firm at No. 9 Wellington
Street. The Company had already been established for twenty-five
years at Chatham* and in London.

Service printing, publishing and stationery had been studied and
specialized in, and the firm became known throughout the British
Army. The printing works was expanded and removed to larger
premises. Then came an event which was destined to have a very
marked influence on the future of the firm—the publication of its
first book. It had been represented to the firm that there was a real
need in the Army for some sort of guide to obtaining certificates of
education. A soldier could not, except in very special circumstances,
be promoted unless he possessed a 3rd Class Certificate, and the firm
commissioned the late Mr. David Morrison, who died in 1930 at
Farnham, but who was then an Army Schoolmaster serving at
Chatham, to write a "Guide to Obtaining a 3rd Class Certificate of
Education." It was but a modest little book and was published at
6d., but its success was immediate; and it was the forerunner of a
series of Army Educational Guides which the firm still publishes.
On this modest foundation was built the publishing side of the business which has issued millions of Army text-books.

The business of Gale & Polden Ltd. continued to expand and many
were the expedients that had to be resorted to to meet the pressure. At
times even the soldier-printers employed in the R.E. Printing Office
at Chatham were "requisitioned" in their spare time to come in and
help cope with the work.

In 1885 the Company built its first factory in Chatham to compete
with the increased business. It was the rapid development of the military business which led to the opening of the branch in Aldershot. The
same enterprise which marked the growth of the firm was again in
evidence in 1893, when it was decided to build a factory in Aldershot.

---

* The firm had its beginnings in the late sixties when a stationer's shop with a
small printing works attached was opened in High Street, Old Brompton, near the
R.E. Depot, Chatham, the business having been founded by the late Mr. James
Gale, a retired naval officer, who was joined in partnership by the late Mr. T.
Ernest Polden and later by his brother, Mr. E. Russell Polden, the present Chairman
of the Board of Directors.

The present site of the Wellington Press at the junction of Birchett Road and The Grove was purchased. The site was then a market garden, noted for its strawberry beds, owned by a Mr. Weybourne, with a stream trickling through it. One of the contractors—Martin, Wells & Co.—then engaged in the building of permanent barracks in South Camp was given the contract for the erection of the building.

The move from Chatham to Aldershot was accomplished in a remarkable manner. The large printing machines at the Brompton Works, Chatham, were kept running until The Grove ground floor wing of the new works was built, and two high-powered gas engines with electrical generating plant were installed at the far end. Then the machines were taken down, loaded into vans which were run straight on to railway trucks, and sent to Aldershot by rail. At Aldershot they were taken straight through the big windows facing The Grove, which had been designedly made large enough for the purpose, and the machines were actually unloaded on the sites they were to occupy. Before the second floor was finished the machines were at work. As each floor became completed in turn it was immediately equipped with machinery and materials transferred from Chatham. The Grove wing was built and occupied by the autumn of 1893, when the Birchett Road wing was still being erected, this leading to a remarkable episode which might well have proved a most serious catastrophe. The wing was nearly completed, and all the roof with the exception of one section at the Cavendish Road end was on, The Grove wing being cut off by a temporary partition. It was a cold and stormy day in October, 1893, and at the height of the gale the wind blew straight under the open portion of the roof and lifted the whole length right up, taking with it the beams and tiles. This first pulled the walls inwards and then they fell outwards with a crash, blocking the yard and Birchett Road with a mass of debris. Fortunately, although this happened in the daytime and the builders were at work and the other wing was occupied, no casualties occurred.

Rebuilding of the wing was at once taken in hand, and as time went on, a third wing in Cavendish Road was added, with the top floor constructed as a photographic studio, this department being opened in 1900. The fourth wing, to complete the quadrangle, was added in 1915.

An important development in the publishing side of the business and to the town as a whole occurred on 23rd June, 1894, when the first number of *The Aldershot News* was published. On 29th March, 1901, the firm first published *The Military Mail*; this was a unique publishing venture—a weekly newspaper produced entirely for the Army—containing sixteen pages for the price of one penny. It had a wide circulation both at home and abroad. It was described as "one of the few newspapers which made no apology for its appearance," adding that "the British Army, caretakers of the grandest Empire the world has ever seen, needed a voice; *Military Mail* supplied it." This Army newspaper had, however, to cease publication on the outbreak of war in 1914.

It was in the spring of 1894 that the late Mr. T. Ernest Polden, then Managing Director of Gale & Polden Ltd., decided to launch a new weekly newspaper in Aldershot, with the intention of its becoming a paper of a high standard giving all the news of the town and district and also a military gazette for the Army at home and throughout the Empire. It took a month to complete the plans for the first number. The military reporter was an enthusiastic young soldier then serving in Aldershot, later to become Colonel F. W. Walker, O.B.E., who in order to join the staff of the paper purchased his discharge and remained with the paper for six years, when he was appointed to be a special correspondent in South Africa for the *Daily Express* during the war.

The policy of the paper was to give full and accurate reports of all news in both camp and town, and in general to put Aldershot more "on the map." *The Aldershot News* was first published on 23rd June, 1894. The paper was an immediate success. In less than twenty-four hours the whole of the first issue of twelve thousand copies had been sold in and around Aldershot. The remaining four thousand copies were held and posted to units of the Army at home and abroad, and for the first time news of Aldershot was being read in every regiment through-out the Empire.

Among the first members of the staff were Wilmott Lewis, later to be knighted and become the Washington Correspondent of *The Times*, and Captain Nicholls, who became "Quex" of the *Evening Standard*. Miss Eleanor Wren was the first woman reporter and in the early days was also the advertisement canvasser.

The Aldershot News, printed in six columns to a page in closely set small type, of eight pages, sold for one penny. One page was devoted to a weekly serial story of a romantic nature. Typical of these were "A Soldier's Sweetheart," by Captain F. M. Peacock, and "A Soldier and a Maid," "Ronald the Fusilier," and other stories. At least one page was devoted to military news under the title "Round the Camp." This weekly feature included such typical items as "1st West Yorkshire Regiment—Departure for Gibraltar," "2nd Cheshire Regiment—Expected move to Ireland"; "1st Seaforth Highlanders (72nd Foot)—Death of Afghan Veteran"; "3rd (King's Own) Hussars—Temperance Branch formed"; "2nd Dragoons (Royal Scots Greys)—Balaclava Day Celebrations," and other news items dealing with personalities, training, sporting and social events. Full details were given of all manœuvres, verbatim reports of speeches at dinners and other functions. No news item, however small, appears to have been missed; full reports were given of all social events in the town.

An interesting annual event in the nineties was the dinner given by *The Aldershot News* to the newsboys engaged in the sale of the paper. This was initiated by Mr. T. Ernest Polden, who gave prizes to the boy who sold the largest number of copies and entertained them to lunch each January at the South-Western Hotel. The first event was a great success as all the newsboys, who were between the ages of twelve and sixteen, with faces washed, hair brushed down and in their Sunday clothes, sat down to this unique luncheon. The function was conducted with all the decorum of such events of the day, although it rather broke down with the ceremonial arrival of the Christmas pudding and the youthful enthusiasm of the newsboys in loudly proclaiming their appreciation. This Newsboys' Luncheon was quite a feature and was looked forward to for many years.

It was in 1895 that *The Aldershot News* Old Folk's Christmas Fund was founded by the first Editor, with the generous support of the late Mr. T. Ernest Polden, the founder of the paper. The fund was started at a time when there was no Old Age Pension. Poor Law relief was sparsely given and the aged poor had a very hard time, experiencing hardships and privations in the evening of their lives. The founding of the fund caused quite a sensation, and received enthusiastic support. The immediate response was such that on the Saturday before Christmas, sixty old men and women sat down to the first *Aldershot News* Old Folk's Tea in the "Tin Hall," at which they all received a gold half-sovereign. The fund was maintained and the tea became an annual event which continues to this day. Year by year the response to the annual appeal has been generous, and still the "Old Folk's Tea" is a feature of the life of the town, an event to which many eagerly look forward as each Christmas comes round.

* * * * *

Some glimpses of the life and times of Aldershot can be gleaned from the displayed advertisements in the issues of *The Aldershot News* in the early nineties.

"Still to the front" reads one announcement. "The Bell Inn, Union Terrace, Proprietor Josh Billings (late of the Royal Dragoons). Smoking Concerts every evening; pianist, Miss Kate O'Neill." A "Picture Gallery" is announced as an additional attraction.

C. Webster advertised as "'Bus, Cab and Fly Proprietor" operating from "The Royal Military Hotel" with "open carriages, Wagonettes,

Broughams and Pony Traps" for hire "By the Day, Hour or Job."

"Theatrical Performances, Nigger troupes, Bicycle Parades, in fact all costume displays attended to with PROMPTITUDE" advertised R. Featherstone, Theatrical Costumier of the Alexandra Hall, who announced that the business had already been established thirty years.

James Williams, "Pharmaceutical, family and dispensing Chemist," of 140, Victoria Road, advertised "Prescriptions and Family recipes dispensed with the purest drugs and chemicals," and also that he was a "Manufacturer of Mineral and Aerated Waters" offering "Special Terms to Messes and Canteens."

H. Webb & Co., Jobmasters, who operated from the Gordon Livery Stables in Gordon Road, with other establishments in Victoria Road and Elms Road, advertised "Chargers, Hunters, Ladies Hacks, Saddle Horses and Cobs at shortest notice," and the fact that they had available "Loose Boxes and Stalls and Good coach houses, etc." all at "moderate charges."

J. W. Jacklett, Photographer, of "The Berlin Studio" at 160, Victoria Road, advertised "Cabinets, *carte de visite*, and Vignette photographs at moderate prices," and "Enlarged permanent portraits in carbon" and "Enlargements on opal, finished in Black and White or Oils." Another photographer, R. W. Elliott, of 93, High Street, advertised "Permanent Platinotype Portraiture at Popular Prices."

Tolley Brothers, of 302, High Street, "Pastrycooks by appointment to the Royal Military College, Sandhurst," advertised as the "Agents for the District for Meaby's Triticumina Bread (Recorded by the Medical faculty as being the finest wholemeal Bread known)."

The South-Eastern Railway Company advertised Special cheap excursions "to London and Back," leaving Aldershot Town at 9.35 a.m. and 4.55 p.m., returning from London at 11.40 p.m. with the "fare there and back 3s. third class."

E. Southon, Undertaker, Funeral Carriage Proprietor and Monumental Mason, of High Street, with works in Sebastopol Road and Crimea Road, advertised "Adults funerals from £2" and "Superior Class Funerals." His scale of charges were detailed and included those for "half or full trimmed coffins, hire of funeral carriage, pall, hat bands and undertakers attendance."

F. J. Hawkins, Army and Family Butcher, of 49 Union Street, supplied "Officers' Messes, Hotels and families at moderate prices with the best quality beef, mutton, pork and veal, slaughtered on the premises."

James Hooper, described as "Italian Warehouseman," of Alexandra Road, advertised the "Finest growths of Teas and Coffees—Breakfast and Luncheon delicacies—Wiltshire Bacon—Ceylon Tea in lead packets," and "New Laid eggs every Wednesday and Saturday."

R. Aylward, Corn and Forage Merchant, of 41, High Street, announced that "having large stores at the Railway Station, he is in a position to supply the Best Quality Forage of all descriptions at short notice, and, at the closest market prices."

W. Store & Son, Military and Hunting Saddlers, of Wellington Street, "patronised by Their Royal Highnesses the Prince of Wales, Duke of Connaught and H.I.M. The Princess Eugenie," advertised "Harness and Saddlery manufactured on the premises by experienced workmen."

Mr. C. H. Saunders, Resident Surgeon Dentist, of Arthur Street, advertised "Painless Dentistry," "Teeth extracted from 1s." and "Artificial teeth from 5s. per tooth."

One gleans from the advertisements, too, that one of the features in the social life of the town was the regular popular concerts, known as the "Weekly Pops," given at the Parish Hall in Church Lane, or the "Tin Hall" in Birchett Road, when entertainment took the form of "Pianoforte duets and solos, choral entertainments, songs and ballads."

*   *   *   *   *

Such was Aldershot as the nineteenth century drew to a close. By then, apart from the military atmosphere which dominated the centre and northern boundaries of the town, it had to a great extent become an ordinary town, typical of Victorian England of the day. The residential areas were quiet, aspidistras at the bay windows, behind the neat trimmed hedges of privet and laurel. Little over fifty years had wrought great changes, many of which were national in character, but possibly more noticeable in Aldershot, where a thriving, orderly, well-organized town had sprung from a village, through a period of bustle and toil, struggles for existence and rapid expansion. Possibly not the least remarkable was the change which had come over the habits and lives of all classes, which in turn had a beneficial effect on the development of this remarkable town, for there is no disputing that it can so be described in the light of its forty-six years progress to the turn of the century.

CHAPTER SIX

ALDERSHOT IN PEACE AND WAR

1902-1921

"PUGNA PRO PATRIA"
The motto of the Borough of Aldershot.

As the war in South Africa drew to a close, so Aldershot began to revert to its peace-time character; for although drafts and reinforcements continued to pass through "The Camp," by 1901 the returning trickle of men from the Cape grew into a steady stream.* The war as far as the public was concerned was over and, although the long-drawn-out operations continued, there were no major troop movements from "The Camp" as had marked the turn of the century. The last troops to leave Aldershot for South Africa were a draft from the Provisional Regiment of Hussars (which was composed of details of the 7th and 18th Hussars and the depot of the 20th Hussars), who entrained at the Government siding the day before peace was concluded.

Preparations for the Coronation of King Edward VII were already afoot before the Boers finally surrendered on 31st May, 1902.

In the following March, King Edward VII and Queen Alexandra were in residence at the Royal Pavilion. On Saturday, 14th June, they attended the Searchlight Tattoo in the grounds of Government House, and there the King contracted a chill. He was taken ill the following day, and was taken back to London. The announcement of the King's indisposition was made known on the Sunday evening, to the consternation and anxiety of the whole nation. The Coronation Review of all the troops in Aldershot had been arranged for Monday, 16th June. It was held despite the King's absence, the salute being taken by Queen Alexandra, and King George V, as Prince of Wales, taking part in the review. He was Colonel-in-Chief of the Royal Fusiliers, and led the 6th and 7th Battalions past the saluting base.

---

* Regiments continued to return to Aldershot throughout 1902 and 1903. The 14th King's Hussars returned to the West Cavalry Barracks (where they had been quartered at the outbreak of war) in May, 1903, and attracted some considerable attention with their baboon mascot "Kruger," which walked beside the band as they marched from the station.

The King's illness took a serious turn, and on 24th June it was announced that the Coronation Ceremony was to be postponed. It did not take place until 9th August.

King Edward's Coronation Day was marked in Aldershot by the firing of a 21-gun salute from six 5-inch howitzer guns of the 130th Battery, Royal Field Artillery, from the top of Redan Hill, the Battery, under command of Major H. Biddulph, parading in full review order. Special services were held in all the churches, and the town echoed to the strains of the National Anthem, played by military bands and sung by choirs.

The festivities which followed included a great children's "treat" in the grounds of Elm Place, and an old folk's tea. The town was gaily decorated with flags and bunting, and the shop fronts in the main streets were illuminated at night, whilst bonfires were lit on the surrounding hills.

Aldershot in Edwardian days was gay and colourful : gay, for it provided for the entertainment of the Army when "off parade" ; colourful, for full-dress uniforms were worn for all ceremonial parades and guards and for "walking out." One has become accustomed today to seeing every soldier in khaki, the only splash of colour being the maroon, green or dark blue berets ; but imagine a crowded Union Street on a Saturday afternoon with all those soldiers in scarlet or dark blue braided jackets, kilted and white-gaitered Highlanders, or the varied colours of the uniforms of the Cavalry, whose walk was accompanied by the jingle of their spurs. Khaki service dress when first introduced was allowed for "walking out" in Aldershot town as an experiment. In March, 1907, it was, however, decided to revert to the wearing of full dress.*

Practically all troop movements were accompanied by the regimental bands, and the roads of "The Camp" and the streets of the town echoed to stirring martial music—the drums and fifes of Infantry and the pipes of the Highlanders, whilst from the barracks adjoining the town, from Reveille to Lights Out, came the hourly trumpet and bugle calls.

Sunday was the great day of the week—for "Sunday in the Camps" never failed to attract and interest crowds of visitors. The weekly scene was unique in its brilliance. Church Parades were held by all units and the troops marched to the three main garrison churches— the old "Red Church" at the top of Wellington Avenue, St. George's

---

* The text of the Aldershot Command Order stated : "N.C.Os. and men when walking out must wear review order in Aldershot town, Lynchford Road and Farnborough ; elsewhere in the Command clean service dress with puttees and waistbelts (mounted corps, puttees, spurs and bandoliers) may be worn."

The familiar uniform of the Infantry of the Line, as seen in Aldershot from the eighties until August, 1914. A Sergeant and Private of The Buffs (The Royal East Kent Regiment), both wearing the Queen's and King's Medals for the South African War (1899-1902). The 1st Battalion of the Regiment was quartered in Badajos Barracks, 1908-1910.

"... but it's 'Thank you, Mr. Atkins,' when the band begins to play ..." RUDYARD KIPLING.

The Connaught Rangers marching to Church Parade along Hope Grants Road. The 2nd Bn. Connaught Rangers were stationed in Aldershot in 1888-9 and again in 1913.

"... but it's 'Special train for Atkins' when the trooper's on the tide ..." RUDYARD KIPLING.

Departure of troops from Aldershot Town Station for South Africa, 1900.

in Queen's Avenue, or the Garrison Church in Marlborough Lines. Units paraded in full dress—Hussars in their braided jackets and busbies, Lancers in their coloured plastron tunics and plumed caps, Dragoons with scarlet tunics and shining helmets, Guardsmen in their tall bearskins, bonneted and kilted Highlanders, Riflemen in their distinctive dark green uniform, and the universal scarlet tunics and spiked helmets of the Infantry of the Line. Led by the bands, the regimental detachments marched to the crowded churches of "The Camp," along routes lined by the civil population and visitors from near and far.

One was in closer touch with the military scene of the day ; columns of cavalry and infantry constantly moved along "The Camp" roads to and from the training areas and, where "The Camp" and town joined, along the line of barracks. The life of the Army constantly merged with that of the town. Most of the business of the town was identified with "The Camp," and the horse-drawn vans of the local traders plied their regular routes through the barrack lines.

Few roads were surfaced, and this led to constant clouds of dust during the summer months, thrown up by the cavalry horses, the marching infantry and the horse-drawn vans, gigs and traps which traversed the town. At this time the roadway of Wellington Avenue lay some two feet below the footpath, a grass verge sloping down between the path and the road, and this was typical of the highways in the area. Trees were more plentiful in the town, and these, in full leaf, lent a brightness to the scene. The tarmac surfacing of the main town roads was first undertaken in 1907.

Building and rebuilding continued. New business premises grew up on the vacant lots which still existed in the town centre, and the shopping area was extended along Grosvenor Road, Victoria Road and elsewhere, and new houses and roads were built to meet the requirements of the growing town. This expansion was to the east from the Redan Hill, to the west from Queen's Road, and south-wards to and beyond Church Lane East.

*   *   *   *   *

The opening of the century saw an increase in the provision of amenities in the town and the establishment of public institutions and services.

The Isolation Hospital was built in 1900, and the town's electricity undertaking was opened on 14th May, 1902, by the G.O.C., General Sir Henry Hildyard, K.C.B. Until 31st March, 1903, the undertaking had been run by the contractors, Messrs. Parker & Co. ; it was then taken over by the Urban District Council.

QI

The Municipal Buildings in Grosvenor Road were opened in 1904, together with the Fire Station, which adjoins the Municipal Offices. The original plans for the Municipal Buildings provided for a large hall at the rear, but the Council of those days were not inclined to incur the additional expenditure. Previous to this date the offices of the Urban District Council had been at No. 122 Victoria Road, the premises occupied by Messrs. Foster, Wells & Coggins. The Municipal Gardens were laid out on what was formerly known as "Clerk's Land" —the land of the Parish Clerk—between the Warren and Grosvenor Road, which was purchased by the Urban District Council from the Parish after some considerable discussion in 1895. On 13th December, 1905, called "Arbour Day," thirty-two young trees were planted in the gardens. A ceremony marked the event, which had been suggested by Mr. C. J. Harland, and was attended by the chairman and members of the Urban District Council. The trees were of all varieties— acacia, ash, lime, prunus, elm, sycamore, willow and walnut—and were given by prominent townspeople, the trees being planted by the donors.

It was in July, 1903, by virtue of the Education Act of 1902, that elementary education became the responsibility of the Urban District Council. This resulted in the formation of the Education Committee. Two years later, in 1905, the Newport Road School was opened, and on 12th September, 1912, the Aldershot County Secondary School was opened by the Earl of Northbrook, then Chairman of the Hampshire County Council.

It was also in 1912, in November, that the Roman Catholic Church of St. Joseph in Queen's Road was dedicated and opened by Bishop Cotter of Portsmouth. In the same year the first Labour Exchange was opened as a sub-office to Guildford, but in July of that year it became a District Office, covering a wide local area.

The first omnibuses had appeared in the streets of Aldershot in 1906. These were two double-deck "bone-shakers" which ran between Aldershot and Farnborough and were run by the Aldershot and Farnborough Motor Omnibus Company.* These replaced in the course of the following year the horse buses which until then plied between Farnham and Aldershot and from the Queen Hotel at the corner of Grosvenor Road to the Queen's Hotel at Farnborough.

The Aldershot and District Traction Company was formed in 1912 and bus routes were opened up between Aldershot, Fleet, Farnborough, Farnham, Ash Vale and Deepcut. The Company's first premises were

---

* These two buses were purchased in St. Leonards-on-Sea and driven to Aldershot, creating quite a sensation along the dusty lanes and in some of the small villages during the journey, which took nine hours.

in Halimote Road on the site now occupied by the N.A.A.F.I. As the Company expanded they acquired more ground, including that now occupied bounded by Grosvenor Road, which was originally a brick-yard, upon which repair shops and garages were erected.

The year 1913 saw the building of the Hippodrome at the corner of Station Road and Birchett Road, and further development of the business area of the town. The Hippodrome replaced a cluster of derelict buildings dating from the late fifties which had been con-demned and left unoccupied, surrounded by a hoarding, for a number of years. Victoria Road and Grosvenor Road, formerly residential property, began to be developed as an extension of the shopping centre, and shop fronts replaced the lower frontages of the villas which had been built in the seventies and eighties. It was in July, 1914, that the Market Arcade leading from Wellington Street to High Street was opened by Messrs. Park & Sparkhall on the site of the old Aldershot Market.

*   *   *   *   *

The Church of St. Augustine, North Town, in Holly Road, was built in 1907 by public subscription, which included a gift of £52 from King Edward VII. The foundation stone, underneath which was deposited an illustrated pamphlet describing the scheme of Aldershot church extension, was to have been laid by H.R.H. Princess Christian of Schleswig-Holstein, who at the last moment was prevented from being present. The nave and aisle of the church were dedicated on 1st November, 1907, by the Bishop of Winchester.

On 29th June, 1914, the foundation stone of St. Augustine's Church Rooms was laid by Princess Henry of Battenberg. The Princess was escorted to the church by a detachment of the 5th Dragoon Guards, and, in the absence of the Bishop of Winchester, the ceremony was conducted by the Vicar in the presence of a large crowd.

*   *   *   *   *

A fair indication of the growth* and amenities of the town in the first ten years of the century may be assessed from the following description of Aldershot taken from "A Guide to Aldershot and District," published by Gale & Polden Ltd. in 1909.

> Few places in the South of England can compare with Alder-shot in the advantages it possesses as a residential district. Situated at a high altitude in the midst of pine and heather, and adjacent to the most beautiful part of Surrey, it is almost unrivalled for health-giving and social facilities.

---

* By 1911 the population of the Aldershot Urban District was 35,175, including 15,711 military personnel in South Camp.

The proximity of the world-famed camp supplies interest and amusement for almost all classes of residents, and both in the town and the district around there are many well-built, conveniently arranged residences, which are let at rents which compare very favourably with other places of less importance and possessing fewer attractions. The rates are low, while the sanitary conditions of the town and the water supply are excellent. It was these circumstances which decided the authorities to make the permanent garrison here, and the health statistics show that their decision was a right and wise one.

Besides the numerous social advantages which appeal especially to those who have interests or associations connected with the Army, the cost of living is a question which may well decide many people in favour of residence in Aldershot.

The fact that the Army needs are so great enables traders to buy in the best markets, and not only can household provisions be bought cheaply, but luxuries of all kinds are always available and at moderate prices. Furniture and drapery establishments, jewellers, and similar traders cater for all classes of customers. Coals and all necessaries of life are comparatively cheap owing to the considerable trade done, and this circumstance may well decide those seeking a place of residence to select Aldershot. In addition there are the undeniable social advantages of Aldershot. Sport of all kinds is constantly going on in "The Camp" and district. The educational resources of Aldershot and the district are being rapidly developed. There are several high-class private schools, and the provision of a large secondary school and teachers' centre will shortly provide the necessary facilities for middle-class education.

New measures have recently been taken by the traders of the town to develop further the commercial possibilities of Aldershot. It is not generally recognized as it should be that the town offers unique facilities for shopping. A new movement which has been set on foot promises speedy developments commercially, and the remarkable growth of Aldershot will no doubt be even more marked in the future than in the past.

Aldershot continued, as it had in Victorian days, to be a centre of military pageantry, and Royal visits to the Army were a regular feature in the life of "The Camp."

In July, 1903, a Royal Review was held on Laffan's Plain, King Edward VII, accompanied by Queen Alexandra, taking the salute, with the Prince of Wales again riding at the head of the 2nd Battalion of his Regiment, the Royal Fusiliers.

In May, 1904, King George V, when Prince of Wales, was in Aldershot, and carried out inspections of troops. On Claycart Hill he watched a demonstration by a Balloon Section, R.E. A small pilot balloon was sent up to test the direction and strength of the wind. This balloon bore the W.D. mark and a request that it should be returned to the Balloon factory by the finder. It was suggested that the Princess of Wales (H.M. Queen Mary) might like to send up similar balloons addressed to the Royal Princes, and this was done, the Princess writing a message to each, these being enclosed in a stout stamped and addressed envelope affixed to the pilot balloons which the Princess released. Three of the four balloons were eventually picked up in widely separated districts in the Midlands.

In the following month the Prince was again in Aldershot when he accompanied the Archduke Frederick of Austria on a review and inspection of the 1st Army Corps.

On 23rd April, 1905, King Edward visited "The Camp," and on 8th June, 1906, the King, accompanied by King Alfonso of Spain, was in Aldershot to review some 20,000 troops of the Aldershot Army Corps. On 6th July King Edward was again in Aldershot to attend the "Aldershot Military Fête," which had then become a two-day annual event, held in the grounds of Government House. The "Military Fête" was the forerunner of the world-famous Aldershot Tattoos which followed in later years. In Edwardian days, however, the event was still very much in the nature of a fête, for in addition to the programme of military displays and sporting events, marquees were erected for refreshments and a "fair" ground was set up. In 1906 one of the main attractions was a "roundabout," described as the "steam galloping horses." An additional attraction was provided by the R.E. Balloon School, which gave ascents to the public in two captive balloons, which were drawn to earth after each ascent by winches driven by steam and petrol engines. During one flight the balloon took off so slowly that it drifted low over the crowds and ballast had to be released over their heads, to the amusement or consternation of the watchers below.

A temporary grandstand was erected with tiers of seats under a large awning, whilst other raised seating accommodation was provided by lines of G.S. wagons. The display events included an officers' jumping competition, a musical ride by the King's Dragoon Guards, an R.H.A. galloping and driving display; the Army Service Corps gave a demonstration of mounting and dismounting wagons. There was a display by the Army Gymnastic Staff, a push-ball competition, and tent-pegging by the cavalry regiment of the garrison.

An unusual (for Aldershot) attraction at the 1906 fête was a display by forty-three petty officers and seamen from H.M.S. *Victory* of life-saving, and later a field gun demonstration on the lines of the Inter-

Port Field Gun Competition as now seen annually at the Royal Tournament. The entertainment concluded with a pageant organized by Lieutenant-Colonel Ferguson, K.D.G., the pageant consisting of a march past of some forty detachments in the appropriate dress and uniforms of Britain's fighting men of all ages : the Crusaders, the archers of Agincourt, the Elizabethan men-at-arms, and so on through the ages to the detachments in the varied full-dress uniforms of the day.

Each evening, as dusk fell, a torchlight tattoo was held with massed bands of over 1,300 performers. After the grand entry of the bands, the pipers of the Highland Regiments played a strathspey and reel ; then the bands marched and countermarched, again accompanied by torch-bearers, each carrying a flaming torch which cast a bright but eerie light over the performers as they marched to the massed drums of the Foot Guards, and the massed bands of the units of the garrison. The First Post was played, followed by the Royal Salute and the National Anthem. The Last Post was then sounded by the Bugles of the Light Infantry and Rifle Regiments, and as the last brassy notes died away in the stillness, every torch was suddenly extinguished, making a dramatic conclusion to the tattoo. Searchlights were turned on to enable the crowds to disperse, who then made their way back to Aldershot and Farnborough on foot or by horse-drawn buses, traps and governess carts which clip-clopped away down the Farnborough Road, past the Officers' Club (which was rebuilt in that year), the bright oil-lit carriage lamps bobbing up and down, looking, from the Queen's Parade, like so many Chinese lanterns glowing in the darkness.

*   *   *   *   *

On 27th July, 1906, King George V, when Prince of Wales, visited Aldershot and inspected the 3rd Bn. King's Royal Rifle Corps in Salamanca Barracks and two R.H.A. Batteries in Waterloo Barracks. From there the Prince of Wales rode to Redan Hill, where he inspected the Heavy Artillery Brigade, Royal Garrison Artillery, commanded by Colonel E. G. Store. The three Batteries were drawn up on the top of the hill on the site of the old battery. The Brigade was armed with 60-pdr. breech-loading guns with a barrel length of 14 feet, the equipment weighing 39 cwt., with projectiles weighing 60 lb.

The Prince took tea on the veranda of the Officers' Club, watching a cricket match between the 2nd Bn. Seaforth Highlanders and the 2nd Bn. Royal Northumberland Fusiliers, before visiting the Balloon Factory of the Royal Engineers and spending the night at Government House as the guest of Lieutenant-General Sir John French, then G.O.C.

There was a considerable disappointment to a large crowd of spectators assembled on Laffan's Plain on the morning of 9th May, 1907, when it was learned that the Royal Review which was to take place that day had been cancelled at a few hours' notice. King Edward VII, accompanied by Prince Fushimi of Japan, was due to arrive at Farnborough in a special train from London, and the troops were already in position on parade when the news came through that the review would not take place, a decision reached in London in consequence of the heavy rain falling there early in the morning. Prince Fushimi did, however, visit Aldershot with the King three weeks later; arriving at North Camp station, the Royal party was met by General Sir John French, then G.O.C., and then moved off to the Fox Hills to watch a "sham fight" by troops of the Command. Returning to Aldershot, lunch was served at the Royal Pavilion, and the afternoon spent in touring "The Camp," visiting the Swimming Bath, where a water polo match was played by teams of the 3rd K.R.R.C., and the "Big Gym," where the Army Gymnastic Staff gave a physical training display; a visit to Blenheim Barracks, and finally to Cove Common to witness a balloon ascent by the R.E. Tea was served at Government House before the Royal visitors left for London from Farnborough station.

On 12th June, 1907, King Edward and Queen Alexandra, accompanied by the Queen of Denmark, inspected 20,000 troops on parade on Laffan's Plain; and on 26th November the King and Queen of Spain visited the 16th Lancers, then stationed in the West Cavalry Barracks, the King being the Colonel of the Regiment. King George and Queen Mary as Prince and Princess of Wales were in Aldershot on Easter Monday, 1907, to witness the final of the Army Football Cup on the Army Athletic Ground. On 16th May they were again in Aldershot when the Princess of Wales presented new Colours to the 2nd Bn. The West Yorkshire Regiment, then quartered in Malplaquet Barracks, on the Queen's Parade. During their stay the Prince and Princess were in residence at Government House, from where they toured the Command, including visits to the Balloon Factory and the Command Gymnasium, and attending an exercise, in which most units participated, in the Fox Hills.

The Annual King's Birthday Parade was held on 28th June on Laffan's Plain, the salute on this occasion being taken by Lord Roberts.

* * * * *

Aldershot has quite naturally been closely associated with every new military development. Chief among these, one may well say, was the advent of the motor-car. The first military car was purchased by the War Office in 1902, and this was dispatched to Aldershot for the use of the General Officer Commanding, Major-General Sir John French. The following War Office letter, addressed to the G.O.C.—

the original of which is still in existence, framed in the office of the G.O.C. at District Headquarters—makes interesting reading :

War Office,
London, S.W.,
21st January, 1902.

Sir,

I am directed by the Secretary of State for War to inform you that it is proposed to purchase a motor car for your use in order to facilitate the inspection of works in progress in the district under your command, and also in order that this class of vehicle may be tried as to its suitability for aiding, by its capabilities of rapid locomotion, the command of troops in the field.

2. The Secretary of the Mechanical Transport Committee has informed me that you consider that a suitable class of car would be one which would carry 6 persons, travel over rough and bad road , and surmount very considerable slopes. Such a car would be somewhat heavy, and would of necessity be one of very considerable horse-power.

3. It has been observed that, although the tendency is to increase the horse-power of cars, yet the heavy type of car carrying a considerable number of passengers is giving way to the "light car" carrying at most 4 persons, including the driver, and it is thought that though the heavy car would possibly be the better for visiting works, yet the light car will probably be found the better for the use of a general officer commanding troops in the field.

4. It is therefore proposed to at first experiment with a car of this description, and such a car is being obtained and will be dispatched to you as soon as possible. I am to ask that you will give it a thorough trial in both the above-mentioned uses, and report as soon as possible as to its capabilities, merits and defects.

I am, Sir,

Your Obedient Servant,
(*signed*) STANLEY.
President, Mechanical Transport Committee.

The use of motor vehicles in the Army had not developed very far by the outbreak of war in 1914. Cars were used only by Staff Officers and by A.S.C. motor transport companies. Civil development had progressed by greater strides, and during the 1914 mobilization many civilian vehicles, cars, vans, lorries and buses were pressed into military service during the early days of the war. There are some interesting photographs taken at the time which show lines of these requisitioned vehicles on the barrack squares and in the Long Valley, with straw-hatted and cloth-capped civilians handing them over to booted and spurred A.S.C. personnel.

It is interesting to note that nearly thirty-six years were to pass from the time of the issue of the first car to the Army in Aldershot to the year when the mechanization of all units in the Command was completed, only four regular horsed cavalry regiments remaining by the outbreak of war in 1939.*

*   *   *   *   *

It was in 1907 that the first military airship—the *Nulli Secundus*—was completed by Colonel J. E. Capper, R.E., and Mr. S. F. Cody,† who, on the 5th October of that year, with Lieut. C. M. Waterlow, R.E., made a world-record flight of 3 hours 25 minutes, from Aldershot to London. After circling St. Paul's, the *Nulli Secundus* headed for Farnborough, but with a speed of only 18 m.p.h. was unable to fight a rising head wind and landed at the Crystal Palace, where the airship was deflated three days later and dismantled. An improved pattern of the original airship—*Nulli Secundus II*—was then built. Its first flight was on the 24th July, 1908, but this lasted only eighteen minutes, and after two further flights the airship was broken up.

The year 1907 was a milestone in British aviation, for it was in that year that S. F. Cody turned his attention to aeroplanes and fitted a kite with a 12-h.p. Buchet engine. With this machine he made a free flight on Laffan's Plain. He was then permitted to borrow the engine from *Nulli Secundus II* and allowed £50 to build a full-size machine, this being called "British Army Aeroplane No. 1." On 16th May, 1908, Cody became the first man in Great Britain to fly, making a flight of fifty feet along a 400-yard clearing on Cove Common. He made five flights that day, the longest being 150 feet. In the same year,

---

* The Life Guards and Royal Horse Guards at Hyde Park and Windsor and The Royals and the Royal Scots Greys in Palestine.

† Samuel Franklin Cody was an American who became a British subject in 1909. He was a distinguished character with his imperial beard and moustache, and is described by Major C. C. Turner in "The Old Flying Days" (Sampson Low, Marston & Co. Ltd.) as an "extremely daring and original character, in turn cowboy, actor, kite inventor, balloonist and aviator. He came to England at the age of thirty-four as a 'Wild West' showman, but a few years later the public tired of this sort of show and Cody became an actor-author of a melodrama. . . ."

While touring the provinces he became interested in kite flying and carried out experiments, and in 1903 succeeded in crossing the channel in a canvas canoe, towed by one of his huge kites. The Admiralty then engaged him to demonstrate his kites for gunnery observation at Whale Island. He then conceived the idea of producing a man-lifting kite for military purposes. He was so successful with his design and his skill in handling it that he convinced the Army of its practicability—Capt. Broke-Smith, R.E., and Leon Cody both reached a height of 3,400 feet in these kites—and in 1906 Cody became Chief Instructor in "Kiting" at the Balloon School at Aldershot, charged with the formation of two kite sections of the Royal Engineers. The sections subsequently formed the nucleus of the Air Battalion R.E., which later became No. 1 Squadron, Royal Flying Corps, and finally No. 1 Squadron, R.A.F.

on 29th September, however, he flew 75 yards, and on 5th October was airborne for 496 yards at a height of 50-60 feet, but ended with a bad smash.

It was then that Mr. Haldane, Secretary of State for War, told him the War Office had decided the aeroplane had no future and that they would rely on airships. Cody's engagement was terminated, but the broken remains of his aeroplane were given to him, less the engine, and he was granted permission to use Laffan's Plain for experiments at his own expense. He set to work and rebuilt the machine, fitting it with two synchronized front elevators and installing a 60-h.p. engine. In this machine, in August, 1909, he carried his first passengers, Colonel Capper and Mrs. Cody, and on 5th September made a world-record cross-country flight of 1 hour 3 minutes. Cody's activities attracted considerable attention, and he made frequent flights over Aldershot, Laffan's Plain and the Long Valley, and on this occasion his trials were watched with interest by the Empress Eugénie accompanied by the Countess Metternich and General Sir Horace Smith-Dorrien, the G.O.C. in Aldershot.

In 1910 Cody built another machine with which he won the Michelin Cup with a flight of 4 hours 47 minutes, and in the following year constructed a smaller machine which was the only British aircraft to complete the round-England race in that year. In this race he finished fourth.

This was the aircraft which, strengthened and fitted with a 120-h.p. engine, won the Military Trials competition on Salisbury Plain in 1912. This competition was held to decide the best aeroplane for military purposes, and Cody's prize money amounted to £5,000, the machine being purchased by the Government.

Shortly after his success in these trials, Cody attended a performance at the Theatre Royal, occupying one of the boxes. At the conclusion of a topical song in which his name was mentioned, the audience called for a speech. Eventually, Mr. Cody was persuaded to step to the front of the box. In his speech he struck a serious note. He intended to go on trying, he said, to endeavour to equip machines which would be suitable in every way for war, although he did not like war; but, he continued, as soon as airmen had furthered their art he believed that they would have done something that would at least frighten people from going to war. He thought that aeroplanes would achieve this, and that was why he would not stop constructing aeroplanes and teaching others the art of flying.* Little did this great pioneer airman know, that night, what the future would bring.

Five years later his youngest son, Samuel Franklin Leslie Cody,

---

* Among his many activities Cody opened a Flying School on Laffan's Plain.

was to be killed in action as a second-lieutenant in the Royal Flying Corps whilst engaging four German aircraft, and during the late war his sons Leon and Vivian, and grandson, were to be engaged in the production of aircraft at the Royal Aircraft Establishment at Farnborough.

Samuel Cody himself was killed on 7th August, 1913, when his aircraft crashed whilst flying over Laffan's Plain. He was buried in the Aldershot Military Cemetery with full military honours, every serving man in the Royal Flying Corps, including the Naval Wing, and members of both Houses of Parliament attending the funeral.

*   *   *   *   *

The year 1910 was marked in Aldershot by a unique event which created widespread interest, for a complete unit of the Canadian Army —the 2nd Regiment of Canadian Militia, The Queen's Own Rifles of Canada—came over to England to undergo training in Aldershot. The regiment went under canvas at Rushmoor, and for a month took an active part in the life of the Command. The arrival of the regiment at gaily decorated Aldershot Town station on 27th August was marked by an official civic reception, headed by Mr. E. A. Underwood, then Chairman of the Aldershot Urban District Council; and an illuminated address of welcome, decorated with the Regimental Badge and the arms of the Dominion and of the Council, was presented to the Canadians, and received on their behalf by the Commanding Officer, Colonel Sir Henry M. Pellatt. The address read:

> We the COUNCIL of ALDERSHOT desire to offer you a cordial welcome to our Town.
>
> We admire your patriotism in coming from the Dominion of Canada to the Military Camp at Aldershot to practise the profession of Arms with the Regular Forces of His Majesty King George.
>
> We are not unmindful of the ready help given to the Mother Country by the forces of Canada in time of need, and you may rest assured that services so nobly rendered in the past were deeply appreciated by Englishmen, and the spirit of unity which was then exemplified gives us the confident hope that if ever our Empire is attacked by foes or the liberty of our Anglo-Saxon race is threatened, England with her Colonies will stand shoulder to shoulder in defending the Empire which we one and all love so well.
>
> We desire in conclusion to wish you all a very pleasant visit and every success in your most patriotic enterprise.

By 1912 the "moving picture" had taken its hold, and the first "Kinema Theatre" was opened in Aldershot at the Masonic Hall in

Station Road. This was followed in 1913 by the building of the Palace Cinema in the grounds of the Aldershot Institute. It was also in this year that the first official film of the British Army was produced. It was a documentary film depicting the military organization of the day, with the object of appealing to potential recruits and giving the citizen a better idea of the life of the Army. The film was "shot" in Shoeburyness, Hythe and Chatham, but with the greater portion in the Aldershot Command. The *première* was held at the Palace Theatre in London in January, 1914, and was attended by a considerable number of troops from Aldershot who had actually participated in its making. The film was divided into two parts, the first depicting the life and training of the soldier, the second dealing with an outbreak of war, commencing with mobilization and leading on to the theatre of operations—the Long Valley and the Fox Hills—where a set-piece battle had been filmed with Maxim guns and artillery in support of infantry, a dashing bayonet charge, and finally cavalry in pursuit.

*   *   *   *   *

King George and Queen Mary, accompanied by Princess Mary, stayed at the Royal Pavilion from 7th May to 22nd May, 1914, and saw much of the troops and the activities of the Command. It was a memorable visit, more especially so, in retrospect, for within three months the majority of the officers and men of the Aldershot Command were in France with the B.E.F. and already in action in the opening stages of the greatest war the world had ever seen.

The following extracts from the full account of the visit published in *The Aldershot News* serve as a record of the Royal interest in the life and training of the Army and give an insight into the military life of Aldershot in the closing months of peace prior to the great struggle which was soon to burst upon the civilized world.

On Sunday, 19th May, the King and Queen attended divine service at the Garrison Church of All Saints.

At the conclusion of the service Their Majesties walked down the hill to the Farnborough Road. The sight there was nothing short of marvellous. From all quarters visitors had poured into Aldershot by the thousand, filling the west end of Wellington Avenue with a dense mass of sightseers who broke into sustained cheers as Their Majesties came into view down the hill.

Taking up a position in the shade of a tree, the King watched the troops march back to the parade, each Corps being headed by a band and the scene being brilliant in the extreme. The bright sunshine playing on burnished brass helmets, waving plumes, gleaming steel and gold appointments, flashing scarlet and vivid blues, brought out the full brilliance of the martial picture, to which the stirring marches and the tramp of men added effect.

On the following Monday a Royal Review was held on Laffan's Plain, described by *The Aldershot News* reporter:

The scene was one of great brilliance and animation; the troops in all their varied uniforms were drawn up in line along the northern side of the plain. Spectators by the thousand filled the enclosure, all being in gay apparel suitable for the occasion.

The parade was a blaze of colour, the Right of the Line being taken by "J" Battery, Royal Horse Artillery, and the glitter of brass helmet with scarlet, gold and blue and crimson denoting the 1st Cavalry Brigade; next in the Line came a mass of blue where the 1st Division Artillery were drawn up, a great splash of scarlet and black fur; next the fur denoting the 1st Infantry Brigade, composed of bear-skinned guardsmen, feather bonneted Highlanders and busbied Fusiliers; another mass of red with a small scattering of green of the 60th Rifles on the flank denoting the Infantry Brigade; and then came the A.S.C.

The 2nd Division in similar order stood next in line, vivid reds and blues topped by gleaming helmet plates and fixed bayonets, carrying the eye on to the end of the line where a business-looking parade of aeroplanes was drawn up; the canvas of the byplanes and monoplanes in the distance striking quite a new feature on the parade.

In one of the enclosures was a contingent of the Officers' Training Corps from Oxford University, among them being the Prince of Wales, now a Lance-Corporal, but as the party were in very ordinary khaki they attracted no attention and the Prince was not recognized as he lay on the grass chatting with his comrades while waiting for the ceremony to open.

The parade followed the usual form with a march past at the end, with the Infantry leading, followed by the Cavalry and Royal Horse Artillery, who finally went past at a gallop—"line after line of charging horsemen sweeping past in an exhilarating charge, the whole plain appearing to be filled by the mass of swiftly moving horsemen."

Among the visitors to the Royal Pavilion during the Royal visit were Prince Leopold and Prince Maurice of Battenberg, both then serving as officers of the King's Royal Rifles; Field-Marshal Earl Haig, then Lieutenant-General Sir Douglas Haig, the G.O.C. Aldershot Command; the G.O.C. of the 1st and 2nd Divisions; the Brigade Commanders and other senior officers of the Command, many of whom—looking through the lists of the guests today—became famous national figures in the Great War which followed within three months.

During the Royal visit the Pavilion guards were mounted by the 2nd Bn. Royal Munster Fusiliers,* 2nd Bn. Highland Light Infantry,

* Disbanded 31st July, 1922.

1st Bn. Royal Berkshire Regiment, 2nd Bn. The Connaught Rangers,* and the 1st Bn. The King's Liverpool Regiment, the subaltern in command of the guard having the honour of dining with the Royal party each evening.

Before departing for London at the conclusion of the visit King George presented Lieutenant-Colonel R. H. K. Butler, who had been in attendance on His Majesty in the field, with signed portraits of himself and Queen Mary. He also decorated Squadron Sergeant-Major Pope, of the Queen's Bays, who had acted as the Royal Standard bearer, with the medal of the Royal Victorian Order, and presented Mr. Burton, the caretaker of the Pavilion, and Mr. Fairchild, the lodge keeper, with jewelled scarf-pins.

During the Royal visit it is recorded that a party of suffragettes from London paraded up and down the Farnborough Road in front of the main entrance to the Pavilion. "So long as they remained there," wrote an *Aldershot News* reporter, "no notice was taken of them except that they were the recipients of some rather rough chaff from the troops who passed them, but when they tried to get round the back of the ground they were effectively prevented by the plain clothes police on duty, who kept them off Government ground."

Their Majesties returned to London on the morning of 21st May, a guard of honour being mounted at the Pavilion by the 1st King's Royal Rifles, with their band and bugles, under the command of Major Hereward Wake, D.S.O.

The "Grand Military Searchlight Tattoo" of 1914 was held in the grounds of Government House for four days in June. The massed bands of 1,500 musicians were the highlight of this event, which was already beginning to attract visitors from all over the country and which was by then established as one of *the* events of the year in Aldershot. The 1914 Tattoo included a musical ride by the 6th Dragoon Guards, a display of Highland dancing by the Black Watch, a club swinging display by the Army Gymnastic Staff, and drill and marching displays by representative composite "guards" of Cavalry, Rifles and Light Infantry, English, Scottish, Welsh and Irish Regiments.

The days of the spectacular historic pageants and episodes in our military history which were the main features of the Aldershot Tattoo of later years were then yet to come.

The pre-war Tattoos relied mainly on the appeal of the military bands and the drilling, marching and counter-marching of troops in the glory of their full-dress uniforms. The Tattoos were even then a great attraction. The setting in the Government House grounds, with its "backcloth" of a belt of trees, formed a natural arena. The

---

* Disbanded 31st July, 1922.

terraces of the gardens were the vantage points, and the only "stands" were provided by rows of G.S. wagons drawn up along the boundaries of the Tattoo ground. Floodlit by the searchlights manned by Royal Engineers, the Tattoo was already a scene of beauty to behold.

It is unlikely, however, that many of the performers in the last of the old Tattoos lived to see the growth and development of the Aldershot Tattoo of post-war years. Eight days after the massed bands had played the National Anthem at the close of the final performance on Saturday, 20th June, in far-off Serajevo Nicholas Princep had fired the revolver shot that killed the Austrian Archduke Francis Ferdinand—a tragedy which led the performers in the Government House grounds on those four nights of June, 1914, to France, to form part of the "Contemptible little Army" which was to stand up to the weight of the attacks of Von Kluck's hordes before many weeks had passed.

The King's Birthday was celebrated in Aldershot in 1914 with a review and march past, the G.O.C., Lieutenant-General Sir Douglas Haig, taking the salute. The ceremony, although strictly in accordance with the prescribed form, and consequently differing but little from similar parades held in other garrisons at home, was, however, as brilliant and attractive as had ever been seen in Aldershot; and, as it transpired, it was the last review to be held in Aldershot of the old army in its full-dress uniforms. The parade, held on Laffan's Plain, was composed of all troops quartered in Aldershot, Deepcut, Blackdown and Woking.

* * * * *

It was at 6.30 p.m. on the evening of 3rd August, 1914, that a soldier came out of the side entrance of the Headquarter offices in Stanhope Lines and hoisted three large black balls up to the top of the tall flagstaff on the lawn outside the H.Q. building. This was the official signal for mobilization.

When the news came for mobilization, Aldershot was already well prepared. A scheme for mobilizing the troops of the Command had formed part of the regular summer training. Never before had preparations been on such an extensive scale or been made so swiftly or secretly.

Reservists poured into the town to join their units, flocking to the barracks, many without the arrival by post of the formal documents recalling them to the Colours, and there was great activity at the station, the Government siding and in the camps adjoining the town. Horses by the hundred moved into the barracks from all parts, nearly every train arriving at the station and the siding having filled horse boxes and cattle trucks attached.

The system of mobilization which had been the outcome of seven years of trial and tests worked smoothly and efficiently.

War was declared on Tuesday, 4th August, and as if by magic the troops disappeared from the streets of the town. It caused comment at the time that at the second house of the Aldershot Hippodrome on that fateful evening not one Service man was present.

The King made a fleeting visit to Aldershot during the early days of mobilization. He arrived by car direct from London, accompanied by Queen Mary, and made a tour of "The Camp" visiting every unit in the Command.

The Aldershot Territorial units were speedily mobilized, the Aldershot Troop of the Hampshire Carabiniers moving off to join their squadron at Basingstoke, and the Hants Brigade Company, A.S.C. (T.F.), joining the Wessex Division. "E" Company of the 4th Bn. The Hampshire Regiment (T.F.), commanded by Captain Hugh Foster,* had the distinction of being the first Territorial unit to be actively employed on mobilization.† The Company took over guard duties at the Royal Aircraft Factory on the day of mobilization from the Royal Munster Fusiliers, who were ordered for duty elsewhere.

Tents and marquees sprang up like mushrooms around the barracks, and the headquarters staffs were fully engaged in the giant task of mobilization.

Mobilization was far from complete when the first units left Aldershot for unknown destinations. Special precautions were taken to prevent any but a very few knowing anything concerning the destination of the troops. Not even the engine drivers taking the troop trains from the Government siding at Aldershot and from Farnborough station were informed of the train's destination until a few minutes before the signal to start was given.

"How different," wrote the Editor of *The Aldershot News*, "were the scenes at the departure of the troops to Flanders to what had been during the dispatch of troops to South Africa! There were no flags, no bands, no crowds, no cheering. There were no bands to play 'Auld Lang Syne,' and the troop trains drew out from the departure platforms with nobody except those on duty to wave them farewell."

---

* Now Sir Hugh Foster, T.D., of Messrs. Foster, Wells & Coggins. President of the Law Society, 1945-1946, and Mayor of Aldershot, 1927-1929.

† The Territorial Force which, created by the Haldane Act of 1907, was at this time represented in Aldershot by a troop of the County Yeomanry, the Hampshire Carabiniers, which had its Squadron Headquarters at Basingstoke, "E" Company of the 4th Hampshire Regiment (T.F.), and the Hants Brigade Company, A.S.C. The units had shared the Territorial Drill Hall which had been opened on Redan Hill in 1912.

In field-service uniform, prior to departure for South Africa—a trooper of the 12th Royal Lancers in the Long Valley.

Inspection of Imperial Yeomanry at Warburg Barracks before they left for South Africa, 1900.

The Royal Scots Greys passing the saluting base, where H.M. Queen Alexandra took the salute, at the Royal Review on Laffan's Plain, 16th June, 1902.

[Copyright : Gale & Polden Ltd.

R

The Army's first car. General Sir John French, General Officer Commanding, with the first car issued for experimental purposes in 1902.

Bishop Taylor Smith dedicating the R.A.M.C. South African War Memorial on Gun Hill prior to its unveiling by H.M. King Edward VII, 24th May, 1905.

H.M. King Edward VII, accompanied by H.M. Queen Alexandra, taking the salute of the 2nd Bn. The Gloucestershire Regiment at the conclusion of a field day, June, 1907.

Church Parade. The Band of The 2nd Bn. Durham Light Infantry leading the Battalion along Queen's Avenue, past St. George's Garrison Church. The 2nd Bn. D.L.I. were stationed in Aldershot on their return from the South African War, in 1902, until 1905.

The Royal Review on Laffan's Plain, 12th June, 1907. General Sir George Higginson, G.C.B., leading the 3rd Bn. The Worcestershire Regiment.

Troops of the 1st Division (4th Bn. The Manchester Regiment) marching out of Aldershot down Eggars Hill to take part in the 1905 manœuvres. Note the slouch hats worn before the introduction of S.D. caps.

". . . An' you're sent to penny fights an' Aldershot it . . ."   RUDYARD KIPLING.

The 1st Bn. Royal Welsh Fusiliers in their trenches during the "sham fight" on the occasion of the visit of Prince Fushimi of Japan, 28th May, 1907.

A push-ball match at the Aldershot Military Fête in the grounds of Government House, 1906.

The Musical Ride at the Aldershot Military Fête, 1906.

A Sergeant and a Band Boy of The Suffolk Regiment, 1904. The "Broderick" Cap they are wearing was introduced in 1902 but was worn for only two years.

Trumpeter, Royal Field Artillery, 1910.

A.S.C. General Service Wagon and Team, Review Order, circa 1908. (Drivers Ragan and Harwood 27th Coy. Army Service Corps.)

Early days of mechanization. A machine gun is fitted to a private car during the 1912 *manœuvres.*

A mobile (horse-drawn) searchlight manned by Royal Engineers, circa 1907.

The 16th The Queen's Lancers passing the saluting base on the Queen's Parade on the King's Birthday Parade, 1912.

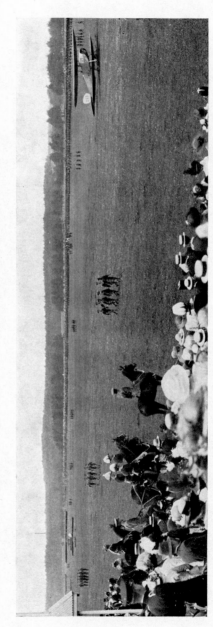

The King's Birthday Parade on the Queen's Parade, 3rd June, 1913. The March Past of the Royal Flying Corps, with the aircraft taxying past the saluting base, with ground crew detachments marching on either side.

H.M. King George V, with Staff Officers of the 1st Division, watching troops on manœuvres above the Long Valley, May, 1914.

H.M. King George V, accompanied by Lieut.-General Sir Douglas Haig, at the Royal Review on Laffan's Plain, Monday, 20th May, 1914.

H.M. King George V, H.M. Queen Mary and H.R.H. Princess Mary (The Princess Royal), accompanied by Lieut.-General Sir Douglas Haig, leaving the (Royal) Garrison Church of All Saints after Divine Service, Sunday, 19th May, 1914.

Men of Kitchener's Army : The 15th (Scottish) Division on parade in Aldershot, September, 1914.

H.M. King George V holding an investiture on the Queen's Parade, 1918. Behind the King are H.R.H. The Duke of Connaught and Sir Derek Keppel, Master of the Royal Household.

H.M. King George V and H.M. Queen Mary taking the salute at a parade of the Women's Auxiliary Army Corps on the Queen's Parade, 1918.

The body of Field-Marshal Sir Evelyn Wood, V.C., guarded by Warrant Officers and N.C.Os. of the 17th Lancers, lying in state in the Royal Garrison Church of All Saints, December, 1919.

The Hussar Brigade passing the saluting base in Queen's Avenue on the occasion of the visit to Aldershot of the Shah of Persia, Monday, 3rd November, 1919.

Captain F. Frere, M.C., leading the detachment of the Royal Tanks Corps in the march past the Shah of Persia in Queen's Avenue.

H.M. King George VI, when H.R.H. Prince Albert, in Royal Air Force uniform, with the Shah of Persia and the G.O.C., General Sir Archibald Murray, leaving the Army School of Physical Training, 3rd November, 1919.

The Rt. Hon. Winston Churchill, accompanied by the G.O.C., General Lord Rawlinson, inspecting the 4th Hussars at Willems Barracks, 4th February, 1920.

By the end of August a constant stream of troops was pouring into Aldershot, and the barracks were filling up with drafts from the various regimental depots. The East and West End Schools were requisitioned to house men of "Kitchener's Army," and the "Tin Hall" became a hostel for soldiers' wives. Already twenty-eight new Regular "service" battalions had been raised in the Command, and these new units were the basis for forming the newly created 8th (Light) Division,* which was raised at Aldershot, under the command of Major-General T. L. N. Morland, early in September, the senior Division in the New Army. The men of Aldershot and the neighbourhood, too, flocked to the colours ; during the month of August a thousand men were enrolled into the County Regiment at a recruiting office set up at the Traction Company's garage.

Three new "Reserve" Cavalry Regiments were also formed and occupied the Cavalry Barracks in Wellington Lines, whilst the camping grounds in the vicinity were occupied by Territorial units. By the end of September four more "New Army" Divisions, the 9th (Scottish), 15th (Scottish), 20th (Light)† and 23rd Divisions, had been formed in the Command.

The 30th August saw the arrival at the Government siding in Aldershot of the first hospital train from Southampton, bringing some two hundred wounded from the first actions in France. The men were taken to the Cambridge and Connaught Hospitals. From these men, Aldershot learnt first hand of the fighting at Mons and of the first days of the retreat.

It was on 8th August, 1914, that "Kitchener's Army" came into being—"Kitchener's Army," a phrase which has lasted to this day, a reminder of the great and astounding achievement, symbolizing the spirit of British determination to rise to the occasion in time of need, in the raising of the New Armies. "Your King and Country Need You," announced the recruiting posters plastered on the hoardings throughout the country. "A Call to Arms—an addition of 100,000 men to His Majesty's Regular Army is immediately necessary in the present grave National Emergency." "Lord Kitchener," the announcement added, "is confident that this appeal will be at once responded to by all those who have the safety of our Empire at Heart." The response was terrific ; it was magnificent. Thousands of men besieged the recruiting offices ; thousands stood in long, winding queues to offer their services, to enlist as soldiers of the King ;

---

* Under Army Order No. 382, dated 11th September, 1914, the 8th (Light) Division, the senior Division of the newly raised First New Army, was renumbered 14th, the reason for this being the formation from Regular troops until then forming part of overseas garrisons of the 8th (Regular) Division.

† Raised under Army Order No. 382, dated 11th September, 1914.

S

thousands waited for hours to reach even the doors of the offices—for the peace-time recruiting procedure was not designed to cope with such an inflow of recruits, and, for that matter, at that stage, neither was the Army.

As may well be imagined, Aldershot became one of the main centres for the reception and initial training of "The First Hundred Thousand," and Aldershot beheld the unusual sight of battalions of men drilling in civilian clothes. Imagine ten thousand men, all of whom had been civilians but a week or so previously, starting from scratch to become soldiers. Never before in the history of the British Army had there been such an influx of recruits. It was impossible to clothe them in uniform and equip them at once, and it took a considerable time to change the battalions of the New Army from the civilian clothes in which they enlisted into khaki. Even then the change was gradual and one saw men in old pre-war blue and scarlet uniforms, some with web equipment, others with buckskin or leather. There were men who were soldiers in every detail but for the head-dress, for a cloth cap or a trilby was still worn in place of the Service cap.

In the case of the 23rd Division, which was raised on 13th September in the Frensham area, and moved to Aldershot in December, "the civilian clothing in which the men joined was in rags by the time that emergency blue clothing was issued in the middle of October." During that month the Division was also issued with a hundred old Lee-Metford rifles to each battalion for drill, and in the following month eight Lee-Enfield rifles and 400 sets of old buff equipment, whilst in December old-pattern water-bottles and white haversacks were received.*

By December, 1914, the artillery of the 20th (Light) Division were partly clothed in full-dress blue uniforms, partly in canvas suits, and partly in thin blue suits ; the issue of khaki did not begin until February, 1915. A few horses had been issued and the available saddlery was a mixture of military, civilian, hunting and colonial. Each brigade had enough harness for only one six-horse gun team and four guns, two French 90-mm. field guns, and two 15-pdrs., but with no sights.*

One can well imagine, therefore, why Aldershot soon heard in consequence the words of a new song, "We are Fred Karno's Army,"† which echoed along the roads to the camp in the late evening as

---

* *Vide* "The History of the Great War—Order of Battle of Divisions" (Part 3A), 1938. (H.M.S.O.)

† Sung to the air of "The Church's one Foundation." Fred Karno was a popular comedian of the day. In his show "The Mumming Birds" his performance raised laughs by its incompetence and imbecility ("Songs and Slang of the British Soldier, 1914-18") (Eric Partridge Ltd.) (1931).

the men, with the irrepressible humour of the Service man, young or old, and with complete disdain for heroics of any kind, made fun of himself in his serious job of becoming a soldier ; but become soldiers they did, and the new Army—Kitchener's Army—grew day by day in strength and stature to take its place in the line in Flanders and on Gallipoli before twelve months had passed.

The King and Queen again visited Aldershot at the end of September, when, accompanied by Lord Kitchener, they spent several days at the Royal Pavilion, and during which time the Royal party visited troops throughout the Command, inspecting the 14th (Light) Division* and the 15th (Scottish) Division on the Queen's Parade on 26th September. This was the first occasion on which the 15th (Scottish) Division had paraded as a formed unit, and, with the exception of the staff, the Division paraded in civilian clothes.†

On his departure the King sent the following message to the General Officer Commanding-in-Chief :

ROYAL PAVILION.
September 30th.

During my stay at Aldershot I have realized with pleasure the keen and thorough spirit animating the daily life and work of the troops. The physical standard is creditable and all ranks are striving to become efficient for the war. All I have seen and heard shows the progress in the training of my soldiers is satisfactory.

On 22nd January, 1915, Field-Marshal Lord Kitchener was in Aldershot, accompanied by M. Millerand, the French Minister of War, and he inspected in heavy rain the 15th (Scottish) Division, commanded by Major-General C. J. Mackenzie, and the 23rd Division, under the command of Major-General J. M. Babington, on the Queen's Parade. On this occasion the 23rd Division paraded in pre-war blue serge uniforms and civilian great coats, whilst the infantry were "armed" with drill-purpose rifles and the 15th Division had sufficient obsolete drill rifles to "arm" the front ranks of the battalions.

In 1915 the King again visited Aldershot and stayed at the Royal Pavilion, the guard being provided by a battalion of National Reserve men then quartered in Blenheim Barracks. The total age of the twenty-five men selected for the guard was 1,191 years, with service aggregating 414 years between them ; they possessed 49 medals with

---

* The Division moved into billets around Guildford and Godalming in November, but returned to Stanhope Lines in February, 1915, where they remained until joining the B.E.F. three months later.

† *Vide* "The History of the Great War—Order of Battle of Divisions" (Part 3A), 1938. (H.M.S.O.)

96 clasps. It was during this stay that the King received Lord Kitchener, who was soon to meet his death at sea.

With the departure of the B.E.F. the forces intended for Home Defence were organized into a group of armies designated "General Force," later changed to "Central Force." This force was made up of a Mounted Division and three Armies, Aldershot being the H.Q. of the Second Army, commanded by Lieutenant-General the Hon. Sir F. W. Stopford, until November, 1914, when it moved to Tunbridge Wells.

As the war years passed by, Aldershot remained unchanged except that its military population came and went. Raw recruits from factories, farms and offices throughout the length and breadth of the United Kingdom arrived in "The Camp," to emerge but a few months later trained and equipped to meet the enemy. In full marching order columns of troops moved down to the railway on the first stages of their journeys to Ypres, the Somme, Gallipoli, Palestine, Salonika and Mesopotamia. The Aldershot military machine was geared into competing with the Nation's requirements to ensure eventual victory. It is recorded that some three million troops were stationed in and around or passed through Aldershot during the war years.

The King and Queen made further visits to Aldershot to inspect troops in the Command in 1916 and again in 1917, when the King held an investiture on the Queen's Parade, when he presented 259 medals and decorations for gallantry. In June, 1918, the King was again in Aldershot and, after inspecting troops in training in the Long Valley and on Laffan's Plain, held an open-air investiture on Queen's Parade when two officers, Major-Generals C. Lowther and H. Tagart, received the accolade of knighthood, and an Aldershot townsman, Captain A. M. Toye, of the Middlesex Regiment, was decorated with the Victoria Cross. It is interesting to record that on this occasion the guard of honour was provided by the Royal Marine Light Infantry and the band by the Portsmouth Division of the Royal Marines.

*   *   *   *   *

At 11 a.m. on 11th November, 1918, "The Camp" siren was sounded to signify the cessation of hostilities. Aldershot had been eagerly awaiting for several hours this official signal of the signing of the Armistice. Flags and bunting held in readiness appeared at the windows of shops and offices, and townsmen came out into the streets, slightly bewildered at the momentous news and the significance of the occasion. Soon groups of soldiers from "The Camp" began to march down into the town, singing and waving flags. Gradually the magnitude of the event dawned upon both townspeople and soldiers,

and the streets began to fill with happy, jostling crowds. By midday
most of the shops had closed, church bells were ringing, the siren of
the Wellington Works was sounding at regular intervals, fog signals
banged from the railway in a *feu de joie*, and civilians and soldiers alike
gave themselves over to unbounded exhibitions of joyous enthusiasm.
Bands played, patriotic songs were sung, there were bursts of cheering ;
the public-houses did an uproarious trade. Vans and cars wending
their way through the town were set upon by cheering crowds who
climbed on to the running boards and roofs to proceed through the
streets, singing and shouting in this outburst of wild and unbounded
joy at the great news. In "The Camp" the G.O.C. came out on the
balcony to address the crowds of troops that thronged around the
Headquarters Offices. His words were drowned in the cheers that
echoed through Stanhope Lines, ending in the spontaneous singing of
the National Anthem.

And so peace came to Aldershot,* but the life of both town and camp
changed but little in consequence. Troops still moved off from the
Government siding, drafts for the Rhine, India, and Ireland ; drafts
to replace the demobilized troops who were returning to England.
There was still the passage of horses, equipment and stores. The
tempo of the military life of Aldershot increased rather than slackened
in the winter of 1918 and the spring of 1919. There was still much for
the Army to do, and much emanated from "The Camp."

*   *   *   *   *

On 6th December, 1919, the funeral of Field-Marshal Sir Evelyn
Wood, V.C., G.C.B., G.C.M.G., took place in Aldershot. He had
died at Harlow, Essex, but was brought to the town to be buried in
the Military Cemetery with his wife, who was buried there when she
died at Government House in 1891 whilst the Field-Marshal was
G.O.C.-in-C. Prior to the funeral his body lay in state in the Royal
Garrison Church of All Saints under guards mounted by the Royal
Horse Guards, 13th Hussars and the 17th Lancers. A salute of nineteen
guns boomed out from a battery on the summit of Redan Hill as the
funeral cortège passed down Wellington Avenue and along High
Street, to the music of the Dead March from "Saul." The coffin,
covered by a Union Jack on which rested the Field-Marshal's plumed
hat and sword, was borne on a gun carriage and was escorted by eight
squadrons of cavalry and six battalions of infantry. Behind the coffin
walked Lord Stamfordham and Lord Tweedsmouth, carrying cushions

---

* A "Welcome Home" Reception and Dinner for the ex-Service men of the
Borough was held in the Maida Drill Hall on 8th May, 1920. The G.O.C., General
Lord Rawlinson, was present, and the Address of Welcome was read by Mr. H.
Ainger.

on which were laid the decorations, insignia and medals of the dead Field-Marshal; following them, a black charger draped in purple cloth, with boots reversed in the stirrups, was led by an N.C.O. of The Blues. Many distinguished soldiers were present, including Field-Marshal Earl Haig and Sir Philip Chetwode, whilst the pall-bearers included Field-Marshals Lord Grenfell and Lord Methuen, General Lord Rawlinson, General Sir Ian Hamilton and General Sir Archibald Hunter.

It was a solemn but impressive occasion, with the dull thud of the muffled black draped drums, the tramp of men slow-marching, with arms reversed, the grand but mournful music of the bands, and the boom of the guns firing their last salute to the great soldier.

The Army paid their last tributes to the only British Field-Marshal to be laid to rest in the home of the British Army.

One of the first ceremonial parades held in Aldershot after the war was on the occasion of the visit of the Shah of Persia, accompanied by H.M. King George VI, when Prince Albert, who on this occasion wore the then new uniform of the Royal Air Force. The Shah arrived in Aldershot, from Buckingham Palace where he stayed during his official visit, on Monday, 3rd November, 1919, an overcast, dreary day which, however, did not detract from the impressive parade and march past in the Shah's honour. He was received by the G.O.C. of the Command, General Sir Archibald Murray, at Government House, where the guard of honour was mounted by the 1st Bn. Northumberland Fusiliers,* and a 21-gun salute was fired from Cove Plateau in the rear of Government House. Proceeding to the Queen's Parade, the Shah took up his position in a small covered stand facing Queen's Avenue, above which flew the Persian Imperial Standard, and here he witnessed the march past and took the salute from a Division commanded by Major-General R. H. K. Butler, K.C.B., K.C.M.G. The Division, of which nearly every man had seen active service in the war, marched past in column of route, led by the Royal Artillery Mounted Band, and a Cavalry Brigade commanded by Brigadier-General J. Vaughan, C.B., C.M.G., D.S.O., and composed of three regiments of Hussars—the 3rd King's Own, the 4th, and the 13th.† The Cavalry were followed by a mixed Brigade of Artillery composed of a battery of 18-pdrs., a battery of 4.5-inch howitzers, a section of 60-pdrs., and a section of 6-inch howitzers, the latter being tractor drawn—a rare

---

* The same battalion which twenty-five years previously had provided the guard of honour at Aldershot station on the arrival of the Kaiser (see p. 102).

† The first Hussar Brigade ever to be quartered in Aldershot. The Brigade was, however, broken up in 1921, when the 3rd Hussars were dispatched to Constantinople, and the 4th Hussars to India (Muttra).

sight even in the year immediately following the 1914-18 war. The Gunners were followed by the 1st Field Company, R.E., with horse-drawn tool carts and pontoons. Three Brigades of Infantry followed,* each of four regular battalions, at full strength, an imposing sight in battle order, wearing web equipment and steel helmets. After rank upon rank of marching infantry had passed by, the rear of the divisional column was brought up by a company of R.A.S.C. and a detachment of the Royal Tank Corps, composed of two green, grey and brown camouflaged tanks, under the command of Captain F. Frere, M.C.

At the conclusion of the march past, the Shah crossed the road to watch a massed gymnastic display in the "Big Gym" by the Army Gymnastic Staff. This was followed by an official luncheon at the Officers' Club before the Royal party left for Farnborough Aerodrome, and later for Sandhurst.

Earlier in the year, in May, H.R.H. Prince Aage of Denmark had spent a five-day visit to the Command; and Aldershot witnessed another Royal visit on 17th May, 1921, when His Imperial Highness the Crown Prince Hirohito of Japan visited the Command and received a welcome that was "equally hearty and cordial as that which he was accorded on arriving in England." The Crown Prince, wearing the uniform of a British General, and his suite arrived in Queen's Avenue by car, the route, strange as it may seem for the great military centre, being lined by men of the Royal Fleet Reserve, who were in camp at Tweseldown following their call up, under the Royal Proclamation, during the labour disorders following the 1921 coal strike. Prince Hirohito was received by the G.O.C.-in-C., Lieutenant-General The Earl of Cavan. As he stepped from his car the Japanese National Anthem was played by the band of the Coldstream Guards. The Japanese Imperial Standard was broken at the masthead of a staff set up near the Royal Stand, and he received the Royal Salute from the guard of honour of the 2nd Bn. Coldstream Guards, whilst a salute of twenty-one guns was fired by the 37th Battery, Royal Field Artillery.

Among the Prince's suite were Prince Kan-in, Admiral Takeshita, Lieutenant-General Takeji Nara, the Marquis Koamatsu, and Count Yoshinori Futara. The Royal visitor inspected the guard of honour and then took the salute as the Battalion under the command of

---

* 1st Brigade, commanded by Brigadier-General H. C. Jackson, C.B., D.S.O., composed of 1st Bn. Royal West Surrey Regiment, 1st and 2nd Bns. Manchester Regiment, and the 2nd Bn. Royal Dublin Fusiliers. 2nd Brigade, under command of Brigadier-General R. O'H. Livesay, C.M.G., D.S.O., made up of four Scottish Battalions, the 2nd Bn. Royal Scots Fusiliers, 1st Bn. Highland Light Infantry, 2nd Bn. Queen's Own Cameron Highlanders, and 2nd Bn. Argyll and Sutherland Highlanders. 3rd Brigade, commanded by Brigadier-General F. W. Ramsay, C.B., C.M.G., D.S.O., composed of the 1st Bn. Lancashire Fusiliers, 1st Bn. South Wales Borderers, 2nd Bn. The Loyal Regiment, and 2nd Bn. The Rifle Brigade.

Lieutenant-Colonel C. P. Heywood, C.M.G., D.S.O., marched past in companies.

The Prince then visited the Headquarters Gymnasium, where the parallel and horizontal bars and vaulting horse were decorated by entwined Japanese flags and Union Jacks, to witness a physical training display. From here he was driven to the Command Supply Depot, and from there to Farnborough Aerodrome. An official luncheon was held at the Officers' Club, after which he departed for Sandhurst after a final Royal Salute from the Coldstream Guards drawn up in front of the Club.

Aldershot was depleted of troops during "The Troubles" in Ireland, and in January, 1921, following the departure of the 2nd Bn. East Surrey Regiment from Mandora Barracks to Ireland, not a single battalion of infantry remained in South Camp, and yet more men in drafts continued to move to the scene of the disturbances. In July of that year possibly the last units of Mounted Rifles ever to be raised were formed in Aldershot: 1st and 2nd Regiments of The Royal Artillery Mounted Rifles, the former composed of Gunners drawn from South Camp and Bordon, the latter from other R.A. units in North Camp and Deepcut. These regiments, each nearly 600 strong, were also dispatched to Southern Ireland.

By the end of the year, however, with the ratification of the Irish peace, troops were returning to Aldershot, and by the spring of 1922 ten Regular infantry battalions were back in "The Camp."

The labour troubles following the great coal strike in 1921 led to the calling up of the Army Reserve on Saturday, 19th April, by a Royal Proclamation which also approved the formation of a Citizens' Defence Force. Over six hundred reservists arrived in Aldershot on the same day. On the Sunday a further 3,600 arrived, followed on Monday by some 4,500. The total number of reservists, mainly Gunners and R.A.S.C., reporting to Aldershot totalled some 11,000 men, and in addition men of the Royal Fleet Reserve were embodied at Tweseldown Camp. This sudden influx of men, in the absence of so many Regular units in Ireland, animated the town. This embodiment, however, had one unfortunate sequel. Among the reservists were a small number of malcontents, and after a time in Aldershot they broke out and rioted in the town. Organized by a small body of extremists, a meeting was held on the evening of Saturday, 7th May, at the foot of Gun Hill, when seditious speeches were made by the agitators and ringleaders. Fanning the ill temper of the extremists, the men, waving a red flag, set off to march through the town, along Union Street, Wellington Street and Victoria Road, leaving a scene of destruction in their wake, damaging property, smashing the plate glass windows of the shops and looting. A bus was set upon and several townspeople and other soldiers hustled and attacked. The rioting was confined to little under two hundred, and the disturbance was quelled by the military and civil police, reinforced by picquets from "The Camp." Precautions were immediately taken to prevent such an occurrence, and on the following day the town was placed "out of bounds," all troops confined to barracks, whilst mounted cavalry picquets patrolled the centre of the town. The prompt action by the military authorities prevented any further trouble, which was proved to have been fermented by a small, dangerous element of reservists from the seat of the troubles.

Unique in the annals of Aldershot was the Naval Review held in the Long Valley on 13th May, 1921, when General the Earl of Cavan inspected the four battalions of the Royal Fleet Reserve embodied under the Royal Proclamation of 9th April, then in camp at Tweseldown—the 1st and 2nd Nore and 1st and 5th Portsmouth Battalions, under the command of Commander Box, R.N. The Bluejackets, wearing their naval uniforms with khaki web equipment, paraded in line of battalions in quarter column and received the G.O.C. with the General Salute. After the inspection the battalions marched past by companies, headed by the battalion naval bands. It was an unusual ceremony for Aldershot, so essentially military, to witness such a naval parade, and it was watched by a more than usually large crowd of interested spectators.

*   *   *   *   *

Slowly the town and camp reverted to peace-time conditions and gradually the life of Aldershot became once again that of the normal pre-war garrison town, with, however, one fundamental change: khaki predominated in the Aldershot scene. Gone for ever, except for the bands and on the occasions of the Tattoos, were the full-dress uniforms. Gone was the ubiquitous scarlet tunic which had been so much a part of the local scene for over sixty years, and with the passing of this military colour went, too, an era of soldiery—the Kiplingesque soldier, who was so true to the type nurtured in Aldershot for over half a century. The post-war army, tempered by war of a different character to any of the past, bore a different stamp which had its effect upon not only the Army but on the town.

The 1921 census showed a population of 28,754, including 9,501 military—the lowest number of troops in "The Camp" for over forty years. The drop in the regular military population was due to the absence of troops in Ireland and the number of troops stationed abroad in overseas garrisons and the armies of occupation following the

1914-1918 war. The drop of 191 in the civil population figures
between 1911 and 1921 was attributed to the absence of wives and
families of soldiers serving abroad and elsewhere, but Aldershot was
taking on a new lease of life, not only in the rebuilding of the post-
war Army but in the strides then being made towards the raising of
the civic status of the town. Aldershot was then on the threshold of
a fuller life, for the town had grown to full stature through three
major wars in the preceding seventy-five years.

CHAPTER SEVEN

THE BOROUGH OF ALDERSHOT
AND ALDERSHOT COMMAND AND DISTRICT
1922-1950

*The Civilian and Military Residents in the newly incorporated
Borough of Aldershot assembled to receive the Charter so
graciously approved by Your Majesty, unanimously resolve to
record their unswerving loyalty, and profound gratitude for the
honour conferred upon Aldershot Town and the great Military
Command within the boundaries of the new Borough.*

From the Charter Day Resolution
proposed on the 21st of June, 1922,
by the Mayor-Elect of Aldershot,
Mr. Arthur H. Smith.

IT was in February, 1917, that a Development Committee was formed,
with the object of developing and promoting the interests of
the town as a residential and trading centre. It was felt by this Committee that steps should be taken to obtain a Charter of Incorporation, and a deputation from the Committee interviewed the Urban
District Council, asking the town authority to take the initial step.
This took the form of the appointment of an Incorporation Committee
composed initially of members of the Council and the Development
Committee. Within a week the Incorporation Committee* held its

---

* The Incorporation Committee was fully representative of all the town's public
bodies. The Chairman was Mr. Arthur H. Smith, the Vice-Chairman Mr. H.
Ainger, the Honorary Secretary Mr. D. Llewellyn Griffiths, O.B.E., and the
Honorary Treasurer Mr. F. A. Darracott. The members were : Councillors J. R.
Attfield, H. Baker, J. Edwards, H. M. Foster (now Sir Hugh Foster), S. Friend,
E. G. Hawkins, W. J. May, M. B. Simes, R. Simmonds, J.P., N. Solomon, R. J.
Snuggs, J.P., E. A. Underwood and A. Willis ; Mrs. Fullbrook, Mrs. Kent, Mrs.
Phelps ; Colonel J. M. Young, C.M.G., D.S.O. ; Major C. B. Walker, O.B.E. ;
and Messrs. W. J. Applin, G. H. Bearcock, R. Barnes, F. Bateman, C. A. L. Calvert,
J. R. Colyer, J. T. Coggins, G. W. Chandler, A. W. Cooke, J. Coombes, S. Danpure,
W. G. Eddy, R. A. Garratt, A. Gregory, J.P., A. D. Gascoigne, J. H. Gilmore,
C. J. Harland, G. Kemp, E. Kingham, H. R. Kipling, A. T. Maling, J. J. Morton,
C. J. Penny, C. F. Roelich, J. Rattray, J. Rogers, C. S. Seager, E. J. Sercombe,
A. H. J. Stroud, C. Snow and F. Watters.

first meeting, and the Committee was then enlarged by the addition of representatives of every organized body in the town. Preliminary work and investigations having been carried out, the committee then ceased its work until the conclusion of the war.

It was on Monday, 26th January, 1920, that a public meeting was held in the Y.M.C.A. Hall in Station Road, and the following resolution was submitted by Mr. Arthur H. Smith, then President of the Chamber of Commerce :

> "That this meeting of ratepayers and inhabitant householders of Aldershot convened by the Chairman of the Aldershot Urban District Council [then Mr. S. Friend, J.P.] is strongly in favour of obtaining a charter of Incorporation for the Urban District of Aldershot, and pledges itself to do all possible in preparing and submitting a petition to His Majesty in Council to grant a Charter of Incorporation creating the Urban District of Aldershot a Municipal Borough and to extend to such Borough and to the inhabitants thereof all the powers, privileges and provisions of the Municipal Corporations Act."

There was an overwhelming vote in favour of the resolution, and in consequence it was decided to proceed with the application.

Having ascertained that the War Office had no objection to the application and that every organization in the town supported the plan, a public meeting was held in January, 1920 ; of an attendance of over three hundred, there were only fifteen votes against the proposal, and sufficient money was guaranteed at the meeting to meet the expenses of promoting the Charter.

In due course the petition was prepared and householders were invited to sign it. There were, at the time, 3,690 householders in the town, of whom 2,366 signed the petition, showing that sixty per cent. of the population were in favour of Incorporation. The petition was then finally prepared and presented to the Privy Council.

A public inquiry was held on 25th February, 1921, by Mr. T. R. Colquhoun Dill, Barrister-at-Law, the commissioner appointed by the Privy Council, the case for Aldershot being conducted by Mr. D. Llewellyn Griffiths, O.B.E., then Clerk to the Urban District Council, the witnesses being Mr. Arthur H. Smith, Chairman of the Incorporation Committee and Mayor-Elect, and Mr. H. Ainger, then Chairman of the Urban District Council and Deputy Mayor-Elect. The petition with the 2,366 signatures was presented, as was also another petition against Incorporation, but this contained only twenty-two signatures.

It was on 23rd March, 1922, that the Charter for the Incorporation of Aldershot as a Municipal Borough was signed by King George V.

The Charter specified the number of Aldermen and Councillors composing the Corporation and their method of election and the order of retirement. It set out the boundaries of the Borough and its division into wards. It was signed by the Lord Privy Seal with His Majesty's seal affixed in red wax. The Charter was printed on parchment and bound with red ribbon. The text was as follows :

GEORGE THE FIFTH by the Grace of God of the United Kingdom of Great Britain and Ireland and of the British Dominions beyond the Seas King, Defender of the Faith :

To all to whom These Presents shall come, Greeting

WHEREAS certain Inhabitant Householders of the Urban District of Aldershot, in the County of Southampton, did in the month of July, One Thousand Nine Hundred and Twenty, Petition Us for the grant of a Charter of Incorporation :

AND WHEREAS such Petition was referred by Us to a Committee of Our Privy Council and one month at least before the same was taken into consideration by the said Committee notice thereof and of the time when the same was to be taken into consideration was duly published in the *London Gazette* and otherwise as directed by the Committee :

AND WHEREAS pursuant to Section 56 of the Local Government Act, 1888, notice of the said Petition was given to the County Council of the County of Southampton, and was also sent to the Minister of Health, and Our Privy Council have considered such representations as were made by the said County Council and the Minister of Health together with the Petition for such Charter :

AND WHEREAS Our Privy Council have recommended Us to grant a Charter of Incorporation to the Inhabitants of the said Urban District of Aldershot :

WE THEREFORE, as well by virtue of Our Royal Prerogative as in pursuance of and in accordance with the Municipal Corporations Act, 1882, or any other Act or Acts, and of all powers and authorities, enabling Us in this behalf, by and with the advice of Our Privy Council, do hereby grant, order and declare as follows :

1. The District comprised within the limits set forth in Part 1 of the First Schedule to these Presents is thereby created a Municipal Borough by the name of the "Borough of Aldershot."

2. The Inhabitants of the said district comprised within the said limits and their successors shall be and are hereby declared to be one Body, politic and corporate, by the name of "The Mayor, Aldermen and Burgesses of the Borough of Aldershot," with perpetual succession and a Common Seal, and may assume Armorial Bearings (which shall be duly enrolled in the Heralds'

College) and may take and hold any lands, tenements and hereditaments which may be vested in them by any Scheme made under Part XI of the Municipal Corporation Acts, 1882, and such other lands, tenements and hereditaments as well without as within the Borough as may be necessary for the site of the buildings and premises required for the official purposes of the Corporation, and other purposes of the Municipal Corporation Acts, provided that such last mentioned lands, tenements and hereditaments shall not exceed in the whole in value £5,000 by the year, according to the values of the same at the time or times when they shall be respectively taken or acquired.

3. The Mayor, Aldermen and Burgesses of the said Borough shall have the powers, authorities, immunities and privileges usually vested by law in the Mayor, Aldermen, and Burgesses of a Municipal Borough, and the provisions of the Municipal Corporation Acts shall extend to the said Borough and the Inhabitants thereof incorporated by this Charter.

4. The number of the Councillors of the Borough shall be twenty-one, which number shall be inclusive of three military representatives appointed on the Council as members thereof by the Secretary of State for War under and by virtue of the powers vested in him by the Public Health Supplemental Act for Aldershot, 1857, and under the powers of this Charter which shall be deemed to confer a power so to appoint.

5. The Borough shall be divided into three Wards with the names, metes and bounds specified in Part II of the first Schedule to these Presents.

6. Each of the Wards shall elect six Councillors.

7. For the purpose of making the Municipal Corporations Act, 1882, applicable, and for the purpose of bringing into full existence and activity the said Corporation and Borough, and completely carrying into effect the Incorporation by these Presents intended, We do hereby, as far only as regards the first election and the first appointment of Town Clerk, and Treasurer for the said Borough, and matters connected therewith, fix and order, direct and declare as follows:

8. If any register of local government electors for any area affected by this Charter is not so framed as to show the persons entitled to vote at an election to be held for a ward or other electoral division the Acting Town Clerk shall make such alteration or rearrangement of the register as may be necessary for the purposes of such election.

9. The outer door of the Municipal Buildings, Aldershot, shall be the place at which any list, notice or document required to be publicly exhibited, exposed or affixed, is to be affixed.

10. Both in relation to the matters aforesaid and also in relation

to any such election as aforesaid which it may be necessary to hold before an election can be held wholly in accordance with the Municipal Corporations Act, 1882, David Llewellyn Griffiths of Aldershot aforesaid Solicitor, or, in the case of his death, inability, refusal, or default, Frederick Hamilton Dominey of Aldershot aforesaid Accountant, shall perform the duties of Town Clerk, and further the said David Llewellyn Griffiths or Frederick Hamilton Dominey (as the case may be) shall be for all purposes whatsoever Town Clerk of the said Borough, and perform all the duties which would be performed by the Town Clerk thereof under any law or statute until a Town Clerk has been duly appointed, in accordance with the Municipal Corporations Act, 1882, and Arthur Herbert Smith of Morningside, Aldershot, Company Manager, or in the case of his death, inability, refusal, or default, Henry Ainger, of 1, Victoria Road, Aldershot, Justice of the Peace, shall perform the duties of the Mayor and Aldermen respectively as Returning Officer, and of the Mayor as Summoner of the first Meeting of the Council, and of the Mayor or Chairman of the meeting for the election of the Mayor and Aldermen, and the appointment of the Town Clerk and Treasurer, and all the said persons shall be substituted in the Municipal Corporations Act, 1882, for the said Town Clerk, Mayor, Aldermen, and Chairman respectively so far as relates to the matters aforesaid and the said persons shall have the like powers and perform the like duties and be subject to the like obligations and penalties in all respects as the officers or persons whose duties they have under the directions aforesaid to perform, by law respectively have to perform and are subject to.

11. The first Meeting of the Council of the Borough shall be held at noon on the Ninth day of November, One thousand nine hundred and twenty-two.

12. The first Councillors of the Borough shall be elected on the First Day of November, One thousand nine hundred and twenty-two, and the first Mayor and Alderman on the Ninth day of November, One thousand nine hundred and twenty-two.

13. The years and the days specified in the second Schedule to these Presents shall be the years and days for the retirement of the first Mayor, Aldermen, and Councillors (other than the three Councillors to be appointed by the Secretary of State for War) who shall retire in the manner and at the times therein designated. The three Councillors to be appointed by the Secretary of State for War shall respectively hold office for the period for which they are appointed.

14. Subject to the provisions and directions of these Presents and the Schedules thereto the provisions of the Municipal Corporations Act, 1882 (so far as unrepealed) and the Acts amending the same and the existing law relating to the registration of local

government electors, and to Electors and Elections in Municipal Boroughs, shall apply to the nominations, elections, and continuance in office of the first Mayor, Aldermen and Councillors, and the appointment and continuance in office of the first Town Clerk and Treasurer, the first meeting of the Town Council, and all matters and things touching and concerning the above ; and the dates and times in the said Act mentioned in that behalf shall be (subject as aforesaid) the dates and times on or during within or for which matters aforesaid and the various acts and things in relation thereto shall take place, be done, be estimated, or be calculated.

15. Except so far as is necessary for carrying out the first election of Councillors for the Borough this Charter shall not come into effect, nor shall the Municipal Corporation Acts extend or apply to the Borough until the first Meeting of the Council.

THE FIRST SCHEDULE

PART I

DESCRIPTION OF THE BOROUGH

The Borough shall comprise the Parish of Aldershot being the present District of the Urban District Council of Aldershot.

PART II

NAMES AND METES AND BOUNDS OF EACH WARD

Ward No. I (or West Ward) shall comprise that part of the Urban District and Parish of Aldershot which is bounded as follows, that is to say, by a line commencing at the point at which a line passing along the middle of the London and South Western Railway (Aldershot Branch) intersects the southern boundary of the said Urban District and Parish, thence proceeding in a north-easterly direction along the middle of the said railway to the point of intersection by a line passing along the middle of Church Lane East, thence proceeding in a north-westerly direction along the middle of Church Lane East to the Junction of Church Lane East with Grosvenor Road, thence proceeding along the middle of Grosvenor Road to the junction of Grosvenor Road with Barrack Road, then proceeding in a southerly direction along the middle of Barrack Road to the junction of Barrack Road with Alexandra Road, then proceeding in a westerly direction along and thereafter following the middle of Alexandra Road to the junction of Alexandra Road with Farnborough Road, thence proceeding in a south-westerly direction along the middle of Farnborough Road to the boundary of the said Urban District

Charter Day Celebrations, 21st June, 1922.
"E" Battery, R.H.A., passing through Wellington Street.

The Band of the 2nd Bn. Grenadier Guards marching along Wellington Street, leading the Charter Day procession to the Manor Park.

T

H.R.H. Prince Henry (H.R.H. The Duke of Gloucester) at the unveiling of the Aldershot War Memorial in the Municipal Gardens, 18th March, 1925.

The unveiling of the War Memorial of the 8th Division in Queen's Avenue.

The unveiling of the 2nd Division War Memorial at the junction of Hospital Hill and Queen's Avenue, December, 1923.

The 1st Bn. Grenadier Guards marching past H.M. King George V and Queen Mary at the main gate of the Royal Pavilion en route to manœuvres, May, 1928. In the foreground is Major F. A. Magnay, M.V.O., commanding No. 3 Company.

A typical Sunday in Wellington Avenue in the early thirties. Detachments, led by the Band, leaving the Royal Garrison Church of All Saints at the conclusion of the 11 a.m. parade service.

An Argyll and Sutherland Highlander (2nd Bn.) in Battle Order on the Parade Ground of Blenheim Barracks, 1920.

Drummer and Company Sergeant-Major of the 4th Bn. The Worcestershire Regiment, 1920, shortly before the Regiment left for the Rhine.

A Lance-Corporal of the 7th Queen's Own Hussars in Field Service Marching Order, 1932.

Changing of the Guard. The 2nd Bn. The East Yorkshire Regiment, Malplaquet Barracks, North Camp, August, 1927.

An Assault-at-Arms. Physical Training Display by the Army Physical Training Corps in the Fox Gymnasium, December, 1935.

SPORT IN THE COMMAND

Out with the Otter Hounds.

The Aldershot Command Beagles moving off from the grounds of the Officers' Club.

Tweseldown Race-course.

The 7th Queen's Own Hussars, in full-dress uniform, on the parade ground of Willems Barracks, 1932. The Regiment was stationed in Wellington Lines, 1931-1933.

"They used to talk about Lancers once,
Hussars, Dragoons an' Lancers once,
'Elmets, pistols an' Carbines once . . ."
RUDYARD KIPLING.

The Departure of the Horses. Artillerymen leading their mounts along Station Road, 1936.

The general view of the Silver Jubilee Review in Rushmoor Arena, Saturday, 13th July, 1935. Infantry of the 1st Division marching past King George V at the saluting base in column of companies.

The Aldershot Show in 1937. A general view of Rushmoor Arena during the Musical Ride by the Royal Scots Greys.

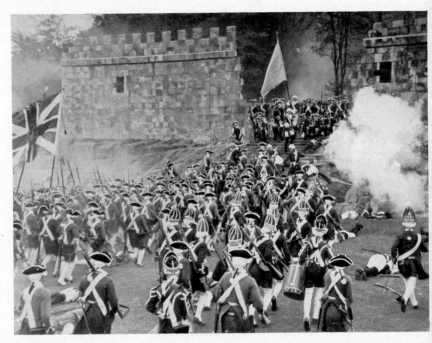

Typical of the many spectacular Tattoo episodes, the Assault and Capture of Fort Moro, Havannah, 1762, re-enacted in Rushmoor Arena in the 1938 Tattoo

The Charge of the Light Brigade, re-enacted for the film "Balaclava," in the Long Valley, 1929.

The Grand Finale of the Aldershot Tattoo.

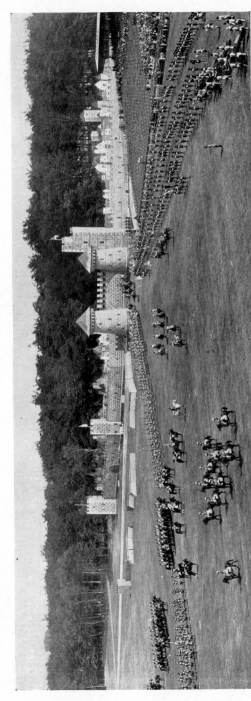

The capture of the fortress of Namur, 1695, re-enacted in Rushmoor Arena in the Aldershot Tattoo of 1934.

The Aldershot Fire Brigade (the word "Volunteer" was dropped in 1930).

The uniform of the Aldershot Volunteer Fire Brigade, 1914. Firemen

The Mayor of Aldershot, Councillor (now Alderman) W. J. North, reading the Proclamation on the Accession of King George VI to the Throne, from the steps of the Municipal Buildings, 1936, supported by members of the Borough Council.

The Right Hon. David Lloyd George, accompanied by the Mayor of Aldershot, Alderman W. M. R. Davis, M.B.E., J.P., in the Manor Park, 12th May, 1935.

H.R.H. Princess Elizabeth and H.R.H. Princess Margaret, accompanied by Lieut.-General Sir John Dill, arriving in Rushmoor Arena for the daylight rehearsal of the Aldershot Tattoo, 1938

H.M. The King, wearing the uniform of the Colonel of the Queen's Own Cameron Highlanders, accompanied by H.M. The Queen and Major-General H. M. Wilson, then G.O.C. of the 2nd Division, walking along Queen's Avenue, in January, 1939, on the occasion of the rededication service of St. Andrew's Garrison Church.

and Parish, thence proceeding in a south-easterly direction along and thereafter following the said last mentioned boundary to the point which is first hereinbefore mentioned.

Ward No. II (or East Ward) shall comprise that part of the Urban District and Parish of Aldershot which is bounded as follows, that is to say, by a line commencing at the point at which a line passing along the middle of the London and South Western Railway (Aldershot Branch) intersects the southern boundary of the said Urban District and Parish, thence proceeding in a north-easterly direction along the middle of the said railway to the point of intersection by a line passing along the middle of Church Lane East, then proceeding in a south-easterly direction along and thereafter following the middle of Church Lane East, Church Lane, Brighton Road, and High Street, to the point of intersection by a line passing along the middle of the London and South Western Railway (Aldershot Branch), thence proceeding in a north-easterly direction along the middle of the said railway to the boundary of the said Urban District and Parish, thence proceeding in a south-easterly direction along and thereafter following the said last-named boundary to the point which is first hereinbefore mentioned.

Ward No. III (or Central Ward) shall comprise that part of the Urban District and Parish of Aldershot which is not included in the Aldershot East and Aldershot West Electoral Divisions.

The Boundaries of the Borough (and of the Wards therein) as above described, are those which are shown on the Ordnance Survey Map (Scale 25 inches to a mile, Edition 1909), one copy of which is deposited at the Office of the Privy Council and the other at the Office of the Town Clerk of the Borough. In the event of any discrepancy between the description and the map the description shall prevail.

If any Councillors in any Ward, or any Aldermen, have obtained an equal number of votes, or have been elected without a poll so that it cannot be determined which of them had the smallest or next smallest number of votes, the Council of the Borough shall at the first Meeting thereof or at the next quarterly meeting following such first meeting and not later, by a majority of votes, or, in case of an equality of votes, by the casting vote of the Chairman, determine who are to go out of office at the times above specified respectively.

In witness whereof We have caused these Our Letters to be made Patent.

Witness Ourself at Westminster the twenty-eighth day of March in the twelfth year of Our Reign.

By Warrant under the King's Sign Manual.

(*Signed*) SCHUSTER.

U

Wednesday, 21st June, 1922, was Aldershot's Charter Day. The Charter arrived by train from London a few minutes after two o'clock, being greeted by a "salute" fired by fog signals placed upon the lines. The Mayor-Elect, Mr. Arthur H. Smith, and the Deputy Mayor-Elect, Mr. H. Ainger, travelled to London in the morning to obtain the Charter. They were met at Waterloo station by the escort to the Charter provided by twelve N.C.Os. and men, under command of R.S.M. Lister, D.C.M., M.M., of the Queen's Westminster Rifles, with which regiment the Mayor-Elect had served as a young man. The escort travelled to Aldershot with the Charter and took part in the celebrations. The Mayor-Elect was accompanied on the return journey by General The Right Hon. J. B. Seely, Lord-Lieutenant of Hampshire, and Lord Wolmer, M.P. for the Aldershot Division. At Aldershot station a guard of honour was mounted by the British Legion, under the command of Major Deacon, D.S.O.

Aldershot presented a gay appearance, the streets in the centre of the town being decked with flags and bunting. The ceremony of the presentation of the Charter took place in Manor Park, and a procession, made up of detachments of every military unit within the limits of the new Borough and every organized body fully representative of the town's activities, marched from the assembly area on the parade grounds of Talavera and Salamanca Barracks along Wellington Avenue and through Wellington Street, Victoria Road and High Street to the Manor Park. The salute was taken by the G.O.C.-in-C., Aldershot Command, Lieutenant-General Sir T. L. N. Morland, K.C.B., K.C.M.G., D.S.O.

The procession was headed by a detachment of both military and civil mounted police, lead by Police Sergeant Bunning. They were followed by the Mounted Band of the 6th Dragoon Guards (The Carabiniers*); a section of "E" Battery, R.H.A. ("The Eagle Troop"), commanded by Lieutenant H. Lumsden; a dismounted detachment of the 12th Brigade, R.F.A., under Lieutenant F. K. Sutton, M.C.; and detachments of R.E., under Lieutenant H. B. Foy, and Royal Corps of Signals commanded by Lieutenant W. V. Tyrrell.

They were followed by a detachment of the British Legion and other Old Comrades' Associations; representatives of local friendly societies wearing full regalia—the Ancient Order of Foresters, the Oddfellows, the Rechabites, Good Templars, Hearts of Oak and the Royal Antediluvian Order of Buffaloes. Next came representatives of the Railway Staff, led by the Station Master, Mr. S. P. Hunt, M.B.E., and the Aldershot Trades and Labour Council.

---

* Amalgamated in 1922 with the 3rd Dragoon Guards (Prince of Wales's). Now the 3rd Carabiniers.

There were two military bands in full-dress uniform, the 2nd Bn. Grenadier Guards and the 2nd Bn. The Queen's Own Cameron Highlanders, and a composite detachment of the 1st Guards Brigade made up of the 2nd Bn. Grenadier Guards, 3rd Bn. Coldstream Guards, 2nd Bn. Scots Guards and 2nd Bn. The Queen's Own Cameron Highlanders.

Then followed over five hundred Cadets, from the County School and the 1st/4th Hampshire Cadet Battalion, Boy Scouts from the 2nd, 3rd, 4th, 6th and 9th Aldershot Troops, and Girl Guides. Following the band of the 2nd Bn. The Royal Scots came a composite detachment of the 2nd Infantry Brigade composed of the 2nd Bn. The Royal Scots and 2nd Bn. The East Surrey Regiment, with detachments of R.A.S.C., R.A.O.C. and R.A.M.C. There was also a Royal Air Force detachment from Farnborough.

Other civil contingents represented the Aldershot Post Office, the Chamber of Commerce, the St. John Ambulance Brigade and the Aldershot Volunteer Fire Brigade. After the procession had passed, the G.O.C. and the Mayor-Elect drove to Manor Park with a mounted escort drawn from the 6th Dragoon Guards (The Carabiniers), the 7th Dragoon Guards* and the 13th Hussars,† under the command of Lieutenant C. D. Phillips of the 7th Dragoon Guards.

It was in the historic Manor Park that Aldershot officially received its Charter. The scene in the park was described by *The Aldershot News*‡ as

> one of brilliant and picturesque animation. The huge oval arena which enclosed the platform for the principal personages figuring in the afternoon's proceedings was a solid mass of expectant townspeople. . . . How many thousands were there it was impossible to say; they were packed too closely to enable anything approximating an accurate guess to be made. . . . Never in its history had Aldershot seen a spectacle such as that provided when the long procession entered the arena. . . .
>
> The khaki of the Guards Brigade, relieved with the scarlet sashes of non-commissioned officers, the khaki and blue of the Scouts, with their troop colours fluttering in the breeze, Girl Guides in blue, the scarlet tartan of Scottish units, the grey of nursing sisters, the light blue of the Royal Air Force, the town and military Fire Brigades, with their scarlet steamers, and the sun reflecting rays of brilliant light from polished helmets, the scarlet and purple fur-lined robes of the visiting Mayors, all

---

* Amalgamated with the 4th (Royal Irish) Dragoon Guards in 1922. Now the 4th/7th Royal Dragoon Guards.
† Amalgamated with the 18th Queen Mary's Own Hussars in 1922. Now the 13th/18th Royal Hussars.
‡ *The Aldershot News*, Charter Day edition, 23rd June, 1922.

combined to form a gorgeous pageant, which passed throug
the serried ranks of spectators with impressive dignity. As ever
section in the vast procession, which took twenty minutes to fil
through the ring, came into view it was greeted by the childre
with hearty cheers.

It was a children's day and the children showed the livelies
interest in the proceedings. While the various units passe
through the ring, the Guides and Scouts returned and forme
an inner ring. The Mayor Elect, with General Seely, Genera
Sir Thomas Morland, the visiting Mayors, Lord Wolmer,* an
other distinguished guests took their places on the platforr
facing the children, and the formal part of the celebration wa
quickly concluded. A vista of deep green trees converging int
an apex at the Church Hill entrance, and circling round th
ground, with just sufficient break to afford a glimpse of the fin
old ivy-covered Manor House. As the Mayor Elect commence
to speak, the children immediately fronting broke into lou
cheering, which was carried along the line and back again wit
real heartiness. Still greater enthusiasm was displayed whe
Mr. Snuggs received from the Mayor-Elect the Charter of Incor
poration and held it up for their inspection. The Chairman of th
Council, the father of a family, entered into the spirit of th
children and waved the Charter aloft, evoking a further torren
of cheering and waving of hands.

The youthful voices were upraised into a fine volume of soun
as the hymn, "O God, our Help in ages past," was sung, th
music being led by the 2nd Infantry Brigade Band. Appreciatio
of the services of the military found juvenile thanks still ready
it seemed as if the children would never cease ; they cheered th
General Officer Commanding, they cheered the Lord Lieutenan
of the County when he wished "Good luck to you all," the
cheered with fervid enthusiasm His Majesty the King and th
Prince of Wales, and only ceased when the dispersal of the plat
form party indicated that the ceremony of presenting the Charte
was at an end.

Before presenting the Charter, the Mayor-Elect addressed th
assembly on behalf of the Incorporation Committee :

First of all I would like to tell you of Aldershot Town and o
Aldershot Camp, what a very great debt of gratitude we owe t
General Sir Thomas Morland for assisting us to make this da
such a successful one. . . . Today is the civic birthday of Alder
shot, and we hope you will remember the 21st of June as th
birthday of the new civic life of Aldershot Borough and remembe
it with as much interest as your own birthdays. When I se
thousands of children before me I stop to wonder as to ho

---

* M.P. for the Aldershot Division.

many will be inspired to try to take their part in the civic life of Aldershot in the future. That is why today concerns you even more than it concerns the older people of our town. You will understand, as you grow up, that it is very difficult to inspire the older people, but we have very good ground with the children. Some of you, perhaps, may imagine that citizenship is not of any great interest to you till you grow up. That is not true. You must train yourselves to become good citizens and good burgesses, and the best way to become good citizens and burgesses is, at your school, at your play, and later in your business life, to give your town and your fellow citizens an absolutely square deal. Those are the places where character is formed, and character is the very foundation of good citizenship. By good citizenship I mean loyalty in its best sense—loyalty to God, loyalty to your King, loyalty to your Empire, and loyalty to your fellow citizens. If you can be inspired and can and will act up to such ideals, the future of Aldershot and of the country is in absolutely safe hands. The Manor House there, the old church behind it, and the grounds surrounding this place is the actual old history of Aldershot, and it is very fitting that this ceremony should take place on the most historic ground in Aldershot, and ground that is the property of the town for ever.

In presenting the Charter to the Chairman of the District Council for safe custody until November, "I sincerely and fervently believe," concluded the Mayor-Elect, "that this Charter granted by the King will be handed down through the centuries to come as unsullied and untainted as we have now received it."

A Military Display was presented in the Park at the conclusion of the ceremony, and in the evening a Commemoration Banquet, attended by over two hundred guests, was held at the Redan Drill Hall, which on this occasion was "beautifully decorated," the walls being "draped in white and pale green, and the tables charmingly arranged, the artistic combination of red, white and blue sweet peas, green trailing smilax and silver candelabra being most effective." Among the guests were the Lord-Lieutenant of the County, the Right Hon. J. E. B. Seely, C.B., C.M.G. ; the G.O.C.-in-C. of the Aldershot Command and Senior Officers of his staff ; the Mayors of Portsmouth, Winchester, Southampton and Guildford ; the Chairmen of the neighbouring Urban District Councils ; the County Court Judge ; and a fully representative assembly of the townspeople, a cross-section of every profession and trade of the new Borough.

* * * * *

Until 1923 the arms of the Urban District Council had been unofficial. The design which had been adopted in the nineties on the formation of the Council had been based on the name Aldershot and could almost be classified as a rebus or pun on the name of the town. These arms were composed of a shield upon which was an alder tree in green and brown on a scarlet background below three piles, each of six round shot in gold on a dark blue background, thus linking the town's name with this symbolism, the alder tree, and the shot, representative of the military associations of the town.

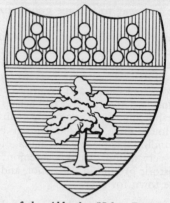

The Arms of the Aldershot Urban District Council

Arms were granted to the Borough on 7th May, 1923, on the application of the Charter Mayor, Mr. A. H. Smith, J.P., the year after the granting of Aldershot's Charter, by the College of Heralds, the arms being passed by the Garter Principal King of Arms, Clarenceux King of Arms and Norroy King of Arms.

Representations had been made to the College of Heralds that the arms, crest and motto should be based on the arms of the Tichborne family, with the addition of special quarterings representative of the Bishopric of Winchester and the military associations of the Borough, and these proposals were approved.*

The Mitre in the first quarter of the Borough Arms represents the Bishops of Winchester, who for many centuries owned the Hundred of Crondall, which included Aldershot, and the Vair in the second and third quarterings, the Lion supporters and the motto are taken from the Tichborne Arms. The military associations of the Borough are recognized by the crossed swords in the fourth quarter. These crossed swords were symbolic of the Army and similar swords form part of the British Army badge.

---

* The first suggestions for the Borough arms—of a simple nature—were not accepted, and it was mainly due to the research and efforts of Mr. R. A. Garratt that the present arms were adopted.

The Tichborne family owned the Manor of Aldershot for a period of approximately two hundred years. In 1599 the Manor was left to two daughters who married two brothers, named Tichborne. These and their heirs held the Manor until about 1750, and by an extraordinary coincidence the family motto of the Tichbornes was "Pugna pro Patria" (Fight for your Country). No motto could be more appropriate to the Borough of Aldershot with its great military tradition and associations.

The Arms of the Borough of Aldershot

The text of the grant of arms was as follows:

TO ALL AND SINGULAR to whom these Presents shall come Sir Henry Farnham Burke, King of Arms, William Alexander Lindsay Esquire, One of His Majesty's Counsel learned in the Law, Clarenceux King of Arms and Gordon Ambrose de Lisle Lee Esquire, Companion of the Most Honourable Order of the Bath, Norroy King of Arms, Send Greeting, WHEREAS ARTHUR HERBERT SMITH Esquire, Mayor of the BOROUGH OF ALDERSHOT, hath represented unto Edmund Bernard Viscount Fitzalan of Derwent, Knight Grand Cross of the Royal Victorian Order, Companion of the Distinguished Service Order, One of His Majesty's Most Honourable Privy Council and Deputy to the Most Noble Bernard Marmaduke, Duke of Norfolk, Earl Marshal and Hereditary Marshal of England, that His Majesty having been graciously pleased by Letters Patent Under the Great Seal of the United Kingdom of Great Britain and Ireland bearing date the Twenty eighth day of March last past, to grant and declare that the Inhabitants of the Urban District of Aldershot in the County of Southampton within the limits set forth in Part One of the first Schedule to the said Letters Patent and their successors, shall be one body politic and corporate by the name of the Mayor Aldermen and Burgesses of the Borough of Aldershot with perpetual succession and a Common Seal and may assume Armorial Bearings (which shall be duly enrolled in the Heralds College). That the Mayor Aldermen and Burgesses of the said incorporated Borough of Aldershot being desirous that the Common Seal to be used by them in their corporate capacity should contain fit and proper Armorial Bearings and be assigned under lawful authority, he therefore requested the favour of his Lordship's Warrant for Our granting and assigning such Armorial Bearings and Supporters as may be proper to be borne by the said Mayor Aldermen and Burgesses and their successors on the Seals Shields Banners or otherwise according to the Laws of Arms AND FORASMUCH as His Lordship did by Warrant under his hand and the Seal of the Earl Marshal bearing date the Third Day of May instant authorize and direct Us to grant and assign such Armorial Ensigns and Supporters accordingly. KNOW YE THEREFORE that We the said Garter Clarenceux and Norroy in pursuance of the aforesaid Warrant and by virtue of the Letters Patent of Our several offices to each of Us respectively granted do by these Presents grant and assign unto the MAYOR ALDERMEN and BURGESSES OF THE BOROUGH OF ALDERSHOT the Arms following that is to say QUARTERLY GULES AND VAIR IN THE FIRST QUARTER A MITRE AND IN THE FOURTH TWO SWORDS IN SALTIRE PROPER POMMELLED AND HILTED OF THE THIRD And for the Crest Issuant out of Mural Crown a Hinds Head with a Spur Rowel Sable as the same are in the margin hereof more plainly depicted And by the Authority aforesaid I the said Garter Principal King of Arms do further grant and assign the Supporters following that is to say on either side a Lion guardant Gules gorged with a Collar Or Pendant therefrom and escutcheon Vair as the same are also in the margin hereof more plainly depicted, the whole to be borne and used for ever hereafter by the said Mayor Aldermen and Burgesses of the Borough of Aldershot and their successors in their corporate capacity on Seals Shields Banners or otherwise according to the Laws of Arms IN WITNESS whereof We the said Garter Clarenceux and Norroy Kings of Arms have to these Presents subscribed Our names and affixed the date of our several Offices this Seventh day of May in the Fourteenth Year of the Reign of our Sovereign Lord George the Fifth by the Grace of God of the United Kingdom of Great Britain and Ireland and of the British Dominions Beyond the Seas King, Defender of the Faith and in the year of Our Lord One Thousand Nine Hundred and Twenty Three.

signed : H. Farnham Burke. Garter.
W. A. Lindsay. Clarenceux.
G. Ambrose Lee. Norroy.

The Aldershot Mayoral Chain, which was made by Mr. F. Phillips,
f Wellington Street, is a fine example of the goldsmith's craft and is
f 18-ct. gold and enamel bearing the London hall-mark. The design
modelled on Elizabethan lines and is distinct in character from the
enaissance style, which is used a great deal for this class of work. The
adge, which bears the arms of the Borough, is vesical in shape, and
ounted on the edge by four scrolls, the scrolls being further sup-
orted by four floral scrolls, which also support an oval quatrefoil
ame upon which the Borough arms are supported. Below the arms
an enamelled ribbon bearing the words "Borough of Aldershot."
he badge is connected to the chain by a centre link made up of a
rolled frame supporting an oval with the initials of Alderman Arthur
. Smith, the first Mayor, in enamel. Above the enamelled monogram
mounted the mural crown. The chain is made up of twelve round
roll shields and is 40 inches in length. The links are cut square and
e in triplicate between each shield.

The Mayoral Chain* is a fine piece of craftsmanship and worthy of
ny borough. It was subscribed for by residents of Aldershot and was
esented to the Mayor on 9th November, 1923, in the Council
hamber by Dr. F. Stroyan, J.P., Deputy Chairman of Directors of
e then Aldershot Gas, Water and District Lighting Company, on
half of the subscribers. The Borough's mace, silver gilt and
namelled, was also made by Mr. F. Phillips and was subscribed
r by the Freemasons of the Borough and was presented to the
ayor on 5th November, 1924, by Mr. John Bowers, Immediate
ast Master of the "Unity Peace and Concord" Lodge, in the presence
representatives of all the Lodges.† The mace bears the inscription
The gift of the Freemasons of Aldershot," and bears the titles of the
bscribing Lodges.‡

In May, 1923, King George V and Queen Mary, whilst resident at
e Royal Pavilion, honoured the new Borough by giving audience
the new Mayor of Aldershot and members of the Council. His
ajesty's action was quite spontaneous and unexpected, which added
the appreciation of the honour conferred upon the leading citizens
the then new Borough. The representative deputation was com-
sed of the Mayor, Alderman A. H. Smith, J.P., Aldermen Colonel

---

* The Chain of Office worn by the Mayoress of Aldershot was purchased in
38 by the Council.
† The Mayor's Robe of Office was presented by the "Aldershot Camp" Lodge
o. 1131.
‡ "Unity, Peace and Concord" Lodge No. 316 (attached to the 2nd Bn. The
yal Scots, then stationed in Aldershot); "Panmure" Lodge No. 723 (named
er Lord Panmure, Secretary of State for War when "The Camp" was established);
ldershot Camp" Lodge No. 1131; "Aldershot Army and Navy" Lodge No. 1971;
d the "Palma Virtuti" Lodge No. 4187.

J. M. Young, S. Friend, J. May, N. Solomon, and Councillors J. R.
Attfield, C. A. L. Calvert, J. Edwards, H. M. Foster, M. B. Simes and
E. A. Underwood, and the Town Clerk, Mr. D. Llewellyn Griffiths,
O.B.E.

The deputation was received by the Master of the Household, the
Hon. Sir Derek Keppel, and the Mayor was first presented to His
Majesty, at whose request he introduced the Aldermen and Councillors
and the Senior Alderman—Alderman Friend—introduced the deputation to Queen Mary and Princess Mary. His Majesty graciously
expressed his pleasure that Aldershot should have been honoured by
the grant of a Charter of Incorporation, and his further pleasure at
being able to convey his congratulations to the Mayor and representatives of the Council, assuring them all of his interest in the Borough
and the great pleasure it gave him to stay at the Royal Pavilion each
year.

In accordance with their custom, dating back to the years before
King George V came to the throne, the King and Queen continued
their regular visits to Aldershot, and in 1923 they spent Whitsuntide
in residence at the Royal Pavilion. They arrived by car and were
greeted by a salute of twenty-one guns, fired on the Queen's Parade by
the 5th Battery, 28th Brigade, Royal Field Artillery. Crowds had
gathered in the Farnborough Road near the entrance to the Pavilion
and gave Their Majesties an enthusiastic welcome. A guard of honour
at the Pavilion was provided by the 1st Bn. The Leicestershire Regiment, and Their Majesties were received by the G.O.C.-in-C., the
Lieutenant-General Sir Philip W. Chetwode.

On Saturday, 19th May, a Royal Review was held on Laffan's Plain
and, despite leaden skies and khaki being for the first time the pre-
dominating colour, the parade was a brilliant spectacle and was witnessed by thousands of spectators.

It was the first Royal Review after the war, and long before the
arrival of the Royal Party the slopes and enclosures facing the long
line of troops, drawn up in line by brigades, were filled with large
crowds, despite the weather, for rain fell steadily for a full half-hour
before the Review, but the arrival of the Royal Party coincided with
a break in the weather.

The most noticeable difference to those who had seen many similar
events in the past was that the blaze of colour which had been the
dominant feature of pre-war reviews had gone. This, however, did
not detract from the effectiveness of the parade. The troops on parade
appeared younger, and for the first time the greater majority were
clean-shaven, a striking contrast to the moustached soldier of pre-war
days, when it was forbidden to shave the upper lip. There were 8,300

all ranks on parade, and also 2,300 horses and mules, 112 guns, 8 tanks and 8 armoured cars.

One of the most interesting features of this review was the march past of the tanks and armoured cars. Taking part for the first time in a Royal Review of this nature, they rolled past in well-kept lines, and the guns in the turrets of the tanks dipped in a simultaneous salute as they passed the saluting base. A Royal Air Force detachment from Farnborough also took part in the parade.

During his stay the King, who always took an active interest in the training of the Army, was to be seen riding his chestnut charger over the Long Valley and over Laffan's Plain, accompanied by his staff. He took particular interest, during this visit, in the series of demonstrations given by the 1st Cavalry Brigade and the 5th Brigade, R.H.A., and a display of bridging over the canal at Eelmore Bridge by the 23rd Field Company, R.E.

At the conclusion of the Royal visit His Majesty wrote to the G.O.C., and his message was published in a special Command Order:

25th May, 1923.

The short stay which the Queen and I have been able to make this year among the troops at Aldershot has been full of interest and enjoyment.

I have been impressed by the progressive nature of the training as it is carried out in your Command, and I am gratified to see that the need for modern methods and equipment is fully appreciated, for thus only can our small Army shoulder its heavy responsibilities. It was, therefore, especially interesting to be present at the demonstrations of Tanks, Pack Artillery, and experimental Motor-drawn Field Artillery.

At the ceremonial parade, I was glad to notice the steadiness under arms of the young soldiers who have now largely replaced the veterans of the war. I am well aware that the complexity of modern training for war leaves little time for ceremonial drill, and this difficulty is accentuated by the present weakness of effectives in many units. The soldierly bearing and precision of manœuvre displayed by all arms was, in consequence, all the more creditable.

The Queen and I bid farewell to you and the troops under your command. We shall look forward to our next visit, and to seeing again as much as possible of the daily life of the Army at Aldershot.

GEORGE R.I.

It was in 1923 that the 2nd Division War Memorial at the top of Hospital Hill was unveiled by General Lord Horne, G.C.B., K.C.M.G., and dedicated by the Rev. Hugh Hornby, who served as a Chaplain with the Division from 1915. The ceremony was attended by representative detachments of the units which composed the Division, "Last Post" and "Reveille" being sounded by the buglers of the 1st Bn. The Queen's Royal Regiment.

The same year marked the Diamond Jubilee of the consecration of the old "Red Church," the Garrison Church of All Saints, the King granting the title of "Royal" in commemoration of the event.

The Aldershot War Memorial in the Municipal Gardens was unveiled on Wednesday, 18th March, 1925, by H.R.H. The Duke of Gloucester, in the presence of a number of distinguished visitors and a large assembly of townspeople. Following a short service, which was accompanied by the band of the 1st Bn. The Gloucestershire Regiment, the memorial was dedicated by the Bishop of Winchester.

After the 1914-1918 war it was decided to build a Church of Scotland church in "The Camp" as a memorial to Scotsmen who had laid down their lives in the war. The site chosen was that then occupied by the old "Iron Church," one of the original churches of "The Camp," which had stood by the canal in Queen's Avenue since 1866. The "Iron Church" was dismantled and removed in 1926, and work commenced on the new Church of St. Andrew, which was opened on 10th December, 1927, by H.R.H. Princess Royal. Although opened in 1927, the church was far from being complete, and additions to the structure were made in later years.

King George VI, when Duke of York, unveiled a memorial window to the late Field-Marshal Earl Haig in the church in 1934, and in the following year a memorial window was unveiled to all ranks of the First Corps who fell in 1914. This window faces the memorial window to Earl Haig. Lady Haig was present at the service, and the window was unveiled by Captain Sir Ian Fraser, then Chairman of St. Dunstan's, and a one-armed soldier employed in the British Legion Poppy Factory.

The building was finally completed in 1939, and on completion, which included redecoration and the extension of the nave by thirty feet, it was reopened on 12th January, 1939, by H.M. The King. A ceremonial parade marked the occasion when the King, wearing the uniform of the Queen's Own Cameron Highlanders, accompanied by the Queen and Major-General H. M. Wilson (later Field-Marshal Lord Wilson of Lybia), attended the ceremony, at which detachments of the four Scottish units then in the Command were on parade—the 1st Bn. The Cameron Highlanders, 1st Bn. The Argyll and Sutherland Highlanders, 1st Bn. Gordon Highlanders, and the 1st Bn. The Royal Scots.

As in the years before the war, Royal associations with the Borough continued in the years between the wars.

During the visit of King George and Queen Mary at Whitsun, 1924, the King held a review of all troops in the Command on Laffan's Plain, and on the following day presented new Colours to the 1st Bn. Devonshire Regiment, 1st Bn. Bedfordshire and Hertfordshire Regiment, 2nd Bn. East Lancashire Regiment, 2nd Bn. Dorsetshire Regiment, and 2nd Bn. Border Regiment. This was a unique ceremony, unusual because of the number of battalions to receive new Colours at the same time. The parade was to have been held on Laffan's Plain, but was transferred to the Headquarters Gymnasium in Queen's Avenue owing to rain.

In 1925 the King was again in Aldershot and presented a new Guidon to the 1st Royal Dragoons, as their Colonel-in-Chief; and in 1931 two battalions stationed in North Camp, the 2nd Bn. Duke of Cornwall's Light Infantry and 2nd Bn. Royal West Kent Regiment, received new Colours, the D.C.L.I. from their Colonel-in-Chief, the Prince of Wales, and the West Kents from the Duke of Gloucester.

While stationed at Talavera Barracks in 1933 the 1st Royal Scots celebrated the 300th anniversary of the raising of the regiment by trooping the Colour. At the parade the Colonel of the Regiment, Lieutenant-General Sir Edward Altham, read a special Order of the Day from the Princess Royal, Colonel-in-Chief; and later in the same year the King and Queen, accompanied by the Princess Royal, visited Aldershot. It was on this occasion that the King bestowed on the pipers of the regiment the right to wear his own personal tartan, the Royal Stuart.

King George VI, as the Duke of York, paid two visits to Aldershot in 1932. On the first visit he saw the 2nd Somerset Light Infantry troop the Colour in commemoration of Jellalabad, and on the second presented new Colours to the 2nd Bn. Queen's Own Cameron Highlanders.

When the King and Queen visited Aldershot in 1934, King George inspected a composite British Infantry Brigade, composed of the 2nd The Queen's Royal Regiment (West Surrey) (England), 2nd Gordon Highlanders (Scotland), 1st Royal Inniskilling Fusiliers (Ireland) and the 1st Welch Regiment (Wales).

The Royal Silver Jubilee in 1935 was celebrated in Aldershot with enthusiasm. The streets, shops, public buildings and private houses were decorated with flags, bunting and garlands. Many thousands attended a Gymkhana held in the grounds of the Manor Park, which concluded in the evening with one of the finest firework displays ever seen in the town. The children of the Borough were treated to a military display on the Recreation Ground and a special tea was arranged for the old folk. A huge beacon was lit on the summit of Hungry Hill—one of the chain of some 2,000 similar fires lit throughout the country—by the local boy scouts and watched by a large crowd, who all joined in singing the National Anthem and three cheers for Their Majesties as the flames leapt up from the blazing pile. Ceremonial parades were held throughout "The Camp," the largest being those of the 2nd and 5th Brigades in North and South Camps respectively; and a Royal Salute was fired near the Wellington Statue by the 84th Field Battery of the 11th Field Brigade, R.A.

One hundred and seventy officers and men drawn from the 1st Cavalry Brigade—The Queen's Bays, 3rd Carbiniers and 4th Hussars—mounted and wearing full-dress uniform, together with a detachment of four guns from the 3rd Brigade, R.H.A., went to London to participate in the procession from Buckingham Palace to St. Paul's Cathedral.

In commemoration of King George V's Silver Jubilee, a number of trees were planted in the Borough. Two oaks were planted in the Manor Park by the Mayor, two by the Chamber of Commerce in the Municipal Gardens, and two tulip trees at the Farnborough Road end of Cranmore Lane by the Aldershot Rotary Club.

Saturday, 13th July, 1935, was the occasion of the great Silver Jubilee Royal Review in Rushmoor Arena, when, standing in front of the flower-decked pavilion, the King took the salute before some 50,000 spectators. It was the first Royal Review to be held in Rushmoor Arena and was undoubtedly one of the most memorable events of the Silver Jubilee year.

The King and Queen drove from Buckingham Palace, arriving in the arena a short while before the Review was timed to start, the Queen driving to the pavilion, where she was received by Viscount Halifax, then Secretary of State for War. With Her Majesty in the pavilion was H.R.H. The Duke of Connaught. After a few minutes of eager anticipation the King, wearing the khaki service dress of a Field-Marshal, came riding into view from among the trees at the far corner of the arena. Behind him, riding in line, were the four Princes, the Prince of Wales wearing the uniform of the Welsh Guards, the Duke of York that of the Scots Guards, the Duke of Gloucester in the uniform of the 10th Hussars, and the Duke of Kent that of the Royal West Kent Regiment. Fifty yards ahead of the King rode Brigadier A. P. Y. Langhorne, D.S.O., M.C., and between the King and the Princes rode the Royal Standard bearer, R.S.M. G. F. Higgs, M.M., of the 4th Hussars. Next in the procession rode three Indian honorary A.D.Cs. and four military members of the Army Council: Field-

Marshal Sir Archibald Montgomery-Massingberd, the Chief of the
Imperial General Staff; Lieutenant-General Sir Harry Knox, the
Adjutant-General ; Lieutenant-General Sir Reginald May, the Q.M.G.;
and Major-General Sir Hugh J. Elles, Master-General of Ordnance.

Immediately the King reached the pavilion he saluted the Queen,
and there was a flashing of steel as the troops drawn up on parade gave
the Royal Salute. The King then took up his position at the saluting
base and the march past commenced.

It was an imposing spectacle. The troops marched in perfect lines,
to the regimental marches played by the massed bands, the Cavalry
making a perfect spectacle—one of the most impressive features of
the parade, the last Royal Review in which a brigade of horsed Cavalry
took part. Two batteries of the 3rd Brigade, R.H.A., were also still
horsed, but the guns of the third battery, "M" Battery, were drawn
by tractors. The 1st Field Squadron, R.E., were still mounted, but
their pontoons and bridging equipment went by on lorries. The
Cavalry Signals passed with their detachments of small wireless cars.
The 1st Cavalry Brigade was played past the saluting base by the
massed mounted bands of the Brigade. The massed bands of the 1st
Division then moved into position opposite the saluting base as the
Division started its march past, followed in turn by the troops of the
2nd Division. The strains of the many famous tunes, the marches of
the various regiments, echoed over the arena as the troops went by
in lines of companies, with Colours flying.

On parade with their regiments were "Taffy VI," the goat mascot
of the Welch Regiment, and "Charlie," the antelope mascot of the
Royal Warwickshire Regiment, with his gold-tipped horns gleaming
in the sunshine.

Among the Gunners that passed were the 1st Light Brigade with
pack mules, the last occasion upon which such a unit paraded at a
Royal Review.

The General Officer Commanding-in-Chief of the Command,
General the Hon. Sir Francis Gathorne-Hardy, dismounted after he
had led the march past and stood behind the King ; and as each
Division and Brigade Commander and Regimental Colonel who had
led his regiment past followed suit, there was, by the end of the parade,
a long line of distinguished soldiers in front of the dais. Whilst the
last units marched past, the Colour parties of the nineteen battalions
on parade formed up in line at the back of the arena in front of the
1st Guards Brigade, with the massed bands of the 1st Division in the
rear. General Sir Francis Gathorne-Hardy then rejoined the parade
and, on his word of command, the parade advanced in review order
with Colours flying. As the parade came to a halt, the order to present

arms was given, the Colours being lowered and the bands playing the National Anthem. The King saluted, and then three rousing cheers were given for His Majesty, led by the General Officer Commanding. Colours were again dipped and arms presented whilst the National Anthem was played again, and so ended the impressive finale of the last Royal Review to be held in Aldershot.*

* * * * *

The death of King George V in January of the following year was marked by the dispatch to Queen Mary of a message from the General Officer Commanding, General the Hon. Sir Francis Gathorne-Hardy, in which he said, "Every man of this Command mourns a great King and a beloved Chief," and by the firing of seventy minute guns—one for each year of the King's life—on the Queen's Parade by a composite battery of the 13th Field Brigade, R.A. Next day a salute of twenty-one guns was fired to mark the accession of King Edward VII. In the town the Proclamation was read from the steps of the Municipal Buildings by the Mayor, Councillor W. J. North, and three thousand troops from Aldershot proceeded to London to line the route on the occasion of the reading of the Proclamation.

In May, 1936, King Edward VIII visited Aldershot to inspect the 3rd Bn. Coldstream Guards and the 2nd Bn. Scots Guards and later to see the latter Battalion off to Palestine.

It was shortly after this that the situation in Palestine was such that it was decided to dispatch the 1st Division to the Middle East. The Division had but recently moved out to participate in exercises in Sussex. The manœuvres were cancelled and the whole formation, less

---

* Some idea of the number of troops in Aldershot at that time, and the number of men actually on parade, may be obtained from the following order of the march past: G.O.C.-in-C. and Staff, H.Q., Aldershot Command; H.Q., 1st Cavalry Brigade; 3rd Brigade, R.H.A.; The Queen's Bays; 4th Queen's Own Hussars; 1st Field Squadron, R.E.; "D" Troop, Cavalry Divisional Signals; G.O.C. and Staff, H.Q., 1st Division; 11th Field Brigade, R.A.; 1st Light Brigade, R.A.; 1st Divisional R.E. and Royal Signals; 1st Guards Brigade—2nd Bn. Grenadier Guards, 1st Bn. Coldstream Guards, 2nd Bn. Queen's Royal Regiment, 2nd Bn. West Yorkshire Regiment; 2nd Infantry Brigade—2nd Bn. Royal Norfolk Regiment, 1st Bn. Welch Regiment, 2nd Bn. Northamptonshire Regiment, 2nd Bn. Wiltshire Regiment; 3rd Infantry Brigade—2nd Bn. The Buffs, 2nd Bn. The Cameronians, 1st Bn. Oxfordshire and Buckinghamshire Light Infantry, Royal Irish Fusiliers; Detachment, 1st Divisional R.A.S.C.; G.O.C. and Staff, H.Q., 2nd Division; 13th Field Brigade, R.A.; 2nd Divisional R.E. and Royal Signals; 5th Infantry Brigade—2nd Bn. King's Own Royal Regiment, 2nd Bn. East York-shire Regiment, 1st Bn. Worcestershire Regiment, 2nd Bn. Queen's Own Cameron Highlanders; 6th Infantry Brigade—2nd Bn. Royal Warwickshire Regiment, 2nd Bn. Duke of Cornwall's Light Infantry, 1st Bn. South Staffordshire Regiment, 1st Bn. Durham Light Infantry; Detachment, 2nd Divisional R.A.S.C. and R.A.M.C.; 10th Field Brigade; 4th Light Brigade and 2nd Medium Brigade, R.A.; 2nd Bn. Royal Tank Corps; 1st Air Defence Brigade; and a Detachment, R.A.O.C.

ts artillery, returned to Aldershot, the transport being supplemented by seventy buses from the Aldershot and District Traction Company. The Division was mobilized, brought up to strength by Class "A" reservists, and departed for Palestine. This move had the desired effect on the troublesome elements of both factions, and although the garrison in Palestine was substantially increased, almost half the Division returned again to Aldershot by the end of the year.

A composite Infantry Brigade left Aldershot to line the route in London on the occasion of the proclamation of King George VI, following the abdication of his brother, whilst in Aldershot, King George's accession was marked by a 21-gun salute, fired by the 24th Field Brigade, R.A., on the Queen's Parade, and the reading of the Proclamation in the town by the Mayor on the steps of the Municipal Buildings.

*   *   *   *   *

As always, Aldershot continued to be included in the itinerary of foreign Royal visitors on the occasion of official visits to the King.

Prince Takamatsu of Japan visited Aldershot on 9th July, 1930, and was greeted by a guard of honour formed by the 1st Bn. The Green Howards, formed up outside the Headquarters buildings, and the firing of a salute by the 13th Field Brigade, R.A., on the Queen's Parade. The Prince's tour included a demonstration by tanks in action near Miles Hill, with air co-operation, and visits to the Command Gymnasium and Baths, the Army Vocational Training Centre and Mons Barracks, the visit concluding with an official luncheon at the Officers' Club.

Wearing his picturesque Eastern robes, the Emir Saud, Crown Prince of Saudi Arabia, visited the Command in July, 1935, and toured "The Camp," showing particular interest in the horses and equipment of the 1st Cavalry Brigade. He later watched troops under training in the area, and saw a Physical Training Display which amused him immensely.

On 17th November, 1938, King Carol of Roumania was in Aldershot ; he drove over from the R.A.F. Station at Odiham, where he had been entertained in the morning, and was received by Lieutenant-General Sir John Dill, the G.O.C.-in-C., and a guard of honour of the 3rd Bn. Grenadier Guards. Proceeding to the Long Valley, King Carol watched a display of mechanized units, including a demonstration by a Carrier Platoon of the 1st Bn. Gordon Highlanders, at the conclusion of which he inspected the units and took the salute at the drive past of the 12th Royal Lancers in their armoured cars, the tractor-drawn 13th Anti-Tank and 4th Medium Regiments, R.A.,

x

the 2nd and 4th Battalions of the Royal Tank Corps, the 6th Anti
Aircraft Regiment, R.A., and the Mobile Searchlights of the 1st A.A
Battalion, R.E.

* * * * *

The geographical position of Aldershot and its accessibility by road
and rail led during the twenties to the development of the town into
a recognized shopping centre. Led by an active Chamber of Commerce
the traders of the town enlarged their old-established business premise
and developed their trade, whilst new shops were opened and new
businesses established. One of the features of the business life of
Aldershot in the post-war years was the holding of an annual "Shop
ping Week." These weeks, inaugurated in 1909, were reintroduce
in 1920, and without doubt became a real benefit both to the buyer
and to the traders of the town and assisted very materially in making
Aldershot the recognized shopping centre for a wide area. The publi
entered fully into the spirit of the Aldershot Shopping Weeks, for, i
addition to improved shopping facilities, some hundreds of free gift
and prizes were offered by the Organizing Committee and individua
business concerns. Prizes were also given for the best decorate
windows and displays of products, all of which encouraged visitor
and brought increased trade to the town.

Aldershot developed to the south and east in the years following
the 1914-1918 war, and later to the west of the town. This developmen
was carried out under the direction of the Borough Council and by
the private enterprise of speculative builders. The local authority was
as has always been the case in the matter of housing, directed by the
Ministry of Health in these matters, the Council acting upon th
powers granted under the Housing Acts passed through Parliamen
from time to time. The first housing programme in Aldershot fol
lowed on the passing of a Housing Act in 1919 and one hundred and
fifteen houses were built on the Aldershot Park Estate. Under a
further Act in 1924 a further three hundred and eighty houses were
built in Aldershot Park and a further twenty-six in other parts of the
town. Further progress was made on the Aldershot Park Housing
Estate under the Housing Act of 1930. Slum clearance was effected
in the early thirties in the area bounding the military lands and new
houses provided as part of this scheme.

Much was done to improve the town by the purchase of open
spaces for recreation grounds in and near the town centre. Until
1920 the present-day Recreation Ground was little more than un
developed heathland, the ground rising from High Street to the top
of Redan Hill in mounds and hillocks of the greyish sand which

typified the area, covered with broom and heather. The present playing pitch had been cleared and levelled in 1905 and used for cricket, but it was very sandy and the grass sparse. Towards the latter years of the 1914-1918 war ground had been purchased by the Council for development as part of the Government plan to cope with the unemployment visualized at the conclusion of hostilities. Local Government bodies had been invited to consider such development plans, being assured that substantial financial assistance would be given to assist in these projects. This area was earmarked as a Recreation Ground and plans were prepared in 1920 by the Borough Surveyor, the late Mr. James Neave ; the plans involved a considerable amount of excavation and levelling of the ground to permit the laying out of a football pitch and gardens. The initial cost of the project was over £10,000, of which three-quarters was borne by the Government grant. The work was completed in 1924. In 1926 the Aldershot Football Club was formed, and the Council were approached to lease the ground for use by the Club for Professional League football. As, in the previous year, the Public Health Act had included a clause permitting local authorities to lease open spaces under their control to clubs for the playing of games on the condition that other land of equal value was acquired by the local authority for the same purpose, approval was given by the Ministry of Health for the leasing of the Recreation Ground to the Aldershot Football Club, but made the condition that some forty acres of Aldershot Park should be laid out for public use in place of the Recreation Ground. This was done and the Recreation Ground was given over to professional sport. By arrangement between the Council and the Aldershot Football Club, the stand, administrative offices, turnstiles and gates were erected in 1926. The stand on the north side of the ground was erected by the Football Club in 1932.

Considerable rebuilding took place in the town. The Midland Bank building in Wellington Street was transferred from the small offices which had been occupied in 1902 by the London Joint City and Midland Bank, and opened in 1923. In 1927 a drastic change was made at the corner of Wellington Street and High Street when the old Royal Hotel, the Tilbury's Hotel of the late fifties, was demolished, and the following year the premises now occupied by Messrs. Montague Burton and Woolworths were opened.

It was in 1930 that the Borough Council purchased from the War Department at a price of £16,500 the site bounded by High Street, the Empire Cinema, Wellington Avenue and Barrack Road, an area known as the "R.E. Yard" with the "R.E.D. (Royal Engineer Department) Huts." The site of the original huts erected in 1854 for the accommodation of the first Engineer Staff responsible for the construction of "The Camp," and from that date the site had been used as an R.E. office and store. This site was cleared ; two cinemas, the Empire and the Ritz, were built on the lower portion and the upper portion converted into a car park and the Princes Gardens. The main project, the erection of a Civic Centre with a large hall and a public library, did not, however, materialize. It was also in 1930 that the Aldershot Swimming Pool was opened in Aldershot Park. This had been a major project undertaken by the Council as part of the plan for the development of the Aldershot Park Estate after its purchase ten years previously.

It was in 1936 that the electrification of the Southern Railway line from Woking to Farnham was completed, and the first electric train was run through Aldershot from Wimbledon to Farnham in December of that year.

Aldershot developed southwards during the late thirties. First there was the Council Estate in Aldershot Park, then the Boxall's Lane Housing Scheme, followed by the Russell Estate which opened up Highfield Avenue in 1936, and then in the years immediately prior to the war the extensive estate covering Jubilee and Coronation Roads was built.

*   *   *   *   *

It was in the early thirties that the great changes began to take place in the Army as a result of the decision to implement the scheme for mechanization. Aldershot felt the effects of this change-over and witnessed the gradual metamorphosis of the barracks as the stables gave way to garages, and horse troughs to petrol pumps. The last mounted parades of many famous cavalry regiments and batteries of Artillery took place on the parade grounds adjoining Wellington Avenue, and the barracks saw many a sad leave-taking of troopers parted from their horses. Orders would come through that a particular unit would be next on the list for mechanization, and the well-groomed and well-cared-for horses were" put on the rough," which meant that they were fed, watered and exercised, but no more. Horse sales were held and the passage of troop horses through the town to the railways and the sale yards became a regular event. Time must perforce bring changes, but this was one change which brought a sadness with it, which is remembered to this day by those who served at the time.

The first cavalry regiment to be mechanized in the United Kingdom was the 11th Hussars, who were at the time stationed in Willems Barracks, and it was on the parade ground of these barracks facing Wellington Avenue that the Regiment's last mounted parade was held on 10th April, 1928. This was the first of many such parades which followed in the ensuing ten years, for the process of mechanization of the Army was slow due in the main to the financial aspect of this great change, for it came at a time when the cries for disarmament and general reduction of our armed forces were gaining increasing support and, in the face of this, expenditure on the Army was kept down. The great change had, however, commenced, and in retrospect the mechanization of "The Cherrypickers" in the spring of 1928 was an epoch-making event.

The mechanization of the Queen's Bays and the 4th Hussars took place in Aldershot in November, 1936, the horses being transferred to regiments that had escaped the change, or sold. "Prince," the drum horse of The Bays, was transferred to The Greys, and "Old Bill," the oldest horse in the Regiment, which had served in the 1914-1918 war, went away to a Blue Cross Home. As the horses left, so in came the light tanks, scout cars and motor-cycles, and the conversion of stables into garages proceeded in step with the great change-over.

It was in 1938 that a major military event, as far as Aldershot was concerned, took place. The 1st Cavalry Brigade, then composed of the 3rd Hussars, 9th Lancers and 10th Hussars, stationed in Warburg, Willems and Beaumont Barracks respectively, was moved to Tidworth* following the complete mechanization of the Brigade. The move was necessary in order that the Brigade could be located more conveniently to the other units of the 1st Armoured Division, but the move was a break in the Brigade's associations with Aldershot which had lasted for eighty-two years.

*   *   *   *   *

One of the great features in the life of Aldershot between the wars was, without doubt, the Aldershot Tattoo, which did much towards making the town even more widely known throughout the country and abroad, and probably did more than anything in the past to emphasize Aldershot's claim to be "The Home of the British Army." The name Aldershot took on a new and wider meaning to the nation as a whole. Beginning, as has been seen, back in the nineties in the form of an annual military fête and torchlight tattoo held in the grounds of Government House, it grew to a magnitude far greater than its original conception, becoming a national event of some major importance, which by 1939 was attracting over half a million spectators each year, coming from every part of the country and from overseas. Vast, enthusiastic audiences crowded into Rushmoor Arena and were thrilled and inspired by the glittering spectacles and the colourful

---

* The 3rd Hussars remained in Aldershot, their place in the Brigade being taken by The Queen's Bays.

panoramas of the grand finales which, with the magnificence of the massed bands and the stirring martial music, made the Tattoos the greatest military displays of all time.* Without its massed bands— massed mounted bands, massed pipe bands, massed drum and fife bands—the Tattoo would not have been The Tattoo. Nowhere in the world except at Aldershot could a moving band of one thousand musicians be seen, marching, counter-marching and wheeling, a kaleidoscope of scarlet, gold and blue, all throbbing, pulsating to the beat and roll of the drum and the stirring martial music, with its predominance of brass. The massed bands, sparkling in the beams of the powerful searchlights, as they moved across the arena were a scene never to be forgotten. Another musical feature, ever popular and equally impressive, was the massed pipe bands of the Highland and Lowland Regiments ; again the rhythmic beat of the drums and the skirl of the pipes, with the feathered bonnets of the Highlanders, the bright tartan plaids and the swinging kilts, made a brave and impressive spectacle.

The Tattoo was revived after the 1914-1918 war as the Grand Searchlight Tattoo and was held on Cove Common, Farnborough, in June, 1922. The Tattoo followed to a great extent the form of the pre-1914 Torchlight Tattoo, for with the exception of the Aeroplane Display by the R.A.F., when three Bristol reconnaissance aircraft from Andover manœuvred in the darkness over the ground,

---

* The Tattoo had its origin in a simple Army routine which was observed as far back as the seventeenth century. It was the practice in those days when operations ceased in the late autumn each year for forces in the field to go into winter quarters in billets in towns and villages. This was the practice of the British Army during the campaign in the Low Countries during the 1690's. As may be expected, the local inns were the only social centres for the troops. In order to get the men to return to their billets at night, the innkeepers had to turn off their beer taps and cease to sell drinks. The time for doing this was between 9.30 and 10 p.m., and this time was notified by a drummer marching through the billeting area beating on his drum.

The drummer was accompanied by the Orderly Officer and Orderly Sergeant. As the sound of the drum beats echoed through the small towns and villages, the innkeepers, on hearing them, remarked "Doe den tap toe," and turned off their beer taps. This was an old Dutch expression which, translated freely into English, means "Turn off the taps."

Authorities are not unanimous concerning the origin of the word "Tattoo," but the general belief is that it was derived from this expression. The word "Taptoe" was used in official documents of the time, and that word has now given place to "Tattoo."

The same custom of rounding up troops for them to return to their billets was observed in this country, and after a period of time a fifer joined the drummer and short tunes were played. Finally the whole corps of drums, fifes or pipes and eventually bands played music for the entertainment of the garrisons, and this was generally known as beating Tattoo or playing Tattoo, the word coming from the old Dutch expression, which had its origin from the simple and practical military routine of the past.—"Military Customs," by Major T. J. Edwards, M.B.E., F.R.Hist.S. (Gale & Polden Ltd.) (1948).

each illuminated with over a hundred coloured electric lamps, the Tattoo was composed of displays by massed bands, Highland piping and dancing, a musical drive by the R.H.A., tent-pegging and jumping by the 7th Dragoon Guards, and a firework display, including "Grand flights of Coloured Rockets, Discharge of Shells, and Thunderbolt Bombardment."

In the following year the Tattoo moved to the newly erected Stadium at Rushmoor Arena, which was the home of the Aldershot Tattoo for the ensuing sixteen years. The 1923 Tattoo was on similar lines to that of the previous year, but an innovation was the first big display in which a "battle" was fought, this item under the title of "Armipotence." It was in two phases. The first, *circa* 1873, depicted a small convoy of horse-drawn wagons with its mounted escort which, having been attacked by savages, proceeded to "laager up" in the arena. In the fight which followed, the convoy, despite suffering heavily in the engagement, finally succeeded in driving off the native hordes. Elated, however, by their partial success, the savages brought the episode to a close by executing a war dance.

The scene and the year changed to 1923 and the episode was reacted under modern conditions; this time the savages attacked a motor convoy escorted by armoured cars. The same defensive measures were taken, but, armed with Vickers and Lewis guns, the convoy beat off the attack with ease, the *coup de grâce* being administered to the tribesmen by tanks and aircraft.

The success of this display led to the inclusion in 1924 of a more ambitious "battle" scene depicting the forcing of a river crossing, in which the retreating enemy blew up the bridge over which they escaped. Mounted cavalry and a light tank arrived to engage the rearguard across the river, and the 18th Pack Battery came into action in support. Under the cover of this fire, sappers from the 12th and 23rd Field Companies, R.E., launched a single-span assault bridge over the "gap." "Hostile" aircraft attacked during these operations, but were picked up by searchlights and engaged by anti-aircraft guns. British planes came on to the scene and drove off the attack. The bridge completed, the river was crossed by cavalry and infantry, with the Pack Battery in support.

The first historical displays were staged in 1925 when, during the playing of the Overture "1812," the outline of burning Moscow appeared above the trees, guns boomed to add effect to the bands, and the smoke of battle drifted across the arena. This was followed by a reconstruction of the Battle of Waterloo, in which the 1st Bn. The Lincolnshire Regiment in the uniform of 1815, representing a composite battalion made up of Guards, Royal Fusiliers, the Welch

Regiment and the Connaught Rangers, played the role of the British squares driving off the attacking "French Cuirassiers," made up of detachments of the 1st Royal Dragoons, 10th Royal Hussars and the 13th/18th Hussars.

The historical display as a feature of the Tattoos was developed in 1926 when an item called "Visions and Realities" was produced. The scene opened with the entry of a detachment of troops, who then camped on the outskirts of an "Oriental village." Whilst the camp slept, visions, wreathed in clouds, appeared, each giving a glimpse into battles of the past—Hastings, Agincourt and Balaclava. This was followed by the "Realities" depicting a battle on modern lines, with artillery, tanks and aircraft in support of infantry in the attack.

The year 1927 saw an innovation in the introduction of community singing, arranged in conjunction with the *Daily Express*, and this accompanied by a Regimental Band became a regular festure of the Tattoos which followed. The singing was conducted the first year by Mr. T. P. Ratcliff, who led the waiting crowds each performance in the popular and traditional songs which through the years have found their niche in our national life.

The main historical display of 1927 was the re-enacting of the Battle of Blenheim in which three cavalry regiments, three infantry battalions and a brigade of R.H.A. took part.

The displays of the 1928 Tattoo included an item depicting the rallying of the Crusaders in 1189, whilst the historic battle re-enacted was the storming of Badajoz in 1812, a brigade of R.H.A. and five infantry battalions participating in the assault on the castle which had been constructed by the 23rd Field Company, R.E. This Tattoo concluded with torchlight evolutions by the 2nd Bn. The East Yorkshire Regiment, the most intricate ever presented at any Tattoo. Each man carried an electric torch, and five hundred and fifty accumulators were required to produce the colour effects. The evolutions concluded with the unfolding of the Union Flag formed by the coloured torches.

The Battle of Waterloo was re-enacted as the main historical feature of the 1929 Tattoo, and in the years which followed Rushmoor Arena became the scene of the reconstruction of the Battle of Dettingen and Queen Elizabeth's visit to Tilbury—this was in 1930. In the following year the Retreat to Corunna and the Roman Invasion of Britain were staged.

It was perhaps appropriate that the Crimean War, which to a great extent was responsible for the final decision to establish a permanent camp at Aldershot, should, nearly eighty years later, provide splendid material for colourful and dramatic episodes in the Tattoos. In 1931 one of the major spectacles was a presentation of the Battle of Inkerman, "The Soldier's Battle" of the Crimea—one of the decisive battles of the war. Two thousand troops, drawn from seven battalions, and a field brigade, R.A., in the 1854 uniforms of British, French and Zouave infantry, with "Russian" Cossacks and infantry, refought scenes from that great battle. It was one of the most spectacular and, numerically, the greatest battle spectacle ever staged in Rushmoor Arena, the episode concluding with a reproduction of the scene portrayed in Lady Butler's famous picture, "The Roll Call," the roll called by a sergeant of the Welsh Guards being a portion of the actual roll of the 3rd Bn. Grenadier Guards after the battle in November, 1854.

The searchlights of the Tattoos continued to floodlight many glorious episodes, not only in our feats of arms, but in the pages of our Empire's history, episodes which have thrilled many generations of our people. The motif of the 1932 Tattoo was "The Flag and Empire," and it did much to revive memories and make many thousands conscious of our national pride.

This Tattoo depicted, in varying scenes, the work, often heroic, often unrecognized, of our soldiers, sailors and administrators, who built up the greatest Empire the world has ever known. Once again the spirit of those great men whom today we are proud to call our forefathers came to life in the floodlit arena, in the wonderful pageant staged by the men of the Aldershot Command. The episodes depicted the landing of Captain Cook in Australia and his planting of the Union Jack on the shores of Botany Bay; a Canadian settlement in the early days of the colonization of the Dominion—an exciting episode this, with the log cabins surrounded by hordes of hostile redskins; and an incident in the Matabeleland Campaign of 1893, when Major Wilson's Shangani Patrol was wiped out by the Matabele after a heroic stand against overwhelming odds. This pageant concluded with a parade of our patron saints and Empire builders, from Drake and Raleigh to Cecil Rhodes and Captain Scott.

The death of General Gordon at Khartoum and the battle of Omdurman were features of the 1933 Tattoo with a great historical tableau depicting Crecy, Waterloo and the Ypres Salient.

The 1934 Tattoo had items in lighter vein, for, in addition to the trick riders of the 16th/5th Lancers in fancy costumes, a giant "Loch Ness Monster" which had featured in an amusing item in the Tidworth Tattoo was brought to Aldershot and moved into Rushmoor Arena by the 11th Hussars, heavily disguised as ancient Britons. The "battle" of the year was a representation of Abercromby's Landing at Aboukir Bay. One of the four regiments taking part in the display—the 1st Bn. Royal Welch Fusiliers, the 23rd Regiment of Foot—having actually taken part in the battle in 1801.

The Silver Jubilee Tattoo in June, 1935, which attracted an attendance of 483,000 spectators, with 62,000 cars and charabancs, and involved 6,300 troops, had as its main theme "The Crown and Empire" and was one of the most brilliant ceremonies which marked the Silver Jubilee of King George V and Queen Mary.

The Tattoo opened with the beating of Tattoo by the Massed Drums, Bugles and Fifes of the Aldershot and Eastern Commands. The mechanization of the Army was already proceeding apace and this gave added interest to the display by the 1st Cavalry Brigade, still mounted, and wearing their full-dress uniforms of the Waterloo period. The display was a Musical Ride performed by The Queen's Bays, 3rd Carabiniers and the 4th Queen's Own Hussars* to the accompaniment of the Massed Bands of the Brigade of Guards and the Royal Artillery. A further touch of pageantry was introduced into this item by the appearance of the Patron Saint of the Cavalry, St. George, and the Knights of the first Brotherhood of St. George,† in the appropriate costumes, followed by a pack of foxhounds racing across the arena in full cry.‡

Two great battle scenes were enacted, one of the Waterloo period, the other "A Modern Encounter Battle," and this was followed by a moving and imposing display of the massed pipe bands of eight regiments.§

The finale was entitled "Long Live the King." A fanfare of trumpets was sounded in the darkened arena, and then, out of the darkness, the Imperial Crown was suddenly and brilliantly lighted up. It was guarded by a detachment of Yeoman Warders and by a detachment of the Brigade of Guards. This was followed by a spectacular pageant of ten sovereigns whose reigns had also reached a silver jubilee, each being accompanied by a personal bodyguard in the costumes and uniform of the reign.

The appropriate theme of the Coronation Tattoo in 1937 was "Loyalty to the Crown," the opening item being a pageant of banners of the British Commonwealth of Nations, carried by men of the 3rd Coldstream Guards. The military episodes which followed gave an insight into the specialized and physical training of the soldier. These included a "battle" demonstrating an operation by a small mechanized

---

* These three regiments celebrated in 1935 their 250th anniversaries.
† Instituted by King Edward III.
‡ "The image of War without its guilt and only five and twenty per cent. of its danger."—JORROCKS.
§ 1st and 2nd Bns. Scots Guards, 1st Bn. The Royal Scots, 2nd Bn. The Royal Scots Fusiliers, 1st Bn. The King's Own Scottish Borderers, 2nd Bn. The Cameronians, 2nd Bn. The Seaforth Highlanders and 2nd Bn. The Queen's Own Cameron Highlanders.

force in the assault crossing of a river, in which two batteries of R.H.A., a Field Company, R.E., an infantry battalion and a battalion of the Royal Tank Corps took part. The massed bands of the Aldershot and Eastern Commands were, as ever, a popular item, with the mounted bands of three cavalry regiments and the R.A. mounted bands, the bands of twenty infantry battalions and the drums and fifes of eight more and the bugles of four light infantry regiments.

The historical episodes were the Lodging of the Colour in the days of King Charles I by three battalions of infantry, and the Passage of the Douro, a reconstruction of the battle in 1809 in which three cavalry regiments, a Field Brigade, R.A., and three infantry battalions participated, wearing the uniform of Wellington's day. In addition, there were evolutions with lanterns, a physical training display, a firework display, and then the grand finale, with a massive Lion of Empire modelled in gold as the centre-piece, with the great arena filled at the conclusion of the pageant by serried ranks in the costume and uniforms of British fighting men throughout the ages.

A spectacular feature of the 1938 Tattoo, involving four regiments of cavalry and twelve battalions of infantry, was the presentation of "The Field of the Cloth of Gold," the pageant depicting the arrival of Henry VIII at the Castle of Guyner in 1520, and the procession of Francois I and his entourage *en route* to the Castle of Ardres, whilst the historic battle scene of this year was the Assault and Capture of Fort Moro, Havana (1762), which was re-acted by a Field Regiment, R.A., and three battalions of infantry.

June, 1939, saw the last of the great pre-war Tattoos. How many among those thousands assembled in Rushmoor Arena on the evening of the last performance on the 17th of June of that year were, within the short space of a few months, to be in uniform themselves! How many were to serve their country in the struggle which in turn may well form the subject of episodes of military pageants of the future! How many realized, as they wended their way back among the crowds to the car parks, that they had witnessed the last Tattoo for many a year to come? The Munich Crisis had come and gone, war had been averted, the precarious peace had been maintained, many thought and hoped for ever, but on that same night soldiers in a different uniform— field grey in colour—in camps and barracks from the Rhine to the Baltic turned in their beds after hearing on the radio the outbursts of their Führer against the outside world that "threatened" them. Theirs were thoughts of a very different nature to those of the men who slept that night in the lines of barracks between Lynchford Road and Wellington Avenue. "Well, an' that's that," quoth a private of the Royal Warwicks; "an' that's the finish of me as a bloomin' Elizabethan pikeman," little dreaming that a year hence he would be back at Aldershot, having fought through a series of battles back to the sand dunes of La Panne—battles which were as vital to our country and Empire as the defeat of the Armada, the historical episode in which he had that night participated.

It was perhaps appropriate and symbolic that the opening item of the 1939 Tattoo, which was held amid its traditional pageantry just eight weeks before the outbreak of war, should have been "The Changing of the Guard," which was "a ceremonial interpretation of the handing over of the duties of national defence by the old Regular Army to the modern mechanized forces." Although the title of the episode suggested "one of Guard Mounting scenes familiar to those who watch the daily ceremonies at the Royal Palaces in London, the Tattoo version of 'changing the Guard' had a much wider significance, for it was an interpretative portrayal of the process by which the scarlet coats and all the brave trappings of the old Regular Army had been replaced by the modern khaki-clad mechanized force, which, though less picturesque, was much more vital to our national require-ments."* The Old Guard was composed of "K" Battery, R.H.A., in full-dress uniforms, with their six-horse gun teams and shining 13-pdr. guns, a detachment of the Royal Horse Guards (The Blues) in ceremonial dress, and a Guard of the 1st Bn. The Black Watch (Royal Highlanders) in review order. "The Old Guard" marched into the arena, and, from the opposite side, in marched "The New Guard," headed by a detachment of the 12th Royal Lancers mounted in six armoured cars; behind them followed the 24th Field Regiment, R.A., with six tractor-drawn guns, and a Guard of the 1st Black Watch in service dress, khaki aprons over their kilts, and wearing steel helmets.

The officer commanding the Old Guard, in his scarlet tunic, feathered bonnet, kilt and plaid, advanced, carrying the National Flag, and handed it over to the khaki-clad officer in command of the New Guard. A verse of the hymn, "O God, our help in ages past," was played by the massed bands† during the ceremony, at the conclusion of which both guards moved off to march past, the Cavalry and Artillery to the music of the R.A. Mounted Band, whilst the two detachments of the Black Watch in the stirring contrast of the uniforms, scarlet and khaki, swung past to their Regimental March, "Highland Laddie," played by the massed pipe bands of four battalions.

---

* Aldershot Tattoo Programme, 1939.
† The massed bands included those of the 1st King's Dragoon Guards, 12th Royal Lancers, 4th/7th Dragoon Guards, and the R.A. Mounted Band, the 1st Royal Scots, 1st Black Watch, 1st Gordon Highlanders and 1st Queen's Own Cameron Highlanders.

The concluding item of this last great pre-war Tattoo was also, as it transpired, a most appropriate one, an adapted and symbolized version of the legend of "Drake's Drum."* In a darkened arena, the waiting audience heard the distant ruffle of the drum, rising in a crescendo before dying away. Then the shrill sound of fifes, and then from the darkness the voice of Sir Francis Drake was heard once again arousing his countrymen to action. The figure of Drake was then seen, floodlit, in the arena, and at several points in the background beacons sprang into flame, beacons such as had burned the length and breadth of England as a warning when the Armada approached. Then the searchlights opened up on the arena to disclose Drake surrounded by the fighting men of his day, pikemen, musketeers, and archers. The arena then filled with all the performers in the Tattoo —some 5,000—massed in a splendid array for the grand finale with the massed bands playing. A great model of the battleship H.M.S. *Queen Elizabeth* appeared at the rear of the arena, flying Nelson's famous Trafalgar signal, and the bands broke into "Rule Britannia," bringing to a close the last of the great Tattoos on a note which was singularly well chosen and appropriate in the light of events so near at hand—events which directed the searchlights of the Tattoo to searching the skies for enemy aircraft, converted Rushmoor Arena into a vast Vehicle Reception Depot, and sent those five thousand performers into action against Hitler's hordes.

As will be appreciated, the vast organization of these great and spectacular Tattoos called for careful planning and direction, organization and administration, from the conception and rough visualization of each item, to the co-ordination, rehearsing and final presentation.

Rushmoor Arena, with its fine natural "backcloth" of green foliage, never presented exactly the same appearance for two successive years. The Tattoo was first held in Rushmoor Arena in 1923, and the Tattoo of that year surpassed in popularity and brilliance those of previous years. All the year round the Committee was occupied with improvements for accommodation, seating, exits and entrances, drainage and a hundred and one other details to ensure the success of each year's display.†

The Tattoos grew in size as each year passed. In 1919, at the first Tattoo held after the Great War, on Cove Common, the public

---

* "Take my drum to England, hang et by the shore,
   Strike et when your powder's runnin' low ;
   If the Dons sight Devon, I'll quit the port o' Heaven,
   An' drum them up the Channel as we drumm'd them long ago."
          SIR HENRY NEWBOLT : *Drake's Drum.*

† The proceeds of the Tattoos were devoted to military charitable funds administered by the Aldershot Command Trust.

attendance was 2,500; by 1938 the attendance at the Tattoo during the eight days was 531,850, and 61,159 vehicles were accommodated in the car parks surrounding Rushmoor Arena. The numbers attending the Tattoo had increased year by year, as this annual spectacle grew in size, stature and importance. It became as integral a part of the life of the nation as the Derby, Ascot, Wimbledon, Henley, the Royal Tournament and other similar events which made up the pattern of the life of the country. The road traffic control was a vast organization and was directed by the Military Police, Civil Police and Special Constabulary and officials of the Motoring Organizations, this combined "force" working together to regulate the remarkable volume of traffic not only in the vicinity of Aldershot but over a considerable portion of Hampshire and the surrounding counties. Over sixty marquees were erected behind the scenes to shelter troops and for use as their "green rooms"; expert dressers were employed to ensure the correctness of dress and other detail for the troops participating in historical episodes. Special precautions were taken to avoid accidents in the battle scenes; even special rubber bayonets with steel sprung cores were manufactured to avoid injuries in the realistic charges and hand-to-hand fighting which took place in the re-enacting of historic battles. A special telephone exchange with over a hundred extensions to various parts of the arena was installed to organize and direct the performances; loud-speakers were set up and wired to relay announcements to the performers and audience. Vast quantities of scaffolding were used for the background scenery, much of which was made by the Royal Engineers. No detailed item was overlooked in order to ensure historical correctness. The whole Tattoo organization, a triumph for the producers, grew into a gigantic task as the years passed by.

By 1938 the number of troops actually participating in the Tattoo was approximately five thousand, and in addition there was an administrative staff of over three thousand five hundred which included some 1,600 troops, 200 Civil Police, and 250 Royal Automobile Club officials.

The Tattoos were a colourful page in the life of the Army and revived much in the brilliant historical episodes of past military glories which left a feeling of emotion, combined with a stimulation of national pride.

*   *   *   *   *

Another local event which through the years between the wars became a national event was the Aldershot Show. The first Show was held in 1918 as the Aldershot Command Horse Show, then described as "the open air Olympia," a one-day affair held on the Aldershot Military Stadium, known at that time as the Army Athletic Ground. There were 23 classes and about 300 entries at this show. The idea of holding it was originated by Captain V. D. S. Williams, a well-known horse-lover and sportsman, who was a familiar figure in many a hunting shire.

In the second year the Show was extended to two days and the trophies included a champion cup presented by King George V, who was one of the original patrons, for the best riding horse in the Aldershot Command, a champion cup presented by H.R.H. The Duke of Connaught for the best horse in the Show, and a £150 challenge cup presented by the Aldershot Chamber of Commerce.

During the next two years the Show, then a three-day affair, was held on the Stanhope Lines Recreation Ground at the junction of Farnborough Road and Fleet Road. The Show transferred to Rushmoor Arena in 1923 and went from strength to strength. It was extended to four days in 1923, and in 1930 changed its title to the more comprehensive one of The Aldershot Show.

In addition to the Horse Show classes, which were in the region of fifty, there was the open Dog Show with over 200 classes, and the Hound Show which became recognized as *the* South of England Show, with famous packs from all over the country entering in both the Foxhound and Beagle Sections. There was the Coaching Clubs' Marathon, the huge Flower Show, and the wide Trades Stands Avenue with the giant marquees which housed the Empire Exhibition and the Army Vocational Training Centre Display. There were musical rides by cavalry in full-dress uniforms, and trick riding displays, and displays and music by massed bands of the Command.

Nowhere in the country could have been found a more enjoyable, spectacular or comprehensive range of competitive shows, displays, exhibitions and entertainments than the brilliant annual Aldershot Show; framed in a delightful setting in the tree-fringed natural amphitheatre of Rushmoor Arena, it was a show of noble proportions.

*   *   *   *   *

From the time of the Munich crisis in 1938 until September, 1939, there was increased activity in military Aldershot. The Government decision to introduce a modified form of conscription in the shape of the Militia led to the construction of additional accommodation and the enlargement and modernization of existing barracks. The labour needed for this work was beyond the scope of local man power, and workmen came into the town each day to swell the numbers working on the new camps. Special trains were run from London to pour these workmen each day into "The Camp." The first militiamen were called up on 15th July, 1939, and many of these young men had their first introduction to army life in Aldershot. Throughout this day train after train brought these militiamen to the town station, to be met and transported to their reception stations in "The Camp."

Up to the declaration of war on 3rd September, 1939, there was considerable troop movement in "The Camp"; the Regular Army was preparing for the war which, despite continental political declarations, was regarded as inevitable. In step with military preparations, both the military and civil authorities turned their attentions to what was known to the Army as "Passive Air Defence" and in civil life as "Air Raid Precautions." In the town a committee was formed to set up a Civil Defence Organization, and a complete system along the lines laid down by the Home Office was developed. This organization was not lacking in support; volunteers came forward to enrol as Wardens and to join the A.R.P. squads. On the same day that the first militiamen arrived in Aldershot the A.R.P. Services paraded for the first time on the Recreation Ground, and were inspected by the Mayor, Councillor A. H. J. Stroud, J.P.

In "The Camp" practical steps taken at the time of Munich were developed. Slit and shelter trenches hastily constructed in October, 1938, were improved and permanent dug-outs and shelters were dug and completed. Each unit in the Command was responsible for the drawing up of a P.A.D. Scheme, and P.A.D. Officers and Squads were formed. These schemes were elaborately designed to compete with air attack by bombs or gas. Anti-gas precautions led to the installation of decontamination and gas cleansing stations; gas-proof rooms were constructed; "Signs, Warning, Gas" were erected, and all the paraphernalia of P.A.D. was issued and put into use. Few at this stage could imagine that, in the event of war, Aldershot would not become a primary target for any hostile attack, and the Army set a lead in organizing its Passive Air Defence precautionary measures.

At the outbreak of war the troops in Aldershot, as has ever been the case, were among the first to mobilize for service with the B.E.F.

The 1st Division then occupied the area south of the Basingstoke Canal, with its Headquarters in Pennefather's Road, Stanhope Lines. It was composed of the 1st Guards Brigade, 2nd Infantry Brigade, both of which had their H.Q. offices in Knollys Road, and the 3rd Infantry Brigade, which was at Bordon. The battalions composing the 1st Guards Brigade were the 3rd Bn. Grenadier Guards at Barrosa Barracks, the 2nd Bn. Coldstream Guards at Albuhera Barracks, and the 2nd Bn. The Cheshire Regiment, which was the Divisional Machine Gun Battalion attached for training at Maida Barracks. The 2nd

The arrival of the 2nd Bn. Scots Guards at Aldershot Town Station on their return from Palestine, December, 1936.

Arrival of the first Militia men to join their units, Aldershot Town Station, 15th July, 1939.

Y

A battalion in Battle Order, the 2nd Bn. The Northamptonshire Regiment, on parade at Oudenarde Barracks, North Camp, October, 1939.

The Canadians march in: *Men of the Royal Regiment of Canada arriving in Aldershot,
4th November,* 1939.

The Prime Minister, The Right Hon. Winston Churchill, inspecting New Zealand troops, the 22nd
Auckland Battalion, 5th September, 1940.

H.M. The King inspecting men of the 1st Canadian Division in Queen's Avenue, January, 1940.

Their Majesties with Canadian troops in Aldershot.

Armour in the Long Valley : Men and tanks of the Fife and Forfar Yeomanry on the occasion of a demonstration watched by members of the Turkish Parliament, May, 1940.

The handing-over ceremony at Talavera Barracks by Brigadier P. G. Phelan to the Mayor, Councillor A. H. J. Stroud, M.B.E., of the Mobile Canteen and Kitchen presented to the Borough by the citizens of Guelph, Ontario, 24th February, 1942.

Admiral of the Fleet Sir William James, K.C.B., the Mayor of Aldershot, Councillor A. H. J. Stroud, M.B.E., J.P., and Major-General R. Evans, C.B., M.C., following the Borough's mace bearer (Mr. W. Davis) at the opening ceremony of Aldershot's Warship Week, 14th-21st February, 1942.

An Aldershot Civil Defence detachment of A.R.P. wardens led by Councillor B. W. Edgoose, Chief Warden, passing the saluting base in the "Salute the Soldier" Week Procession, 1944.

American troops in Aldershot : A detachment of U.S. infantry marching along High Street, at the foot of Ordnance Road, during the "Salute the Soldier" Week Procession, 22nd July, 1944.

"C" (Aldershot Town) Company of the 27th (Hampshire) Bn. Home Guard marching past the saluting base at the Recreation Ground during the Borough's V.E. Day Celebrations, May, 1945.

The Presentation of the Freedom of the Borough to the Canadian Army overseas, 26th September, 1945.

The Contingent of the Canadian Women's Army Corps marching up Victoria Road.

The Presentation of the Freedom of the Borough to the Royal Hampshire Regiment, 11th September, 1945. The Colours of the 1st Battalion passing down Barrack Road headed by "Fritz," the Regimental Mascot, led by the "Dog Major."

The County Regiment on parade, with the Colours of seven Battalions, at the Recreation Ground.

A passing-out parade, in the presence of H.R.H. The Duke of Gloucester, of the Officer Cadet Training Unit at Mons Barracks.

THE XIV OLYMPIAD, 1948.

Events in the Modern Pentathlon, held in Aldershot.

Major H. A. Larkos, of Finland, participating in the Equestrian Event at Tweseldown.

Captain A. Grut, of Sweden, winning the Swimming Event in the Aldershot Bathing Pool.

Lieut. Morrot Coehlo, of Brazil, and Captain Moreiras Lopez, of Spain, fencing at the Army School of Physical Training.

H.R.H. *The Duchess of Gloucester unveiling the Heroes' Shrine in the Manor Park on Friday, 5th May, 1950. In the foreground are the Bishop of Guildford and Alderman G. Roberts, J.P., then Mayor of Aldershot.*

H.R.H. The Duchess of Gloucester, escorted by Lieut.-Colonel H. N. Cole, O.B.E., T.D., R.A. (T.A.), commanding 667 Heavy Anti-Aircraft Regiment, Royal Artillery (Hampshire) (T.A.), inspecting the Guard of Honour of Aldershot Territorials mounted outside the Manor House on 5th May, 1950.

The Dedication Ceremony.

The Coaching Marathon, a popular event at the annual Aldershot Horse Show.

A Motor-cycle Scramble on Hungry Hill.

H.M. The King presenting Colours to the 1st, 2nd and 3rd Battalions The Parachute Regiment on Queen's Parade, Aldershot, on Wednesday, 19th July, 1950.

Infantry Brigade was made up of the 1st Bn. The Loyal Regiment, quartered in Salamanca Barracks, the 2nd Bn. The North Staffordshire Regiment in Badajos Barracks, and the 1st Bn. The Gordon Highlanders in Talavera Barracks ; the 2nd Bn. The Hampshire Regiment at Corunna Barracks and the 1st Bn. The Argyll and Sutherland Highlanders—the Corps Machine Gun Battalion—at Mandora Barracks were attached to the Brigade for training.

The Divisional Artillery had its H.Q. in Pennefather's Road ; the 2nd and 19th Field Regiments were stationed at Bordon and Deepcut, and the 24th Field Regiment and 21st Anti-Tank Regiment in Waterloo Barracks, Wellington Lines.

The Divisional R.E., made up of the 23rd and 26th Field Companies, R.E., and the 6th Field Park Company, R.E., were all stationed in Gibraltar Barracks. The Divisional Signals were at Mons Barracks, and the Divisional R.A.S.C., composed of the 7th Divisional Supply, 40th Divisional Petrol and 42nd Divisional Ammunition Companies, at Clayton Barracks.

The 2nd Division was located in the area north of the Canal, the Headquarters being in Marlborough Lines. This Division was made up of the 5th and 6th Infantry Brigades, the former composed of the 2nd Bn. The Royal Warwickshire Regiment in Ramillies Barracks, the 1st Bn. The Queen's Own Cameron Highlanders in Malplaquet Barracks, and the 2nd Bn. The Manchester Regiment in Tournay Barracks, and the 6th Brigade, made up of the 2nd Bn. Dorsetshire Regiment at Oudenarde Barracks and three other battalions stationed at Blackdown and Woking. The Divisional Artillery were at Ewshot and Deepcut, and the 13th Anti-Tank Regiment at Lille Barracks, North Camp. The Divisional Engineers, the 5th, 11th and 38th Field Companies, were at Gibraltar Barracks and the Divisional Signals at Mons Barracks, and the R.A.S.C., composed of the 8th, 24th and 29th Companies, were in Clayton Barracks.

These two Divisions were speedily mobilized and formed the major portion of the original B.E.F. which unobtrusively moved out of Aldershot to embark for France, the men travelling for the most part from Southampton to Cherbourg and the vehicles and stores from Southampton to Brest and Nantes.

The departure of the Regular Army from Aldershot left a gap in the military accommodation, but this was gradually filled by the increase in the number of training battalions, Officer Cadet Training Units and other establishments which came into existence.

In December, 1939, the G.O.C., Lieut.-General C. N. F. Broad, C.B., D.S.O., informed the Mayor, Councillor A. H. J. Stroud, M.B.E., J.P., that Aldershot had been selected as the Headquarters of

z

the Canadian Army, and invited him to initiate a scheme for the founding of a Service Club in the town designed for the exclusive use of
Dominion troops. The Mayor made an appeal to the burgesses of the
Borough, and as a result a sum of over £1,500 was raised within
fourteen days.

The Foleys, in Cargate Terrace, owned by the War Department, was allotted for the establishment of the Club, and this was
officially opened by the G.O.C. on 26th January, 1940. In the Committee Room at the Municipal Buildings there hangs today a hand-
painted and decorated notice which was painted in July, 1943, by a
Canadian soldier—A. Dickerson Silverman—and hung in the Club
until it was closed in February, 1946. This reads :

DOMINION SOLDIERS' CLUB

ALDERSHOT

As a gesture of appreciation and a sincere welcome to all
Dominion Troops this Club was opened on 26th January, 1940.

It is operated entirely by a voluntary staff of helpers, is financed
through proceeds of the canteen.

. . . for the duration of the conflict the War Office has kindly
donated this home and grounds for the enjoyment of you men
from—

Canada, Australia, Union of South Africa, New Zealand and
Crown Colonies.

Through the generosity of the people of Aldershot, the Mayor
raised a fund which furnished and equipped this Club.

The Club was visited on 19th April, 1941, by Lady Patricia Ramsay
when she opened a new recreation hut erected in the grounds. She
was received by a guard of honour of Canadian troops drawn from
her own regiment, Princess Patricia's Canadian Light Infantry, and the
Mayor, Councillor A. H. J. Stroud, and the Rt. Hon. R. B. Bennett,
Chairman of the Canadian Red Cross. Every day throughout the war
years, from January, 1940, until February, 1946, the Club remained
open, staffed entirely by voluntary helpers.

It was on 17th December, 1939, that the first great convoy of five
famous liners steamed into the Clyde from the Dominion. These ships
brought the first contingents of the 1st Canadian Division. The second
"flight" of the Division landed on 30th December, and the third,
made up mainly of ancillary troops, arrived on 7th February.

The 1st Canadian Division, on disembarkation, was moved to
Aldershot, where it was concentrated and immediately commenced

training, and training hard. When the Division arrived at Aldershot it had received only elementary training, and as soon as the troops had settled into their quarters a training syllabus was prepared to take the men through individual basic training, followed by unit and finally formation training.

On 9th April news was received that the German forces had attacked Norway. A few days later the Commander of the Canadian Army in the United Kingdom was asked to provide troops to participate in the operations of the North-Western Expeditionary Force then being assembled. The Canadian response was to organize an assault force of 1,300 all ranks from the 1st Division, which moved to Scotland. The troops were standing by to embark for Trondhjem when the operation was cancelled and the Canadians returned to Aldershot, keenly disappointed at missing the opportunity of seeing action against the enemy.

Hopes ran high again, however, the following month, when the War Office informed General McNaughton, the Canadian Commander, that they proposed to allot the task of restoring the communications between the main force of the B.E.F. and the Channel ports to Canadian troops. The 1st Canadian Infantry Brigade was moved from Aldershot to Dover, where it stood by waiting to embark. The situation on the Continent was worsening rapidly, and finally it was decided that no useful purpose would be served in landing more troops in the vicinity of Boulogne, Calais and Dunkirk. This was another disappointment for the Canadians, and the Brigade returned once again to Aldershot.

The general situation at this time was such that it was evident to the G.O.C. the Canadian Division that the immediate task of the formation was to prepare for the active defence of this country. With this object in view the Division was reorganized into "a highly mobile, quick acting, hard hitting reserve, ready to move in any direction against an enemy who might now conceivably decide to attack England herself."* As May, 1940, drew to a close this force, known as "Canadian Force," moved from Aldershot to Northamptonshire, and here they stood by during the evacuation from Dunkirk.

Thousands of troops of the B.E.F. evacuated from Dunkirk were poured into Aldershot in train-loads from the coastal ports. They were housed in the barracks, in the new hutted camps, and on all the old-established camping grounds in the area from Wellington Lines to Tweseldown and Crookham which were opened as Rest Camps. Here for days the men, many completely exhausted, lay in the warm sunshine, sleeping and resting, whilst arrangements were being

---

* *Vide* "The Canadians in Britain, 1939-1944." (Ministry of National Defence, Ottawa.)

made for them to be equipped and clothed, sorted out and reorganized.

Following the withdrawal from Dunkirk, the German attack was directed against the French armies and the British lines of communication, then defended only by the 1st Armoured Division, the 51st (Highland) Division, and a number of *ad hoc* formations raised from L. of C. units. It was decided to send out further troops to support France, then almost on the point of collapse. The 1st Canadian Division was among the few formations available for this task. Back to Aldershot they came. On 8th June they were visited by Their Majesties the King and Queen in the barracks and camps around the town. By the evening of the following day the Division again moved out of Aldershot for Plymouth and Falmouth, where eventually the 1st Infantry Brigade Group embarked, landing at Brest on 13th and 14th June. The Canadians pushed forward to Rennes and Le Mans. By that time the German advance was pressing onwards ; Paris had fallen and organized resistance in France was almost at an end. In consequence it was decided to withdraw all troops from the Continent. The Canadian Brigade was withdrawn from France and, together with the rest of the Division, which had not embarked, once again returned to Aldershot, bitterly disappointed at the turn of events. On its return to Aldershot the Division was again reorganized to form a mobile force and again moved from the area to a central position in Oxfordshire.

It was on 18th June, 1940, that Mr. Winston Churchill said : "What General Weygand called the Battle of France is over. I expect that the Battle of Britain is about to begin." Shortly after this a secret conference was held in London of representatives of the local authorities of cities and towns which, in the view of the military authorities, would be targets for German air attack. The main South Coast ports and Aldershot were considered to be certain targets for the Luftwaffe. Portsmouth and Southampton were early targets, but Aldershot escaped any direct attack. It is perhaps one of the mysteries of the war that Aldershot should have escaped almost unharmed by air attack. Although in 1940 bombs actually fell in the Aldershot area, only on two occasions were there any casualties, and the town suffered no major material damage at all.

The first bomb to cause any casualties fell on Salamanca Barracks in Wellington Avenue on the afternoon of Saturday, 6th July, 1940, killing three Canadian soldiers and wounding one officer and 28 men of the Royal Canadian Ordnance Corps. These casualties were the first to be sustained as a direct result of enemy action, by the Canadian Army Overseas. It was not until 11th October that any further casualties were sustained, when two soldiers died from their injuries when a single bomb was dropped on the Farnborough Road near Cranmore Lane.

Whilst the B.E.F. was fighting its way back to the beaches of Dunkirk, the new citizen army of the Home Guard, first called the "L.D.V." (Local Defence Volunteers), was raised and organized.

It was on the evening of 14th May that the historic broadcast was made by Mr. Anthony Eden, calling for men to join the organization of "Local Defence Volunteers"—The L.D.V.*

The following day a party of local men met at the police station, with the result that an organization was formed and a Headquarters established in the Mews in Little Wellington Street. The volunteers were formed into squads and immediately commenced training with but few arms and little equipment. The squads were drilled on the police square and on the waste ground in Little Wellington Street by ex-officers and N.C.Os. with service in the 1914-1918 war, and the men were soon ready to assume guard and security duties at the Waterworks, the Gasworks, the A.R.P. Centre and at other important points.

In the early days no uniforms were worn and the men were distinguished by a khaki arm-band bearing the black letters "L.D.V." Denim battledress and khaki "fore and aft" caps were issued soon afterwards, and on 15th June the L.D.V. Organization began to take a more military shape. The Aldershot Contingent became No. 9 Platoon of the Rotherwick Company, L.D.V., and by this time was several hundred strong.

It was on 15th September, 1940, that the Home Guard was formed from the L.D.V. and the Aldershot L.D.V. Platoon became No. 6 (Aldershot) Company of the 25th (Rotherwick) Bn. Hampshire Home Guard, commanded by Major C. J. Brockbank, O.B.E., with Captain S. H. Wheble as Second-in-Command, and the Aldershot Home Guard Headquarters was moved to Elm Place, in Church Lane.

The Aldershot Home Guard grew into a very strong unit, and by the time the Company had reached some six hundred strong they were transferred from the 25th to the 27th Bn. Hampshire Home Guard and allotted to a section of the outer defences of Farnborough Aerodrome, the Company taking over posts at Eelmore Bridge, Puckeridge Camp and Claycart Bridge. By this time the Home Guard were fully equipped for their role, but owing to the operational commitments of the Company being outside the town area their

---

* Within two months the total number of volunteers who came forward in response to this appeal was 1,060,000. By October, 1940, the Home Guard numbered one and a half million.

activities were not always before the public eye ; but many hours of hard training, in addition to hours of work on wiring and on weapon pits, trenches and the construction of other defensive works, were carried out by these part-time volunteer soldiers.

It was on 7th September, 1940, that the code word was sent out for all troops to stand to, as it was felt that the threat of invasion was imminent. The following order issued to the members of the Aldershot Home Guard now makes interesting reading and gives an insight into their local operational role :

"C" COMPANY, 27TH HAMPS. BN. H.G.

ACTION STATIONS

1. A General Mustering of this Company has been ordered.

2. You will *immediately* proceed to your Battle Headquarters and report to your Platoon Commander for duty.

3. You are required to bring with you the following :
    (a) Nat. Reg. Identity Card.
    (b) Sufficient food to last 24 hours.
    (c) Knife, Fork and Spoons.
    (d) Drinking Mug.
    (e) An enamel plate (if possible).
    (f) Towel.
    (g) Soap.
    (h) Comb.
    (i) Shaving Material.

4. You will proceed fully armed and in Battle Order, *i.e.*
    (a) Steel Helmet with Camouflage Net.
    (b) Respirator (at the alert).

5. If you proceed on a bicycle, it must be immediately hidden on your arrival at your Battle Station.

6. Men who have not been posted to a platoon will report to Coy. rear H.Q. at Elm Place, Church Lane East, Aldershot, for orders.

COY. BATTLE H.Q.	PUCKERIDGE CAMP.
Company Commander	Major C. J. Brockbank, M.B.E.
Second in Command	Captain S. H. Wheble.
Intelligence Officer	Lieut. S. Prior.
Liaison Officer	Lieut. E. F. Yandle.
Company Adjutant	2/Lieut. W. Hyland.

Platoon	Pl. Commander	Location of Battle Headquarters
No. 1	Lieut. V. L. McGrath	Claycart.
No. 2	Lieut. E. L. Ponsford	Puckeridge Camp.
No. 3	Lieut. F. R. Killick	Eelmore.
No. 4	Lieut. A. J. A. Rumble	Gas Works, Aldershot.
No. 5	Lieut. A. C. Dundas, O.B.E.	"Avenue House," Cargate Avenue, Aldershot.

Signal Section	
Intelligence Section	Puckeridge Camp.
H.Q. (Mobile) Platoon	

At the time that the moves of the 1st Canadian Division were taking place, the 2nd Canadian Division was arriving in the country. The main bodies arrived on 2nd August and 5th September and proceeded to Aldershot to take over the quarters vacated by the 1st Division.

All this time Aldershot was a hive of military activity. New training establishments were formed, new units raised, and there was a rising flow of troops in and out of the town and camp. The roads for miles around echoed to the tramp of marching men ; their transport stirred up the dust of the Long Valley and Laffan's Plain and filled the roads over a wide radius from the central huts of Aldershot ; the tat-tat-tat of automatic weapons and the continuous plop-plop of the rifle fire echoed over the town from the nearby ranges, followed by the thuds and cracks of explosions during exercises in the training areas, whilst at night the sky was lit by the flashes of "thunder flashes," and bright Very lights as they soared up from positions in the country beyond the Farnborough Road.

The streets of the town were packed with troops—British and Dominion troops from all corners of the Empire, and French troops from the French Training Centre which had been established at Camberley. The town's centres of amusement were always crowded—the theatres, cinemas, restaurants and public-houses. New businesses sprang up to cater for the military influx : new military tailors and outfitters and small shops catering for the needs of the soldier from cap-badges to enamel cups, from shoulder-flashes to souvenirs of all types. Khaki uniforms and accessories were to the fore in practically every shop window where it was possible to provide for the requirements of the vast number of men of all ranks who thronged the town in their off-duty hours.

In September, 1940, three Canadian Reinforcement Groups were formed in Aldershot. Each Group was composed of several R.H.Us. (Reinforcement Holding Units) organized by arms and services. This organization was the start of the Canadian Reinforcement System branch in Aldershot, which eventually became a Major-General's responsibility, to ensure an adequate supply of trained reinforcements of officers and men for the Canadian Army in the United Kingdom and later in the Italian and North-Western Europe theatres of operations. This was the primary role of these Reinforcement Groups, but in addition they assumed an operational role in providing mobile columns to combat airborne landings and in manning local defences with the Home Guard. Many of the local military establishments were taken over by the Canadians, including the Connaught Hospital. In November, 1942, the first contingent of the C.W.A.C. (Canadian Women's Army Corps) arrived in England, and in May of the following year a company of C.W.A.C. was allotted to the Canadian Reinforcement Units in Aldershot.

Further evidence of the Dominion's links with Aldershot was shown on 24th February, 1942, on the parade ground of Talavera Barracks, when a mobile canteen and kitchen presented by the citizens of Guelph, Ontario, to Aldershot was handed over to the Mayor by Brigadier P. G. Phelan, on behalf of the High Commissioner of Canada.

In addition to the Canadian Divisions, Aldershot was also the training centre of troops from New Zealand and South Africa, and men from most of the Colonies at some time passed through "The Camp." In addition, Aldershot saw French and Polish troops, and although no American troops were actually stationed in "The Camp," they were in camp in the area, and the streets of the town were often filled with men of the United States Forces, and a detachment of G.Is. participated in the "Salute the Soldier" Week procession in the town in July, 1944.

Troops of the Royal Netherlands Army were trained in Aldershot, and after the liberation of Holland when the Dutch were faced with the task of re-establishing, organizing and equipping their Army, this was carried out in Aldershot.

Recruitment of the Auxiliary Fire Service in Aldershot had been opened in 1937. Progress was slow at the start, but in the spring of 1938 the first two Home Office trailer pumps were issued and training commenced. By the outbreak of war nearly 150 men had completed or were undergoing training. Seven members of the old Aldershot Volunteer Fire Brigade and 32 A.F.S. enrolled for full-time service in September, 1939, and two auxiliary fire stations were equipped and manned. One was in Vick's Garage in Church Lane West, the other at the Park Garage in High Street, near Aldershot Green. These stations later moved, the former to the Army and Navy Co-operative Society's premises in Beechnut Road and the latter to Messrs. Harwood's premises in Ash Road. Delivery of trailer pumps and other equipment was speeded up and steps were taken to increase the availability of water supplies. Several 5,000 gallon steel tanks were erected in strategic positions in the town, and a huge tank with a clay-lined basin with a capacity of 270,000 gallons was constructed at Talavera Barracks to serve both the town centre and Stanhope Lines.

On the outbreak of war the Chief Officer of the Aldershot Fire Service was appointed District Officer, and Aldershot became the headquarters of No. 5 District of the Home Office Regional Reinforcement Scheme. This district consisted of Aldershot, Basingstoke, Farnborough, Alton, Farnham, Camberley and neighbouring rural areas, and during the early part of 1940 several communication and mobility exercises were carried out to test the scheme, the value of which was definitely proved when it later became necessary to put the scheme into operation in real earnest.

The first call for assistance to a blitzed town was received on 7th September, 1940, when the district was called upon to send nine pumps and crews to London, two of which were provided by Aldershot. From then onwards, appliances and crews were sent to the assistance of Birmingham, Southampton, Bristol, Manchester, London, Bath, Portsmouth, Exeter and Plymouth, to some of them on several occasions. On many occasions also appliances and crews were sent to various rendezvous points in close proximity to blitzed areas to stand by in the event of raids, and pumps and crews from Aldershot and neighbourhood were standing-by continuously for several weeks in the neighbourhood of Portsmouth and Southampton.

The voluntary fire-watching organization came into being in 1941 and groups of fire watchers were formed in the town to operate in the larger business premises; and in June, 1942, compulsory fire-watching was applied to the Borough by a Home Office Order. Under this order all male civilians between the ages of 18 and 60 were compelled to enrol for fire-watching duties unless exempted in consequence of other commitments with the Home Guard, Police, N.F.S. or Civil Defence. Compulsion was not applied to the women of the Borough, but many of the fire-watching parties in the residential areas were composed entirely of women volunteers.

Aldershot, strangely enough, was never subjected to the air attack which was directed against many other towns and boroughs. Never did the town become a main target for the bombers of the Luftwaffe. The reason will perhaps never be known. It is thought that perhaps the German High Command never realized that the great military centre still continued to function; perhaps they thought that we should never maintain a large concentration of troops in a world-famous garrison. Alternatively, as was proved by their activities, perhaps they preferred the direct attack on industrial areas, centres of communication or against the civil population, feeling that the discipline and P.A.D. measures of the Army were such that their attacks would be of little avail. Or, lastly, was Aldershot earmarked in the Nazi plan for the housing of their own armies of occupation ? If so, they may have refrained from damaging what they themselves required for future use.

However, whatever the reason, Aldershot was spared the horrors of bombing of the magnitude which befell many other towns ; the streets were never seen, in the grey light of dawn, littered with the debris of shattered buildings, blocking the roadways. Aldershot was spared and Aldershot was thankful. Night after night when the blackout shut out the life of the town the sirens wailed their warning of the approach of hostile aircraft. Night after night came the drone of bombers speeding their way across the skies above the town, but they were intent on targets elsewhere. The Civil Defence Organization, ever on the alert in the light of this constant and very real danger, was keyed up for any emergency. Regular exercises, to maintain a high pitch of efficiency, were held and these had a marked effect on perfecting the A.R.P. Services. In all during the war years Aldershot experienced nine raids, twenty-eight bombs falling in the Borough, resulting in eighty-one civilian casualties, of whom four people were killed and seventy-seven injured. A total of 1,760 civilian properties sustained damage of varying degrees of severity.

The National Fire Service came into existence in August, 1941,* when all Fire Brigades and Auxiliary Fire Services throughout the country were amalgamated to form one national force. At that time 275 men, 30 women and 40 messengers had been enrolled in the local fire service.

Aldershot became the headquarters of "A" Division of No. 14 Fire Force Area, and the Chief Officer of Aldershot was appointed to command the Division, which consisted of 28 fire stations and over 100 fire appliances covering a large area of Hampshire, including the Boroughs of Aldershot and Basingstoke, the Urban Districts of Farnborough, Fleet, Alton, Petersfield, and Havant (including Hayling Island), and the Rural Districts of Hartley Wintney, Basingstoke, Kingsclere and Whitchurch, Alton, and Petersfield. The Divisional Headquarters were set up at "Stoneycroft," in Church Lane West, where a fire control room was established and short-wave wireless

---

* The National Fire Service ceased to exist in April, 1948, when the fire service was again placed under local control and Aldershot became the Headquarters of "A" District of the Hampshire Fire Service.

installed to keep in touch with the headquarters of the Fire Force Area at Portsmouth.

Considerable attention was given to improving the water supplies in the Borough, and a number of static tanks, each containing from 10,000 to 30,000 gallons of water, were constructed at strategic points. Six-inch steel piping was laid from the "Gravel Pit" lake behind Boxall's Lane to the water basin at Talavera Barracks, and from the lake in Manor Park to the Post Office corner, and connected to static supplies on these routes.

As the routine of the town went on with its war-time duties and commitments superimposed on its business and domestic life, military activities were for ever on the increase—continuous movement of troops, arrivals, departures, exercises and every form of training—and many were the distinguished visitors to see the men preparing for their task of defeating the enemy.

The King and Queen were regular visitors and were constantly among the Dominion troops stationed in the area.

On 1st July, 1941—Dominion Day—the King presented Colours to the Carleton and York Regiment, commanded by Lieutenant-Colonel Lawson, and the Edmonton Regiment, commanded by Lieutenant-Colonel Wilson ; and on 24th October, 1941, the Queen presented Colours to the Saskatoon Light Infantry, commanded by Lieutenant-Colonel Scott Dudley. "Remember," wrote His Majesty in a special message to these Canadian Regiments, "that wherever you may be called on to meet, and beat, the enemy you will be defending your own homes as surely as if you were fighting on the very soil of New Brunswick and Alberta."

The Canadian troops in Aldershot formed the greater portion of the force which participated in the Dieppe Raid on 22nd August, 1942, the story of which was later told in many an Aldershot home. Men whom the people of Aldershot had come to know as their own sons and brothers disappeared suddenly, their departure shrouded in the cloak of security. There were many who never returned from the beaches on which they fought, but others did, many of them months afterwards, having returned to Aldershot from the French coast via military hospitals, and it was from these men that Aldershot learned something of the task facing the soldier in carrying the war into the enemy's country.

The war had by now, however, become world wide, and security measures were to a certain extent relaxed in Aldershot, inasmuch as troops were seen to leave their barracks with bands playing and with the men equipped for service in the tropics. Glimpses of khaki drill and topees were obtained as men marched out destined for service in the

Western Desert, in India and Burma. Throughout 1943 formations came, stayed for a while whilst completing their mobilization, and went. The tide of war was on the turn; the successes in North Africa were already having their effect on the Army and on the Nation.

The following year was one of expectancy and anticipation. "The Second Front" were words on everyone's lips, and Aldershot possibly more than most towns was "in the secret." Aldershot could see daily the vast preparations that were being built up. The town was filled with military activity possibly more so than at any other stage of the war. Tanks and vehicles rumbled through the town to marshalling areas. Static units and training establishments were moved out to make room for the great concentration of troops who were collecting in battalions at Gibraltar Barracks—the home of the Sappers in Aldershot; were moved north to Ayrshire to leave their quarters vacant for the invasion forces, and many other such moves took place. The preparations for D Day included the strengthening of fire-fighting resources in the south of the country by the transfer of appliances and crews from the North, and a new temporary fire station was erected in York Road to accommodate reinforcements from Lancashire.

After months of preparation the day approached and even more and more troops moved in or passed through.

On the main roads to the south of the town and especially along the Hog's Back the tanks and vehicles of the great assault force were lined up, end to end, miles of them, ready for the move to the ports of embarkation. A large part of the invading forces passed through the Borough and, as "The Day" drew near, Grosvenor Road was on one occasion closed to all traffic for twelve hours whilst the 11th Armoured Division passed through.

The town seemed strangely empty in the weeks following the Normandy landings. Aldershot had lived up to its reputation as a great training ground for British arms, and now that training was being put to the test.

It was at this time that Aldershot had its first experience of the flying bombs. The first fell in June in the gardens below Hillside Road, a second fell in August behind Cranmore Lane, whilst others fell in the W.D. lands in the area. Again Aldershot was lucky as in no case did these bombs fall on buildings, and there was no loss of life. Although the bombs fell on comparatively soft ground, damage of varying degree was, however, sustained by over two thousand properties.

Like all other cities and towns, Aldershot played its part in the great National Savings Campaigns. Warship Week, held in

February, 1942, brought Admiral Sir William James, K.C.B., to the town to make an appeal and to take the salute with the Mayor on the occasion of the procession which marched through the Borough. The procession included a detachment from H.M.S. *Collingwood*, together with W.R.N.S. from Portsmouth and also detachments of Free French troops, then stationed at Camberley, R.A.F. from Odiham, Canadian troops and A.T.S., W.A.A.F., and the Aldershot Home Guard and the Civil Defence Units. A special concert was given at the Garrison Theatre by the Concert Party of H.M.S. *Kestrel*. In consequence of Warship Week the town adopted a submarine, H.M.S. *Tuna*, and a replica of the submarine's crest on a commemorative plaque was presented to the Council.

The "Wings for Victory" Week was held in 1943, the town having set a target of £200,000 for the purchase of four Lancaster bombers and sixteen troop-carrying gliders. The final figure reached was £244,101, providing nearly enough funds to purchase a fifth bomber. The week was opened by Mr. Oliver Lyttelton, M.P. for the Aldershot Division, and the programme included a procession through the town of the same pattern as that of Warship Week except that in this instance the Royal Air Force detachments played a major role.*

This was followed in July, 1943, by Merchant Navy Week, which raised a sum of £3,122, and in the same year the Mayor's appeal for the Hampshire Regiment's Prisoner of War Fund raised £737.

Then came V.E. Day. A military parade and display was held on the Recreation Ground, watched by some ten thousand people. Town and camp united in an impressive thanksgiving service, at the conclusion of which the salute at the march past was taken by the District Commander, Major-General H. O. Curtis, C.B., D.S.O., M.C., and Major-General D. C. Spry, D.S.O., M.C., the G.O.C. of the Canadian Reinforcement Units. Thousands danced and sang and celebrated on the Recreation Ground in the evening. The joy, exultation and relief of the populace knew no bounds. These immediate celebrations were followed by planned Victory Parties, which included many street parties where, below flags and bunting stretched across the roads from house to house, the children of the Borough sat down to tea at long tables set down in the middle of the roadways. Fifty Aldershot Service men, released from prison camps in Germany, most of them flown home from airfields on the Continent, were the guests of the Aldershot Trades Council at a "Welcome Home" dinner at Darracott's Restaurant, and many other public celebrations of the cessation of hostilities in Europe were held throughout the Borough.

---

* The Borough had already subscribed sufficient funds for the purchase of a Spitfire.

With the cessation of hostilities in North-Western Europe one of the first effects upon Aldershot came as a result of the setting up of a large Dispersal Centre in Talavera and Waterloo Barracks. To this centre came the officers and men released in accordance with their Age and Service groups. Many hundreds of thousands of men passed through this centre and spent the last night of their service under the roofs of these old original Aldershot barracks. They usually arrived late in the evening, were fed, given accommodation, and the following day passed through the documentation rooms before being transported to Woking, where a clothing depot was established to equip them for their return to civil life.

The Canadian Reinforcement Groups changed their role, and the Cavalry Barracks which they occupied became a Repatriation Depot for the Canadian Army Overseas. Practically the whole of the Canadian Army passed through Aldershot on its return to the Dominion, and this Depot functioned until the beginning of 1947.

Throughout the war the Mayoralty of the Borough was held by Councillor A. H. J. Stroud, M.B.E., J.P., C.C. In addition to holding the office of Mayor he was also Chairman of the Emergency and Invasion Committees, and the town owes much to his energy, drive and leadership during the war years.

The Town Clerk, Mr. D. Llewellyn Griffiths, O.B.E., combined his duties with that of Civil Defence Controller, and to him also the town owes a debt of gratitude.*

On 11th September, 1945, the Freedom of the Borough was conferred on the County Regiment. The Hampshire Regiment, four hundred strong, under the command of Lieutenant-Colonel J. M. Lee, D.S.O., made up of detachments of the 1st, 2nd, 1st/4th, 2nd/4th, 5th, 7th, 11th and 14th (Holding) Battalions, together with detachments from the 14th Infantry Training Centre and the 147th (Hants) Regiment, R.A., headed by "Fritz," the mascot of the Regiment,† marched to the Recreation Ground for the ceremony, bayonets fixed and Colours flying. The King's and Regimental Colours of seven battalions were carried on the parade, making it a unique ceremony.

---

* A practical expression of the town's gratitude for the Town Clerk's services to the Borough was made on 7th May, 1947, when the Borough Council unanimously passed a resolution conferring upon him the Freedom of the Borough.

† " 'Fritz,' the mascot of the Royal Hampshire Regiment, a handsome St. Bernard, was a German police dog. When the regiment made its attack on Arromanches on 7th June, 1944, the dog was seen in the heat of the battle trotting around in the forward area. Later, when a batch of German officer prisoners arrived in England, 'Fritz' was with them. The dog was 'sentenced to death,' but Leading Wren V. Elgar took pity on him and paid his quarantine fees. Hearing that the Royal Hampshire Regiment had an interest in him, she made him a special present to the Regiment who adopted him as their mascot."—"Military Customs," by Major T. J. Edwards M.B.E., F.R.Hist.S. (Gale & Polden Ltd.) (1948).

After a formal address by the Town Clerk a silver casket, containing the parchment scroll of the Freedom, was handed over by the Mayor, Alderman J. W. White, J.P., to the Colonel of the Regiment, General Sir George Jeffreys.

This ceremony was followed on 26th September, 1945, by the presentation of the Freedom of the Borough to the Canadian Army Overseas, which also took place on the Recreation Ground. It was a unique ceremony as it was the first occasion upon which such a compliment had been paid to an Overseas Army. Aldershot has had long associations with the Canadian Army, dating back through two world wars to even earlier years, and it was in consequence of the unanimous decision of the Council that the Freedom of the Borough was handed over to Lieutenant-General The Hon. P. J. Montague, C.B., C.M.G., D.S.O., M.C., of Canadian Military Headquarters, by Alderman J. W. White, J.P., the Mayor of the Borough. The Freedom took the form of a parchment scroll, which was read by the Town Clerk as follows :

> To Lt.-General the Hon. P. J. Montague, C.B., C.M.G., D.S.O., M.C., Officers and Men of the Canadian Army Overseas.
>
> It is with great pride that the Burgesses of Aldershot invite the Canadian Army Overseas to accept conferment of the Freedom of the Borough.
>
> Aldershot is not an ancient town and has little civic history behind it, but for nearly one hundred years it has been the traditional home of the British Army, and for nearly six years many thousands of the men of your Overseas Army have been stationed in our Camp.
>
> Your very distinguished and brilliant achievements both in the Great War of 1914-18 and in the war just concluded have added new lustre to the name of Canada.
>
> Your men recruited from every part of your great Dominion gained imperishable fame by their feats of arms in the war of 1914-1918 and in the present war that magnificent record has been still further enhanced.
>
> Vimy Ridge, Passchendaele, Ypres, Dieppe, Ortona, Ravenna, Falaise and Nijmegen are names in the history of the Army that will never be forgotten in the homes of Canada.
>
> It is with these thoughts in mind that we invite you to accept from this military Borough the highest honour which it is in our power to bestow.
>
> At a meeting of the Borough Council held on 5th September, 1945, at 10 a.m., the following Resolution was passed unanimously :

"CANADIAN ARMY OVERSEAS.

"That the Mayor, Aldermen and Councillors of the Borough
of Aldershot now assembled, bearing in mind the fact that
the great majority of the Overseas Army have served in the
Aldershot Military District and have been our guests since
the outbreak of war, and in recognition of the very distinguished and devoted service in every part of the world
rendered to this country and the Empire, hereby confer upon
the Army the

FREEDOM OF THE BOROUGH."

Aldershot gave a warm welcome to the representative contingent
of the Canadian Army at the ceremony, which concluded with the
playing of the National Anthem and the Canadian national hymn,
"O Canada."

Aldershot was still to see much of the Canadian Army, for the role
of the Reinforcement Units was changed to that of "Repat" Units, and
every Canadian soldier returning from the Continent passed through
Aldershot on his return to the Dominion. Not a day passed without
its arrivals from Europe or its departures for the ports from which
the Dominion troops sailed for Canada and home. Sometimes whole
battalions entrained, but the steady flow of home-bound Canadians
continued. The farewell parade of the Canadian Army in Aldershot
was held in December, 1945. It was not entirely a military parade and
it was likened to a scene from a Western film. The parade was watched
and received by enthusiastic crowds, and the procession was made up
of many troops in the costume of cowboys and cowgirls, Indians and
their squaws, and various tableaux including an old transcontinental
stage coach of the early pioneering days; there were bands, and
military detachments representative of all arms of the Canadian
Army.

On 4th December the Princess Royal visited Aldershot and presented five new Company flags to the 1st Bn. Canadian Scottish at
Badajos Barracks, and at Christmas the Canadian Army made their
last Christmas in Aldershot memorable by the number and magnitude
of their children's parties for the young folk of the Borough; for six
years the Canadians had given similar parties, but those of 1945
reached the greatest heights of festivity, entertainment and generosity.

The last of the Canadian Army Units left Aldershot by the spring
of 1946; by January of that year 60,000 of the 97,000 Canadians who
were on active service in Europe at the end of 1945 had passed through
Aldershot on their way home. In January, Field-Marshal Lord
Alexander, then Governor-General Designate of Canada, visited
Aldershot to present new Colours to the Lake Superior Regiment.

In June, 1947, Aldershot celebrated the Silver Jubilee of its Charter of Incorporation, and a week of celebrations included a civic service at Holy Trinity Church, attended by representative detachments of every organization in the Borough, and a Mayoral Banquet, and concluded with a ceremony on the Recreation Ground, when before a large crowd the Mayor, Alderman C. Porter, J.P., presented the Town Clerk, Mr. D. Llewellyn Griffiths, O.B.E., with the Freedom of the Borough and an inscribed silver salver, in recognition of his thirty-one years' service to the town. The script of the Freedom was read by Alderman W. North :

> To David Llewellyn Griffiths, Officer of the Most Excellent Order of the British Empire, upon this twenty-fifth anniversary of the grant of a Charter of Incorporation to the Borough of Aldershot, and in recognition of your Eminent Services to the Borough as its Town Clerk during the whole of that period (and for six years previously as Clerk to the Urban District Council), the Corporation takes pride and pleasure in conferring upon you the Freedom of the Borough, whose interests it has always been your endeavour to preserve and enlarge.
>
> Your services to the Town, both official and voluntary, during the critical years of two World Wars will long be gratefully remembered ; as will your contribution in the sphere of education ; while in the fields of sport, drama, and the arts, among the ex-servicemen, and not least in the varied activities of Youth, your initiative, energy and leadership have earned for you the most affectionate regard of the townspeople of all ages.
>
> At a Meeting of the Borough Council held on 7th May, 1947, the following Resolution was passed unanimously :
>
> "That the Freedom of the Borough of Aldershot be conferred upon Mr. D. Llewellyn Griffiths, O.B.E., Town Clerk, in appreciation of the eminent services rendered by him to the Borough of Aldershot since his appointment as Clerk to the Urban District Council in 1916 and as Town Clerk since the year 1922."

At the conclusion of the ceremony, a drill display was given by the Parachute Holding and Training Battalion, and a demonstration of Airborne troops in action by the Parachute Regiment Training Centre.

In April, 1948, the King and Queen made their first post-war visit to Aldershot to attend the Army Football Cup final at the Aldershot Military Stadium. Their Majesties were cheered by large crowds who lined the route on their return from the match, their car driving slowly through the town. Over two thousand children were massed in High Street between Gun Hill and Ordnance Road, and the crowds

2A

extended through High Street and the Ash Road to the Borough boundary.

The match had ended in a draw, and the replay the following week was marked by an unusual tragedy. A freak thunderstorm broke near the ground and most of the players were bowled over by a vivid flash of lightning, two of the players receiving fatal injuries. It was decided not to replay the match a second time, and the teams from the Royal Armoured Corps Training Centre at Bovington and the 121st Training Regiment, Royal Artillery, Oswestry, each held the cup for six months.

The King was again in Aldershot in July when he visited over a thousand cadets of the Junior Training Corps in camp at Bourley.

On 1st November, 1944, a resolution had been unanimously passed by the Borough Council to confer the Honorary Freedom of the Borough upon the great war-time Prime Minister, the Right Honourable Winston Churchill. At the time it was not possible for a number of reasons for Mr. Churchill to make the journey to Aldershot to receive the Freedom, and he ultimately consented to the ceremony taking place in London.

The presentation of the Honorary Freedom was conferred on Mr. Winston Churchill at the Dorchester Hotel, Park Lane, London, on Tuesday, 6th July, 1948. The luncheon was attended by some four hundred Aldershot residents, fully representative of the Army and professional and commercial life of the town.

On arrival at the Dorchester Hotel, Mr. Winston Churchill was received by the Mayor, Alderman George Roberts, J.P., and he inspected a guard of honour formed by a composite detachment of Aldershot Territorials,* under the command of Captain P. B. Fox, M.B.E., R.A. (T.A.), drawn from 667 Heavy Anti-Aircraft Regiment, R.A. (T.A.), the 4th (T.A.) Bn. Royal Hampshire Regiment, 354 Engineer Equipment Workshop, R.E.M.E. (T.A.), and 667 H.A.A Workshop, R.E.M.E. (T.A.).

After the ceremonial luncheon the Mayor called upon the Town Clerk, Mr. David Llewellyn Griffiths, O.B.E., to read the text of the

---

* The 1st of May, 1947, saw the re-formation of the Territorial Army. From 1923 until 1939 Aldershot had maintained only one company of Territorial Infantry —a company of the County Regiment with its H.Q. at the Redan Hill Drill Hall— but the requirements of the post-war Territorial Army called on Aldershot to raise a Heavy Anti-Aircraft Regiment two R.E.M.E. units, and a company of the Royal Hampshire Regiment. To these units, in 1948, were added a company of the 14th Bn. Parachute Regiment (5th Bn. Royal Hampshire Regiment) (T.A.) and three platoons of W.R.A.C. (T.A.), and a major portion of Beaumont Barracks, the old South Cavalry Barracks, was handed over to the Hampshire Territorial and Auxiliary Forces Association as a local T.A. centre.

script containing the resolution passed by the Town Council on 1st November, 1944. The wording of the script was as follows :—

BOROUGH OF ALDERSHOT

To The Rt. Hon. Winston Spencer Churchill, C.H., F.R.S., M.P., Prime Minister, First Lord of the Treasury, Minister of Defence, and Lord Warden of the Cinque Ports. It is with immeasurable pride that the Burgesses of Aldershot invite you to accept conferment of the Freedom of the Borough. Aldershot is not an ancient town and has little civic history behind it, but for nearly one hundred years it has been the centre of the British Army. Your brilliant and adventurous career as a statesman, soldier, orator and author has earned you undying fame and has also made you the outstanding personality not only in the British Empire, but throughout the whole world. Your early military service was spent in this Borough, and therefore Aldershot has a peculiar interest in your after career. Your leadership has been an inspiration to all concerned, whether in the Fighting Services or on the Home Front, and your unwearying confidence has been an invariable tonic to those who, during times of crisis, might have lost faith in ultimate Victory. It is with this thought in mind that we hail you as our Leader and we invite you to accept from this military Borough the highest honour which it is in our power to bestow. At a Meeting of the Borough Council held on 1st November, 1944, at 10 a.m., the following Resolution was passed :

"FREEDOM OF THE BOROUGH

"That the Freedom of the Borough of Aldershot be conferred on The Rt. Honourable Winston Spencer Churchill, C.H., F.R.S., M.P. Prime Minister, First Lord of the Treasury, Minister of Defence, and Lord Warden of the Cinque Ports, in appreciation of the unique and most distinguished service rendered by him on behalf of the Nation in the prosecution of the War."

The Seal of the Aldershot
Borough Council.

A. H. J. STROUD,
Mayor.
D. LLEWELLYN GRIFFITHS,
Town Clerk.

The Mayor then asked Mr. Churchill to accept the casket containing the illuminated script conferring the Freedom of the Borough. Mr. Churchill accepted the casket and script and then signed the Roll of Honorary Freemen, and made the customary declaration.

His declaration was as follows:

"I, Winston Leonard Spencer Churchill, do solemnly and sincerely declare that I will well and truly serve our Sovereign Lord George the Sixth, of the United Kingdom of Great Britain and Ireland and of the British Dominions beyond the Seas, King, Defender of the Faith, his heirs and successors, Kings and Queens of Great Britain, as a free and franchised man of the Borough of Aldershot.

"I will preserve the peace and tranquillity of the said Borough so far as in me lieth and if I know of any unlawful conventicles or assemblies against the State thereon I will forthwith disclose the same to the Mayor of the said Borough for the time being whom I will aid by my best counsel and advice, and I will defend the customs and privileges of this Borough in every just and lawful cause."

*   *   *   *   *

In 1948 Aldershot was chosen as one of the venues for events of the XIV Olympiad. The Equestrian events were held on the Command Central Ground (later in the year redesignated the Aldershot Military Stadium), and the Riding, Fencing and Swimming events of the Modern Pentathlon, the Riding taking place on Tweseldown Race-course, the Fencing in the Gymnasium in Queen's Avenue, and the Swimming in the Aldershot Municipal Bathing Pool. Over three hundred horses and grooms were accommodated in the old Cavalry Barracks, Warburg Barracks, which for a brief time captured some of the old atmosphere of the days prior to mechanization, and townspeople saw in the streets a number of new and strange uniforms worn by the foreign competitors and their soldier grooms.

The Equestrian events of the Olympic Games brought a large influx of foreign visitors to Aldershot. The first three days were devoted to dressage competitions on the Command Central Ground. Nineteen riders from nine different countries—Argentine, Austria, France, Mexico, Portugal, Spain, Sweden, Switzerland and the U.S.A.—competed in the first event, which ended in a win for Switzerland by Captain Hans Moser. The competition was a test of memory as well as horsemanship, for it comprised thirty-three tests, in which each competitor was allowed thirteen minutes, which were carried out by memory ; the tests being carried out at the walk, a trot and canter in an arena 60 metres long by 20 metres wide, enclosed by white fencing in the centre of the ground. Forty-five riders took part in the dressage events which followed, which ended in a win for France by Colonel A. R. Jousseaume, the second place being gained by A. S. Buhler for Switzerland, and the third by the Marchese Fabio Mangilli for Italy.

The endurance, speed and cross-country event commenced on the Queen's Parade, the competitors starting at five-minute intervals. From here they rode to Tweseldown Race-course and completed the steeplechase course before covering 15 kilometres over tracks, roads and paths to the Royal Military Academy Sandhurst, where the cross-country section of the event was carried out over Old Dean Common to Saddleback Hill, a course which included thirty-four jumps. The time limit for this whole course was 2 hours 2 minutes 18 seconds.

The final Equestrian event of the Olympic Games was the jumping, which was also held on the Command Central Ground, witnessed by nearly 5,000 spectators. A French officer, Captain Bernard Chevallier, won the Individual Championship of the three-day event, with Lieutenant-Colonel F. S. Henry, of the U.S.A., gaining second place and Captain J. R. Selfelt, of Sweden, third.

At the conclusion of the jumping, a member of the Mexican team, wearing a wide brimmed sombrero, gave a clever display of "free style" riding as used by cow punchers, and Colonel A. Podhajsky of Austria gave a display of "high school" horsemanship.

Seventeen nations competed in the Modern Pentathlon—Argentine, Belgium, Brazil, Chile, Cuba, Czechoslovakia, Finland, France, Great Britain, Hungary, Italy, Mexico, Sweden, U.S.A., Uruguay, Spain and Switzerland—and to welcome these competitors to the Borough a Mayoral Luncheon was held in the Traction Hall, on 28th July, attended by officers of the seventeen different countries and a large gathering of townspeople. The luncheon was presided over by the Mayor, Alderman George Roberts, J.P., with the G.O.C. Aldershot District, Major-General J. A. Baillon, C.B., C.B.E., M.C., the Chairman of the XIV Olympiad Committee, and the Chairman of the International Committee of the Modern Pentathlon.

During the week that the Pentathlon was held, the Mayor gave a ball in the Maida Gymnasium in honour of the visiting officers. It was a truly international gathering. The crowded dance hall had unusual splashes of colour from the gay uniforms of many of the foreign guests. It was a unique occasion, and one without parallel in the history of the town—white dress tunics, scarlet, field grey, green and khaki, mingled with the blue patrols of the British officers and the formal evening dress of the civilian guests.

The first event of the Pentathlon was the Riding event, held at Tweseldown Race-course, where forty-five competitors rode over a 5,000-metre course containing twenty-two jumps. The riders set off at five-minute intervals, and nine of them scored full points. There was one accident—to Captain L. Karacson, a Hungarian competitor, who fractured a collar bone but insisted in carrying on with the competition as best he could, competing in the fencing and shooting with his arm strapped to his side.

On the following day the Fencing contests were held in the "Big Gym" off Queen's Avenue. There were eight "pools" in the Gymnasium; 1,980 bouts were fought and special electrical apparatus was used to record the hits. Captain W. O. G. Grut of Sweden and Lieutenant Morrot Coelho of Brazil tied for the first place, each with twenty-eight wins to his credit.

On the next day the shooting events were held on the N.R.A. Ranges at Bisley, and these were followed by the Swimming contest, which took place in the Swimming Pool in Aldershot Park. Here Captain Grut of Sweden was the winner in the 300-metre free-style race, his time being 4 minutes 17 seconds for the course. The last event of the Pentathlon, the Cross-country run over a 4,000-metre course, was held at the Royal Military Academy Sandhurst and was won by Lieutenant K. S. Wehlin of Sweden.

The Modern Pentathlon was won by Captain W. O. G. Grut, a thirty-four-year-old Swedish Artillery officer, with an aggregate of 16 points. This was the best aggregate ever made in the Olympic Games, and Captain Grut the first competitor ever to win three out of the five events. Major G. B. Moore, an American officer, was the runner-up, whilst Lieutenant G. Gardin of Sweden came third.

* * * * *

The N.A.A.F.I. Soldiers' Club at the foot of Gun Hill was opened by H.R.H. The Duke of Gloucester on Wednesday, 17th November, 1948. The guard of honour, wearing for the first time on a ceremonial occasion the new dark blue berets, was drawn from the Army Catering Corps. The Royal visitor was received by the late Lord Portal, then Lord-Lieutenant of Hampshire; Admiral Sir Harold Burrough, Commander-in-Chief, The Nore, who was then President of the N.A.A.F.I. Council; Major-General J. A. Baillon, the G.O.C.; and the Mayor of Aldershot (Alderman G. Roberts), who later presided at the opening ceremony in the ballroom when the building was dedicated by the Bishop of Guildford.

The birth of H.R.H. Prince Charles was marked in Aldershot at one o'clock on Monday, 15th November, 1948, by the firing of a 21-gun Royal Salute on Jubilee Hill by a troop of 25-pdr. guns manned by Royal Artillery Cadets from the Mons Officer Cadet School, the first occasion on which a Royal Salute has been fired in Aldershot other than by a Regular R.H.A. Field or Medium Regiment.*

---

* The only Regular Artillery stationed in Aldershot at the time was the 44th Heavy Anti-Aircraft Regiment at Lille Barracks, North Camp.

The year 1949 was marked by the reintroduction of the King's Birthday Parade, which was held on the Queen's Parade on Thursday, 9th June. There was considerable enthusiasm and interest in this return to the military pageantry of yore which, although shorn of much of the former splendour of such events, was impressive and spectacular, one of the most interesting features being the fact that with but few exceptions the troops on parade were National Service men. It was a brilliant day and the long line of khaki topped with dark blue relieved only by the glint of bayonets and the maroon berets of the Airborne troops, stretched from opposite the Iron Bridge to far beyond the Military Stadium. The troops were drawn up by units each of three companies, each company of three ranks of twenty-five files.

The Officer Commanding the Parade, Brigadier A. de L. Cazenove, C.B.E., D.S.O., M.V.O., A.D.C., and the Garrison Adjutant were mounted, as were also the G.O.C. and his staff. The G.O.C., Major-General W. A. Dimoline, C.B., C.B.E., D.S.O., M.C., rode on to the parade and was received with the General Salute; riding along the ranks, he inspected the parade before assuming command. At a given signal the Royal Standard was broken from the masthead, the Royal Salute was given as the National Anthem was played, and guns manned by the R.A. Wing of the Mons Officer Cadet School fired a 21-gun salute from a position near Blenheim Barracks.

Caps and berets were waved aloft as General Dimoline gave three cheers for the King; then, as the Royal Standard was slowly lowered, the Royal Salute was repeated.

Then followed the march past along Queen's Avenue, the G.O.C. taking the salute outside St. George's Garrison Church as the solid files of khaki swung past to the stirring regimental and corps marches.

*   *   *   *   *

And so this story of Aldershot ends, rightly so, on a martial note, this last vignette in the history of the town and camp being on the historic parade ground of the British Army in the heart of Aldershot Camp—non-existent a hundred years ago, but now a military centre renowned throughout the world as the home of the British Army. As one watched the khaki-clad files of National Service men marching, proudly and with precision, past their G.O.C., one could not but reflect upon the countless thousands of British soldiers who had trod that route before them, men who have carried the name of Aldershot to every corner of the globe, men who have gone forth to fight their country's battles to win undying fame and honour for British arms in the cause of God, King and Country. Aldershot is proud of its contribution to our Nation's fame and glory.

THE PAST YEAR

The year 1950 was marked by two unique and historic occasions, the unveiling of the Heroes' Shrine and Garden—the Borough's War Memorial—and the presentation by H.M. The King of the first Colours to the three Regular Battalions of the Parachute Regiment.

What was rightly described by Sir Frederick Rowland, the Lord Mayor of London, as a wonderfully memorable and historic occasion took place in Aldershot on Friday, 5th May, when H.R.H. The Duchess of Gloucester unveiled the Heroes' Shrine and Garden in the Manor Park. The Shrine, shaded by the branches of a huge deodar tree, looked beautiful, with multi-coloured flowers growing in the two rockeries formed of fifty-six stones from bomb-damaged cities and towns of Britain, which made the Shrine a national rather than a local memorial. The afternoon unveiling ceremony was preceded by a Mayoral Luncheon in the Traction Hall, where the guests were received by the Mayor of Aldershot, Alderman George Roberts, J.P., who later presided over the luncheon.

When the Duchess of Gloucester arrived at Manor Park House, a composite guard of honour drawn from Aldershot units of the Territorial Army gave a Royal Salute, and the Royal Artillery Mounted Band played the National Anthem. Her Royal Highness was received by the Duke of Wellington, Lord-Lieutenant of Hampshire, who presented the Mayor of Aldershot, Alderman George Roberts, J.P. The Mayor than presented the Mayoress and Deputy Mayor, Major-General W. A. Dimoline, the G.O.C. Aldershot District, and Mrs. Dimoline, the Bishop of Guildford, Air Marshal Sir Arthur and Lady Barratt, Mr. Oliver Lyttelton, M.P. for the Aldershot Division, General Sir Robert Haining, Lord-Lieutenant of Surrey, the Town Clerk, Mr. D. Llewellyn Griffiths, O.B.E., and Mr. F. W. Taylor, the Borough Surveyor. Lieut.-Colonel H. N. Cole, O.B.E., T.D., commanding the guard of honour, was then presented to the Duchess, who inspected the Territorial guard, five officers and fifty other ranks strong, drawn from 667 H.A.A. Regiment, R.A. (T.A.), the Support Company, 4th (T.A.) Bn. Royal Hampshire Regiment, 354 Engineer Equipment Workshop, R.E.M.E. (T.A.), and 667 Workshop Detachment, R.E.M.E. (T.A.).

Two processions were formed at the Manor House, the first consisting of the thirty visiting Lord Mayors, Lady Mayoresses, Mayors and Mayoresses, the Lord-Lieutenant of Surrey, Mr. Oliver Lyttelton and the Service guests ; while in the second, the Duchess was accompanied by the Duke of Wellington, the Bishop of Guildford and the

Mayor and Mayoress of Aldershot, with members of the Borough Council.

At the Memorial the standard bearers of ten local branches of ex-Service organizations, carrying the standards, faced the Memorial. With them were massed choirs of St. Michael's, Holy Trinity, Royal Garrison, St. Augustine's and Aldershot Methodist Churches.

The service was opened by the Mayor : "Your Royal Highness, My Lords, Lord Mayors and Mayors of many towns and cities and burgesses of Aldershot, we are met together this day," he said, "in pride and sacred purpose. Here in this quiet place are the emblems of a nation's endurance in a great ordeal, and over all there stands the figure of Him in whose will alone we find our peace. I bid you join with me in hallowing the memory of those men and women who in the defence of their country and their homes, in battle on the sea, on the land, in the air or in the burning cities of our land, gave their lives that we might live."

The hymn "O Valiant Hearts" preceded the unveiling, for which the Mayor walked forward with the Duchess, and when the Duchess pulled a cord the Union Jack fell away to reveal the imposing figure of Christ, carved in Portland stone and enclosed by four pillars. The memorial was then dedicated by the Bishop of Guildford to the glory of God and in memory of the fallen.

Standards were dipped slowly as a bugler of the King's Royal Rifle Corps sounded the Last Post, and were raised again when another bugler, posted on the opposite side of the Memorial, sounded the Reveille. As Chaplain to the British Legion, the Rev. A. G. Kick then recited the Legion's exhortation : "They shall grow not old, as we that are left grow old : age shall not weary them, nor the years condemn. At the going down of the sun and in the morning we will remember them," with the response "We will remember them" from a congregation numbering upwards of two thousand. The hymn "O Brother Man, fold to thy heart thy brother," sung to the tune of "The Londonderry Air," was followed by the lesson, read by the Rev. Alan Cook, Vicar of Holy Trinity Church, telling the story of Christ stilling the storm, prayers by the Rev. A. L. E. Hoskyns-Abrahall, Vicar of Aldershot, the hymn "O God, our help in ages past," and the Blessing, given by the Bishop.

The King's Birthday Parade was again held on the Queen's Parade on Thursday, 8th June, when the General Officer Commanding Aldershot District, Major-General W. A. Dimoline, C.B., C.B.E., D.S.O., M.C., inspected the parade composed of eighty per cent. of the troops stationed in Aldershot. A twenty-one-gun salute was fired as the Royal Standard was broken at the flagstaff ; and after the

G.O.C. had called for "Three cheers for His Majesty," he took the salute at the march past, to the regimental marches played by the massed bands. The traditions and the high standard of drill which has always marked troops stationed in Aldershot were maintained that day as the long, close marching ranks swung past the saluting base.

Wednesday, 19th July, was a great day for Aldershot, a historic occasion for both town and camp, for on that day H.M. The King presented, on the Queen's Parade, the first Colours to the three Regular Battalions of the Parachute Regiment, and later, accompanied by H.M. The Queen, drove through the beflagged centre of the town on his return to London.

Arriving at Government House, the King and Queen were met by the Duke of Wellington, Lord-Lieutenant of Hampshire, Lieut.-General Sir Ouvry Roberts, G.O.C.-in-C. Southern Command, and Major-General W. A. Dimoline, G.O.C. Aldershot District. From Government House Their Majesties drove in an open car to the Queen's Parade, arriving at the saluting base, where they were received by Field-Marshal Viscount Montgomery, Colonel Commandant of the Parachute Regiment, and Brigadier W. F. H. Kempster, Commanding the 16th Independent Parachute Brigade Group, as the last round of the twenty-one-gun salute was fired by the 33rd Airborne Light Regiment, R.A.

Drawn up in close column of parade were the 1st, 2nd and 3rd Battalions of the Parachute Regiment, nearly one thousand strong, with the massed bands and drums of the three battalions, under the command of Colonel K. T. Darling.

His Majesty was accompanied by Field-Marshal Montgomery during his inspection, and meanwhile the Chaplains moved in procession from the saluting base to the raised stand, where the Colours were resting, in readiness for the consecration service. The two senior majors of each unit handed the King the King's and Regimental Colours, and subalterns came forward to receive them on bended knee.

His Majesty addressed the Regiment after the presentation of Colours. "I am glad to be here today," he said, "to give you your first Colours and to inspect the Parachute Regiment for the first time. I have been deeply impressed by what I have seen and I congratulate you on your fine bearing and drill. This has been no surprise to me, for I have watched the growth of your regiment from its earliest days and I recognize in this parade the keenness and spirit which have brought you through the perils of so many difficult operations. Yours has not been a long history. Only a short time separated your first raids on the Tragino Aqueduct and the Bruneval radar station from the fighting in North Africa and Sicily. Very soon afterwards, with the 6th Airborne Division, you were adding your weight to those great blows which fell upon the enemy in Normandy, at Arnhem and on the Rhine, and which brought the European war to an end.

"There were other battles and much varied training, for you had to fight not only as parachutists but often for months at a time as infantrymen. The volunteers who came from all arms of the Service to fill your ranks had much to learn; they learnt it quickly and they learnt it well.

"These Colours which I have just presented to your three battalions are the traditional symbol of a soldier's loyalty. The qualities which they represent and call forth are those which are common to and, indeed, essential to all good soldiers in all ages. They are qualities which you have shown that you possess alike in war and peace. I am fully confident that you will maintain the high standard which you have already established and that these Colours will always be safe in your hands."

After Colonel Darling had replied on behalf of all ranks, the Colours were given the General Salute and were carried to join their battalions in slow time while the National Anthem was played. After the King had taken the salute during the march past, the Regiment advanced in review order and gave a Royal Salute, followed by three cheers for His Majesty.

From the parade ground Their Majesties drove along Queen's Avenue to the Regimental Museum in Maida Barracks, where the King inspected the contingent of old comrades of the Regiment. After lunch in the Officers' Mess at Talavera Barracks the Mayor and Mayoress of Aldershot (Alderman Lieut.-Colonel H. D. Tanner, O.B.E., and Mrs. Tanner) were presented to Their Majesties outside the Mess, and drove behind the Royal car through Grosvenor Road, Victoria Road, High Street and Ash Road. Many hundreds of people lined the route and cheered the King and Queen as they drove slowly through the town to the Borough boundary.

A month later, on 15th August, the Queen's Parade resounded to the salute of twenty-one guns fired by the Field Troop of the Mons Officer Cadet School on the occasion of the birth of Their Majesties' second grandchild, H.R.H. Princess Anne Elizabeth Alice Louise—a Royal Salute, the military tribute on the occasion of a royal birth, which in the crack of the 25-pdr. guns echoed the greetings not only of the Army in Aldershot but of the Burgesses of the loyal Borough which owes its greatness to its growth in step with the armed forces of the Crown, with whom its past and its future are so closely identified.

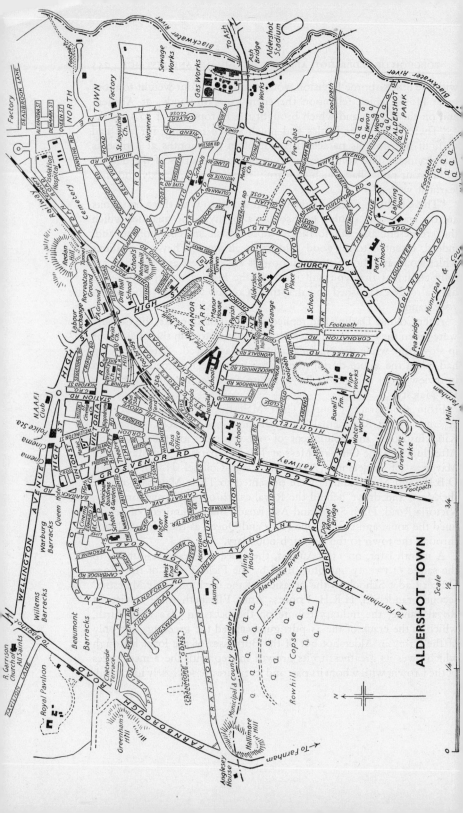

ALDERSHOT TOWN

CHAPTER EIGHT

ALDERSHOT TODAY

LET us now look at Aldershot today, which we will approach by the old coach road from Guildford along the Hog's Back. From this high ground the town can be seen for many miles. As one approaches, it begins to take shape, clustering as it does below the line of hills which divides the town and camp and below the dominating feature of Caesar's Camp, which rises six hundred feet above sea-level, and is of chalk, forming the outlying bastion of the North Downs of Hampshire. Below Caesar's Camp the area covered by the Long Valley and Aldershot Heath or Common is the southern boundary of the Bagshot Sands, which form a large portion of West Surrey. These sands reach their highest elevation at this point, some four hundred feet above sea-level.*

The landmarks which catch the eye as one nears the town are the large gasholder in the foreground, the tower of the Cambridge Hospital, the Cargate water tower, the spire of the Royal Garrison Church and the tower of the Methodist Church. As will be seen later, Aldershot town lies in a saucer-shaped depression. This is more evident when exploring the town, for there is an inner ring of high ground running along Knollys Road to Redan Hill and Windmill Hill on the north ; Chetwode Terrace, Ayling Hill and Cargate to the west, and Church Lane to the south. The town centre lies within these boundaries, from all points of which one can catch glimpses of the cluster of streets and buildings of the old town.

To reach Aldershot one turns off the Hog's Back down through Tongham village, on the boundaries of which lies the Aldershot Stadium, which, although bearing the town's name, is actually over the Surrey border. Here is a greyhound racing track and a motor-cycle speedway. The road continues until one joins the old Ash Road at a T-junction and turns westward. To the left lies some waste ground, a site for travelling fairs, and a hundred yards along the road

---

* The summit of Greenham's Hill is 413 feet above sea-level.

one crosses a small bridge, Ash Bridge, which spans the River Black-water, at this point a stream but a few feet in width, the boundary between Hampshire and Surrey and the Municipal boundary of Aldershot, it being locally known as "The County Stream."

On both sides of the road lie the Gas Works of the former Mid Southern Utility Company, which was founded in 1865 on this site as the Aldershot Gas Consumers' Company. This private Company was reconstituted, by an Act of Parliament, in the following year and became the Aldershot Gas and Water Company. After several changes of title it became, in 1932, the Mid Southern Utility Company, which, under the Gas Act of 1948, became, on 1st May, 1949, part of the Nationalized Gas Industry, as the Aldershot and District Gas Undertaking (Southern Gas Board).

Commencing on a small scale, designed to supply gas to the growing town, the Company expanded as the years passed by and absorbed the smaller gas works at Odiham, Hartley Wintney and South Farnborough. These works were closed and all gas was supplied from the Aldershot works. The huge gasholder which dominates the Gas Works and this part of the town, and is a landmark for many miles, stands 200 feet high. Its gas capacity is 3,000,000 cubic feet when fully inflated. It has five lifts or rising sections above the basic steel tank. The frame consists of twenty steel standards of plate construction braced with steel girders, rods and stays. Its over-all weight is approximately 3,000 tons. It was built in 1926-7 by Messrs. Newton, Chambers & Co., of Sheffield, after the first turf on the site had been cut on 30th December, 1925, by the then Mayor of Aldershot, the late Alderman J. May, J.P.

Today these works supply gas over an area of some one hundred and fifty square miles, including most of Camberley and as far afield as Yateley, Greywell, Elstead and Blackdown. The extensive yards to the south of the Ash Road are bounded by a high castelated wall, erected in 1922, which shut out the view of the sidings and dumps of fuel which were then bounded only by a wide, overgrown ditch. The pavement along the line of the wall has been planted with plane trees which in summer leaf improve this industrial site. Set in the wall near where it turns into Lower Farnham Road stands Brook House, which is shown on the map of Aldershot of 1856, today converted into two houses, 152 and 154 Ash Road. Behind the Gas Works, to the north, lies the Borough Sewage Works with its tank and filter beds.

The first turning to the right is North Lane, which runs through the district of Aldershot called North Town, the lower portion of which is one of the older parts of the town, developed in the late fifties in consequence of its position on the Ash Road and, later, the building of the Gas Works. At the lower end of North Lane is a row of neat cottages, named North Place, which bear the date 1856. On the opposite side of the road is a large wooden hall opened in 1947 as the headquarters of the Salvation Army.

North Lane runs northwards through an area which has gradually developed as the town has grown; it is, in consequence, patchy, with undeveloped ground and allotments leading away to the east. At the junction of Holly Road and North Lane stands St. Augustine's Church.

The church, a red brick building designed by Sir T. G. Jackson, R.A., was erected in 1907 in a modern style, and its interior still gives the impression of being newly built. The church has no spire or tower, and the church bell hangs from the apex of the roof, outside the building, high above the west door. The church has no stained glass windows, the windows being of plain leaded diamond-shaped panes; there is a row of similar gable windows set into the roof on either side. The only pews are those used by the choir, rows of chairs being provided for the congregation.

Just inside the main entrance, which is by the south door under a porch facing Holly Road, is a wall plaque commemorating the dedication of the church by "Henry Edward, Lord Bishop of Winchester, on All Saints' Day 1907 A.D.," and on the opposite side is a wall memorial to the memory of Emma Greenwood, "for twenty-one years a faithful worker in this district of North Town," who died in 1906. There is also an oak war memorial bearing 58 names of "men of this District" who fell during the 1914-1918 War.

The church has a quiet dignity, and, standing as it is in an open area, its interior is light and bright. Adjoining the church is the well-appointed Church Hall, on the east wall of which is a stone plaque bearing the inscription: "To the Glory of God and for the Work of Christ's Church, This stone was laid on June 29th 1914 By H.R.H. Princess Henry of Battenberg."

The first turning off North Lane to the left, opposite North Place, is Lower Newport Road, and here stood, until 1923, the then smallest inhabited house in Aldershot, on a tiny triangular piece of land. The house, only about twelve feet by fifteen feet, surrounded by a hedge, was built of wood, with a tiled roof and a small porch. It dated back to 1850, having been originally used for the purpose of storing turf which was cut on the common and where South Camp was built, by the tenants of Giles' Cottages, then the only houses in North Lane, as was their traditional right dating back to the days of the Crondall Customary. The old cottage was purchased by the Council and demolished in order to facilitate traffic movement in the area. At the junction of North Lane and Newport Road lie Yew Tree Farm and a group of old cottages which have retained their rural appearance, with their typical flowered cottage gardens. Yew Tree Farm as such no longer exists, the farmyard area now being a builders' yard. A hundred years ago the farm possessed a hop kiln, the top of which was removed about twenty years ago, but the rounded wall of the kiln remains, now joined to the main farm buildings. To the right lies Herrett's Farm, named after William Herrett, who farmed in Aldershot in the early fifties, a neat, white-fronted old house with a long paved path leading through well-kept lawns and fruit trees. At the rear of the house are the buildings of the Holly Dairies, equipped with a modern pasteurization plant which was installed in 1949, and the garages and stables of the Dairy, the latter being the original stables of the old farm, the pasture land of which, until recent years, ran back towards Holly Road, and on which stands the Council housing estate of Friend Avenue* and Calvert Close.†

Continuing along North Lane one can judge the period of the houses from the names of the roads which lead off to the left and right—Queen Street, Denmark Street, Alexandra Street (in which stands the Havelock Baptist Mission Hall,‡ which serves North Town), and Canning Road. Here too are two public-houses whose names link them with the time of their building—the "Heroes of Lucknow" and the "Prince Albert"—whilst to the left of the road lies the Aldershot Isolation Hospital, which was built in 1900 and extended in 1938.

---

* Named after the late Alderman Samuel Friend, who was born in Southwark and came to Aldershot in 1876, articled to Mr. James Galsworthy, then Surveyor to the Local Board of Health. In 1882 he started in practice as an architect and surveyor in the town, and in 1894 was elected to the local Board. He was later Chairman of the Aldershot U.D.C. on three occasions, and was one of the first six Aldermen of the Borough. The Freedom of the Borough was conferred on Alderman Friend in April, 1931.

† Named after the late Alderman Charles Augustus Lees Calvert, who came to Aldershot in the early 1890's, after eight years in the Royal Navy. He bought his discharge and joined the London Salvage Corps. Four years later he went to Australia, but soon returned to England and to Aldershot, where he started in business. He was elected to the Aldershot U.D.C. in 1900 and became an Alderman of the Borough in 1925. The Freedom of the Borough was conferred on him in April, 1931.

The practice of naming roads after prominent townsmen has recently been continued. On the Aldershot Borough Housing Estate built at Ash on the Borough's boundary just over the Surrey border are: Underwood Avenue, named after the late Alderman E. A. Underwood, Mayor of Aldershot, 1926-7; May Crescent, after the late Alderman J. May, J.P., Mayor, 1925-6; Attfield Close, after the late Alderman J. R. Attfield, who gave many years' public service to the town; and Robertson Way, after the late Mr. W. T. Robertson, J.P., C.C., one-time Chairman of the Aldershot Magistrates and a great benefactor and President of the Aldershot Hospital for many years.

‡ Here in the latter years of last century the Band of Hope did much good work, over a hundred children regularly attending the Sunday and Mission Schools.

North Lane ends at the railway line, but the road continued under the line until recent years; it then became but a footpath leading across a stretch of gorse-covered sandy ground in the apex formed by the Government Siding and the main line. Today a new concrete road links North Lane with the roads which run from "The Camp" to serve the Government Siding and the R.A.O.C. Depot and the Command Workshops.

The North Town area has been scheduled for further development, a decision reached in 1943 when an area of eighty-seven acres was "zoned" for light industry. Evidence of this can already be seen, for on the ground to the immediate south of the railway stands the new factory of Messrs. Timothy White & Taylors Ltd. This large, well-lighted and heated modern warehouse, set in seventy acres of land, was first opened for packing and distribution on 3rd May, 1948. This warehouse was built in consequence of the destruction by enemy action during the war of the Company's pre-war premises at Portsmouth. Aldershot was selected as a possible area for the construction of the post-war warehouse; negotiations with the Borough Council were opened in 1945, and in June of that year agreement was reached on the purchase of the site. The warehouse accommodation covers over 115,000 square feet, whilst there is an additional 30,000 square feet occupied by garages. This large distributive warehouse, which employs some 300 people, is the focal distribution point for this well-known firm. From here some five hundred branches of the Company are kept supplied with every item of the chemists' products and household stores retailed by the branch stores. Goods are received here from manufacturers all over the country and stored ready to meet the demands of the branches. These requirements are made up as needed, packed and taken by electric trollies to the distribution bays, from where they are loaded on to the Company's delivery vans for direct delivery.

Beyond the boundary of Timothy White's premises, which runs along Deadbrook Lane,* lies a stretch of low-lying marshy ground, known as Deadbrook Pond.† This is bounded by the Basingstoke Canal, which at this point runs above the level of the surrounding country, the banks rising steeply several feet from the low-lying waste land to the level of the canal water, which at this point is thick with weeds. Away to the right lies Deadbrook Farm and open fields which

---

* Deadbrook Lane, today but a footpath, is among the oldest roads in Aldershot. At one time, in the days prior to the establishment of the camp, it was the only road leading from Aldershot to South Farnborough, and therein was an inn called the "New Found Out," patronized by farmers, drovers and bargees. The old inn was converted in the early 1880's into three cottages.

† Mentioned in the Crondall Customary of 1568 as "Dedbroke."

2B

run down to the straggling line of the Blackwater River, locally known
as the "County Stream." Pleasant meadowland, leafy lanes and quiet
footpaths adjoin the river, along which runs the Municipal Borough
Boundary, and the "County Stream" is crossed by a small footbridge
on the site of a ford along the old route from North Town to Shawfield
at Ash.

In North Lane itself are the premises of Messrs. Thomas Christy &
Co. Ltd., manufacturers of proprietary medicines and cosmetics, whose
original premises in the City of London were completely destroyed
in 1941. Temporary accommodation was found at Hale and in
Farnham and in Church Lane until the present site was purchased and
the new premises opened in 1949. Here also is the factory of the
Godalming Fur and Skin Company, process fur manufacturers, and
the sites acquired for the building of factories for Messrs. N. Como
& Co. Ltd., briar pipe manufacturers, and Messrs. A. R. Wade
electrical furnace manufacturers. Near by, opposite the "White Swan,"
lies an old farm-house, a low red-brick building within a walled
garden, which dates from the days before the building of "The
Camp."

Continuing along Ash Road to the town centre one observes the
varying styles of buildings which are typical of the older roads of the
town; the cottages of the late fifties mingle with the solid Victorian
houses of the seventies, the Edwardian villas and the modern style
of semi-detached houses. There are terraces, houses with basements
and steps rising to the door, houses with front doors that open direct
on to the pavement, detached houses standing in pleasant gardens, and
small shops sandwiched in between the residential blocks. This
mixture has been brought about by the gradual expansion of the
town.

As a whole, the development has been rapid, but in detail it has taken
a hundred years to make up the present-day pattern of the town.
Although the town centre grew rapidly, the outer areas grew gradually.
For many years the rural character of the town persisted, and houses
and cottages were built wherever a farmer would sell his land. This
led to a straggling town, but as the years went by the gaps between the
cottages were filled by the more solid and pretentious residences;
in turn other gaps were filled by the urban villas, and today the last
gaps are being filled in by the modern buildings of red brick or rough
cast rendered walls.

At 215 Ash Road stands the old Ash Bridge House, which is shown
on the map of Aldershot of 1856, and at the corner of Ash Road and
Lower Newport Road is Cross House, which is shown on the same
map. Today it is a butcher's shop. Between the modern frontage of

the shops at 159 and 163 Ash Road runs a narrow passage leading to the entrance of the Rechabite Hall.

To the left of Ash Road lie Herrett Street, which takes its name from Herrett's Farm, and Brighton Road, formerly Red Lion Lane. Then comes Elston road, named after Mr. John Elston,* one of the original landowners in the area, who in 1860 lived in Aldershot Lodge.

At the junction of Ash Road and Herrett Street is the red brick Ash Road Methodist Church, "The Ebenezer," built in 1885. Following the custom of the time, this church bears six foundation stones, all dated 14th October, 1885. In Herrett Street by the east door are the stones laid by the Ash Road and Victoria Road Primitive Methodist Sunday Schools, and facing Ash Road those laid by C. Palmer, Esq., J.P., of Reading, Mrs. Allden, Herbert Dodsworth Terry and Sergeant G. Musselwhite. The interior of the church, with a Sunday school at the rear, is simple in design and decoration. The organ bears a brass plaque recording that it is dedicated to the memory of Frederick William Winter, organist of the church from 1912 until April, 1932.

To the right of Ash Road lie Institute Road and Coleman Road. It is possibly a mystery to many why Institute Road is so called, for no such building exists therein or near by. The road takes its name from the fact that on the site of this road and Coleman Road, before the houses were built, was the original sports ground of the Aldershot Institute, the gift of the late Mr. William Allden. The ground was described as "a lovely place with a first-class cricket ground and fine tennis courts and magnificent oak trees providing ample shelter." Eventually, however, the site had to be sold, and it was purchased in 1890 by a Mr. Coleman of Farnham, who disposed of it in building plots, the two roads built on the ground being named after the Aldershot Institute and the purchaser.

At the point where Ash Road joins Brighton Road stands the "Red Lion" public-house. The present building is but little over twenty years old, but it occupies the site, and has inherited the name, of one of the two inns which flourished in Aldershot village for many years prior to the establishment of "The Camp."

Ash Road continues into High Street and takes on this name at the Red Lion, just before Aldershot Green, the original village green of Aldershot. Today this is a triangular piece of grass with its base bounding High Street and its apex in Church Hill. May trees have been planted on the green, and in the centre in a small enclosure is a sundial on which is the inscription "I Count the Bright Hours Only." The sundial stands on an ornamental stone plinth upon which are the words, "To my native town—Walter Finch—1922," it having been given

---

* First Chairman of the Aldershot Burial Board, 1860.

in that year to the Borough by Mr. Walter Finch of Ayling Barn, Ayling Lane.*

Opposite the Borough Green a group of seventeen cottages known as Ivy Cottages lie back from the road. These cottages are built on three sides of a square with a small communal, well-cultivated garden in the centre. Each cottage, too, has its small front garden in which cluster in profusion ferns, privet, irises, lupins and roses.

On the left of the road lies the Manor Park, of which the Borough is justly proud.

The Manor Park has proved a valuable asset to the Borough since its purchase by the Council in 1919.† It has spacious playing fields for children, pleasant walks and beautiful vistas, a large nursery and a charming ornamental lake.

There is a fine avenue of trees dividing the park proper from the playing fields. This avenue leads from the footpath—Manor Walk—running along the south boundary to the main High Street gateway at the St. Michael's Road end. This avenue was planted by the late Major Newcome when owner of the Manor House and estate. Every tree in the avenue, which is known as "The Major's Walk," was brought home by him at different periods on his return from service overseas, It is a unique avenue with some fourteen different varieties of trees.

Here in the Park amid delightful surroundings stands the Manor House, which was built in 1670. The house has undergone structural alterations both exterior and interior as the years have passed by, but it remains in a fine state of preservation in its eighteenth-century form with its nineteenth-century additions. Above the staircase leading from the tiled entrance hall are two stained glass windows depicting St. Peter and St. Paul. On the west gable still hangs the Manor House bell. The house was also purchased by the Council in 1919, when they took over the estate, and today it is used as the Child Welfare, Ante-Natal and Diphtheria Immunization Clinics. It is also the offices of the Hampshire County Council Registration District, and the Registrar of Births and Deaths for the Aldershot Sub-District. Here also the Maternity and Child Welfare, Guardian and Assessment Committees hold their meetings.

To the left of the house among the trees stand the old stables, coach-house and yard, used today as one of the depots of the Parks

---

* Mr. Walter Finch's father was among the first business men who came to Aldershot in the middle fifties and established a builder and undertaker's business in High Street.

† This also led to the High Street Improvement Plan, which involved the clearing of trees along the northern boundary of the Park, the filling in of the old wide ditch which had acted as a drain, and the widening of the main eastern approach to the town to thirty feet.

Department; and near by are two large huts erected during the war, now used as the headquarters of the Aldershot Company of the 2nd Cadet Battalion The Parachute Regiment, A.C.F.

To the south of the footpath leading from Church Lane East along the southern boundary of the Park to St. Michael's Road stand the new modern buildings of the Manor Park School opened in 1949.

Between the Manor House and the Parish Church the park has been laid out and cultivated; shrubs, trees and flower-beds have been planted with seasonable flowers so that the gardens are always a joy to behold. It is indeed a secluded and peaceful retreat. In the lower grounds bordering upon Church Lane lies the "Heroes' Garden" in memory of those who fell in the First World War. Here stands a rough granite memorial upon which is a plaque bearing the inscription "Their Name liveth for Evermore, 1914-19." The stone stands on a rough square of crazy-paving set in which is a mosaic bearing the words "The Heroes' Garden." To the right of the main path from the Manor House stands an ornamental stone flower-bowl in which bulbs, geraniums and other flowers are planted according to the season. The bowl is supported by four cherubs standing on a plinth which bears the names and dates "Omar Harland 1854—C. J. Harland 1917."* Omar Harland, who had a building business in Wellington Street in the early fifties, was one of the earliest traders in the town.

Behind the Manor House, below the branches of a large deodar tree, is the walled, sunken Heroes' Shrine and Rock Garden, Aldershot's National Memorial to those who lost their lives in the Second World War, which was unveiled by H.R.H. The Duchess of Gloucester on 5th May, 1950.

The inception of the memorial was largely due to Mr. J. E. A. Thomas, of Evelyn Avenue, Aldershot, President of the Aldershot Branch of the Royal Air Forces Association, who submitted a suggestion to the Mayor and the Town Clerk that a memorial should be erected in Aldershot as a tribute to those who took part in the Battle of Britain and to the people of the "blitzed" cities and towns, and that it should take the form of a Memorial Shrine, with rockeries composed of stones from famous buildings which had been destroyed by air attack. This proposal was considered by the Borough's War Memorial Committee, and was approved with the addition of the idea that it

---

* The Memorial was a gift to the Borough by Mr. C. J. Harland, of York Crescent, to commemorate the year in which his father held civic office in the early days in the town, and the year that he himself was chairman of the Urban District Council, also the fact that it was during his chairmanship of the Council that he opened the negotiations which led to the purchase, by the Council, of the Manor House and Park.

should take the form of a National Memorial, as it was considered fitting that such a memorial should be erected in a town which is the home of the British Army and one which escaped the full force of the enemy air attacks.

Invitations were sent to the Lord Mayors and Mayors of the cities and boroughs which had suffered the most severe damage from the air attacks during the war, inviting them to co-operate in the plan. Eighteen cities and thirty-four boroughs responded to the invitation, and each sent a stone, or several stones, from their most famous war-damaged buildings. Among those received, which now form part of the rock gardens, were those from Coventry Cathedral ; the Tower of London ; the Priory Church of the Venerable Order of St. John of Jerusalem ; the Guards' Chapel, Wellington Barracks ; the fourteenth-century Guildhall of York ; Holy Trinity Church in H.M. Dockyard, Portsmouth ; St. John's with St. Peter's, Brighton ; and the George Street Baptist Church, Plymouth.

The memorial, which was designed by the Borough Surveyor, Mr. F. W. Taylor, has as its main feature a huge Portland stone figure of Christ stilling the storm, which stands in the centre under a small dome supported on four columns. Around the base is the inscription :

HE COMETH IN RIGHTEOUSNESS TO JUDGE THE WORLD
WITH HIS TRUTH, HE REBUKED THE WIND AND THE SEA, HE
MAKETH WAR TO CEASE IN ALL THE WORLD.

The actual stone from which the figure is carved is a block rejected by Sir Christopher Wren in the building of St. Paul's Cathedral, owing to a flaw which it was possible to eliminate when the figure was carved by the famous sculptor, Josephina de Vasconcellos (Mrs. D. Banner). The statue was presented to the Borough through the Central Council for the Care of Churches.*

On the wall on either side of the central figure are panels on which are carved the names of the cities and boroughs, whilst in four alcoves are set four oak seats, each bearing a small plaque with the inscription :

THESE FOUR SEATS ARE DEDICATED TO THE MEMORY OF
ROTARIAN FLIGHT LIEUTENANT RICHARD JOHN KINGHAM, R.A.F.
KILLED IN ACTION 6TH AUGUST 1944
PRESENTED BY THE ROTARY CLUB OF ALDERSHOT

---

* The memorial was constructed by Messrs. Perryman & Co. Ltd., of Woking, at a cost of £3,200. The inscriptions on the panels of the Shrine and the carving of the names of the cities and towns upon the stones of the rockeries were carried out by Messrs. E. Finch & Sons, of High Street.

The main inscription of the memorial is on a stone slab resting on the lawn before the figure of Christ, which reads :

1939-1945. TO THE GLORY OF GOD AND AS A TRIBUTE TO THE MEN AND WOMEN OF BRITAIN WHO GAVE THEIR LIVES IN THE HOUR OF NEED, FIFTY-FOUR BOROUGHS SENT STONES FOR THIS ROCKERY FROM RUINS OF CHURCHES AND HISTORIC BUILDINGS DESTROYED IN THE BATTLE OF BRITAIN. SPECIAL HONOUR IS PAID TO THE PEOPLE OF OUR DEVASTATED CITIES AND TOWNS, WHO, IN THE DARK DAYS OF INVASION BY AIR, MAINTAINED UNFAILING COURAGE, CHEERFULNESS IN ADVERSITY AND THEIR FAITH IN GOD. MANY THOUSANDS OF OUR YOUNG MEN AND WOMEN WHO HAD THEIR MILITARY TRAINING IN ALDERSHOT DIED IN THE DEFENCE OF THEIR HOMES AND HERITAGE. WE REMEMBER THEM WITH PRIDE AND SORROW. "THOU SHALT NOT BE AFRAID FOR ANY TERROR BY NIGHT ; NOR FOR THE ARROW THAT FLIETH BY DAY."
PSALM XCI 5.

On each side of this stone are the two large rockeries composed of the fifty-six stones from the bomb-damaged cities and towns.* The stones, embedded in rubble, are symbolic of the devastation brought about by air attack. The main and larger stones are carved with the name of the city or town from whence they came. The three from Bermondsey are also carved with charges of the Borough arms.

*   *   *   *   *

From Aldershot Green to St. George's Road East the road runs along the north borders of Manor Park, and the ornamental lake, which with its water-fowl is a source of attraction to the children, lies in the north-east corner of the park. On the west of High Street, opposite the lake, at the junction with Waterloo Road, within a low-walled, well-cultivated cottage garden, stand Manor Cottages, which bear

---

* The cities of London, York, Bristol, Canterbury, Cardiff, Coventry, Exeter, Leeds, Liverpool, Manchester, Norwich, Portsmouth, Plymouth, Rochester, Salford, Sheffield, Westminster and Kingston-upon-Hull.

The County Boroughs of Bootle, Brighton, Croydon, Eastbourne, Grimsby, Great Yarmouth, Hastings, Middlesbrough, Southampton, Sunderland, Swansea, South Shields and Southend-on-Sea.

The Boroughs of Bodmin, Chatham, Ealing, Folkestone, Wimbledon, Gosport, Maidstone, Margate, Ramsgate, Tottenham and Weston-super-Mare.

The Metropolitan Boroughs of Bermondsey, Bethnal Green, Greenwich, Hammersmith, Kensington, Poplar, St. Marylebone and Woolwich, and the Urban District of Cowes.

the date on the gable—1851. These attractive cottages, standing amid well-tended flowers and vegetables, are of red bricks, with clematis and roses climbing over the porches and up the walls. Beyond these cottages stands the Manor Park Pavilion Cinema, and then, behind a high brick wall, Campbell House, which is shown on the map of Aldershot of 1854. Waterloo Road rises steeply to the south of Windmill Hill, and was part of the early residential area of the town and is composed of typical early Victorian villas, with basements. Among them are "Pugh's Buildings," which bear the date 1861, with the initials "J.H." Next to these houses lie two public-houses which are converted private houses, the bars being built out from the frontages of the original buildings. One of these, which in its day was known as the "Bricklayers," has now been reconverted into residential use. On the opposite side of the road lies Raglan Road, the shortest road in Aldershot. Although named,* there are no houses in it except for the side entrance to a domestic store which is 37 Waterloo Road. Raglan Road is only forty-five feet in length, and contains only four lock-up garages, the end being blocked by fencing, below which lie a number of allotment gardens.

At the top of the hill Waterloo Road runs into Mount Pleasant Road and opposite to Staff Road, at the corner of which stands the Royal Staff Hotel. At the lower end of Waterloo Road, Newport Road, which was originally known as Malt House Lane, runs off to the right and leads into the Chrismas Estate. This is an extensive housing estate developed in 1933, when 268 houses were built, and takes its name from the Chrismas family, who farmed Park Farm for three generations. Park Farm House still stands in its original form at the junction of Newport Road and Wolfe Road and opposite Chrismas Avenue. The old barns and outbuildings of the farm remain at the rear of the old house. This estate of modern, well-planned small houses with pleasant gardens covers some 196 acres. The names of the roads are appropriate to the town, being named after famous military leaders—Wolfe, Clive, Haig and Roberts; also Anglesey Road, which takes its name from Anglesey House, the well-known residence of the former commanders of the Cavalry Brigade.†

Lower down Newport Road stands the Newport Road School, built in 1905. To the left of Waterloo Road lies one of the first named roads of the town, Wyndham Street, which is shown on the 1856

---

* After Field-Marshal Lord Raglan, Commander-in-Chief of the Forces in the Crimea in 1854-5, who, as Lord Fitzroy Somerset, had lost an arm at the battle of Waterloo.

† See pp. 299 and 379.

map of Aldershot. There is a track leading off on the right half-way along this street which leads up to the open grassy slopes of Windmill Hill, which takes its name from the old mill of Aldershot village, which stood on this hill in the eighteenth century. This hill is shown on a map of the area published in 1792 as Windmill Clump. Windmill Hill is a pleasant open space with a row of small houses at the summit, and others in Windmill Hill Road facing the hill in the style of houses built round a village green. A fine view of the town and the country beyond is obtained from the hill. Immediately below lies the wooded Manor Park, and farther afield, in a semi-circle, the view extends to the Hog's Back and to Caesar's Camp, with the Methodist Church, the Roman Catholic Church and the Cargate water tower rising above the streets of the town.

On the north side of the hill is Windmill Road, which runs up from High Street. To the top, on the right, stands the East End School, and, beyond, the buildings of one of Aldershot's laundries, whilst to the left the road is flanked by the Redan Hill Gardens, which are bounded on the north by Redan Road, until 1948 called Redan Hill. Below this road is the cutting in which lies the railway, which runs at this point through a tunnel under Redan Hill. Redan Hill is now an open space under the control of the Parks Committee of the Borough Council. Its grass slopes are traversed by paths and on the top is an asphalt square. This was the site of the old Aldershot Fort and saluting battery, hence its designation,* and it is interesting to record that at one period of the late war this was a temporary site for a troop of light anti-aircraft guns. A very fine view is obtained from this hill, the view extending in a semi-circle which embraces, as does Windmill Hill, the outlying country from the Hog's Back to Caesar's Camp, but also takes in on the east the Ash Ranges, the butts being clearly visible, Ash Church and the Hog's Back Hotel; to the south, Crooksbury Hill; and to the west, the panorama of Aldershot is laid before the viewer. Immediately below the hill lie the huts and sheds of the Field Stores and the Government Siding, beyond which lies the military cemetery on Thorn Hill, whilst the Aldershot Cemetery lies beyond the railway line to the south-east.

At the foot of the Redan Hill stand Bateman's Cottages and the forage stores of Messrs. Bateman & Sons, the corn merchants and forage contractors, who were in business in Aldershot in the late fifties, the cottages being shown on the Aldershot map of 1856 with their present designation.

Leading down to the right is Holly Road, which runs through at

* Redan: a fieldwork (field fortification) with two faces forming a salient angle (Fr.).

the back of East End to North Town and joins North Lane by St. Augustine's Church. Holly Road takes its name from Holly Farm, the buildings of which still remain beside the Holly Nursery at the rear of 65-75 Holly Road. Holly Farm existed for several years before the establishment of "The Camp," and Holly Road, which was developed between 1890 and 1910, was built across the farm lands.

Leading off Holly Road to the north-east is Belle Vue Road, so named from the fine view obtained from the crest of the high ground above Ash. In this road, in a railed enclosure bordered with fir and holly trees, stands the Roman Catholic Church of St. Mary. This is a green-painted, corrugated-iron building with a small tower, standing at the end of a gravel, tree-lined path which crosses a lawn. This was the original Roman Catholic Church in Aldershot which stood on the site of St. Joseph's Church in Queen's Road until the latter was built in 1912. The church was originally brought to Aldershot from Southampton, and was moved to its present site to provide a place of worship for the Roman Catholics of the North Town area when the permanent church was built. It is a small church. On the walls are a series of framed pictures of the Crucifixion, and above the main door is a large oil painting, a reproduction of Leonardo da Vinci's "Last Supper." There are figures of the Holy Virgin and the Sacred Heart, and the altar is flanked by six tall silver candlesticks.

Lower down Holly Road is Highland Road, still unmade, and typical of the roads of the residential area of the town prior to the days of tarmacadam surfacing. At the junction of Highland Road and Belle Vue Road stands one of the estates of prefabricated houses built in 1947 to ease the housing problem.

Redan Road continues from the top of the hill down to North Lane, running between the main cemetery and a cemetery strip adjoining the railway. Aldershot Cemetery, covering thirty acres, is well cared for; the trees, grass and paths are well tended. Some of the earlier graves lie in the area bounding the fence between the main gates. There are two mortuary chapels in the cemetery; these are conjoined on either side of a roadway. The chapels were built in this manner to allow one for the Church of England, the other for Nonconformists.

At the east end of the cemetery is the walled Jewish cemetery. Two tablets—one in Hebrew, the other in English—were fixed on the gate pillars inside the cemetery when it was opened in 1864, and where they remain to this day, to commemorate the consecration of the ground. The Jewish cemetery is small and well kept, the tombstones bearing inscriptions in both Hebrew and English, with the names of many well-known Jewish families who have been associated with the growth of the town. In addition to these is one tombstone bearing the inscription "In memory of Pte. David Cott-Scot, 2nd Dragoon Guards (The Queen's Bays), killed while preventing a comrade from committing suicide. September 6th 1900— Age 20." There is also a grave with the standard military head-stone to mark the resting-place of 113551 Pte. S. Solomomski of the 8th Canadian Mounted Rifles, who died in Aldershot in December, 1916.

At the top of Redan Road in the apex formed by this road and Windmill Road lie the Redan Hill Gardens,* well laid out with a children's playground and hard tennis courts. Lower down Redan Road stands the Redan Drill Hall, built in 1912, which is the head-quarters of the Aldershot Territorial Army Company of the County Regiment, today the Support Company of the 4th (T.A.) Bn. The Royal Hampshire Regiment, and a company of the 14th Parachute Regiment (The 5th Royal Hampshire Regiment) (T.A.). It is also the local Army Cadet Force Centre where, under the direction of H.Q., Aldershot District, Hampshire and Surrey units of the A.C.F. undergo week-end training under experienced Regular Army and T.A. instructors. The Drill Hall is modern and well appointed, with a fine hall, canteen, messes, administrative offices, stores and an armoury to implement the needs of the Territorials and Cadets ; additional huts and garages have been erected in the grounds. The regimental flag of the County Regiment flies proudly from the staff outside the main entrance.

At the foot of Redan Road facing High Street stand the National Schools, one of Aldershot's earliest schools, the appearance of which is still that of the village school of Victorian days. It was built in 1872 as the Church of England school. The foreground of the school is an open space with evergreens and traversing pathways. A little farther back along High Street at the junction of Pound Road, which ends at the foot of a wooded slope at the rear of the Redan Hill Gardens, stands the "Beehive" public-house, which, together with the "Red Lion," made up the only two inns in Aldershot before "The Camp" was built.† Pound Road takes its name from the fact that here, from 1880 to 1922, on the left of the road opposite the "Beehive," was

---

* These gardens were opened in 1930 and were laid out on a sand-hill.

† At the opening of the Aldershot Institute in 1860, General Knollys, the first General Officer Commanding "The Camp," referred to his early days in Aldershot, saying that when he first came to the town he stayed at the "Beehive" until his first temporary quarters were built.

the Aldershot Pound where straying animals were kept in safe custody until claimed by their owners.*

To the left of High Street in this area lie St. George's Road, St. George's Road East and St. Michael's Road, the latter two roads backing on to the Manor Park. In the north corner of the Park in St. George's Road East is the Hampshire Education Committee's Clinic, a well-appointed building. St. George's Road and St. Michael's Road are residential areas. Until July, 1939, a forge stood on the site of 2 St. Michael's Road, premises occupied by blacksmiths since the earliest days of the town. The building was, however, demolished as it had become unsafe.

St. George's Road runs parallel with the line of the railway; it is crossed by East Station Road, which leads to the footbridge over the railway to the station, and farther up, by St. Joseph's Road, at the junction of St. Joseph's and St. George's Roads, stands a new pre-fabricated R.C. school which was built in 1948 on the site of some allotment gardens. In St. George's Road, between Nos. 60 and 62, stands Harland Hall, the headquarters of the Aldershot and District Boy Scouts and Girl Guides Association.† This was formerly a church, having been built and opened in 1901 as Christ Church of the Reformed Episcopal Church of England. This church was, however, transferred to the Rotunda Church, the Primitive Methodist Church of Aldershot, in Victoria Road, on the amalgamation of the Methodist Churches.

Opposite Redan Road in High Street stands the Fricker's Hotel, formerly known (in 1859) as Boulter's Hotel, from which Boulter's Road, which runs at its side, takes its name. A few yards farther on the

---

* The Pound was originally located in the area of the present-day Recreation Ground, then a stretch of sandy common land. The Pound was fenced from the rest of the common and was the property of, and was controlled by, the Crondall Ecclesiastical Court. The Keeper of the Pound was appointed by this Court, the last keeper being a Mr. T. Bennett, whose family held the post for a considerable number of years. The official charge payable to the Pound Keeper was "eight-pence for turning the key to admit stray cattle; fourpence for turning it to let them out." A shilling a day was charged for animal feeding and a penny per day watering. Stable fees in addition were charged for horses. Any person taking a stray animal to the Pound received payment of one shilling, which was charged to the owner. The majority of the animals impounded were horses and cattle which had been turned out to graze without permission on the W.D. lands. Some-times large numbers would be rounded up by the Military Police and driven to the Pound, the M.Ps. collecting a further 2s. 6d. per beast from the owner in addition to the Pound charges, this money being sent to the Provost Marshal's office. There were sometimes lively scenes at the Pound, when irate gypsies tried to get the animals away without paying the fees, or owners would come at night to release their beasts when the Pound-keeper was asleep.

† The Hall was presented, in memory of the Chief Scout and as a tribute to the great movement, by Mr. C. J. Harland to the Aldershot Boy Scouts and Girl Guides Association, in May, 1941.

road passes under the railway bridge, and on the right is the Aldershot Recreation Ground, with its fine football ground and the grand stands and club buildings of the Aldershot Football Club. The ground is reached through turnstiles set on the lawns and shrubberies which abut on to the road.

The Aldershot Football Club, which has reached the fifth round of the F.A. Cup on one occasion, has brought professional football to the town since 1928. At first the Club competed in the Southern League, winning the championship of this competition two seasons later. Since then the club has competed with varying success in Third League football.

Above the football ground is an open space used on occasions for fêtes and fairs, and higher up, below the slopes of Redan Hill, are hard tennis courts. Adjoining the Recreation Ground is the Labour Exchange, and this in turn adjoins the start of the military lands where stands a large N.A.A.F.I. building at the lower end of Parsons Barracks in Ordnance Road. Opposite the Recreation Ground, Victoria Road leads off to traverse the centre of the town. "The Cannon" public-house stands on the corner, and adjoining this is the Liberal Club, which was opened in 1914 on the site of the old "Cricketers'" inn. Beyond the club is an open space, behind which is a public-house called the "Crimea" standing at the corner of Crimea Road, which, as its name and that of the next road, Sebastopol Road, imply, dates from the earliest days of the town's development. The present-day public-house dates from the nineteen-thirties when the old inn was rebuilt. During the rebuilding an old Miné rifle, used in the Crimea, was removed from above the main doorway, where it had hung since the late fifties of last century.

From here onwards High Street sweeps round, facing the barracks, although along this line of road they are obscured by a long line of chestnut trees. The only town buildings are on the left of the road and these are mainly warehouses, shops and cafés. Near the point facing Ordnance Road, which leads off to the Field Stores, stands the British Legion Club, and the headquarters of the Aldershot Branch of the British Legion, which is unique inasmuch as it is the only branch which has as its President a serving soldier. The General Officer Commanding in Aldershot always occupies the President's chair during his tour of command. The club, originally called the Ex-Service Men's Club, was opened on 27th May, 1922, by Field-Marshal Earl Haig. The club was reconstructed in 1938 and renamed the United Services Club, and as such was opened by the G.O.C., then Lieut.-General Sir John Dill. It became the British Legion Club in 1947.

For many years the junction of the roads High Street, Wellington Avenue, Station Road and Gun Hill had proved a danger spot and a traffic bottle-neck, and in consequence it was decided to construct a roundabout at this junction. Work commenced on the site in the spring of 1948 and it was completed by the end of the year. The result has been to improve greatly this area both for traffic and for appearance. The roundabout, thirty feet across, stands three feet up, the centre being turfed and planted with beds of flowers. The whole is surrounded by six lamp standards which throw down their light on to the crossings.

At the foot of Gun Hill facing the roundabout stands the imposing modern N.A.A.F.I. Club, which was built on the site of the guard room of Waterloo Barracks West, and opened by H.R.H. The Duke of Gloucester in September, 1948.

High Street continues to the west, but still with shops and offices only on the left of the road. On the right lie the Police Station and the Court House. The Court is a quiet, dignified building, with two court rooms, retiring room for the Justices, barristers and solicitors, and waiting rooms. The Court is connected to the Police Station by a corridor. Beyond Court Road stand two large cinemas, the Empire and the Ritz, and beyond is the Municipal Car Park and the pleasantly laid-out Princes Gardens which lie between Wellington Avenue and High Street. Along the south side of High Street run rows of shops, many new and modern, others dating back almost a hundred years. One can clearly see the line of buildings much as they stood in the late fifties of last century, the centre of the trading community which had grown along "The Camp" boundary. Some of the names of the traders have appeared on the fascia boards throughout those years.

The oblong area bounded by High Street, Station Road, Victoria Road and Grosvenor Road, traversed by Wellington Street, Union Street and Cross Street, is the commercial centre of the town, and much of it remains, with its old houses tucked away in side streets and alleys, as it did in the early days of the town's development. Many of the old houses have been demolished to make way for modern buildings ; many more were demolished as part of the Borough's slum-clearance plans, for this was a crowded, over-populated area with homes, shops and offices in the old small cottage dwellings which sprang up behind High Street between 1854 and 1860. There is, however, still sufficient evidence to give the observer a good indication of the centre of Aldershot in those early days. There are mews, stables, small cottage gardens and small houses tucked away in the side streets, chief among which are Alfred Street and Little Wellington Street.

Here is the Arcade Mews, which in the days before the coming of the motor-car and the bus provided stabling for the town centre. In 1907 the Mews was advertised as "First Class stabling for fifty horses with private loose boxes and stalls." Today it is a garage. Between this and the arcade which runs from Victoria Road into Wellington Street stand a number of old cottages which adjoined the farm of Richard Lloyd, who owned a market garden in the area of Wellington Street before "The Camp" was built. These old buildings can be reached through a passage-way which leads from an unpretentious doorway in the Arcade, few realizing that behind this door is a typical scene of Aldershot as it was some ninety years ago.

In Wellington Street are the premises of Mr. F. Phillips, Manufacturing Silversmiths and Medallists, one of the oldest businesses of the town, being established in High Street in 1856. The firm moved to Wellington Street in 1901, and is well known for its specialization in the manufacture of trophies and medals for countless unit and sports associations throughout the Empire.

Between Wellington Street and Station Road runs a portion of Victoria Road. At the corners of Wellington Street, Victoria Road and Gordon Road stand three banks—Lloyds, Westminster and National Provincial—and the George Hotel, one of the oldest hotels in the town. Lloyds Bank was built on the site of a farm-yard which adjoined the Victoria Hotel—a Trust House—in the courtyard of which, at the rear of the hotel, are still portions of the rough stone farm walls. The bank was built in 1881, but high up on the wall in the apex of the roof there is an inscription, "Founded 1834"; this refers to the old Capital and Counties Bank, which was taken over in Aldershot by Lloyds in 1914.

To the right of the Bank runs Gordon Road, off which leads Fir Tree Alley, originally called Burchett Close, which is referred to in the Crondall Customary of 1568, and is part of the original road through Aldershot.

Just past the Victoria Hotel, known in its earlier days as "Churchward's Hotel,"* is the Church of England Soldiers', Sailors' and Airmen's Institute. This Institute, which is much larger than most people imagine, was opened in 1881. With the exception of its entrance, the frontage is now occupied by Messrs. Godfrey's music shop, but until the 1930's this was the main coffee-bar of the Institute.

---

* The original Victoria Hotel in the town was situated at the corner of Cambridge Road and Alexandra Road, on the site of St. Anthony's Convent. In 1859 the proprietor, J. Williams, was advertising "Genuine Wines and Spirits, and fine ales. ... Dinners etc. on the shortest notice ; an excellent Billiard Table, Good Stabling, and horses taken into Livery."

On the east wall of the building overlooking the little front garden of the adjoining warden's house is a commemorative tablet bearing masonic signs and the badge of the House of Schleswig-Holstein, and the inscription : "The foundation stone of this wing was laid by the R. W. Bro. Sir Augustus Webster, Bart., Provincial Grand Master and the Provincial Grand Lodge officers of Hampshire and the Isle of Wight on the 24th February 1904 and the wing opened by H.R.H. Princess Christian of Schleswig-Holstein on the 14th July, 1904." In the spacious entrance hall the word "Welcome" is set in the floor tiles, and on the wall are a pair of crossed lances, with their red and white pennants, below which are three brass plaques erected by past and present members of the 12th Royal Lancers, each bearing the regimental badge, to the memory of Corporal William John Nicholls and Privates George Andrews Greenham and J. W. Cox, all of whom gave their lives for their country in South Africa in April and May, 1900, and June, 1901, respectively.

There is another wall plaque* in memory of the Rev. John Wilson Pickance, M.A., LL.D.,† who took holy orders in order to be appointed warden of the Institute, a post he held from November, 1892, until his death at the age of seventy-five on 29th January, 1920. On the staircase which leads from the hall there is a fine, almost life-size, oil painting of him in cassock and surplice.

The entrance hall leads into a spacious coffee-bar, the walls of which are decorated by a fine collection of pouch and belt ornaments and helmet and cap badges, together with old pistols, rifles and powder horns, one of which is a real horn bearing the regimental inscription, "64th Regt."‡ On the first floor is a well-lit, bright, well-equipped library and reading room, and a fine, spacious billiard room with three tables. These rooms, the Walters, Holkum and Sedgwick Rooms, are named after early benefactors of the Institute.

On the wall of the reading room is an early photograph of the Duke of Wellington in civilian dress, seated on a horse. Interest is added to this picture by the fact that the mount is autographed by the Duke. On the landing is an old iron plaque bearing the date 1684 ; this comes from the gateway of the palace built at Winchester by King Charles II which later became Winchester Barracks and was destroyed by fire in 1894.

On the top floor are cubicles, bedrooms and bathrooms provided for the convenience of soldiers, whilst beyond, above the billiard

---

* Unveiled on 8th May, 1921, by Major J. Clisham.

† The Rev. J. Pickance, who lived at "The Foleys" in Cargate, was described as "A true friend to the Soldier, who found in him not only a spiritual adviser but a real friend in every meaning of the word."

‡ Now the 1st Bn. The North Staffordshire Regiment (The Prince of Wales's).

A general view of Aldershot today from Hungry Hill.

2C

Aldershot from the air.

The Blackwater River, the "County Stream." The rural scene, south of Deadbrook Farm.
The left bank, in Hampshire, being the Borough as well as the County boundary.

The Carved Oak Fireplace, dated 1714, *in the hall of Aldershot Park Mansion.*

The Manor House, from Manor Park.

The narrowest house in Aldershot: No. 19 Queen's Road.

Wellington Street.

Union Street.

The Western approach, High Street.

Victoria Road, looking west, with the Methodist Church in the distance.

The Lake, Aldershot Park.

The Municipal Gardens.   The 1914-1918 War Memorial Cenotaph.

In the Manor Park. The Heroes' Garden, with the 1914-1918 War Memorial, and, in the background, the Heroes' Shrine and Rock Garden, Aldershot's National Memorial for the 1939-1945 War.

The Ornamental Lake, Manor Park.

The Aldershot Football Club Ground in the Recreation Ground, High Street.

The Bathing Pool, Aldershot Park.

The General Post Office, at the junction of Station Road and Victoria Road.

The Municipal Buildings in Grosvenor Road, Aldershot, with, on the right, the Fire Station and the Methodist Church.

The Presbyterian Church, in Victoria Road.

Holy Trinity Parish Church from Albert Road.

The Tichborne Memorials in Aldershot Parish Church. On the left is that to Lady Ellen Tichborne, who died in 1606, and on the right that to Lady Mary Tichborne, who died in 1620.

The Parish Church of St. Michael the Archangel from the junction of Church Lane East and Church Hill, seen in all its architectural stages. From left to right are seen the sixteenth-century Tower, the eighteenth-century Nave (now the South Aisle), the twelfth-century Lady Chapel, and the twentieth-century extension.

The Lady Chapel of the Parish Church : all that remains of the original twelfth-century Parish Church.

The division of Town and Camp. Princes Gardens, dividing High Street from Wellington Avenue and Talavera Barracks with, on the left, Barrack Road and Hospital Hill

room, is the famous Gordon Chapel. This small but well-cared-for chapel was erected in memory of General Charles George Gordon— "Gordon of Khartoum"—and is used for voluntary services, meditation and prayer. There is a small marble bust of Gordon above the door. The light filters in through nine stained-glass windows behind the altar and on either side. All these windows bear inscriptions to the memory of soldiers who have worshipped in the chapel or who have been associated with the Institute in supporting its aims, objects and maintenance.

One window is in memory of Major James B. MacMillian, D.S.O., killed in action in France on St. Andrew's Day, 1917, and to Sergeant I. R. L. Kerr, of the 5th Cameron Highlanders, killed on 8th December, 1915. Another window is a memorial to Colonel Llewellyn Wavel,* late Bengal Staff Corps, the third son of Major-General Wavel, born on 15th November, 1839, who died on 27th November, 1910. Colonel Wavel was elected to the Committee of the Institute in 1885 and was Honorary Secretary from 1892 until his death.

Another window is in memory of General Gordon and of David Bowie Clarke, priest and chaplain to the forces, who died in May, 1894, and to all soldiers who fell in the Omdurman Campaign of 1898.

A pair of windows on either side of the altar were "given by many who knew and loved him" in memory of Colour-Sergeant Douglas George Huntley, who died at sea in May, 1888.

On the opposite side of the road are the offices occupied by Messrs. Foster, Wells and Coggins, formerly used by the Aldershot Local Board before the construction of the Municipal Buildings. Next to these offices is the small, grey limestone Strict Baptist Church, which was built in 1862, with its oak, iron-studded door. The interior is rather bare, but the rows of wooden pews with the light streaming in through the leaded Gothic windows give the little church a quiet dignity—a peaceful haven in the busy thoroughfare.

Between 124 and 126 Victoria Road is a passage-way which leads to the Conservative Club, a well-appointed modern building with a fine secluded bowling green, with four rinks, within a walled garden. The building was erected in 1931 and was opened on 30th September of that year by the President, the Right Hon. Viscount Wolmer, P.C., then M.P. for the Aldershot Division.

At the corner of Victoria Road and Station Road is the Aldershot Institute, and on the opposite corner the General Post Office. The Aldershot Institute, built in 1887, is now used mainly as a social club,

---

* See also reference to the Llewellyn Wavel Memorial Chapel in the Church of England Soldiers', Sailors' and Airmen's Institute in North Camp, p. 353.

2D

containing assembly rooms, lounge, buffet, billiard room and a library. To the left, Station Road leads on to the roundabout; on the right is an imposing building built in 1899 at a cost of £4,000 as a Masonic Hall, the site having been bought for £600. It is now in use as a Y.M.C.A. Before being taken over as a Y.M.C.A. Club, the Masonic Hall was used as a "Motion Picture Theatre," and it was here that the first "movies" were seen in the town.

Just below the junction of Station Road and Victoria Road, next to a piece of vacant ground surrounded by a low brick wall, the site of Ivy Lodge which was demolished to make room for a building site a few years before the late war, stands the Presbyterian Church. Farther down the road, lying between Victoria Road and Albert Road, stands Holy Trinity Church, an imposing edifice which to a great extent is lost in its surroundings; it is constructed in the Gothic style of architecture in brick and bargate stone facings. A feature of the church is the Gothic chancel arch. The nave and side aisles and chancel are in Bath stone. The vestry was added in 1890. The iron gates leading from Victoria Road were erected in 1949 in memory of Frederick Ernest Jerome and his wife Ellen.

The church, which has accommodation for 800, contains some fine stained-glass windows, the great west window above the altar being installed as a memorial to the fifty-three men of the parish who fell during the 1914-1918 war. The names of the men are recorded on a tablet on the south wall, which bears the inscription:

> To the glory of God. This tablet contains the
> names of the men of this Parish who gave their
> lives during the Great War 1914-19 to whose
> memory the West Window was erected.

There are nine stained-glass windows in groups of three on the south wall, each group being a memorial: The first to the memory of Madge, daughter of Henry and Maude Stone, "of this town," who died in December, 1893. The second in memory of Kate Wallis, born May, 1849, who died in August, 1925, and Edward Wallis, born June, 1850, who died in October, 1929. The third window is a memorial to Thomas Benham, who died on All Saints' Day, 1891, and to his wife Elizabeth, who died in February, 1927. Between these windows is an oak board which commemorates the consecration of the church on 14th October, 1878, and bears on the centre panel the names of the Members of the Committee and the Patrons who raised the funds and erected the church. On either side are panels bearing the lists of Vicars, Vicars' Wardens and Parish Wardens since 1878.

On the north wall is another stained-glass window, erected by

Richard Bateman in memory of his wife, Sarah Frances Bateman, August, 1881.

By the organ, which was rebuilt, renewed and rededicated on 6th April, 1925, is a brass memorial plaque erected to the memory of Richard Allden, who died on 4th October, 1879. "He was the donor of the site of this Church," reads the inscription, "and a liberal subscriber to the funds for erecting the edifice and honorary treasurer of the building Committee."

Above this brass is a wooden tablet dedicated on Ascension Day, 1925, in memory of Nellie Andrews, L.L.C.M., who died in November, 1924, a devoted worker for many years "in connection with this Church, its music and its Sunday School."

There are several other brasses on the walls, including one in memory of Sister Maria (Maria Whitty), who devoted sixteen years of her life to rescue work in Aldershot and died in Portsmouth in January, 1901, and another erected by brother firemen and fellow townsmen "in affectionate memory" of Reginald Hughes and Leonard Perks, who lost their lives on duty at the Fire Station on 18th January, 1911.

Other wall memorials include a marble panel bearing, in bronze, the badge of the Royal Welch Fusiliers, erected to the memory of Charles Gilbert Lawes, Lieutenant, 9th Bn. R.W.F., second son of James Edward and Emma Lawes, of Aldershot, who was killed in action on the Somme on 17th October, 1916. There are also memorials to Charles Greenwood, born 1819, who died in 1889, and his wife and daughter, and to Henry McDonald, who died in 1883, and to Elizabeth, wife of Henry Stone, who died in 1880.

The imposing brass lectern was presented to the church by Jane McDonald in memory of her husband, Henry McDonald, who died in October, 1883. A carved wooden font cover bears the carved inscription, "In Memory of Hellena Riley at rest November 18, 1924. From friends in Aldershot"; and the dignified reredos in dark oak is a memorial to W. J. Snuggs.

By the north door is another wall-brass which commemorates the jubilee of the church on 14th October, 1928, and the fact that the roof, fabric and interior was entirely restored and redecorated by the congregation and friends of the church.

Although not one of the military churches, Holy Trinity had strong ties with the Army during the late war, especially the Canadian Army Overseas, whose own chaplains conducted parade services in the church for troops quartered in Wellington Lines, and it became a practice for drafts leaving Aldershot to join the Canadian formations on the Continent to hold their communion in this church before

entraining for the theatres of war. Evidence of these services remain
in the deep scratches on the rows of pews caused by the equipment
and side arms of the soldiers who came to Holy Trinity for their last
service in Aldershot on the eve of their departure.

Lower down Victoria Road at the corner of Albert Road stands the
Rotunda Church. It is unique in its construction and in the number
of commemorative plaques surrounding its walls. There are eight
separate foundation stones, four facing Victoria Road and four
facing Albert Road. All these stones bear the date 22nd March, 1876.
On the Victoria Road frontages three were laid by Mrs. Samuel Terry,
William Allden, Esq., and W. Francis, Esq., of Ramsgate, respectively.
On the Albert Road side they were laid by Mr. William Massley,
William Beehworth, of Leeds, and R. D. Catchpole, of Reading. The
remaining two stones are chipped and defaced.

Adjoining the church in Albert Road is Christ Church Hall, which
also has four foundation stones laid on 15th December, 1874, one by
William Terry, one by Mary Allden, a third by the scholars of the
Methodist Sabbath School. The fourth stone is defaced and the
inscription now illegible.

Adjoining Christ Church in Victoria Road is the old Primitive
Methodist Soldiers' Home and Institute, the two foundation stones of
which were laid on 6th April, 1887, one by Mrs. S. Terry, the other
by C. Palmer, Esq., of Reading. This Institute contained a refreshment bar, writing and reading rooms and bedrooms, and on the wall
by the staircase is a stained glass window depicting the Children of
Israel gathering together at Shiloh to go up to war against the Children
of Reuben and Gad and the tribe of Manasseh (Joshua xxii). The
building, now called "Rotunda House," is, however, no longer in
use as such and is now the Women's Department of the Employment
Exchange, whilst the upper floors have been converted into five flats.

In Albert Road, which runs behind Victoria Road and backs on to
the railway goods sidings, are the flour mills of Messrs. W. & J.
Simmonds.

Station Road runs from Victoria Road past the Aldershot Hippodrome, a spacious theatre erected in 1913. The Hippodrome provides
for a class of entertainment in the form of touring revues, variety acts
and pantomimes which cannot be seen elsewhere for many miles
around, for it is the only variety theatre in the old music-hall style in
this part of the country, the nearest to Aldershot being Reading and
Kingston. The popularity of the Hippodrome can be assessed by the
fact that it never succumbed to becoming a cinema during the lean
years of variety between the wars, and has continued to keep going
in the old tradition of the music-hall of the days in which it was built.

Opposite the Hippodrome, occupying an extensive site bounded by The Grove, Birchett Road, and Cavendish Road, stands the Wellington Press, the Printing and Publishing House of Gale & Polden Ltd., and the offices of *The Aldershot News*.

On the opposite corner is the Aldershot Bus Station, a large yard, with its waiting room and inquiry office, from which there is a constant flow of the familiar green buses of the Aldershot and District Traction Company which operates over a wide area of Hampshire and Surrey, and with services which bring passengers from even farther afield. Beyond the Bus Station the road leads on to the Railway Station, which, although not a big station, carries a very considerable amount of passenger and goods traffic in addition to a vast amount of military traffic. For many years there has been agitation for the construction, for the convenience of townspeople, of a subway under the station, but still only a wooden footbridge exists to enable people to cross over from the town centre to the now thickly populated area east of the line. This footbridge was brought to Aldershot by the old London and South-Western Railway Company from Woking Station, where it served for many years prior to the building there of the existing bridge over the line.

From Station Road the road leads on into The Grove, one of the oldest residential roads in Aldershot, which took its name from the row of trees growing on the west side, now so lopped that the name alone indicates the reason for its choice in mid-Victorian times. In the Grove is the Holy Trinity Vicarage and the Municipal Day Nursery, whilst on the opposite side of the road on the open ground above the railway are the headquarters of the Hants 200 British Red Cross Detachment, which were opened by the Countess of Malmesbury in 1947, and farther along the headquarters of the Aldershot Division of the St. John Ambulance Brigade.

From The Grove one can look across to the rising ground along which runs Church Lane East, and in the distance can be seen the old fabric of the Parish Church of St. Michael the Archangel.*

The Parish Church most certainly dates from the twelfth century, possibly earlier, as it was originally built as a "Chapel of Ease" at the time when the nearest church was at Crondall. The original church was enlarged in 1865, when, following the rapid increase in the

---

* The parish forms part of the Diocese of Guildford. When it was founded in 927, with its twin diocese of Portsmouth, out of the old, historic Diocese of Winchester, a dozen parishes on the north-east corner of Hampshire (of which Aldershot and Farnborough are the largest), together with the whole of West Surrey, came into the Diocese of Guildford. With the exception of Guildford itself and its neighbourhood and the Borough of Epsom and Ewell, Aldershot and Farnborough together are the largest and most important part of the Diocese.

population, it was found to be inadequate to minister to the spiritual needs of the enlarged parish. The old twelfth-century nave was demolished and the church reconstructed by the addition of the north arcade, north aisle and the chancel arch between the old chancel and the newly built nave.

Further additions and alterations were made in the early years of this century. From designs by Sir Thomas Jackson, R.A., a new nave and chancel and a new north arcade were added.

The castellated tower of the church is unusual, being a mixture of stone and brick building.* On the south wall of the tower a memorial tablet is let into brown sandstone. This stone was laid on 22nd July, 1910, by Harriet Sarah, Lady Wantage, "in unfading memory of the interest in British soldiery taken by her husband, Robert Loyd Lindsey, Lord Wantage, V.C., K.C.B."

The church lies back from the road in the south-east corner of the Manor Park at the junction of Church Hill and Church Lane East. It stands in a well-tended churchyard, with firs, yews, cypresses, roses and shrubs. The gravestones in the churchyard date from 1740 and among them are those dated 1767, 1797, 1820, 1823, 1828 and 1833. The latest grave is dated 1947, but the churchyard is no longer in general use as a burial ground.

By the south door of the church there are three graves of the Begent family, each bearing unusual inscriptions which are clearly visible on the tombstones. Side by side are those of John Begent, who died at the age of sixty on 27th February, 1775, and of his wife Esther

---

* "The foundations are of large blocks of sarsen stone, laid apparently on the surface of the ground, providing a precarious support for a heavy building on a London clay subsoil, and there are inside the church indications of possible rebuilding of the north wall of the tower.

"As we see it today the tower is of three stages divided horizontally by projecting courses of brick. The stone used is a beautiful golden-brown sandstone, rather roughly dressed. In the mortar between the courses small pieces of the same stone are inserted, a form of decoration known locally as garneting. Other instances of it are to be seen in Surrey villages. The upper embattled storey and the four angles of the tower are of brick, the bricks used being thinner than modern bricks and of varied colour. This unusual mixture of stone and brick perhaps was adopted to make a lighter and stronger building. . . . Inside the ground storey of the tower, in the soft stone head of the window a number of grooves have been cut, evidently by a bell rope passed through the window in order to ring the bell from the church-yard. There are a few much shallower grooves on the heads of the west door and the door into the church. Similar grooves have been observed in other churches. It is not known when or why a bell was rung from the churchyard, and it must have been for many years to make such deep grooves. One suggestion is that the bellringer, being in the churchyard, could watch for the arrival of the chaplain riding from Crondall along Church Lane to take the service : or, the bellringer being outside, there would be more room inside the tower for the assembly of mourners at funerals."—"The Parish Church of St. Michael the Archangel, Aldershot," by Dr. J. H. Gibson (The British Publishing Company) (1948).

who died at the same age twenty-two days before him. On the former stone is the inscription :

> Grieve not for him that lieth here
> Though gone and left a daughter dear
> For though his body turned to dust
> His soul doth live among the just.

Whilst the latter bears the words :

> In Heaven her soul with God above
> Her body resteth here
> When to this world she bid adieu
> I left a parent dear.

It would appear that these tributes were probably written by their surviving daughter Ann, who possibly also wrote her own epitaph prior to her death, for inscribed on an adjoining headstone above the grave of Ann, wife of James Coules, daughter of John and Esther Begent, who died on 5th January, 1788, at the age of fifty-one, is the following :

> Stay Paffenger that paffeth by,
> As you are now for once was I,
> And as I am for muft you be
> Prepare for death and follow me.

Near by are six graves of the Guden family, dated between 1812 and 1856, and three graves of the Allden family, dated from 1813 to 1836. Opposite the bell tower is one of the first graves identifying Aldershot village with the military camp. It is that of "Elizabeth, beloved wife of Sergeant Henry Frisby of the Hertfordshire Regiment of Militia," who died in April, 1856, and of their daughter, who died at the age of seven, in October, 1855. This tombstone bears the epitaph :

> Their trials are past,
> Their work is done,
> And they are fully blest,
> They fought the fight
> The Victory won
> And entered into rest.

The stone was erected by Lieutenant-Colonel Smith-Dorrien and the officers of the Hertfordshire Militia "as a token of respect to Sergeant Henry Frisby."

At the rear of the church, hard by the iron railings which divide the churchyard from the Manor Park, are four other soldiers' tombstones. The Military Cemetery on Thorn Hill was not enclosed until the end of 1856, and although a number of soldiers were buried on that site prior to that year, others and their families were interred in the churchyard of the village parish church. Here in a row are the head-stones of the son of William McIntyre, Quartermaster-Sergeant of the Bedfordshire Militia, who died in October, 1885, and that of Private Henry Woodwards, drowned whilst bathing with his regiment, the 1st Bn. Coldstream Guards, 30th June, 1856. The inscription on the stone tells that "the deceased left.England with his Regiment in February 1854 and was through the Crimean Campaign and present at the Battle of Inkerman and Balaclava and the siege of Sebastopol." Next is the gravestone of "Colour Sergeant William Garner (formerly of H.M. 69th Regiment of Foot) of the King's Own Staffordshire Light Infantry Regiment of Militia who died in the Camp at Aldershot on the 1st day of September 1855," and that of Private William Baker of the Royal Sussex Light Infantry Militia, "a native of the Parish of Sompting in the County of Sussex who died at Aldershot Camp on the 15th of May 1856. Age 21." The gravestone was erected "at the expense of Colonel The Duke of Richmond to mark the sense of worth of the deceased as a good man and a faithful soldier."

Also at the rear of the church in the north-east corner of the church-yard overlooking the former family home—the Manor House—are five graves of the Newcome family.

On the south wall of the Lady Chapel is a tablet in memory of Joseph Hart, who died at the age of seventy-eight in 1820, and of his wife, who died in May, 1829, and their two daughters, Elizabeth and Ruth, who died in 1787 and 1789.

The interior of the church is best seen from the west door, from which one looks down the nave to the chancel. To the right is the Lady Chapel, the remaining original portion of the Church, and in the north aisle is the Children's Chapel. The carved oak reredos behind the high altar* is decorated with scenes depicting the Nativity and the Resurrection, and is surmounted by six small carved figures. The reredos bears a small brass plate recording its dedication to the "Glory of God in thanksgiving for the life of Anna Camilla Hoyle, by many friends within and without our Parish who loved her—December 23rd 1912." The north side panel bears an inscription in memory of George Newcome, who was killed in action in East Africa in March, 1916.

In the north wall of the sanctuary are two stained-glass windows, memorials to members of the Newcome family : Cecilia, widow of

---

* The church plate includes a chalice dated 1887, a paten of 1888 and a flagon dated 1841.

Henry Newcome, born 1807, died 1896 ; and Henry George Newcome, who died in 1895.

At the west end of the south aisle stands the font, the carved oak cover of which is a memorial to Harold Conway Jay, born in May, 1892, who "gave his life in the Great War, July 9th, 1916." On the wall on either side of the door leading to the ringing chamber of the belfry, carved oak decorated panelling forms the memorial to those men of the parish who lost their lives on service in the 1914-1918 war. The memorial contains 176 names, and in a glass case below is the Book of Remembrance, compiled and written by Mrs. Frances Gibson, listing the names of those who served.

The pulpit bears a small brass tablet in memory of Isaac Hoyle (1828-1911), a "generous benefactor to the Church," and the canopy and panelling of the pulpit were erected in 1926 "To the Glory of God and in Loving Memory of Robert Lloyd 1840-1919, Ann Lloyd, his wife, 1841-1926, and their sons Richard Omar Lloyd 1868-86 and Frederick John Lloyd 1872-1922." The church organ on the north of the chancel was rebuilt and restored in 1930 as a gift to the church by Mrs. Daniel.

At the entrance to the Lady Chapel stands the carved oak figure of St. Michael the Archangel—three feet in height—erected in 1936 as a memorial to Lilian Bunbury. On the wall on the opposite side of the entrance is a memorial tablet to Captain Thomas Newnham of the Royal Navy, who died in August, 1795, and to Elizabeth, "Relict of the above and wife of the Rev. James Piggott, Vicar of Wigston, Leicestershire," who died in October, 1809. Below is the inscription :

Could but this silent stone distinctly show,
The virtues she possessed who sleeps below,
Forth from the reader's breast would steal the sigh,
Lamenting so much worth should ever die.

The east window of the Lady Chapel is a memorial to Captain George Newcome, J.P., who died in November, 1884. The window is in three portions, the first depicting St. Gabriel, then St. Michael, and the centre the Good Samaritan. On either side of the window behind the altar hang the helmets of Sir John White and his son Robert, which were hung there at the times of their funerals.

There are two more stained-glass windows in the south wall of the chapel, one of which depicts the figures of St. John and St. Paul, being a memorial to Henry James West, who died in September, 1893.

The panelling of the Lady Chapel is a memorial erected by his wife to Richard Simmonds, J.P., of Elm Place, who died in June, 1923, at the age of seventy-nine, after long and devoted service to the town.

On the north wall of the new chancel, having been removed from the north wall of the old chancel, is a memorial to Robert White's elder daughter, Lady Ellen Tichborne, depicting her kneeling. Below the figure is a tablet bearing the inscription :

Erected by Sr. Richard Tichborne, Knight, to ye
memory of his dearest wiefe the Lady Ellen Tichborne,
eldest daughter of Robt. White of Aldershot, Esq. who
godly departed thys lyfe the 18 day of May, in the
year of our redemption 1606, and of her age 27.

Who lived (and now is dead)
a life prepared for dying,
Who died (and now she lyves)
a death prepared for lyving.
So well she both profest,
That she in both is blest.

Still in its original position on the south wall of the old chancel, now the Lady Chapel, is a memorial to Lady Mary Tichborne, Robert White's younger daughter. The memorial contains in the foreground her kneeling figure, and in the background on the left the figures of seven kneeling boys, her sons ; on the right six kneeling girls, her daughters. Below are two tablets bearing inscriptions in Latin and English, the latter reading :

Here lieth Ye body of Ye Lady Mary Tichborne, Ye wife
of Sr. Walter Tichborne, Knight, who was married to
him Ye 7 of May 1597, and deceased Ye 31st of Ianuary
1620, leaving issue now living, Benjamin, Francis, Iohn,
Walter, Iames, Richard White, Lionell, Theophila,
Frauncis, Marie, Elizabeth, Charitie, Bridgett, and had
also issue one other Iames yt deceased in Ye year 1615,
which both wer Ye godsonnes of Ye King by his favour
and grace

On the same wall is the armorial memorial brass erected to the memory of Sir John White, who died in June, 1573. Along the top of the brass plaque are the words "Morire mundo, vivas Deo" ("To die to the world, is to live for God"). In the centre of the brass is the complete achievement of shield, helmet, crest, mantling and motto ("In God is my trust") of Sir John White, flanked by the shields of the arms of his two wives. Below the shields are the christian names of his children : on the right, Thomas, Robert, William, Benjamin, Margaret, Mary and Jane ; on the left, John, Thomas and Katherine.

At the base of the brass is a five-lined inscription :—

> Here under lyeth buried ye body of Syr John White, Knyght,
> Alderman, Cityzen and Grocer of London, who departed thys
> present lyff wyth a wylling mynde, commytting his body and
> soule to the eternal God through Christ our Lord ye.........
> day of .... ao 15.........

The day, month and year are strangely absent. It may have been that
Sir John White chose his own memorial brass and epitaph before his
death and when erected the inscription was never completed.

On the south wall of the nave is a memorial of marble, which was
removed from the north wall of the old nave ; on this is the inscription :

> Near this place lie deposited the remains
> of Charles Viner Esq.* Barrister at law,
> who died June 5th, 1756, aged 78 years.

His widow, Mrs. Raleigh Viner, died 3rd January, 1761, aged seventy-
nine years. Also of John Elwes Weekes, Esqr., who died 6th January,
1762, and ordered this monument to be erected "To perpetuate the
memory of him and his beloved sister. The first a generous benefactor
to the University of Oxford, the last two kind and charitable to their
neighbours."

On the same wall are memorial tablets to Richard John Stovold,
of Ayling House, who died in December, 1877 ; John Allden, who
died in January, 1829 ; and a bronze memorial tablet to Annie Chalwin,
who died in March, 1906, erected by parishioners "that her loving
service of forty years in this Parish may not be forgotten" ; and a
marble tablet in memory of the Rev. James Dennett, Pastor of Aldershot from 1853 to 1865, with the inscription :

> He was a faithful and assiduous pastor in this parish and
> beloved by the parishioners and all who knew him. During
> his Ministry, the Church was enlarged and rebuilt, schools
> were erected and many useful agencies organized for the
> benefit of the parish.

St. Michael's possesses a very fine light ring of eight bells, the
tenor with a note of A flat, weighing just under 8¼ cwts. Although
not containing the weight of metal used in many notable peals of bells,
they have claim to distinction inasmuch as they contain, as the 3rd,
4th and 5th bells of the present octave, three very old bells. These

---

* Charles Viner, a leading figure in his profession in the eighteenth-century, was
the founder of the Vinerian Scholarship at Oxford University.

were the church's original three chiming bells. The smallest is of
fifteenth-century origin and bears the lion's face, coin and foliate
stamp of the group of bells that came from the Wokingham Foundry.
The second was cast by E. Knight, of Reading, and is dated 1624.
It has an elaborate foliate band around the crown. The largest of the
three (the present 5th bell) was cast in 1611, and has the founder's
mark of three bells on a shield between the initial W and Y, showing
it as having been cast by William Yare, of Reading.

It was not until the church was enlarged in 1911 that an actual
ringing peal of bells was installed. The number of bells was increased
to six, the present 6th, 7th and tenor being cast by Messrs. Mears and
Stainbank, of Whitechapel. The tenor is a memorial to William
Fludder, verger and parish clerk, who died in 1910. Several peals
were rung on the six bells, mostly under the conductorship of Mr.
Charles Edwards.

After the 1914-1918 war the six bells were augmented to the present
eight by the addition of two light trebles. These were subscribed for
and cast as a memorial to soldiers who fell in the First World War,
and are known as "soldiers' bells." They were dedicated on 9th May,
1920. The inscription on the treble reads : "These two trebles were
added by soldiers in memory of their comrades who fell in the Great
War." The late Captain A. J. Mayne, and the late Mr. James Mann—
who served for many years in the Royal Engineers—were the prime
movers in this scheme, and a tablet to the memory of Mr. Mann hangs
in the ringing chamber.

The bells are hung in plain bearings in a combined iron and oak
frame, and normally require little attention, but have recently been
placed in the hands of expert bell-hangers for a well-deserved overhaul
at a cost of £157. The old fixed crown staples have been drilled out
from the 4th and 5th bells and new independent staples fixed.

Local legend has it that an illegitimate child of Nell Gwynn is
buried under the yew tree by the churchyard gate. Nell Gwynn is
said to have given birth to the child whilst *en route* from Farnham to
London, at the old "Fox and Hounds" inn—the old houses in Weybourne Road, opposite Ayling Lane.* This legend is supported by a
"fact" passed down among local residents that the Parish Church still
receives an annual grant, which has been paid since the days of King
Charles, as long as the yew tree remains undisturbed. This "fact" is,
however, a fallacy, and there is no record in existing archives of the
church to support this.

Opposite the Parish Church stands the Vicarage, at the corner of
Croft Road and Church Lane, whilst on the other corner stands the

* See p. 7.

Parish Hall. On the Vicarage corner is an old building which until recent years had a thatched roof and diamond-shaped leaded windows, and which was Aldershot's first school, opened in the early 1820's. Croft Road continues but a short way before becoming a rural, tree-lined footpath which turns away to the right behind "The Croft" on the right, and on the left the gardens of the houses in Evelyn Avenue. This path follows the route of the original footpath which led across the fields from Farnham to Aldershot village. Today much of this ancient footpath has been lost, but it exists from Croft Road to High-field Gardens,* and is picked up again leading from Highfield Avenue to the railway bridge at the junction of Boxall's Lane and the foot of Eggar's Hill.

Below this footpath after leaving Croft Road lies the comparatively recently built estate composed of Evelyn Avenue, Coronation and Jubilee Roads. Until 1938 this area, as far down as Boxall's Lane, was open fields, but it was developed as a residential area in the years immediately preceding the late war. Coronation Road, however, does not take its name from the 1937 Coronation; it dates back to 1911, for from that date until the building of the estate there were two houses—Coronation Villas (35 and 37 Coronation Road)—standing alone in an unmade, rough road which ended in a footpath across the fields.

At the foot of Coronation and Jubilee Roads lies Boxall's Lane, which takes its name from Boxall's Farm, the southern boundary road of the Borough, which runs from Lower Farnham Road to Weybourne Road. Until 1933 this was nothing but a tree-lined country road, but in that year the building of the first hundred houses in the lane was sanctioned by the Council and yet another portion of rural Aldershot was replaced by bricks and mortar.

At the junction of Church Hill, which runs up to the Parish Church from Aldershot Green and Church Lane East, this latter road becomes Church Lane, one of the original roads of the village that was Alder-shot; it winds to this day in the bends that denote its origin as a country lane. Between Church Lane and Croft Road behind the Vicarage stands the Grange, reached by a carriage drive through pleasant, secluded wooded grounds; lower down, on the left, close to the road, but secluded by a high wall and its wooded gardens, is Aldershot Lodge, with its imposing carriage house and stables with a small bell tower which can be seen from the gateway; and opposite stands Elm Place, one of the oldest residences in Aldershot, occupying the site of an older building in which, local legend has it, King John

---

* Named after the "Highefeald" area of the Tithing of "Aldrisshott" (Aldershot) in the Crondall Customary, 1568.

slept, in 1215, on his way to Runnymede to sign Magna Carta. The present house has been taken over by the Council for flats and its grounds have now become overgrown and have fallen into disrepair. There is still a fine, although disused, large conservatory and the red brick carriage houses and stables, now the store of a commercial enterprise, which tell the story of the days when Elm Place was numbered among the fine residences of the town. The grounds extend over some 13 acres and lead back to the rear of Coronation Road, and are flanked on the south by Park Road. Most of this ground is now occupied by allotments and a new school, the Church of England School, built in 1939 and enlarged in 1948, which is sited off the footpath which leads from Croft Road, behind Coronation Road, to the Lower Farnham Road.

Church Lane joins Elston Road and Brighton Road, which was originally known as Red Lion Lane. Off Brighton Road is one of Hooper Struve's mineral water factories, originally the factory of Allen & Lloyd, which was founded in Aldershot in 1857. This firm adopted as its motto "We follow the troops," for in these early days horse-drawn and hand carts followed the marching men to refresh them at the halts. Dubbed "Fizzer wallahs" by the troops after the sparkling "pop" they purveyed, they became part of the life of "The Camp" in those days. Today this factory has an output of some 20,000 bottles of minerals a day—some six million each year—which gives an indication of the growth of the business. Elston Road and Brighton Road were developed as a housing estate in the early thirties, long before a concrete road took the place of the old tree-lined lane. Church Lane continues on, flanked by villas of the late Victorian and Edwardian age, until it joins the Lower Farnham Road at "The Heron" public-house, which takes its name from Heron Wood, at the northern end of Aldershot Park between Whyte Avenue and the county boundary.

The whole of the area to the south of the Lower Farnham Road as far as the border of Hampshire and Surrey is occupied by a large Council Housing Estate, developed after the 1914-1918 war. At the lower end of the road Gloucester Road (named after the Duke of Gloucester, who had had many associations with the Borough), and Morland Road (named after Lieutenant-General Sir T. L. N. Morland, K.C.B., K.C.M.G., D.S.O., the G.O.C. at the time of the grant of Aldershot's Charter of Incorporation) turns off to the left towards Aldershot Park Mansion. Opposite "The Heron" the Avenue leads in the same direction. This, until the building of the housing estate, was the avenue which led to the main entrance to the park, lined by stately oaks and elms. The old trees were cut down after the road was built, but the Avenue has still a pleasing appearance ; the houses lie back from the road, and well-kept grass verges lie between the pavements and the highway, and a new avenue of trees has been planted. Between the Avenue and Gloucester Road is an open space of nearly eight and a half acres in which stand two Council schools, known as the Park Schools. These are well-lighted, modern, single-storeyed buildings surrounded by playgrounds and lawns.

Along the lower boundary of the school fields lies Pool Road, from which leads the entrance to the Aldershot Bathing Pool, one of the biggest open-air swimming pools in the country, containing over a million and a half gallons of water, the clarity of which is beyond reproach, the water being a clear blue. The pool is situated in pleasing and picturesque surroundings in the Aldershot Park Estate, which was purchased by the Council in 1920, and gradually developed in the years that followed.* In the grounds of the estate was a lake, which had deteriorated since the eighties, when the house was owned by Mr. Charles D'Oridant and it was described as a "fine sheet of water," for in 1920 it was overgrown with weeds, the banks had crumbled, and it was overhung with trees. The Borough Council decided to convert it into a Bathing Pool and this was one of the Council's major improvement projects of the twenties. The old lake was drained, considerable excavations were made, and the pool connected with the necessary filtering plant, dressing rooms and other amenities, including the pleasant lawns and terraces around the pool, at a cost of nearly £20,000.

The depth of the Bathing Pool varies from a few inches to ten feet, thus enabling even the smaller children to bathe in perfect safety. At the shallow end a sloping runway enables bathers to walk into the water, the depth from here to a central boom being from a few inches to 4 ft. 6 in. On the other side of the boom is a straight course, 55 yards in length, with an average depth of 6 feet, which can also be

---

* Aldershot Park, which occupies an area of 154¼ acres, was purchased by the Council in 1920 for £21,000. The original plans for the development of the Aldershot Park estate, which were prepared in 1919 by Mr. J. Neave, the Town Surveyor, were very much on the lines of the satellite town projects of today, and incorporated many of the present-day features of town planning. The layout of the proposed estate incorporated the then existing tree-lined avenue which led up to the house. The lake was to be the centre of a public garden in the middle, and the old mansion was to be demolished. On the south-east of the public garden were sites for a church, a school and a public hall, and provision was made for a cemetery, a small shopping centre, allotment gardens, and small holdings. There were to have been some seven roads, and the most distinctive feature of the scheme was the construction of an arterial road which cut through the estate. It was planned that this road should start at Aldershot Green and run in a direct line over the Blackwater, through Tongham, and thence straight up to the Hog's Back, thereby joining the main Portsmouth Road with the centre of Aldershot.

used for polo matches. The diving stage is equipped with Olympic spring-boards, the greatest diving height being 16 feet 3 inches (5 metres). The Pool is immensely popular in the summer months, large numbers of bathers from many miles around making good use of this popular amenity of the Borough. Many interesting inter-club competitions are held here, and it was in this pool that the swimming event of the Modern Pentathlon of the XIV Olympiad took place in June, 1948.

Ample dressing-room accommodation is provided, and alongside the pool are gymnastic apparatus and grass tennis courts.

Aldershot Park Mansion, with its pillared porchway which over-looks the pool, still has an air of quiet Georgian dignity despite the changes wrought on its surroundings. The old house is now in use as flats in the Council Housing Scheme.

In the main hall of the Mansion, today the communal hall, stands an unusual, massive and ornate carved oak fireplace, which remains from the days when the house was a private residence. It was offered for sale by the Council in 1920, but no purchaser was forthcoming. The fireplace, which bears the date 1714, is just over nine feet in height and eight feet in length. Above the mantelpiece, which is supported by two figures thought to be St. Peter and St. Paul, are three hand-carved Biblical scenes, depicting the Shepherd's Vision, the Nativity, and Jesus in the Temple, the latter two containing nine and ten figures. Above are carved the letters "I.N.R.I." Below the mantelshelf in separate panels are the words, "East or West Hames Best," whilst immediately above the grate are carved two shields, that on the right being the shield of the arms of the City of London, that on the left being a shield depicting an oak tree the trunk of which is superimposed on a salmon proper with its head to the dexter side of the shield. The fireplace is an imposing and interesting example of the craftsman's art. Unfortunately, the carving is now damaged, several of the figures and ornamentations having been chipped and broken, and the wood worm is at work.

From the well hall a fine staircase leads to the upper floor, and above is a glass roof, the walls leading to it decorated with hand-painted designs.

To the west side of the house, facing Pool Road, the large coach-house and stables, with a wooden clock tower surmounting the roof, remain, now used as commercial premises.

To the north of the Park lies the Council Housing Estate, made up of the Avenue, Guildford Road, Chetwode Place (named after General Sir Philip Chetwode), Allden Avenue (after Richard Allden), Whyte Avenue (after the Whyte family, who lived in Aldershot in the sixteenth and seventeenth centuries), Newcome Place (after the Newcome family who owned the Manor House until 1919), and Tichborne Place, recalling the association with Aldershot of the Tichborne family, on whose arms those of the Borough are based. At the lower end of Guildford Road one enters the pleasantly wooded outer portion of the original Aldershot Park. To the right lies the ground of the Aldershot Cricket Club, on the left a laid-out pleasure ground with a large oblong paddling pool and children's playground; this portion of the park is bounded on the north and east by a wide, pleasant stretch of water, which on the opposite side is bounded by Heron Wood. This was originally the boating lake of the park, and although it has now been enclosed and its banks built up, to guide its course, it retains much of its natural beauty and a glimpse along either of the reaches gives the impression of a natural, unspoiled country stream, with its grassy banks overhung with bushes and set off against the tall elms and oaks of Heron Wood. Below the wood lies an expanse of grass-land, now a sports ground of some nineteen acres with two pavilions, leading down to the Blackwater River, which forms the county boundary. To the south-west is another stretch of woodland known as Kiln Copse. To the north of Heron Wood runs a footpath leading from Tongham Road, which is a turning off the Lower Farnham Road by Parkside Farm-house, across the meadows and over the Blackwater to the Surrey village of Tongham. A little farther to the north is another footpath running in the same direction. This is the area which, although not marked as such on the Ordnance Survey Map, is locally known as "Smokey Hole."* This old name dates from the days when, both in this area and by Kiln Copse, there were a number of lime kilns, the chalk being brought down from along the Hog's Back, and the smoke and fumes given off from the kilns gave rise to the local designation which has lasted to this day. The old kilns were demolished in the early twenties, but the name they gave to this area remains.

Parkside Farm-house, which lies behind a tidy hedge back from the road where Tongham Road joins the Lower Farnham Road, is not an old building, but it stands on the site of one of the early farms in the district. It is a double-fronted farm-house with a large outbuilding adjoining upon which the name of the contractor and the date are shown up on the wall in large letters formed by the bases of a number of green bottles set into the red bricks, "George Greenwood 1887." Behind the farm-house are a number of outbuildings, and between the

---

* Originally known as "Smokey Hall," and marked as such on the map of the Hundred of Crondall published in the "Crondall Records," Part I, compiled by Francis Baigent in 1891.

farm and the rear of the Gas Works yards and sidings on the Ash Road, and along the line of the Blackwater, is one of the Council estates of "prefabs," built on a sports ground in 1945.

On the west of the Lower Farnham Road at its junction with Ash Road is the "Prince of Wales" public-house, shown on the map of 1859, and on the corner of Stone Street, which took its name from the gravel pit (now used as a Borough Council "tip" and yard) behind Herrett Street, to which it leads, is the "White Lion," also marked in the early maps of the town. From the south end of Herrett Street a footpath runs through to Brighton Road. This path, until 1938, bordered a large orchard which covered some ten acres of ground in this area. It was in that year that the housing estate comprising Orchard Way and Gardens and Gillian Avenue and Close was built.

At the point where Lower Farnham Road meets Boxall's Lane, the former leads down to the line of the Blackwater River, which at this point is but a narrow stream. The Municipal boundary conforms to the river line, and on crossing Pea Bridge over the Blackwater one leaves Aldershot and Hampshire, to enter Surrey and Badshot Lea.

Boxall's Lane runs parallel with the river and leads under the railway at the point where it joins Eggar's Hill and becomes Weybourne Road. At the rear of the gardens on the south of Boxall's Lane, and to the west of Pea Bridge, is an extensive pond known as "Aldershot Lake" or the "Gravel Pit Lake," originally a large gravel pit. This was marked on the maps of 1930 as "Aldershot Stadium" and, on earlier maps, as an Athletic Ground.* This was flooded in 1938. There were many plans for its future—for it to be developed as a boating lake and a pleasure ground—but these did not materialize. It has now been stocked with fish and is a preserve of the Farnham Angling Society, who have purchased the lake.

To the north of Boxall's Lane, at the rear of Jubilee Road, at the foot of a shrub-strewn steep hill lies a brick and tile works, today the premises of Carwood, Wharton and Co. Ltd., manufacturers of Porex Pipes. The old kilns stand on the site of brickworks which have existed for over two hundred years on this site, the brick kilns being shown on the map of 1856, and were known during the latter part of last century as "Kemp's Brickworks," after the Aldershot builder of that name. To the left of the brickworks is Boxall's Farm,†

---

* The use of this old pit for either of these purposes never materialized. Projects for development of the gravel as such were shelved. It was, however, for a time used as a motor-cycle "dirt track."

† Boxall's Farm comprises three cottages, a farmyard and outbuildings, and in the sale sheet issued by the auctioneers when the farm was sold in February, 1922 was described as a "very compact small holding with sufficient ground for pig and poultry farming" comprising 1¼ acres with "a capital barn, cowsheds and piggeries."

the original buildings of which remain, and adjoining is a large field, formerly a playing field, which bounds the southern edge of a housing estate comprising Highfield Gardens and Highfield Close, which was built in 1938-9 and is still being developed, the roads taking in the old footpath which ran from Farnham to Guildford through the villages, a part of the old Pilgrims' Way. This footpath, which still exists in parts, ran at a diagonal from Boxall's Lane near the foot of Eggar's Hill, behind the lower portion of Highfield Avenue and across the fields, to the rear of Evelyn Avenue, where it joined Croft Road and led on to the Parish Church. The footpath is picked up again off Waterloo Road, and a portion of it still runs behind Haig Road. The footpath which today runs from North Lane to the Blackwater River is a continuation of this old way.

To the south of Boxall's Lane in the area bounded on the west by the railway and on the south by the Blackwater River lie the Aldershot Waterworks of the former Mid Southern Utility Company, with the pumping station and storage tanks. The water undertaking was transferred on 3rd January, 1950, to the Mid-Wessex Water Company.

To the east of the railway and at the rear of Highfield Avenue lies the site of Manor Lodge, now demolished, which stood in just over three acres of pleasantly wooded grounds backing on to Bridge Road ; the old lawns and gardens are now overgrown and derelict and only the foundations of the old house remain, half covered by long grass and weeds. Adjoining the railway embankment on the west is Eggar's Hill, named after Samuel Eggar,* who owned a considerable part of the land in Aldershot which was sold to the Government for the establishment of Aldershot Camp. At the foot of the hill leading to the west is Weybourne Road, which is the main road out of Aldershot to Farnham. To the south of the road near the railway bridge stands Vine Cottage, which was shown on the map of 1856 as "Aldershot Cottage," and at the rear are the well-laid-out sports grounds of the Aldershot and District Traction Company. Here are an excellent cricket ground, bowling green and tennis courts, with a well-appointed pavilion, and adjoining the line of the river is an athletic sports ground and grandstand, the whole covering some seven and a half acres.

At the foot of Ayling Hill, opposite the "Duke of York" public-house, built in 1912, set back from the road, are a row of attractive old-world cottages which have been modernized and are well cared for. These cottages are among the oldest buildings in Aldershot, and date back to Stuart days, and are shown on several old maps as "Aldershot Buildings." They were, for many years, known as "The Dog Kennels," for at the end was a small inn called the "Fox and Hounds." Eighty

* See p. 5.

yards on, one again reaches the municipal boundary where the Black-water runs under the road through a culvert and forms the boundary between Hampshire and Surrey.

Ayling Lane runs northwards up from the Weybourne Road, and is undoubtedly the most rural road remaining in Aldershot. The road is lined with trees and the original hedges of the lane form the hedges of the front gardens of the houses on either side. On the left of the road at the lower end it is still agricultural land, and corn is still grown in this farm land within the Borough. The last harvest was, however, probably reaped in August, 1949, for this area is now threatened by development, and a housing estate has been planned where, for many hundreds of years, crops have grown. Near the top of the hill stands Ayling House, one of Aldershot's early farm-houses, which dates from the seventeenth century, and on the open ground which slopes away to the left is a belt of trees known as the Grove. Between Ayling Lane and Eggar's Hill lies a residential area, traversed by Hillside Road, Manor Road and Winton Road, which joins the latter with Church Lane West. Here are a number of fine houses standing amid well-laid-out wooded grounds and gardens, from the rear of which a fine view is commanded—a view which reaches out across the Surrey countryside to Hindhead. This area lies on the ground rising from Weybourne Road, immediately behind which, amid pleasant surroundings, is the Underwood Bowling Club with its fine green, and the hard tennis courts of the Methodist Church Tennis Club.

To the right of Ayling Hill, at the junction with Church Lane West, stands the unfinished Church of the Ascension, which was con-secrated on 23rd April, 1945, by the Bishop of Guildford. The building of the church ceased in 1939, the foundation stone having been laid on St. Mark's Day of that year. The remaining half of the nave, in which will be a gallery for the choir, an organ, and a tower, has yet to be built. At the foot of the path leading to the church is a wooden calvary which originally stood outside the Mission Church of St. Aidan in King's Road, one of the two mission churches serving the West End of Aldershot prior to the building of the Church of the Ascension. The Ascension district became a separate parish in 1949.

The unfinished church, in red brick, has a corner-stone foundation stone near the west door ; on one side is a cross Pattonce, on the other an inscription commemorating the fact that the stone was placed in position on St. Mark's Day, 1939, by John, Bishop of Guildford, and the words "Ye are God's Building." Above the west door the church bell hangs on the outside wall of the church in the position the tower will occupy when it is built.

The interior of the church is in modern-style architecture, the leaded windows of the south wall catching the light which floods across the pews in the south aisle and the nave. On the south wall is the one stained-glass window, of modern design, bearing the inscription at the base, "A.M.D.G." and "in memory of Alfred William Ker Spence and Mary Lucy Spence—MCMXLVIII." Behind the altar is an oil painting of the Virgin Mary, the child Jesus and St. Peter, and the aisles contain several small shrines. In the north aisle is a shrine, the figure of Our Lord set on an oak plinth bearing a brass tablet upon which is the inscription, "In memory of my dear husband Ronald Ernest Kimber age 31 years. Squadron Leader R.A.F., killed in action on the night of August 11th-12th 1942." The oak lectern bears a plaque commemorating this gift to the church "from her daughter Blanche" in memory of Emily Crittwell, who died in March, 1943.

Near the west door is a small wall tablet brought to the church from the old Mission Church of St. Aidan. The tablet records the "grateful record of the Ministry of Robert Trevor Morgan Curate of Aldershot 1901-05, Curate of Belair, South Australia 1906," who died in that post in the same year.

At the foot of Ayling Hill is a cross-roads; to the right is York Road, to the left Cranmore Lane, which takes its name from the Cranemore of the Customal and Rental Roll of St. Swithun's Priory, 1287.*

The first houses on the left of Cranmore Lane are a group of five alms-houses (3, 5, 7, 9 and 11 Cranmore Lane), built in 1879, bearing a plaque on which is the inscription, "Erected in Memory of Richard John Stovold Esq., of Ayling House," who farmed in Aldershot in the middle of last century in the lands adjoining Ayling Hill.

On the right of the lane just below "Alverstoke" another house bears a plaque above the porch. The building, which is divided into two portions, is known as "Salter's Thanksgiving Houses," and is composed of two rest homes for the aged, erected in 1923 by the late Mr. J. O. Salter. Over the central entrance, facing Cranmore Lane, is a tablet upon which is the bust of Mr. Salter in profile, and carved on the woodwork the inscription :

AD. MAJOREM DE GLORIAM.

These Homes of Rest have been erected and endowed
by James Oliver Salter as a thanksgiving for
Blessings received through life. June, 1923.

The houses were consecrated and officially opened by the Rev.

---

* Cranmore Lane and "a wood called Cranmore" are referred to as such in the Crondall Customary, 1568.

Garth Ireland, then Vicar of Aldershot, at a simple ceremony. The houses have been described as "an antique gem in a modern setting, an old-world building of oak and brick set between diminutive lawns and kitchen gardens." The rooms are all on the ground floor with a covered passage-way connecting the two houses, each of which contains a living room, bedroom, scullery, bathroom and coal store, the walls of the two main rooms being panelled with oak and fitted with cupboards. Let into the walls between the living rooms and bedrooms is a draw-out shelf containing a Bible, and a book of family prayer, so fitted that they can be obtained from either room. Surmounting this shelf is the text, "Seek and ye shall find."

A number of older houses are situated in the lane, among which is Cranmore House, approached by a carriage drive. In the sale sheet of the residence published by Messrs. Alfred Pearson & Son when the house, then the property of Captain W. S. C. Crawshay, of the 8th Hussars, was put up for auction in 1911, it was described as "very suitable for an officer serving in the Aldershot Command" and "occupying a high and healthy position." Among the features of the house were "Two excellent Wine Cellars," and garages and stabling with loose boxes and a hay store.

At the west end of this residential road, where it joins the Farnborough Road, is Hallimore Hill, known to older inhabitants as "Foxes' Den," and beyond is Rowhill Copse, which lies over the Surrey border within the bounds of the Farnham U.D.C. Negotiations were opened up, in 1949, between the Borough Council and the Farnham Council which resulted in the purchase of the southern slopes of Hallimore Hill and the Copse, thereby adding over fifty acres to the Borough. It was decided to leave this land in its natural wooded state with the object of its forming a "green belt" between the boundaries of Aldershot and Farnham.

Amid the trees and undergrowth, near the footpath at the foot of Hallimore Hill, just over eighty yards from the end of Cranmore Lane, stands a moss-covered boundary stone, marking both the County and the Borough boundaries. The Hallimore Hill–Rowhills Copse area is encircled by War Department boundary stones, marking the extent of the Government lands. The County boundary is shown on the Ordnance Map as running in a straight line over Hallimore Hill to a point where another boundary stone used to stand by the spring which is the source of the River Blackwater. From here the rivulet runs down the wooded hillside to wind away to south-east and east, broadening into the stream which forms the boundary between Hampshire and Surrey.

On the opposite side of the Farnborough Road, set back among wooded grounds, stands Anglesey House,* built in the late fifties as the residence of the Cavalry Brigade Commander.

The open country to the north of Cranmore Lane, until recently occupied only by an extensive nursery, which lay below a plantation at the rear of Pavilion Road, is now being rapidly developed as a housing estate lying to the west of King's Road, below Pavilion Road, which takes its name from its proximity to the Royal Pavilion. King's Road leads up from the junction of Cranmore Lane with Ayling Hill and York Road, at the corner of which stands the old West End Farm, the buildings outwardly having the same appearance as they did a hundred years ago when Mr. Stovold farmed the whole of this area, and when Cranmore Lane was but a footpath through hop-fields.

Sandford Road forks off King's Road just above West End Farm, and in the apex of the fork stands the now-disused Mission Church of St. Aidan, a red brick building with a small wooden tower, whose congregation has now been absorbed into the new Parish of the Ascension. The church, with its church hall, stands back from the road behind a row of lime trees and is now used as a Youth Club. Farther up Sandford Road stand West End Cottages, which housed the workers on the old West End Farm, and Rock House, which, as Rock Place, is shown on the map of 1856.

At the top of the road is the Methodist Mission Hall, a commodious corrugated iron building where meetings and Sunday schools are held.

Immediately before one, at the junction of Sandford Road and Alexandra Road, is the unusually high brick wall of the South Cavalry Barracks, which rises some forty feet from the roadway, for the level of the barrack area is high above the town roads which lie below.

Next to the "Rifleman" public-house, which stands at the bend of Alexandra Road, is one of the last two remaining blacksmith's forges in the town. The town's smithies have, as the years have passed, gradually closed down, but here the glowing forge and the ring of the

---

* The name of Anglesey House may be thought to have been taken from the association of the Earls of Anglesey with the neighbourhood. The Anglesey family was connected with the district between 1652 and 1761, when Farnborough Place was one of the family residences, used as a hunting seat. It is more probable, however, that the house, which from 1861 until 1938 was always the residence of the Officer Commanding the Cavalry Brigade, takes its name from the first Marquis of Anglesey (1768-1854), the distinguished cavalryman who, as Henry William Paget, commanded the whole of the Cavalry and Artillery, under Wellington, at Waterloo He had previously served in the Peninsular War, and commanded an Infantry Division in the Walcheren Expedition of 1809, and was Colonel of the 7th Light Dragoons from 1797 to 1842, when he exchanged to the Royal Horse Guards. He was twice Master-General of Ordnance, on the last occasion from 1846 to 1852, and at one time Lord-Lieutenant of Ireland.

anvil may still be heard as a reminder of the days, not so far distant, when the streets echoed to the sound of the clop-clop of horses' hooves.

Away to the left runs Queens Road, which leads through to the top of Victoria Road. Here, at No. 19, stands the narrowest house in Aldershot, the whole house being but eight feet wide and having an unusual appearance, its three storeys being sandwiched into a gap between two of the normal type of villa house.

Turning off Queen's Road and running through to Alexandra Road, which follows the line of the high wall of the Cavalry Barracks, is Cambridge Road, named after H.R.H. The Duke of Cambridge, in which stands St. Anthony's Convent. At the junction of Cambridge Road and Alexandra Road, on the convent wall at the first-floor level, is a statue of St. Anthony and the Holy Child, and on the red brick wall facing Cambridge Road is a tiled circular plaque bearing the figure of the Infant Christ. The entrance to the convent is in Cambridge Road. One passes through a lych gate ; under the porch is a carved and painted figure of St. Anthony in monk's robes, bearing in his hand an open Bible on which stands a small child with open arms. Beyond the porch lies a peaceful and pleasantly laid out garden, with lawns, shrubs and flower-beds and a shrine in rough stone in which stands a statue of the Virgin Mary, before her a figure kneeling in prayer.

At the junction of Queen's Road and Perowne Street stands the Palais de Danse, and beyond this the old mission church of St. Alban, which since it ceased to be used as such has been in turn an Oddfellows' Hall, a store and a club. In Queen's Road are two of the Borough's schools, the West End Schools, which were opened in November, 1873, and Queen's Road New Infants' School, opened on 3rd October, 1898, the former backing on to the Municipal Gardens, the latter with its spacious buildings and playgrounds fronting on to York Road.

The area known as Cargate, which takes its name from "Cartgate," the old western approach to Aldershot village,* lies to the south of Queen's Road and runs down to Church Lane West. Cargate covers the high ground occupied by Cargate Hill, Cargate Grove, Terrace and Avenue, a residential area built in the seventies and eighties with fine houses in well-laid-out grounds and ample plantations. At the top of Cargate Hill stands the reservoir of the former Mid Southern Utility Company and the water tower built in 1907, which is a dominating landmark for many miles. At the lower end of Cargate runs the tree-lined residential Church Lane West, which is connected

---

* "Cargate feald" and "A close called the Carte gate" are referred to in the Crondall Customary, 1568.

to Lansdowne Road by a rural lane, known as Frog Lane, one of the last country footpaths in the Borough, with its hedgerows and tall trees, the leaves and boughs of which join across the old path. Church Lane West joins the top of Eggar's Hill at the junction of Grosvenor Road opposite the "Five Arch" Bridge over the railway. Some of Aldershot's most pretentious residences lie in Church Lane West and on Eggar's Hill, standing in their own grounds, reached by carriage drives. Most of these were built in the late seventies, and command fine views of the Surrey highlands as far as Hindhead. There is an unobstructed view from the junction of these two roads overlooking the railway cutting, and in 1949 two oak seats were set up on this site by the Aldershot Rechabites. Carved on the seats are the words "Rest and be Thankful," and each seat bears a brass plaque with the inscription :

This seat was presented to Aldershot by the Military
District of Rechabites No. 111 in thanksgiving for
return of peace after the 1939-45 War.

On the east of the "Five Arch" Bridge—so named locally when it was first built from the five brick arches of which it is composed—lies Church Lane East, which runs through to the Parish Church. This leads into a residential area. Beyond the bridge are two old public-houses, the "Garden Gate," reminiscent of the days when a market garden stood behind the inn (a few old cottages still cluster in a secluded alley at the rear of the present public-house), and the "Wheatsheaf," for there were cornfields in the area now occupied by Upper St. Michael's, Northbrook, Southmead, Brockenhurst and Avondale Roads. Turning to the right lies Highfield Avenue, at the top of which is the modern, well-equipped and well-sited County High School, which was opened in 1912. On the left of Church Lane East, in St. George's Road, stands Aldershot Hospital, opened in August, 1897, by H.R.H. The Duke of Connaught. The hospital today is a large red brick building with red tile roofs and gables. It started, however, in a modest way as a small cottage hospital, extensions having been added to the original building as the years passed. In the main entrance porch is a small bronze tablet, set over the foundation stone, which commemorates the laying of the stone by H.R.H. The Duchess of Connaught and Strathearn on 28th July, 1896.

On the wall of the entrance hall are two oak tablets bearing the names of the Life Governors of the hospital and four smaller wooden plaques erected to the memory of William Wren, Honorary Secretary to the hospital for forty-six years, A. J. Andrews, Honorary Treasurer for forty-eight years, Dr. J. Cohen, a member of the honorary medical staff from 1904 until 1946, and Alderman Underwood, Chairman of the Hospital Board from 1929 to 1942 and President from 1938. The wards of the original hospital building bear brass tablets inscribed in script with the names of those generous donors of the past whose names are closely associated with the development of the town. These are the "Richard Eve," "Newcome" and "Robertson" Wards and the "Underwood" Block. In the main corridor by the Out-Patients' entrance is a new and modest little wooden tablet on which, in blue painted lettering, is the inscription which commemorates the service of voluntary workers prior to the taking over of the hospital by the State in 1948 :

> In tribute to the Workers of the West Surrey
> and Aldershot Hospital League for their devoted
> Service to the Voluntary Hospital and to the
> Community 1928-1948.

This corridor leads into a wing which bears a foundation stone on which is the inscription, "Laid by Frederick Arthur Simmonds Esq. in May 1934—a friend of Children and a generous supporter of the Hospital."

Facing into St. Michael's Road on the wall of one of the extensions is a plaque commemorating the laying of the foundation stone of this wing on 3rd October, 1928, by the Countess of Selborne, and the opening of the Wing, on 10th July, 1929, by Lieutenant-General Sir David G. M. Campbell, K.C.B., the then G.O.C. the Aldershot Command. Beyond this wing is a later extension, now the Maternity Unit, and the Physiotherapy Department.

Continuing along Church Lane East beyond St. Michael's Road, the north side runs along the edge of the Manor Park, and in the area bounded by Manor Walk, which connects Church Lane East with St. Michael's Road, stand the new Manor Schools, built last year. Beyond, is the Parish Church of St. Michael the Archangel.

From the "Five Arch" Bridge, at the Eggar's Hill end of Church Lane West, Grosvenor Road leads down into the centre of the town.

To the right lie the extensive garages and repair shops of the Aldershot and District Traction Company, and the administrative offices and booking offices, standing at the junction of Grosvenor Road and Halimote Road, which were built in 1924. At the rear is the "Traction Hall," which is let for dances and other social occasions, and here many of the leading events of the town have been held, the hall being the venue of many civic functions in recent years.

The Traction Company was formed in 1912 to operate local services. Today, although adhering to its original title, the services maintained extend far beyond the area covered by its name, and the familiar green double- and single-decker buses carry the name of Aldershot over ninety-seven routes which they traverse as far afield as London, Bognor, Reading, Horsham and Winchester.

On the left of Grosvenor Road, at this point, is Cavendish Mews, with its disused stables behind the cottages, and small houses which run up to join Frog Lane at the rear of Cargate Avenue. Among the houses is one bearing a name board announcing it to be "St. Agnes Lodge," a small welfare centre and maternity home.* Next come Lysons Road and Upper Lysons Road, which take their name from General Sir Daniel Lysons, K.C.B., the General Officer Commanding in Aldershot from 1880 to 1883 ; and beyond are Elms Road and Upper Elms Road, in which stands the Baptist Tabernacle at the junction of Vine Street.

At the next cross-roads are Laburnum Road and Birchett Road. In Birchett Road, at the point where it intersects Gordon Road, stands the Theatre Royal, built in 1891.† Originally a music-hall, the theatre has alternated between the legitimate stage and variety and is now the home of Repertory in Aldershot. Here a first-class company, with a change of programme each week, produce both classical and modern plays, which have given a stimulus to the appreciation of drama in the Borough. A Playgoers' Society was formed in the town in 1946, and a year later this organization took over the lease of the theatre, a company being formed to deal with the business side of the theatre, and another non-profit-making company established at the same time to deal with the local aspect of the management.

At the junction of Elms Road and Birchett Road there stands, in the former, Birchett Hall, the Aldershot National Spiritualist Church, and lower down is the large corner building used as the Aldershot Youth Club.

Laburnum Road is bounded on the north by the Municipal Gardens, and on the opposite side of the road behind the "Bank Tavern," so named from the days when Grosvenor Road was called Bank Street, runs Laburnum Passage, containing a row of twelve typical village cottages with small well-kept gardens. Continuing along the road one comes to the yard of the Borough Engineer's and

---

* St. Agnes Lodge celebrated its jubilee in 1930, and during those fifty years, as it does today, the staff of the Lodge had carried on magnificent work in preventive and rescue work among women in the district, the Lodge dealing with all aspects of welfare work, from maternity cases to providing the occasional night's shelter to needy women. St. Agnes Lodge is affiliated to the Guildford Diocesan Council for Moral Welfare.

† The theatre was sold on 28th February, 1939, and was described in the prospectus as having "seating accommodation for about 750 in stalls, circle and gallery, three bars, six dressing rooms, offices and workshops."

Surveyor's Department, adjoining which are the Ambulance Station and the Electricity Works. At the top of Laburnum Road a footpath runs between the Municipal Gardens and a children's playground to The Warren.

Adjoining Laburnum Road are the well-laid-out Municipal Gardens, which were opened up in 1904 on the site of the former Parish Clerk's land, which was bought by the local authority in 1898. The gardens, which lie on the side of a slope running down from the rear of Queen's Road, extend back to The Warren and the playgrounds of Queen's Road New Schools and the Municipal children's playground at the rear of Cargate Hill. At the entrance of the Municipal Gardens is a fountain, around the border stone of which is the inscription, "To the Memory of Minnie, Wife of Nathaniel Solomon"—who was Mayor of Aldershot, 1924-5.* Beyond the fountain, within a low chain fence, stands the imposing obelisk of grey Cornish granite on a granite base, which is Aldershot's War Memorial of the 1914-1918 war. The memorial, which was unveiled by H.R.H. The Duke of Gloucester on 18th March, 1925, bears the inscription, "Borough of Aldershot— This memorial was erected in grateful memory to those who gave their lives to their country in the Great War 1914-1919, and in the World War 1939-1945."† Until 1940, two captured field guns, one German, one Turkish, flanked the memorial.‡

At the top of the rising grass slope at the rear of the Municipal Buildings overlooking the entrance to the gardens is a pleasantly situated brick and tile shelter, with seats along its frontage and an inner room, heated in winter by a stove. This shelter was presented to the Borough by Alderman W. J. North, J.P., when Mayor of Aldershot, 1935-1937, "for the use and comfort of the aged residents of the Borough," a fact which is commemorated by a small plaque inside the building.

These well-established wooded gardens are well situated, providing a peaceful, small and compact park for the residents in the town centre, as well as tennis courts and a children's playground with swings and see-saws, which is a feature of all the parks in Aldershot. The gardens contain an unusual variety of trees—acacia, ash, lime, prunus, walnut, elm, mountain ash, chestnut, silver birch, sycamore and willow—most of which were given to the Borough and planted by their donors at a ceremony on 13th December, 1905.

---

* The fountain was unveiled by Alderman Solomon on Friday, 13th May, 1921.

† The inscription relating to the late war was added in November, 1950.

‡ These remained from a collection of eight captured field guns and howitzers, four German and four Turkish, which was displayed in the Municipal Gardens in November, 1919.

At the north-east corner of the gardens, facing Grosvenor Road, stand the Municipal Buildings, which were built in 1904. In recent years the expansion of the functions of the Borough Council has outgrown the building, and the houses on the opposite side of the road have been taken over as offices for the Public Health Department, the Sanitary Inspector, the Housing Officer and the Citizens' Advice Bureau.

The red brick Municipal Buildings have a tiled entrance hall. On the walls of the staircase leading to the first floor are two commemorative plaques presented to the Borough in recognition of the "Salute the Soldier" and "Wings for Victory" Weeks held in 1944 and 1945. There is also a large framed coloured and autographed print of our great war-time Premier, whose associations with Aldershot date from the time when he was a subaltern in the 4th Hussars. Below this portrait is a coloured reproduction of the crest of the submarine H.M.S. *Tuna*, enclosed in a grommet and surmounted by a Naval Crown. Below is a small brass plaque commemorating the adoption of the *Tuna* by the Borough during Warship Week, February, 1942. The crest was presented to the town by the Lords Commissioners of the Admiralty. In the Mayor's Parlour is a miniature replica of the submarine, made by one of the crew.

On the first floor of the building is the Council Chamber, a pleasant, well-lighted room. Over the entrance above the public seats is a glass domed roof, and on either side are the Councillors' Retiring Room and the Lady Councillors' Room. The Council Chamber itself has a central domed roof, and is occupied by two rows of semi-circular tables facing in to the long top table, occupied, when the Council is sitting, by the Mayor, Deputy Mayor and the Town Clerk. Behind this table stands the Mayoral Chair, on the back of which are carved the old arms of the Aldershot Urban District Council, the alder tree below three piles of shot. Before the Mayor's place at the Council table stands a large carved wooden inkstand, which also bears on the sides the arms of the old U.D.C. and the coat of arms of the Worshipful Company of Butchers, and the inscription "Amiez Loyaulte," the family motto of the Marquess of Winchester. The stand is surmounted by the carved wooden figure of a bull, which is accounted for by the inscription on a silver plate affixed to the stand which reads, "Presented to the Mayor and Corporation of Aldershot in 1922 by the Master Butchers of Aldershot and District." The presentation actually took place in May, 1923.

The windows of the Council Chamber look out on to the pleasantly wooded slopes of the Municipal Gardens. On the walls are the photographs of Aldershot's fourteen Mayors in their robes of office,

and also a large photo of Henry Wells, J.P., C.C., Chairman of the
Aldershot U.D.C., 1895-6; an aerial view of Aldershot, presented
to the Council by Councillor H. T. Reeves to mark the completion of
his tenth year of public service; a group of the Incorporation Committee, taken in 1922; and a photo taken in the Council Chamber
in February, 1921, on the occasion of the Inquiry by the Special
Commission before the granting of Aldershot's Charter. There is also
an interesting Ordnance Survey Map of Aldershot, printed in
1873-1875.

Also on the first floor is the Committee Room, the Town Clerk's
Office and the Mayor's Parlour, on the walls of which hang photo-
graphs of the first military Borough Councillor and Captain Alfred
Maurice Toye, V.C., M.C., an Aldershot man who won his Victoria
Cross near Eterpigny, south of Peronne, on 25th March, 1918, whilst
serving with the 2nd Bn. Middlesex Regiment. Here also is a large
silver salver presented to the Borough by Councillor A. H. J. Stroud,
Aldershot's war-time Mayor. In the Mayor's Parlour is the Borough's
Distinguished Visitors' Book, which was commenced on the occasion
of the grant of Aldershot's Charter of Incorporation in 1922. This
interesting book contains a number of notable signatures. Among the
early entries is the signature "Henry," being that of H.R.H. The Duke
of Gloucester, commemorating his visit to Aldershot to unveil the
War Memorial in 1925. There are the signatures of two Prime
Ministers, the Rt. Hon. Winston Churchill and the Rt. Hon. David
Lloyd George, and five Field-Marshals, Viscount Montgomery, Sir
John Dill, Sir Cyril Deverell, Lord Milne and Andrew McNaughton.
There, also, may one see the signatures of the Bishop of Winchester,
the Lord-Lieutenants of the County, several former Cabinet Ministers,
the G.Os.C. of the Aldershot Command and District, and four V.Cs.,
together with those of a number of other distinguished personages
who have officially visited the Borough.

In the upper hallway, on either side of the entrance to the Council
Chamber, stand two glass-covered cabinets* containing sections of the
Aldershot copy of the Crondall Customary. These ancient documents,
written partly in Latin and partly in English, and dating from 1568,
were placed in this position in January, 1950, after having been
restored by the Keeper of the Manuscripts of the British Museum,
following the handing-over of the Customary to the Council to hold
on trust for the people of Aldershot.

Adjoining the Municipal Buildings is the Fire Station, built

---

* The polished oak cabinets containing the parchments were made by Mr.
C. H. Southon, an employee of the Council at the Laburnum Road Depot, from a
tree felled in Aldershot Park.

in 1904. Here stand the bright red engines, with their highly polished brass, of the Hampshire Fire Service. On the nearby walls hang the boots, equipment and helmets of the firemen ready for instant use. Behind the building is an open yard for exercises, and adjoining the garage is the firemen's rest room and canteen, and the administrative offices. On the walls of the garage are three brass plaques, two bearing the inscriptions, "Aldershot Volunteer Fire Brigade." One is "In memory of members of the Brigade who lost their lives on Fire Brigade Service and in the service of their country during the Great War 1914-18," and bears the names of three killed on fire service and whilst on war service. The other bears the names and units of the members of the Brigade who served with His Majesty's Forces during the 1914-1918 war. The third plaque, which was unveiled in 1950, bears the inscription :

A.F.S.—Aldershot Fire Service—A.F.B.—A.F.S.—N.F.S.

In memory of members who lost their lives in the service of their Country in the World War, 1939-1945. Messenger L. F. C. Day, killed on War Service in Holland, 12th June, 1943. Patrol Officer R. J. Kingham, killed on flying duties over France, 6th August, 1944. Fireman M. J. M. Cox, killed on war service in Holland, 28th October, 1944. Leading Fireman W. L. Bennett-Snell, killed on Fire Service duties, 17th August, 1945.

A few yards beyond the Fire Station is a cross-roads ; to the right runs Victoria Road, to the left Queen's Road, at the corner of which are the premises of Messrs. George Potter & Co., Drum and Fife Manufacturers. Their shop windows are attractive and befitting to a military town, for although today their business, which was established in the town in 1859,* has been extended to deal with all forms of musical requirements, they are primarily the manufacturers of drums. The shop is a virtual museum of military drums, many of which are of historical interest. The firm had its origin in the original company formed by Samuel Potter, sometime Coldstream Guards, who opened his first business in the 1790's to supply drums to the Army. Samuel Potter had two sons, Henry and George, the former establishing a similar business in London, the latter founding, out of the parent company, the present business in Aldershot. In the windows are many old drums, of many corps and regiments, cavalry and infantry, regular,

* In 1859 George Potter, in an advertisement in "Sheldrake's Guide," begged "respectfully to acquaint Commanding Officers of Regiments that he had taken premises in High Street, Aldershot (next door to the Alliance Hotel) for the purpose of supplying Regimental necessaries for musical instruments. Repairs of every description, both brass and wood, done on the premises including drum heads, cords, sticks, &c. Publisher of the Regulation Drum, Bugle, Fife Duty Books, Drum and Flute Journal &c."

militia and volunteers. Among these are the bass and side drums of the old Royal Anglesey Light Infantry. Within the shop the walls, and even the ceilings, are decorated with the heraldic panels of bass and side drums straightened out and mounted. Here one may see the badges, crests, mottoes and battle honours of many famous regiments borne on the drum panels, many of the regiments now disbanded, or bearing the old titles and regimental numbers in use before the Cardwell reforms of 1881. Among the interesting old drums is a bass drum carried at the Battle of Waterloo by the Coldstream Guards, a Russian side drum brought home from the Crimea, and a number of others bearing the dates of manufacture, 1840, 1854 and 1863. There is also the exact replica of Drake's Drum made by the firm for use in the Aldershot Tattoo in 1939.

Above the shop are the workrooms where the drums are made by hand by skilled craftsmen, the panels of wood rounded and seasoned, the skins stretched and fixed, and then the painting and emblazoning by hand of the badges and regimental appointments in full heraldic colours. The firm are specialists in this class of work, and have supplied, and still are supplying, drums to regiments at home and overseas. One of their specialities is the manufacture of silver drums, and it is their claim that more silver drums have been made by the firm, in their Aldershot workshops, than any other firm in the country. It is appropriate and fitting that drums carried by regimental bands in every corner of the globe in the past ninety years should have been made in Aldershot, a fact of which the craftsmen who make them are justly proud.

On the opposite corner stands the imposing Methodist Church, built in 1874 at a cost of £10,000, with its fine hundred-foot tower which can be seen for many miles and is a local landmark, and its clock which was erected by the family and friends of the Rev. Edward Pearce Lowry, Honorary Chaplain to the Forces of the Aldershot Command, 1892-1919, in his memory; a fact which is commemorated by a brass memorial in the vestibule of the church, which was unveiled in January, 1929, "as a tribute to the love and esteem in which he was held by all ranks of the Army and by all classes in the Borough of Aldershot."

The church is a fine building with seating accommodation for 1,250. The main feature of the interior is the nave, supported by columns of cast iron with caps and bases of Bath stone. In the chancel facing the east door is a memorial window erected in "grateful memory of General Sir James Hope Grant, G.C.B., by Wesleyan soldiers and friends October 24th 1876."

Behind the altar below three stained-glass windows is a reredos in mosaic and tiles, bearing the Ten Commandments and the Lord's Prayer. The reredos is a memorial to Frances Penelope Wharton Middleton, daughter of Lieutenant-Colonel Lewis Watson, who served as a Major in the 69th Regiment at Waterloo. This is commemorated on a brass plaque, dated 29th January, 1880, at the base of the reredos which was erected by her husband, Richard Wharton Middleton, of Leasingham Hall, Lincolnshire, late of the 71st Highlanders, "mourning the loss of his companion of 56 years and waiting in extreme old age a blissful reunion in the rest which remains into which she through faith in her forerunner entered September 1st 1878." On one of the columns of the chancel arch is the foundation stone laid on 19th November, 1875, by Alderman W. McArthur, M.P. To the right is the fine organ which bears a small plaque, "To the memory of James Englebert Vanner, one of the founders of the Church," the organ being presented in his memory in 1906 by his sisters, Mrs. Charles Early and Mrs. George Stringer-Rowe. To the left of the chancel is the pulpit, given to the church by Mr. and Mrs. Wharton. The pulpit, in carved oak, is set upon a stone plinth, around which is the inscription, "In memory of their Kinsman Sir Henry Havelock, K.C.B. and in token of their interest in the spiritual welfare of the British soldier." In 1950 a conductor's oak music stand, made by Lee Bros. of Aldershot, was installed as a memorial to Walter Gad Curry, who for forty years was choir-master of the Church.

The church contains two war memorials in the form of wall tablets. One marble tablet commemorates the "heroism and sacrifice of those from this congregation who took part in the Great War 1914-18." There is a central panel bearing the names of eighteen men who lost their lives, and on either side panels bearing the names of seventy-six other members of the congregation who served in His Majesty's Forces.* The War Memorial tablet of the 1939-1945 war was erected in 1948 "in grateful and proud memory of five members of the church who gave their lives for their King and Country."

At the rear of the church is the Wesley Hall, which stands on the corner of Barrack Road and Queens Road, and adjoining the church in Grosvenor Road is Wesley House and a row of shops ; but above the shop fronts the buildings are in the same style of ecclesiastical architecture, and of the same grey stone, as Wesley House and the church, whilst continuing round into Alexandra Road one sees, above a furniture shop, the large Gothic window of what was once another church hall behind Wesley Hall, which faces into Queen's Road at the

---

* The memorial was designed by Mr. Walter Finch, and was unveiled on 16th January, 1921, by Field-Marshal the Earl of Cavan, then G.O.C.-in-C. Aldershot Command.

2F

rear of the church. The encroachment of commerce into buildings built in ecclesiastical style is most noticeable when, standing at the top of Union Street, one lifts one's eyes above the line of the shop fascias. These shops occupy the lower floor of what was originally the Wesleyan Soldiers' Home.

On the corner of Edward Street and Barrack Road stands the famous Miss Daniell's Soldiers' Home, the oldest institution of its kind in the country. It is an imposing building of grey stone with Gothic windows, gables and porchways, which bears the date 1863. One side abuts Edward Street, but the main entrance lies back from Barrack Road beyond a gravel drive and line of trees. In the entrance hall are two brass memorial plaques "In Remembrance of Louisa, widow of Captain Daniell, H.E.I.C.S. who established the Aldershot Mission in 1862 and opened this Soldiers' Home in October 1863, and carried on with untiring energy and devotion until her death 16th September 1871." On the opposite wall is a similar plaque. "In remembrance of Georgina Fanny Shipley Daniell, daughter of Captain Daniell . . . she laboured much in the Lord and extended her Mother's work by establishing branch homes at Colchester, Plymouth, Chatham, Windsor, London and Okehampton. She entered unto rest June 24th 1894." This Institute contains reading and recreation rooms, with facilities for billiards and bagatelle, a coffee-bar and refreshment room, a Bible book depot and a large lecture hall, capable of accommodating five hundred, where religious services are conducted. On the floor above are bedrooms and baths for the convenience of soldiers. The Home is open every day and the great work founded eighty-seven years ago is still carried on, a lasting memorial to the founder and her daughter. Large photographs of both decorate the walls of the reading room. The official title is the Mission Hall and Soldiers' Home and Institute, but it is universally known to countless soldiers, past and present, by the name which has endured, "Miss Daniell's Home,"; for a home it really has been to many soldiers, old and young, who have spent their off-duty hours within a few yards of the barracks, but in an atmosphere of homeliness and friendship.

Opposite Miss Daniell's Soldiers' Home at the apex of Queen's Road and Edward Street is the Roman Catholic Church of St. Joseph, which was opened in 1912 and replaced an iron building* which had stood on this site for many years. It is a fine building of singularly beautiful architectural design following that of Italian churches of the tenth and eleventh centuries, the high altar being at the end of the nave, which is divided from the aisles by brick arches. It is a dignified

---

* Removed to Belle Vue Road when St. Joseph's Church was built, and now known as St. Mary's Roman Catholic Church. See p. 270.

building and although based on ancient design is executed in modern style. It has seating accommodation for 600 and adjoins the St. Joseph's Schools, which face the West End Schools in Queen's Road.

The Romanesque design of the church, with its imposing lines and unusual external features, is uncommon and there is no church in England quite like it. In the centre of the high red brick wall facing Victoria Road stands a statue of St. Joseph, below which is the inscription, "Thy Church Protect." The plan for the church was the outcome of necessities, for it was a difficult triangular site on which to build, and the problem was to provide as large a church as possible, symmetrical in design and within the compass of the funds available. The church is of red brick and tile, stone being only introduced into the floors and doorways. At the west end of the church, at which there are entrances from Queen's Road and Edward Street, and the Presbytery, there is a narthex, and here are two altars, one of Our Lady, the other of Holy Souls ; this smaller chapel occupies the full width of the site at this end. There is a graduated decrease in the width of the building towards the high altar, which occupies the semi-circular portion of the eastern end of the church. The sanctuary is raised high above the level of the nave. The altar is of greyish-green marble, beautifully marked, and the communion rails are of the same marble relieved with a band of deep yellow sienna marble and bordered with black marble. A beautiful effect is given by a semi-circle of five columns of black marble with capitals of finely carved white marble, above which are smaller open arches. The main decorative effect within the church has been achieved by the use of coloured bricks and tiles.

Barrack Road runs down to join Grosvenor Road at an apex, by the entrance of Warburg Barracks, on which stands the Imperial Hotel, one of the oldest in the town ; and on the opposite corner is the Queen Hotel, which also dates from the early days of the growth of Aldershot. Next door in High Street is a public-house, "Uncle Tom's Cabin," which probably takes its name from one of the old rough, cabin-like beer-houses which sprang up in the town whilst "The Camp" was being built and became "Uncle Tom's Cabin," again probably because the proprietor's name was Tom, and so linked with the name of the famous book. Last year when this house was being redecorated and renovated a number of old swords, bayonets and carbines were found hidden in the loft and rafters. These were probably souvenirs of the Crimea and at one time decorated the walls of the bars. These arms were presented to the Borough and are to be cleaned and hung on a wall in the Municipal Buildings.

In the area bounded by Barrack Road, High Street and Wellington Avenue lie Princes Gardens, a well-laid-out park which provides a pleasing approach to the town from Wellington Lines. This open space, with its lawns, flower-beds, shrubberies, footpaths and seats, forms a restful and pleasant spot amid the bustle of this busy area where the town joins "The Camp."

It was in 1930 that the Borough Council purchased from the War Department the site bounded by High Street, Court Road, Wellington Avenue and Barrack Road, an area then known as the "R.E. Yard," with the "R.E.D. (Royal Engineer Department) Huts." This was the site of the original huts erected in 1854 for the accommodation of the first engineer staff, responsible for the construction of "The Camp," and from that date the site had been used as an R.E. office and store. This site was cleared, two cinemas, the Empire* and the Ritz, were built on the lower portion, and the upper portion converted into a car park and the Princes Gardens. The main object, the erection of a Civic Centre, with a large hall and a public library, did not, however, materialize.

In Alexandra Road, just off Barrack Road, is the Alexandra Cinema, which stands on the site of one of the town's early music-halls. From Grosvenor Road down to Wellington Street run the shopping streets of Victoria Road and Union Street. Leading off the former and connected by a passageway to Wellington Street stands the Market Place, which is almost the central point of the Borough.

The town centre has the outward appearance of the shopping area of any provincial town or metropolitan suburb. There are the usual run of shops of the distributive trades, and although these include the branches of numerous multiple stores whose names have become household words, the names of private traders dominate the fascias. These are the shops which have brought a considerable amount of local fame to the town during the past thirty years as a popular shopping centre—a fact which is not only due to the enterprise of the private trader and the branch managers, and to the virile direction of the Chamber of Commerce and local branches of the many local trade organizations, but to the very character of the town. Aldershot is a friendly town, the newcomer is welcomed and assisted on his way, for Aldershot has a way with the visitor, and this is reflected in the shopping centre. This attitude and atmosphere is undoubtedly attributable to the effect of the constantly changing population, possibly not so much today as in the past; but with the presence of some 20,000 troops with their wives and families on the doorstep of the town one can well imagine the comings and goings throughout the years as the

---

* The Empire Cinema was opened on 1st August, 1930, announced at the time as "The only cinema in the District built for the 'Talkies'." The total seating accommodation is 1,550. The interior of the hall is 80 feet by 100 feet.

regiments have changed stations. The Aldershot trader may at any time be dealing with a housewife whose last purchases were made in an Eastern bazaar, in a N.A.A.F.I. families' shop in a distant garrison, in Gibraltar, or Germany, Catterick or Cairo. The shifting population for many years outweighed the regular customer, and it was up to the traders of the town to do their best for all comers ; and they did, thereby creating a tradition which holds to this day.

That is the Aldershot on the surface. It is, however, in the alley-ways and in the yards behind the roads of the town centre that the old Aldershot remains almost unchanged after some ninety years. The out-ward appearance is new ; the universal frontage which makes the town at first sight like so many other provincial towns is but the façade which hides what remains of Aldershot of the early days. Behind the present frontage lie many small houses and cottages with small walled gardens. There are mews with coach-houses and stables, lofts, cobbled yards and outhouses, all of which make up the pattern of the old town which clustered as close to "The Camp" as land would permit in the days when the sole purpose in the life of the town was the service of the Army.

There are also, as may be expected in a Borough which has within its boundaries a Royal residence, a number of shops bearing the Royal Arms, showing the firms to be holders of the Royal Warrant.

There are, naturally, a number of military tailors and outfitters, their windows occupied by displays of uniforms, caps, and accessories, and a number of smaller shops specializing in military requisites from camp beds to cap-badges, medal ribbons and insignia, belts and blanco, the needs of the soldier being catered for as is befitting to a military centre. All these shops have their military interest beyond the wares they sell, for most of them have been established for many years, and goods which were of common purchase in the years gone by are now of value as relics of the age in which they were first displayed. There are cases of medals and cap-badges, full-dress uniforms, helmets and busbies, swords and sashes and old military prints, all of which add to the traditions of these established traders who serve the Army.

One of the noticeable features of the town is still the number of licensed houses. In the area bounded by High Street, Wellington Street, Grosvenor Road and Victoria Road there are still some four-teen hotels and public-houses.

It was recorded in 1859 that there were twenty taverns and some forty beer-houses in the town, compared with the two inns which existed in 1854 before the establishment of "The Camp." This number increased even more in the sixties.

In recent years, however, the number of licensed houses has

decreased and several have been closed or demolished in the course
of the town's planned expansion, including the famous Royal Hotel
at the junction of High Street and Wellington Street, and the Royal
Camp Hotel near the corner of High Street and Station Road; but
even so there are today a total of fifty-four licensed houses in the
Borough, and of these a high proportion have names of a military
flavour reminiscent of the days of the beer-houses which sprang up in
the late fifties. We still have the "Hussar," the "Rifleman" the
"Cannon," the "Crimea," the "Heroes of Lucknow," the "Lord Clive,"
the Royal Military,* and others with a military and patriotic flavour.
These names have set a tradition which still obtains, for in 1949
"Dibden's Bar" in High Street was renamed "The Pegasus," and now
displays as its sign the well-known badge of our Airborne Forces,
Bellerophon astride a Pegasus, in pale blue on the familiar maroon
background, which in years to come will, as have the older names which
have associations with the days following the Crimea and the Mutiny,
have a link with the men of Arnhem.

There is an old "chestnut" concerning the number of licensed houses
in the town which bears repeating. It was in the eighties that a senior
staff officer from London arrived rather late for an inspection, and,
being a stranger to Aldershot, missed the road to the scene of the
parade. Accordingly, he stopped a soldier, a recruit who had been left
behind in the camp. "Where is the Duke of Cambridge?" he inquired.
The soldier stood to attention and saluted. "I don't know, sir," was
his answer, "I've only just joined and I'm a teetotaller myself; but I'll
ask the canteen-sergeant, he knows all the pubs in the garrison!"

*   *   *   *   *

The Borough of Aldershot today stands in the centre of a beautiful
and healthy country district, occupying an area of 4,178 acres. It is
still situated in the ancient Hundred of Crondall, the Diocese of
Guildford, the County Court District of Aldershot and Farnham, and
the Petty Sessional Division of Odiham. The height above sea-level
varies from 230 feet at its lowest to 393 feet, and the air is pure and
bracing, and Aldershot proudly claims to be one of the healthiest town
in Great Britain. The birth rate is high, the death rate low; prior to
and even during, the war the death rate compared favourably with
that of the rest of the country.

Aldershot is a focal point from which radiates the fine system of
public road travel operated by the Aldershot and District Traction
Company Ltd. The railway services of Aldershot are particularly

* It was at the rear of this building, as late as the nineties, that there was still
'Rat Pit," where the record kill by "The Aldershot Terrier" was 196 rats in te
minutes.

good, with a half-hourly service to and from London. Connections with Reading, Alton, Winchester, Guildford and London give the travelling public facilities for easy rail communications with all parts of the country.

The electricity supply of Aldershot, which before the nationalization of the industry in 1948 was under the control of the Borough Council, formerly came from current made at its own generating station, but is taken now from the national grid system. The use of electricity in the Borough has shown a remarkable increase in recent years, and it is now extensively used for lighting, heating, cooking and business purposes. Current is supplied on both A.C. and D.C. systems. The gas supply of the Borough is provided by the Aldershot and District Gas Undertaking (Southern Gas Board). The gasworks is equipped with the most up-to-date plant for the manufacture of high-quality gas, and the recovery of such important by-products as coke, tar, breeze, etc.

The Mid-Wessex Water Company now owns the water supply of Aldershot, which is managed with equal efficiency. The water is obtained from semi-artesian borings and is pumped to reservoirs from which it is distributed by gravitation. Special high-pressure mains are laid which enable the Company at very short notice to divert supplies to any part of the town for fire-fighting purposes. The water supply has proved itself equal to all demands, including droughts and war periods. The depth of the supply source and the system of purification ensure an exceptionally high standard of bacteriological purity.

For many years the name Aldershot was only associated in the minds of many people with a large military camp. Today it is known to countless thousands as a centre of enterprising and progressive traders, who have made Aldershot an excellent shopping centre, where the public can obtain good value for their money. It is the boast of Aldershot shops that almost everything that is required by the residents can be provided at prices which compare very favourably with those in any other town of its size in the country.

The cultivation and performance of the Arts in Aldershot have shown a marked increase in recent years. A very successful Choral Society was formed in 1943, and since that date has given frequent concerts in co-operation with the Aldershot Symphony Orchestra, formed in 1945. Each year also since 1943 a Festival of Music and Art has been held in Aldershot and has gone from strength to strength. Numerous entries are received not only from Aldershot but also from a wide area surrounding for choral singing, madrigals, solo singing, pianoforte and string playing, drama, folk dancing, needlework, and numerous other classes.

The Aldershot Playgoers' Society have also, as part of their cultural programme, organized various very successful concerts at the Theatre Royal on Sunday afternoons. A big step to stimulate the appreciation of drama in the Borough was the formation of the Playgoers' Society at the beginning of 1946. Last, but by no means least, the Aldershot Welsh Society have produced three most successful Eisteddfods, and it can now be claimed to be an annual cultural effort in Aldershot.

*   *   *   *   *

Such is the town of Aldershot today, a town the life of which in the past has been primarily bound up with the life of the Army, but which today, although still co-operating to the full with the Army, is desirous of growing to full stature with eventually all the facilities and amenities of a County Borough.

It has been felt for many years that it was desirable to plan and integrate the Aldershot area as a whole. With this in view, the Aldershot Corporation submitted proposals of a far-reaching nature to the Boundary Commission, to take over the administration of a very wide area which included part of Farnham and Camberley Urban Districts, part of Hartley Wintney Rural District, and the parishes of Tongham, Normandy and Ash in the Rural District of Guildford. This would have increased the area of the Borough from 4,178 acres, of which 2,746 acres is military land, to approximately 30,000 acres, and would have meant that the population of the enlarged Borough would be well over 100,000 as against the present figure of approximately 26,000. The object of this proposal was not purely territorial aggrandisement of the area, but to bring under a unified control the complementary parts of what is, in effect, an economic and topographical entity. This proposal was a highly controversial subject and has been temporarily shelved in consequence of the winding-up of the Boundary Commission. But Aldershot is looking to the future with vision and enthusiasm. . . .

CHAPTER NINE

"THE CAMP" TODAY

"Bare and dusty are the Parade Grounds but they are thick with
memories. . . . Here the young recruit drills ; the warrior puts on
his medal, the old pensioner steals back to watch them, and the
soldiers' children play. . . ."
—*Mrs. Juliana Horatia Ewing in "The Story of a Short Life"* (1885).

r is the wall of the old Cavalry Barracks which today forms that
harp line of demarcation between town and "Camp." From the main
ates of the East Cavalry Barracks—Warburg Barracks—in Barrack
Road, facing Princes Gardens and High Street, the barrack wall runs
outh along Barrack Road, then westwards along the full length of
Alexandra Road, and bears right along Chetwode Terrace. At one
oint it reaches a height of forty feet.

Beaumont Barracks, originally known as the South Cavalry Bar-
acks, occupy a dominating position facing Chetwode Terrace, high
bove the town, affording from the upper windows of the barrack
locks an uninterrupted view of Crooksbury Hill and beyond, so that
n clear days the wireless pylons above the Devil's Punch Bowl at
Hindhead are clearly visible.

The Cavalry Barracks extend from the East Gate, facing High
treet, to the gates of the West Cavalry Barracks—Willems Barracks
—on the Farnborough Road. These barrack gates are impressive,
omposed of four brick pillars with stone dressings, surmounted by
amps. Carved in the masonry is the Royal monogram, "VR."

These three blocks of barracks, which were built in 1856 and
ompleted in 1859, were the original quarters of the 1st Cavalry
Brigade, and remained so until 1938, when, following mechanization,
he Brigade moved to Tidworth to be closer to the other units of the
st Armoured Division (which was then spread out over the Salisbury
lain area), thereby breaking an association with Aldershot which
ad lasted eighty years.

The barracks are spacious and all follow the same plan, each block
eing composed of five barrack blocks to accommodate the Regimental Headquarters and the four squadrons. The blocks were built

317

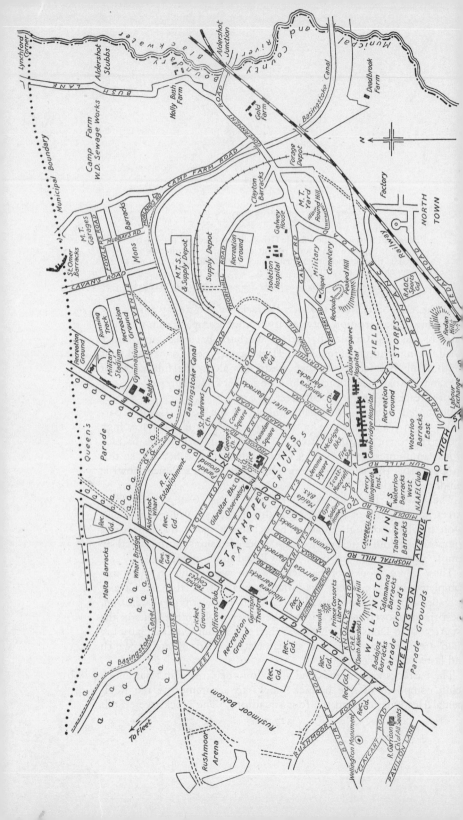

with the men's accommodation above the stables, the barrack rooms being reached by a central stairway, and with a veranda running along the front of each building.

Originally these blocks had two lengthy barrack rooms on either side of the central stairway, but for comfort and convenience these were subsequently divided into smaller rooms with a central passage running between them.

During the late war the barracks were occupied by the Canadian Army Reinforcement Units, later by the "Repat. Depots" of the Canadian Army Overseas; and following the departure of the Dominion troops, the barracks were used to house several thousand German prisoners of war who were formed into P.W. Companies working under the Pioneer Corps. Today a large portion of Beaumont Barracks has been handed over to the Hampshire Territorial Army and Auxiliary Forces Association for use by Aldershot's Territorial Anti-Aircraft Gunners, R.E.M.E. Workshops and W.R.A.C. (T.A.). The local squadron of the Air Training Corps also has its headquarters in these barracks. The Cavalry Barracks have, since the war, housed the 3rd Carabiniers and the 13th/18th Hussars, but are now occupied by training units.

In addition to the stables and barrack rooms, each barracks had its imposing officers' mess block* and parade grounds, and its own riding school—massive, impressive buildings of rusticated brickwork with projecting piers, each building 180 feet by 60 feet wide, where many thousands of officers and men spent many thousands of hours in the eighty years which passed from the time the first cavalry regiments jingled into their then new quarters : hours during which, amid the dust from the deep covering of tan on the floor, they rode around the schools, trotting, cantering and jumping, and making half figures of eight, whilst in the centre the Riding Masters and Rough Riding Sergeant-Majors reigned supreme. How often have those walls echoed to their commands ! "Ride—ter-er-ot ! Ride—cross stirrups. . . . All except the leading file, fold yer arms. . . . Ride—Can-ter ! . . . Now then, Trooper Smith, what the —— do you think you're doing? That's it—go on ; sit down in your saddles. Grip with yer knees, Trooper Jones ! I'm here to make you ride, not to watch you bobbing round like a sack of oats on a wagon. . . ." At last the ride halts, and comes that unique order—known only to the British Army— "Make much of your horses." Those old Riding Schools are alive today with the ghosts of the officers, Riding Masters, N.C.Os. and

---

* Described by William Sheldrake in 1859 as having noble façades with "dressings of cut stone, with a handsome pediment in the centre with stone pilasters, and surmounted by a very fine carving in solid stone of the Royal Arms."

troopers of every regiment of Dragoons, Hussars and Lancers in the Army List.

In those barracks the great changes of the late thirties took place, for here a number of famous cavalry regiments held their last mounted parades, followed by the sad leave-taking of their "long-nosed friends" as the horses were finally led away, to be replaced by the cars and light tanks with which the cavalry were equipped on mechanization. Forage stores and stables gave way to garages and petrol pumps took the place of the horse-troughs.

With the passing of the years there were many additions to the barracks : married quarters for N.C.Os. and men, most of which bear the name of some foreign station—"Egypt Quarters," "Iraq Quarters," "Kohat Quarters," and so on ; schools for the soldiers' children ; N.A.A.F.I. Institutes ; and fine, tree-bordered recreation grounds were laid out between the barracks. The East and West Cavalry Barracks face on to the world-famous Wellington Avenue,* which runs through an avenue of chestnut trees from the Farnborough Road to the foot of Gun Hill. On the north side of the Avenue stand three blocks of barracks built between 1854 and 1856,† the first permanent barracks in Aldershot. They are all named after Wellington's victories. At the west end stand Badajos Barracks, next come Salamanca Barracks, and in line, divided from Salamanca by Hospital Hill and facing Princes Gardens, stand Talavera Barracks. These barracks lie back from the Avenue at the rear of the parade grounds. Chestnut and plane trees line the barrack squares. Each barracks has its own guardroom and administrative buildings and a central officers' mess block, with gardens in the foreground which run down to the road.

When these barracks were first built an unusual feature of their construction was the joining of the two main blocks, which stand one behind the other, by a large, high iron and glass roof,‡ which thereby provided cover between the blocks for a whole battalion to parade. The blocks are of three storeys, each storey being reached by an iron staircase on the outside of the building, the barrack rooms being entered from long verandas which run the full length of the buildings. The glass roofs were removed in 1922.

At the rear of Badajos Barracks is Red Hill, a wooded slope now dotted by terraces of married quarters and soldiers' allotment gardens. It was on this hill that the huts used by the Secretary of State for War

---

* Formerly known as "The Avenue" or "The Avenue Road."
† Designed for the accommodation of three infantry battalions, each composed of 47 officers and 1,400 men.
‡ Likened by William Sheldrake, in 1859, to the roof construction of the Crystal Palace.

were built when "The Camp" was first established in 1854. The rising
ground at the rear of Salamanca Barracks is also occupied by terraces
of quarters for soldiers' families, institutes, stores and other administrative buildings, and an R.E. Yard; and the same obtains in the case
of the ground behind Talavera Barracks, where Campbell Road and
Rutland Terrace are occupied by red brick-built married quarters.
A barrack road runs through the line of Infantry Barracks from the
Farnborough Road end of Badajos Barracks to the entry to Talavera
Barrack Square, and here at the rear of Badajos stands the hut, marked
over the door by the Star of David, which serves as the military
synagogue for soldiers of the Jewish faith.

On the north of the barrack road, near to Hospital Hill, stands one
of the Camp cinemas; adjoining is Wellesley Hall and All Saints
Church Room and Institute. Here also is a chapel, open to all for
private prayer and meditation and where communion services are
held. It is but a small room, with seating accommodation for about
twenty. There is an altar, with communion rails, and the room is lit
by a stained glass window which bears the unusual inscription—
unusual for no specific regiment is mentioned—"In memory of
Lancers who fell in the Boer War 1899-1902." Adjoining the Institute
are the offices of the Senior Chaplain of Wellington Lines.

To the east of Talavera Barracks lie Waterloo Barracks, two
extensive blocks known as Waterloo Barracks East and West respectively. These barracks were among the first permanent quarters to be
built and date from 1855. The West Barracks were until 1939 always
occupied by a Brigade (later Regiment) of Royal Horse Artillery,
whilst the East Barracks on the opposite side of Gun Hill Road were
occupied by a Brigade (later Regiment) of Field Artillery. Here the
barrack blocks are of similar construction to the old Cavalry Barracks,
with barrack rooms above the stables, now converted into garages
and stores.

This line of barracks, which stretches just over three-quarters of a
mile in length from the Farnborough Road to Ordnance Road, is
intersected by three roads leading up from Wellington Avenue into
South Camp; they all slope upwards to the line of the high
ground which separates the rest of "The Camp" from Wellington
Lines.

The first of these roads is Hospital Hill and leads up between
Salamanca and Talavera Barracks from the point where Barrack Road
meets Wellington Avenue. It was here that for many years stood a
stone drinking fountain, one of the features of this part of "The
Camp"; it stood nearly twelve feet in height, with the water gushing
from the mouths of two fish set on either side. The fountain was

severely damaged in a traffic accident in the early twenties and, being beyond repair, was demolished and removed.

On the left of the road is the oldest building in Aldershot "Camp." It is now used as the District Pay Office, formerly the Command Pay Office. It has been used as such since the seventies.

The building, which existed when "The Camp" lands were purchased, was taken over by the Military Authorities in 1855 and converted into a hospital, which, together with a row of huts on the opposite side of Hospital Hill, was known for many years as the 2nd Station Hospital. This is the answer to the naming of Hospital Hill, which no longer contains or leads to a hospital—a fact not realized by newcomers to Aldershot today. It is Gun Hill which leads to the Cambridge Hospital.

The District Pay Office, before being included in "The Camp" and taken over by the Army, was the old Union Workhouse, and when taken over in 1855 it was a Union School for pauper children. The school was moved to Crondall when the building was taken over by the Military Authorities. It has been recorded that the building probably dates back to 1680. The building has a distinctive character and some of the old walls still exist; although it has undergone many changes, additions and alterations, it still to a great extent remains much as it was. When a fire occurred in the building in February, 1907, the authorities planned to rebuild on more modern lines better suited for use as a military office, but it was then realized that the building had been originally acquired by the War Department under a deed containing reservations, and in the light of these clauses the building had to be reconstructed and restored to its original form.

Few realize that this somewhat unpretentious military office tucked away on the side of Hospital Hill, behind huts and the outbuildings of Salamanca Barracks, is, in fact, the oldest building in "The Camp" and one of the oldest in Aldershot.

*   *   *   *   *

At the junction of Hospital Hill, Knollys Road* and Queen's Avenue, the 1914-1918 War Memorial to the 2nd Division stands on a high grass bank, with a background of larches and birches, overlooking the road. The memorial was designed by Captain J. B. Scott, M.C., an officer of the Division. It consists of a pillar, surmounted by a Gothic cross, and is inscribed, "Grant them, O Lord, eternal rest" and "I have fought a good fight; I have finished my course; I have kept the Faith." It also bears the titles of the units

---

* Knollys Road takes its name from the first General Commanding "the Camp at Aldershot"—General Sir William T. Knollys, correctly pronounced "Noles," but referred to, in Aldershot, for many years as "Nollies."

which formed the Division during the 1914-1918 war. The divisional sign is carved on the rear panel of the base of the Portland stone Gothic cross, and in addition the Memorial stands on a base which depicts the sign, which was a black oval with a large central eight-pointed red star, flanked by a white eight-pointed star on either side. The two white stars stood for the Second Division, and the red star for the 1st Corps—"The second Division of the First Corps." The base of the Memorial is rarely seen except by those who go to the top of the mound to see the oval design in flint, the smaller stars in white stone, and the central red star, upon which the Memorial Cross stands, in red bricks.

The Memorial was unveiled on 1st December, 1923, by General Lord Horne, G.C.B., K.C.M.G., in the presence of a representative company gathered to pay tribute to the memory of those who fell serving with the 2nd Division in the Great War.

Between Talavera Barracks and Waterloo Barracks West runs Middle Hill. At the entrance to the Hill outside the guardroom of Waterloo Barracks West stands a brass gun, the wooden wheels of which are now rotting inside the iron tyres. The piece bears the Royal monogram "VR" and the date 1859. It also bears a monogram "LH" in a garter on which is the motto "Une je serviray," and the name F.M. Eardley-Wilmot.

On the left of the hill stands Queen Mary's Home for Children, which is managed by a ladies' committee of which the wife of the G.O.C. Aldershot District is President. The home is provided for the purpose of caring for soldiers' children whose mothers, through sickness or other reasons, are temporarily unable to look after them. Children of officers, W.Os., N.C.Os. and men serving in the Aldershot District are admitted ; boys up to the age of eight years, girls up to the age of eleven years and, in cases of emergency, infants under nine months are admitted. Above the Children's Home are the offices and stores of the D.C.R.E., South Aldershot.

On the opposite side of the road is a small grove in which swings and see-saws have been erected to form a playground for the children from the married quarters.

Between Waterloo Barracks West and East runs Gun Hill, which took its name from the old saluting gun which stood there, alongside the "Sebastopol Bell," from the late fifties until the early seventies, when it was removed to a site on Thorn Hill.*

At the foot of Gun Hill stands the modern N.A.A.F.I. Club, which occupies the site of the old guard-room of the R.H.A. Barracks,

* See p. 54.

and was built in 1947-8. The club was opened by H.R.H. The Duke
of Gloucester on 28th October, 1948.

The N.A.A.F.I. Club is an imposing building, erected at a total
cost of £70,000, which can, from its well-chosen site, be seen to
advantage from every approach. It has been constructed on modern
lines with extensive use of glass to secure the maximum of natural
lighting. One of its features is its central tower, on which is a large
clock, the face of which is illuminated after dark. The tri-coloured
N.A.A.F.I. flag flies from the staff on the lawn outside the building.

One enters the club through a spacious and imposing lounge hall,
and one is immediately struck with the interior decorations in pastel
shades, which are worthy of a first-class London hotel; and the club
is luxuriously equipped with soft carpets and comfortable chairs and
sofas.

The many amenities of the club include a large ball-room with a
sprung floor, which accommodates 400 dancers, or can also be used
as a concert hall; a tavern and bar which would be in keeping with
the surroundings of a luxury hotel at some popular resort; games
and billiard rooms; reading and writing and quiet rooms; a hair
dressing saloon, shower baths, an information bureau, and a sales
kiosk. A feature of the ball-room and annexe is that they can be
completely closed off from the rest of the club on the occasion of
special dances.

There are thick pile carpets on the floors of the lounge and tea
rooms on the first floor, and not only is a grand piano provided but
also one of the latest television sets.

This Aldershot club, in which the N.A.A.F.I. have spared nothing
in order to provide the young soldiers with every comfort and
amenity, was the fifth such club to be opened in this country. It can
accommodate nearly two thousand at any one time. Such clubs are
an innovation in the life of the soldier, for it was from the lessons
learned during the late war, and the successes of the temporary clubs
and welfare centres established at home and overseas, that the idea
materialized for the modern N.A.A.F.I. clubs of today as exemplified
by the Aldershot club.

It was in the N.A.A.F.I. Club on 4th April, 1949, that military
history was made, when thirty-seven auxiliaries of the A.T.S. were
attested as members of the then newly formed W.R.A.C., the attesta-
tion being performed by the G.O.C., Major-General W. A. Dimoline,
C.B., C.B.E., D.S.O., M.C., in the presence of Alderman G. Roberts,
J.P., Mayor of Aldershot. This was the first time in the history
of the British Army that there had been a regular corps of
women.

Major-General Dimoline, in welcoming and thanking the Mayor for his attendance, said it was very significant that the Mayor of Aldershot should be present, as the town was the traditional home of the British Army, and that his presence typified the close bond between "The Camp" and the town.

General Dimoline stressed the solemnity of the occasion as the first ceremony of its kind in the district. To the girls he said : "You are the first regular members of the W.R.A.C. to be attested here. The oath you have just taken has great historical significance. It is exactly the same oath that has been sworn since 1871, and has been taken by British soldiers in every part of the world." He pointed out that the W.R.A.C. would, as well as inheriting the traditions of the Army, be able to build their own traditions, which as a new corps were in their own hands.

Until the building in 1948 of the N.A.A.F.I. Club, which necessitated the demolition of the guard-room of Waterloo Barracks (West) off Gun Hill, two brass guns, which dated from about 1750, stood at the entrance to the barracks before this guard-room. The guns were placed there in 1925. They came from the armouries of the Tower of London and were used by the 1st Brigade R.H.A., then quartered in Waterloo Barracks, in the Aldershot Tattoo of 1925. At the conclusion of the Tattoo application was made by the R.H.A. for the retention of these guns so that they would be available for use in future Tattoos. The Curator of the Tower Armouries, Major Charles ffoulkes, visited the brigade to formally hand them over and at the same time lend to the R.H.A. some armour and old weapons which were used to decorate the walls in the Institute in Waterloo Barracks East, then occupied by a Field Brigade.* During the late war the two brass guns were removed to the Field Stores, and they have recently been claimed by "G" Battery (Mercers Troop), R.H.A., as being guns used by that unit at Waterloo.

Near the top of Gun Hill stands the "Percy Illingworth" Institute, erected by "the Baptist Union of Great Britain and Ireland," now the Home for all soldiers of the United Board, and equipped with a large coffee-bar, billiard room, and reading and writing rooms. One of the features of the Institute is the mural paintings in the spacious hall on the first floor which is used for worship and cultural and recreational activities, the murals representing two years' work by Tom Luzny, a Canadian soldier from Winnipeg, one-time cartoonist on the staff of the Canadian Army newspaper, *The Maple Leaf*. These murals were unveiled in June, 1948, by Major-General J. A. Baillon, C.B., C.B.E., M.C., the then G.O.C. Aldershot District, before a company of

* *Vide The Gunner Magazine*, July, 1949.

2G

distinguished visitors, including the Assistant High Commissioner for Canada and the President of the Baptist Union.

The ten panels have a religious significance as well as decorative value ; they are intended to express the truth that meaning is to be found in man's existence on this earth only when the whole of life—secular as well as sacred—is offered to God. The main panel at the back of the stage depicts Our Lord blessing the bread and the fish. Thus the Son of Man is offering up what is both a gift of God and the outcome of man's toil. Here, too, the Son of God reveals His care for the ordinary people and their everyday common needs. The outstretched hands to bless are the hands outstretched to save mankind, for Christ's attitude foreshadows the Crucifixion. Symbolically, the tree against which He stands, the branches of which sweep out encircling as it were all people, means Life through the Cross.

The eight side panels portray men engaged in their ordinary and essential work—fishing, building, harvesting, timber-cutting, quarrying, making pottery and transporting produce. Some know only weariness, frustration and disappointment in their toil, others achievement and satisfaction, but never complete satisfaction, and this is the point of the last seven panelled murals depicting a minister, with the word of God in his hands, standing not only amid the fruits of man's labour but also against the background of his sin—symbolized by the apple tree. By hearing and obeying God's word the whole of man's temporal existence would be enriched and his "immortal longings" would be satisfied in the certainty of the City of God where there shall be no more sin, sorrow and death.

At the top of Gun Hill on the grass bank to the left of the road stands the Royal Army Medical Corps War Memorial to those members of the Corps who were killed or died on service during the South African War. The memorial was unveiled by H.M. King Edward VII on Empire Day, 24th May, 1905, and this is commemorated by a small plaque lying before the steps of the memorial. The centre of the memorial is a column bearing the R.A.M.C. badge and the inscription :

R.A.M.C.

TO THOSE WHO GAVE THEIR LIVES FOR THEIR COUNTRY

Before the column is a group of three figures in bronze depicting a wounded soldier held in the arms of an R.A.M.C. orderly, whilst his leg is bandaged by a Medical Officer. The figures stand on a plinth bearing the inscription "South Africa." The memorial is semicircular, with fourteen bronze panels bearing the names of one Colonel and two Surgeon Lieutenant-Colonels of the Militia Medical

Staff Corps, six Majors, five Captains, five Lieutenants, two Quarter-masters, two Sergeant-Majors, nine Staff Sergeants, nine Sergeants, five Lance-Sergeants, eighteen Corporals, five Lance-Corporals and two hundred and forty-three Privates. Three steps lead up to the memorial, upon which is the inscription, "Erected by the Officers, Warrant Officers, Non-Commissioned Officers and Men of the Royal Army Medical Corps in memory of their Comrades of the Corps."

Beyond Waterloo Barracks lies Ordnance Road, on the right of which, abutting on High Street on the south, are Parsons Barracks, occupied by the Royal Army Ordnance Corps, which adjoin the "Field Stores," the name which has persisted for many years to describe the large Ordnance Depot. The depot, which covers a considerable area, lies to the south of Peaked Hill on the site where it was first established nearly a hundred years ago. Here, too, are the extensive Command Workshops (13 Command Workshops, R.E.M.E.), employing a large number of military and civilian technicians and skilled workers engaged in the maintenance of technical equipment. Ordnance Road swings away to the right, where it joins Louise Margaret Road and runs along the southern fence of the Ordnance Depot and the Workshops, continuing south of the military cemetery. The railway runs into the Depot, to the Government Siding, which branches off from the main line just over half a mile from the Redan Hill tunnel. On both sides of the line to the south of Round Hill are acres of store sheds and workshops.

Between Peaked Hill and Round Hill, to the south of Thorn Hill, lies the Aldershot Military Cemetery, and adjoining the cemetery boundary fence at the top of Peaked Hill is the site of an old redoubt, its lines of earthworks amid the sand, gorse, broom and bushes being clearly visible. The tactical value of this site was again exploited during the late war, for there today stand two brick and concrete "pill bores" which were built as local defence posts in 1940.

The Military Cemetery, which was opened in 1865, is extensive and it lies on the north and east slopes of Thorn Hill and Peaked Hill. The graves are set amid well-kept grounds, traversed by gravel paths. The whole cemetery is well wooded with oaks, pines, firs and chestnut trees, with laurel hedges, and with bracken and heather bordering the close-cut turf. Before the cemetery was opened in 1865 it was typical of the Aldershot countryside, as it was in the days before "The Camp" was built, and it has retained its character. Here amid surroundings so familiar during their soldiering days are the graves of men of all ranks who have died in Aldershot, many of them in the military hospitals from wounds or disease contracted on active service.

One enters the cemetery from Thorn Hill Road, near where the old time-gun stood. Here is the Cemetery Chapel which was built in 1879 to replace the old wooden chapel erected, when the cemetery was opened, lower down the slopes. This wooden building was burnt down, and the present chapel was built on additional ground, towards the summit of Peaked Hill, taken over at the time. A fine view of the whole district is obtained from this point, the view stretching for miles over the town and camp. It was on this high ground that a redoubt was constructed when "The Camp" was built, and this later became a signal station for semaphore and helio, the signallers practising the sending of messages to other detachments located on Caesar's Camp, Hungry Hill, Crooksbury Hill, and Hindhead.

The cemetery grounds—covering some fifteen acres—are still to a great extent in their natural state, lending a peaceful, calm atmosphere to the surroundings. The graves are either scattered on the hillside under trees or in quiet corners, or are grouped in rows, which in the case of many of the military graves lends a regimental appearance, as though the still graves were on parade in military formation. This is most noticeable with the standardized low headstones provided by the Imperial War Graves Commission, bearing in each case the regimental or corps badge of the deceased, the name, rank, regiment and date of death, and a plain cross. These gravestones were introduced during the 1914-1918 war, and so those of earlier years follow the styles of the age, the military tombstones, which bear the names of men of all ranks of nearly every unit of the Army, being mainly of Gothic cross design. Many of the stones date back to the late sixties and seventies, the regimental titles of the inscriptions being the old titles in use prior to the Cardwell Reforms, such as 5th Fusiliers, 22nd Regiment, and 92nd Highlanders.

The cemetery is also open for the interment of wives and families of all ranks, and there are a number of family graves in consequence, and also for some civilians who have spent their lives with the Army. Near the north boundary of the cemetery below a wooded slope two graves stand alone on a little mound. On one, below a plain cross, is the inscription :

TO the memory of LOUISA, widow of Capt. Daniell
H.E.I.C.S.
founder of the Aldershot Soldiers' Mission Hall
died at Malvern September 1871. Age 62 years.
Erected by Officers of the Army to the best interest of
which she devoted many years of her life.

This is also the grave of her daughter, who "died at the Mission Hall and Soldiers' Home June 1894."

The adjoining grave is that of Kate Hanson, for twenty-six years a worker and Honorary Lady Superintendent of Miss Daniell's Soldiers' Home, who died in 1913.

Near by, within a low hedge, is a simple grave surmounted by a plain stone cross which bears the simple inscription :

> EVELYN WOOD V.C.
> FIELD MARSHAL
> BORN 9 FEB. 1839
> DIED 2 DEC. 1919

This is also the grave of his wife and brother, who was Colonel of the Northumberland Fusiliers.

To the right are the graves of fifteen Canadian soldiers who died in Aldershot during the 1914-1918 war, each with a standard headstone bearing the maple leaf, together with the grave of one Newfoundland gunner who died in 1941 ; whilst not far distant is another grave, on the stone of which is the Springbok, where a private of the 2nd Regiment of South African Infantry lies buried. Below this group of graves are those of twenty-one Polish soldiers and members of the Polish Resettlement Corps who have died in the district since the war, whilst farther along are three graves of Belgian soldiers who died in Aldershot in 1914. The stones on these graves bear inscriptions in French, reproductions of the Belgian Order of Leopold, and a circular coloured plaque in the Belgian national colours—red, yellow and black.

This portion of the cemetery lies in a little valley, the ground then rising steeply to a point overlooking the Government Siding and away to the Fox Hills and the Ash Ranges, where stands a simple stone cross on which is a bronze unsheathed sword conforming to the arms of the cross. Around the base above the narrow steps of the plinth is the inscription, "Their Name liveth for Evermore." This memorial—the Cross of Sacrifice—is identical with that which is used in all the cemeteries established and cared for by the Imperial War Graves Commission. The hillside slopes sharply downwards from this memorial on ground, enclosed by a low hedge, containing the graves of men of all ranks and regiments who died on service in the Great War.

Near to this war memorial are a group of private graves, one surmounted by an imposing figure of Christ erected over the tombstone which bears an inscription recalling the pioneering days of aviation in Aldershot :

> In Loving Memory of
> SAMUEL FRANKLIN CODY
> who was killed while flying
> over Laffan's Plain 7 August 1913.

At the foot of the grave is an additional memorial to Second Lieutenant Samuel Franklin Leslie Cody, R.F.C., his youngest son, "who fell in action fighting four enemy machines" on 23rd January, 1917.

There is also a tall column in red stone in memory of Lieutenant Roy Maurice Gzowski, of the Queen's Own Rifles of Canada, "who died whilst doing duty in the Mother Country" in Aldershot in September, 1910. On the base of the memorial is the badge of his regiment and the inscription :

> ERECTED BY THE OFFICERS OF THE ALDERSHOT
> COMMAND IN TOKEN OF THE FELLOWSHIP WHICH
> BINDS ENGLAND TO CANADA AND ALL SOLDIERS
> OF THE EMPIRE TO ONE ANOTHER.

Beyond this grave is that of Captain de la Poer Beresford, R.E., who was killed in 1910 near the corner of Scarletts Road.*

The cemetery runs down the sloping hillside to a point below the old magazine where a number of the earlier graves, dating from the sixties, lies below the pines and cedars. At the foot of the hill where the cemetery is bounded by Ordnance Road lie the graves of one German officer and fifteen soldiers who died whilst prisoners of war during the 1914-1918 war. Their graves are marked by granite plaques in place of the normal headstone. Behind, on a stretch of grass, are the graves of sixty-two Germans who died in Aldershot as prisoners of war in 1944-1946. Here one may read the names of two officers and a doctor of the German Army, of eight members of the Luftwaffe and four German sailors. All the graves are marked by plain white-painted wooden crosses bearing the cipher of the Imperial War Graves Commission, the initial letters entwined, and surmounted by the Imperial Crown, the rank, name and arm of the service of the deceased, and date of death.

In another part of the cemetery is another group of graves of German and Italian prisoners of war. These are the graves of the Roman Catholics, a group of forty-nine wooden crosses marking the last resting-place of twenty-four Italian soldiers and one Italian sailor, sixteen German soldiers, three sailors and five airmen. Among the German graves, marked by the same plain wooden cross as the others, is the grave of General Feldmarschall E. B. W. Busch, of the German General Staff, who died at Amersham, Bucks, on 17th July, 1945. He lies between the graves of two German Lance-Corporals, Gefreiter† K. Pawlowski, of the German Army, and Gefreiter K. H. Kirch, of the German Air Force. The funeral of Feldmarschall Busch was

---

* See pp. 344 and 362.
† Lance-Corporal.

attended by a number of senior German officers, then prisoners of war ; among them was Feldmarschall Rundstedt.

Another group of graves, marked with the official headstones bearing the regimental or corps badges, are those of eighty-eight British soldiers who died during the late war. Among the graves is one to a private of the A.T.S., who died in 1946, which also has an additional memorial inscribed :

From the Officers and Auxiliaries of "G" Company
A.T.S. at Keogh Barracks, Mytchett.

In this group there are also a few wooden crosses, one marked in memory of "F. J. Side served as Pte. J. Monk—National Defence Corps 9.10.39," and others to soldiers of allied armies, two of the Royal Netherlands Army, one of the Polish Army, and one Russian, Private W. Lukjanow, who died in May, 1945.

The Aldershot Military Cemetery is unlike any other in this country, for not only is it an unusual site set on hills and small valleys in natural surroundings, but here, at rest, lie fighting men of nine nations, soldiers who have served and died in Aldershot over the past eighty-four years.

*　　*　　*　　*　　*

The line of demarcation between Wellington Lines and the remainder of South Camp runs from the Farnborough Road along Knollys Road. To the north of the road, facing the Farnborough Road, set back amid beds of rhododendrons and in a grove of firs, beech, larch and chestnuts,* stands the Prince Consort's Library, used today by officers and cadets. The library was built in 1859 and opened in the following year ; it was constructed to the design of Captain F. Fowke, R.E.,† the architect of the Albert Hall in London, and was the gift of Albert, the Prince Consort. Carved in stone on the wall above the main entrance is the Prince's coat of arms, with the motto "Treu und Fest" on a scroll below.

---

* Many of these trees and bushes undoubtedly date from the laying out of the grounds following the building of the Library. In the Royal Archives at Windsor Castle is the original estimate prepared by John Standish of Bagshot, dated 13th April, 1860, submitted to, and approved by, the Prince Consort for the "Plants and Planting out of the ground around the library." The total cost amounted to £38 9s. od. The estimate included full details : 40 rhododendrons for an oval bed, £2 10s. od. ; 150 juniper plants for two kidney-shaped beds, £3 15s. od. ; 80 plants, Arbor-vitæ, £3 os. od. ; and a further 300 rhododendrons, 8 magnolias and 22 other trees (Royal Archives, Windsor).

† Captain Francis Fowke was commissioned in the Royal Engineers in 1842. He was Secretary of the British Commission at the Paris Exhibition and later designed the Edinburgh Museum of Science and Art and the Dublin National Gallery. He died in 1865. (Dictionary of National Biography.)

The building is composed of the main library hall surrounded by a balcony. The librarian's office is near the entrance, and next door is a quiet reading room; above is another reading room containing valuable military records and reference books. The walls of the library above the bookcases are decorated with trophies of arms and armour, and from the balcony of the library hang a number of masonic banners, for the library is the venue of the periodical meetings of several military masonic lodges.

At the far end of the library hangs a fine life-sized oil painting of Albert, the Prince Consort, painted in 1868 by Mayall,* and presented to the library in January, 1920, by Captain J. Reeves, of the 3rd Bn. The London Regiment (Royal Fusiliers). There is also a head-and-shoulders painting of the Duke of Cambridge, whilst there is a fine collection of Ackermann military prints.† Among the other items of interest in the library is a stone shot dating from the fifteenth century, which was discovered in 1863 at Eelmore Common, three feet below the surface. It is mounted on a stand made from bog wood found on the same moor.‡

In the reading-room are a number of interesting prints and water-colour reproductions of views of "The Camp" in its early days, taken from the originals which hang in the royal collection at Windsor Castle. Adjoining the library is a large lecture hall, which is used from time to time for military studies and indoor exercises.

Behind the library, facing the Officers' Mess of Barrosa Barracks, is one of the few tumuli in the Aldershot area. This tumulus is sur-rounded by a circle of trees, and the top has been flattened so that it can be used as a bandstand. Farther along Knollys Road one over-looks Red Hill, and a fine vista of Aldershot Town is seen. Here on the south of the road stands the Catholic Soldiers' Club and Knollys Hall and a school for officers' children. The institute was built in 1907 and was designed by W. Bevan, F.R.I.B.A., former Chief

---

* There is no trace of the artist Mayall in either Bryant's "Dictionary of Painters and Engravers" or in "Thieme-Becker Kunstler Lexikon" (Allgemeines Lexikon de Bildenden Kunster), but there are references to Mayall, an American photographer, in Queen Victoria's Journal of 1855. So it may be assumed that the photographer turned painter to execute this portrait in oils of the Prince Consort after his death, possibly from one of his own photographs.

† Among the original purchases between 1857 and 1861 made for the Library by the Prince Consort (Royal Archives, Windsor).

‡ Reference is made to this shot in a letter in the Royal Archives at Windsor from Colonel Simmons, dated 31st December, 1864, to a Major Elphinstone, in which he stated that the shot was in his possession, and suggesting that he could think of no better place to house it than the Prince Consort's Library. He refers to other "curiosities" dug up on Cove Common at the same time as the shot was discovered, but adds that most of them (unfortunately not described) were taken away by the workmen.

Government Architect in the Transvaal. The club, with its white walls and green-painted doors and windows, has the distinct style of "colonial" architecture. Inside the club is a large "coffee bar" and recreation room, with facilities for table tennis and billiards, whilst Knollys Hall is available for dances and other social events.

At the point where Knollys Road joins Hospital Hill and Queen's Avenue, Pennefathers Road* runs off to the left to the Farnborough Road. At the corner stands the N.A.A.F.I. officers' shop, a well-equipped general and provision store, and on the opposite side of the road is the officers' mess block of Corunna Barracks, now in use as the Airborne Forces Museum. A little farther along are the pre-war Headquarters of the 1st Division.

On the opposite side of Queen's Avenue lies Hospital Road, which until 1949 was a continuation of Knollys Road and runs along the high ground above Middle Hill and Gun Hill, at the junction of which stands one of the Military Fire Stations; and on the right is the large and imposing Cambridge Hospital, built in 1873, with its central tower which dominates the surrounding buildings and is a landmark for many miles.

The tower is 109 feet in height, surmounted by a clock tower, the face of the clock being eight feet in diameter. Within the clock turret is the "Sebastopol Bell," which was moved from its site at the top of Gun Hill to its present position when the hospital was built. This bell, together with two smaller bells, formed a chime which used to strike at the hours and the quarters. The two smaller bells bear the inscription "Cast by Gillett, Bland and Co. Clockmakers to her Majesty. Croydon 1878 London."

The hospital wards, high and well windowed, flank the central structure and are connected by covered corridors. The Leishman Laboratory, where much valuable research work in combating tropical diseases has been carried out, was opened by Lady Leishman in 1932 in memory of the work of her husband, Lieut.-General Sir William Leishman. At the rear of the hospital, terraced gardens have been cut in the slope of the hill which drops down to a recreation ground. Here convalescent patients can rest and walk in the shade of the trees which grow on the grassy slopes. In the south-east corner of the grounds of Cambridge House, by the Cambridge Hospital, is an oak tree reputed to have been planted by Queen Victoria on the occasion of one of her early visits to Aldershot to review troops on their return from the Crimea. Alongside the oak is a weeping willow, also said to have been planted by the Queen in memory of the Prince Consort.

To the east of the Cambridge Hospital stands the Louise Margaret

* See p. 362.

Hospital, named after H.R.H. The Duchess of Connaught and Strathearn, who laid the foundation stone on 1st March, 1897, when H.R.H. The Duke of Connaught was commanding the Aldershot District. This is the hospital for soldiers' wives and children. In 1926 an extension was added, and this is commemorated by a plaque on the wall bearing the inscription :

This Extension to Louise Margaret Hospital
was erected for wives and children of officers
by voluntary effort and was personally named
The Queen Mary's Wing by Her Majesty, a generous
subscriber, on the 21st May, 1926.

Opposite the Louise Margaret Hospital stands the wooden Roman Catholic Church of St. Michael and St. Sebastian, which has changed but little since it was first erected in the late fifties. It is a lofty building, the roof supported by wooden pillars. The organ is situated in a small gallery erected above the main door. The walls of the church are decorated by painted crosses and a series of modernistic plaques depicting in bas-relief scenes leading to the Crucifixion. Near the high altar affixed to the wall is a brass shield bearing the inscription :

To the honor of God and the Glory of Mary
Immaculate this statue was given by the
Catholics of the 1st Batt. South Wales Borderers
in memory of their Comrades of the 24th Regt.
who fell gloriously at Isandhlwana 22nd January
1879. On their souls sweet Jesus have mercy.
Mary, Mother of God, pray for them.
Xmas 1892.

There are also brass plaques erected to the memory of Private Thomas Killacky of the 13th Hussars, who died in Mesopotamia, 28th July, 1916 ; and to Anne Russel Fergusson, a benefactress of the church, who died on 27th November, 1905. There are also two brass plaques bearing the badge of the R.A.S.C. and the following inscription :

The Stations of the Cross in this Church of
St. Michael and St. Sebastian have been
erected by the Catholic Officers of the Royal
Army Service Corps to the Glory of God and in
commemoration of all those officers and men of
the Corps who laid down their lives in the War
of 1939-1945.
Requiescant in Pace.

At the rear of the church is a memorial to members of the Catholic Soldiers' Association killed in action.

To the north of Knollys and Hospital Roads lie Stanhope Lines, named after Mr. J. Stanhope, who was Secretary of State for War, 1887-1892, during the period of the building of these barracks to replace the old wooden hutted camp. Here are Albuhera, Barrosa, Corunna, Maida* and McGrigor Barracks, and the married quarters of Scott-Moncrieff and Jerome Squares. This area is separated from the northern portion of Stanhope Lines by a line of parade and recreation grounds ending at Mandora Barracks, which form the eastern end of these lines.

Between Thornhill Road and Mandora Road lie Mandora Barracks and Buller Barracks, headquarters of the Royal Army Service Corps.

Facing Mandora Barracks is a red brick building with a tower above the entrance; this is the St. Andrew's Soldiers' Home and Club, one of the features of which are the badges of all the Scottish regiments in full colours in stained glass set into the leaded windows. Adjoining the club is the St. Andrew's Hall, with fine panelled walls, timbered roof, and stage. The walls are decorated with panels of clan tartans and framed reproductions of the colours of Scottish regiments. On the wall is a memorial plaque: "In grateful memory of Alexander Hugh Bruce, Lord Balfour of Burleigh, P.C., K.T., G.C.M.G., G.C.V.O., to whose efforts and care the erection and maintenance of the club is largely due."

At the junction of Mandora Road and Buller Road is the Headquarter Office of the R.A.S.C. Training Centre, on the side wall of which is a small enclosure of Portland stone, with iron gates bearing the scrolled letters "R.A.S.C." Against the wall is the Royal Army Service Corps War Memorial, which was dedicated and unveiled by Lieutenant-General Sir Frederick Clayton, K.C.B., K.C.M.G., on 29th April, 1923. At the top of the memorial is the Corps badge in colours, and below is the inscription:

IN MEMORY OF 280 OFFICERS AND 8187
WOS, N.C.OS AND MEN OF THE ROYAL
ARMY SERVICE CORPS WHO LAID DOWN
THEIR LIVES FOR THEIR COUNTRY DURING
THE GREAT WAR 1914-18.

At the base is a similar inscription in memory of the 286 officers and 8,871 other ranks who were killed in action or died in service during

---

* At the rear of the guard room of Maida Barracks is an oak brought from Jerusalem and planted by General Gordon. General Gordon also brought back two cedar trees from the Lebanon, one of which was planted in the grounds of what is now the R.A.M.C. Officers' Mess.

the 1939-1945 war. The similarity of the total casualty figures of the wars is most noticeable.

On the centre of the memorial is another inscription commemorating the fact that, in addition to this tangible memorial, "a memorial fund has been raised and is being devoted to helping in the educational expenses of sons and daughters of all ranks of the Royal Army Service Corps and assisting members of the Corps suffering from illness and the effects of wounds."

The present-day R.A.S.C. establishment is a mixture of old and new. As would be expected, there are large garages, machinery sheds and instructional rooms for the care and maintenance of the Mechanical Transport of the Corps, but in addition there is the large Riding School, the last in Aldershot to be in use, of the Animal Transport Wing. The R.A.S.C. Training Centre and the Royal Military Police Training Establishment are the only military establishments in Aldershot to have their horses to this day. A visit brings back to many an old soldier nostalgic memories of days not so long ago. Here are the lines of stables, the jumps, the familiar smells of the forage, the stables and the tan of the riding school. The brass-buttoned service dress of the men, with pantaloons, puttees and spurs, takes one back to the Aldershot of the days between the wars. There is the clip-clop as the horses are led from the stables to water; there are the N.C.Os., whips under their arms as of old, and the line of the stables, and the old familiar rattle of the halters; the clack of horses moving in the loose-boxes—all the sights and sounds of a past era are kept alive in the Animal Transport Wing of the R.A.S.C. today.

In contrast, on the next square are rows of three-ton lorries, tended by the greasy, blackened hands of the young soldiers in denims as they bury themselves under the bonnets or lie beneath their vehicles, engaged on the maintenance task of the day. Not for nothing is the Corps motto "Nil Sine Labore."

*   *   *   *   *

Beyond the buildings of the R.A.S.C. establishment stands the Camp's Power Station, with its tall chimney-stack, which dominates this area. On the west side of the road the ground rises steeply up the slopes of Thorn Hill. Part of this hillside is still in its natural state, and the gorse bushes run down to the rear of the line of married quarters in Thorn Hill Terrace. Off Thorn Hill Road are the buildings of the former Army Vocational Training School, where in pre-war days regular soldiers in their last six months' service received instruction in their chosen trade to fit them for civilian life. On the slopes of Thorn Hill are also the R.A.V.C. School and Laboratory.

The R.A.V.C. School celebrated its jubilee in June, 1930, the occasion being marked by the unveiling of a commemorative tablet on the north wall of the building by Major-General W. S. Anthony, C.B., C.M.G., then Director-General of Army Veterinary Services, recording the fiftieth anniversary of the school, which had been opened on 1st June, 1880. In those fifty years over five thousand officers and men of combatant units received instruction there in animal management both in health and disease. The school had during the same period developed the research wing.

* * * * *

Stanhope Lines continue northwards between Steeles Road, named after General Sir Thomas Steele, K.C.B., who commanded in Aldershot from 1875 to 1880, and the Basingstoke Canal. Stanhope Lines are divided by the famous Queen's Avenue, which runs from the top of Hospital Hill straight through "The Camp" for over a mile and a half until it joins Lynchford Road, Farnborough, at the extreme end of North Camp. Queen's Avenue is a fine thoroughfare, lined on both sides by an avenue of trees. It is the main artery of "The Camp" and the main road between South Farnborough and Aldershot Town.

At the Aldershot end of the Avenue opposite Corunna Barracks stands the Smith-Dorrien Methodist Soldiers' Home, a tall red-brick building with entrances below two towers. In the centre of the building is a large stained glass window bearing the regimental crests of the R.A., R.E., R.A.M.C., A.S.C., and the Duke of Cornwall's Light Infantry. This home, equipped with recreation rooms, coffee bar and other amenities, takes its name from Lieutenant-General Sir Horace Smith-Dorrien, K.C.B., D.S.O., G.O.C.-in-C. when he laid the foundation stone on 4th March, 1908. Adjoining this institution is the Command Central Gymnasium, familiarly known as the "Maida Gym," a spacious building, the scene of many leading military and civil social functions. On the opposite side of the Avenue, at the junction with Scarletts Road, is one of the Garrison Theatres, the Stanhope Theatre, which stands near the site of the original Camp Theatre built in 1859.

At the junction of Queen's Avenue and Steeles Road stand the Headquarters buildings, set back from the road behind lawns which face the Avenue, and on which stands a flagstaff from which flies the Union Jack and the pennant of Aldershot District. Built in 1894-5 of red brick, now to a great extent covered by creeper, the main entrance of the building is in Steeles Road, flanked by two old muzzle-loading cannons, bearing the dates 1806 and 1811, and the name of the makers —I. and J. King. The Headquarters building has an imposing entrance under a porch supported by four stone columns. At the doorway is the foundation stone of the building, laid on 28th March, 1894, by H.R.H. The Duke of Connaught, then commanding the Aldershot District, whilst above the porch, which forms a small balcony, are the Royal Arms above the motto "Dieu et Mon Droit," and above two flanking windows the letters "V" and "R" surmounted by crowns. In the entrance hall is an oak board bearing the names of the forty General Officers who have commanded in Aldershot since 1854, and set in the tiles is the monogram "VR" and the date 1895. The main stairway is flanked by two shells, two small brass saluting cannons bearing the date "MDCCCI" and two piles of round shot, whilst the pillars either side are decorated by lances with red and white pennants, and two with green pennants bearing the District sign. The walls on either side of the stairway are hung with trophies of arms. Immediately above the main entrance is the office of the General Officer Commanding, around the walls of which are the photographs of every G.O.C. in Aldershot from General Sir William T. Knollys (1854-1859) to Major-General J. A. Baillon (1947-1949). The Headquarters Staff Offices lead off from the two main corridors which run along the ground and first floors of the building.

Adjoining the Headquarters offices is the Stanhope Lines Post Office, built in 1896, from which the military postal business of "The Camp" is conducted.

Opposite the Headquarters building, at the junction of Queen's Avenue and Steeles Road, stands a circular small red brick building with a green-painted domed roof. This is the observatory, which bears on the side a small metal plaque, in each corner of which is a small six-pointed star, and in the centre the inscription :

PRESENTED TO THE ALDERSHOT ARMY CORPS
BY PATRICK V. ALEXANDER ESQ. 1906.

The building contains a nine-inch refracting telescope, the gift of Mr. P. V. Alexander of Mytchett, who for many years had carried out astronomical research at his home and on the Chobham Ridges, and who, on leaving the district in April, 1906, presented the telescope and equipment to the "Aldershot Army Corps." The observatory was opened on 22nd December, 1906, by Lieutenant-General Sir John French, then G.O.C.-in-C.

The 1914-1918 War Memorial of the 8th Division, an imposing structure, surmounted by a bronze figure of a lion, stands at the north-east corner of the parade grounds opposite the Headquarters building. On three sides of the monument appear the names of the regiments which composed the Division, and on the front is the inscription : "To the glorious memory of all Officers, Warrant Officers, Non-commissioned Officers and Men of the 8th Division who fell in France and Belgium in the Great War, 1914-1918."

To the left of Queen's Avenue stand Gibraltar Barracks, the home of the Royal Engineers in Aldershot, composed of twelve barrack blocks with messes, institutes and administrative buildings. The officers' mess, set back among lawns and a belt of trees, stands at the Farnborough Road end of the barracks. Gibraltar Barracks are divided from what is known as the "R.E. Establishment" by Alisons Road, which is named after Lieutenant-General Sir Archibald Alison, Bt., G.C.B., who commanded in Aldershot, 1883-1888, and runs from the Farnborough Road to the foot of Thorn Hill Road. The R.E. Establishment occupies the whole of the area bounded by Alisons Road, Queen's Avenue, the Farnborough Road and the Canal. Here are the workshops of the Corps, the machinery shop, foundry, joiners', carpenters' and blacksmiths' shops, and the training establishments for the divers R.E. trades. Here, too, are the old stables, wagon sheds and riding school, and the Pontoon and Field Works Stores and the "Q" Stores. The R.E. guard-room stands in Alisons Road, and the R.E. Theatre, near which on the wall of one of the office buildings is a small metal plaque bearing the inscription :

BALLOON SQUARE
The School of Ballooning
which was then a branch of the
Royal Engineers
was founded here in
1892.

Beyond lie spacious recreation grounds and sports pavilions. At the east end of the R.E. Establishment is a large tree-lined parade ground where the R.E. flag flies from the staff opposite the west door of St. George's Garrison Church. Here on the verge of the parade ground of Gibraltar Barracks facing the church stands a stone obelisk —the memorial erected to the memory of Lieutenant Reginald Archibald Cammell, of the Air Battalion, Royal Engineers, who lost his life on 17th September, 1911, "while flying an aeroplane at Hendon." This memorial was erected by his brother officers "in recognition of his services to military aviation." At the rear of the obelisk is the Royal Engineer monogram surmounted by the crown, with the R.E. mottoes "Ubique" and "Quo fas et Gloria ducunt" on scrolls above and below.

On the opposite side of the Avenue stands St. George's Garrison Church—an imposing edifice of red brick with Portland stone facings and a dominating spire which is a landmark in "The Camp." The tower and spire rise above the west door which faces Queen's Avenue. Above the door, sculptured in relief, is the kneeling figure of St. George by the slain dragon, and below the inscription NON NOBIS DOMINE NON NOBIS SED NOMINI TVO DA GLORIAM. The foundation stone of the building, which was laid by Queen Victoria in June, 1892, is set into the east wall behind the altar and bears the inscription :

TO THE GLORY OF GOD AND IN HONOUR OF ST. GEORGE
THIS STONE WAS LAID ON THE XXVII DAY OF JUNE MDCCCXCII
BY HER MAJESTY QUEEN VICTORIA
EMPRESS OF INDIA.

Inside the porch of the west door, mounted in a small glass case above a commemorative plaque, are the actual trowel and mallet used by Queen Victoria at the foundation stone ceremony.

The church has an impressive interior, with its high nave, flanked by Gothic arches leading to the north and south aisles, and its wide chancel. There is a gallery above the west door, and the font stands immediately below. The church is rich in stained-glass windows ; there are twenty-six in all, the large east window, together with the central mosaic panel of the reredos, having been erected to the memory of all ranks of the Army Service Corps who fell during the South African War.

In the south aisle is a window erected in memory of Lieutenant-Colonel W. A. F. Williamson, of the Army Service Corps, who died in June, 1911 (the window being erected by his brother officers) ; and another to the memory of Lieutenants T. E. Martin-Leake and W. T. McC. Caulfield, of the Royal Engineers, who were drowned at sea on 28th May, 1907, in H.M. Balloon *Thrasher*, this memorial being erected by past and present officers of the Balloon School. A third window in this aisle was erected in October, 1911, in memory of three Lance-Corporals of the Military Mounted Police and four Lance-Corporals of the Military Foot Police who lost their lives in the South African War.

In the north aisle is a stained glass window erected to the memory of William Brian Watson, Chaplain of St. George's, who served in the Dongola and Nile Expeditions and the South African War and who died, as Vicar of Hornby, Yorks, in 1912 ; another, "erected by his comrades," is in memory of Colonel James Laird Irvine, C.B., late Royal Engineers, who served many years in Aldershot and died in August, 1911 ; whilst a third is in memory of another R.E. officer, Lieutenant-Colonel John Baker Lindsell, who served for seven years in Aldershot and died in May, 1898. In this aisle is also the memorial

Military Aldershot today.

" I smelt the smell o' the barracks,
I 'eard the bugles go,
I 'eard the feet on the gravel,
The feet o' the men what drill . . ."

RUDYARD KIPLING.

THE DISTRICT BADGE

The formation badge of Aldershot District is a shield, symbolic of the military nature of the sign. The background of the shield is evenly divided—the upper portion blue, representative of a summer night sky, the lower half the green of a grass field ; across the sky are two white crossed searchlight beams, all symbolic of the Aldershot Tattoo, which was so closely associated with the pre-war Aldershot Command in the minds of a very wide section of the population.

Superimposed on this background is a yellow torch, with red flames—the Torch of Learning. This has a double significance : firstly, as a further association with the Torchlight Tattoos of the past, and secondly the role of Aldershot District today, which is primarily one of training and teaching, the majority of units in the District being Training Units or Establishments and Schools of Instruction for all ranks.

The introduction of this badge in July, 1947, saw the passing of the familiar badge which was worn by troops in Aldershot from 1944, a white-winged figure of Victory set on a saxe-blue background representing sea and sky, and before her the white points of the Needles.

This was originally the badge of Hants and Dorset District of Southern Command, and it was introduced in 1943, for it was in the coastal area of that District that a high proportion of the D-Day concentrations of troops were assembled, and it was from the District's South Coast ports that the invasion fleets set sail for Normandy in June, 1944. On the reorganization of the Southern Command consequent upon the disbandment of South-Eastern Command in 1944, this area was redesignated Aldershot and Hants District, its boundaries being altered to include those of the pre-war Aldershot Command and the war-time Aldershot District, less the territory which lay within the county of Dorset.

In 1947 the designation of the District was changed again, and it became known as the Aldershot District. The war-time badge which had been inherited from the original Hants and Dorset District had, therefore, lost much of its significance. The new badge, however, was considered more appropriately associated with Aldershot District, its past activities and its role today. The badge was designed by Major-General J. A. Baillon, C.B., C.B.E., M.C., G.O.C. Aldershot District, 1946-1948.

"An Acre of Barren ground, ling, heath, brown furze, anything . . ."—*The Tempest, Act I, Scene I.*
The general view of Caesar's Camp and the Long Valley.

Headquarters, Aldershot District, facing Steeles Road.

The Headquarter Mess of the Royal Army Service Corps, Buller Barracks.

The Officers' Mess Block, Warburg Barracks, the old East Cavalry Barracks, from Wellington Avenue.

BARRACKS, OLD AND NEW

The A.C.C. Training Centre, St. Omer Barracks, Aldershot, the largest cookery training establishment in the world.

St. George's Garrison Church, Stanhope Lines, from Queen's Avenue.

St. Andrew's Garrison Church (Church of Scotland) from Transport Road.

The Royal Garrison Church of All Saints (The "Red Church)" from the Farnborough Road.

St. Alban's Garrison Church, Marlborough Lines, North Camp.

The plaque on the wall facing Alisons Road in the Gibraltar Barracks area.

Queen Victoria's cipher above the entrance to Willems Barracks, the old West Cavalry Barracks, on the Farnborough Road.

To the Memory of
LIEUTENANT GENERAL THE HON.
SIR JAMES YORKE SCARLETT, G.C.B.
COMMANDER OF THE LEGION OF HONOUR
&c., &c., &c.
COLONEL OF THE 5TH DRAGOON GUARDS.
HE COMMANDED
THE HEAVY CAVALRY BRIGADE AT BALACLAVA
ON THE 25TH OF OCTOBER 1854,
AND WAS CONSECUTIVELY
LIEUT. GOVERNOR OF PORTSMOUTH,
ADJUTANT GENERAL OF THE FORCES
AND
COMMANDER OF THE ALDERSHOT DIVISION.

HE WAS 2ND SON OF
JAMES, FIRST LORD ABINGER,
AND WAS EDUCATED AT ETON,
AND TRIN. COLL. CAMBRIDGE.
HE ENTERED THE ARMY IN 1818,
AND WAS APPOINTED CORNET
IN THE 18TH HUSSARS,
AND AFTERWARDS TO THE 5TH DRAGOON GUARDS
WHICH REGIMENT HE COMMANDED
FOR UPWARDS OF 14 YEARS.

THIS MONUMENT IS ERECTED
BY SOME OF HIS NUMEROUS FRIENDS
AND COMPANIONS IN ARMS,
WHO KNEW AND RESPECTED HIS WORTH,
HIS GALLANTRY, AND HIS KINDLY NATURE.
BORN 1ST FEB. 1799, DIED 6TH DECR. 1871.

The Memorial in the Royal Garrison Church of All Saints to Lieut.-General Sir James Yorke Scarlett, Commander of the Aldershot Division, 1865-1870, who commanded the Heavy Brigade at Balaclava.

The Central Panel of the Lazny Murals in the Percy Illingworth Institute on Gun Hill.

The R.A.S.C. War Memorial, Mandora Road.

The Prince Consort's Library.

Hospital Hill, leading down to the town.   On the bank at the right is the 1914-1918 War Memorial of the 2nd Division.

The Cambridge Hospital.

The N.A.A.F.I. Club.

Queen's Avenue, leading from Aldershot to Farnborough. In the distance can be seen the spire of St. George's Garrison Church and the flagstaff in the grounds of the Headquarter Offices.

The Royal Pavilion, Aldershot : The main entrance, a photograph taken in July, 1914, showing sentries of the 2nd Bn. Royal Munster Fusiliers.

[Copyright: Gale & Polden Ltd.

The view looking north from the terrace of the Royal Pavilion.

Major-General W. A. Dimoline, C.B., C.B.E., D.S.O., M.C., General Officer Commanding Aldershot District, inspecting the Parade accompanied by Brigadier A. de L. Cazenove, C.B.E., D.S.O., M.V.O., A.D.C., the Deputy District Commander, on the occasion of the King's Birthday Parade on the Queen's Parade, 10th June, 1950.

window to Lieutenant-General Sir Robert Grant, C.B. (born August, 1837; died January, 1904).

The west windows, which bear representations of "The Good Shepherd" and St. George, the former including in the design the badge of the Royal Army Chaplains' Department, the latter the Royal Arms, are memorials to John Cox Edghill, D.D., Chaplain to the Forces and Chaplain-General of the Forces, 1885-1901, who was responsible for the idea of the building of St. George's.

In the sanctuary are four memorial windows, all erected by their brother officers, to two R.E. and two R.A.S.C. officers: Major-General Sir Howard Elphinstone, who was drowned at sea off Ashanti in March, 1890; Lieutenant-Colonel John Jervois, R.E., who died in Aldershot in May, 1895; Lieutenant-Colonel Bernard Hengate, A.S.C., who was accidentally killed whilst hunting in December, 1898; and Colonel Guthrie Jessop, R.A.S.C., who died from the effects of a carriage accident in Cape Town in November, 1902.

Along the north aisle is a series of marble tablets erected to the memory of former members of Army Medical Staff and R.A.M.C., including a tablet to the memory of two Surgeon Lieutenant-Colonels of the Militia Medical Staff Corps who died in South Africa in 1900, two Warrant Officers and two hundred and eighty-six N.C.Os. and men of the R.A.M.C., and thirteen N.C.Os. and men of the Militia Medical Staff who lost their lives during the campaign. There are two other panels containing the names of twenty-two sisters of the Army Nursing Service and Army Nursing Service Reserve who died in South Africa during the war 1899-1902. A further three tablets contain the names of nineteen officers of the R.A.M.C. who were killed in action or died in South Africa. Another tablet has been erected in memory of Captain Charles Arbeiter, Quartermaster of the Army Medical Staff, who died at Las Palmas from illness contracted while serving with the Ashanti Expedition of 1895-6.

There is a similar series of tablets in the north aisle erected to the memory of sixty-seven of all ranks of the Army Service Corps who lost their lives between 1884 and 1904: in the Nile campaign of 1884-5; at Suakim, 1885-6; the Ashanti, 1895; the Dongola Expedition, 1896; in Crete, 1897; in the Sudan, 1898; West Africa, 1898; and Somaliland, 1904.

Here also is the 1939-1945 War Memorial of the Army Catering Corps, which was dedicated on Sunday, 9th July, 1950, by the Bishop of Guildford, the Rt. Rev. H. C. Montgomery-Campbell, and unveiled by Major-General C. M. Smith, C.B., C.B.E., M.C., Director of Supplies and Transport at the War Office, whilst a Book of Remembrance was entrusted to the Church by Colonel R. A. A. Byford,

21

M.V.O., O.B.E., Controller of the Army Catering Corps. The Memorial is constructed of polished English marble, and is surmounted by the Regimental Crest, carved in relief, and finished in the heraldic colours of the Corps. Within a recess, behind the gilded bronze doors, is placed the Book of Remembrance, bound in black morocco leather, with the crest embossed in gilt and colour. The book contains 775 names of all ranks of the Corps in whose memory the memorial is erected.

On a panel below the recess is engraved the inscription : "In memory of the officers, N.C.Os. and men of the Army Catering Corps who gave their lives in the World War 1939-1945. Their names are recorded in this Book of Remembrance." Above the memorial is hung the Regimental Flag of the Army Catering Corps.

There are two small side chapels, that at the end of the north aisle containing a fine memorial in mosaic depicting the arrival of the three kings with tributes to the infant Christ, held in the arms of the Holy Virgin. This memorial was erected to the memory of the Chaplains to the Forces who "laid down their lives in the service of their country in the South African War, 1899-1902."

In this chapel is a wall plaque surmounted by the old badge of the Army Medical Staff, in memory of Surgeon-General Sir William Taylor, K.C.B., M.D., K.H.P., Director-General of the Army Medical Service, 1901-1904, who died at Windsor in 1917, having during his career served on the Canadian Frontier, 1865, in the Jowaki Expedition of 1877, the Burmese War of 1885-6, the Chino-Japanese War 1894-5, the Ashanti Expedition of 1895-6, and the Sudan campaign of 1898.

The chapel is lit from three stained-glass windows, one to the memory of David Barrie Clark, Chaplain to the Forces, who died in Aldershot in 1894, another to Sophia Waller, a Sister of the Guild of St. Helena, and the third to Arthur Cecil Somerset Durnford, Second Lieutenant of the West India Regiment, who died at Cape Coast Castle in 1897.

The proximity of St. George's to the Royal Engineer and Royal Army Service Corps Establishments has made St. George's the spiritual home of these two Corps, as may be seen from the numerous memorials. Latterly those of the R.A.S.C. have predominated, and the church is known to the R.A.S.C. as "The Corps Cathedral." Set into the tiles of the sanctuary are two tablets commemorating the fact that in the sanctuary and the chancel of the church are the memorials dedicated "to the Glory of God and in memory of all ranks of the R.A.S.C." who died during the South African War and the 1914-1918 war, and the fact that the communion rails are a memorial to those members of the Corps who fell in the 1939-1945 war.

On either side of the altar are the Corps flags of the Royal Engineers and the Royal Army Service Corps, and on the high altar rest the cross and two candlesticks, the gift of H.R.H. The Duke of Connaught, who was commanding in Aldershot when the church was opened.

In a wooden case, set in the wall by the communion rails, are two Books of Remembrance containing the names of all ranks of the R.A.S.C. who fell in the 1914-1918 and 1939-1945 wars. The case is decorated with wood carving depicting the rose, the oak, the thistle, daffodil and shamrock, with the letters "R.A.S.C." entwined, and the Corps badge in full colours. On the south wall of the chancel are three panels with mosaic borders erected in memory of those members of the Army Service Corps who lost their lives during the South African War. This memorial contains the names of nineteen Officers, six Warrant Officers, thirty-eight Staff Sergeants and Sergeants, sixty-three Corporals, one hundred and sixty Drivers, seventy-nine Privates, five Shoeing and Carriage Smiths and two Trumpeters; also two Officers and fourteen Other Ranks who died at home on their return from the campaign.

On the walls of the sanctuary and chancel are a series of marble tablets of standard size separated by mosaic. There are one hundred and six of these tablets, all of them individual memorials to officers of the R.A.S.C.

The carved oak lectern and the pulpit were originally in use in the old "Iron Church." The former is a memorial to Lieutenant-Colonel Charles Cornwallis Chesney, R.E., and the latter to the memory of Assistant-Commissariat-General Ruben Hill Powell of the Commissariat and Transport Staff, who died during a passage home from Singapore in October, 1884.

In a small chapel at the chancel end of the south aisle are four more small stained-glass windows: one a memorial to Mrs. Ewing,* the children's story-writer of the middle years of last century, which bears the inscription, "In grateful recollection of Juliana Horatia Ewing, sometime resident at Aldershot Camp, who served God in

---

* Mrs. Juliana Horatia Ewing was born in 1841 near Sheffield, the daughter of Dr. and Mrs. Alfred Gatty. Her mother, Mrs. Margaret Gatty (1809-1873), was well known as a writer for children, the most popular of her works being "Aunt Judy's Tales." Following in her mother's footsteps, Mrs. Ewing's first story was published in July, 1861. In 1867 she married Major Alexander Ewing, of the Army Pay Department, and soon after sailed for New Brunswick, but later came to Aldershot, where her husband was stationed for a number of years. Among her best-known works are "The Land of Lost Toys" (1869) and "A Flat Iron for a Farthing" (1873). It was in 1872 that she wrote her first soldier story, "The Peace Egg," and this was followed by "Lob-lie-by-the-Fire," the well-known "Jackanapes" (1884) and "The Story of a Short Life" (1885). She also helped to edit the children's magazine, *Aunt Judy's Magazine*, started by her mother. Mrs. Ewing died at Bath in May, 1885. There is a signed photograph of her hanging in the Vestry.

her writings and illustrations of the soldiers' life, this window is dedicated."

Of the other three windows, one was erected by his comrades of the 7th Company, R.E., to the memory of Lieutenant Percy Trevor Bourne, R.E., who was drowned at Malta in June, 1893 ; another is in memory of Captain W. H. T. Gunthorpe of the 1st Bn. The Yorkshire Regiment, who died of fever in the Sudan in September, 1907 ; a third window erected by his brother officers in Aldershot is a memorial to Lieutenant William Grant Stairs, R.E., who died in June, 1892, at Chinde, East Africa, "shortly after promotion into the Welsh Regiment."

Wall tablets and plaques are numerous. On either side of the west door are two large tablets. One is to the memory of the N.C.Os. and Men of the Bridging Battalion, R.E., who died on service during the South African War. This contains the names of twelve men of "A" and seven of "C" Pontoon Troops, two men of the Royal Monmouthshire R.E., and one of the Royal Anglesey R.E. The other tablet is to the memory of the Officers, N.C.Os. and Men of the Commissariat and Transport Corps who died in Egypt in 1882.

On the walls of the aisles are other tablets : one to the memory of Captain John Laird Gallwey Irvine, of the Argyll and Sutherland Highlanders, killed in action at the age of twenty-six at Grispot, France, on 8th July, 1915, "when helping some wounded men to a place of safety." This memorial was erected "as a token of affection and admiration to a gallant nephew" by Lieutenant-Colonel Sir H. L. Galway, K.C.M.G., D.S.O. Near by is a tablet to the memory of Captain de la Poer Beresford, commanding the 1st Field Troop, R.E., who died in Aldershot saving the life of a comrade,* and another in memory of Colonel Charles Frederick Cobbe Beresford, R.E. (born May, 1844 ; died December, 1925).

The church is imposing, the architecture dignified, and the lighting of the sanctuary, chancel and side chapels so designed as to show these portions of the building to advantage.

Leaving St. George's Church, one crosses a parade ground, on the east of which is a building in use as a Youth Club, called the "Dimoline Youth Centre," to Buller Road, beyond which lies a large R.E. Yard.

On this side of Buller Road, facing Queen's Avenue, behind a grove of plane trees, stands the Garrison Church of St. Andrew of Scotland, which occupies the site of the old "Iron Church" which stood here from the 1850's until 1926. St. Andrew's Church is of red brick with Portland stone facings, and above the porch of the west door is the Cross of St. Andrew in stone above a large lantern.

* See pp. 330 and 362.

The interior of the church, which was designed by Sir Robert Lorimer, is plain, but the high, dark oak-roofed transept is impressive, leading up to the apse at the east end of the church, in which is a stained glass window—Scotland's tribute to the memory of Field-Marshal Earl Haig—which was unveiled on 18th November, 1934, by King George VI, when Duke of York.

In the south transept is a stained-glass memorial window, unveiled on 23rd November, 1930, by Major-General J. G. Cameron, C.B., C.M.G., Colonel of the Queen's Own Cameron Highlanders. This window, which bears the figure of St. Andrew and the badge of the regiment, was presented to the church by the 1st Bn. The Cameron Highlanders to replace the window which the battalion erected in the old "Iron Church" in memory of the battalion's stay in Aldershot, 1909-1913.

Above the west door is another stained-glass window, the gift of Countess Haig, in memory of all ranks of the 1st Corps who fell in 1914. This was unveiled on 29th September, 1935, by Captain Sir Ian Fraser, Chairman of St. Dunstan's. Below the window is an oak wall panel bearing the names of the twenty-eight Senior Chaplains of the Church who have held the post since 1856.*

The church contains only two wall memorials, one a small bronze tablet near the pulpit erected in memory of Brigadier-General Leslie Warner Yule Campbell, C.M.G., "One time Elder of this Kirk"; the other a brass plaque bearing in relief at the top the badge of the Royal Inniskilling Fusiliers, and below a service revolver. The plaque, which is bordered with a design of thistles, is affixed to a column at the corners by four bolts with unusual heads, the top two bolts being covered by two ordinary brass buttons bearing the cipher "GRI" and the Imperial Crown and the words "Indian Army," the lower bolts being covered by large reproductions of officers' rank stars. The plaque bears the inscription:

IN LOVING and Proud Memory
2nd Lieutenant Alfred Douglas Wingate, Indian Army
only surviving son of Sir Andrew Wingate K.C.I.E.
and Lady Wingate. Born at NASIK, India June 1894
Passed out of Sandhurst August 1914.
Killed in action at Richbourg L'AVOVE
May 16th 1915 leading the Bombers of the
2nd Royal Inniskilling Fusiliers.

---

* There are thirty-one names, but three are duplicated, having held the post on separate occasions at different times. Until 1892, when St. George's Church was built, the old "Iron Church" which stood on this site was used for parade services by both the Church of England and the Church of Scotland, the services being at different times.

Below the inscription is the text which was found in his notebook, "Remember God has been there before you and has chosen the place for you."

Leaving St. Andrew's Church, one crosses the Basingstoke Canal over the "Iron Bridge." The bridge marks the site of the pontoon which was built by the Royal Engineers in 1854 to connect the North and South Camps.

Over the bridge Queen's Avenue runs northwards through an avenue of trees. To the left, beyond a thirty-yard range, lies the expanse of green sward, stretching across to Farnborough Road, which is known as "The Queen's Parade," for it was here that Queen Victoria carried out her annual inspections and reviews of the garrison. Here is the polo ground of the former Aldershot Command Polo Club, and other sports grounds. In the centre, amid a cluster of trees, stands a pavilion for the use of teams using the grounds. Across the stretch of grass at a diagonal from Cavans Road to the Farnborough Road just south of Vine Cottage runs a W.D. ride. On the right lies Princes Avenue, which leads away to Mons Barracks, built in 1926-7, and until 1940 the Headquarters, in Aldershot, of the Royal Corps of Signals. During the construction of these barracks a change was made in "The Camp" landscape by the levelling in 1926 of Smallshot Hill, a dominating feature of this area, where at one time stood the lofts of the carrier pigeons of the old R.E. Signals Unit, the forerunners of the Royal Signals. This was a gigantic task involving the excavation and removal of 250,000 tons of soil. During the late war Mons Barracks were occupied by an Officer Cadet Training Unit which later, on the reduction of these Establishments, became the Basic O.C.T.U., and in 1948 was formed into the Mons Officer Cadet School. This is the counterpart of the Royal Military Academy Sandhurst, which trains officers for the Regular Army, whereas the Mons Officer Cadet School trains the National Service officer of all arms of the Service with the exception of Infantry, R.A.O.C. and R.E.M.E. The Mons Officer Cadet School was formed by the amalgamation of the Basic O.C.T.U. with the R.A.C. O.C.T.U. which during the war years was at Bovington and a second R.A. O.C.T.U. from Deepcut.

The Mons Officer Cadet School is designed to give basic and special arms training to potential National Service officers of the R.A.C. and R.A. and basic training of other arms of the Service. National Service officers spend two years with the Regular Army and now go on to the Territorial Army for three and a half years. The Mons Officer Cadet School is therefore responsible for the training of a very high proportion of Army officers.

Intakes to the school arrive about twice a month and they pass out at the same intervals. The capacity of the school allows for the training of over 700 cadets at any one time, and it functions throughout the whole year and does not work in terms as is the case at Sandhurst.

The standard of training and discipline at the school is very high, and great importance is attached to the turn-out of cadets, who are distinguished by the wearing of white gorget patches on their battle-dress.

The drill standard is high and this today is in the hands of R.S.M. Brittain, M.B.E., of the Coldstream Guards, who during some sixteen years' service as a drill instructor at Sandhurst and at Mons Barracks has probably drilled more potential officers than any other warrant officer or N.C.O. in the British Army.

The end of each course is marked by a passing-out parade. A Battalion Parade is held and the troop which is passing out takes its place on the right of the line, and the ceremony which follows is conducted on the same lines as the Sovereign's Parade at the Royal Military Academy Sandhurst, with the exception of the march past in slow time. A Senior Officer takes the parade on each occasion and presents the prize to the best cadet of the passing-out troop. This prize now takes the form of a silver-mounted cane, which replaces the pre-war Sword of Honour as used at Sandhurst and the war-time Belts of Honour given at the various O.C.T.Us.

The final phase of the passing-out parade follows the form of that carried out at Sandhurst. The men passing out slow march off parade and up the steps while the band plays "Auld Lang Syne," followed by the Adjutant mounted on his charger.

*   *   *   *   *

In the area lying between the Basingstoke Canal, at the point where it turns southwards by Morlands Road at the south-east corner of Mons Barracks, and the County boundary, which conforms to the line of the Blackwater, is a wide expanse of open country. Running parallel with the canal is Camp Farm Road, with Government Road leading off to the right from Gasworks Bridge, above Gold Farm, which takes its name from the low-lying marsh and osiers on the south side of the railway known as "The Gold." Beyond Gold Farm lies Holly Bush Farm, to the north of which is the area known as "Aldershot Stubbs," and beyond this the Municipal boundary runs from west to east to a bend in the river known as Lynchford Corner, the north-western extremity of the Borough. On the west of Government Road lies Camp Farm, the War Department Sewage Works, with its sludge and settling tanks, pumping stations and filter-beds.

Camp Farm Road, which runs between Mons Barracks and the Camp Farm, merges into Kitcheners Road just below the Municipal boundary, and here, on the left, on the high ground which prior to 1926 led up to Smallshot Hill, stands an imposing modern building which is reached from Cavans Road, the Officers' Mess of St. Omer Barracks, between which and the Marlborough Lines Garrison Church are the officers' quarters of Mons Lodge, Mons House, Sedgemore House and Connaught House.

St. Omer Barracks, the Army Catering Corps Training Centre and Headquarters, were completed in 1940. The spacious building covers an area of some 10,000 square feet and it is equipped with all the latest types of cooking equipment, which is installed in modern kitchen class-rooms. These training facilities within the building are linked with field kitchens, where instruction is given in improvisation and the use of cooking equipment in the field.

It is here that instructional courses are held covering all aspects of catering in the Army. Some 4,000 men pass through the Centre on instructional courses each year. The main object of training at the Centre ensures that the soldier-cook can take his place in the field, trained to compete with any situation.

Near the junction of Princes Avenue and Queen's Avenue is one of "The Camp" cinemas, and beyond stands the Aldershot Command Swimming Bath, now called the Aldershot Military Bath. On the side of the building facing the Avenue, in large metal letters, is the Royal Cipher "VR" surmounted by a crown and the date of the building— 1900. The baths are reached through the entrance at the side where, in the tiled hall under a cupolar roof, is a series of photographs of past Army and Inter-Service Swimming Teams.

Next to the baths, lying back from the road, stands the imposing creeper-covered red-brick Gymnasium, which was also built in 1900, above the north door being a large metal monogram "VRI" above two large crossed swords, the badge of the Physical Training Corps. This is known as the "Big Gym," and is equipped with every form of gymnastic-apparatus—beams, ropes, benches, box horses, wall bars, jumping standards, horizontal bars—all the aids for the training of the Army Physical Training Corps. It was here that the fencing events of the Modern Pentathlon of the XIV Olympiad were held in 1948. This is the Army School of Physical Training, which was established in 1860, and here the Physical Training Instructors of the Army are made, to go out as unit instructors to every unit of the Army.

Next to the Gymnasium stands the Aldershot Military Stadium, formerly known as the Command Central Ground. Behind the corrugated iron walls is a fine stadium with a football ground and running track, a covered grandstand capable of seating 1,500, and a number of open stands, a well-appointed and equipped pavilion, and other buildings for control staffs and administrative personnel. It is here that the Army Athletic Championships are held and also the Army Football Championship. In 1948 and 1949 the Stadium was the venue of the Aldershot Horse Show, and in 1948 was the scene of the equestrian events of the Olympic Games, attended by horsemen of eighteen nations.

Continuing along the Queen's Avenue, some sixty yards north, one crosses the Aldershot Municipal boundary and enters the Farnborough Urban District. This Municipal demarcation is, however, unnoticed, dividing as it does Military Aldershot; for "The Camp" is, and must be, regarded as a whole. It is Marlborough Lines, North Camp, Aldershot, to the world, and not North Camp, Farnborough, which would be strictly correct; but Aldershot is Aldershot to the Army, and for that matter to the outside world, and Farnborough, although having a large portion of the W.D. lands within its boundaries, must perforce allow Aldershot to take precedence in nomenclature. No soldier stationed in Ramillies, Oudenarde, Malplaquet or Blenheim Barracks ever says he is stationed in Farnborough. No—he is in Aldershot, and to the soldier Aldershot Camp knows no municipal bounds.*

At the point where Cavans Road crosses Queen's Avenue one enters North Camp proper in the barrack area known as Marlborough Lines, with the barracks named after Marlborough's victories. To the right, in Cavans Road, stand the former Headquarter offices of the 2nd Division, for in the pre-war Aldershot Command it was the troops quartered in North Camp which made up the bulk of this formation.

To the right of Queen's Avenue lie Ramillies Barracks and to the left Oudenarde Barracks. Beyond Oudenarde, to the left, lie Malplaquet and Blenheim Barracks, the latter now occupied by one of the wings of the Staff College, Camberley. The officers' messes of these barracks are in Duke of Connaughts Road and face the parade grounds between the blocks. These barracks all conform to the old barrack blocks of the original hutted camp and, although open and to the casual observer seemingly all one, each block of buildings is complete with its own accommodation, guard room, institutes, miniature ranges, workshops, stores and other administrative buildings for a battalion. Barrack blocks are still numbered A1, A2, A3, B1, B2, B3 and so on, conforming almost identically to the numbering of the huts in the original hutted camp.

---

* On the Ordnance Survey Map it will be seen that the boundary line between the Borough and the Farnborough U.D.C. at one point actually runs diagonally through the Officers' Quarters of the St. Omer Barracks Officers' Mess.

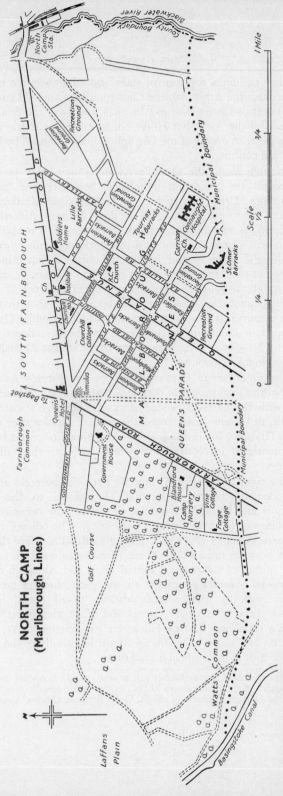

NORTH CAMP
(Marlborough Lines)

[Copyright: *Gale & Polden, Ltd.*]

North Camp is dissected by Evelyn Woods Road, Duke of Connaughts Road, Redvers Bullers Road and Cavans Road, all named after former G.Os.C. of Aldershot. At the east end of Evelyn Woods Road, on rising ground, stands the Marlborough Lines Garrison Church, now called the Garrison Church of St. Alban, one of the first three churches to be erected in "The Camp" in the middle fifties. This church serves North Camp and in the early days dominated the area, for it stands on rising ground, and then towered above the low wooden huts. The church has changed but little as the years have passed. It is constructed of wood, a large spacious building, its overhanging roof supported by eight wooden pillars on brick bases. It has been popularly supposed, for many years, that the church was originally constructed for use as a hospital in the Crimea, but the war ended before it could be dispatched and it was retained in Aldershot for use as a "temporary church," and owing to this the church was not dedicated until 24th September, 1949, when a Service of Dedication was conducted by the Chaplain-General to the Forces. No major structural alterations have taken place since it was first erected on its present site, and this background knowledge of its origin accounts for the general appearance of the interior, which could well be that of a drill hall of early Victorian days. The interior of the church was, however, considerably improved by interior decorations in 1949.

The altar, which was small and out of proportion to the width of the church, was enlarged and moved forward. The floor of the Chancel and Choir was covered by grey carpet which, in conjunction with the red velvet curtains which now hang in a semi-circle from either wall behind the altar, adds richness and beauty which the church had, in the past, so sadly lacked. A red velvet pelmet runs along the top of the curtain behind which are electric lights, throwing the subdued lighting down into the chancel, whilst the altar Cross is lit up by a spot light affixed to a beam over the choir stalls. The walls, which were painted and rather patchy, are covered in beaver board, and much of the ceiling struture and slats similarly concealed.

The church, which has a seating capacity of 850, is well lighted by eight windows and, above the altar, a circular stained-glass window. The church is still heated by coke stoves set at intervals along the side walls. To the left of the nave stands the organ, presented in 1945 by General Sir Richard Haking, G.B.E., K.C.B., K.C.M.G., then Colonel of The Royal Hampshire Regiment, in memory of his wife, Rachel Violet Haking. When the improvements to the church were carried out in 1949 the organ was electrified, the large pipes removed from above it and hidden from view behind the red velvet curtains of the chancel. This organ had replaced a smaller one which stood on the right of the church and was removed in March, 1949. It had formerly been in use in the Garrison Church at the Curragh and was installed in the Marlborough Lines church in 1922.

The oak communion table, chairs, candle-sticks and two church-wardens' wands, were presented to the church in August, 1941, by the Royal Corps of Signals, who occupied Mons Barracks from the time of their construction until the late war, "to commemorate their long association with the Church." The font was given to the church by the Marlborough Lines branch of the Sisters of the Guild of St. Helena on 8th May, 1912, a fact which is commemorated by a small brass tablet, whilst the wooden font cover was presented by the Band of the 1st Norfolk Regiment in June, 1912, and the brass lectern was given at Easter, 1892, by the South Staffordshire Regiment. Owing no doubt to the fact that the church was for many years regarded as but a temporary building, it lacks the memorials which are a feature of the Royal Garrison Church of All Saints and St. George's and St. Andrew's Garrison Churches. The first wall plaque was erected on the south wall in 1950, and bears the inscription :

TO THE GLORY OF GOD
IN GRATEFUL MEMORY OF THE GENEROUS HOSPITALITY
BESTOWED ON THE NETHERLANDS SAILORS, SOLDIERS AND
AIRMEN DURING THEIR STAY IN THE UNITED KINGDOM
ANNO DOMINI 1940-47.
THIS TABLET IS PRESENTED BY THE PROTESTANT CHURCHES
OF THE NETHERLANDS
"I was a Stranger and you took me in."

Behind the church stands the Connaught Military Hospital, which faces Duke of Connaughts Road, on the opposite side of which lie Tournay Barracks. To the rear of Tournay Barracks in Redvers Bullers Road, and between this and North Road, lies the married quarters in Grant Square and Somerset Square, and the now-disused Military Detention Barracks, familiarly known in former days as "The Glass House"; for behind the high, forbidding walls stood the large, grim brick buildings in which soldiers under sentence for military crimes were detained. The buildings had a large glass roof covering the central hall, around which ran three storeys of cells leading off an open iron passageway and reached by open iron stairways.

In Redvers Bullers Road stands the Roman Catholic Church of St. Patrick, and an Infants' School, behind which lie the former Head-quarter offices of the pre-war 5th Infantry Brigade of the 2nd Division.

The Roman Catholic Church of St. Patrick is not one of the official garrison churches, although it serves North Camp. The altar of the church is of recent installation. It was first erected in March, 1947, in the Church of Christ the King at Sarafand in Palestine by the Catholic soldiers of the garrison. The altar was brought home and re-erected in its present position at the end of the British Mandate in Palestine, a fact which is commemorated by a small brass tablet. One of the features of interest in the church is a very large, and very old, oil painting depicting the taking down of Our Lord from the Cross. The canvas originally hung behind the altar and now occupies almost the whole width of the rear of the church above the entrance.

Eastwards from Redvers Bullers Road, behind the Connaught Hospital and Tournay and Lille Barracks, lies a stretch of waste sandy ground, broken by recreation grounds.

North Camp ends along the line of Lynchford Road, Farnborough. To the south of the road lies North Camp, but the north side of the road is occupied by the shopping centre of South Farnborough, which developed along the same lines as High Street, Aldershot, when the camps were first built. The pattern of Lynchford Road has changed but little in the passing years, and the "Elephant and Castle," a wooden-fronted building, appears today as it undoubtedly did in the late 1880's. A glance at the names on the shop fascias shows that a number of the Aldershot traders, with an eye to business among the troops of North Camp, established branches of their businesses in South Farnborough to cater for the needs of the Army.

At the north end of Queen's Avenue, on the right of the road, stands the Methodist Soldiers' Home, which was renamed in 1933 "The Harington Home." This is a single-storeyed red-brick building with two small towers, with spires, above the entrances.

In Lynchford Road, to the west of Queen's Avenue, stands the Church of England Soldiers', Sailors' and Airmen's Institute, equipped with coffee-bar and recreation and billiard rooms ; and also in this building is the Llewellyn Wavel Memorial Chapel, which is open all day for private prayer, and where services are held by the warden of the Institute. It is a small but dignified chapel with seating accommodation for forty, and a small harmonium, and with six stained-glass windows, three above the altar, the centre window depicting St. George, below which is the inscription :

To my beloved husband Llewellyn Wavel, Colonel

to whose beloved memory this room was dedicated January 21st 1911. Served with the 1st Bengal European Fusiliers throughout the Indian Mutiny, served in the China War 1862, Afghanistan 1879. Born November 15th, 1839, passed away at Camborne, Farnborough, November 27th, 1910.

On either side are other memorial windows to the younger son of Colonel Llewellyn Wavel and Mrs. Emily Wavel, who died in 1880, and his eldest son, who died in 1873 ; and to the infant son of Colonel Arthur Henry Wavel of the Welch Regiment, who died in 1887. The fifth window is in memory of Major Arthur John Byng Wavel, M.C., F.R.G.S., of the Welch Regiment, who commanded the Arab Rifles and who fell in action in January, 1916, near Mwele, in British East Africa. The last window was erected to the memory of Colonel Arthur Henry Wavel, of the Welch Regiment, eldest son of Major-General Arthur Goodall Wavel, K.F., K.C.S., F.R.S., who died in January, 1891, and his wife, who died in 1918. There is a wall plaque commemorating the fact that the reredos in the chapel was erected in May, 1932, in memory of Emily Ann Maria Wavel, widow of Colonel Llewellyn Wavel, who died the previous year and to whom the inception of the little chapel was due. A small brass tablet records that the room was furnished in 1910 by the Sisters of the Marlborough Lines Guild of St. Helena.

*   *   *   *   *

Turning west along Lynchford Road one passes the married quarters of Napier Square, officers' quarters in Avenue House, Churchill House and more married quarters, known as Queen's Quarters, and eventually reaches, on the north side of the road, the Queen's Hotel, which stands at the junction of the Farnborough Road and Lynchford Road opposite the tumulus known as Cockadobby Hill.* This tumulus was opened, about the middle of last century, at the instigation of a Mr. Greene, who had served as a junior officer at Waterloo and came to live at The Lodge, Farnborough, soon afterwards. He lived there until 1887 and was an enthusiastic antiquarian. Nothing of any importance was discovered in this Anglo-Saxon burial mound. Before it was filled in, however, some current coins, copies of *The Times*, and some samples of pots and pans locally manufactured (in the pottery established by William Smith, who farmed Street Farm, Farnborough, over a hundred years ago) were buried in suitable containers so as to be of some interest to any future antiquarian who might cause the tumulus to be opened in later years.†

Here, by the tumulus, at the north-west corner of "The Camp" stands a memorial in the form of a pillar and fountain, behind which is a stone seat reached by steps on either side. On the pillar is the

---

* See p. 13.
† "Jottings from a Farnborough Notebook," by Jessie Challacombe (Gale & Polden Ltd.) (1923).

simple and anonymous inscription, "In Memory of one who died for his country," and in Roman numerals the date 1901. This memorial was erected in September, 1903, but to this day remains nameless. The site was given by the War Department and the water for the fountain provided by the Farnborough Urban District Council. The architect was Miss Clotilde Brewster, of Barton Street, Westminster, and it was built by Mr. Hammond, of Elm Grove, Farnborough, but there is no indication of the donors or to whose memory the memorial was erected. The secret has been kept for nearly half a century locked away in the files of the War Office and the Farnborough U.D.C., and the hearts of those concerned with its construction. In *The Aldershot News* in September, 1903, the Editor wrote : "Someone in particular fell. Some friends in particular were bereaved, but it stands there at the cross-roads, that nameless fountain in the quiet dignity of an impersonal symbol to the valiant. From the true to those who strive from those who love. No more suitable or significant memorial could have been thought out by the anonymous donors."

* * * * *

Here one turns down the main road, the Farnborough Road, which is the dividing line between "The Camp" and the W.D. lands to the west. This is the old London–Winchester turnpike road and runs northwards through Farnborough to Frimley and southwards to Farnham. An avenue of chestnuts runs along the Queen's Parade side of the road, and at intervals there are groups of three or four tall pines which have stood for many years and marked the line of the old road.

On the right of the road, hidden from view by the plantations of trees, stands Government House, its entrance marked by two sentry-boxes outside the fence and a small lodge at the main gate. From the date of its erection in 1883 until 1939, this was the official residence of the General Officer Commanding at Aldershot. Today it is "A" Mess of Headquarters, Aldershot District. The house is reached up a gravel drive ; it stands on high ground, the garden dropping down in terraces to a stretch of green sward and a belt of firs. It was on this ground that the first military fêtes and torchlight tattoos were held, which subsequently grew into the renamed Aldershot Tattoo. There is a gap between the trees which gives a direct line of sight from the upper terrace to the top of the grandstand at Rushmoor Arena, and through this gap signals were made to the Tattoo ground from Government House when the King and Queen were in residence to warn the ground of the arrival or departure of the Royal Family.

Most members of the Royal Family through five reigns have visited or stayed in Government House, which, although not a big house, is pleasantly situated and has spacious accommodation. In what is now the ante-room is a large water-colour of a review in the Long Valley in Queen Victoria's day.

Farther down the Farnborough Road on the right, opposite the Queen's Parade, standing back among the trees in its own grounds, is Blandford House, until 1950 the residence of the General Officer Commanding Aldershot District. Prior to 1939, when the G.O.C.-in-C. of the Command resided in Government House, Blandford House was occupied by the Major-General in Charge of Administration of the Command. Below the grounds of Blandford House stands Vine Cottage, one of the first officers' residences built in "The Camp," and occupied throughout the years by the senior Royal Engineer Officer in Aldershot. The house is no longer in use, but adjoining the south wall is a conservatory in which grows the large vine from which the house presumably took its name. To the south of the garden of the house a number of modern houses have recently been built for use as Officers' Married Quarters.

Farther down the road is a recreation ground, on the west side of which are the old huts and buildings of the Army School of Farriery with its stores, offices and forge workshops.

Behind this old school runs a narrow road named Shoe Lane, which runs from the Farnborough Road at the rear of the gardens of Vine Cottage and Government House, and along this road runs the Municipal boundary. It is a pleasant road, flanked on the west side by woodlands of firs and pines, whilst on the Aldershot side beyond Forge Cottage lies "The Camp Nursery." Near the top of the road the Aldershot Command Golf Course stretches away to the left, the Club-house lying just off Shoe Lane. At the end of the lane one turns to the right along Government House Road back to the main road.

A footpath leads between trees from the Farnborough Road to the north of the old School of Farriery and continues westwards, conforming to the northern line of the Municipal boundary between the Borough of Aldershot and the Farnborough Urban District. On this path to the north of Wharf Copse is a boundary stone, marked on the Ordnance Map as "Green Stone B.S.,"* and marked by the conventional sign of the "Site of an Antiquity."† Just under half a mile westwards along the same path, below Watt's Common, where it joins Laffan's Road, another boundary stone, known as "Watt's Boundary Stone," is similarly marked.

---

* B.S.—Boundary Stone.   †   ⚬⊹

The Municipal boundary turns south-west below Berkshire Copse to Claycart Bridge over the canal, and at the point where Puckeridge Hill Road joins the canal bridge there is another such site marked as "Tichborne's B.S." From this point the Municipal boundary runs in a straight line north-east to cross the canal in the lower reach of Puckeridge Flash, and *en route* it passes another boundary stone in Puckeridge Camp on Puckeridge Hill, marked with the same conventional sign as "Burte's B.S." North of the canal, to the north-western apex of the Borough boundary at Norris Hill East, the boundary line passes four more such boundary stones, named "Evelyn's," "Porter's," "Wheeler's" and "Streets'."

Although each of these eight boundary stones is marked on the map as a "Site of an Antiquity," they are not in fact antiquities as far as can be ascertained. These stones are thought to mark the old boundaries between the parishes of Aldershot and Farnborough or, even earlier still, the boundary of the old Hundred of Crondall; for although Farnborough is recognized today as being within the old Crondall Hundred, there is evidence of this fact having, in the past, led to dispute, and it is on record that at one time the Parish of Farnborough paid a fee to the Parish of Crondall in order to ensure its identity. Crondall, in exchange for the payment, waived its claim to Farnborough being included in its jurisdictional boundaries.

When the boundary was originally perambulated in 1868 for the purpose of Ordnance Survey, only three of these boundary stones were in place; the sites where the others previously stood being pointed out by local inhabitants to the surveyors, who recorded the accepted local names.*

From the north-western extremity of the Borough boundary the boundary runs southwards between Norris Hill East and Miles Hill, through Miles Copse and along the eastern slopes of Long Hill on the western extreme of the greyish sandy wastes of the Long Valley. This wild, wind-swept stretch of unusual terrain is bounded on the north by Eelmoor Hill, Spur Hill and Ravine Road.

Beyond the Recreation Ground before the old School of Farriery one again crosses the Basingstoke Canal over the old Wharf Bridge, which takes its name from the old "Farnham Wharf," as it was known in the days before "The Camp" was built.

---

* The "Object Name Book" of the Archæology Branch of the Ordnance Survey Office which covered this area was destroyed during the late war by enemy action, and thus have been lost records which may have existed with regard to the origin of these stones and sites. The names of White, Titchborne, Nicholas Watts, and Thomas Weeller (Wheeler ?) are, however, signatories (as tenants in the Crondall Hundred) to an agreement dated 9th September, 1672, as to fees payable to the steward of the Dean and Chapter of Winchester ("The Crondall Records," Part I) (Warren & Son, Winchester) (1891).

2K

The canal* has, in the past, played an important role in the military
and social life of Aldershot. In the former role it has enabled several
generations of Sappers to practise bridging and pontooning, and,
although as the years passed by it became unsuitable for the latter
form of training, the "wet gap" still provided the sites for bridging
operations, the semi-permanent constructions in several cases remaining as permanent bridges over the canal.

The only bridge over the canal in the Aldershot area at the time of
the establishment of "The Camp" was the Wharf Bridge, then on the
old London–Winchester turnpike road. The first military bridge was
a pontoon built on the site of the present-day "Iron Bridge" which
crosses the canal in Queen's Avenue.

Fifty years ago there were several boat-houses along the banks
which provided skiffs, punts and canoes for the recreation of troops
and the civil population. As the canal gradually fell into disuse, and
the weeds and water plants which grew in profusion in the water
narrowed the stream, boating in the canal in "The Camp" area lost
much of its attraction. Today the nearest functioning boat-houses
are at Ash Vale and Fleet, and the canal between these points has been,
in recent years, unfrequented as a navigable highway.

There are a number of small properties along the canal banks where
the canal runs through the Borough from Deadbrook Pond to the
Wharf Bridge on the Farnborough Road. Near the junction of
Government Road and Camp Road, adjacent to "Gasworks Bridge,"

* The construction of the Basingstoke Canal was commenced in about 1778
under powers granted by a special Act of Parliament, entitled "The Basingstoke
Canal Act." The Canal was constructed with the object of linking the rising
industrial town of Basingstoke with the Thames. The Engineer would appear to
have been a Mr. Jessop and the Contractor a Mr. Pilkington. A plan of "The
Intended Navigable Canal from Basingstoke to the River Wey," published about
the same year from a survey by one Joseph Parker, shows Aldershot and, to the
north of the village, the line of the canal running through "Great Heath" to the
county boundary along a stretch named "Dead Brook."
The necessary funds for the construction of the canal were publicly subscribed,
the original capital of the undertaking being £86,000 divided into £1 shares.
The shareholders included the Earls of Dartmouth and of Portsmouth with 4,000
shares each and the Corporation of Basingstoke with 500 shares. An early prospectus showed that the annual estimated tonnage would be over 30,000 tons, and
that tolls were expected to amount to some £7,785 per year, and a dividend of
7½ per cent. was anticipated.
The construction of the Canal presented a number of complicated problems of
engineering, but the work, once started, proceeded steadily and was completed
in fourteen years, the Canal being opened for public transport in 1792. Trade
flourished until the advent of the railways, from which time its prosperity declined
although the entire length of the Canal was in use until 1906. Gradually parts of the
Canal fell into disuse commercially and today only the stretch from Woking to
Byfleet is operated, and this mainly for the transport of timber. (*Vide* the Sale
Prospectus of the Basingstoke Canal issued in February, 1949, by Messrs. Alfred
Pearson & Son Ltd., Auctioneers, of Victoria Road, Aldershot.)

on the south side of the canal is a small bungalow called Lock Cottage, whilst on the west side of Wharf Bridge stands an old red-brick building in use as a shop, café and dwelling-house, known as "Boat House Café," and a large disused boat-house, 75 feet in length, built of timber, with a slated roof. On the opposite side of the road is a brick-and-tile building called Wharf House with a warehouse adjoining, 87 feet in length, with several store rooms and stabling.

The canal provides many pleasant walks along its tow-paths; it abounds in wild life, and is a delight to naturalists and fishermen. Bordered with rushes, flags, loosestrife and sedges, and with trees and shrubs hanging over the water's edge, the narrow path leads along a route with ever-changing scenery. The canal abounds in places with water lilies, water plants and weeds which, in the summer sunlight, can be seen moving gently under the water's surface. The falling into disuse enhanced the natural beauties of the canal and its surroundings. Large blue and green dragon-flies skim along over the water; the squawk of the moorhen is heard as the little birds swim along through the rushes; the gay kingfishers make their nests in the rising banks; even the water-voles, with their keen, piercing eyes, and ears pricked at the alert, are acceptable in this sanctuary of waterside life. Water shrews; smooth, crested, and palmate newts; frogs and toads—all have their homes along the canal; whilst fish abound in the waters—from roach, chub, minnows and sticklebacks to pike. The canal has a fascination, and is an attraction to many who derive considerable pleasure from its natural attractions.

The Basingstoke Canal received nation-wide publicity in the early months of 1949 when public notices appeared announcing that the whole of the canal, with its wharves and lock-keepers' cottages, would be sold by auction on 1st March. The canal had been owned for many years by the Harmsworth family, but as soon as the sale was announced a public meeting, supported by the Inland Waterways Association, was held at Woking which resulted in a committee being formed to see what action could be taken to save the canal, as considerable anxiety was felt regarding its future. The committee consisted of local persons and members of the Inland Waterways Association, and from it was formed a separate purchasing committee. A public meeting was held in Aldershot and an appeal for its preservation was made in the National Press. The notice of the sale was too short for action by the local authority, though the Hampshire County Council appointed a committee with powers to purchase, but whose interest was only in that portion which ran through their county. The object of the purchasing committee in conjunction with the Inland Waterways Association was to restore the whole of the canal as an inland waterway and to convert it into a public amenity for public boating and fishing. They achieved their aim by purchasing the canal and preventing it from passing into the hands of business speculators, whereby much of its beauty would doubtless have been destroyed— for example, by the felling of trees and neglect through lack of proper maintenance. There was even the risk of its being drained and filled in. Funds were in the main raised privately, but the purchase was greatly assisted by considerable public enthusiasm and support.

The Basingstoke Canal purchase committee was unable, however, owing to legal difficulties, to float its own limited liability company to project its original aims, but two private companies, the New Basingstoke Canal Co. Ltd. and Waterways Properties Ltd., have been launched to implement the plans of the committee to maintain the canal as an inland waterway : the top portion being used for fishing and pleasure boating ; the centre section being used by the Nature Conservancy, set up by the Government, and for fishing ; whilst the lower part of the canal would be used for water contracts, commerce, pleasure, boating, mooring and fishing.

After crossing the canal one sees, on the right, one of the now disused boat-houses which plied a busy trade up to some twenty years ago, and to the left the cottages of Aldershot Wharf where, in days gone by, cargoes for the canal barges were taken on or off-loaded.

Beyond the bridge on either side of the road are recreation grounds : those of the R.E. Establishment on the left, whilst on the right lie the tennis courts of the Officers' Club, bounded by Clubhouse Road, at the corner of which is the site of the old "Row Barge" Inn which thrived in the early days of "The Camp."

The grounds of the Officers' Club are extensive, with a bandstand, twenty grass and four hard tennis courts, a hockey ground and a first-class cricket ground, where some excellent cricket can be seen played in ideal surroundings.

At the south-west corner of the cricket ground stands the pavilion, a substantial, well-built red-brick building built in 1935. It was built on the site of an old wooden pavilion which had been in use since the eighties. This old building bore a commemorative plaque which is now on the wall of the main room and records the fact that the original pavilion "was designed and built in 1887 by Quartermaster Maguire of the Divisional Staff out of funds contributed as follows : Major-General W. Cooper, Commanding 1st Infantry Brigade, £50 ; Major G. M. Fox, Assistant Inspector of Gymnasia, £50 ; Colonel R. Harrison, C.B., C.M.G., Commanding R.E., £20 ; and the Race Committee, £50." The first turf for the foundations of the new pavilion was cut in December, 1935, by Brigadier Bullock-Marsham, D.S.O., M.C., and it was opened on 2nd July, 1936, by the G.O.C., General Sir Francis Gathorne-Hardy, G.C.B., G.C.V.O., C.M.G., D.S.O., A.D.C., a fact which is commemorated on a companion plaque to that taken from the original pavilion. The clock on the top of the building was taken from the first pavilion. The present building has an eighty-foot frontage with dressing rooms in the wings, and is equipped with showers and baths. Inside the pavilion is a series of interesting photographs of the members of the Aldershot Command Cricket Club and of the Army v. Australia matches in 1934 and 1936. There are also photos showing the pavilion in use as offices by the A/Q Staff of 1st Corps during mobilization in September, 1939.

The club-house stands back from the road at the junction of Fleet Road and Farnborough Road. In many ways its general appearance has varied but little from the days when the club was first built in the late fifties of last century, but the building has undergone structural alterations and modernization as the years have passed, the last major alterations having been effected in the early nineteen-thirties.

The building contains fine lounges and a first-class dance hall with a spring floor. The walls are decorated with shields on which are the regimental crests and badges of units which have been stationed in "The Camp" in recent years. Among these military badges are two R.A.F. crests, of the 4th and 13th Army Co-operation Squadrons, and one Canadian badge—that of the Royal Regiment of Canada.

In the dining-room, which overlooks pleasant lawns, hangs an original oil painting by Lady Butler entitled "A halt on a forced march during the retreat to Corunna," which was painted in 1892 and has been lent to the club by her daughter, Mrs. Elizabeth Kingscote. Lady Butler,* famous for her striking paintings of military subjects, was the wife of Lieutenant-General The Right Hon. Sir William Butler, G.C.B., P.C.,† who commanded the 2nd Infantry Brigade in Aldershot from 1893 to 1896. Lady Butler had her studio in a large wooden hut set in a clump of trees at the north end of the Queen's Parade, and it was there that she painted several of her well-

---

* Lady Butler, formerly Elizabeth Southerden, married Lieutenant-General The Right Hon. Sir William Butler in 1877. Lady Butler was already a distinguished artist who had had her oil paintings hung in the Royal Academy and had studied art in Florence and Rome. Many of her paintings have become famous and hundreds of reproductions have graced the walls of countless messes, institutions and schools. Possibly the most well known, apart from those mentioned here, are "The Roll Call," "Floreat Etona" and "Scotland for Ever." Lady Butler died in Ireland in 1933.

† He later became, from September, 1900, to January, 1901, G.O.C. at Aldershot.

known pictures, including "Dawn of Waterloo" in 1895, and "Steady the Drums and Fifes" in 1896.

On the walls of other rooms in the club are a number of pictures from the officers' messes of the 19th and 20th Hussars,* and a fine set of Ackermann prints of military types.†

In the entrance hall of the club there is a small brass tablet recording that in February, 1914, a grant of £4,000 was made by the South African Garrison Institutes to enable the mortgage on the club to be paid off.

It is here that many of the main military social functions are held throughout the year.

The club-house faces Hope Grants Road, named after General Sir James Hope Grant, G.O.C. in Aldershot from 1870 to 1875, which runs between Albuhera and Barrosa Barracks and the large parade grounds which lie to the north of Steeles Road. Lower down the Farnborough Road on the left is the Garrison Theatre and the Aldershot Boxing Stadium, which are bounded by Scarletts Road, named after Lieutenant-General The Hon. James Yorke Scarlett, G.C.B., who commanded the Heavy Brigade at Balaclava and was G.O.C. in Aldershot, 1865-1870.

At the junction of Scarletts Road and the Farnborough Road stands a small drinking-fountain bearing the letters "R.E.," which recalls a tragedy of forty years ago, for the inscription thereon reads : "Near this spot on the 30th May 1910 Captain Charles Claudius de la Poer Beresford, Royal Engineers, was killed in a brave attempt to stop a runaway horse."‡

At the lower end of the Albuhera and Barrosa Barrack§ blocks runs Pennefathers Road, which takes its name from the second G.O.C. in Aldershot, Lieutenant-General Sir John Pennefather, K.C.B., who commanded "The Division at Aldershot," 1860-1865. In this road are the old Headquarter offices of the 1st Division, and on the opposite side are the officers' messes of Albuhera and Barrosa.

Beyond, set back from the main road, in a plantation of firs, birches, pines and chestnuts, stands the Prince Consort's Library.

Opposite the library are recreation grounds, and Bourley Road and Rushmoor Road turn off into the W.D. lands, the latter leading to

---

* In 1922 the 19th Royal Hussars (Queen Alexandra's Own) were amalgamated with the 15th The King's Hussars to become the 15th/19th Hussars, and the 20th Hussars amalgamated with the 14th King's Hussars to become the 14th/20th King's Hussars.

† From the collection in the Prince Consort's Library.

‡ See p. 344.

§ Many of the trees planted around Albuhera, Barrosa and Corunna Barracks were brought from Windsor Great Park and planted at the direction of General Sir Linthorn Simmons, who was Chief Engineer.

Rushmoor Arena, which covers some thirty-seven acres, with its corrugated iron fence and grandstands, in recent years deserted and derelict, the arena overgrown with lank grass and weeds, recalling but a memory of the glory of the spectacular Tattoos of pre-war days.*

Back on the main road one sees, in the distance, through the trees† on the mound known as Round Hill, the imposing equestrian statue of the Duke of Wellington, which was erected on this site in 1885. The statue represents the Duke of Wellington as he appeared at Waterloo, mounted on his favourite horse "Copenhagen," wearing the customary short cloak which the artist skilfully draped so as to give it something of the grace of classic costume. The Duke sat for the sculptor,‡ Mr. Matthew Coles Wyatt, at his studio in the Harrow Road, London, and the initials of the artist's name, Matthew Coles Wyatt—M.C.W.—form the embroidery of the saddle cloth.

The statue stands on the top of Round Hill, the slopes of which are covered with rhododendron bushes, fir and silver birch trees. These, planted in 1887, grew up through the years and, by 1946, had almost obscured the statue from view. In 1947 the military authorities had some of these trees and bushes cut back so that once again the impressive monument can be clearly seen from the Farnborough Road and Wellington Avenue. The statue stands upon a red corshill stone plinth—on either side of which is the single word "Wellington"—which is surrounded by a circle of sixteen cannon barrels sunk into

* Early in June, 1950, public attention was focused on Rushmoor Arena when it was learned that contractors were engaged in cleaning up, repairing and renovating the famous arena and its stands. In July it was officially announced that the Aldershot Tattoo would be revived in 1951 as part of the Army's contribution to the Festival of Britain, and so the famous Rushmoor Arena would once again revert to its pre-war glories. In November, however, it was announced by the Secretary of State for War that the Tattoo would not take place after all owing to the Army's commitments in 1951.

† The belt of firs on the west of the Farnborough Road was planted at the instigation of the Prince Consort to prevent sand blowing from the Long Valley across the hutted camp.

‡ There would, however, appear to be some doubt about this fact. The General Committee formed at the invitation of King Edward VII when Prince of Wales in 1884, to consider the future of the statue had the authority of the 2nd Duke of Wellington to state "his illustrious father did *not* sit to Wyatt for the statue and that the horse was modelled, *not* from 'Copenhagen,' but from a thoroughbred named 'Recovery,' three years after the death of the famous charger" (*The Times*, 28th March, 1884). But the Duke of Rutland, writing to *The Times* (dated 29th March, 1884) referring to this statement, quoted a letter from himself to Lord Melbourne (then Prime Minister), dated May, 1839, wherein it stated that it was "The intention to represent His Grace as he appeared on the evening of the 18th of June, 1815, towards the close of the Battle of Waterloo, and His Grace has been so obliging as to meet our wishes by sitting to the artist in the costume he then wore"; and stated further that a report of the Sub-Committee (of the Wellington Statue Committee, dated 14th July, 1839, recorded ". . . and in order to render the drawing as perfect as the nature of such a design would admit, His Grace has been so good as to honour Mr. Wyatt with several sittings" (*The Times*, 29th March, 1884).

the ground and linked by an iron chain affixed to wooden balls sunk into the mouths of the cannons. At the foot of the front of the plinth is a plaque bearing the inscription :

> 1846   Erected at Hyde Park Corner, London.
> 1885   Re-erected here and handed over to the
> charge of the Aldershot Division by
> H.R.H. Prince of Wales by order of
> H.M. Queen Victoria.
>   Matthew Coles Wyatt, Sculptor.

Round Hill is surrounded by an iron fence, and by the entrance gate is a notice which reads :

> These Grounds and all in them are placed
> under the protection of the Troops and
> Inhabitants who are requested to assist
> in preserving them.

The statue has stood now on its present site for sixty-four years and it is without doubt Aldershot's most famous landmark. Its site was appropriately chosen, and it has throughout the years been a symbol of Aldershot's progress. The symbolism of the Duke's arm pointing out towards the military training areas, as if ordering "Forward," has been an inspiration to all those who have passed below the monument. Some six generations of soldiers have marched past the statue to train for their primary task of defending our country and our Empire in time of war. Many thousands of troops throughout the years have looked up at "The Duke" and cannot have been unconscious of the inspiration the statue has conveyed.

Helmeted Dragoons, Hussars in their plumed busbies, Lancers with their fluttering pennants, have trotted by amid the jingle and metallic rattle of appointments and accoutrements. With the rumble and scrape of the wheels of their guns and limbers on the sand and gravel, Artillerymen have ridden by ; column after column of scarlet-coated Infantry, with their shakos and spiked helmets, have crunched past on the road to the Long Valley. Every arm of the Service in the bright martial colours of days of yore have marched that way. With the changing years, khaki-clad columns have passed, still the crunch of marching men, still the jingle of trotting cavalry and then, later, the columns of dark green vehicles, the tracks of the carriers and the metallic rattle of the armour, as Churchill tanks follow the well-trodden military path still overlooked by the statue of the great man who led our armies to victory in India, Portugal, Spain and the Low Countries nearly a hundred and fifty years ago.

On through the sixty-four years men have passed "The Duke," passed him *en route* to every quarter of the globe, many of them to rest for ever in the sands of the Nile valley, the rock-strewn mountains of the Tirah, the acrid veldt of the Transvaal, the mud of Passchendaele, the foothills of Judea, the farmlands of Picardy, the Lybian wastes, the Burmese jungle and the beaches of Normandy. "The Duke" has "seen" them all—standing on that hill which overlooks the great military centre of the Empire, which is Aldershot, fulfilling the wish expressed by a writer in the *Illustrated London News* in 1846 when describing the erection of the statue at Hyde Park Corner— "destined we trust for centuries to commemorate the bravery of the British hero, the skill of the British Artist and the gratitude of the British Nation."

Surely today the symbolic statue of the Duke has, in consequence of the site on which it stands, taken on a fuller meaning ; for identified with it today is the ever-green memory of those countless British soldiers who have marched passed "The Duke" to earn the eternal gratitude of the nation for the part they have played throughout the years in keeping our country and Empire safe against all comers.

To the south of the road which winds below the Wellington statue, on rising ground, stands the Royal Garrison Church of All Saints. It is an imposing edifice. Its dominating tower, with a pyramidal roof, is 121 feet high and is one of the landmarks of "The Camp." It has for many years been familiarly known as the "Red Church" from the red brick from which it is built. Time, however, has dulled the original brightness of the brick, and the tower and walls are now mellowed, and a bright creeper has grown up its sides which, as its leaves change with the seasons, adds dignity to the building. One can appreciate the reason for its being known among both soldiers and civilians as the "Red Church," for it must have been a great contrast to the surrounding barrack buildings of yellow brick with grey slate roofs, and in the days before it became almost obscured by the trees within its precincts it was a dominating feature of "The Camp." Old prints and engravings give the church more prominence than it has in fact today, for, although it stands on rising ground, it does not stand out as it did in the latter half of last century.

The church is reached from the Farnborough Road opposite Wellington Avenue by a gravel path leading between an impressive avenue of cedar trees, flanking lawns on either side. At the top of the path below the east window is a stone memorial cross erected in memory of Colonel Bonar Millet Dean, Deputy Adjutant-General at the Cape of Good Hope, formerly commanding the 1st Bn. 19th

Princess of Wales's Own Regiment,* who was killed at the age of forty-six while "gallantly leading the attack at Laing's Nek on the 18th of January 1881." The memorial was erected by his brother officers and friends "in remembrance of a good and brave officer."

One enters the church through the porchways on the north and south of the building, the south entrance being known as the 1st Division Porchway, for here is a large wooden, iron-bound cross, a memorial on which is carved the inscription : "In memory of officers, N.C.Os. and Men of the 1st Division killed in action near High Wood during September, 1916."

This wooden cross was originally constructed and erected in High Wood by the 23rd Field Company, R.E., as a memorial to the officers and men of the Division who fell on the Somme. The cross was made from timber obtained from ruins in Bazentin. In the summer of 1927 the cross was brought to England and set up outside the Aldershot Headquarter offices of the 1st Division in Pennefathers Road. In January, 1939, the 23rd Field Company, R.E., then stationed in Gibraltar Barracks, reconstructed the porchway of the church and moved the cross to its present position. The story of the cross is told on a small brass tablet on the inside wall of the porch.

The impressive interior of the church is rich in military history, its memorials recalling many a campaign and action now almost forgotten, deeds of heroism, famous battles and regiments, and individual officers and men who served their country well.

In the chancel hang the Colours of the 37th,† 62nd‡ and 70th§ Regiments, now but pieces of faded, ragged silk clinging to the network on which they are sewn—one of those of the 37th Regiment being but a remnant, a shred some eighteen inches in length, truly an example of those described in Sir Edward Hamley's famous lines :

A moth-eaten rag, on a worm-eaten pole,
It does not look likely to stir a man's soul.
'Twas the deeds that were done, 'neath that moth-eaten rag,
When the pole was a staff, and the rag was a flag.

The two Colours of the 37th Regiment are those actually carried during the Indian Mutiny, and this is commemorated in the great stained-glass east window above the high altar, which is a memorial to the "Officers, Non Commissioned Officers and Privates of the 37th North Hants Regiment" who were killed or died on service during

---

* Now The Green Howards (Alexandra, Princess of Wales's Own Yorkshire Regiment).
† Now 1st Bn. The Royal Hampshire Regiment.
‡ Now 1st Bn. The Wiltshire Regiment.
§ Now 2nd Bn. The East Surrey Regiment.

the Mutiny, 1857-1858. The design of the window incorporates the Regimental Crest and a reproduction of the Colours as they were at the time.

The Colour of the 62nd Regiment, now the 1st Bn. The Wiltshire Regiment, lodged in the church in May, 1865, was carried by the Regiment in the Crimea. It was presented to the 62nd at Winchester in April, 1848, by Major-General Lord Fitzclarence.

On both sides of the altar is the memorial of the Royal Army Chaplains' Department, to the memory of the chaplains to the forces of all denominations who lost their lives during the 1914-1918 war. The memorial is in the form of oak and alabaster panelling the alabaster portions bearing in the centre the badge of the Department in purple and gold mosaic. Set into blue mosaic work along the top of the panels is the inscription, "To the Glory of God and in Memory of the Officers of the Royal Army Chaplains' Department who gave their lives in the Great War 1914-18." The oak panels bear the names of 172 chaplains. This memorial was unveiled by General the Earl of Cavan, then Chief of the Imperial General Staff, and dedicated by the Right Rev. Bishop J. Taylor Smith, then Chaplain-General to the Forces, on All Saints' Eve, 31st October, 1923. In the tiled floor of the sanctuary are inlaid sixteen memorial tiles, also to Chaplains to the Forces. A stained glass window on the north wall of the chancel is a memorial to Lieutenant James Fergusson, Adjutant of the 21st Royal North British Fusiliers,* who was lost in the mail steamer *Chebuba* between Calcutta and Rangoon, in 1869.

By the chancel steps stands the brass lectern given to the church by Colonel Samuel Bowen Bevington of the 3rd Volunteer Battalion of the Queen's Royal Regiment, in memory of Captain Samuel Bevington of the 2nd Bn. The Queen's, who died in March, 1896. Opposite is the oak pulpit, a memorial to Major-General Sir James Alleyne, Royal Engineers (1849-1899), and in the centre stands an oak faldstool bearing the carved inscription :

In memory of the gallant men of the
25th Division who gave their lives for
England in France and Flanders in
1916-17-18. 623 Officers, 12663 Other
Ranks—I have fought a good fight
I have kept the faith.

At the end of the nave, below the west window (which is a memorial to General Sir John Pennefather, Colonel of the 22nd Regiment,† Governor of Chelsea Hospital and G.O.C. of the Division at

---

* Now The Royal Scots Fusiliers.
† Now The Cheshire Regiment.

Aldershot, 1860-1864, who died in 1872), stands a life-sized marble bust of Lieutenant-General the Hon. Sir James Yorke Scarlett. The bust is on a stone plinth flanked by two life-sized figures in the full-dress uniforms of troopers of the 5th Dragoon Guards and the 18th Hussars, regiments in which General Scarlett served. Both figures are wearing the V.C., the Crimea War Medal and the Long Service and Good Conduct Medal. On the plinth is a central panel bearing the inscription :

To the Memory of
Lieut. Gen. the Honble
Sir James Yorke Scarlett G.C.B.
Commander of the Legion of Honour
&c.   &c.   &c.
Colonel of the 5th Dragoon Guards
He commanded
The Heavy Cavalry Brigade at Balaclava
on the 25th of October 1854
and was consecutively
Lieut.Governor of Portsmouth
Adjutant General to the Forces
and
Commander of the Aldershot Division
He was 2nd Son of
James, first Lord Abinger
and was Educated at Eton
and Trinity College, Cambridge.
He entered the Army in 1818
and was appointed Cornet
in the 18th Hussars
and afterwards to the 5th Dragoon Guards
which he commanded
for upwards of 14 years
This monument is erected
by some of his numerous friends
and Companions in Arms
who knew and respected his work
His gallantry and his kindly nature
Born 1st Feb. 1799 Died 6th Decr 1871.

On the right and left of this monument are groups of memorial wall plaques of cavalry regiments and memorials to individual cavalry-men. These plaques are grouped by regiments, and there is a group of seven erected by the 10th Royal Hussars. One is a marble plaque with a mosaic border in memory of those who lost their lives in Afghanistan, 1879, which includes the names of thirty-eight who died from cholera in June, 1879, forty-seven drowned in the Cabul river on 31st March in the same year, and sixteen others who died elsewhere in the campaign. There is a similar plaque in memory of one officer and twenty-seven N.C.Os. and men killed in action in South Africa, 1899-1902, and one officer and fifty N.C.Os. and men who died of disease during the campaign. A third plaque bears the names of two officers and four N.C.Os. and men killed in the Sudan Campaign of 1884. Above these memorials runs a narrow strip of mosaic erected by the regiment in memory of Henry Cornish, M.D., late 10th Royal Hussars, killed at Majuba Hill, and Corporal Thomas David Hawkins and Privates John Evans, Hobert Dengate and Henry Milner, who died serving with the Light Camel Corps during the Nile Expedition of 1884-1885.

Near by are the brass plaques in memory of 9th Lancers killed in the Afghan War in the Chardeh Valley on 11th December, 1879, and on the Siah Sung Heights two days later, and also those who died on service during the South African War.

Among the other Cavalry regimental memorials is a large brass plaque on which are engraved a sword, carbine, pouch-belt and busby of the 4th Hussars, and the names of five officers, twenty-one W.Os. and N.C.Os., three trumpeters and sixty-three privates who died in India between 1867 and 1878. On another brass memorial bearing the crest and battle honours of the 12th Lancers are inscribed the names of five officers and sixty W.Os., N.C.Os. and privates who died in South Africa, 1899-1902.

There is a group of regimental memorials of the 17th Duke of Cambridge's Own Lancers, each bearing the silver skull and crossbones badge; two are similar in style, one in memory of the six officers and ninety-three other ranks killed or died on service during the South African War, the other* to the eleven officers and one hundred other ranks who fell in the 1914-1918 war and to eighteen members of the regiment who lost their lives serving in other regiments into which they were commissioned during the war. Between these two memorials is a smaller plaque erected* to the memory of three officers and one N.C.O. "Killed on Active Service in Ireland 1920-22," whilst near by is a small oval marble memorial on which is the regimental crest set above crossed lances, erected in 1881 in memory of two officers and five other ranks who "fell or died in Zululand 1879." The regimental memorial of the 1939-1945 war hangs near by, and this takes the form of a framed handwritten list giving the names of nineteen officers and one hundred and thirty W.Os., N.C.Os. and men, together with the names of six attached personnel, who lost their lives during the late war.

---

* Unveiled by Field-Marshal Earl Haig in 1922.

Among the many wall tablets of marble and brass is a memorial to
Julian Henry Layard, Lieutenant of the 37th North Hants Regiment,*
Military Attaché to the British Embassy, Constantinople, who died
of fever in September, 1877, whilst serving with the Turkish forces
under Suleiman Pasha in the Shipka Pass. Near by, in the chancel,
are memorials to John George Drake, Esq., of the 4th Royal Irish
Dragoon Guards, who died in Aldershot in 1868; Captain Arthur
Bennet Mesham of the Royal Dragoons (1864-1891); Captain
Arthur William Barron, who served seventeen years with the 1st
Staffordshire Regiment; Lieutenant de Lander W. de M. Thullier,
of the Cameronians, who died in 1885; and Major and Brevet Colonel
Charles Lavsada Thesiger Barron, D.S.O., Second-in-Command of
the 2nd Bn. The Cameronians, who served in Afghanistan, 1880, in
Egypt, 1882, the Sudan, 1885, and died at Brindisi in 1892 on his way
home to England.

On the wall by the vestry door is a brass erected by the N.C.Os.
and men of the 32nd Light Infantry† "in affectionate memory" of
Captain and Quartermaster Edward Vaughan of that Regiment, who
died in South Camp in 1881; and a tablet in memory of Lieutenant
Napier Burnett Lindsay, Adjutant of the 1st Bn. The Royal Irish
Fusiliers, who was killed whilst hunting near Odiham in 1909. Wall
tablets have been erected along both the north and south aisles, and in
the former these include a marble tablet inscribed:

Sacred to the memory of
Gnr. Jos. Tubb and Bombr Jno. McDermott
who died on 29th Octr and 30th Novr. 1862
Armr Sergt Jno Venn who died
5th Novr 1865 Gnr Saml Browning
Drvr G. H. A. Crocker who died on
the 24th March 1866 Gunr Thos Grigmiles
who died 21st Jany 1867 of G Batty
8th Bde Royal Regt of Artillery.

This tablet was erected by their comrades. Above is another tablet
in memory of Br. Collar Maker Phillip Mason, two gunners and one
driver, all of "I" Battery, R.H.A., who died on service in Ireland,
1886-1889.

In this aisle are other memorials—to Lieutenant Edward Conduit
Bicknell, of the 38th (1st Staffs) Regiment, who died in Aldershot in
1870; Major-General Sir George Henry Marshall, K.C.B., who
commanded the Royal Artillery in the South African War, and who
died in Camberley in 1909; and a large brass memorial tablet to

---

* Now 1st Bn. The Royal Hampshire Regiment.
† Now 1st Bn. The Duke of Cornwall's Light Infantry.

Major-General Sir John Eardley Wilmot Inglis, K.C.B., Colonel of the 32nd Regiment, commander of H.M. Forces in the Ionian Islands, "who by his enduring fortitude and preserving gallantry in the defence of the residency at Lucknow for eighty seven days against an overwhelming force maintained the honour of the British Arms and contributed to the triumph of his Country over a cruel and treacherous enemy." He died in Homburg in September, 1862, and the tablet was erected by his brother officers serving in the Ionian Islands "in just admiration of his public services and in affectionate remembrance of his private worth."

Near by is the 1914-1918 war memorial to all ranks of the 2nd Division, and a brass in memory of Colonel Joseph Noble Beasley, Lieutenant-Colonel Commanding the 1st Bn. Royal Irish Fusiliers, in which he served for twenty-nine years, and died in Egypt in 1882, and to the memory of nineteen N.C.Os. and men of the Battalion who died during the Egyptian Campaign.

Along the aisle is the 1914-1918 memorial of the 19th Hussars (Queen Alexandra's Own) and a brass tablet to the memory of four officers and seventy-eight N.C.Os. and men of the 19th Hussars who fell at Brockhurst Spruit in the Transvaal on 20th December, 1880, and sixty N.C.Os. and men who lost their lives in the campaigns in South Africa, 1879-80.

There is also a small brass memorial to Lance-Sergeant William Clark and Privates Mark Healey and William Barnes of the 19th Hussars, who were "drowned at Aldershot doing their duty on the 4th of June, 1912. The two former lost their lives trying to save their comrade."*

The stained-glass windows of the north aisle are all memorials, one being erected "In memory of Percy Harry Stanley Barrow C.B., C.M.G. Colonel Commanding the 19th Hussars by his comrades in the march across the Bayuda Desert for the relief of Khartoum in January and February 1885 as a record of his heroism and devotion." Below the window is also a tablet erected in his memory by the N.C.Os. and men of the 19th Hussars "in token of their grief for his loss" when he died in Cairo in January, 1886, from wounds received in action with the regiment at El Teb. Another window is a memorial to two officers, one sergeant, one trumpeter and fourteen privates of the Royal Dragoons, who lost their lives in the Nile Expedition of 1884-5.

A guidon of The Royals, placed in the church in October, 1926, is affixed to the wall near this window.

There are a window and a tablet "In memory of a soldier a gentleman

---

* This tragedy occurred at the "Horse Swimming Pool." See p. 380.

and a Christian," General Sir Henry Dalrymple White, K.C.B., Colonel
of the 6th Inniskilling Dragoons, who joined the Regiment in 1838
and "commanded it with distinguished gallantry in the Heavy Cavalry
charge at Balaclava and through the Crimea." He was later A.A.G.
of Cavalry, 1863-1865, and commanded the Cavalry Brigade at The
Curragh and in Aldershot, 1866-1871. Another window is in memory
of General Robert Wardlaw, C.B., and was erected by his old comrades,
officers, N.C.Os. and private soldiers of the Royal Dragoons in which
he served thirty-two years, during twelve of which he was in command.

In the south aisle are the stained-glass memorial window erected by
all ranks of the 89th Princess Victoria's Regiment in 1867 to the
memory of those who died serving their country under the old Colours
deposited in this church, and a new window depicting the figures of
St. Helen and St. Dorothy erected in 1947, with a memorial tablet to
Helen Peirce, O.B.E., "who for forty years devoted her life and labours
to the Welfare of soldiers and their families." These memorials were
erected by "all regiments and Corps of the British Army and her
many friends and admirers."

A third window, with a tablet below, is a memorial to five officers
of the Control Department who died on the West Coast of Africa
"during the campaign against the King of Ashantee 1873-4."

There are a number of wall tablets and plaques along the walls of
the aisle, including one of the earliest of the memorials in the church—
to Henry Carline, Esq., who was for thirteen years assistant surgeon
to the Carabiniers, and died at Ballincollig Barracks in September,
1851. There is a marble tablet with a dragoon's helmet, trumpet,
sword and two guidons in relief erected by his brother officers in
memory of Lieutenant Archibald Douglas Monteath, of the 3rd
Dragoon Guards, who died in Dublin in 1853. Near by is a brass
tablet on which is engraved an officer's helmet set on crossed swords
which was erected "by the N.C.Os. and Soldiers of 'E' Company
in remembrance of their captain"—Captain Charles Whittle, of the
1st Bn. The Leicestershire Regiment, who was killed in a hunting
accident in January, 1886.

Along the aisle is a marble tablet with a mosaic border in memory
of one officer, two N.C.Os. and eleven privates of the 5th Dragoon
Guards who died whilst serving as volunteers in the Sudan, 1882-
1885, and brass memorial tablets to Major Charles Cobry, of the 68th
Durham Light Infantry, who died near Allahabad in March, 1884;
Eric Barnes, late of the 13th Hussars, who served in South Africa,
taking part in the relief of Ladysmith; Lieutenant-Colonel Arthur
Hames Nixon, who "had served with distinction and gallantry in
the Crimea and the Indian Mutiny" and who died in Aldershot in 1875

whilst commanding the 3rd Rifle Brigade; Lieutenant Henry Charlton Chatworth Mustrrs, of the 3rd King's Own Hussars, who died on active service in West Africa with the Royal Niger Company in February, 1897; and Captain Mervyn Crawshay, of the 5th Dragoon Guards, who fell in action near Ypres in October, 1914. There is also a memorial, erected by his parents, to Lieutenant Henry Thomas Renny, of the Argyll and Sutherland Highlanders, who died in West Africa in 1897; and next to it a tablet in memory of his father, General Henry Renny, C.S.I., Colonel of the 81st Regiment, who died in 1900.

Among this group of memorials is a brass in memory of General Sir James Hope Grant, who died in March, 1875, whilst in command of the Aldershot Division, and a brass tablet, a memorial to thirty-six N.C.Os. and men of the 6th Dragoon Guards who died in the Afghan War of 1879-1880. The names include a sergeant instructor of fencing, a farrier-major and two hospital sergeants.

Other memorials in the south aisle are to Godfrey Knight Robinson, Quartermaster of the 5th Lancers, who died in 1888; W. B. Edmons, Veterinary Surgeon of the 9th Lancers, who died in 1876; Captain William Clayton Clayton of the same regiment, who died at Delhi on Christmas Day, 1876; and Lieutenant-General Richard Buckley Prettejohn, C.B., who died in 1891 when Colonel of the 13th Hussars. This memorial was erected by officers of the 14th King's Hussars, with whom he served in "the South Mahratta Country," 1844-1845, in the Punjab, 1848-1849, at Ramnuggur "with the charging Squadrons," Chillianwallah, and Goojerat, and elsewhere in India. Here, also, are the regimental memorials of the 13th Hussars to those who fell in the South African War and the Great War.

At the east end of the south aisle is the Warriors' Memorial Chapel of St. Michael, which contains the oak panelled memorial bearing the inscription, "To honour and perpetuate the memory of those officers and other ranks of the 5th Princess Charlotte of Wales's Dragoon Guards who gave their lives in the Great War." The panels bear the crest, badge and battle honours of the regiment and the names of fourteen officers and one hundred and eighty-two W.Os., N.C.Os. and men who fell. Two guidons of the regiment hang above the memorial panels. Also from the walls hang the two Union Flags which covered the coffin of Field-Marshal Lord Roberts when he died in Flanders in 1914.

The oak altar of the chapel is a memorial to Captain Francis Mussenden Whitmore-Smith, M.C., of the Queen's Bays, who died in Cairo in February, 1924, and was given by his brother officers. The communion rails of this side chapel were presented by the 19th

2L

(Queen Alexandra's Own) Hussars, and the prayer desks were the gift of the Royal Artillery Mounted Band.

On the walls of the chapel are a number of memorial tablets, one in memory of Major Thomas Trout, who served in Spain during the Carlist War, 1836-1837, with the British Legion under Sir de Lacy Evans, and with the 7th Hussars during the Canadian Rebellion, 1838. Major Trout was for over twenty years Provost Marshal in Aldershot and died in 1881. There is another oval marble tablet to Lieutenant-Colonel Barton Parker Brown, who died at Bath in June, 1889, at the age of ninety-one. He was then one of the few surviving officers who fought at Waterloo, where he had served as a cornet in the 11th Light Dragoons, remaining with that regiment until 1838. Below is an inscription : "This tablet is placed here by a few old comrades and other officers who served or are serving in the regiment now the 11th Prince Albert's Own Hussars." Near by is a brass tablet, a memorial to Major-General John Douglas of Glenfinart, Argyllshire, C.B., Officer of the Legion of Honour and Knight of Medjide, who commanded the 11th Hussars in the charge of the Light Brigade at Balaclava, and who died in May, 1871, whilst in command of the Cavalry Brigade at Aldershot. In the chapel are also the memorial tablets to Godfrey Munday, of the 11th Hussars, who died in October, 1874, and Captain Francis Grenville Doyle, of The Bays, who died in December, 1882.

Beyond the Warriors' Chapel is one of the two south doors of the church, and in the passage-way leading to it are two small wooden wall tablets bearing the names of the twenty-six "chaplains in charge" of the church since 1863. Above the door which leads into the verger's room is a panelled memorial, surmounted by a statuette of St. George killing the Dragon, and flanked by two statuettes of St. Michael. The centre of the memorial is occupied by a marble bust of Lieutenant-General Sir Charles Crawford Fraser, K.C.B., V.C., below which is the inscription in the words of Whyte Melville :

> Wounded, Helpless, Sick, Dismounted,
> Charlie Fraser, well I knew,
> Came the worst I might have counted
> faithfully on you.

The "Red Church" holds much which is dear to the Army and to Aldershot. It is here that the annual Remembrance Services of the South African War Veterans' Association, the Old Contemptibles and the British Legion are held ; it is here, under the spreading yew trees, that the Legion's Garden of Remembrance of little wooden crosses and Flanders poppies is laid out each November.

A soldiers' church in a soldiers' town, where the regimental bands take the place of the organ at parade services, and the spirit and traditions of the British Army in its service of God, King and Country dominates the very atmosphere ; and here the singing of Sullivan's great hymn, "Onward, Christian Soldiers," and Kipling's famous "Recessional" are heard with greater feeling and emotion than perhaps in any other similar surroundings throughout the world. The Royal Garrison Church holds something which is difficult to express, for it holds something of the soul of the Army. . . .

*   *   *   *   *

Passing between the Wellington Monument and the "Red Church," with on the left Wellesley House, the residence of the G.O.C., one comes along a tree-lined road past a recreation ground—one of the original grounds laid out for the garrison in the early days of "The Camp." It was on this ground that the first Army Athletic Championship Meetings were held. The west end of the ground lies along Bourley Road, which we now follow to a junction of the road and several tracks, at the north end of which is the Royal Pavilion enclosure. These grounds are bounded on the south by the Farnborough Road and face the barrack walls and west gates of Willems and Beaumont Barracks, the main entrance to Aldershot's Royal residence lying opposite the former.

The Royal Pavilion has changed but little in the passing years. The iron railings and outbuildings and, by the main entrance, the guard-room and stables, now infrequently used, are somewhat forlorn, and are all in need of renovation. The trees and rhododendron bushes have grown and thickened, but one can still sense the atmosphere of the past as one enters by the carriage drive which winds through the well-timbered grounds and lawns edged with beds of heather. It was in deference to Queen Victoria's wishes that no attempt was made at cultivation of the grounds at the Pavilion. The tall bracken, purple foxgloves and heather grew unchecked. The tall pine trees served a double purpose : they screened the low Pavilion from the sun and intercepted the clouds of dust from the Long Valley.

One enters the Royal Pavilion from the Farnborough Road, through the iron gates, to behold a scene which appears much as it did in its earliest days. To the left are the stables, containing a row of stalls and another of loose boxes, and by the entrance is the harness room, and a covered stand where in former days the horses of visiting officers could be tethered.

On the right of the entrance is the porter's lodge, a wooden building surrounded with an overhanging roof supported by pillars, around which rambler roses are entwined. Beyond the lodge is the guard-room, another wooden building with a projecting roof. The building accommodated a guard of eight N.C.Os. and men. Whilst the Royal Family were in residence two sentries were usually posted, one at the main entrance, the other on the terrace outside the main entrance to the Pavilion.

It is interesting today to see the scratched inscriptions on the rear window of the guard-room which prove that the same glass is in place as existed as far back as 1884, and now identifies some of the regiments who have provided the Pavilion guards. These inscriptions have been scratched with a knife or some sharp-pointed instrument on the pane by soldiers idling the time away between sentry duties. Among the men and units so identified are "Francis J. O'Shea, 18th Royal Irish,* 1881," who appears to have been the most in-dustrious of those who have left their marks to this day; "T. Newman, 97th Regt."†; "2nd Bn. Rifle Brigade, Oct. 6th 1884"; "8th King's"‡; "3rd Royal Fusiliers"; and the 44th,§ 48th‖ and 88th¶ Regiments. Following on this precedent created by the "Privates of the Line" of the eighties, there stands today, also at the rear of the guard-room, a disused sentry-box containing the pencilled or carved titles of some dozen or so regiments of the Canadian Army who used the Pavilion during the war years.

The Pavilion, a single-storeyed building of bungalow style, is built in the shape of an E without the centre arm. Its pine-wood walls are painted white, whilst the pair of shutters to each window is in green. The main entrance is below a porch leading from the quadrangle, which is actually in the rear of the building. In the entrance of the tiled quadrangle is a square goldfish pond, which was installed whilst the Duke and Duchess of Gloucester were in residence from the end of 1935 until 1939, at the time when the Duke was a student at the Staff College. The principal front of the building faces north. The central room, with a large bay window, was the main reception room, now the ante-room of the officers' mess of the 13 Command Workshops, R.E.M.E. Leading from this to the right is the room which was the Royal drawing-room, now the main ante-room of the mess. On the left of the reception room is a room that was used once by the Prince Consort as a study.

At the rear of these rooms is a long passage-way which links the

---

* The Royal Irish Regiment: disbanded July, 1922.
† Now 2nd Bn. Queen's Own Royal West Kent Regiment.
‡ Now The King's Regiment.
§ Now 1st Bn. The Essex Regiment.
‖ Now 1st Bn. The Northamptonshire Regiment.
¶ Later 1st Bn. The Connaught Rangers; disbanded July, 1922.

wings of the building, and from which open a number of small rooms now used for officers' accommodation.

The west wing was originally the private rooms of the Royal Family, and the east wing contains the dining-room, forty feet in length, now the officers' mess.

There has been but little change made in the decoration of the Pavilion, since the Queen decided, on the formation of "The Camp," to have the residence built on the same lines as those provided for the soldiers. Some striped chintz hangings were used; the furniture, which was mostly of deal, plainly but solidly built, was still in use until recent years.

The kitchen and servants' quarters are situated in detached buildings which are sited to the right rear of the east wing at a lower level down the slope from the plateau on which the main building is sited. The kitchen is connected to the pavilion by an underground passage, which half-way along has a glass roof; it is along this passage that the food is carried to a lift which comes up to the servery behind the dining-room.

The carriage drive winds in a gradual ascent of about thirty feet to the terrace where the Pavilion stands. The main entrance faces south and overlooks a belt of firs. From the north terrace a lawn, bounded by rhododendron bushes, falls away to a copse, and through the gaps in the trees the view extends over the sand, heather and firs of the Long Valley.

During the late war the Royal Pavilion was turned over to the care of Aldershot District and it became an officers' mess, to help accommodate the influx of officers which stretched existing accommodation to its limits between 1940 and 1944. The pavilion was occupied by various units of the Canadian Army Overseas. From March, 1944, until they moved off on 10th June to participate in the operation on Normandy beach-head, the Pavilion was occupied by the H.Q. of the 11th Armoured Division. They were followed by the H.Q. of the 1st Polish Armoured Division for a few days—the 18th to 30th July, 1944. From November, 1944, until June, 1946, the Pavilion became "B" Mess of H.Q., Aldershot District. It was then, from January to July, 1948, the officers' mess of the 2nd Royal Tank Regiment, which was stationed in Badajos Barracks at the west end of Wellington Avenue.

In July, 1948, the Regiment moved to Cove, and on 21st July the 3rd Bn. Coldstream Guards marched into Badajos Barracks and the officers took over the mess established in the Royal Pavilion, thereby having the distinction of being the first unit of the Household Brigade to so occupy this Royal residence. When the Guards left Aldershot for Windsor in May, 1949, the pavilion became the officers' mess of 13 Command Workshops, R.E.M.E.

Behind the grounds of the Pavilion to the left lies Pavilion Hill, and from this rising ground one looks across the stretch of sand hills, covered with bracken, gorse and firs.* Beyond Cheese Hill, Brown Loaf Hill, Skirmishing Hill and Windy Gap Hill rise the steep slopes of Caesar's Camp, with the cluster of firs known as Jubilee Clump, planted to commemorate Queen Victoria's Jubilee in 1887, crowning the crest of this dominating feature. Caesar's Camp forms a natural safety guard behind the rifle ranges which lie along Steep Bottom below Steep Hill, south of the Bourley Road. These ranges run back to the six-hundred-yard firing points and were among the first ranges to be laid out in the Aldershot training area. It was here that the first Championship Meetings of the Army Rifle Association were held in the days before the opening of the N.R.A. Ranges at Bisley.

To the south lie several ancient earthworks, and to the north-wets lies the expanse of sandy waste of the Long Valley† and Eelmore Plain, an unusual stretch of loose sand broken only occasionally by a small plantation and clumps of coarse grass, heather and bracken. The training ground of many thousands of British soldiers, this area has been used for exercises for almost a hundred years. The sand is now marked by the criss-cross patterns left by tank tracks and wheels where once cavalry and horse-drawn artillery rode and manoeuvred amid the clouds of dust driven up by the galloping hooves.

Moving on to the rising ground of Rushmoor Hill and looking westward, one has a clear view of Jubilee Hill, Jubilee Plantation and across country to the camping grounds at Firs Hill. As far as the eye

---

* Described by Queen Victoria in her Journal, 30th July, 1856, as "so Scotch looking" (Royal Archives, Windsor).

† The resemblance between the Long Valley and the valley of the Alma led to its choice in 1929 as the location for the re-enacting of the charge of the Light Brigade in the Gainsborough film "Balaclava," first shown in 1930, which starred Cyril McLaglen, Benita Hume, Alf Goddard and Miles Mander. The charge was directed by Captain H. Oakes-Jones, M.B.E., F.S.A., the producer of the Aldershot Tattoos, who acted as the official military adviser to Gainsborough films. The officers, men and horses came from the 1st Cavalry Brigade, and every effort was made to ensure accuracy in military and historical detail. The soldier-actors entered into the spirit of the occasion, and there were numerous touches of realism which added to the authenticity of the scenes. Dummy men and horses were carried among the charging ranks so that when the Russian "shells" burst among the galloping horses the dummies were dropped, to be seen lying among the drifting smoke. Other dummies in Russian uniforms were propped against the guns ; these were marked with labels so that they could be pierced by the lances or cut down by the swords of the charging cavalry. Trick riders fell from their horses before the cameras, and "shell bursts" were detonated by electricity and fired by "dead" men lying on the battlefield. The same area was once again chosen in 1950 for the filming of battle scenes for the film "Lili Marlene."

can see to the south and west lies the wild heathland which is typical of the area. The country has an all-the-year-round attraction, for the gorse, broom and firs are green at all times. The birches and silver birches and larches, too, have an attraction, whether in leaf or when they have been shorn of their foliage by the winds which sweep across the open country in the winter months. In spring the heathland is brightened by the yellow bloom of the gorse and broom; in summer, the bright purple of the clumps and stretches of heather; and in the autumn, the brown, red and gold tints of the dying birch leaves and bracken, mingled with the constant green of the firs and gorse.

Continuing along the track at the foot of Rushmoor Hill one is overlooking, on the left, the depression of Claycart Bottom. Here amid a stretch of firs and birches lies Batt's Hog Stye, the site of an ancient pre-Roman encampment. This ancient earthwork is difficult to find without the aid of a map or careful direction. It lies to the immediate north of a camping ground—the permanent camp constructions and corrugated iron administrative installations adjoining the boundary wire fence which encloses the site. The ancient earthwork is obscured by birch and fir trees and covered with heather and bracken. The site is marked at three of the corners by small notice boards, which contain a notice prohibiting digging for any purposes. The earthwork is in the shape of a square, rounded at the corners, with four distinct mounds conforming to this shape around the centre, which is approximately two hundred feet square. The outline of the earthwork is clearly marked by the mounds, and a footpath runs across the north-west corner.

Back to the Farnborough Road again, the old London–Winchester turnpike road, one passes southwards along the line of railings and hedges of the Royal Pavilion and the yellow-grey walls of the old Cavalry Barracks. Away to the right the bush, heather, and gorse-covered country leads away to the original Aldershot Heath. On the east lies Chetwode Terrace, and below, behind Cranmore Lane, work is proceeding on a new housing estate, and bricks and mortar are claiming the old nursery and kitchen gardens.

As one approaches the County and Borough boundary, Anglesey House* is seen on the right of the road, lying back behind a tree-lined fence. Today the house is the official residence of the Deputy District Commander, and was formerly that of the Commander of the Cavalry Brigade quartered in Beaumont, Willems and Warburg Barracks. The house is an imposing residence, with its lawns and gardens, and stables in the rear of the house, which stands at the foot of Hungry Hill, which is on the Surrey side of the county boundary. The County

* See p. 299.

boundary runs along the south side of the grounds of Anglesey House, along the foot of Hungry Hill, across a line of ancient earthworks which straddle Windy Gap, and continues along a footpath which traverses Long Bottom from the Farnborough Road, commencing just north of Anglesey House. This path becomes but a track of loose stones and flints as one passes the house and it winds upwards, bordered by gorse and broom, to join a well-marked footpath leading down from Greenham's Hill. This path was known locally and unofficially for many years as "The King's Way," for in the early part of the century it was cleared and widened to enable King Edward VII to drive along this route from the Royal Pavilion to watch the sending of messages by the R.E. Signals from one of the first wireless installations in Aldershot and to witness the cavalrymen swimming their horses in the "Horse Swimming Pool." This "pool," covering over two and a half acres, was a pond situated just off the pathway in Long Bottom and was used for this form of cavalry training for many years. The pool has now dried up, but there are small patches of water still lying among the young birch trees and shrubs which have grown up over its bed.

In all directions from this point the heather, gorse, sandhills and firs extend as far as the eye can see—the Military lands, unchanged by the passage of time—a vista which is a setting for all phases in local history: the drovers with their herds ; the turf cutters ; the gipsies ; the lone horsemen wrapped in their cloaks as they ride along the old tracks from Odiham to the turnpike road ; Cromwell's cavalry patrols ; Regiments of Foot, Hussars, Dragoons, Lancers, in file or in echelon or single vedettes ; the scarlet-coated soldier and his lass a-walking on a summer's eve ; khaki-clad infantrymen in Bren carriers, tanks—all set against the unchanging scene throughout the years.

The County and Borough boundary continues from Long Bottom in a south-easterly direction amid the gorse, broom, bracken, and sandy footpaths to a point some 150 yards north of Sandy Hill, and then turns sharply north-west to cut across the promontory of Caesar's Camp at the northern end of Bricksbury Hill.

On the Surrey side of the boundary the ground rises steeply to Hungry Hill, which on the Ordnance Survey maps is marked as the site of a redoubt and is 559 feet above sea-level, and the line of high ground along the 550-foot contour leading westward to Sandy Hill.

From the summit of Hungry Hill, by a concrete pillar which is an Ordnance Survey Triangulation Station, one can obtain one of the most magnificent views in the South of England, giving an uninterrupted all-round panorama of the country for many miles radius.

To the north-west, Caesar's Camp juts out its long plateau, dominating the area; northwards, the Long Valley stretches away over the typical Aldershot country to Cove Common and Farnborough Aerodrome; to the north-east is the belt of firs and pines of the Royal Pavilion enclosure, and the tower of the "Red Church"; to the left lie the lines of barracks of South Camp; then, turning eastwards, Aldershot Town clusters in the dip below the high ground. Farther afield the panorama embraces Hindhead to the south and Finchampstead Ridges to the north.

One experiences a feeling of exhilaration, having reached this point of vantage, high up above the surrounding country, the fresh winds blowing on one's face, to look down on to Aldershot. For miles around as far as the eye can see there is an uninterrupted view. It was to this point that many have climbed in days gone by to view the exercises and "sham fights" conducted by the "Division at Aldershot." One can visualize the scene : the thin red lines of advancing infantry ; the red dots of the skirmishers, bobbing about among the broom and heather ; the swirl of dust as the squadrons of cavalry trotted into position ; the sounds of the trumpet and bugle calls carried on the breeze ; and the rattle of musketry giving the spectators a bird's-eye view of a typical battle scene of the day. Such are the sights and sounds conjured up as one rests on this dominating feature, from which Aldershot, both Town and "Camp," can be seen laid before one like a model.

*   *   *   *   *

Such is the history of Aldershot—a past, full of achievement, which can be looked upon with pride. And such is Aldershot today—a progressive town and still a great military centre. May the years to come justify the ambitions and the anticipation for the progress of the Aldershot of the future !

*   *   *   *   *

"OUR YESTERDAYS FOLLOW US ; THEY CONSTITUTE OUR LIFE, AND THEY GIVE CHARACTER AND FORCE AND MEANING TO OUR PRESENT DEEDS."—*J. Parker.*

CHAPTER TEN

THE OTHER ALDERSHOTS

THERE are but very few, including Aldershot's own residents, who know that the English Aldershot has already given its name to three other places in the British Commonwealth : a military camp in Nova Scotia; a hamlet in Ontario ; and a township in the Wide Bay District of Queensland. It is perhaps fitting in this volume to record the following notes about the Canadian and Australian Aldershots, which have taken their name from the Borough whose story has now been told. It is with some pride, and sensibility of that feeling of brotherhood which links all peoples of our great Commonwealth of Nations, that these facts about the other Aldershots are included, as they justly should be, in this story of Aldershot.

ALDERSHOT CAMP, NOVA SCOTIA, CANADA

Aldershot Camp is one of Canada's older military training areas. It is situated just outside the town of Kentville, seventy miles west of Halifax in the province of Nova Scotia. It was first established in 1870 as a rifle range, but later developed into a military camp and was named "Aldershot Camp" after the then already famous military centre of the British Army in England.

As early as 1882 it was used as a Brigade Camp, and was then considered the most convenient and suitable ground for a large military camp in any of the Maritime Provinces of Canada. Its use as a summer training camp for militia units has continued ever since.

During the 1914-1918 war, Aldershot Camp was greatly expanded as a training area for units of the Canadian Expeditionary Force and later for men called up for service under the Military Service Act, 1917. In the years of peace following the First World War, Aldershot Camp reverted to its pre-war role as a summer training camp for units of the Militia, and the rifle range was also used by Provincial Rifle Associations.

Following the outbreak of war in 1939, steps were taken for the organization of an Infantry Training Centre at Aldershot Camp, and during the war years the camp functioned both as a training and a staging camp for troops moving overseas. When hostilities ceased it served again as a staging camp for troops returning from service in Europe.

The present area of Aldershot Camp is approximately 2,800 acres. and it has a network of paved roads and more than a hundred buildings. Once again it has reverted to its peace-time role of a summer training camp for units of the Canadian Army Reserve Forces.

ALDERSHOT, ONTARIO, CANADA

Aldershot, Ontario is situated in East Flamborough township of Wentworth county. It is a hamlet with a population of some three hundred, straddling one of the main highways of Ontario two miles from the outskirts of the city of Hamilton ; a row of residential and business houses fronting the wide dual "Highway No. Two" which at this point is a continuation of "The Queen Elizabeth Way," which connects Toronto, forty-three miles away, with Hamilton and runs parallel with and not far from the waterfront of Lake Ontario, Aldershot itself lying but a mile or so from the shore.

Although not incorporated as a village, Aldershot, Ont., has a railway station on the Canadian National Railway, a post office and telegraphic agency and a sub-branch of the Royal Bank of Canada.

The village of Aldershot lies at the main highway end of "Aldershot Road," which runs down from Waterdown, situated on Highway No. 5 at the top of the escarpment at the end of the "Snake trail" which leads out from Hamilton near the famous sunken rock gardens and through beautiful countryside. "Aldershot Road," which connects the parallel Highways No. 5 and 2, runs past rushing creeks and waterfalls, around curves and up and down hills—scenery which is typical of the natural beauty spots which have been preserved in the environs of Hamilton in its unusually beautiful situation at the western tip of Lake Ontario on the land-locked Burlington Bay, now named Hamilton Harbour.

ALDERSHOT, QUEENSLAND, AUSTRALIA

Aldershot, Queensland, is now but a very small freehold township situated six miles north of Maryborough, in Burrum shire in the Wide Bay area of Queensland. In the last published Commonwealth Census taken in 1933 the population of the township was given as thirty-six persons.

There is, however, a railway station on the North Coast Railway, which was opened when the township was the site of an important

Aldershot Camp, Nova Scotia.
National Defence Photograph, Canada. [Copyright.]

Aldershot Station, Ontario, on the Canadian National Railway.
This picture and that overleaf were specially photographed for "The Story of Aldershot," by the Ontario Department
of Travel and Publicity.

ce p. 384

Highway No. 2, Aldershot, Ontario.

smelting and metallurgical works known as the Aldershot Smelting Works, operated by a London company which in about 1899 named it after Aldershot, England. The township was formed in that year when a freehold portion of the parish of Walliebum in the county of March was subdivided into sections.

The Aldershot Smelting Works which operated during the latter part of last century and until 1906, treated silver, lead and copper ores and gold concentrates from all parts of Queensland. The plant was composed of lead blast, calcining, and power-driven ore-roasting furnaces ; a circular copper matteing furnace, softening and refining plant for lead bullion ; zincing kettles and zinc retorting and cupelling furnaces. During the time that the plant was in full operation this works employed a very large number of men working three shifts per day throughout the year. The works, however, were closed down in March, 1906, owing to the fact that there were insufficient tonnages of ore available to keep the furnaces continually at work.

When the works closed down, the bulk of the buildings and residences in the vicinity were dismantled and at the present time there is very little evidence of the former existence of the important industry and thriving centre of population which grew up following the opening of the works in 1899. All that remains today is the railway station and a few residences, but it continues to bear the name which was given to it by the London company who opened and developed the area just over fifty years ago.

THE GENERAL OFFICERS COMMANDING AT ALDERSHOT

1855 TO THE PRESENT DAY

1855—1860	LIEUT.-GENERAL SIR WILLIAM T. KNOLLYS.
1860—1865	LIEUT.-GENERAL SIR JOHN L. PENNEFATHER, K.C.B.
1865—1870	LIEUT.-GENERAL HON. JAMES YORKE SCARLETT, G.C.B.
1870—1875	GENERAL SIR J. HOPE GRANT, G.C.B.
1875—1880	GENERAL SIR THOMAS M. STEELE, K.C.B.
1880—1883	GENERAL SIR DANIEL LYSONS, K.C.B.
1883—1888	LIEUT.-GENERAL SIR ARCHIBALD ALISON, BT., G.C.B.
1889—1893	LIEUT.-GENERAL SIR H. EVELYN WOOD, V.C., G.C.B., G.C.M.G.
1893—1898	GENERAL H.R.H. THE DUKE OF CONNAUGHT, K.G., K.T., K.P.
1898—1899	GENERAL THE RIGHT HON. SIR REDVERS BULLER, V.C., G.C.B.
1899	MAJOR-GENERAL KELLY KENNY.
1899—1900	GENERAL SIR A. G. MONTGOMERY MOORE, K.C.B.
1900—1901	LIEUT.-GENERAL SIR W. F. BUTLER, K.C.B.
1901 (Oct. 23-24)	MAJOR-GENERAL L. J. OLIPHANT, M.V.O.
1901	GENERAL THE RIGHT HON. SIR REDVERS BULLER, V.C., G.C.B.
1901—1902	LIEUT.-GENERAL SIR HENRY J. T. HILDYARD, K.C.B.
1902—1907	GENERAL SIR JOHN FRENCH, G.C.V.O., K.C.B., K.C.M.G.
1907—1912	LIEUT.-GENERAL SIR HORACE SMITH-DORRIEN, K.C.B., D.S.O.
1912—1914	LIEUT.-GENERAL SIR DOUGLAS HAIG, K.C.B., K.C.I.E., K.C.V.O.
1914—1916	MAJOR-GENERAL A. HAMILTON GORDON, C.B.
1916—1917	GENERAL SIR W. ARCHIBALD HUNTER, G.C.B., G.C.V.O., D.S.O.
1917—1919	GENERAL SIR ARCHIBALD MURRAY, G.C.M.G., K.C.B., C.V.O., D.S.O.
1919—1920	GENERAL LORD RAWLINSON, G.C.B., G.C.V.O., K.C.M.G., A.D.C.
1920—1922	GENERAL THE EARL OF CAVAN, K.P., G.C.M.G., G.C.V.O., K.C.B., A.D.C.
1922—1923	LIEUT.-GENERAL SIR T. L. N. MORLAND, K.C.B., K.C.M.G., D.S.O., A.D.C.

1923—1927	GENERAL SIR PHILIP CHETWODE, BT., K.C.B., K.C.M.G., D.S.O.
1927—1931	GENERAL SIR DAVID G. M. CAMPBELL, K.C.B., A.D.C.
1931—1933	GENERAL SIR CHARLES H. HARRINGTON, G.C.B., G.B.E., D.S.O., D.C.L., A.D.C.
1933—1937	GENERAL HON. SIR FRANCIS GATHORNE-HARDY, G.C.B., G.C.V.O., C.M.G., D.S.O., A.D.C.
1937—1939	LIEUT.-GENERAL SIR JOHN DILL, K.C.B., C.M.G., D.S.O.
1939—1940	LIEUT.-GENERAL C. N. F. BROAD, C.B., D.S.O.
1940	LIEUT.-GENERAL M. G. H. BARKER, C.B., D.S.O.
1940—1941	MAJOR-GENERAL D. G. JOHNSON, V.C., C.B., D.S.O., M.C.
1941—1944	MAJOR-GENERAL R. EVANS, C.B., M.C.
1944	MAJOR-GENERAL C. W. NORMAN, C.B.E.
1944—1945	MAJOR-GENERAL H. O. CURTIS, C.B., D.S.O., M.C.
1945—1946	MAJOR-GENERAL R. K. ROSS, C.B., D.S.O., M.C.
1946	MAJOR-GENERAL SIR NOEL G. HOLMES, K.B.E., C.B., M.C.
1946—1948	MAJOR-GENERAL J. A. BAILLON, C.B., C.B.E., M.C.
1948—	MAJOR-GENERAL W. A. DIMOLINE, C.B., C.B.E., D.S.O., M.C.

APPENDIX II

THE MAYORS OF ALDERSHOT

1922—1950

The Charter of Incorporation of the Borough was granted on 28th March, 1922. It came into operation on 1st November of that year when the first Borough Council was elected.

1922—1923	ALDERMAN ARTHUR H. SMITH, J.P.
1923—1924	ALDERMAN H. AINGER, C.C., J.P.
1924—1925	ALDERMAN N. SOLOMON, C.C., J.P.
1925—1926	ALDERMAN J. MAY, J.P.
1926—1927	COUNCILLOR E. A. UNDERWOOD, J.P.
1927—1929	COUNCILLOR (NOW SIR HUGH) FOSTER, T.D., J.P.
1929—1932	COUNCILLOR R. W. EDWARDS, C.C., J.P.
1932—1933	ALDERMAN J. A. DINES, J.P.
1933—1935	ALDERMAN W. M. R. DAVIS, M.B.E., J.P.
1935—1937	COUNCILLOR (NOW ALDERMAN) W. J. NORTH, C.C., J.P.
1937—1944	COUNCILLOR A. H. J. STROUD, M.B.E., C.C., J.P.
1944—1946	ALDERMAN J. WHITE, J.P.
1946—1947	ALDERMAN C. PORTER, J.P.
1947—1950	ALDERMAN G. ROBERTS, J.P.
1950—	ALDERMAN LIEUT.-COLONEL H. D. TANNER, O.B.E., J.P.

BIBLIOGRAPHY

A GUIDE TO ALDERSHOT AND ITS NEIGHBOURHOOD, by W. Sheldrake, late Colour Sergeant, Coldstream Guards (Sheldrake's Printing Press, Aldershot) (1857). (Wm. May & Co. Ltd., Aldershot.)

ALDERSHOT AND ALL ABOUT IT, by Mrs. Young (G. Routledge, London) (1857).

ALDERSHOT AND DISTRICT GUIDE (Gale & Polden Ltd.) (1909).

ALDERSHOT CALLING (Gale & Polden Ltd.) (1947).

ALDERSHOT AND THE WAR, 1939-1945 (Gale & Polden Ltd.) (1947).

ALDERSHOT—A RECORD OF MRS. DANIELL'S WORK AMONG SOLDIERS AND ITS SEQUEL, by Her Daughter (Hodder & Stoughton) (1879).

ALDERSHOT MUNICIPAL CHRONICLE, May 1947—July 1950.

ALDERSHOTTANA, OR CHINKS IN MY HUT (Ward, Lock & Co. Ltd.) (1859).

ALDERSHOT TATTOO PROGRAMMES, 1922-1939.

AN INTRODUCTION TO FIELD ARCHÆOLOGY AS ILLUSTRATED BY HAMP-SHIRE, by Dr. J. P. Williams Freeman, M.D. (Macmillan & Co. Ltd.) (1915).

BLACK'S GUIDE TO HAMPSHIRE (A. & C. Black Ltd.) (1919).

BOROUGH OF ALDERSHOT OFFICIAL GUIDE (Gale & Polden Ltd.) (1930).

CONCISE OXFORD DICTIONARY OF ENGLISH PLACE NAMES, by Eilert Ekwall (Oxford University Press) (1936).

COUNTY TOPOGRAPHIES: "HAMPSHIRE." Edited by E. R. Kelly, M.A., F.S.S. (Kelly & Co., London) (1875).

DICTIONARY OF NATIONAL BIOGRAPHY (Oxford University Press).

DREW'S ALDERSHOT AND FARNBOROUGH DIRECTORY AND ALMANAC (John Drew (Printers) Ltd.) (1932).

FLYING, by Claude Grahame White (Chatto & Windus) (1930).

FOLLOWING THE DRUM, by Horace Wyndham (Andrew Melrose Ltd.) (1914).

FROM MIDSHIPMAN TO FIELD-MARSHAL, by Field-Marshal Sir Evelyn Wood, V.C. (Methuen & Co. Ltd.) (1906).

GEORGE, DUKE OF CAMBRIDGE—A MEMOIR OF HIS PRIVATE LIFE, by Edgar Sheppard, C.V.O., D.D. (Longmans, Green & Co. Ltd.) (1906).

HAMPSHIRE WITH THE ISLE OF WIGHT. Edited by Arthur Mee (Hodder & Stoughton) (1939).

HARK BACK, by Colonel Wilfrid Jelf, C.M.G., D.S.O. (John Murray) (1935).

HISTORY OF THE ARMY PHYSICAL TRAINING CORPS: PART I. THE ARMY GYMNASTIC STAFF, 1860-1914, by Lieut.-Colonel E. A. L. Oldfield (Gale & Polden Ltd.) (1949).

HISTORY OF THE CORPS OF ROYAL ENGINEERS, Vol. III, by Colonel Sir Charles M. Watson, K.C.M.G., C.B., M.A. (R.E. Institution) (1915).

HISTORY, GAZETTEER AND DIRECTORY OF HAMPSHIRE AND THE ISLE OF WIGHT, 1859.

HISTORY OF THE ROYAL DRAGOONS, 1661-1934, by C. T. Atkinson.

JOTTINGS FROM A FARNBOROUGH NOTEBOOK, by Jessie Challacombe (Gale & Polden Ltd.) (1923).

KING EDWARD VII—A BIOGRAPHY, by Sir Sidney Lee (Macmillan & Co. Ltd.) (1925).

LIFE OF HIS ROYAL HIGHNESS THE PRINCE CONSORT, by Sir Theodore Martin, K.C.B. (Smith, Elder & Co.) (1879).

LOB-LIE-BY-THE-FIRE, by Mrs. J. H. Ewing (Geo. Bell & Sons) (1874).

MILITARY CUSTOMS, by Major T. J. Edwards, M.B.E., F.R.Hist.S. (Gale & Polden Ltd.) (1948).

MURRAY'S HANDBOOK FOR TRAVELLERS IN HAMPSHIRE (John Murray) (1894).

MY EARLY LIFE, by the Right Hon. Winston Churchill, C.H., M.P. (Odhams Press Ltd.)

PHOTOGRAPH ALBUM OF ALDERSHOT TOWN AND CAMP (Gale & Polden Ltd.) (1900).

"PUNCH," 1882, 1883, 1884.

ROCK'S ALBUM OF ALDERSHOT (Rock Bros. Ltd., London) (*circa* 1880).

SIXTY YEARS A QUEEN, told by Sir Herbert Maxwell, M.P., and Alfred C. Harmsworth (Harmsworth Bros.) (1897).

SKETCHES OF THE CAMP AT ALDERSHOT (Andrews & Lucy, Farnham) (1858).

SOME HISTORICAL PARTICULARS OF THE PARISH OF CROOKHAM, HANTS, by Grace Lefroy, C.B.E. (reprinted from the *Crookham Church Parish Magazine*, 1923).

SOUVENIR ALBUM OF VISIT OF 2ND REGT. QUEEN'S OWN RIFLES OF CANADA (Gale & Polden Ltd.) (1910).

"THE ALDERSHOT NEWS," 1894-1949.

"THE ALDERSHOT NEWS" SPECIAL ISSUES :

Diamond Jubilee Supplement, 26th June, 1897.
General Buller Number, 10th November, 1900.
Special Coronation Number, 11th August, 1902.
Coronation Number, 23rd June, 1911.
Shopping Supplement, 15th November, 1912.
Special Charter Day Edition, 23rd June, 1922.
Charter Day Supplement, 23rd June, 1922.
Shopping Week Supplement, 10th October, 1924.
Golden Jubilee Number, 23rd June, 1944.

THE CANADIAN ARMY AT WAR : NO. 1. THE CANADIANS IN BRITAIN, 1939-44 (Ministry of National Defence, Ottawa) (1946).

THE CIVIL WAR IN HAMPSHIRE, 1642-45, by Rev. G. N. Goodwin (J. & E. Bumpus Ltd., London) (1904).

THE CRONDALL RECORDS : PART I. HISTORICAL AND MANORIAL, by
Francis Joseph Baigent (Hampshire Record Society) (1891)
(Warren & Son Ltd., Winchester).

"THE GUNNER" (July, 1945).

THE HAMPSHIRE PARISH RECORDS : VOL. II, edited by W. P. W. Phillimore and S. Andrews (The Hampshire Record Society) (1900).

THE HISTORY OF AERONAUTICS IN GREAT BRITAIN, by J. E. Hodgson
(Oxford University Press) (1924).

THE HISTORY OF THE GREAT WAR—ORDER OF BATTLE OF DIVISIONS
(H.M.S.O.) (1938).

"THE ILLUSTRATED LONDON NEWS," 1846, 1855-1869.

THE LETTERS OF QUEEN VICTORIA. A Selection of Her Majesty's
correspondence between the years 1837 and 1861. Published by
Authority of His Majesty The King. Edited by Arthur Christopher
Benson, M.A., and Viscount Esher : 3 Vols. (John Murray)
(1907).

THE LIFE AND CUSTOMS IN WHITE'S, COBBETT'S AND KINGSLEY'S
COUNTRY, by J. A. Eggar (Simpkin Marshall Ltd.).

THE MILITARY LIFE OF H.R.H. GEORGE, DUKE OF CAMBRIDGE, by
Colonel Willoughby Verner, late Rifle Brigade, assisted by
Captain Erasmus Darwin Parker, late Manchester (63rd) Regi-
ment (John Murray) (1905).

THE OLD FLYING DAYS, by Major C. C. Turner (Sampson Low, Marston
& Co. Ltd.).

THE PARISH CHURCH OF ST. MICHAEL THE ARCHANGEL, ALDERSHOT,
by Dr. J. H. Gibson (The British Publishing Co. Ltd.) (1948).

THE PRINCE CONSORT, by Roger Fulford (Macmillan & Co. Ltd.)
(1949).

THE STORY OF A SHORT LIFE, by Mrs. Horatia Ewing (Society for
Promoting Christian Knowledge) (1885).

THE STORY OF THE ROYAL GARRISON CHURCH OF ALL SAINTS, ALDERSHOT,
by Frederick Ingall Anderson (Wm. May & Co. Ltd., Aldershot)
(1924).

"THE TIMES," 1884.

"THE TIMES" HISTORY OF THE WAR, VOL. I (1914).

TRADITIONS ABOUT ALDERSHOT, by C. S. Herve (W. Straker & Co.,
London) (1881).

VICTORIA COUNTY HISTORY OF HAMPSHIRE, Vol. IV (1911).

WELLINGTON, by Richard Aldington (Wm. Heinemann Ltd.) (1946).

INDEX

GENERAL INDEX

INDEX TO MILITARY UNITS AND FORMATIONS

Cavalry

Foot Guards

Regiments
(in alphabetical order)